Audio files in MP3 format and electronic text in PDF format are available for free at

JACOBELIGOODSONS.COM

The files are in .zip folders for ease of transfer
Utilize the audio with the paper text and electronic text

SPANISH BASIC COURSE

UNITS 16-30

ROBERT P. STOCKWELL -- J. DONALD BOWEN
ISMAEL SILVA-FUENZALIDA

FOREIGN SERVICE INSTITUTE
WASHINGTON, D.C.
1961
DEPARTMENT OF STATE

jacobeligoodsons.com For Free Audio

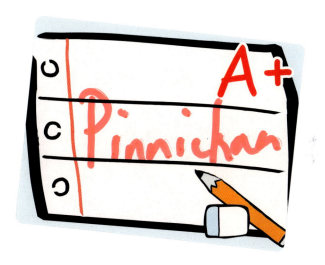

jacobeligoodsons.com For Free Audio

SPOKEN SPANISH   CONTENTS

Table of Contents

16.1	Basic sentences - Sightseeing..	16.1
16.2	Drills and grammar..	16.6
16.21	Pattern drills..	16.6
16.21.1	Redundant constructions with indirect clitic pronouns......................	16.6
16.21.2	Question intonation patterns - No questions................................	16.14
16.22	Replacement drills..	16.18
16.23	Variation drills..	16.24
16.24	Review drill - Masculine demonstrative forms...............................	16.28
16.3	Conversation stimulus...	16.30
16.4	Readings..	16.35
16.40	Introduction and list of cognate loan words................................	16.35
16.41	Los Nuevos Vecinos..	16.37
17.1	Basic sentences - Social life in Surlandia.................................	17.1
17.2	Drills and grammar..	17.6
17.21	Pattern drills..	17.6
17.21.1	Past I tense forms of regular verbs..	17.6
17.21.2	Question intonation patterns - Affirmative confirmation questions............	17.20
17.22	Replacement drills..	17.23
17.23	Variation drills..	17.29
17.24	Review drill - Possessive phrases with /kyén/..............................	17.33
17.3	Conversation stimulus...	17.34
17.4	Readings..	17.38
17.41	Comentando..	17.39
18.1	Basic sentences - Discussing Carmen's work.................................	18.1
18.2	Drills and grammar..	18.5
18.21	Pattern drills..	18.5
18.21.1	Past II tense forms of regular verbs.......................................	18.5
18.21.2	Past II tense forms of irregular verbs.....................................	18.16
18.21.3	Question intonation patterns - Negative confirmation questions...............	18.22
18.22	Replacement drills..	18.25
18.23	Variation drills..	18.31
18.24	Review drill - Word order in information questions.........................	18.35

jacobeligoodsons.com For Free Audio

CONTENTS   SPOKEN SPANISH

18.3	Conversation stimulus...	18.36
18.4	Readings...	18.40
18.41	Comentando (continued)...	18.41
19.1	Basic sentences - Visit to Air Mission.............................	19.1
19.2	Drills and grammar...	19.4
19.21	Pattern drills...	19.4
19.21.1	Past I and past II in the same construction........................	19.4
19.21.2	Question intonation patterns - Echo questions......................	19.15
19.22	Replacement drills...	19.19
19.23	Variation drills...	19.25
19.24	Review drill - Spanish simple tense for English verb construction in interrogations.................................	19.29
19.3	Conversation stimulus..	19.30
19.4	Readings...	19.35
19.41	Los Robinson...	19.36
20.1	Basic sentences - Visit to Air Mission (continued).................	20.1
20.2	Drills and grammar...	20.5
20.21	Pattern drills...	20.5
20.21.1	Direct and indirect clitics in the same construction..............	20.5
20.21.2	Exclamatory /ké, kómo/...	20.14
20.21.3	Question intonation patterns - Choice questions....................	20.18
20.22	Replacement drills...	20.24
20.23	Variation drills...	20.30
20.24	Review drill - Postposed full-form possessives....................	20.34
20.3	Conversation stimulus..	20.35
20.4	Readings...	20.39
20.41	La Primera Visita..	20.40
21.1	Basic sentences - The weather......................................	21.1
21.2	Drills and grammar...	21.4
21.21	Pattern drills...	21.4
21.21.1	Irregular past I verb forms - an /-ár/ verb taking regular /-ér-ír/ endings..	21.4
21.21.2	Irregular past I verb forms - verbs with extended stems...........	21.10
21.21.3	Irregular past I verb forms - verbs with modified stems...........	21.20

0.2

jacobeligoodsons.com For Free Audio

SPANISH SPOKEN   CONTENTS

21.21.4	Irregular past I verb forms - verbs with suppleted stems.....................	21.35
21.21.5	Statement intonation patterns - Deliberate statements........................	21.42
21.22	Replacement drills...	21.49
21.23	Variation drills...	21.55
21.24	Review drill - Theme class in past II tense forms............................	21.59
21.3	Conversation stimulus..	21.60
21.4	Readings...	21.64
21.41	Plan de Estudiar...	21.65
22.1	Basic sentences - Mrs. Harris wants to go to the market......................	22.1
22.2	Drills and grammar...	22.2
22.21	Pattern drills...	22.4
22.21.1	Present tense irregular verbs - stem vowel changing.........................	22.4
22.21.2	Statement intonation patterns - Sentence modifiers..........................	22.18
22.22	Replacement drills...	22.21
22.23	Variation drills...	22.27
22.24	Review drill - Theme class in past I tense forms.............................	22.31
22.3	Conversation stimulus..	22.32
22.4	Readings...	22.36
22.41	Jane and Ruth..	22.37
23.1	Basic sentences - Shopping at the market.....................................	23.1
23.2	Drills and grammar...	23.5
23.21	Pattern drills...	23.5
23.21.1	Present tense irregular verbs - velar stem extensions.......................	23.5
23.21.2	Present tense irregular verbs - mixed stem-vowel changing and velar stem extensions..	23.15
23.21.3	Present tense irregular verbs - mixed miscellaneous /kaér, traér/, /oír/, /aşér, deşír/, /sabér/................................	23.23
23.21.4	Statement intonation patterns - Leavetakings................................	23.33
23.22	Replacement drills...	23.36
23.23	Variation drills...	23.42
23.24	Review drill - The obligatory clause relator /ke/...........................	23.46
23.3	Conversation stimulus..	23.47
23.4	Readings...	23.50
23.41	¿Quién Rompió los Platos?..	23.51

0.3

jacobeligoodsons.com For Free Audio

CONTENTS

SPOKEN SPANISH

24.1	Basic sentences - Shopping in the stores..	24.1
24.2	Drills and grammar...	24.5
24.21	Pattern drills...	24.5
24.21.1	Reflexive clitic pronouns..	24.5
24.21.2	Reflexive clitic pronouns with progressive and	
	periphrastic future verb constructions...	24.15
24.21.3	Expressions for time of day..	24.31
24.22	Replacement drills...	24.34
24.23	Variation drills...	24.40
24.24	Review drill - Gender class assignment of certain nouns - I....................	24.44
24.3	Conversation stimulus..	24.46
24.4	Readings...	24.50
24.41	Los Fuentes se Despiden..	24.50
25.1	Basic sentences - A visa interview...	25.1
25.2	Drills and grammar...	25.4
25.21	Pattern drills...	25.4
25.21.1	Reflexive and indirect clitic pronouns in the same construction................	25.4
25.22	Replacement drills...	25.14
25.23	Variation drills...	25.20
25.24	Review drill - Verb-subject order in certain dependent clauses.................	25.24
25.3	Conversation stimulus..	25.25
25.4	Readings...	25.29
25.41	Señora Sistemática...	25.30
26.1	Basic sentences - A visa interview (continued).................................	26.1
26.2	Drills and grammar...	26.4
26.21	Pattern drills...	26.4
26.21.1	Reflexive and direct clitic pronouns in the same construction..................	26.4
26.21.2	Reflexives with no designated agents...	26.9
26.22	Replacement drills...	26.14
26.23	Variation drills...	26.20
26.24	Review drill - Gender class assignment certain nouns - II......................	26.24
26.3	Conversation stimulus..	26.25
26.4	Readings...	26.29
26.41	Día de Mercado...	26.29

0.4

jacobeligoodsons.com For Free Audio

SPOKEN SPANISH   **CONTENTS**

27.1	Basic sentences - Sports...	27.1
27.2	Drills and grammar..	27.5
27.21	Pattern drills...	27.5
27.21.1	Formal command forms for regular verbs..................................	27.5
27.21.2	Formal command forms for irregular verbs................................	27.15
27.21.3	Familiar command forms for regular verbs................................	27.27
27.21.4	Familiar command forms for irregular verbs..............................	27.35
27.22	Replacement drills...	27.47
27.23	Variation drills...	27.53
27.24	Review drill - Nominalized possessives...................................	27.57
27.3	Conversation stimulus..	27.58
27.4	Readings...	27.63
27.41	La Técnica de Comprar..	27.63
28.1	Basic sentences - At the golf course.....................................	28.1
28.2	Drills and grammar...	28.4
28.21	Pattern drills...	28.4
28.21.1	Indirect command forms - regular and irregular..........................	28.4
28.21.2	Hortatory command forms...	28.17
28.22	Replacement drills...	28.29
28.23	Variation drills...	28.35
28.24	Review drill - Review of past I tense forms.............................	28.39
28.3	Conversation stimulus..	28.43
28.4	Readings...	28.47
28.41	Ciudades Latinoamericanas..	28.48
29.1	Basic sentences - At the tennis court....................................	29.1
29.2	Drills and grammar...	29.4
29.21	Pattern drills...	29.4
29.21.1	Clitic pronouns with command forms......................................	29.4
29.21.2	Clitic pronouns in constructions with infinitives and with /-ndo/ forms...	29.14
29.22	Replacement drills...	29.25
29.23	Variation drills...	29.31
29.24	Review drill - Review of present perfect construction...................	29.35
29.3	Conversation stimulus..	29.37
29.4	Readings...	29.40
29.41	El Barrio Viejo de Las Palmas..	29.41

jacobeligoodsons.com For Free Audio

CONTENTS   SPOKEN SPANISH

30.1	Basic sentences - Bullfighting...	30.1
30.2	Drills and grammar..	30.4
30.21	General review..	30.4
30.21.1	Verb review...	30.4
30.21.11	Translation-substitution drill - verb forms................................	30.4
30.21.12	Translation-substitution drill - Verb construction.........................	30.8
30.21.2	Response drill - Clitic pronoun review.....................................	30.10
30.22	Replacement drills..	30.19
30.23	Variation drills..	30.25
30.3	Conversation stimulus...	30.29
30.4	Readings..	30.33
30.41	En el Mercado...	30.35
A II	Appendix II...	AII.1
A II.1	Vocabulary..	AII.1
A II.2	Index...	AII.41

0.6

jacobeligoodsons.com For Free Audio

SPOKEN SPANISH   UNIT 16

16.1   BASIC SENTENCES.   Sightseeing.

        Molina and the Harrises are driving around the city in Jose's car.

ENGLISH SPELLING   AID TO LISTENING   SPANISH SPELLING

        the sector, section   èl‑sèktór↓   el sector

        commercial   kòmérşyál↓   comercial

Molina   éstę |èąèlsèktór |kòmérşyál↓   Molina
    This is the business section.   Este es el sector comercial.

        better, best   mèhór↓   mejor

        the store   lá‑tyéndá↓   la tienda

        the city   lá‑şyúdád↓   la ciudad

    The best stores in the city are here. (1) àkięstán |làzméhorestyéndaz |dèlaşyúdád↓   Aquí están las mejores tiendas de la
                                                                                       ciudad.

        to her   sé↓ lé↓   se (le)

Harris   ombrè↓ nó |selodiga |àmięspósá↓   Harris
    Man, don't tell my wife that. (2)   ¡Hombre! ¡No se lo diga a mi esposa!

Mrs. Harris   pórkenó↓   Sra. Harris
    Why not?   ¿Por qué no?

        the people   lá‑hènté↓   la gente

UNO   16.1

jacobeligoodsons.com For Free Audio

UNIT 16   SPOKEN SPANISH

What a lot of people on the street. What's   kékantiɗá |ɗéhèntę |ènlàká꞉꞉yè↓ képásà↓   ¡Qué cantidad de gente en la calle!
happening?   ¿Qué pasa?

        special   èspéꞩyá´l↓   especial

        to stroll   pàséar↓   pasear

Molina   náɗą |ènèspèꞩyál↓ èstámpaseándò↓   Molina
    Nothing special. They're just strolling.   Nada en especial. Están paseando.

        today   óy↓   hoy

        to finish   àkábar↓   acabar

        to have just...(3)   àkàbar—dè↓   acabar de...

        the Mass   là—mìsà↓   la misa

Today is Sunday and they've just come out   óyézɗómiŋgo |Ʇákábaŋ |dèsálìrɗemísà↓   Hoy es domingo y acaban de salir de misa.
    of church.

        the church   lą—iglesyà↓   la iglesia

Mrs. Harris   keꞱglésyꝺesakéꞋyà↓   Sra. Harris
    What church is that?   ¿Qué iglesia es aquélla?

        the cathedral   lá—kátèɗrá´l↓   la catedral

Molina   éz |làkàtèɗrá´l↓   Molina
    It's the cathedral.   Es la catedral

16.2   DOS

SPOKEN SPANISH															UNIT 16

the ministry	èl‑ministeryò↓	el ministerio
the relation	là‑rrèlàṣyòn↓	la relación
exterior	è(k)stèryòr↓	exterior
the Foreign Affairs Office	èl‑ministeryo |dèrrèlàṣyones‑ e(k)steryòrès↓	el Ministerio de Relaciones Exteriores.
And that's the Foreign Office.	ɪesè |èsélministeryo |dèrrèlàṣyones e(k)steryórès↓	Y ése es el Ministerio de Relaciones Exteriores.
the cafe	èl‑kàfé↓	el café
so	tán↓	tan
full	ᵑyènò↓	lleno

Harris
Jean, see how full the cafes are? —— yìn↓ bèzloskafes |tanᵈyenòs↓ —— **Harris** Jean, ¿ves los cafés tan llenos?

seen (to see)	bistò↓ bér↓	visto (ver)
from appearances, apparently	pòr‑ló‑tistò↓	por lo visto
here (4)	àkà↓	acá
to take, to drink	tómàr↓	tomar
the coffee	èl‑kàfé↓	el café

Mrs. Harris
Yes, apparently they drink more coffee here than in the U. S. —— sì↓ pòrlòbisto |àka |tómánmáskafé | kènlòsèstádòsùnìdòs↓ —— **Sra. Harris** Sí. Por lo visto, acá toman más café que en los Estados Unidos.

TRES

jacobeligoodsons.com For Free Audio

16.3

UNIT 16   SPOKEN SPANISH

the pretext, excuse	èl—prète(k)stó↓	el pretexto
to get together, assemble	rrèwnírsè↓	reunirse
to converse, to chat	kòmbèrsár↓	conversar

Harris
It's just an excuse to get together and talk.   é(s)sóloụmpretèk̞sto |pàràréwnirsẹ

akombersár↓   Es sólo un pretexto para reunirse a
                                                 conversar.

(I) would like (to want) [5]   kisyèrà↓ kèrér↓   quisiera (querer)

old, ancient   àntirwó↓   antiguo

Mrs. Harris   *Sra. Harris*
I'd like to see the old part of the city.   yokisyèrɔ̀er |làpártẹàntiꞬwà |dèlàṣyùɕáɕ↓   Yo quisiera ver la parte antigua de la
                                                                                       ciudad.

Molina   *Molina*
It's not worth the trouble.   notẹlelapéná↓   No vale la pena.

the year   èl—aꞬyò↓   el año

it makes... that it is; it has been... for   àẹe....kẹ—está↓   hace... que está

neglected (to neglect, abandon)   àbàndònaɕò↓ àt̬àndónar↓   abandonado (abandonar)

It's been neglected for years.   áẹẹaꞬyos |késtá |muyat̬andonáɕà↓   Hace años que está muy abandonada.

nonsense   ke—t̬á↓   qué va

magnificent   màᴣnifikó↓   magnífico

Harris   *Harris*
What do you mean! It's magnificent!   kètá↓ é7 |màᴣnifikà↓   ¡Qué va! Es magnífica.

16.4   CUATRO

SPOKEN SPANISH   UNIT 16

(I) was (to be)	èstubé↓ éstár↓	estuve (estar)
(a few days) ago	aşę—unoz—días↓	hace (unos días)
I was there a few days ago.	yǫęstubęai̯ |aşęunozdías↓	Yo estuve ahí hace unos días.
the foot	èl—pyé↓	el pie
to go by foot	ir—a—pyé↓	ir a pie
Some other day we'll *walk* through it.	otrodia |bamos̬apyé↓	Otro día vamos a pie.
because	porkè↓	porque
narrow	èstrechò↓	estrecho
Because the streets there are very narrow.	pórkèlàskal̬l̬yes |al̬l̬i |sónmuyéstréchâs↓	Porque las calles allí son muy estrechas.

16.10   Notes on the basic sentences

(1) Several times in previous notes the differences between the distributions (and therefore meanings) of certain Spanish prepositions and their English counterparts have been called to your attention. In this sentence there occurs a conspicuous example of such difference: English has 'the best stores *in* the city,' Spanish has 'the best stores *of* the city.'

(2) In the build-up the item /se/ *se* is identified as belonging with /le/ *le*, the indirect clitic pronoun with which you are already familiar. A full explanation of the replacement of /le/ by /se/ under certain conditions will appear in Unit 20. In the meanwhile, simply note that two clitic pronouns both beginning with /l/ never occur in sequence together: the first one is always replaced by /se/. Thus in this sentence the impossible /lelo/ *le lo* has become /selo/ *se lo*.

(3) Special attention should be called to this construction, since it is quite different from anything in English but is very common in Spanish. The only way in which 'to have just done something' is normally translated into Spanish is by this idiom: /akabár—de/ plus the infinitive of the verb.

CINCO   16.5

UNIT 16   SPOKEN SPANISH

(4) While it is hazardous to generalize about the complex distributional differences that make up the difference in meaning between this item /aká/ *acá* and a very similar item /akí/ *aquí*, in many occurences such as this one it may rightly be pointed out that /aká/ means 'around here , in this general area, hereabouts' as against /akí/ which means 'right here, in this specific area.'

(5) The form /kɪsyéra/ *quisiera* belongs with past subjunctive forms, which will not be examined until Unit 49. It is, however, very frequent in this particular meaning, and this usage is simply special to this one form, not associated with the customary past subjunctive usages.

16.2   DRILLS AND GRAMMAR

16.21   Pattern drills

16.21.1   Redundant constructions with indirect clitic pronouns

A. Presentation of pattern

ILLUSTRATIONS

—————————	1	àmɪ |tráygame |sopadelegúmbrès↓	*A mí tráigame sopa de legumbres.*
Does it suit *you?*	2	àtí |tekómbyéne↑	*¿A ti te conviene?*
Does it suit *you?*	3	aùstéɖ |lekómbyéne↑	*¿A Ud. le conviene?*
Does it suit *him?*	4	ael |lekómbyéne↑	*¿A él le conviene?*
Does it suit *her?*	5	ae^ya |lekómbyéne↑	*¿A ella le conviene?*
ugly		féó↓	*feo*
It seems ugly *to us.*	6	ánósótròz |nospareṣeféó↓	*A nosotros nos parece feo.*

16.6   SEIS

SPOKEN SPANISH   UNIT 16

It seems strict *to you all?*   7 aùsteɖez |lespareşerriġurosó†   *¿A ustedes les* parece riguroso?

It seems strict *to them(m).*   8 ae͠yoꜩ ae͠yoꜩ |lespareşerriġurósò↓   *A ellos les* parece riguroso.

It seem wonderful *to them(f)λ*   9 ae͠yaꜩ !lespareşestupéndò↓   *A ellas les* parece estupendo.

EXTRAPOLATION

	Indirect clitic	Redundant construction
1 sg	me	a‑mí
2 fam sg	te	a‑tí
2 - 3 sg	le	a‑ustéd
		a‑él
		a‑éⁿya
1 pl	nos	a‑nosótros
2 - 3 pl	les	a‑ustédes
		a‑éⁿyos
		a‑éⁿyas

NOTES

a. Redundant relator phrases, composed of /a/ plus a pronoun,
    are used to restate the indirect clitic pronoun.

b. Such redundant phrases are used with 2 - 3 clitics to clarify
    their reference, or with any clitics for contrastive emphasis.

SIETE   16.7

UNIT 16   SPOKEN SPANISH

16.21.11 Substitution drills -- Person-number substitution

1 ámi |mefaltaumbaúl↓

   ànósótroz_____↓   ànósotroz |nosfaltaumbaúl↓

   ákármèn_____↓   ákármen |lefaltaumbaúl↓

   ąeⁿyoz_____↓   ąeⁿyoz |lesfaltaumbaúl↓

   ąústéd_____↓   ąústéd |lefaltaumbaúl↓

2 ąel |legustaelkóché↓

   ànósótroz_____↓   ànósotroz |nozgustaelkóché↓

   ąústédez_____↓   ąústédez |lezgustaelkóché↓

_____

        1 *A mí* me falta un baúl.

           A nosotros_____.   A nosotros nos falta un baúl.

           A Carmen_____.   A Carmen le falta un baúl.

           A ellos_____.   A ellos les falta un baúl.

           A Ud._____.   A Ud. le falta un baúl.

        2 *A él* le gusta el coche.

           A nosotros_____.   A nosotros nos gusta el coche.

           A Uds._____.   A Uds. les gusta el coche.

16.8   OCHO

SPOKEN SPANISH   UNIT 16

àmí _____↓   àmí |megustąelkóchè↓
ąéⁿya _____↓   ąéⁿya |legustąelkóchè↓

3 ánòsotroz |nosparegegrándè↓
    àhóse _____↓   àhóse |leparegegrándè↓
    áhwanɟamaría _____↓   áhwanɟamaría |lesparegegrándè↓
    àmí _____↓   àmí |meparegegrándè↓
    àtí _____↓   àtí |teparegegrándè↓

A mí _____.   A mí me gusta el coche.
A ella _____.   A ella le gusta el coche.

3 A *nosotros* nos parece grande.
    A José _____.   A José le parece grande.
    A Juan y a María _____.   A Juan y a María les parece grande.
    A mí _____.   A mí me parece grande.
    A ti _____.   A ti te parece grande.

NUEVE   16.9

UNIT 16

SPOKEN SPANISH

Number substitution

1 àmı̀ |mefáltalabísà↓

ànósótroz |nosfaltalabísà↓

2 àe͡ʸàz |lespareşeŋkáràs↓

àe͡ʸa |lepareşeŋkáràs↓

3 ànósotroz |nozgustaelwíski↓

àmı̀ |megustaelwíski↓

4 àústeɗ |nolegustanáɗà↓

àústeɗez |nolezgustanáɗà↓

5 àmı̀ |mebàmuymál↓

ànósotroz |nozbamuymál↓

6 àel |lekombyénelpréşyò↓

àe͡ʸoz |leskombyénelpréşyò↓

7 ànósotroz |nospareş̧eamábl̀e↓

àmı̀ |mepareş̧eamábl̀e↓

---

1 *A mí* me falta la visa.

A nosotros nos falta la visa.

2 *A ellas* les parecen caras.

A ella le parecen caras.

3 *A nosotros* nos gusta el **whiskey**.

A mí me gusta el whiskey.

4 *A Ud.* no le gusta nada.

A Uds. no les gusta nada.

5 *A mí* me va muy mal.

A nosotros nos va muy mal.

6 *A él* le conviene el precio.

A ellos les conviene el precio.

7 *A nosotros* nos parece amable.

A mí me parece amable.

16.10

DIEZ

SPOKEN SPANISH

UNIT 16

16.21.12 Response drill

	1	ǫusteđ↓ lėpàréşė͡ᵐlíbrŏbwénǫ↑omálò↓	ȧmɨ |mėpàréşė |mủybwénȯ↓
	2	ǫusteđės↓ lézǫústạėlẉiskɪ↑olȧşẹrbéşà↓	ȧnȯsótroz |nȯzgústạėlẉiskɪ↓
[ǫusteđ↓]	3	ȧkyénlėgústạ |ėlẉískɪ↓	ȧmɨ |mėgústạ |ėlẉískɪ↓
[ȧmɨ↓]	4	ȧkyénlėgústan |lazgáfàs↓	ǫusteđlėgústán↓
[ạė͡ᵐyà↓]	5	ạél |lėfáltarrópa↑	nó↓ ạélnó↓ ạė͡ᵐyà↓
[ǫusteđės↓]	6	ạė͡ᵐyoz |lespàréşẹlẉiskɪ |baráto↑	nó↓ ạė͡ᵐyoznó↓ ȧnȯsótrȯs↓

---

	1 A Ud., ¿le parece el libro bueno o malo?	A mí me parece muy bueno.
	2 A Uds., ¿les gusta el whisky o la cerveza?	A nosotros nos gusta el whisky.
(a Ud.)	3 ¿A quién le gusta el whisky?	A mí me gusta el whisky.
(a mí)	4 ¿A quién le gustan las gafas?	A Ud. le gustan.
(a ella)	5 ¿A él le falta ropa?	No, a él no, a ella.
(a Uds.)	6 ¿A ellos les parece el whisky barato?	No, a ellos no, a nosotros.

ONCE

[ǎústéd↓] 7 ǎel|lebámál|akí↑   no↓ ǎelnó↓ àmí↓

8 àtı|tequstaeledifıșyo|delkámpo↑   sí↓ ámımequstamúchó↓

9 ǎústéđez|lezqustalaeskwéla↑   sí↓ ánósotroz|nozqustamúchó↓

10 ǎel|lebabyénakı↑   sí↓ ǎel|lèbá|muybyénakí↓

11 àtı|tepareșekármem|boníta↑   sí↓ ámı|mèpáréșè|muybonítá↓

(a Ud.) 7 ¿A él le va mal aquí?   No, a él no, a mí.

8 ¿A ti te gusta el Edificio del Campo?   Sí, a mí me gusta mucho.

9 ¿A Uds. les gusta la escuela?   Sí, a nosotros nos gusta mucho.

10 ¿A él le va bien aquí?   Sí, a él le va muy bien aquí.

11 ¿A ti te parece Carmen bonita?   Sí, a mí me parece muy bonita.

SPOKEN SPANISH   UNIT 16

16.21.13 Translation drill — Paired sentences

1 He sends me the newspaper.   mèmándạ |elpèryódìkỏ↓   Me manda el periódico.

   He sends *me* the newspaper.   àmı |mèmándạ |elpèryódìkỏ↓   A mí me manda el periódico.

2 He's given us the furniture.   nósạdạdo |lozmwéblès↓   Nos ha dado los muebles.

   He's given *us* the furniture.   ànósotroz |nósạdạdolozmwéblès↓   A nosotros nos ha dado los muebles.

3 I speak to them in English.   lésạblọeninglés↓   Les hablo en inglés.

   I speak to *them* in English.   ạéṇyoz |lésạblọeninglés↓   A ellos les hablo en inglés.

4 I write her in Spanish.   léskríbọenespanyól↓   Le escribo en español.

   I write *her* in Spanish.   ạéṇya |léskríbọenespanyól↓   A ella le escribo en español.

5 She cleans the apartment for him.   lélímpyạ |elapartaméntỏ↓   Le limpia el apartamento.

   She cleans the apartment for *him*.   ạél |lélímpyạ |elapartaméntỏ↓   A él le limpia el apartamento.

6 He brings us the car.   nóstrạelkárrỏ↓   Nos trae el carro.

   He brings *us* the car.   ànósotroz |nóstrạelkárrỏ↓   A nosotros nos trae el carro.

7 He writes me very little.   méskríbemuypókỏ↓   Me escribe muy poco.

   He writes *me* very little.   àmı |méskríbemuypókỏ↓   A mí me escribe muy poco.

TRECE   16.13

UNIT 16   SPOKEN SPANISH

8 He helps her to clean.   leáyuḍalımpyár↓   Le ayuda a limpiar.

   He helps *her* to clean.   aé^ya |leáyuḍalımpyár↓   A ella le ayuda a limpiar.

9 She washes their (the) shirts for them.   léžlàbàlàskamísàs↓   Les lava las camisas.

   She washes their (the) shirts for *them*. aé^yòz |léžlàbàlàskamísàs↓   A ellos les lava las camisas.

B. Discussion of pattern

The 2 - 3 forms of the indirect clitic pronouns are ambiguous in their reference, since they can correspond to any of three subject pronoun forms. If this ambiguity is not clarified in the context of the sentence or situation, it will be clarified by a 'redundant construction'. The construction is really not redundant, of course; the term is used to designate a construction which restates the reference of a clitic pronoun.

The redundant construction consists of the relator /a/ plus an appropriate nonclitic pronoun. It has considerable freedom of occurrence in a sentence, appearing before or after the clitic-verb combination, though not necessarily *immediate*ly before or after.

This relator phrase, as well as clarifying a 2-3 clitic form, may appear with *any* clitic pronoun to supply emphasis or contrast. Clitic pronouns normally appear unstressed and are not emphasized by a shift in word stress as is usual in English; emphasis is given by the addition of a redundant phrase, which *can* appear under strong stress and / or a higher pitch. Thus, 'He sends me the newspaper' would be /memánda |elperyódiko↓/ but 'He sends *me* the newspaper' would be /amí |me mánda |elperyódiko↓/

16.21.2   Question intonation patterns – No questions

   A. Presentation of pattern

                                              ILLUSTRATIONS

                                                                                  2   2 2↑
                                         1   tyeneunlapiş↑   ¿Tiene un lápiz?

   Don't you have a pencil?   nótyeneunlapiş| 2 2   3 1 |
                                                                                  ¿No tiene un lápiz?

16.14   CATORCE

                        jacobeligoodsons.com For Free Audio

SPOKEN SPANISH   UNIT 16

————————————   2   èstáẹstudyando↑   1 2   2 2↑
                                                                            ¿Está estudiando?
        Isn't she studying?
                                          noẹstaẹstuḍyandò| 2 2   3 1|
                                                                                 ¿No está estudiando?

————————————   3   byenenẹmbarko↑   2   2 2↑
                                                                            ¿Vienen en barco?
     Aren't they coming by boat?
                                          nóbyénenẹmbarkò| 2 2   3 1|
                                                                                 ¿No vienen en barco?

                                  EXTRAPOLATION

Yes-no question	No (with surprise)
/1222↑/	/no/ + /2231 |/

                                       NOTES

a. A negative question with a /2231 \|/ pattern usually
   anticipates a negative answer, expressing surprise on
   the part of the questioner.

QUINCE

UNIT 16   SPOKEN SPANISH

16.21.21 Substitution drill – Pattern substitution

1 kyérg̣untragó↑   nokyérg̣untragó|

2 tyénelekipahé↑   notyénelekipahé|

3 áblg̣espaɲyól↑   ng̣ablg̣espaɲyól|

4 é(s)suyalg̣ídeá↑   ng̣e(s)suyalg̣ídeá|

5 légustalabitaçyón↑   nolégustalabitaçyón|

6 légustanlozmwéblés↑   nolégustanlozmwéblés|

| | 2   2 2↑ |
| 1 | ¿Quiere un trago? |

| | 2   2 2↑ |
| 2 | ¿Tiene el equipaje? |

| | 2   22 ↑ |
| 3 | ¿Habla español? |

| | 1 2   22↑ |
| 4 | ¿Es suya la idea? |

| | 1 2   22↑ |
| 5 | ¿Le gusta la habitación? |

| | 1 2   2 2↑ |
| 6 | ¿Le gustan los muebles? |

2   2   3 1|
¿No quiere un trago?

2 2   3 1|
¿No tiene el equipaje?

2 2   31 |
¿No habla español?

2   2   31|
¿No es suya la idea?

2   2   31|
¿No le gusta la habitación?

2   2   3 1|
¿No le gustan los muebles?

16.16   DIECISEIS

SPOKEN SPANISH   UNIT 16

7 kyerehamon↑   nokyerehamon|

8 kyerelmenu↑   nokyerelmenu|

9 kabelmaletın↑   nokabelmaletın|

10 éstaǫkupaðo↑   noǫstaǫkupaðo|

11 tyenelcheke↑   notyenelcheke|

---

                2   22↑   2   2   31|
7 ¿Quiere jamón?   ¿No quiere jamón?

                2   22↑   2   2   31|
8 ¿Quiere el menú?   ¿No quiere el menú?

                2   22↑   2   2   31|
9 ¿Cabe el maletín?   ¿No cabe el maletín?

            1 2   2 2↑   2   2   3 1|
10 ¿Está ocupado?   ¿No stá ocupado?

                2   2 2↑   2   3 1|
11 ¿Tiene el cheque?   ¿No tiene el cheque?

B. Discussion of pattern

    A question pattern of /2231|/ which is cast in the negative anticipates a negative answer which is a cause of surprise to the questioner. Often the question will also show modifications in pronunciation beyond the regular intonation features, such as openness or laxness and / or a stretching of the pitch intervals.

DIECISIETE   16.17

UNIT 16   SPOKEN SPANISH

16.22   Replacement drills

A   éstę |eşelsektorkomerşyál↓

1   _____bonító↓   éstę |eşelsektorbonító↓

2   _____son_____↓   éstos |sonlo(s)sektorezbonítós↓

3   _____partez_____↓   éstas |sonlaspartezbonítás↓

4   éstą_____↓   éstą |ezlapartebonítá↓

5   _____trankílá↓   éstą |ezlapartetrankílá↓

6   _____una_____↓   éstą |eşunapartetrankílá↓

7   _____kañyes_____↓   éstas |sónúnàskañyestrankílàs↓

_____

A   Este es el sector comercial.

1   _____bonito.   Este es el sector bonito.

2   _____son_____.   Estos son los sectores bonitos.

3   _____partes_____.   Estas son las partes bonitas.

4   Esta _____.   Esta es la parte bonita.

5   _____tranquila.   Esta es la parte tranquila.

6   _____una_____.   Esta es una parte tranquila.

7   _____calles_____.   Estas son unas calles tranquilas.

16.18   DIECIOCHO

SPOKEN SPANISH   UNIT 16

B   àkię́stan | làzmèhórestyéndàs↓

1 _____apartaméntòs↓   àkię́stan | lòzmèhóres,apartaméntòs↓

2 ái_____↓   áię́stan | lòzmèhóres,apartaméntòs↓

3 _____otél↓   áię́sta | ẹlméhorotél↓

4 _____otro_____↓   áię́sta | ẹlotrotél↓

5 dónde_____↓   dóndesta | ẹlotrotél↓

6 _____seŋyóràs↓   dóndestan | lasọtra(s) seŋyóràs↓

7 komọ_____↓   komọ̀estan | lasọtra(s) seŋyóràs↓

B   Aquí están las mejores tiendas.

1 _____apartamentos.   Aquí están los mejores apartamentos.

2 Ahí_____.   Ahí están los mejores apartamentos.

3 _____hotel.   Ahí está el mejor hotel.

4 _____otro_____.   Ahí está el otro hotel.

5 ¿Dónde_____?   ¿Dónde está el otro hotel?

6 ¿_____señoras?   ¿Dónde están las otras señoras?

7 ¿Cómo_____?   ¿Cómo están las otras señoras?

DIECINUEVE   16.19

UNIT 16   SPOKEN SPANISH

C ke̦igle̦sya̦ |e̦șak6ʼya̦↓

1 ──se̦k̦șyón──────↓   ke̦se̦k̦șyón |e̦șak6ʼya̦↓

2 ────────éșa̦↓   ke̦se̦k̦șyon̦e̦șéșa̦↓

3 ──e̦skwélaș──────↓   ke̦skwéla(s)son̦éșáș↓

4 kwántaș──────────↓   kwántașe̦skwélaș |son̦éșáș↓

5 ──────baúleș──↓   kwántozbaúleș |son̦éșóș↓

6 ────────súyóș↓   kwántozbaúleș |sonsúyóș↓

7 kwál──────────────↓   kwálbaul |e(s)súyó↓

──

C ¿Qué iglesia es aquélla?

1 ¿──sección──────?   ¿Qué sección es aquélla?

2 ¿──────────ésa?   ¿Qué sección es ésa?

3 ¿──escuelas──────?   ¿Qué escuelas son ésas?

4 ¿Cuántas──────?   ¿Cuántas escuelas son ésas?

5 ¿──baúles──────?   ¿Cuántos baúles son ésos?

6 ¿──────────suyos?   ¿Cuántos baúles son suyos?

7 ¿Cuál──────────?   ¿Cuál baúl es suyo?

16.20   VEINTE

SPOKEN SPANISH   UNIT 16

D   yı́n↓ bézloskafés |tánʸyénos↑

1 _____ká^ʸes _____↑   yı́n↓ bézlaskáʸes |tánʔyénas↑

2 _____ estréchas↑   yı́n↓ bézlaskáʸes |tanestréchas↑

3 _____ aké^ya _____↑   yı́n↓ bés |aké^yaká^ʸe |tanestrécha↑

4 _____ párte _____↑   yı́n↓ bés |aké^yapárte |tanestrécha↑

5 _____ antígwa↑   yı́n↓ bés |aké^yapárte |tanantígwa↑

6 __ rrékwerɗas _____↑   yı́n↓ rrékwerɗas |aké^yapárte |tánantígwa↑

7 sényorés _____↑   sényorés↓ rrékwerɗan |aké^yapárte |tán
                                                     antígwa↑

_____

D   Jean, ¿ves los cafés tan llenos?

1 __, ¿ __ calles _____?   Jean, ¿ves las calles tan llenas?

2 __, ¿ _____ estrechas?   Jean, ¿ves las calles tan estrechas?

3 __, ¿ __ aquella _____?   Jean, ¿ves aquella calle tan estrecha?

4 __, ¿ __ parte _____?   Jean, ¿ves aquella parte tan estrecha?

5 __, ¿ _____ antigua?   Jean, ¿ves aquella parte tan antigua?

6 __, ¿recuerdas _____?   Jean, ¿recuerdas aquella parte tan antigua?

7 Señores, ¿ _____ ?   Señores, ¿recuerdan aquella parte tan
                                                     antigua?

VEINTIUNO

UNIT 16   SPOKEN SPANISH

E   yokisyéraḅer |làpárteantígwà↓

1   _____ konoşer _____ ↓   yokisyéra |konoşer |làpárteantígwà↓

2   _____ komerşyál↓   yokisyéra |konoşer |làpártekomerşyál↓

3   _____ bárryo _____ ↓   yokisyéra |konoşer |èlbárryokomerşyál↓

4   _____ ír |à _____ ↓   yokisyéraᶅir |àlbárryokomerşyál↓

5   _____ mazbonítò↓   yokisyéraᶅir |àlbárryo |mazbonítò↓

6   _____ séktor _____ ↓   yokisyéraᶅir |àlséktor |mazbonítò↓

7   _____ bibir |én _____ ↓   yokisyéra |bibir |énélséktor |mazbonítò↓

E   Yo quisiera ver la parte antigua.

1   _____ conocer _____ .   Yo quisiera conocer la parte antigua.

2   _____ comercial.   Yo quisiera conocer la parte comercial.

3   _____ barrio _____ .   Yo quisiera conocer el barrio comercial.

4   _____ ir a _____ .   Yo quisiera ir al barrio comercial.

5   _____ más bonito.   Yo quisiera ir al barrio más bonito.

6   _____ sector _____ .   Yo quisiera ir al sector más bonito.

7   _____ vivir en _____ .   Yo quisiera vivir en el sector más bonito.

SPOKEN SPANISH   UNIT 16

F pórkèlàskáⁿyés |aⁿyi↑sònmúyestréchàs↓

1 _____antígwàs↓   pórkèlàskáⁿyés |aⁿyi↑sònmúyantígwàs↓

2 _____èðifiṣyos_____↓   pórkèlósèðifiṣyos |aⁿyi↑sònmúyantígwòs↓

3 _____àki_____↓   pórkèlósèðifiṣyos |aki↑sònmúyantígwòs↓

4 ____muchos_____↓   pórkèmuchos₤ðifiṣyos |aki↑sònmúyantígwòs↓

5 _____súṣyòs↓   pórkèmuchos₤ðifiṣyos |aki↑sònmúysúṣyòs↓

6 ___kásàs_____↓   pórkèmúchaskásàs |aki↑sònmúysúṣyàs↓

7 ____hentę_____↓   pórkèmúchahéntę |aki↑ęzmúysúṣyà↓

_____

F Porque las calles allí son muy estrechas.

1 _____antiguas.   Porque las calles allí son muy antiguas.

2 _____edificios_____.   Porque los edificios allí son muy antiguos.

3 _____aquí_____.   Porque los edificios aquí son muy antiguos.

4 ____muchos_____.   Porque muchos edificios aquí son muy antiguos.

5 _____sucios.   Porque muchos edificios aquí son muy sucios.

6 _____casas_____.   Porque muchas casas aquí son muy sucias.

7 _____gente_____.   Porque mucha gente aquí es muy sucia.

VEINTITRES

UNIT 16   SPOKEN SPANISH

16.23   Variation drills

A   kékantidád |dehéntę |ènlàká̂ỳè↓   ¡Qué cantidad de gente en la calle!

    1 What a lot of cars on the street!   kékantidád |dęáwtós |ènlàká̂ỳè↓   ¡Qué cantidad de autos en la calle!

    2 What a lot of kids in the park!   kékantidád |deníŋyòs |ènélpárkè↓   ¡Qué cantidad de niños en el parque!

    3 What a lot of Americans in the cafés!   kékantidád |dęamerikánòs |ènlóskàfés↓   ¡Qué cantidad de americanos en los cafés!

    4 What a lot of stores in the commercial   kékantidád |detyéndàs |ènélséktór   ¡Qué cantidad de tiendas en el sector
       section!   kómérçyál↓   comercial!

    5 What a lot of baggage in the custom's   kékantidád |dekipáhę |ènládwánà↓   ¡Qué cantidad de equipaje en la aduana!
       office!

    6 There sure is a lot of work in the   kémobimyéntǫ |ènlàsèkşyóŋkònsúlár↓   ¡Qué movimiento en la sección consular!
       consular section!

    7 How cheap!   kebarátò↓   ¡Qué barato!

B   óyèzdòmiŋgo |ḻàkában |dèsálirdemísà↓   Hoy es domingo y acaban de salir de misa.

    1 Today is Friday and they've just come   óyèzbyérnes |ḻàkában |dèsálirdelạeskwélà↓   Hoy es viernes y acaban de salir de la
       out of school.   escuela.

16.24   VEINTICUATRO

SPOKEN SPANISH   UNIT 16

2 Today is Thursday and they've just come   óyèshwébes |ₗàkában |dèꟙyègarƌꟙànápòlis↓   Hoy es jueves y acaban de llegar de
  from Annapolis.   Anápolis.

3 Today is Monday and we've just practiced   óyézlúnes |ₗàkábamoz |dèpráktikárespaŋyól↓   Hoy es lunes y acabamos de practicar
  Spanish.   español.

4 Today is (the) first and I've just   óyèsprimero |ₗàkábo |dꟙàlkilárunꟙapartaméntò↓   Hoy es primero y acabo de alquilar un
  rented an apartment.   apartamento.

5 He's just returned from Cuba.   àkába |dèbólberƌekúbá↓   Acaba de volver de Cuba.

6 They've just bought a house.   àkában |dèkómprárunakásá↓   Acaban de comprar una casa.

7 They've just begun.   àkábandempeşár↓   Acaban de empezar.

C àká |tómànmàskafé |kènlòsêstáƌòsꟙúniƌòs↓   Acá toman más café que en los Estados
                                                                                   Unidos.

1 Here they drink more Coca-Cola than   àká |tómànmáskokakola |kenmaƌríƌ↓   Acá toman más Coca-Cola que en Madrid.
  in Madrid.

2 Here there're more stores than in Caracas.   àká |áymástyéndas |keŋkarákàs↓   Acá hay más tiendas que en Caracas.

3 There're more taxis in Washington than   èŋwáshiŋton |áymástáksis |kenrríchmòn↓   En Washington hay más taxis que en
  in Richmond.   Richmond.

VEINTICINCO   16.25

UNIT 16   SPOKEN SPANISH

4 A Cadillac is more expensive than a   úŋkádilak |ézmaskáro |kẹumbwík↓   Un Cadillac es más caro que un Buick.
  Buick.

5 A Buick is less expensive than a   úmbwik |ézmazbaráto |kẹuŋkádilák↓   Un Buick es más barato que un Cadillac.
  Cadillac.

6 A Buick is bigger than a Chevrolet.   úmbwik |ézmazgránde |kẹunchebrolé↓   Un Buick es más grande que un Chevrolet.

7 The Hotel Statler is nicer than the   élótéléstatler |ézmazbonito |kelotél El Hotel Statler es más bonito que el Hotel
  Hotel Bristol.   brístól↓   Bristol.

D é(s)solọumprete(k)sto |pảrárréwnirsẹakombersár↓   Es sólo un pretexto para reunirse a
                                                                conversar.

    1 It's only an excuse to begin to dance. é(s)solọumprete(k)sto |pảrạempéṣarabaylár↓   Es sólo un pretexto para empezar a bailar.

    2 It's only an excuse to be able to go.   é(s)solọumprete(k)sto |pảrápóderír↓   Es sólo un pretexto para poder ir.

    3 It's only an idea to practice more.   é(s)solọunạidea |pảrápráktikarmás↓   Es sólo una idea para practicar más.

    4 It's only an idea to study better.   é(s)solọunạidea |pảrạéstúdyarmehór↓   Es sólo una idea para estudiar mejor.

    5 It's only an idea to do that well.   é(s)solọunạidea |pảráṣeresobyén↓   Es sólo una idea para hacer eso bien.

16.26   VEINTISEIS

SPOKEN SPANISH   UNIT 16

6 It's only an idea to see everything.   e(s) sólọunạidéa |pàràbertódọ↓   Es sólo una idea para ver todo.

7 It's only a joke to tease.   e(s) sólọunabroma |pàrámòlèstar↓   Es sólo una broma para molestar.

E   áṣẹạnyos |késtámúyàbàndonáḋà↓   Hace años que está muy abandonada.

1 She's been married for years.   áṣẹạnyos |kestákasáḋà↓   Hace años que está casada.

2 It's been rented for a year.   áṣẹúnạnyo |kestálkiláḋà↓   Hace un año que está alquilada.

3 They've been together a short time.   áṣẹpókotyémpo |kestạnhúntòs↓   Hace poco tiempo que están juntos.

4 I've been waiting for two days.   áṣèḋoₒdías |kespérò↓   Hace dos días que espero.

5 I've been studying Spanish for two months. áṣèḋozméses |kèstuḋyọespạnyól↓   Hace dos meses que estudio español.

6 I've been living in this section for a long áṣèmuchotyémpo |kébibọenẹstebárryó↓   Hace mucho tiempo que vivo en este
   time.   barrio.

7 I've been buying in that store for twenty   áṣèbeyntẹạnyos |kèkómprọenẹsatyéndà↓   Hace veinte años que compro en esa
   years.   tienda.

VEINTISIETE   16.27

UNIT 16   SPOKEN SPANISH

F   yóęstubęai |ášęunozďíàs↓   Yo estuve ahí hace unos días.

   1 I was here a year ago.   yóęstúbęaki |ášęunáɲyòs↓   Yo estuve aquí hace un año.

   2 I was in Madrid two years ago.   yóęstubenmaďriď |ášęďosáɲyòs↓   Yo estuve en Madrid hace dos años.

   3 I was with my girl friend a month ago. yóęstubekonminobyą |ášęúnmés↓   Yo estuve con mi novia hace un mes.

   4 I was with my friends a short time ago. yóęstube|konmis‚amigos |ašępókò↓   Yo estuve con mis amigos hace poco.

   5 Jose came a long time ago.   hòsebinǫ |ášęmuchotyémpò↓   José vino hace mucho tiempo.

   6 He learned English many years ago. élaprendyoịnglés |ášęmuchosáɲyòs↓   El aprendió inglés hace muchos años.

   7 They told me that a moment ago. mědiheronęsǫ |ášęúnmómentò↓   Me dijeron eso hace un momento.

16.24 Review drill — Masculine demonstrative forms

   1 This present is mine.   éstèrrégalǫezmíô↓   Este regalo es mío.
      These presents are mine.   éstòzrrégalos |sonmíôs↓   Estos regalos son míos.

   2 This book is mine.   éstèlibrǫezmíô↓   Este libro es mío.
      These books are mine.   éstòzlibros |sonmíôs↓   Estos libros son míos.

16.28   VEINTIOCHO

jacobeligoodsons.com For Free Audio

SPOKEN SPANISH   UNIT 16

3 This suit is pretty.   éstétrahezbonító↓   Este traje es bonito.

    These suits are pretty.   éstóstrahes |sombonítós↓   Estos trajes son bonitos.

4 This pencil is green.   éstèlapiş |ezbérđè↓   Este lápiz es verde.

    These pencils are green.   éstózlapişes |sombérđés↓   Estos lápices son verdes.

5 This ashtray is small.   éstèşénişerọ |espekéŋyò↓   Este cenicero es pequeño.

    These ashtrays are small.   éstó(s)şénişeros |sompekéŋyòs↓ Estos ceniceros son pequeños.

6 That trunk is mine.   ésèbàulezmíŏ↓   Ese baúl es mío.

    Those trunks are mine.   ásòɾbàules |sonmíòs↓   Esos baúles son míos.

7 That newspaper is mine.   ésèpèryoɗikọezmíŏ↓   Ese periódico es mío.

    Those newspapers are mine.   ésóspéryoɗikos |sonmíòs↓   Esos periódicos son míos

8 That gentleman is American.   ésèséŋyor |esamerikánó↓   Ese señor es americano.

    Those gentlemen are American. ésò(s)sèŋyores |sonamerikánòs↓ Esos señores son americanos.

9 That hotel is inexpensive.   ésẹótelezbarátó↓   Ese hotel es barato.

    Those hotels are inexpensive. ésósóteles |sombarátòs↓   Esos hoteles son baratos.

10 That's my son.   esezmịíhò↓   Ese es mi hijo.

    Those are my children.   eso(s)sonmisíhòs↓   Esos son mis hijos.

VEINTINUEVE   16.29

UNIT 16   SPOKEN SPANISH

11 That trunk is small.   ésébáulespekéŋyó↓   Ese baúl es pequeño.

    Those trunks are small.   ésózbáules |sompekéŋyòs↓   Esos baúles son pequeños.

16.3   CONVERSATION STIMULUS

                                          NARRATIVE 1

1 Saturday evening at the Harrises.   élsábado |pòrlánoche↑ènlákasadelos El sábado por la noche en la casa de
                                        hárris↓   los Harris.

2 Colonel Harris, Bob, is talking with ė̇córónelhárriz↑ bòb↑ èstáblándokon El coronel Harris, Bob, está hablando
   his wife.   sụespósà↓   con su esposa.

3 He tells Jean that tomorrow they're   eⓃlediҙҙayin |kémáŋyána |banapasҙar | El le dice a Jean que mañana van a pasear
   going out for a ride.   enáwtò↓   en auto.

4 Jean thinks it's a splendid idea.   áyin |lepareҙe |kèsúnҙidegestupéndà↓ A Jean le parece que es una idea estupenda.

5 They don't have a car.   eⓃyoz |notyéneŋkárrò↓   Ellos no tienen carro.

6 But Molina is going to take them in his. pérómólina |báⓃyèbárlos |eṇeldél↓   Pero Molina va a llevarlos en el de él.

7 He wants to take them sightseeing (to elkyéreⓃyebárlos |àkónóҙérlaҙyudád↓ El quiere llevarlos a conocer la ciudad.
   know the city).

16.30   TREINTA

SPOKEN SPANISH																			UNIT 16

8 How kind that friend of Bob's is! Don't you think?

kẹamáblẹ |èșésẹàmígóơèbób↓ nólèspárẹ̀sẹ↑

¡Qué amable es ese amigo de Bob! ¿No les parece?

DIALOG 1

Jean, pregúntele a Bob que qué van a hacer Uds. mañana.

kèbamoșașer |maŋyáná |bób↓

Jean: ¿Qué vamos a hacer mañana, Bob?

Bob, contéstele que van a pasear en auto. Pregúntele que qué le parece la idea.

bámòșàpásẹarenáwtó↓ kèteparẹ̀sẹ |lạ̀iơéá↓

Bob: Vamos a pasear en auto. ¿Qué te parece la idea?

Jean, contéstele que a Ud. le parece estupenda. ¿Pero en cuál auto?, pregúntele. Uds. no tienen, dígale.

ámí |mépárẹ̀șèstúpendá↓ pèrọènkwaláwtó↓ nòsotroz |nótènemòs↓

Jean: A mí me parece estupenda. ¿Pero en cuál auto? Nosotros no tenemos.

Bob, contéstele que en el de Molina. Que él quiere llevarlos a conocer la ciudad.

énẹ́ldèmólìná↓ èlkyérè꜔꜔ɣebárnos | àkònòșerlașyuơáơ↓

Bob: En el de Molina. El quiere llevarnos a conocer la ciudad.

Jean, dígale a Bob que qué amable es ese amigo de él.

kẹamáblẹ |èșésẹàmígótúɣó↓

Jean: ¡Qué amable es ese amigo tuyo!

NARRATIVE 2

1 Sunday morning.

èldòmiŋgoporlamaŋyáná↓

El domingo por la mañana.

2 Bob says they can't go to church today.

bòbơìsẹ |kènópweơenír |ámìșạ |óy↓

Bob dice que no pueden ir a misa hoy.

3 And he has a good excuse this time.

ityénẹ |úmbwèmpreté(k)ștọ |éstàbéș↓

Y tiene un buen pretexto esta vez.

TREINTA Y UNO																			16.31

jacobeligoodsons.com For Free Audio

UNIT 16　　　　　　　　　　　　　　　　　　　　　　　　　　　　　　　　　　SPOKEN SPANISH

4　Molina just called.　　　　　　　mólina |akabaḍe͡ʸyamár↓　　　　　Molina acaba de llamar.

5　He's coming over here right away.　byénèpáràka |ɛnsegíḍà↓　　　　Viene para acá en seguida.

6　Sure, Bob can ask Molina if he can　klaro↑ bob |pwéḍèprègúntarlɛ |àmólina↑　Claro, Bob puede preguntar a Molina
　　take them to church.　　　　　　　sịɛl |pwéḍe͡ʸyèbárlosamísà↓　　　si él puede llevarlos a misa.

7　But he is sure Molina isn't going to　pèrọel |estaségúro |kɛàmòlina |nólebaǥustár↓　Pero él está seguro que a Molina no le
　　like (it).　　　　　　　　　　　　　　　　　　　　　　　　　　　　va a gustar.

8　Because Molina never goes to church.　pórkèmólina |nuŋkabamísá↓　　Porque Molina nunca va a misa.

DIALOG 2

Bob, dígale a Jean que hoy no pueden ir a　oy |nopoḍemos |ịramísá |yín↓　Bob: Hoy no podemos ir a misa, Jean.
　misa.

Jean, pregúntele que cuál es el pretexto　kwales,elpreté(k)stọ |éstèḍómíŋgồ↓　Jean: ¿Cuál es el pretexto este domingo?
　este domingo.

Bob, contéstele que Molina acaba de llamar.　mólina |akabaḍe͡ʸyamár↓ byéneparaká |　Bob: Molina acaba de llamar. Viene para
　Que viene para acá en seguida.　　　　ɛnségíḍà↓　　　　　　　　acá en seguida.

Jean, pregúntele si no le puede preguntar a　nólèpweḍes |preguntarạel |sinóspweḍe　Jean: ¿No le puedes preguntar a él si
　él si los puede llevar.　　　　　　　͡ʸyebar↑　　　　　　　　　nos puede llevar?

Bob, contéstele que está bien. Pero Ud. está　éstabyén↓ pèrọestóységúro |kènóleba　Bob: Está bien. Pero estoy seguro que no
　seguro que no le va a gustar, dígale.　ǥustár↓　　　　　　　　　　le va a gustar.

16.32　　　　　　　　　　　　　　　　　　　　　　　　　　　　　　　　　　TREINTA Y DOS

SPOKEN SPANISH   UNIT 16

Jean, pregúntele que por qué no le va a gustar.   pórké |nolebagustár↓   Jean: ¿Por qué no le va a gustar?

Bob, contéstele que porque Molina nunca va   pórkémólina |nuŋkabamísà↓   Bob: Porque Molina nunca va a misa.
   a misa.

                                        NARRATIVE 3

1 Molina is here. He just arrived.   mòlinaestakí↓ àkabadeˇyegár↓   Molina está aquí. Acaba de llegar.

2 The Harrises are ready.   lósharrisestánlístós↓   Los Harris están listos.

3 But they haven't been (gone) to mass yet.   péró |noanidoamísà |tòdàbíà↓   Pero no han ido a misa todavía.

4 Mr. Molina says he has to go to mass also.   èlséŋyormolina |diṣekel |tyénékęírà   El Sr. Molina dice que él tiene que ir a
                                        misà |tàmbyén↓   misa también.

5 The Colonel doesn't say anything.   èlkòrónel |nodiṣenádà↓   El coronel no dice nada.

6 Jean would like to go to the Cathedral.   yiŋkisyęrąir |àlàkàtèdrál↓   Jean quisiera ir a la Catedral.

7 The Cathedral is an old church, but it's   làkàtèdral |ésùnąiglesya |muybyéhà↓   La Catedral es una iglesia muy vieja,
   very nice.   pèrǫę́ʳmuybonítà↓   pero es muy bonita.

8 The Colonel hasn't seen (doesn't know)   èlkòrónél |nokonoṣę |esąiglésyà↓   El coronel no conoce esa iglesia.
   that church.

9 Because he hasn't been to a church for a   pòrkę́áṣemuchotyémpo |kélnòbá |ąùnąiglésyà↓   Porque hace mucho tiempo que él no va
   long time.   a una iglesia.

TREINTA Y TRES   16.33

UNIT 16   SPOKEN SPANISH

DIALOG 3

José, dígales a los señores 'buenos días'
y pregúnteles si están listos.

bwénózdíàs |sènyórès↓ èstánlistos↑

José: Buenos días, señores. ¿Están
listos?

Jean, contéstele que sí, pero que Uds. no
han ido a misa todavía.

sí↓ pèrónósotroʔ |noémósídoàmisà|
tódàbíà↓

Jean: Sí, pero nosotros no hemos ido
a misa todavía.

José, dígale a Jean que magnífico, que
Ud. también tiene que ir.

mágnifikó↓ yòtámbyén |téŋgókęír↓

José: Magnífico. Yo también tengo
que ir.

Jean, dígale a Bob, que si no ve. Que el
Sr. Molina tiene que ir a misa también.

nóbeʔ |bob↑ èlsènyormolina |tyénèkęír
àmisà |tàmbyén↓

Jean: ¿No ves, Bob? El señor Molina
tiene que ir a misa también.

Bob, no conteste nada.

— — — — — — —

Bob: _____

José, pregúntele a Jean que a cuál
iglesia quieren ir ellos.

àkwaliglésya |kyérenạirustédès↓

José: ¿A cuál iglesia quieren ir ustedes?

Jean, contéstele que dicen que la catedral
es una iglesia muy antigua y muy bonita.
Que Ud. quisiera ir allí.

diçeŋ |kèlàkàtédral |èsúnạiglésya |
muyantigwạ |imuybonítà↓ yókisyérạirạlyí↓

Jean: Dicen que la catedral es una iglesia
muy antigua y muy bonita. Yo
quisiera ir allí.

José, pregúntele al coronel si él conoce
la catedral.

ústédkónoçelakatédral |koronél↑

José: ¿Ud. conoce la catedral, coronel?

Jean, contéstele al Sr. Molina que no, que
hace mucho tiempo que su esposo no va
a una iglesia.

nó |sènyormolínà↓ áşèmúchò |tyémpo |kè
mįésposo |nobạunạiglésyà↓

Jean: No, Sr. Molina. Hace mucho tiempo
que mi esposo no va a una iglesia.

16.34   TREINTA Y CUATRO

jacobeligoodsons.com For Free Audio

SPOKEN SPANISH   UNIT 16

16.4   READINGS

16.40   Introduction and list of cognate loan words.

Probably all of the reading you will do in Spanish for a long time to come will present problems of new vocabulary, since writers will be drawing on the tremendous lexicon of the entire Spanish language and not just on the limited vocabulary of this basic course. The potential proportions of this problem are reduced for an English speaker learning Spanish by the considerable number of cognate loan words which English received from French (a sister language to Spanish) particularly between the 12th and 14th centuries, when French was the language of the ruling class in England.

Some of these cognates are spelled identically in English and Spanish, such as *color, capital*. Others show only minor differences, especially in the endings. These words are usually also similar in meaning, though sometimes they can be deceptive. For example *gracioso* means 'funny', 'cute'; it does not mean 'gracious'.

The similarities are sufficiently numerous, however, that a few generalizations can profitably be made about the differences in form that will help a student recognize cognate loan equivalents in Spanish. For one thing, Spanish words tend to end in a vowel. Many Spanish words resemble English cognate loans except that they have an additional final vowel: *americano, defecto, típico, república, decente, importante,* etc.

Of course, symbols that represent English sounds which are not in the inventory of Spanish sounds will be different: thus the *t* in *norte* corresponds with English *th* in *north*. Often, however, a single symbol will stand for one sound in English and another in Spanish, as does the *x* in *Mexico*, and recognition of certain words is as easy from the spelling as from the sounds.

Recognizing the form class (and hence the function) of a word is often helpful in grasping meanings from context. It is worthwhile remembering that nouns usually appear with articles-if one sees an article, he should look for a following noun to associate it with.

Adjectives also frequently have gender marking endings which are helpful clues as to what items in a stream of words are closely associated. In the following sentence: *La señorita de los Estados Unidos es muy bonita*, the final *a* of *bonita* indicates that the pertinent relationship is with *señorita*, not the nearer *Estados Unidos*. Also the appearance of the modifier *muy* helps identify the following word as an adjective which then has to be related elsewhere in the sentence.

Verbs have their characteristic endings in both languages, but certain sets can be correlated. The *-ada* of *situada* is comparable to the *-ed* of *situated*, and this correlation can be extended to many other verbs. Likewise the *-ando* of *comentando* can be associated with the *-ing* of *commenting*, and this correlation also can be extended to many other verbs. Infinitives in English do not have characteristic endings as they do in Spanish; thus the identification of the semantic relationship of pairs like *discutir* and *discuss* is facilitated by dropping off the *-ir* of the Spanish verb. Such correlations cannot, of course, be analyzed each time one occurs; but the habit of making them is as useful to reading skill as good pronunciation habits are to speaking ability.

Reading involves interpreting a symbolization of speech which is less than complete and less than perfect. Intonation, phrasing, voice quality and so forth are at best only roughly hinted at on the printed page by commas, question marks, periods, italics, and similar devices. Yet these features are often as important to understanding as are the vowels and consonants. With intonational features absent, grammatical relationships are even more important in recreating a meaningful vocal *or* silent reproduction of the phonological elements to assure that they will convey the meanings their author intended.

TREINTA Y CINCO   16.35

jacobeligoodsons.com For Free Audio

UNIT 16   SPOKEN SPANISH

A student is well advised to get used to looking for *word groups*, rather than single words, as the basic building blocks of full sentences. Single words are the spokes, phrases are the wheels, and the utterance is the vehicle. Useful movement of the vehicle is attained only when the wheels turn. The spokes are there and functioning, but not individually or independently; they hold the hub and the rim together so that the wheel as a whole can function as an integral part of the vehicle.

Below is a list of the cognate loan words that have not occurred before their appearance in the reading selection which follows. Be sure that you can identify their meaning, and ask your instructor about any that are not clear to you.

la capital	lá-kápitál↓
la república	lá-rrèpúblikà↓
típico	tipíkò↓
latinoamericanas	làtínọàmèrikanâs↓
el norte	èl-nórtè↓
situada (situar)	sitwàdà↓ sitwár↓
el color	èl-kólór↓
el defecto	èl-dèfektô↓
decente	dèşèntè↓
norteamericano	nórtẹàmérikanò↓

16.36   TREINTA Y SEIS

SPOKEN SPANISH   UNIT 16

16.41   Reading selection

Los Nuevos Vecinos

En las afueras de la ciudad de Las Palmas, capital de la república de Surlandia, hay un barrio nuevo llamado Barrio Bellavista. Es ahí donde vive don Ricardo Fuentes con su esposa y seis hijos, cuatro varones y dos niñas. Es una familia bastante grande, pero eso es típico de las familias latinoamericanas.

En la parte norte del barrio hay un parque y detrás de ese parque, en la esquina de la Calle Diez y la Avenida Colón, está situada la casa de los Fuentes. Es una casa nueva, de dos pisos, color verde, muy bonita, y sólo tiene el defecto de ser un poco pequeña para una familia tan grande como la de ellos. Por esta razón, don Ricardo ha estado pensando alquilar otra un poco más grande, pero hasta la fecha no ha podido encontrar; las dos o tres casas todavía sin alquilar en ese barrio son, o iguales a la de él o más pequeñas. Claro, ellos pueden mudarse a otra parte de la ciudad, pero no quieren porque Bellavista les gusta mucho y están muy contentos; toda la gente que vive ahí es gente buena y muy decente, y el barrio es nuevo, muy limpio, y sobre todo, muy tranquilo.

Una de esas dos o tres casas nuevas que todavía no han sido alquiladas en este barrio está situada en la misma Calle Diez y casi enfrente de donde viven los Fuentes. Es una casa igualita a la de ellos y mucha gente ha venido a verla. A todos les gusta mucho, pero nadie la quiere por la misma razón: la casa no tiene muebles.

Pero, por fin, la agencia ha podido alquilarla esta semana a la familia de un señor norteamericano que acaba de llegar a Surlandia para trabajar en la Embajada de los Estados Unidos. Esta es la familia Robinson, los nuevos vecinos de los Fuentes.

16.42   Response drill [1]

1 ¿Cuál es la capital de Surlandia?

2 ¿En qué parte de Las Palmas está el Barrio Bellavista?

3 ¿Quién vive en ese barrio?

4 ¿Cuántos hijos tienen los Fuentes?

5 ¿Cuántos varones y cuántas niñas?

6 ¿En qué parte del barrio está situada la casa de ellos?

TREINTA Y SIETE   16.37

jacobeligoodsons.com For Free Audio

UNIT 16   SPOKEN SPANISH

7 ¿Cómo es la casa de ellos?

8 ¿Cuál es el defecto que tiene esa casa?

9 ¿Por qué no alquilan otra, entonces?

10 ¿Por qué les gusta este barrio a los Fuentes?

11 ¿Es la casa de enfrente más grande o más pequeña que la de ellos?

12 ¿Por qué no han podido alquilar esa casa hasta ahora?

13 ¿Ha venido mucha o poca gente a verla?

14 ¿Quién la ha tomado por fin esta semana?

15 ¿Qué va a hacer el Sr. Robinson en Surlandia?

---

(1) The response drills which accompany this and subsequent reading selections are intended primarily as written assignments to be completed outside of class hours. Hence responses should be in the form of full utterances, so that scoring each sentence will not require reference to the stating of the question.

16.38   TREINTA Y OCHO

SPOKEN SPANISH

UNIT 17

17.1   BASIC SENTENCES.   Social life in Surlandia.

Molina and Carmen are at the cocktail party which John White has invited them to.

ENGLISH SPELLING

AID TO LISTENING

SPANISH SPELLING

(it) went (to go)

fwé↓ ír↓

fué (ir)

White
And the Harrises. How did they make out?

įàlósharris↑ komolesfwé↓

White
Y a los Harris, ¿cómo les fué?

(I) left (to leave)

déhé↓ déhár↓

dejé (dejar)

Molina
Okay. I left them at their house.

muybyén↓ lòzdèhensukásà↓

Molina
Muy bien. Los dejé en su casa.

(it) seemed (to seem)

pàrèşyó↓ pàrèşér↓

pareció (parecer)

White
How did the city strike Mrs. Harris?

keleparèşyo│laşyudad│àlàsèɲyóráhárris↓

White
¿Qué le pareció la ciudad a la señora
Harris?

(it) pleased (to please)

gùstó↓ gùstár↓

gustó (gustar)

(she) put (to put, place)

pusó↓ pónér↓

puso (poner)

herself (she) got (to get, become)

sè-pusó↓ pónersé↓

se puso (ponerse)

nervous

nèrbyósó↓

nervioso

to get nervous

pónerse-nerbyósó↓

ponerse nervioso

UNO

17.1

UNIT 17   SPOKEN SPANISH

the traffic   èl—trafikó↓   el tráfico

the noise   èl—rrwidó↓   el ruido

Molina   *Molina*
She liked it a lot, but she got nervous with   lègustomúchó↓ pérósépuso |nèrbyosa| Le gustó mucho, pero se puso nerviosa con
  the traffic and the noise.   kònèltrafiko |ỵélrrwidó↓   el tráfico y el ruido.

(it) happened (to happen)   pásó↓ pàsár↓   pasó (pasar)

(I) arrived (to arrive)   ()yège↓ ()yègár↓   llegué (llegar)

passed (to pass)   pàsàdó↓ pàsár↓   pasado (pasar)

last month   èl—mes—pasádó↓   el mes pasado

White   *White*
The same thing happened to me when I   àmi |mépàsólómizmo |kwándó()yège| A mí me pasó lo mismo cuando llegué el
  arrived last month.   ḙlmespasádó↓   mes pasado.

to accustom   àkòstúmbrár↓   acostumbrar

to accustom oneself   àkòstúmbrarsè↓   acostumbrarse

I'm beginning to get used to...   yá—bóy—àkòstúmbrándòmè↓   ya voy acostumbrándome

But now I'm getting used to everything. pèróỵaboy |àkóstúmbrandomḙatódó↓   Pero ya voy acostumbrándome a todo.

even   áún↓   aún

Even to so many parties.   áún |àtàntasfyéstàs↓   Aún a tantas fiestas.

(it) turned out (to result, turn out)   rrèsúlto↓ rrèsúltár↓   resultó (resultar)

17.2

SPOKEN SPANISH   UNIT 17

 fantastic   fàntastikó↓   fàntástico

Carmen   ápropósitó↓ làdélotrodía↑   Carmen
By the way. That one the other day turned out   rrèsúlto|fàntastiká↓no↑   A propósito. La del otro día resultó
 to be quite something, didn't it? (1)   fantástica, ¿no?

 at least   pòr—ló—menós↓   por lo menos

 ourselves (we) entertained (to enjoy)   nòz—dìbèrtimós↓ díbértirsè↓   nos divertimos (divertirse)

Molina   pòrlómenoz|nósotroz|nòzdìbèrtimozmúchò↓   Molina
At least *we* enjoyed ourselves thoroughly.   Por lo menos nosotros nos divertimos
                                                                                            mucho.

 (you) left (to leave)   dèharòn↓ dèhár↓   dejaron (dejar)

 to leave off, to skip, to miss   dèhar—dé↓   dejar de

 not even   ni↓   ni

 the piece (of music)   là—pyeşà↓   la pieza

White   ústedez|nódèháròndèbàylár|nṇunapyéşà↓   White
You all didn't miss dancing a single number.   Ustedes no dejaron de bailar ni una pieza.

 (we) were (to be)   fwimós↓ sér↓   fuimos (ser)

 last   última↓   último

Molina   ifwimoz|lósultimos|enírnós↓   Molina
And we were the last to leave.   Y fuimos los últimos en irnos.

 myself (I) put to bed (to retire)   mę—àkósté↓ àkóstársè↓   me acosté (acostarse)

TRES   17.3

UNIT 17   SPOKEN SPANISH

myself (I) got up (to arise)   mé—lébánté↓ lèbàntàrsè↓   me levanté (levantarse)

the pain   èl—dòlòr↓   el dolor

the head   là—kàbèşà↓   la cabeza

the headache   èl—dòlòr—de—kabéşà↓   el dolor de cabeza

horrible   órrìblè↓   horrible

Carmen   *Carmen*
I went to bed at four and got up at eleven with   yo |mè̞ákòstéa̞láskwàtró↓imélèbánté| Yo me acosté a las cuatro y me levanté
a horrible headache.   a̞lásònşe |kónu̞ndolòr |dèkàbèşa̞ |órrìblè↓   a las once, con un dolor de cabeza
                                                                                      horrible.

less injury, luckily; it could have   ménoz—mál↓   menos mal
 been worse

there was, there were (to have)   àbìà↓ àbèr↓   había (haber)

it was necessary to... (2)   àbìa—ké↓   había que

Molina   *Molina*
Well, at least we didn't have to go to work. (3)   menozmál |kènɡábìa |kètràbàhár↓   Menos mal que no había que trabajar.

(I) began (to begin)   èmpéşé↓ émpéşa̞r↓   empecé (empezar)

Carmen   *Carmen*
I started off the day badly.   yo̞èmpeşemál |èldíà↓   Yo empecé mal el día.

itself (it) fell (to fall)   sè—kàyó↓ káersè↓   se cayó (caerse)

itself to me (it) dropped   sè—mè—kàyó↓   se me cayó

17.4   CUATRO

jacobeligoodsons.com For Free Audio

SPOKEN SPANISH   UNIT 17

the cup   là‑tàṣà↓   la taza

itself (it) broke (to break)   sé‑rròmpyó↓ rròmpérsè↓   se rompió (romperse)

itself to me (it) broke   sé‑mè‑rròmpyó↓   se me rompió

I dropped a cup of coffee and broke the cup. (4)   sémékàyo |ynàtàṣàcekafe |iṣémèrrómpyó↓   Se me cayó una taza de café y se me rompió.

the woman   là‑múhèr↓   la mujer

don't yourself complain (to complain)   nó‑te‑kéhés↓ kèhàrsé↓   no te quejes (quejarse)

(it) was (to be)   fwé↓ sér↓   fué (ser)

Molina   Molina
  Oh, well, don't complain. That was nothing.   bwénó |múhér↓ nótekéhés↓ éso |nófwénàdà↓   Bueno, mujer, no te quejes. Eso no fué nada.

worse   péór↓   peor

(it) made (to make)   iṣó↓ àṣér↓   hizo (hacer)

the damage, hurt   él‑dàɲò↓   el daño

to harm, to be harmful   àṣér‑dáɲò↓   hacer daño

the breakfast   él‑dèsàyunó↓   el desayuno

Things went worse with me. Something I ate for breakfast made me sick.   àmi |mèfwépéór↓ mèiṣódàɲọ |èldèsàyunó↓   A mí me fué peor. Me hizo daño el desayuno.

CINCO   17.5

jacobeligoodsons.com For Free Audio

UNIT 17   SPOKEN SPANISH

17.10   Notes on the basic sentences

(1) The word /fantástiko/ *fantástico*, literally the equivalent of English *fantastic*, is used with a good deal less restraint than is the English word. It will be heard in contexts where it can hardly be translated as meaning anything more than 'interesting', 'nice', 'pleasant', or some other slightly-more-than-lukewarm expression.

(2) /abía—ke/ *había que* is the only past tense form of /áy—ke/ *hay que*. /áy—ke/ and /abía—ke/ are fully idiomatic units whose meanings cannot be analyzed out of the component parts /abér/ and /ke/. They should therefore be learned carefully as unit lexical items, in the meaning of impersonal compulsion: 'it is (was) necessary to...', 'one has (had) to...'

(3) Even though it is not built up as a separate word /ke/ homonymous with other occurrences of /ke/, the student should note that in this sentence the word /ke/ *que* which appears after /ménos—mál/ *menos mal* means 'since' or 'because', not 'that' or 'what' as it has in previous occurrences. That is, literally the sentence means something like 'The fact that you got up with a terrible headache wasn't quite such a catastrophe since it wasn't necessary to go to work'.

(4) It may occur to some observant individual that this particular example is rather loaded with constructions of a type which will subsequently need a bit of explanation and drill. Such needs will be filled in Unit 25, and the student should not worry himself about the apparent absence of parallel this construction shows with others he is familiar with. If a literal translation will help, the utterance says, 'A cup of coffee dropped itself with respect to me and broke itself with respect to me'.

17.2   DRILLS AND GRAMMAR

17.21   Pattern drills

17.21.1   Past I tense forms of regular verbs

A. Presentation of pattern

ILLUSTRATIONS

_____	1	yoͤempeṣé │málͤeldíá↓	Yo *empecé* mal el día.
Did you need many things?	2	néṣésitaste │muchaskósas↑	¿*Necesitaste* muchas cosas?
_____	3	ladͤelotrodía │rrͤesúltófantastíká↓	La del otro día *resultó* fantástica.

17.6   SEIS

jacobeligoodsons.com For Free Audio

SPOKEN SPANISH   UNIT 17

We sent the clothes yesterday.   4   màndámoz larropayér↓   Mandamos la ropa ayer.

_____   5   ústéɗez |noɗeharondebaylár↓   Ustedes no *dejaron* de bailar.

I ate very little.   6   yó |kòmí |muypókò↓   Yo *comí* muy poco.

Where did you eat yesterday?   7   dondekomísteay ér↓   ¿Dónde *comiste* ayer?

_____   8   dondeloaprendyó↓   ¿Dónde lo *aprendió?*

We learned a lot.   9   áprèndimozmúchò↓   *Aprendimos* mucho.

    the student   èl—èstúɗyàntè↓   el estudiante

    the lesson   là—lèkşyón↓   la lección

The students learned the lesson.   1o lòsèstúɗyantes |áprèndyéronlalekşyón↓   Los estudiantes *aprendieron* la lección.

EXTRAPOLATION

| | —ár | —ér | —ír |
	abl—ár	kom—ér	bɪb—ír
1 sg	abl—é	kom—í	bɪb—í
2 fam sg	abl—áste	kom—íste	bɪb—íste
2-3 sg	abl—ó	kom—yó	bɪb—yó
1 pl	abl—ámos	kom—ímos	bɪb—ímos
2-3 pl	abl—áron	kom—yéron	bɪb—yéron

NOTES

a. There are two sets of past tense forms in Spanish; the set here presented is called past I.

b. Past I tense forms of regular verbs have strong-stressed endings.

c. There is no distinction in the sets of endings for /—ér/ or /—ír/ verbs.

c. The 1 pl forms of /—ár/ and /—ír/ verbs are identical in past I and present tenses.

SIETE   17.7

UNIT 17   SPOKEN SPANISH

17.21.11 Substitution drill — Person-number substitution

1 yonokomprenáđà↓
   karmen_____↓   nokompronáđà↓
   lwísaɪantónyo_____↓   nokompraro(n)náđà↓
   ántonyoɪyo_____↓   nokompramoznáđà↓
   ústeđ_____↓   nokompronáđà↓

2 éˇya |ʎyégoanóchè↓
   karmeniyo_____↓   ʎyègamosanóchè↓
   ústeđez_____↓   ʎyègaronanóchè↓

_____

1 *Yo no compré nada.*

   Carmen_____.   No compró nada.
   Luisa y Antonio_____   No compraron nada.
   Antonio y yo_____   No compramos nada.
   Ud._____.   No compró nada.

2 *Ella* llegó anoche.

   Carmen y yo_____.   Llegamos anoche.
   Uds._____.   Llegaron anoche.

17.8   OCHO

SPOKEN SPANISH   UNIT 17

àntónyo_____↓   λyègoạnóchè↓
yó_____↓   λyègeạnóchè↓

3   àntónyọáblokonẹlseɲyór↓
yó_____↓   áblekonẹlseɲyór↓
tú_____↓   áblastekonẹlseɲyór↓
lwísạ_____↓   áblokonẹlseɲyór↓
elìyó_____↓   áblamoskonẹlseɲyór↓

_____

Antonio_____.   Llegó anoche.
Yo_____.   Legué anoche.

3   *Antonio* habló con el señor.

Yo_____.   Hablé con el señor.
Tú_____.   Hablaste con el señor.
Luisa_____.   Habló con el señor.
El y yo_____.   Hablamos con el señor.

NUEVE   17.9

UNIT 17   SPOKEN SPANISH

4 élkomyó |múytárðè↓
   elílwisa_____↓   kómyérón |múytárðè↓
   àntónyǫiyó_____↓   kòmímòz |múytárðè↓
   yo_____ ___↓   kòmí |múytárðè↓
   tu_____↓   kòmístè |múytárðè↓

5 àntónyǫiyó |àpréndímòs̯èspáŋyol |àkí↓
   e^yas_____↓   àpréndyéróṇèspáŋyol |àkí↓
   ùstéð_____↓   àpréndyóęspáŋyol |àkí↓

──

        4 *El* comió muy tarde.

           El y Luisa_____.   Comieron muy tarde.
           Antonio y yo_____.   Comimos muy tarde.
           Yo_____.   Comí muy tarde.
           Tú_____.   Comiste muy tarde.

        5 *Antonio y yo* aprendimos español aquí.

           Ellas_____.   Aprendieron español aquí.
           Ud._____.   Aprendió español aquí.

17.10   DIEZ

SPOKEN SPANISH   UNIT 17

       hwánṭustéḍ_____↓   áprèndyéróné̩spàŋyol|àkí↓

       yó_____↓   áprèndíe̩spàŋyol|àkí↓

6 kármen|ábryólozrregálòs↓

      yo_____↓   ábrílozrregálòs↓

      kármeṇiyó_____↓   ábrimozlozrregálòs↓

      lwís̩a_____↓   ábryolozrregálòs↓

      ústeḍes_____↓   ábryéronlozrregálòs↓

      Juan y Ud._____.   Aprendieron español aquí.

      Yo_____.   Aprendí español aquí.

6 *Carmen* abrió los regalos.

      Yo_____.   Abrí los regalos.

      Carmen y yo_____.   Abrimos los regalos.

      Luisa_____.   Abrió los regalos.

      Uds._____.   Abrieron los regalos.

ONCE

UNIT 17   SPOKEN SPANISH

7 yóbíbíá⌐yi |dósáŋyós↓
   àntónyọílwísa_____↓   bíbyéronai |dósáŋyós↓
   lwísa_____↓   bíbyóậⁿyi |dósáŋyós↓
   lwísạiyó_____↓   bíbímosai |dósáŋyós↓
   éⁿyóz_____↓   bíbyéronai |dósáŋyós↓

_____

7 *Yo viví ahí dos años.*

   Antonio y Luisa_____ .   Vivieron ahí dos años.
   Luisa_____ .   Vivió ahí dos años.
   Luisa y yo_____ .   Vivimos ahí dos años.
   Ellos_____ .   Vivieron ahí dos años.

17.12   DOCE

SPOKEN SPANISH   UNIT 17

Tense substitution

1 álkilaundormitóryò↓   álkiloundormitóryò↓

2 èstudyodosóràs↓   èstúdyedosóràs↓

3 dèhanlakwéntà↓   dèharonlakwéntà↓

4 kòmbèrsamozdemasyádò↓   kòmbèrsamozdemasyádò↓

5 màndòmuchaskósàs↓   màndemuchaskósàs↓

6 kàmbyanloschékès↓   kàmbyaronloschékès↓

7 làbalaskamísàs↓   làbólaskamísàs↓

8 bèbobínò↓   bèbibínò↓

9 àprendèmbastántè↓   àprèndyerombastántè↓

---

1 *Alquila* un dormitorio.   Alquiló un dormitorio.

2 *Estudio* dos horas.   Estudié dos horas.

3 *Dejan* la cuenta.   Dejaron la cuenta.

4 *Conversamos* demasiado.   Conversamos demasiado.

5 *Mando* muchas cosas.   Mandé muchas cosas.

6 *Cambian* los cheques.   Cambiaron los cheques.

7 *Lava* las camisas.   Lavó las camisas.

8 *Bebo* vino.   Bebí vino.

9 *Aprenden* bastante.   Aprendieron bastante.

TRECE

UNIT 17   SPOKEN SPANISH

10   bárrelasálá↓   bàrryolasálá↓

11   kómemos̩enͅunrrestorán↓   kòmimos̩enͅunrrestorán↓

12   metolapátà↓   mètilapátà↓

13   subenͅelas(ş)ensór↓   sùbyoeͅnͅelas(ş)ensór↓

14   biboaí↓   bìḷiaí↓

15   èskribimospókò↓   èskrìbimospókò↓

16   abrenlatintorería↓   àbryéronlatintorería↓

17   àprèndemos̩espaŋyól↓   àprèndimos̩espaŋyól↓

_____

10 *Barre* la sala.   Barrió la sala.

11 *Comemos* en un restorán.   Comimos en un restorán.

12 *Meto* la pata.   Metí la pata.

13 *Sube* en el ascensor.   Subió en el ascensor.

14 *Vivo* ahí.   Viví ahí.

15 *Escribimos* poco.   Escribimos poco.

16 *Abren* la tintorería.   Abrieron la tintorería.

17 *Aprendemos* español.   Aprendimos español.

17.14   CATORCE

SPOKEN SPANISH   UNIT 17

17.21.12 Response drill

            1   ànóche |ùstédèstúdyo↑osalyó↓   ànóchèstúdyé↓

            2   ànóche |éˇyòsèstúdyaron↑osalyérón↓   ànóchèstúdyarón↓

            3   ànóche |élèstúdyo↑osalyó↓   ànóchèstúdyó↓

            4   ànóche |ùstédèsèstúdyaron↑osalyérón↓   ànóchèstúdyamòs↓

[àkí↓]   5   dóndekomyoŷustéd |àyér↓   kómiąkí↓

[ènèlşéntrò↓]   6   dóndekomyéronéˇyòs |àyér↓   kòmyéronenęlşéntrò↓

[énsùkásà↓]   7   dóndekomyoél |àyér↓   kòmyoęnsukásà↓

---

            1 ¿Anoche Ud. estudió o salió?   Anoche estudié.

            2 ¿Anoche ellos estudiaron o salieron?   Anoche estudiaron.

            3 ¿Anoche él estudió o salió?   Anoche estudió.

            4 ¿Anoche Uds. estudiaron o salieron?   Anoche estudiamos.

(aquí)   5 ¿Dónde comió Ud. ayer?   Comí aquí.

(en el centro)   6 ¿Dónde comieron ellos ayer?   Comieron en el centro.

(en su casa)   7 ¿Dónde comió él ayer?   Comió en su casa.

QUINCE

UNIT 17   SPOKEN SPANISH

[ákí↓]   8   dondekomyéronustédès |àyér↓   kómimos.akí↓

[únàmàlétà↓]   9   kekomprástetú |àyér↓   kómprɛynamalétà↓

[rrópà↓]   10 kekompráronustédès |àyér↓   kòmpramozrrópá↓

[únáplumá↓]   11 kekompróél |àyér↓   kómproynaplúmà↓

[rrópà↓]   12 kekompráronéỵós |àyér↓   kómpraronrrópá↓

[únáplumà↓]   13 kòmpróel |unamaleta↑   nó↓ kòmproynaplúmà↓

[pókó↓]   14 èstúdyaronustédez |muchoeldomíŋgo↑   nó↓ èstúdyamospókó↓

_____

(aquí)   8 ¿Dónde comieron Uds. ayer?   Comimos aquí.

(una maleta)   9 ¿Qué compraste tú ayer?   Compré una maleta.

(ropa)   10 ¿Qué compraron Uds. ayer?   Compramos ropa.

(una pluma)   11 ¿Qué compró él ayer?   Compró una pluma.

(ropa)   12 ¿Qué compraron ellos ayer?   Compraron ropa.

(una pluma)   13 ¿Compró él una maleta?   No, compró una pluma.

(poco)   14 ¿Estudiaron Uds. mucho el domingo?   No, estudiamos poco.

17.16   DIECISEIS

SPOKEN SPANISH   UNIT 17

[àkí↓] 15 àlmórȿaronéʎyos |enelȿentrọayer↑   nó↓ àlmórȿaron̩akí↓

        16 sàlistetú |ẹldomiṇgo↑   sí↓ sàlí↓

        17 sàlyeronụstedes |eldomiṇgo↑   sí↓ sàlimòs↓

        18 sàlyeronéʎyos |eldomiṇgo↑   sí↓ sàlyerón↓

        19 sàlyóel |eldomiṇgo↑   sí↓ sàlyó↓

        20 légùstoẹstalekȿyon↑   sí↓ mègústomúchò↓

        21 lèpàrèȿyofaȿil↑   sí↓ mèpárèȿyó |muyfáȿil↓

(aquí)   15 ¿Almorzaron ellos en el centro ayer?   No, almorzaron aquí.

         16 ¿Saliste tú el domingo?   Sí, salí.
         17 ¿Salieron Uds. el domingo?   Sí, salimos.
         18 ¿Salieron ellos el domingo?   Sí, salieron.
         19 ¿Salió él el domingo?   Sí, salió.
         20 ¿Le gustó esta lección?   Sí, me gustó mucho.
         21 ¿Le pareció fácil?   Sí, me pareció muy fácil.

DIECISIETE   17.17

UNIT 17   SPOKEN SPANISH

17.21.13 Translation drill

1 They arrived here a year ago.   éǒyoz |(0)yègárónàkı |àȿȿunáŋyó↓   Ellos llegaron aquí hace un año.

2 I arrived here two weeks ago.   yó |(0)yéȿèȿkí |áȿèdo(s)semánàs↓   Yo llegué aquí hace dos semanas.

3 I rented a comfortable apartment.   àlkilé |ynápàrtàméntokómòdó↓   Alquilé un apartamento cómodo.

4 Carmen helped me a lot.   kármen |mȩáyúdomúchò↓   Carmen me ayudó mucho.

5 On Sunday they took a walk around the èldómíŋgọ†éǒyòspàsȩarom |pórèl   El domingo ellos pasearon por el sector
  business section.   sèktorkomerȿyál↓   comercial.

6 They didn't see the Ministry of Foreign éǒyoz |nobyéron |èlministéryo | Ellos no vieron el Ministerio de Relaciones
  Affairs.   dèrrèláȿyonesȩsteryórès↓   Exteriores.

7 We saw the cathedral.   bímoz |làkàtédrál↓   Vimos la catedral.

8 We found a very large store.   èŋkòntrámos |ùnàtyénda |múygrándè↓   Encontramos una tienda muy grande.

9 I bought a suit.   yó |kómpreyntráhè↓   Yo compré un traje.

10 She bought many things.   éǒya |kómprómuchaskósàs↓   Ella compró muchas cosas.

17.18   DIECIOCHO

SPOKEN SPANISH   UNIT 17

11 We ate across (the street) from the   kòmimos |èmfrèntedelatyéndà↓   Comimos enfrente de la tienda.
    store.

12 Did you go out last night?   sàlyoustéd |anóche↑   ¿Salió Ud. anoche?

13 I didn't go out last night.   yónosalí |anóché↓   Yo no salí anoche.

14 I wrote a lot.   èskribimúchò↓   Escribí mucho.

15 He studied two hours.   él |èstúdyo |dosóràs↓   El estudió dos horas.

B. Discussion of pattern

    Spanish has two sets of endings to express past time. These, referred to as past I and past II, reflect an important difference in the way of thinking about events in the past by Spanish speakers. A more complete discussion of the implications of this difference will be presented in Unit 19. For the present, remember that the past I tense forms drilled in this unit do not equate fully with the verbs in the English translations.

    Past I forms (sometimes called 'preterit' forms) carry the idea of specificity, in time or in extent. For example, past I forms express a single action completed at a given point of time in the past, or an action repeated a specific number of times within a given period of time. There is an inherent unity implied in any action or event which is reported in past I; that is, the action is regarded as a whole happening or incident, with its beginning, course, and ending equally in view.

    The forms of regular past I tense patterns characteristically have strong stress on their endings, a fact which distinguishes all but 1 pl from present tense patterns. In the /–ár/ and /–ír/ theme classes, the 1 pl forms are identical in past I and present tenses, as are the present and past forms of some English verbs like 'cut, put'. The time reference in such verbs must be inferred from the context they appear in. In past I, as in all tenses except present, the /–ár/ and /–ír/ theme classes fall together; that is, they take the same set of endings.

DIECINUEVE   17.19

UNIT 17   SPOKEN SPANISH

17.21.2 Question intonation patterns — Affirmative confirmation questions

    A. Presentation of pattern

ILLUSTRATIONS

Is it bigger?	1 ézmazgrandé↑	1 2 2 2↑ ¿Es más grande?
―――――――	ézmazgrándè |nó↑	1 2 1 1 |22↑ Es más grande,¿no?
Did it turn out unusually well?	2 rrésúltofantástiko↑	1 2 2 2↑ ¿Resultó fantástico?
―――――――	rrésúltofantástikó |nó↑	1 2 1 1 | 22↑ Resultó fantástico, ¿no?
―――――――	3 yátyénekasá↑	2 2 2 2↑ ¿Ya tiene casa?
You already have a house, don't you?	yátyénekásá |nó↑	2 2 1 1 | 22↑ Ya tiene casa, ¿no?

EXTRAPOLATION

Yes-no question	Affirmative confirmation
/1222↑/	22↑ /1211 | nó /

NOTES

    a. When a speaker wants an affirmative confirmation of what he is asking, he follows
                           22↑
    the /1211 \|/ pattern with /nó /.

SPOKEN SPANISH

UNIT 17

17.21.21 Substitution drill — Pattern substitution

1 tràbahamúcho↑   tràbahamúchò |no↑

2 buskakàsa↑   buskakásà |no↑

3 tyenenóbya↑   tyenenóbyà |no↑

4 ablaespaɲyol↑   ablaespaɲyól |no↑

5 kréeso↑   kreésò |no↑

6 byenemaɲyana↑   byenemaɲyánà |no↑

7 barretambyen↑   barretambyén |no↑

---

   1 2   2 2↑   1 2   1 1 | 22↑
1 ¿Trabaja mucho?   Trabaja mucho, ¿no?

   2   2 2↑   2   1 1 | 22↑
2 ¿Busca casa?   Busca casa, ¿no?

   2   2 2↑   2   1 1 | 22↑
3 ¿Tiene novia?   Tiene novia, ¿no?

   2   22 ↑   2   11 | 22 ↑
4 ¿Habla español?   Habla español, ¿no?

   2 2 2 ↑   2 1 1 | 22↑
5 ¿Cree eso?   Cree eso, ¿no?

   2   2 2↑   2   1 1 | 22 ↑
6 ¿Viene mañana?   Viene mañana, ¿no?

   2   22 ↑   2   11 | 22 ↑
7 ¿Barre también?   Barre también, ¿no?

VEINTIUNO

17.21

UNIT 17   SPOKEN SPANISH

8 lábabyén↑   lábabyén |nó↑

9 kyér̦e̦agwa↑   kyér̦e̦águwá |nó↑

10 kyéresópa↑   kyéresópà |nó↑

11 éstálísto↑   èstálístó |nó↑

```
       2    22 ↑                                              2    11 |  22 ↑
8  ¿Lava bien?                                          Lava bien, ¿no?

       2   2 2 ↑                                             2   1  1↑  22 ↑
9  ¿Quiere agua?                                         Quiere agua,  ¿no?

       2    22 ↑                                             2    11 |  22 ↑
10 ¿Quiere sopa?                                         Quiere sopa, ¿no?

      1 2 2 2  ↑                                          1 2 1 1 |  22 ↑
11 ¿Está listo?                                          Está listo, ¿no?
```

B. Discussion of pattern

A question which anticipates an affirmative confirmation in its answer will usually be structured on the pattern /1 2 11 |22↑/, with the last part consisting of
the word /nó²²↑/. This /nó²²↑/ is the equivalent of a number a phrases used in a similar way in English, such as: 'don't you', 'isn't she', 'won't they', 'doesn't it', etc.

17.22   VEINTIDOS

SPOKEN SPANISH   UNIT 17

17.22   Replacement drills

A   ¿àlósharris↓ komolesfwé↓

1   _____ ketal _____↓   ¿àlósharris↓ ketal|lesfwé↓

2   _____ pareşyó↓   ¿àlósharris↓ ketal|lespareşyó↓

3   _____ ke_____↓   ¿àlósharris↓ kelespareşyó↓

4   ¿àtí_____↓   ¿àtí↓ ketepareşyó↓

5   _____ gustó↓   ¿àtí↓ ketegustó↓

6   ¿àéῆyòs_____↓   ¿àéῆyòs↓ kelezgustó↓

7   _____ pasó↓   ¿àéῆyòs↓ kelespasó↓

_____

A   Y a los Harris, ¿cómo les fué?

1   _____ , ¿qué tal ____?   Y a los Harris, ¿qué tal les fué?

2   _____ , ¿ _____ pareció?   Y a los Harris, ¿qué tal les pareció?

3   _____ , ¿qué _____?   Y a los Harris, ¿qué les pareció?

4   Y a ti_____ , ¿ _____?   Y a ti, ¿qué te pareció?

5   _____ , ¿ _____ gustó?   Y a ti, ¿qué te gustó?

6   Y a ellos____ , ¿ _____?   Y a ellos, ¿qué les gustó?

7   _____ , ¿ _____ pasó?   Y a ellos, ¿qué les pasó?

VEINTITRES   17.23

UNIT 17   SPOKEN SPANISH

B   kéleparęęyó |laęyudád |àlàsènyórà↓

1   kétal_____↓   kétal |leparęęyolaęyudád |àlàsènyórà↓

2   _____sènyórès↓   kétal |lesparęęyolaęyudád |àló(s)sènyórès↓

3   _____ésa_____↓   kétal |lesparęęyo |ęsaęyudád |àló(s)sènyórès↓

4   _____edifíęyòs_____↓   kétal |lesparęęyeron |esos,edifíęyós |àló(s)

                                                    sènyórès↓

5   _____ęllyòs↓   kétal |lesparęęyeron |esos,edifíęyòs |ąęllyòs↓

6   _____embahádą_____↓   kétal |lesparęęyo |esąembahádą |àęllyòs↓

7   _____tí↓↓   kétal |teparęęyo |esąembahádą |àtí↓

_____

B   ¿Qué le pareció la ciudad a la señora?

1   ¿Qué tal_____?   ¿Qué tal le pareció la ciudad a la señora?

2   ¿_____señores?   ¿Qué tal les pareció la ciudad a los señores?

3   ¿_____esa_____?   ¿Qué tal les pareció esa ciudad a los señores?

4   ¿_____edificios_____?   ¿Qué tal les parecieron esos edificios a los señores?

5   ¿_____ellos?   ¿Qué tal les parecieron esos edificios a ellos?

6   ¿_____embajada_____?   ¿Qué tal les pareció esa embajada a ellos?

7   ¿_____ti?   ¿Qué tal te pareció esa embajada a ti?

17.24   VEINTICUATRO

SPOKEN SPANISH   UNIT 17

C   àmı |mèpásólomízmó↓

1   ạel_____↓   ạel |lèpásólomízmó↓

2   _____nòs_____↓   ànósotroz |nòspásólomízmó↓

3   _____pàrèşyo___↓   ànósotroz |nòspàrèşyolomízmó↓

4   àtı_____↓   àtı |tèpàrèşyolomízmó↓

5   _____dìheron___↓   àtı |tèdìheronlomízmó↓

6   àhwàn_____↓   àhwàn |lèdìheronlomízmó↓

7   _____prègùntaron_____↓   àhwàn |lèprègùntaronlomízmó↓

_____

C   A mí me pasó lo mismo.

1   A él_____.   A él le pasó lo mismo.

2   _____nos_____.   A nosotros nos pasó lo mismo.

3   _____pareció___.   A nosotros nos pareció lo mismo.

4   A ti_____.   A ti te pareció lo mismo.

5   _____dijeron___.   A ti te dijeron lo mismo.

6   A Juan_____.   A Juan le dijeron lo mismo.

7   _____preguntaron___.   A Juan le preguntaron lo mismo.

VEINTICINCO   17.25

UNIT 17   SPOKEN SPANISH

D   làdèlótròdia |rrèsùltófàntastìkà↓   làdèlótròdia |sàlyófàntastìkà↓

1   _____ sàlyó_____ ↓   èldèlótròdia |sàlyófàntastìkò↓

2   èl_____   èldèànoche |sàlyófàntastìkò↓

3   _____ ànoche_____ ↓   èldèànoche |sàlyóbyén↓

4   _____ byén↓   èldèàyer |sàlyóbyén↓

5   _____ àyer_____   lòzdèàyer |Ⓜyègárómbyén↓

6   _____ Ⓜyègáróm_____ ↓   làzdèàyer |Ⓜyègárònmalàs↓

7   _____ malàs↓

D   La del otro día resultó fantástica.   La del otro día salió fantástica.

1   _____ salió_____ .   El del otro día salió fantástico.

2   El_____   El de anoche salió fantástico.

3   _____ anoche_____ .   El de anoche salió bien.

4   _____ bien .   El de ayer salió bien.

5   _____ ayer_____   Los de ayer llegaron bien.

6   _____ llegaron_____ .   Las de ayer llegaron malas.

7   _____ malas .

17.26   VEINTISEIS

jacobeligoodsons.com For Free Audio

SPOKEN SPANISH   UNIT 17

E   yo̧ȩmpeȩ |maleldía↓

1   nòsótros————————↓   nòsótros |èmpèȩamoz |maleldía↓

2   ————————áṇyò↓   nòsótros |èmpèȩamoz |maleláṇyò↓

3   ————————byén————↓   nòsótros |èmpèsámoz |byénɛláṇyò↓

4   ——åkàbåmoz————↓   nòsótros |åkåbåmoz |byénɛláṇyò↓

5   eͫyos————————↓   eͫyos |åkåbårom |byénɛláṇyò↓

6   ————————————més↓   eͫyos |åkåbårom |byénɛlmés↓

7   ——påsó————————↓   el |pasó |byénɛlmés↓

_____

E   Yo empecé mal el día.

1 Nosotros————————.   Nosotros empezamos mal el día.

2 ————————año.   Nosotros empezamos mal el año.

3 ————————bien——.   Nosotros empezamos bien el año.

4 ——acabamos————.   Nosotros acabamos bien el año.

5 Ellos————————.   Ellos acabaron bien el año.

6 ————————mes.   Ellos acabaron bien el mes.

7 ——pasó————————.   El pasó bien el mes.

VEINTISIETE   17.27

UNIT 17   SPOKEN SPANISH

F   àmí |mefwepeór↓

1   àtí _____ ↓   àtí |tefwepeór↓

2   _____ mehór↓   àtí |tefwemehór↓

3   _____ nos _____ ↓   ànòsótroz |nosfwémehór↓

4   _____ salyo _____ ↓   ànòsótroz |no(s)salyomehór↓

5   àùstèḍez _____ ↓   àùstèḍez |le(s)salyomehór↓

6   _____ fantástikó↓   àùstèḍez |le(s)salyofantástikó↓

7   _____ rresultarom _____ ↓   àùstèḍez |lezrresultaromfantástikós↓

F   A mí me fué peor.

1   A ti _____ .   A ti te fué peor.

2   _____ mejor.   A ti te fué mejor.

3   _____ nos _____ .   A nosotros nos fué mejor.

4   _____ salió ____.   A nosotros nos salió mejor.

5   A Uds. _____ .   A Uds. les salió mejor.

6   _____ fantástico.   A Uds. les salió fantástico.

7   _____ resultaron _____ .   A Uds. les resultaron fantásticos.

SPOKEN SPANISH   UNIT 17

17.23   Variation drills

A   lózdéhénsukásà↓   Los dejé en su casa.

1 I left them at their apartment.   lózdéhe |ensyapartaméntò↓   Los dejé en su apartamento.

2 I found them on the street.   lòsénkòntré |enlakáłyè↓   Los encontré en la calle.

3 I waited for them in the living-room. lòséspèré |enlasálà↓   Los esperé en la sala.

4 I took them to the airport.   lòzⁿyèbe |alaeropwértò↓   Los llevé al aeropuerto.

5 I looked for them (f) in the restaurant. làzbùské |enelrrestorán↓   Las busqué en el restorán.

6 I found them (f) in the bathroom.   làsénkòntré |enélkwartòdebáŋyò↓   Las encontré en el cuarto de baño.

7 I washed them (f) this afternoon.   làɤlàbestatárdè↓   Las lavé esta tarde.

B   sèpúsònèrbyósa |kónéltrafiko |ɤèlrrwidò↓   Se puso nerviosa con el tráfico y el ruido.

1 She got nervous with the party and the people.   sèpúsònèrbyósa |kònlàfyestạ |ilàhéntè↓   Se puso nerviosa con la fiesta y la gente.

2 She got nervous with so many people.   sèpúsònèrbyósa |kòntántahéntè↓   Se puso nerviosa con tanta gente.

VEINTINUEVE   17.29

UNIT 17   SPOKEN SPANISH

3 He got nervous with all that.   sèpúsónérbyóso |kòntoỏgésỏ↓   Se puso nervioso con todo eso.

4 She was very gay with the drinks.   sèpúsókóntenta |kònlòstragòs↓   Se puso contenta con los tragos.

5 She was very pleased with the car.   sèpúsókóntenta |kònélawtỏ↓   Se puso contenta con el auto.

6 He was very happy with the house.   sèpúsókóntento |kónlàkásà↓   Se puso contento con la casa.

7 He was very happy with the glasses.   sèpúsókóntento |kónlàzgafàs↓   Se puso contento con las gafas.

C   pòrlòménòz↑nòsótroz |nózdibértimozmúchó↓   Por lo menos nosotros nos divertimos mucho.

1 At least we dressed right away.   pòrlòménoz↑nósótroz |nózbèstimos,ensegídà↓   Por lo menos nosotros nos vestimos en
                                                                                    seguida.

2 At least we got together yesterday.   pòrlòménoz↑nósótroz |nózrrèwnimos,ayér↓   Por lo menos nosotros nos reunimos ayer.

3 At least we took a bath last night.   pòrlòménoz↑nósótroz |nózbànyamos,anóchè↓   Por lo menos nosotros nos bañamos anoche.

4 At least we shaved this morning.   pòrlòménoz↑nósótroz |nósáfèytamós |éstà   Por lo menos nosotros nos afeitamos esta
                                          màŋyánà↓   mañana.

5 Luckily we got used to it soon.   mènozmál |kènósótroz |nós,àkòstúmbramospróntò↓   Menos mal que nosotros nos acostumbramos
                                                                                    pronto.

6 Luckily we didn't complain.   mènozmál |kènósótroz |nónoskehámós↓   Menos mal que nosotros no nos quejamos.

17.30   TREINTA

SPOKEN SPANISH   UNIT 17

7 Luckily we didn't move.   ménozmál |kènòsótroz |nónozmuɗámós↓   Menos mal que nosotros no nos mudamos.

D   ùsteɗez |nóɗèháróndèbàylár |nɪ̧unàpyéṣà↓   Ustedes no dejaron de bailar ni una pieza.

1 You (pl) didn't miss practicing a single day.   ùsteɗez |nóɗèháróndèpràktikár |nɪ̧undíà↓   Ustedes no dejaron de practicar ni un día.

2 They (f) didn't stop talking a single minute   éⱡⱨaz |nóɗèháróndèkómbèrsar |nɪ̧unmoméntò↓   Ellas no dejaron de conversar ni un momento.

3 Joseph and Manuel didn't miss going out   hòséⱨmanwèl |nóɗèháróndèsàlir |nɪ̧unanóchè↓   José y Manuel no dejaron de salir ni una
  a single night.   noche.

4 The girl never missed straightening up the   làmúchacha |nuŋkaɗeho |ɗⱨarreglarelkwártó↓   La muchacha nunca dejó de arreglar el
  room.   cuarto.

5 My wife and I never missed going out on   mⱨèspósaⱨyò |nuŋkaɗehamoz |ɗèsàlírloz   Mi esposa y yo nunca dejamos de salir los
  Sundays.   ɗomíngòs↓   domingos.

6 My friend Joseph never stopped drinking.   mⱨàmígòhóse |nuŋkaɗehoɗetomár↓   Mi amigo José nunca dejó de tomar.

7 We never stopped buying there.   nòsótroz |nuŋkaɗehamoz |ɗèkómprarái↓   Nosotros nunca dejamos de comprar ahí.

E   fwímoz |lósu̧ltimosenírnòs↓   Fuimos los últimos en irnos.

1 We were the last to get dressed.   fwímoz |lósu̧ltimos |embestírnòs↓   Fuimos los últimos en vestirnos.

TREINTA Y UNO   17.31

UNIT 17   SPOKEN SPANISH

2 We were the last to complain.   fwímoz |lós̬ṵltimos |eɲkehárnós↓   Fuimos los últimos en quejarnos.

3 We were the last to sit down.   fwímoz |lós̬ṵltimos |ensentárnós↓   Fuimos los últimos en sentarnos.

4 Joseph was the last one to get sea sick. hóse |fwélúltimo |enmare̯árse̩↓   José fué el último en marearse.

5 Betty was the last one to bathe.   béti |fwélạultimạ |embaɲyárse̩↓   Betty fué la última en bañarse.

6 He was the first one to notice (it).   él |fwélprimero̩ |emfihárse̩↓   El fué el primero en fijarse.

7 She was the first one to get used to (it). eɲ̣ya |fwélápriṃerạ |enạkostumbrárse̩↓   Ella fué la primera en acostumbrarse.

F menozmál |keṇɡabía |ketrạbạhár↓   Menos mal que no había que trabajar.

1 Luckily we didn't have to (it wasn't   menozmál |keṇɡabía |kestuḍyár↓   Menos mal que no había que estudiar.
  necessary to) study.

2 Luckily we didn't have to (it wasn't   menozmál |keṇɡabía |kebaylár↓   Menos mal que no había que bailar.
  necessary to) dance.

3 Luckily we didn't have to (it wasn't   menozmál |keṇɡabía |kesperár↓   Menos mal que no había que esperar.
  necessary to) wait.

4 Luckily we didn't have to (it wasn't   menozmál |keṇɡabía |kelabár↓   Menos mal que no había que lavar.
  necessary to) wash.

5 At least we didn't have to (it wasn't   pòrlómenoz |ṇɡabía |kebarrér↓   Por lo menos no había que barrer.
  necessary to) sweep.

17.32   TREINTA Y DOS

SPOKEN SPANISH   UNIT 17

6 At least we didn't have to (it wasn't   pòrlòmenoz |nọabía |kẹablár↓   Por lo menos no había que hablar.
   necessary to) talk.

7 At least we didn't have to (it wasn't   pòrlòmenoz |nọabía |kesalír↓   Por lo menos no había que salir.
   necessary to) leave.

17.24   Review drill -- Possessive phrases with /kyén/

1 Whose is this?   dèkyénẹsẹéstó↓   ¿De quién es esto?

2 Whose is that?   dèkyénẹsẹésó↓   ¿De quién es eso?

3 Whose ashtray is that?   dèkyén |esẹesẹẹeniṣéró↓   ¿De quién es ese cenicero?

4 Whose key is that?   dèkyén |esesaĉyábé↓   ¿De quién es esa llave?

5 Whose book is that?   dèkyén |esẹeselíbró↓   ¿De quién es ese libro?

6 Whose suitcase is that?   dèkyén |esẹesamalétà↓   ¿De quién es esa maleta?

7 Whose sheet is that?   dèkyén |esẹesasábànà↓   ¿De quién es esa sábana?

8 Whose photo is that?   dèkyén |esẹesafótò↓   ¿De quién es esa foto?

9 Whose trunk is that?   dèkyén |esẹesebaúl↓   ¿De quién es ese baúl?

10 Whose dollar is that?   dèkyén |esẹesedólàr↓   ¿De quién es ese dólar?

11 Whose table is that?   dèkyén |esẹesamésà↓   ¿De quién es esa mesa?

TREINTA Y TRES   17.33

jacobeligoodsons.com For Free Audio

UNIT 17   SPOKEN SPANISH

17.3   CONVERSATION STIMULUS   *NARRATIVE 1*

1   Juan liked the party last night.   àhwán |légùstólafyéstạ |ànóchè↓   A Juan le gustó la fiesta anoche.

2   He thought it was terrific.   lèpárèşyo |fántàstikà↓   Le pareció fantástica.

3   They throw these parties very often here. àkidan |esàsfyestaz |muyamenúdó↓   Aquí dan esas fiestas muy a menudo.

4   You've got to go to at least three parties áykẹir |pòrlómènos |àtresfyestas |porsemánà↓   Hay que ir por lo menos a tres fiestas por
    a week.   semana.

5   But Juan says he can't go to that many.   péròhwàndişẹ |kélnòpweḍẹir |atántàs↓   Pero Juan dice que él no puede ir a tantas.
    It'll make him sick.   lẹaşẹdáņyò↓   Le hace daño.

6   Jose thought the same thing when he   lómizmopensohosé |kwándọèmpèşọạtrabahar | Lo mismo pensó José cuando empezó a
    started to work in the Embassy.   enlạembaháḍà↓   trabajar en la Embajada.

7   But he's used to it now.   pérọáorạ |estákostumbráḍò↓   Pero ahora está acostumbrado.

8   And he likes it a lot.   ilègustà |muchò↓   Y le gusta mucho.

17.34   TREINTA Y CUATRO

jacobeligoodsons.com For Free Audio

SPOKEN SPANISH   UNIT 17

DIALOG 1

José, pregúntele a Juan si le gustó la
fiesta anoche.

tègùstólafyestạ |anóche |hwán↑

José: ¿Te gustó la fiesta anoche, Juan?

Juan, contéstele que le pareció fantástica.
Pregúntele si dan esas fiestas aquí a
menudo.

mèpàrèẹyó |fántastikȧ↓ dán |ésasfyestas
aki |ạmenudȯ↑

Juan: Me pareció fantástica. ¿Dan esas
fiestas aquí a menudo?

José, dígale que claro. Que aquí hay que
ir por lo menos a tres fiestas por semana.

klaró↓ ȧki |aykẹir |pórlòmenos |ȧtrés
fyestạs |porsemánȧ↓

José: Claro. Aquí hay que ir por lo menos
a tres fiestas por semana.

Juan, dígale que Ud. no puede ir a tantas.
Que le hace daño.

yónópwềṛọ |írȧtantás↓ mẹȧṣẹdạŋyó↓

Juan: Yo no puedo ir a tantas. Me hace
daño.

José, dígale que lo mismo pensó Ud. cuando
empezó a trabajar en la Embajada.

lòmızmopenseyó |kwándọẹmpèṣẹạtrabahár |
enlạembạhádȧ↓

José: Lo mismo pensé yo cuando empecé a
trabajar en la Embajada.

Juan, pregúntele si ahora ya está acostumbrado.

ịȧorȧ↓ yạẹstás |akostumbradọ↑

Juan: Y ahora, ¿ya estás acostumbrado?

José, contéstele que sí, claro, y que le
gusta mucho.

sí |klȧró↓ ìmégustạ |múchȯ↓

José: Sí, claro, y me gusta mucho.

NARRATIVE 2

1 By the way, Juan did all right with his
girl.

àprópósitó↓ àhwán↑lềfwé |múybyeŋ |
konsuchíkȧ↓

A propósito, a Juan le fué muy bien con su
chica.

2 They didn't miss a single dance.

ẹ̃́yoz↑nòdèharon |dèbáylár |nịunapyéṣȧ↓

Ellos no dejaron de bailar ni una pieza.

TREINTA Y CINCO   17.35

jacobeligoodsons.com For Free Audio

UNIT 17   SPOKEN SPANISH

3 And they got home all right after the
  party.

ìⁿyèɡárómbyén |àlàkàsa |ɗespwéʐɗela

fyéstà↓

Y llegaron bien a la casa después de
la fiesta.

4 Jose and Carmen left the party
  before ten.

hóseɪkármen |sàlyérondelafyestạ |

àntezɗelazɑɣéʂ↓

José y Carmen salieron de la fiesta
antes de las diez.

5 They didn't wait for Juan and his girl.

nǫesperarón |àhwanɪasuchíkà↓

No esperaron a Juan y a su chica.

6 Because Carmen began to feel a horrible
  headache.

pórkèkármen |èmpèʂoạsentir |ùndólorɗe

kabeʂạ |órriblè↓

Porque Carmen empezó a sentir un dolor
de cabeza horrible.

7 Something she ate made her sick.

algokekomyo |lɛɪʂoɗáɲyó↓

Algo que comió le hizo daño.

DIALOG 2

José, dígale que a propósito, que cómo le
fué con la chica de él, pregúntele.

àpróposìtò↓ komotefwé |kontuchíkà↓

José: A propósito, ¿cómo te fué con tu
chica?

Juan, contéstele que muy bien, que no dejaron
de bailar ni una pieza.

múybyén↓ noɗehamoʐ |ɗébáylár |nɪunapyéʂạ↓

Juan: Muy bien, no dejamos de bailar ni
una pieza.

José, pregúntele si llegaron bien a la casa
después de la fiesta.

ⁿyéɡarombyén |alakasa |ɗespwéʐɗelafyesta↑

José: ¿Llegaron bien a la casa después
de la fiesta?

Juan, dígale que sí, pero por qué no los
esperaron a Uds., pregúntele.

sí↓ pero |pòrké |nonos.esperáròn↓

Juan: Sí, pero ¿por qué no nos esperaron?

17.36   TREINTA Y SEIS

SPOKEN SPANISH   UNIT 17

José, dígale que Uds. salieron de la   nòsotros |sàlimoz |delafyèsta | José: Nosotros salimos de la fiesta
fiesta antes de las diez.   antezdelazdyéş↓   antes de las diez.

Juan, pregúntele que por qué, que qué   pòrké↓ képasó↓   Juan: ¿Por qué?, ¿qué pasó?
pasò.

José, contéstele que Carmen empezó a sentir   kármen |èmpèşòasentir |ùndólor |dèkàbèşa   José: Carmen empezó a sentir un dolor de
un dolor de cabeza horrible. Que algo que   orríblè↓ algokekomyo |lèışodáŋyò↓   cabeza horrible. Algo que comió
comió le hizo daño.   le hizo daño.

NARRATIVE 3

1 Juan is very sorry about what happened   hwan |syéntèmuchò |lókélèpàsó |akármèn↓   Juan siente mucho lo que le pasó a Carmen.
   to Carmen.

2 Jose took her home right away.   hósé |láⁿyèboalakasa |ènsègìdà↓   José la llevó a la casa en seguida.

3 He took her in a taxi.   láⁿyèboenuntáksi↓   La llevó en un taxi.

4 He returned to the party afterwards to   dèspwéz |bolbyoalafyésta |pàràbisarlè   Después, volvió a la fiesta para avisarle
   let Juan know about it.   ahwán↓   a Juan.

5 He looked for him, but didn't find him.   lòbúsko |pèrónoloeŋkontró↓   Lo buscó, pero no lo encontró.

6 There were so many people there.   àbia |tantahéntè |àⁿyí↓   Había tanta gente allí.

TREINTA Y SIETE   17.37

jacobeligoodsons.com For Free Audio

UNIT 17   SPOKEN SPANISH

DIALOG 3

Juan, dígale que lo siente mucho. Pregún-   lòsyéntomuchó↓ láῆyèbàstҫ|àlàkàsҫ| Juan: Lo siento mucho. ¿La llevaste
tele si la llevó a la casa en seguida.   ènsègìdàↈ   a la casa en seguida?

José, contéstele que sí, que la llevó en un   sì↓ láῆyèbènùntáksì↓   José: Sí, la llevé en un taxi.
taxi.

Juan, pregúntele que por qué no le avisó   pòrkènomҫabìsáste↓   Juan: ¿Por qué no me avisaste?
a Ud.

José, dígale que Ud. volvió a la fiesta des-   yòbòlbí|ҫlàfyèstà|dèspwéstìtè   José: Yo volví a la fiesta despúes y te
pués y lo buscó, pero no lo encontró. Que   bùské↓ pèrónotèŋkòntré↓ àbíà|tántàhéntè↓   busqué, pero no te encontré.
había tanta gente.   Había tanta gente.

Juan, dígale que tiene razón, que había   tyènezrràҫón↓ àbìa|múchìsìmà↓   Juan: Tienes razón. Había muchísima.
muchísima.

17.4   READINGS

17.40   List of cognate loan words

          comentando (comentar)   kòméntàndó↓ kòméntár↓

       la   persona   là—pérsònà↓

             puntual   púntwál↓

             exactamente   ésàktàménté↓

17.38   TREINTA Y OCHO

jacobeligoodsons.com For Free Audio

SPOKEN SPANISH   UNIT 17

el minuto   èl-minútó↓

importante   impórtantè↓

interrumpió (interrumpir)   intèrrúmpyó↓ intèrrúmpír↓

discutir   diskútír↓

insignificantes   insignifikàntès↓

el tono   èl-tonó↓

el sarcasmo   èl-sàrkazmò↓

el teléfono   èl-tèlefónó↓

exclamó (exclamar)   èsklámó↓ èsklàmár↓

delicioso   dèlişyosó↓

17.41   Reading selection

Comentando

       Es la una de la tarde y don Ricardo, que siempre va a su casa a almorzar, acaba de llegar en su carro. El es una persona muy puntual y siempre llega exactamente a esa hora, ni un minuto antes ni un minuto después. Al bajarse del carro, ve a varios hombres que están metiendo mesas, sillas, camas, sofás, etc., a la casa de enfrente.

       —Veo que por fin han podido alquilar esa casa —le dice a Marta, su esposa, que al oír llegar el carro ha salido a encontrarlo. —¿Sabes quiénes son los nuevos vecinos?

       —Creo que es una familia americana —contesta ella. —Dicen que son unos señores Robinson. Parece que este señor viene a trabajar con la Embajada de los Estados Unidos y que es una persona muy importante.

       —¿Cómo sabes tú? ¿Has hablado con ellos?

       —No, pero me lo dijeron las señoritas Martínez, ésas que viven a la vuelta.

TREINTA Y NUEVE   17.39

UNIT 17   SPOKEN SPANISH

—Esas viejas siempre lo saben todo.

—Ay, Ricardo, no digas 'esas viejas', es muy feo decirles así.

—'Señoras', entonces; son demasiado viejas para poder pensar yo en ellas como 'las señoritas Martínez'.

—Pero Ricardo—interrumpió Marta—señoras son las mujeres casadas, ellas son solteras. Por favor, tú no debes....

—Bueno, bueno, no vamos a discutir por cosas tan insignificantes. En fin, ¿qué más te dijeron las 'señoritas' Martínez?—preguntó Ricardo con cierto tono de
    sarcasmo.

—Eso fué todo, sólo que hablé un momento con ellas por teléfono porque estaba muy ocupada cuando me llamaron. Bueno, vamos a sentarnos —exclamó Marta
    hablando de otra cosa—¿tienes mucha hambre?

—Tengo una hambre horrible, ¿qué hay de comer?

—Lo que más te gusta a ti, chuletas de puerco. Y de postre te tengo un pastel de manzana delicioso.

17.42   Response drill

    1 ¿Don Ricardo va siempre, o sólo de vez en cuando a almorzar a su casa?

    2   ¿A qué hora llega a almorzar?

    3 ¿Por qué llega siempre exactamente a esa hora?

    4 ¿Qué están haciendo unos hombres en la casa de enfrente?

    5 ¿Quiénes son los nuevos vecinos de los Fuentes?

    6 ¿Cómo sabe Marta quiénes son?

    7 ¿Dónde viven las señoritas Martínez?

    8 ¿Por qué no le gusta al señor Fuentes llamarlas 'señoritas'?

    9 ¿Son ellas casadas o solteras?

    10 ¿Qué más le dijeron las Martínez a Marta de los nuevos vecinos?

    11 ¿Cuánto tiempo habló Marta con ellas por teléfono?

    12 ¿Por qué habló sólo un momento?

    13 ¿Qué le preguntó Marta a su esposo entonces para hablar de otra cosa?

    14 ¿Qué tenían de comer ese día?

    15 ¿Y de postre?

17.40   CUARENTA

jacobeligoodsons.com For Free Audio

SPOKEN SPANISH

UNIT 18

18.1   BASIC SENTENCES.   Discussing Carmen's work.

Jose Molina, Carmen del Valle y John White continue talking in White's apartment.

ENGLISH SPELLING	AID TO LISTENING	SPANISH SPELLING
the company	là⁀kòmpàɲyìà↓	la compañía
White		*White*
What company do you work for, Carmen? [1]	éŋkèkompàɲyìà ǀtràáhàùstéd ǀkármèn↓	¿En qué compañía trabaja usted, Carmen?
the airline	là⁀àèrólìnèà↓	la aerolínea
national	nàsyònál↓	nacional
Carmen		*Carmen*
For National Airlines.	ènàèrólìneaz ǀnàsyònálès↓	En Aerolíneas Nacionales.
White		*White*
For quite a while? [2]	dèzrgàsè ǀmùchotyémpò↑	¿Desde hace mucho tiempo?
(I) worked, was working (to work)	tràbàhàbà↓ tràbàhár↓	trabajaba (trabajar)
the office	là⁀ófìsìná↓	la oficina
(they) paid, were paying (to pay)	págàbàn↓ pàsár↓	pagaban (pagar)
Carmen		*Carmen*
No. I used to work in an office, but they didn't pay me enough.	nó↓ ántes ǀtràbàhàbàenùnàofìsìná↓ péró ǀnomepagàbam ǀbastántè↓	No, antes trabajaba en una oficina, pero no me pagaban bastante.
(it) suited, was suiting (to suit, to be advantageous)	kòmbènìà↓ kòmbènír↓	convenía (convenir)

UNO

18.1

jacobeligoodsons.com For Free Audio

UNIT 18   SPOKEN SPANISH

(you) did (to do)   iṣiste↓ àṣer↓   hiciste (hacer)

Molina   Molina
If it didn't suit you, you did well to leave it.   si⌐ótèkómbènia↑iṣiste̱byenen |dehárló↓   Si no te convenía, hiciste bien en dejarlo.

to be difficult   kóstár↓   costar

Carmen   Carmen
It was hard for me to do.   mèkósto |bàstánte↓   Me costó bastante.

the boss, chief, manager   èl—héfè↓   el jefe

(he) was, was being (to be)   érà↓ sér↓   era (ser)

the person   là—pèrsonà↓   la persona

(I) saw, was seeing (to see)   bèìà↓ bér↓   veía (ver)

to tell him it   dèṣirséló↓   decírselo

The boss was a very nice guy, and I couldn't   èlhéférà |muybwénapersóna̱ |inobeia | El jefe era muy buena persona y no veía
see a way to tell him about it. (3)   komodeṣírsèló↓   cómo decírselo.

Molina   Molina
Another matter... (4)   áblando |dȩotrakósá↓   Hablando de otra cosa.

to invite   imbitár↓   invitar

to visit   bísitár↓   visitar

the mission   là—misyón↓   la misión

the Air Force   là—fwérṣa̱—aérȩà↓   la Fuerza Aérea

18.2   DOS

jacobeligoodsons.com For Free Audio

SPOKEN SPANISH   UNIT 18

Harris invited us to visit the Air Mission.   hárriz |nòsimbitó |ạbisitár |lâmisyón | Harris nos invitó a visitar la Misión de la
                                                     dèlâfwerṣạérẹà↓   Fuerza Aérea.

        (it) would please (to please)   gústàrià↓ gústár↓   gustaría (gustar)

White   *White*
I'd like to go.   ámɪ |mêgústárɪạír↓   A mí me gustaría ir.

        (he) said (to say)   dihò↓ dèṣɪ́r↓   dijo (decir)

        (we) could, were able (to be able)   pódɪàmòs↓ pòḋér↓   podíamos (poder)

        that comes, next   kè‑ɩ̯yenè↓   que viene

Molina   *Molina*
He said we could come this Saturday or next. **(5)** diho |kèpóḋɪamosɪr |estesábaḋo | Dijo que podíamos ir este sábado o el que
                                                     ọelkebyénè↓   viene.

Carmen   *Carmen*
I'm not going to be able to go this   yo |nobóy |àpóḋér |estesábàḋò↓   Yo no voy a poder este sábado.
Saturday.

        the purchase   là‑komprà↓   la compra

        to go (of) shopping   ɪr‑dé‑kómprás↓   ir de compras

I have to go shopping with Mrs. Harris.   teṇgokẹɪr |ḋèkompras |kònlàsèṇyorahárris↓   Tengo que ir de compras con la señora
                                                                                                          Harris.

        the next **(6)**   èl‑ótró↓   el otro

White   *White*
We can leave it for the next one, then.   póḋemozḋeharló |pàrạẹlótrọ |èntónṣès↓   Podemos dejarlo para el otro, entonces.

        don't yourself stay (tostay,   no‑se‑kéḋèn↓ kèḋarsè↓   no se queden (quedarse)
        remain)

TRES   18.3

UNIT 18   SPOKEN SPANISH

Carmen   *Carmen*
No, don't stay away because of me.   noↄ pórmi |nosekéↄenↄ   No, por mí no se queden.

    go (to go)   bayànↄ írↄ   vayan (ir)

You all go.   báyanùstec̣èsↄ   Vayan ustedes.

    (I)'ll call (to call)   Uyàmàréↄ Uyàmárↄ   llamaré (llamar)

Molina   *Molina*
Then I'll call the Colonel.   éntonşes |Uyàmáre |alkoronélↄ   Entonces llamaré al Coronel.

    to agree to, decide on   kèↄar—ènↄ   quedar en

We'll settle for going this Saturday at eleven.   kèↄamos |ènkébamos |èstèsaↄaↄçalasⓞnşèↄ   Quedamos en que vamos este sábado
                                                                                                               a las once.

18.10   Notes on the basic sentences

    (1) Notice the correlation of /en/ *en* with English *for* in this sentence. 'To work for' and /trabahár—en/ *trabajar en* are semantically equivalent.

    (2) Literally, of course, 'Since it makes much time?' 'Since some time ago?' The Spanish phrase measures duration from a starting point, its English equivalent measures length of time without respect to a starting point.

    (3) The form and meaning of Past II will be discussed subsequently in this unit, but it may be pointed out here that /beía/ *veía* is an occurrence of the Past II in a meaning that must be considered rather secondary. It should mean something like 'I didn't see' or 'I wasn't seeing', but here it must be translated 'I couldn't see'.

    (4) This is a specific transition utterance: it signals 'I'm changing the subject now'.

    (5) The common way of talking about next week, month, or year, is to refer to it as the one that is coming: 'tomorrow' is, of course, /manyána/ *mañana*, 'day after tomorrow' is /pasádo—manyána/ *pasado mañana*, and anything after that is the one that 'is coming', as in /la—semána—ke—byéne/ *la semana que viene* 'next week'.

    (6) Your present annotator finds this expression one of the most remarkably difficult to keep straight of all that he knows. You start to enter a classroom and your companion says, 'No, the other' /nóↄ el—ótroↄ/ *No. El otro*, and your years of reacting as an English speaker take control of your carefully cultivated Spanish habits and you wonder 'Which other?' — when all he means is 'The next room.' All this is by way of saying: Note this usage carefully or you too will be confused some day.

18.4   CUATRO

jacobeligoodsons.com For Free Audio

SPOKEN SPANISH   UNIT 18

18.2   DRILLS AND GRAMMAR

18.21   Pattern drills

18.21.1 Past II tense forms of regular verbs

    A. Presentation of pattern

                                              ILLUSTRATIONS

—————————————————   1   yoȩstaba|limpyandomelozdyéntès↓   Yo *estaba* limpiándome los dientes.

You always treated us well.   2   syempre|nostratabazbyén↓   Siempre nos *tratabas* bien.

She was working in an office.   3   é^yatrabahaba|enụnạofiȿínà↓   Ella *trabajaba* en una oficina.

    tired (to tire)   kánsadó↓ kánsár↓   cansado (cansar)

We were tired.   4   èstábamoskánsáɗòs↓   *Estábamos* cansados.

—————————————————   5   nomepaçabambastántè↓   No me *pagaban* bastante.

—————————————————   6   yokreía|kèlòsâmèrikanos|éràn   Yo *creía* que los americanos eran más
                                      mastraŋkílós↓   tranquilos.

You were right.   7   tuteniaっrraȿón↓   Tú *tenías* razón.

—————————————————   8   sinotekombeniạ|iȿístèbyenȩndehárló↓   Si no te *convenía*, hiciste bien en dejarlo.

CINCO   18.5

jacobeligoodsons.com For Free Audio

UNIT 18   SPOKEN SPANISH

_____   9 diho |kèpóđíamosir |estesábàđò↓   Dijo que *podíamos* ir este sábado.

They were right.   10 é^yos |teníanxraşón↓   Ellos *tenían* razón.

EXTRAPOLATION

| | -ár | -ér-ír | |
	abl—ár	kom—ér	bíb—ír
1-2-3 sg	abl—ába	kom—ía	bíb—ía
2 fam sg	abl—ábas	kom—ías	bíb—ías
1 pl	abl—ábamos	kom—íamos	bíb—íamos
2-3 pl	abl—ában	kom—ían	bíb—ían

NOTES

a. The other set of past tense forms, presented above, is called past II.

b. Past II tense forms of regular verbs have strong stressed endings, always the first syllable of the ending.

c. There is no distinction in the sets of endings for /—ér/or/—ír/ verbs.

18.6   SEIS

jacobeligoodsons.com For Free Audio

SPOKEN SPANISH   UNIT 18

18.21.11 Substitution drills — Person-number substitution

1   yoẹstuḍyaba͡ʼyí↓

    márịa_____↓   èstúḍyaba͡ʼyí↓

    àntonyọịyó_____↓   èstúḍyabamosa͡ʼyí↓

    é͡ʼyos_____↓   èstúḍyabana͡ʼyí↓

    ùsteḍ_____↓   èstúḍyaba͡ʼyí↓

2   é͡ʼya|syémpre͡ʼyeġabatárḍè↓

    nósotros_____↓   syémpre͡ʼyeġabamostárḍè↓

    tú_____↓   syémpre͡ʼyeġabastárḍè↓

_____

    1 *Yo* estudiaba allí.

       Maria_____.   Estudiaba allí.
       Antonio y yo_____   Estudiábamos allí.
       Ellos_____.   Estudiaban allí.
       Ud._____.   Estudiaba allí.

    2 *Ella* siempre llegaba tarde.

       Nosotros_____.   Siempre llegábamos tarde.
       Tú_____.   Siempre llegabas tarde.

SIETE   18.7

UNIT 18   SPOKEN SPANISH

lwisₐikármen_____↓   syémpre^ÿegábantárđè↓
yo_____↓   syémpre^ÿegábatárđè↓

3 é^ÿaz|límpyabantóđò↓

karmen_____↓   límpyabatóđò↓
ùsteđez_____↓   límpyabantóđò↓
nòsotroz_____↓   límpyabamostóđó↓
yo_____↓   límpyabatóđò↓

Luisa y Carmen_____.   Siempre llegaban tarde.
Yo_____.   Siempre llegaba tarde.

3 *Ellas* limpiaban todo.

Carmen_____.   Limpiaba todo.
Uds._____.   Limpiaban todo.
Nosotros_____.   Limpiábamos todo.
Yo_____.   Limpiaba todo.

SPOKEN SPANISH   UNIT 18

4 yokomía |enlaşyuđáđ↓
   ústeđ_____↓   kómía |enlaşyuđáđ↓
   àntonyǫikármeņ_____↓   kómían |enlaşyuđáđ↓
   kármeniyo_____↓   kómiamos |enlaşyuđáđ↓
   éˇya_____↓   kómía |enlaşyuđáđ↓

5 nòsotros |tráiamoseláwtó↓
   el _____↓   tráiŋeláwtó↓
   lwísa_____↓   tráiŋeláwtó↓
   lwísaịantónyo_____↓   tráiaņeláwtó↓
   yo_____↓   tráiŋeláwtó↓

_____

4 *Yo* comía en la ciudad.
   Ud._____.   Comía en la ciudad.
   Antonio y Carmen_____.   Comían en la ciudad.
   Carmen y yo_____.   Comíamos en la ciudad.
   Ella_____.   Comía en la ciudad.

5 *Nosotros* traíamos el auto.
   El _____ .   Traía el auto.
   Luisa_____ .   Traía el auto.
   Luisa y Antonio_____ .   Traían el auto.
   Yo_____ .   Traía el auto.

NUEVE

UNIT 18   SPOKEN SPANISH

6 éⁿyas |tràdúşıanmehór↓

   yo _____↓   tràdúşıamehór↓

   tu _____↓   tràdúşıazmehór↓

   ùstedes _____↓   tràdúşıanmehór↓

   karmenıyo _____↓   tràdúşıamozmehór↓

7 lwisa |súbıąenęlas(ş)ensór↓

   yo _____↓   súbıąenęlas(ş)ensór↓

   nósotros _____↓   súbıamos |enęlas(ş)ensór↓

   ùsteɗ _____↓   súbıąenęlas(ş)ensór↓

   éⁿyas _____↓   sùbıan |enęlas(ş)ensór↓

---

6 *Ellas* traducían mejor.

   Yo _____ .   Traducía mejor.

   Tú _____ .   Traducías mejor.

   Uds. _____ .   Traducían mejor.

   Carmen y yo _____ .   Traducíamos mejor.

7 *Luisa* subía en el ascensor.

   Yo _____ .   Subía en el ascensor.

   Nosotros _____ .   Subíamos en el ascensor.

   Ud. _____ _____ .   Subía en el ascensor.

   Ellas _____ .   Subían en el ascensor.

18.10   DIEZ

SPOKEN SPANISH   UNIT 18

Tense substitution

1   nèşèsito |unlápiş↓   nèşèsitaba |unlápiş↓

2   èspèramos |alasekretáryà↓   èspèrábamos |alasekretáryà↓

3   pàsean |lozdomíngòs↓   pàsęaban |lozdomíngòs↓

4   kobra |demasyádò↓   kòbraba |demasyádò↓

5   nokomotántò↓   nokomıatántò↓

6   subemporaí↓   sùbıamporaí↓

7   metelapátà↓   mètıalapátà↓

8   mirǫ |aesamorénà↓   miraba |aesamorénà↓

9   àblamos |konsyíhà↓   àblabamos |konsyíhà↓

10   bàrrelkwártò↓   bàrrıaelkwártò↓

11   èmpèşamos |alaznwébè↓   èmpèşabamos |alaznwébè↓

_____

1   *Necesito* un lápiz.   Necesitaba un lápiz.

2   *Esperamos* a la secretaria.   Esperábamos a la secretaria.

3   *Pasean* los domingos.   Paseaban los domingos.

4   *Cobra* demasiado.   Cobraba demasiado.

5   No *como* tanto.   No comía tanto.

6   *Suben* por ahí.   Subían por ahí.

7   *Mete* la pata.   Metía la pata.

8   *Miro* a esa morena.   Miraba a esa morena.

9   *Hablamos* con su hija.   Hablábamos con su hija.

10   *Barre* el cuarto.   Barría el cuarto.

11   *Empezamos* a las nueve.   Empezábamos a las nueve.

ONCE

UNIT 18   SPOKEN SPANISH

18.21.12 Response drill

                1   èláɲyópàsàdọ |ùstéċtràbàhàbà↑ọestuɖyábà↓   èláɲyópàsàɖo |tràbàhàbà↓

                2   èláɲyópàsàdọ |ùstéċéstràbàhàbàn↑ọestuɖyábán↓   èláɲyópàsàɖo |tràbàhàbàmós↓

                3   èláɲyópàsàdọ |éltràbàhàbà↑ọestuɖyábà↓   èláɲyópàsàɖo |tràbàhàbà↓

                4   èláɲyópàsàdọ |éℓyóstràbàhàbàn↑ọestuɖyábán↓   èláɲyópàsàɖo |tràbàhàbàn↓

[èŋkàlifórnyà↓] 5   dondebibiànℓyós |ántèz̧ẹ̀bèníràkí↓   bíbiànẹŋkàlifórnyà↓

[èŋkàlifórnyà↓] 6   dondebibiàstú |ántèz̧ẹ̀bèníràkí↓   bíbiạẹŋkàlifórnyà↓

[èŋkàlifórnyà↓] 7   dondebibiànụstéɖès |ántèz̧ẹ̀bèníràkí↓   bíbiàmos |èŋkalifórnyà↓

[èŋkàlifórnyà↓] 8   dondebibiạél |ántèz̧ẹ̀bèníràkí↓   bíbiạẹŋkàlifórnyà↓

---

                1   ¿El año pasado Ud. trabajaba o estudiaba?   El año pasado trabajaba.

                2   ¿El año pasado Uds. trabajaban o estudiaban?   El año pasado trabajábamos.

                3   ¿El año pasado él trabajaba o estudiaba?   El año pasado trabajaba.

                4   ¿El año pasado ellos trabajaban o estudiaban?   El año pasado trabajaban.

(en California) 5   ¿Dónde vivían ellos antes de venir aquí?   Vivían en California.

(en California) 6   ¿Dónde vivías tú antes de venir aquí?   Vivía en California.

(en California) 7   ¿Dónde vivían Uds. antes de venir aquí?   Vivíamos en California.

(en California) 8   ¿Dónde vivía él antes de venir aquí?   Vivía en California.

18.12   DOCE

SPOKEN SPANISH   UNIT 18

[ènlàkása↓]   9   kwándoustedestudyábà |kòmiạẹnụnrrestoran↑   no↓ kòmiạẹnlakásà↓

[ènlàkása↓]   lo   kwándọẹ´yos,estudyábàn |kòmiạẹnụnrrestoran↑   no↓ kòmianẹnlakásà↓

[ènlàkása↓]   11   kwándoustéṛes,estudyábàn |kòmiạẹnụnrrestoran↑   no↓ kòmiamos |enlakásà↓

[ènlàkása↓]   12   kwándọelestudyábà |kòmiạẹnụnrrestoran↑   no↓ kòmiạẹnlakásà↓

              13   téniạustedawtọ |antes↑   si↓ antes |teniáwtô↓

              14   téniạnụsteṛes,awtọ |antes↑   si↓ antes |teniamos,awtô↓

              15   tèniạnẹ´yos,awtọ |antes↑   si↓ antes |tenianáwtô↓

(en la casa)   9 Cuando Ud. estudiaba, ¿comía en un restorán?   No, comía en la casa.

(en la casa) 10 Cuando ellos estudiaban, ¿comían en un restorán?   No, comían en la casa.

(en la casa) 11 Cuando Uds. estudiaban, ¿comían en un restorán?   No, comíamos en la casa.

(en la casa) 12 Cuando él estudiaba, ¿comía en un restorán?   No, comía en la casa.

              13 ¿Tenía Ud. auto antes?   Sí, antes tenía auto.

              14 ¿Tenían Uds. auto antes?   Sí, antes teníamos auto.

              15 ¿Tenían ellos auto antes?   Sí, antes tenían auto.

TRECE

jacobeligoodsons.com For Free Audio

UNIT 18   SPOKEN SPANISH

18.21.13 Translation drill

1 Louise never washed anything.   lwísánuŋka |labⁿabanáða↓   Luisa nunca lavaba nada.

2 The shirts were always dirty.   láskámisas |syemprestabansúşyàs↓   Las camisas siempre estaban sucias.

3 We used to send them to the laundry.   nósótroz |lázmándabamos |alalabanderíá↓ Nosotros las mandábamos a la lavandería.

4 I took them myself.   yómizmó |làzˆ‸yèbábà↓   Yo mismo las llevaba.

5 There were always a lot of people there. syémpre |àbíámuchahénte |à‸yí↓   Siempre había mucha gente allí.

6 Louise lived previously in the outskirts. lwisa |bibⁿiantes |ènlàsàfwerás↓   Luisa vivía antes en las afueras.

7 She worked in the business district.   trábàhabə |ènèlsèktorkomerşyál↓   Trabajaba en el sector comercial.

8 The traffic made her nervous.   èltrafiko |làpònianerbyósà↓   El tráfico la ponía nerviosa.

9 The noise didn't bother us.   ànósótros |èlrrwido |nonozmolestábà↓ A nosotros, el ruido no nos molestaba.

10 We always had something special to do. syémpretenłamos |algoespeşyál |keáşér↓ Siempre teníamos algo especial que hacer.

11 I used to have an old desk but a good   yoteniə |uneskritóryobyéhò |péròⁿwenò↓ Yo tenía un escritorio viejo pero bueno.
   one.

18.14   CATORCE

SPOKEN SPANISH   UNIT 18

12 I liked it a lot.   mégústabamúchò↓   Me gustaba mucho.

13 Every day at four Louise brought us   tódoᴦloᴦdías |àlàskwátro |lwísa | Todos los dias a las cuatro Luisa nos
    coffee.   nòstráiakafé↓   traía café.

14 We also ate apple pie.   kómiamos |pasteldemanşáná |tàmbyén↓ Comiamos pastel de manzana también.

15 Carmen and Louise washed the cups.   kármenilwísa |lábabanlastáşàs↓   Carmen y Luisa lavaban las tazas.

16 On Fridays nobody brought anything.   lóᴦbyérnez |naᵭyetraianáᵭà↓   Los viernes nadie traía nada.

17 They (f) were all tired.   tóᵭas |estábaŋkansáᵭàs↓   Todas estaban cansadas.

B. Discussion of pattern

      The second set of endings to express past time in Spanish is referred to as past II. These are always distinguished from past I forms in the sense that they 'mean'
something different. A full comparison of past I and past II is presented in Unit 19.

      Past II forms (sometimes called 'imperfect' forms) carry the idea of indefiniteness, in time or in extent. For example, past II forms express actions (or processes) of
extended or undetermined duration or an action repeated an indefinite number of times. There is inherently an aspect of indefinite extension in any action or process which is
reported in past II; that is, the course of the action is emphasized, rather than its beginning or ending.

      The forms of regular past II tense patterns have two or three syllable endings with stress on the first syllable of the ending. There is no distinction between 1 sg
and 2-3 sg. Also the /-ér/ and /-ír/ theme classes fall together throughout their past II formation.

QUINCE   18.15

jacobeligoodsons.com For Free Audio

UNIT 18   SPOKEN SPANISH

18.21.2   Past II tense forms of irregular verbs

    A.   Presentation of pattern

ILLUSTRATIONS

————————————————   1   nobéía│komoḍeşírsélô↓   No veía cómo decírselo.

You couldn't see a way to tell him about it?   2   nobéías│komoḍeşirseló↑   ¿No veías cómo decírselo?

We couldn't see a way to let him know.   3   nobéíamos│komᶐabisárlê↓   No veíamos cómo avisarle.

They didn't see how they could get used   4   nobéíaŋ│komᶐakostumbrársê↓   No veían cómo acostumbrarse.
    to it.

————————————————   5   élhefẹ│érâmuybwénapersónâ↓   El jefe era muy buena persona.

Before, you were more calm.   6   antes│érâzmastraŋkíló↓   Antes eras más tranquilo.

In those days we were good friends.   7   énẹsozdías│érâmózmuyamígós↓   En esos días éramos muy amigos.

————————————————   8   lòsámérikanos│érânmastraŋkílós↓   Los americanos eran más tranquilos.

————————————————   9   íbaḍarmẹ│unaḍúchâ↓   Iba a darme una ducha.

You previously went by boat?   10   antes│íbasembárko↑   ¿Antes ibas en barco?

18.16   DIECISÉIS

jacobeligoodsons.com For Free Audio

SPOKEN SPANISH   UNIT 16

We always went by plane.   11   syémprę |íbamosporabyón↓   Siempre íbamos por avión.

Beside, they went with   12   ádėmás↑íbàŋkómpèrmisò↓   Además, iban con permiso.
(had) permission.

EXTRAPOLATION

	b—ér	s—ér	—ír
1-2-3 sg	be—ía	—éra	—íba
2 fam sg	be—ías	—éras	—íbas
1 pl	be—íamos	—éramos	—íbamos
2-3 pl	be—ían	—éran	—íban

NOTES

a. There are only three verbs in Spanish with irregular past II tense forms.

b. Of these, /bér/ is irregular only in having the stem /be—/ instead of the stem /b—/.

c. /sér/ and /ír/ have no stems in past II, only an irregular set of endings.

d. The /ír/ forms are noteworthy as the ancestral forms of /—ír/ past II endings: /íba/
   resembles /ába/ by having the /—b—/ that is missing from the /—ía/ endings.

DIECISIETE   18.17

UNIT 18   SPOKEN SPANISH

18.21.21 Substitution drills — Person-number substitution

1   yoᵉramigoᵈél↓
    ústeᵈes_____↓   eran |ámigozᵈél↓
    ántonyọịyó____↓   eramos |ámiọozᵈél↓
    lwísạ_____↓   eramịgaᵈél↓
    eꞈyos_____↓   eran |ámiọozᵈél↓

2   eꞈyá |syémprẹịbạsusfyéstás↓
    yo_____↓   syémprẹ |íbạsusfyéstás↓
    eꞈyas_____↓   syémprẹ |íbạṇạsusfyéstás↓

──

1   *Yo* era amigo de él.

    Uds._____ .   Eran amigos de él.
    Antonio y yo_____ .   Eramos amigos de él.
    Luisa_____ .   Era amiga de él.
    Ellos_____ .   Eran amigos de él.

2   *Ella* siempre iba a sus fiestas.

    Yo_____ .   Siempre iba a sus fiestas.
    Ellas_____ .   Siempre iban a sus fiestas.

18.18   DIECIOCHO

jacobeligoodsons.com For Free Audio

SPOKEN SPANISH   UNIT 18

    ántonyo̧iyó_____↓   syémprȩ |íbamo̧s̯asusfyéstàs↓

    lwís̯a̧ihóse_____↓   syémprȩ |íban̯asusfyéstàs↓

3 nósotroz |bȩ́iamozlasfótòs↓

    eⁿya_____↓   bȩ́ialasfótòs↓

    hwánilwísa_____↓   bȩ́ianlasfótòs↓

    hwániyo_____↓   bȩ̀iamozlasfótòs↓

    yo_____↓   bȩ́ialasfótòs↓

    Antonio y yo_____.   Siempre íbamos a sus fiestas.

    Luisa y José_____.   Siempre íban a sus fiestas.

3 *Nosotros* veíamos las fotos.

    Ella_____.   Veía las fotos.

    Juan y Luisa_____.   Veían las fotos.

    Juan y yo_____.   Veíamos las fotos.

    Yo_____.   Veía las fotos.

DIECINUEVE

jacobeligoodsons.com For Free Audio

UNIT 18   SPOKEN SPANISH

Tense substitution

1	somozgórdòs↓	eramozgórdòs↓
2	boyapyé↓	ibapyé↓
3	benasusamígòs↓	béìanasusamígòs↓
4	soyamigosúyò↓	éràmigosúyò↓
5	bámóstodozlozdíàs↓	íbàmóstodozlozdíàs↓
6	beomuybyén↓	béìamuybyén↓
7	sónmuynerbyósòs↓	érànmuynerbyósòs↓
8	banenáwtò↓	ibanenáwtò↓
9	bétodomál↓	béíàtodomál↓

1	*Somos* gordos.	Eramos gordos.
2	*Voy* a pié.	Iba a pié.
3	*Ven* a sus amigos.	Veían a sus amigos.
4	*Soy* amigo suyo.	Era amigo suyo.
5	*Vamos* todos los días.	Ibamos todos los días.
6	*Veo* muy bien.	Veía muy bien.
7	*Son* muy nerviosos.	Eran muy nerviosos.
8	*Van* en auto.	Iban en auto.
9	*Ve* todo mal.	Veía todo mal.

18.20

SPOKEN SPANISH   UNIT 18

18.21.22 Translation drill

1 We were very good friends of the Garcías.   nósótros |érámó?muyamigo? |delozgarṣíá↓   Nosotros éramos muy amigos de los García.

2 Alice was a friend of theirs also.   áliṣyạ |èràmígádéⁿyòs |tàmbyén↓   Alicia era amiga de ellos también.

3 We always went to the stores together.   syémprẹibamos |álástyéndashúntòs↓   Siempre íbamos a las tiendas juntos.

4 Alice went with us.   áliṣyạ |ibako(n)nosótrós↓   Alicia iba con nosotros.

5 We saw many pretty things.   béıamoz |muchaskósazbonítạs↓   Veíamos muchas cosas bonitas.

6 Alice looked at lots of suits.   áliṣya |bèıamuchostráhès↓   Alicia veía muchos trajes.

7 We went to lots of parties with the   ibamos |ámuchasfyéstas |konlozgarṣíá↓   Íbamos a muchas fiestas con los García.
   Garcías.

8 Their daughter never went with us.   lạihadéⁿyo? |nuṇkạibako(n)nosótrós↓   La hija de ellos nunca iba con nosotros.

9 Alice and her fiancé went only once in   áliṣyạisunóbyo |solọiban |dèbeṣẹ̣ṇkwándò↓   Alicia y su novio sólo iban de vez en
   a while.   cuando.

10 Alice was very pretty.   áliṣyạ |éràmuybonítạ̀↓   Alicia era muy bonita.

11 Her fiancé was (an) American.   élnóbyọ̀éⁿyạ |erámerikánò↓   El novio de ella era americano.

VEINTIUNO   18.21

UNIT 18   SPOKEN SPANISH

8.21.3 Question intonation patterns — Negative confirmation questions

A. Presentation of pattern   ILLUSTRATION

                                                                                      2   2 2 ↑
Is it worth while?   1   balelapéna↑   ¿Vale la pena?

    the truth   lā—bérđáđ↓   la verdad
                                                                                     2 2   1 1 │ 1 22↑
It isn't worth while, is it?   nobalelapéná │bèrđađ↑   No vale la pena, ¿verdad?

                                                                                   1   2   2 2 ↑
———————————   2   ezmuykaro↑   ¿Es muy caro?

                                                                                        2   2 1 │ 1 22 ↑
It isn't very expensive, is it?   noezmuykaró │bérđáđ↑   No es muy caro, ¿verdad?

                                                                                   2   2 2 ↑
Does it have a bedroom?   3   tyeneđormitoryo↑   ¿Tiene dormitorio?

                                                                                        2 2   1 1 │ 1 22 ↑
It doesn't have a bedroom, does it? notyeneđormitóryó │bèrđađ↑   No tiene dormitorio, ¿verdad?

                                        EXTRAPOLATION

Yes-no question	Negative confirmation
/1222↑/	/nó/ + /2211 │ 1 22↑/ berdád

a. When a speaker wants a negative confirmation of what he is asking, he follows the
                                                      1   22
    /2211 │/ pattern which includes the word /nó/ with /berdád↑/.

18.22   VEINTIDOS

jacobeligoodsons.com For Free Audio

SPOKEN SPANISH   UNIT 18

18.21.31 Substitution drill — Pattern substitution

1 baylamúchó↑   nobaylamúchó |bérdad↑

2 byenestanóché↑   nobyenestanóché |bérdad↑

3 balabóda↑   nobalabóda |bérdad↑

4 kyeremaságwa↑   nokyeremaságwà |bérdad↑

5 dapropína↑   nodapropína |bérdad↑

6 kambyachékes↑   nokambyachékèz |bérdad↑

7 trabahaestasemana↑   notrabahaestasemánà |bérdad↑

---

        2   2 2↑   2 2   1 1 | 1 22↑
1 ¿Baila mucho?   No baila mucho, ¿verdad?

        2   2 2↑   2 2   1 1 | 1 22↑
2 ¿Viene esta noche?   No viene esta noche, ¿verdad?

        2   2 2↑   2 2   1 1 | 1 22↑
3 ¿Va a la boda?   No va a la boda, ¿verdad?

        2   2 2↑   2 2   1 1 | 1 22↑
4 ¿Quiere más agua?   No quiere más agua, ¿verdad?

        2   2 2↑   2 2   11 | 1 22↑
5 ¿Da propina?   No da propina, ¿verdad?

        2   2 2↑   2 2   1 1 | 1 22↑
6 ¿Cambia cheques?   No cambia cheques, ¿verdad?

       1 2   2 2↑   2   2   11 | 1 22↑
7 ¿Trabaja esta semana?   No trabaja esta semana, ¿verdad?

VEINTITRES

UNIT 18   SPOKEN SPANISH

8 éstakonténtó↑   noẹstakonténtò |bèrďadí↑

9 belos,anúnṣyos↑   nóbelos,anúnṣyóʐ |bèrďaďí↑

10 komprạelperyóďiko↑   nókomprạelperyóďikò |bèrďaďí↑

11 debeďemasyáďo↑   noďebeďemasyáďò |bèrďaďí↑

───

```
        1 2    2 2↑                              2  2    1 1 | 1 22↑
8  ¿Está contento?                          No está contento, ¿verdad?

        2     2 2↑                              2 2    1 1 | 1 22↑
9  ¿Ve los anuncios?                          No ve los anuncios, ¿verdad?

        2       2 2↑                             2 2       1 1 | 1 22↑
10 ¿Compra el periódico?                      No compra el periódico, ¿verdad?

        2      2 2↑                              2 2     1 1 | 1 22↑
11 ¿Debe demasiado?                           No debe demasiado, ¿verdad?
```

B. Discussion of pattern

    A question which anticipates a negative confirmation in its answer usually will be cast in the negative (/nó/ will appear before the verb) and will be structured on

the pattern /2211 |122↑/, with the last part consisting of the word /berdád↑/. The confirmation element is often expanded to /noẹsberdád↑/.

    Equivalent English expressions are: 'are you', 'does it', 'has he', 'did they', or 'aren't you', 'doesn't it', 'hasn't he', 'didn't they', etc.

18.24   VEINTICUATRO

SPOKEN SPANISH   UNIT 18

18.22   Replacement drills

A   éŋkekompaŋyíà|tràbáhạùstéʧↆ

1   _____ ʉ́stéʧès↓   éŋkekompaŋyíà|tràbáhànụstéʧès↓

2   __kwàl_____↓   éŋkwàlkompaŋyíà|tràbáhànụstéʧès↓

3   _____tràbàhában___↓   éŋkwàlkompaŋyíà|tràbàhábànụstéʧès↓

4   _____hòsé↓   éŋkwàlkompaŋyíà|tràⱡàhábàhòsé↓

5   __şyuʧáʧ_____↓   éŋkwàlşyuʧáʧ|tràbáhábàhòsé↓

6   _____bibíà_____↓   éŋkwàlşyuʧáʧ|bibíàhòsé↓

7   _____nòsótròs↓   éŋkwàlşyuʧáʧ|bibíàmòznòsótròs↓

_____

A   ¿En qué compañia trabaja usted?

1 ¿ _____ ustedes?   ¿En qué compañia trabajan ustedes?

2 ¿__cuál_____?   ¿En cuál compañia trabajan ustedes?

3 ¿ _____trabajaban ___?   ¿En cuál compañia trabajaban ustedes?

4 ¿ _____José?   ¿En cuál compañia trabajaba José?

5 ¿ ____ciudad _____?   ¿En cuál ciudad trabajaba José?

6 ¿ _____vivía _____?   ¿En cuál ciudad vivía José?

7 ¿ _____nosotros ?   ¿En cuál ciudad vivíamos nosotros?

VEINTICINCO   18.25

UNIT 18   SPOKEN SPANISH

B   èlhéfę |èràmúybwénàpersónà↓

1   lòs_____↓   lóshéfes |èrànmúybwénaspersónàs↓

2   _____amígòs↓   lóshéfes |èrànmúybwénos‚amígòs↓

3   ___chìkas_____↓   làschìkas |èrànmúybwénas‚amígàs↓

4   _____màlàs_____↓   làschìkas |èrànmúymàlas‚amígàs↓

5   àké'‚yàs_____↓   àké'‚yàschìkas |èrànmúymàlas‚amígàs↓

6   _____ombres_____↓   àké'‚yòs‚ombres |èrànmúymàlos‚amígòs↓

7   _____héfès↓   àké'‚yòs‚ombres |èrànmúymàloshéfès↓

_____

B   El jefe era muy buena persona.

1   Los_____ .   Los jefes eran muy buenas personas.

2   _____amigos.   Los jefes eran muy buenos amigos.

3   ___chicas_____ .   Las chicas eran muy buenas amigas.

4   _____malas_____ .   Las chicas eran muy malas amigas.

5   Aquellas_____ .   Aquellas chicas eran muy malas amigas.

6   ___hombres_____ .   Aquellos hombres eran muy malos amigos.

7   _____jefes .   Aquellos hombres eran muy malos jefes.

18.26   VEINTISEIS

SPOKEN SPANISH

UNIT 18

C   àmí |mègùstàrìaír↓

1   ‗nòsotroz_____↓   ànósotroz |nòzgùstàrìaír↓

2   _____tràbahár↓   ànósotroz |nòzgùstàrìatràbahár↓

3   _____gústàba_____↓   ànósotroz |nòzgùstàbatràbahár↓

4   ‗éˆyoz_____↓   ạeˆyoz |lèzgùstàbatràbahár↓

5   _____ırɗekómpràs↓   ạeˆyoz |lèzgùstàbạ |ırɗekómpràs↓

6   _____gùstạ_____↓   ạeˆyoz |lèzgùstạ |ırɗekómpràs↓

7   naɗyè_____↓   ànaɗyè |lègústạ |írɗèkómpràs↓

C   A mí me gustaría ir.

1   ‗nosotros_____.   A nosotros nos gustaría ir.

2   _____trabajar.   A nosotros nos gustaría trabajar.

3   _____gustaba_____.   A nosotros nos gustaba trabajar.

4   ‗ellos_____.   A ellos les gustaba trabajar.

5   _____ir de compras.   A ellos les gustaba ir de compras.

6   _____gusta_____.   A ellos les gusta ir de compras.

7   ‗nadie_____.   A nadie le gusta ir de compras.

VEINTISIETE

UNIT 18   SPOKEN SPANISH

D   yó |noboyapodér |éstèsábàdò↓

1   _____ díás↓   yó |noboyapodér |éstózdíàs↓

2   nòsótroz_____↓   nòsótroz |nobamosapodér |éstózdíàs↓

3   _____tárdè↓   nòsótroz |nobamosapodér |éstàtárdè↓

4   _____benír_____↓   nòsótroz |nobamosabenír |éstàtárdè↓

5   _____íbamos_____↓   nòsótroz |noíbamosabenír |éstàtárdè↓

6   _____àké⌒yà___↓   nòsótroz |noíbamosabenír |àké⌒yàtárdè↓

7   él_____↓   él |noíbabenír |àké⌒yàtárdè↓

_____

D   Yo no voy a poder este sábado.

1   _____días.   Yo no voy a poder estos días.

2   Nosotros_____.   Nosotros no vamos a poder estos días.

3   _____tarde.   Nosotros no vamos a poder esta tarde.

4   _____venir_____.   Nosotros no vamos a venir esta tarde.

5   _____íbamos_____.   Nosotros no íbamos a venir esta tarde.

6   _____aquella___.   Nosotros no íbamos a venir aquella tarde.

7   El_____.   El no iba a venir aquella tarde.

18.28   VEINTIOCHO

SPOKEN SPANISH   UNIT 18

E   pòdemoz |dèhárlo |pàrǎélótrò↓

1   pwédo_____↓   pwédo |dèhárlo |pàrǎélótrò↓

2   _____hwébès↓   pwédo |dèhárlo |pàrǎélhwébès↓

3   _____ése_____↓   pwédo |dèhárlo |pàrǎésehwébès↓

4   pódía_____↓   pódía |dèhárlo |pàrǎésehwébès↓

5   _____áșérlo_____↓   pódía |àșérlo |pàrǎésehwébès↓

6   _____díá↓   pódía |àșérlo |pàrǎésedíá↓

7   _____ótro____↓   pódía |àșérlo |pàrǎótrodíá↓

E   Podemos dejarlo para el otro.

1   Puedo_____.   Puedo dejarlo para el otro.

2   _____jueves.   Puedo dejarlo para el jueves.

3   _____ese____.   Puedo dejarlo para ese jueves.

4   Podía_____.   Podía dejarlo para ese jueves.

5   _____hacerlo_____.   Podía hacerlo para ese jueves.

6   _____ día.   Podía hacerlo para ese día.

7   _____otro____.   Podía hacerlo para otro día.

VEINTINUEVE

UNIT 18   SPOKEN SPANISH

F   èntonṣez |ᴺy̌ámáreạlkoronél↓

1 _____héfè↓   èntonṣez |ᴺy̌ámáreạlhéfè↓

2 nuŋka_____↓   nuŋka |ᴺy̌amareạlhéfé↓

3 _____chíká↓   nuŋka |ᴺy̌amareạlachíkà↓

4 _____ésa_____↓   nuŋka |ᴺy̌amare |ạesachíkà↓

5 dèspwéz_____↓   dèspwez |ᴺy̌amare |ạesachíkà↓

6 _____seɲórès↓   dèspwez |ᴺy̌amare |ạeso(s)seɲórès↓

7 àora_____↓   àora |ᴺy̌amare |ạeso(s)seɲórès↓

F   Entonces, llamaré al Coronel.

1 _____ jefe.   Entonces, llamaré al jefe.

2 Nunca _____.   Nunca llamaré al jefe.

3 _____ chica.   Nunca llamaré a la chica.

4 _____ esa____.   Nunca llamaré a esa chica.

5 Después _____.   Después llamaré a esa chica.

6 _____ señores.   Después llamaré a esos señores.

7 Ahora_____.   Ahora llamaré a esos señores.

18.30   TREINTA

jacobeligoodsons.com For Free Audio

SPOKEN SPANISH   UNIT 18

18.23   Variation drills

A dèzdeaşe |muchotyémpò↓   Desde hace mucho tiempo.

   1 For such a long time.   dèzdeaşe |tántotyémpò↓   Desde hace tanto tiempo.

   2 For so many years.   dèzdeaşe |tántosáŋyòs↓   Desde hace tantos años.

   3 For many years.   dèzdeaşe |múchosáŋyòs↓   Desde hace muchos años.

   4 For many days.   dèzdeaşe |múchozdíàs↓   Desde hace muchos días.

   5 For some days.   dèzdeaşe |únozdíàs↓   Desde hace unos días.

   6 For five days.   dèzdeaşe |şıŋkodíàs↓   Desde hace cinco días.

   7 For five months.   dèzdeaşe |şıŋkomésès↓   Desde hace cinco meses.

B nó↓ ántes |tràbàhabạ |enuŋaofişínà↓   No. Antes trabajaba en una oficina.

   1 No. Before, I was working at an agency.   nó↓ ántes |tràbàhabạ |enụnahénşyà↓   No. Antes trabajaba en una agencia.

   2 No. Before, I was working in the   nó↓ ántes |tràbàhabạ |enlạembaháɗà↓   No. Antes trabajaba en la embajada.
       Embassy.

   3 No. Before, I was in the Embassy.   nó↓ ántes |lạembaháɗà↓   No. Antes estaba en la embajada.

TREINTA Y UNO   18.31

UNIT 18   SPOKEN SPANISH

4 No. Before, I was in California.   nó↓ ántes |èstábạeŋkalifórnyà↓   No. Antes estaba en California.

5 Yes. Before, I was living in California.   sí↓ ántez |bibịạeŋkalifórnyà↓   Sí. Antes vivía en California.

6 Yes. Before, I was living here.   sí↓ ántez |bibiakí↓   Sí. Antes vivía aquí.

7 Yes. Before, I used to eat here.   sí↓ ántes |kómiakí↓   Sí. Antes comía aquí.

C áblandodẹọtrakósà↓   Hablando de otra cosa.

1 Speaking of other things.   àblandodẹọtraskósàs↓   Hablando de otras cosas.

2 Speaking of another person.   àblando |dẹọtrapersónà↓   Hablando de otra persona.

3 Speaking with another person.   àblando |kónọtrapersónà↓   Hablando con otra persona.

4 Eating with some friends.   kómyendo |kónụnósámigòs↓   Comiendo con unos amigos.

5 Going out with some friends.   sályendo |kónụnósạmigòs↓   Saliendo con unos amigos.

6 Conversing at the office.   kómbèrsando |enlạofiṣínà↓   Conversando en la oficina.

7 Arriving at the office.   Ịyègando |alạofiṣínà↓   Llegando a la oficina.

18.32   TREINTA Y DOS

SPOKEN SPANISH   UNIT 18

D hárriznosimbitó|ạbisitárlamisyón↓   Harris nos invitó a visitar la misión.

1 Harris invited us to visit his house.   hárriznosimbitó|ạbisitársukásạ↓   Harris nos invitó a visitar su casa.

2 Molina invited us to visit the stores.   mólinanosimbitó|ạbisitárlastyéndàs↓   Molina nos invitó a visitar las tiendas.

3 Juan invited us to see (get acquainted with)   hwá(n)nosimbitó|ạkònóşèrlaşyuḍáḍ↓   Juan nos invitó a conocer la ciudad.
   the city.

4 Mary took us to see (get acquainted with)   màrianozảyebó|ạkònóşèrlaşyuḍáḍ↓   María nos llevó a conocer la ciudad.
   the city.

5 Paul took us to see the downtown (section).   pablonozảyebó|ạbérelşéntró↓   Pablo nos llevó a ver el centro.

6 He took us to buy some things.   élnozảyebó|ạkòmprárunaskósàs↓   El nos llevó a comprar unas cosas.

7 Someone invited us to go out.   álgyen|nosimbitóạsalír↓   Alguién nos invitó a salir.

E téŋgokẹir|ḍekómpras|kònlàsẹŋyorahárris↓   Tengo que ir de compras con la señora
                                                                                Harris.

1 I have to go shopping this afternoon.   téŋgokẹir|ḍekómpras|ẹstátardẹ↓   Tengo que ir de compras esta tarde.

2 I have to go out shopping this afternoon.   téŋgokẹsalír|ḍekómpras|ẹstátardẹ↓   Tengo que salir de compras esta tarde.

3 I have to go out to eat tonight.   téŋgokẹsalír|akomér|ẹstảnochẹ↓   Tengo que salir a comer esta noche.

4 I have to come to work tonight.   téŋgokẹbenír|atrabahár|ẹstảnochẹ↓   Tengo que venir a trabajar esta noche.

TREINTA Y TRES   18.33

UNIT 18   SPOKEN SPANISH

5 I have to come tomorrow.   téŋgo |kébènirmaŋyánà↓   Tengo que venir mañana.

6 I have to return tomorrow.   téŋgo |kébólbermaŋyáná↓   Tengo que volver mañana.

7 I have to return (some) other day. téŋgo |kèʋólbérotrodíà↓   Tengo que volver otro día.

F bamos |éstèsàbadǫalasónṣé↓   Vamos este sábado a las once.

1 Let's go this Saturday at twelve o'clock.   bamos |éstèsàbadǫalazdóṣè↓   Vamos este sábado a las doce.

2 Let's go this Sunday at twelve o'clock.   bàmos |éstèdòmiŋgǫalazdóṣè↓   Vamos este domingo a las doce.

3 Let's go this Monday at three o'clock.   bàmos |éstèlunes,alastrés↓   Vamos este lunes a las tres.

4 Let's go this Thursday at one o'clock.   bàmos |éstèhwèbes,alạúnà↓   Vamos este jueves a la una.

5 Let's go this Thursday at two o'clock.   bᵃmos |éstèhwèbes,alazdós↓   Vamos este jueves a las dos.

6 Let's go this Friday at two thirty.   bàmos |éstèbyérnes |àlàzdos,imédyà↓   Vamos este viernes a las dos y media.

7 Let's go this week.   bàmos |éstasemánà↓   Vamos esta semana.

18.34   TREINTA Y CUATRO

jacobeligoodsons.com For Free Audio

SPOKEN SPANISH   UNIT 18

18.24   Review drill — Word order in information questions

1 Where is he?	dondestaél↓	¿Dónde está él?
2 Why is he coming?	pòrkébyenél↓	¿Por qué viene él?
3 When is he coming?	kwàndobyénél↓	¿Cuándo viene él?
4 What are you studying?	kestúdyaustéd↓	¿Qué estudia Ud.?
5 When does he arrive?	kwàndoḷyegaél↓	¿Cuándo llega él?
6 Where does he live?	dóndebibél↓	¿Dónde vive él?
7 What does he have?	kétyenél↓	¿Qué tiene él?
8 How does he talk?	komoablaél↓	¿Cómo habla él?
9 How does he write?	komoeskribél↓	¿Cómo escribe él?
10 Where do you work?	dondetrabáhaustéd↓	¿Dónde trabaja Ud.?
11 How much do you owe?	kwántodébeustéd↓	¿Cuánto debe Ud.?

TREINTA Y CINCO   18.35

UNIT 18   SPOKEN SPANISH

18.3   CONVERSATION STIMULUS

NARRATIVE I

1 Jose has been at the Embassy for a long time.

ásęmuchotyémpo |kèhòsèstaęnląèmbaháḍà↓

Hace mucho tiempo que José está en la Embajada.

2 He started to work there five years ago.

élempeşo |ątràbàhara͡íỵi↑áşèşiŋkọáŋyòs↓

El empezó a trabajar allí hace cinco años.

3 He didn't work before that. He was in school.

antezḋeso |notrabaháḃà↓ éstaḃaęnląeskwélà↓

Antes de eso no trabajaba. Estaba en la escuela.

4 It wasn't in school where he met Carmen.

nòfwenląeskwélà |ḋòndèkònòşyóąkármèn↓

No fué en la escuela donde conoció a Carmen.

5 He met her only a year ago, when she was working as a secretary.

làkónòşyo |áşęąpènas |unáŋyó↓

kwándòtrábáhaba |komosekretáryà↓

La conoció hace apenas un año, cuando trabajaba como secretaria.

DIALOG 1

Juan, pregúntele a José cuánto tiempo hace que él está en la Embajada.

kṿántotyémpọ |aşękestás |enląembaháḍà|

hòsé↓

Juan: ¿Cuánto tiempo hace que estás en la Embajada, José?

José, contéstele que Ud. empezó a trabajar allí hace cinco años.

émpéşe |ątrạbahara͡íỵi↑áşèşiŋkọáŋyòs↓

José: Empecé a trabajar allí hace cinco años.

Juan, pregúntele en qué trabajaba antes.

èŋketrabahabasántès↓

Juan: ¿En qué trabajabas antes?

18.36   TREINTA Y SEIS

SPOKEN SPANISH   UNIT 18

José, dígale que Ud. no trabajaba. Que   notrabahábà↓ èstabạ |ènlạéskwelà↓   José: No trabajaba. Estaba en la escuela.
estaba en la escuela.

Juan, pregúntele si fué allí donde conoció   fwégỵ̀i |dondekonoṣiste |akármen↑   Juan: ¿Fué allí donde conociste a Carmen?
a Carmen.

José, contéstele que no. Que a Carmen Ud.   nó↓ àkármen↑làkónóṣi |áṣẹàpenas | José: No. A Carmen la conocí hace apenas
la conoció hace apenas un año, cuando   únạṇyó↓kwándòtràbàhaba |kómòsèkrètaryạ |en   un año, cuando trabajaba como
trabajaba como secretaria en una oficina.   unạofiṣínà↓   secretaria en una oficina.
                                                           NARRATIVE 2

1 She was very happy in that job.   ẹ⁽ⁿ⁾yạ |èstábàmuykonténtạ |ènéṣètràbáhò↓   Ella estaba muy contenta en ese trabajo.

2 But she quit because it didn't suit her.   pérólòdèho |pórkènolekombenía↓   Pero lo dejó porque no le convenía.

3 They paid her very little.   lèpàgàbàn |muypókò↓   Le pagaban muy poco.

4 She did the right thing in quitting that   íṣòbyen |endèhar |eṣetrabáhọ |èntónṣès↓   Hizo bien en dejar ese trabajo, entonces.
job, then.

5 Besides, she's soon going to be Mrs.   àdèmàs |prontobaser |làsèṇyoradèmolínà↓   Además, pronto va a ser la señora de
Molina.   Molina.

6 But it was hard for her to quit her job.   pérólèkósto |dèhareltrabáhò↓   Pero le costó dejar el trabajo.

7 Because she liked the people she worked   pórkèlègùstàbamucho |làhente |koṇkyen   Porque le gustaba mucho la gente con
with very much.   trabahábà↓   quien trabajaba.

TREINTA Y SIETE   18.37

UNIT 18   SPOKEN SPANISH

DIALOG 2

Juan, pregúntele a José, a propósito, por qué dejó ella ese trabajo. Que si no estaba contenta.

apropósitó↓ porke |dehoeⓊya |esetrabáhó↓ noęstabakontenta↑

Juan: A propósito, ¿por qué dejó ella ese trabajo? ¿No estaba contenta?

José, contéstele que sí, pero que no le convenía. Que pagaban muy poco.

sí↓ peronolekombeníá↓ lépàgaban | muypókò↓

José: Sí, pero no le convenía. Le pagaban muy poco.

Juan, dígale que entonces hizo bien. Que además, pronto va a ser la Sra. de Molina.

entonçes |işobyén↓ àdėmas |prontobaser | làsènyoraḍemolínà↓

Juan: Entonces hizo bien. Además pronto va a ser la señora de Molina.

José, dígale que así es. Pero le costó dejar el trabajo, dígale.

àsiés↓ péròlèkòstò |ḍehárèltràbáhó↓

José: Así es. Pero le costó dejar el trabajo.

Juan, pregúntele que cómo, que por qué.

komó↓ pòrke↓

Juan: ¿Como? ¿Por qué?

José, dígale que porque le gustaba mucho la gente con quién trabajaba.

pórkélėgústabamucho |làhente |kòŋkyén trabahábà↓

José: Porque le gustaba mucho la gente con quién trabajaba.

NARRATIVE 3

1 Changing the subject, Harris invited Jose and Carmen to visit the Air Force Mission.

àblando |ḍęotrakosa↑harrisįmbito |ahòse įakarmen |àbisitarlamisyon |dèlàfwerşaéreà↓

Hablando de otra cosa, Harris invitó a José y a Carmen a visitar la Misión de la Fuerza Aérea.

2 He invited Juan as well, but didn't tell him what day.

imbitoąhwán |tàmbyém↓péronoledího |keḍíà↓

Invitó a Juan también, pero no le dijo qué día.

18.38   TREINTA Y OCHO

SPOKEN SPANISH   UNIT 18

3 He told Jose this Saturday or the next.

àhòséledího|késtesàbado|ǫelkèbyéne̊↓

A José le dijo que este sábado o el que
viene.

4 Juan would like to go the next.

àhwán|lègústàriǫir|èlkèbyéne̊↓

A Juan le gustaría ir el que viene.

5 Carmen would, too.

àkármentambyén↓

A Carmen también.

6 Because this Saturday she has to go
   shopping with somebody.

pórkéstesàbadǫ|eǫyatyénekǫir|dekómpràs|
kònálgyèn↓

Porque este sábado ella tiene que ir de
compras con alguien.

DIALOG 3

Juan, hablando de otra cosa, pregúntele a
José si Harris lo invitó a visitar la
Misión de la Fuerza Aérea.

àblandǫdǫǫotrakósà↓ àtitǫimbitohárris|
abisitarlamisyón|delafwerǫaereà↑

Juan: Hablando de otra cosa, ¿a ti te invitó
       Harris a visitar la Misión de la
       Fuerza Aérea?

José, contéstele que sí, que lo invitó a Ud.
y a Carmen también.

sí↓ mǫimbitǫami|ǫàkármentambyén↓

José: Sí, me invitó a mí y a Carmen también.

Juan, dígale que a Ud. también lo invitó,
pero no le dijo qué día.

ámìtambyen|mǫimbitó↓pèrónomediho|kédíà↓

Juan: A mí también me invitó, pero no me dijo
       qué día.

José, contéstele que a Ud. le dijo que este
sábado o el que viene.

ámimediho|késtesàbado|ǫelkebyéne̊↓

José: A mí me dijo que este sábado o el que
       viene.

Juan, dígale que a Ud. le gustaría ir el que
viene.

ámì|mègústàriǫir|èlkèbyéne̊↓

Juan: A mí me gustaría ir el que viene.

José, dígale que a Carmen también porque
este sábado ella quedó en ir de compras
con alguien.

àkármentambyém↓pórkéstesàbadǫ|
eǫyakedó|ǫnirdekómpràs|kònálgyèn↓

José: A Carmen también porque este sábado
       ella quedó en ir de compras con
       alguien.

TREINTA Y NUEVE   18.39

jacobeligoodsons.com For Free Audio

UNIT 18   SPOKEN SPANISH

18.4   READINGS

18.40   List of cognate loan words

          la continuación   là—kòntínwàsyóṅ↓

          general   hènèrál↓

          excepto   ès(ṣ)éptò↓

          la manera   là—mànerà↓

          diferente   difèréntè↓

          francamente   fràŋkaméntè↓

          directamente   dírektaméntè↓

          superior   sùpéryór↓

          por ejemplo   pòr—èhemplò↓

          irritada (irritar)   irritàdà↓ irritár↓

          formar   fòrmár↓

          la opinión   là—òpinyóṅ↓

          la forma   là—formà↓

          tímido   timídò↓

18.40   CUARENTA

SPOKEN SPANISH   UNIT 18

18.41   Reading selection

Comentando (continuación)

Después de almorzar, los niños se levantaron de la mesa, pero don Ricardo y su esposa se quedaron conversando como lo hacían siempre. Después de hablar de otras cosas, don Ricardo volvió al tema de los nuevos vecinos.

——Americanos, ¿eh? ——exclamó—— ¿Qué piensas tú de los americanos en general?

——Yo no sé, pero me parece que deben ser gente igual a nosotros, excepto que ellos hablan inglés y nosotros español, y que su manera de vivir puede ser un poco diferente a la nuestra——contestó ella.—— ¿Por qué?, ¿qué crees tú de ellos?

——Francamente no sé qué decir porque nunca los he tratado directamente; sólo hablo de vez en cuando con ellos cuando llegan a la oficina a preguntar cualquier cosa. Pero te pregunto porque a don Manuel, el jefe mío, no le gustan. Dice que todos los americanos creen que son superiores a nosotros; que, por ejemplo, a la vuelta de su casa vive una familia desde hace más de seis meses, y que hasta la fecha ni él ni los otros vecinos del barrio han podido conocer a esa gente. Dice que muchas veces se ha encontrado con ellos en la calle y ha querido hablarles, pero que ellos nada: no dicen ni 'buenos días' ni 'buenas noches' y eso lo hacen porque se creen superiores. Y así como es esa familia son todos los americanos, todos son iguales......eso dice don Manuel, yo no——agregó don Ricardo al ver que su mujer lo miraba un poco irritada.

——¿Cómo puede ese jefe tuyo formarse una opinión general de la gente así en esa forma? ¿Cómo sabe él si la razón por la cual esos americanos que viven cerca de su casa no hablan con nadie es porque no saben hablar español, o porque son muy tímidos, o por muchas otras razones?

——Tienes toda la razón. Don Manuel hace mal en hablar así de los americanos. Pero tú sabes que él es mi jefe y yo no puedo decirle nada. A propósito, ¿no sabes si estos señores de enfrente hablan español?

——No, no sé, pero debemos ir a visitarlos y ver si podemos ayudarles en algo. En todo caso, si no hablan español, tú sabes un poco de inglés.

——Hace mucho que no hablo, necesito practicar. Pero vamos esta noche, si quieres.

——No, Ricardo, esta noche no. Mejor mañana; ellos acaban de mudarse y todavía deben tener todo sin arreglar.

——Muy bien——exclamó don Ricardo, levantándose de la mesa—— Así tengo tiempo de estudiar un poco esta tarde. Voy a llevarme el libro a la oficina. ¿Dónde está?

18.41

jacobeligoodsons.com For Free Audio

UNIT 18   SPOKEN SPANISH

18.42   Response drill

1 ¿Qué hacían siempre Ricardo y Marta después de almorzar?

2 Después de hablar de otras cosas, ¿a cuál tema volvieron?

3 ¿Qué pensaba Marta de los americanos en general?

4 ¿Por qué no sabe don Ricardo cómo son los americanos?

5 ¿Qué le parecen al jefe de don Ricardo?

6 ¿Por qué tiene él la opinión de que los americanos creen ser superiores?

7 ¿Dónde vive esa familia de quién él habla?

8 ¿Cuánto tiempo hace que esa familia vive allí?

9 ¿Hace bien don Manuel en hablar así de los americanos?

10 ¿Por qué no puede don Ricardo decirle a él que hace mal?

11 ¿Cuándo van a ir los Fuentes a visitar a los Robinson?

12 ¿Por qué es mejor no ir esta noche?

13 ¿A dónde va a llevar don Ricardo el libro de inglés?

14 ¿Para qué va a llevarlo allí?

15 ¿Cuánto tiempo hace que él no practica el inglés?

18.42   CUARENTA Y DOS

SPOKEN SPANISH   UNIT 19

19.1   BASIC SENTENCES.   Visit to Air Mission.

         Molina and White go to visit the Mission and are met by Coronel Harris.

ENGLISH SPELLING   AID TO LISTENING   SPANISH SPELLING

     pardon (to pardon)   pèrdonè↓ pèrdònár↓   perdone (perdonar)

     that (we) might arrive (to arrive)[1]   kè-˄yègàràmòs↓ ˄yègá̀r↓   que llegáramos (llegar)

     on time   à—tyémpò↓   a tiempo

Molina   Molina
Coronel, excuse us for not arriving on time.   kòrònèl↓pèrdòne|kèno˄yègáramos,atyémpò↓   Coronel, perdone que no llegáramos a
                                                                                  tiempo.

     don't yourselves worry (to worry)   no-sè-preokúpèn↓ prèòkúparsè↓   no se preocupen (preocuparse)

Harris   Harris
Don't give it a thought. What happened?   nosepreokúpèn↓ kelespasó↓   No se preocupen. ¿Qué les pasó?

     it got late on us   sè—nòs—ìṣo—tárdè↓   se nos hizo tarde

     to become late   àṣerse—tárdè↓   hacerse tarde

     (we) could, were able (to be able)   púdimòs↓ pòdér↓   pudimos (poder)

     to communicate ourselves (to communicate)   kòmúnikàrnòs↓ kòmúnikàrsè↓   comunicarnos (comunicarse)

Molina   Molina
It got late on us and we couldn't get in touch   sènòs,ìṣotárdè↑inopudimos|kòmúnikàrnòs| Se nos hizo tarde y no pudimos comunicar-
  with you.   nos con usted.
                                              kònústéd↓

     the line   là—linèà↓   la línea

UNO   19.1

jacobeligoodsons.com For Free Audio

UNIT 19   SPOKEN SPANISH

White
We called but the line was busy.

Çyàmamos │pèrólàlinęa │estabạokupáđà↓

White
Llamamos pero la línea estaba ocupada.

Harris
You're right.

tyenerrąşón↓

Harris
Tiene razón.

    about, around

kómó↓

    como

    the attaché [2]

èl‑ágrégađó↓

    el agregado

    aerial

áérèó↓

    aéreo

I was nearly an hour talking with the Air Attaché.

èstube │kómǫúnąorạ │àblando │kônélágrégadǫ áérèó↓

Estuve como una hora hablando con el Agregado Aéreo.

    to pertain, to belong

pèrtènèşe'r↓

    pertenecer

Molina
This building here....Does it belong to the American Mission?

estedifíşyó↓ pèrtènęşęalamısyon̦amerikana↑

Molina
Este edificio, ¿pertenece a la Misión Americana?

    the war

là‑gérrà↓

    la guerra

    the War Department

èl‑ministéryo‑de‑gérrà↓

    El Ministerio de Guerra

    the country

èl‑páís↓

    el país

Harris
No. It belongs to the War Department of this country. [3]

nó↓èzđélministéryo │đègérra │đéstèpáís↓

Harris
No, es del Ministerio de Guerra de este país.

    only

sólaméntè↓

    solamente

We only have three rooms here for our offices.

sólaménte │tènémósạki │treskwartos │para nwestrasǫfişínàs↓

Solamente tenemos aquí tres cuartos para nuestras oficinas.

SPOKEN SPANISH   UNIT 19

forty   kwàrentà↓   cuarenta

to land   àtèrrişàr↓   aterrizar

White   *White*
Look at that C-47 coming in.   mirạeseşe|kwaréntạisyétè|kèstàterrişándò↓   Mira ese C.47 que está aterrizando.

to take off (4)   dèspègàr↓   despegar

Molina   *Molina*
Isn't it the same one that was taking off when nọeșelmizmo|kec̦espegaba|kwandobeniamos↑   ¿No es el mismo que despegaba cuando
  we were coming?   veniamos?

the motor, engine   èl—mòtòr↓   el motor

Harris   *Harris*
Yes. They're testing the engines.   si↓èstámpròbàndo|lo—motórès↓   Sí, están probando los motores.

(we) would be able (to be able)   pòdrìàmòs↓ pòdér↓   podríamos (poder)

Molina   *Molina*
Could we go see it?   pòdriàmos|ịrabérlo↑   ¿Podríamos ir a verlo?

Harris   *Harris*
Sure.   klarò↓   ¡Claro!

the base   là—bàsè↓   la base

Afterwards I'll introduce you to the base commander. dèspwéz|lèsprésénto|àlhefecᵈelàbásè↓   Después les presento al jefe de la base.

several   bàryòs↓   varios

TRES   19.3

UNIT 19   SPOKEN SPANISH

the pilot   èl—pìlótò↓   el piloto

And also to some of the pilots.   ìtàmbyén ¦àbàryòz ¦dèlòspìlótòs↓   Y también a varios de los pilotos.

19.10   Notes on the basic sentences

(1) This form is a past subjunctive. It will be dealt with in units 49 and following.

(2) Usage varies in different countries. For instance, in Chile, /adíkto/ *adicto* is frequently used.

(3) Note /és—de/ *es de*, literally 'it is of.' In the present context this expression translates 'it belongs to'.

(4) Instead of /despegár/ *despegar*, another item, /dekolár/ *decolar* is regularly heard in Peru, and occasionally in other Latin American countries.

19.2   DRILLS AND GRAMMAR

19.21   Pattern drills

19.21.1 Past I and past II in the same construction

A. Presentation of pattern

ILLUSTRATIONS

_____	1	⌢yàmàmós ¦pèrólàlíng̩a ¦estàḅg̩okupádà↓	*Llamamos*, pero la línea *estaba* ocupada.
_____	2	sìnótekòmbènìa↑ ịs̩ístèbyénèndèhárló↓	Si no te *convenía, hiciste* bien en dejarlo.
When I called, he wasn't in.	3	kwándòyò⌢yàmé↑ g̩lng̩ẹstábà↓	Cuando yo *llamé, él* no estaba.
I opened a suitcase that wasn't mine.	4	àbrịŋnàmàléta ¦kèng̩ẹramíà↓	*Abrí* una maleta que no *era* mía.

19.4   CUATRO

jacobeligoodsons.com For Free Audio

SPOKEN SPANISH   UNIT 19

I went out with a girl that spoke Spanish.   5   sàli |kònúnàsèŋyòrita |kẹ́áblábạẹspạŋyól↓   *Salí* con una señorita que *hablaba* español.

_____   6   diho |kẹ̀pòdíamos,ir |éstẹsábádò↓   *Dijo* que *podíamos* ir este sábado.

while   myẻntràs↓   mientras

While I was studying, she went downtown.   7   myẻntràzyóẹstudyábạ́f ė̀·yafwẹ̀ạlşẻntrò↓   Mientras yo *estudiaba*, ella *fué* al centro.

EXTRAPOLATION

	Past I	Past II
Singly	↓ ⟋	⋯⋯ ⟋
	↓↓↓↓ ⟋	↓ n^{th} ⟋
In combination	↓ ⋯⋯⋯ ⟋	

NOTES

a.   ∧   means present
          ⟋ means past
        ⟋   means future

b. Past I implies definiteness in time or number.
    Past II implies indefiniteness in time or number.

c. In combination, an action in past I occurs during the background of
    an action in past II.

CINCO

UNIT 19   SPOKEN SPANISH

19.21.11 Translation drills — Contrastive translation [1]

1 I worked (for a time) at the Embassy.   tràbàhenlạembahádà↓   Trabajé en la Embajada.

   I was working (at that time) at the   tràbáhabạenlạembahádà↓   Trabajaba en la Embajada.
   Embassy.

2 I went down (once) in the elevator.   bàhenẹlas(s)ensór↓   Bajé en el ascensor.

   I went down (customarily) in the elevator.   bàhabạenẹlas(s)ensór↓   Bajaba en el ascensor.

3 I couldn't find the house.   nọeŋkontrabalakásà↓   No encontraba la casa.

   I didn't find the house.   nọeŋkontrélakásà↓   No encontré la casa.

4 I left late (that time).   sàlitárdè↓   Salí tarde.

   I left late (customarily).   sàliatárdè↓   Salía tarde.

5 I lived there with my family (at that time).   bibìa|kònmifàmílyạ|á()yí↓   Vivía con mi familia allí.

   I lived there with my family (for a time).   bibi|kònmifàmílyạ|á()yí↓   Viví con mi familia allí.

6 I drank beer (all day).   tòmeşerbéşà↓   Tomé cerveza.

   I drank beer (every day).   tòmabaşerbéşà↓   Tomaba cerveza.

_____

   (1) For the purpose of this drill, the contexts have been kept minimal. Notice, however, that the implications of the choice of forms in Spanish can often be expressed
in English only by an additional (here parenthetical) notation. Something akin to these parenthetical meanings is inherently present in the past I or past II Spanish verb.

19.6   jacobeligoodsons.com For Free Audio   SEIS

SPOKEN SPANISH   UNIT 19

7 I wrote very little (that time).   èskríbimuypókǫ̀↓   Escribí muy poco.

   I wrote very little (as a rule).   èskríbiàmuypókò↓   Escribía muy poco.

8 I ate chops (once).   kòmichulétàs↓   Comí chuletas.

   I ate chops (regularly).   kòmiàchulétás↓   Comía chuletas.

9 I rented the house (that time).   álkilélakásà↓   Alquilé la casa.

   I was renting the house (at that time).   álkilábalakásà↓   Alquilaba la casa.

                                    Mixed past tenses [1]

1 When I arrived, he wasn't there.   kwándǫ̀ỳ̀ẹ̀gè↑èlnǫèstábǫ̀|àí↓   Cuando llegué, él no estaba ahí.

2 I saw an apartment that didn't have (any) bí|ỳnàpàrtàmento|kènòteniàmwéblès↓   Vi un apartamento que no tenía muebles.
   furniture.

3 I met a lady who was a friend of his.   kònǫ́ṣì|ạùnàsèŋyora|kéràmìgadél↓   Conocí a una señora que era amiga de él.

4 I spoke to the girl that I wanted to meet. áblé|kònlàmúchacha|kèkèrìàkonoṣér↓   Hablé con la muchacha que quería conocer.

5 She swept the room that was dirty.   bàrryó|ẹ̀lkwàrto|kèstàbasúṣyò↓   Barrió el cuarto que estaba sucio.

6 I went out with a girl that didn't speak sàlí|kònǜnàmúchacha|kènǫàblàbạ̀inglés↓   Salí con una muchacha que no hablaba
   English.   inglés.

_____
[1] Each of the sentences in this drill is constructed to require one verb in past I and one verb in past II. Notice that the selection is not simplified by construc-
tional contrasts in English such as 'did go' vs 'was going.'

SIETE   19.7

UNIT 19   SPOKEN SPANISH

7 We saw the lady that wanted to buy the house.

bímos |àlásèŋyóra |kèkèríakömprárlakásà↓

Vimos a la señora que quería comprar la casa.

8 He bought a car that didn't cost much.

kömproʊn̯awto |kénokostábamúchò↓

Compró un auto que no costaba mucho.

9 I opened a trunk that wasn't mine.

àbriʊmbaúl |kénǫeramíó↓

Abrí un baúl que no era mío.

10 We cleaned the windows because they were dirty.

limpyámoz |lázbèntánas↑pórkèstabansúsyàs↓

Limpiamos las ventanas porque estaban sucias.

11 We repeated the sentence because he didn't understand it.

rrèpètímoz |láfrase↑pórkél |nolǫentendíà↓

Repetimos la frase porque él no la entendía.

12 While I was having lunch, Juan wrote the letter.

myéntràzyoạlmorṣaba↑hwaṇeskribyólakártà↓

Mientras yo almorzaba, Juan escribió la carta.

13 While I was there, nobody went out.

myéntràzyo |ęstabaⱷⱴꭓ↑nosalyónáɗyè↓

Mientras yo estaba allí no salió nadie.

Contextual translation [1]

1 We arrived from Cuba two years ago.

ⱷyègámoz |ɗèkubạ |áṣèɗosáŋyòs↓

Llegamos de Cuba hace dos años.

2 When we lived there, we didn't speak Spanish.

kwándòbíbìamos |áⱷꭓ↑nǫablábamosẹspaŋyól↓

Cuando vivíamos allí no hablábamos español.

---

[1] The sentences in this drill, though numbered separately, are contextually related. In each case, the context determines whether the verb will occur in a past I or a past II form.

19.8   OCHO

SPOKEN SPANISH   UNIT 19

3 Every week we went to parties.   tóðazla(s)semanas|íbanosˌafyéstàs↓   Todas las semanas íbamos a fiestas.

4 We used to have lots of fun.   nózðibèrtiámòʐ|múchò↓   Nos divertíamos mucho.

5 At that time we had only one child.   èntónʂes|téníámòs̯uníhò|sólàméntè↓   Entonces teníamos un hijo solamente.

6 We had a girl that took care of him.   téníamos|ùnámùchacha|keloatendía↓   Teníamos una muchacha que lo atendía.

7 When we arrived in Cuba, we bought a   kwándòˊyègámos|akuba↑kómprámos̯unakásâ↓   Cuando llegamos a Cuba compramos una
   house.   casa.

8 It was very large.   éràmuygrándê↓   Era muy grande.

9 It had five bedrooms.   téníáʂiŋkoↄormitóryòs↓   Tenía cinco dormitorios.

10 Before leaving there, I fixed it up.   ántez|ðèsàlírdˌeàˊya↑larreglé↓   Antes de salir de allá la arreglé.

11 A friend of mine bought it.   únàmígomiolakómpró↓   Un amigo mío la compró.

12 Actually, he didn't pay me very much.   ènrrẹàlíðaↄ↑nomepagómúchò↓   En realidad no me pagó mucho.

13 We lived in Cuba five years.   bíbimós|èŋkuba↑ʂiŋkọáɲòs↓   Vivimos en Cuba cinco años.

14 And we liked it a lot.   inòzgústo|múchò↓   Y nos gustó mucho.

15 We left there two years ago.   sàlímozðẹaↄya↑ạ̀ʂèðós̯aɲòs↓   Salimos de allá hace dos años.

NUEVE   19.9

B. Discussion of pattern

English and Spanish have both developed from what 3000 years ago was a single language. The effects of this relationship can be seen in the many structural features the two languages have in common, such as number in nouns, person and case in pronouns, and tense in verbs. However, 3000 years is a long time, and the resultant differences are now as apparent as the similarities. For example, there is no gender agreement in English, the case distinctions of the pronouns are not the same, and the concept of tense in verbs is different, which is the subject of the present discussion.

In terms of form, the English verb system differentiates only what we call *past* from something we can best refer to negatively as *nonpast*. This nonpast can be differentiated structurally on the construction level into *present* and *future* (i.e., future can be expressed only through a *construction*: 'goes' vs 'will go'; there is no *tense* to express futurity.)

So English verbs differentiate three periods of time:

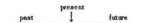

The present is represented as a point on the time line moving at a constant rate from past toward future.

For Spanish, the concept of *past* must be divided into two ideas that might be labelled *aspects*. For convenience these are referred to as past I and past II. Thus the Spanish concept of chronology must be represented:

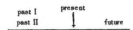

Note that the relationship between the **two past tenses is not** a temporal one. They could not be shown in a linear sequence one after the other, since both are represented in relation to present and future.

Note also that the presence of two categories in past time means that the choice of *one or the other is always* obligatory. One *cannot be noncommittal*; the speaker must choose between past I, with implications of unity and definiteness inherent in such a choice, and past II, with implications of extended duration and indefiniteness inherent in that choice. In other words, *past* is possible only when one selects between the 'I' and the 'II', unlike English where the selection of the additional implications is not forced with every reference to past time.

This choice does not greatly trouble a Spanish speaker. He has lived with the distinction since childhood, and he automatically makes the aspect distinction when he makes the time distinction. Indeed, he may feel at a loss in a language like English, because the available past tense forms do not say everything that he wants them to.

An English speaker learning Spanish, however, must make the additional aspect choice *every time he uses past tens*, and until he builds the distinction into his usage so it operates below the level of awareness, as it does for Spanish speakers, he will likely find the choice difficult and burdensome. This is not strange; English speakers completely lack experience in making such a choice.

Nor can an error in the choice of past I or past II be lightly dismissed as a 'slight' error (after all, they're both *past*). Past I is distinguished from past II by as great a difference as either is from present or future tenses, and the wrong choice will be just as conspicuous.

In fact, it may result in greater confusion for one important reason: without distinguishing context, past I can appear in almost any sentence past II can appear in, but with the important consideration that it *means* something different. This is why it is especially important to get a 'feel' for the difference between past I and past II.

An analogy to photography may help in understanding how past I differs from past II. Photography is a visual method of recording past time. A snapshot is like past I in recording a single event distinct from other similar events, and it has the unity of its single occurrence. The emphasis is on the event as separate and complete. A motion picture is more like past II in recording an extension of time with emphasis on moving action and continuity. The temporal limits of the action are hazy, and we are aware of the intimate relation to what precedes and follows as being part of the action at any point. The key words in this analogy are 'event' and 'action'; the event in past I implies 'what happened', and the action in past II implies 'what was going on'.

The following diagrams may be helpful in differentiating the two past tenses:

/anóche-(l)yegó-hwán↓/   /hwán-syémpre|salía-de-nóche↓/

'John arrived last night.'   'John always went out at night.'

Past I is a unit event of momentaneous or specifically limited duration. Past II is an action of indefinitely extended duration. However, length of duration in the past is not absolute, but highly relative. The determining thing is the attitude of the speaker toward the situation as a discrete unit or as an extension. Several centuries can be thought of as a single event, or a minute may provide background extension for a more limited event:

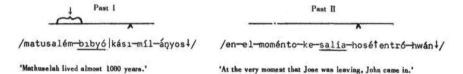

/matusalém-bibyó|kásı-míl-áɲyos↓/   /en-el-moménto-ke-salía-hosé↑entró-hwán↓/

'Mathuselah lived almost 1000 years.'   'At the very moment that Jose was leaving, John came in.'

If the degree of definiteness or indefiniteness is in terms of the number of times an action is repeated, the distribution can be charted as follows:

/fwímos-kwátro-béşes↓/   /ántes|íbamos-tódos-los-días↓/

'We went four times.'   'Previously, we went every day.'

ONCE

UNIT 19   SPOKEN SPANISH

In the first example the four 'goings' are considered as discrete, sequential events, and they are therefore reported in past I. Note the following two sentences, which show that a context can be established to convey the concept of duration or the concept of discreteness (even though the exact number of repetitions is not stated) merely by the choice of past tense forms.

/en—ése—tyémpo |fwímos—múchas—béşes↓/   /ántes |íbamos—múchas—béşes↓/

'At that time, we went many times.'   'Previously, we went many times.'

Other specific examples and contrasts follow.

Past I is typically used for narration of sequential events (what happened), each thought of as dissociated from preceding and following events, and as having equal grammatical status:

/el—seŋyór—salyó↑ fwé—a—un—rrestorán↑ ı—komyó—múcho↓/

'The gentleman went out, went to a restaurant, and ate a lot.'

Separation into distinct events may be sequential or just conceptual; i.e., nonsequential actions (or conditions) may also be thought of as isolated and distinct:

/los—días—fwéron—bonítos↓ syémpre—işo—sól |kwándo—fwímos—al—kámpo↓/

'The days were beautiful; it was always sunny when we went to the country.'

By way of contrast, and regardless of translation, past II is used for background description (what was going on). Therefore, a sentence which has a past II form rarely makes sense if uttered in isolation (/el—seŋyór—komía↓/The gentleman was eating') unless the specific conditions under which such background information occurred are made explicit, because the very occurrence of a past II form creates a context which strongly implies another event happening against the backdrop of that context. This other event may be specifically stated (in past I) or it may be suggested by the overall context:

/el—día—estába—boníto↓ por—éso |fwímos—a—la—pláya↓/

'The day was pretty; so, we went to the beach.'

/entónşes |bıbíamos—en—karákas↓/

'Then, we were living in Caracas.'

19.12   DOCE

SPOKEN SPANISH   UNIT 19

Most important for the drills in this section is the relationship of verbs in past I and past II in the same sentence. If one action is in progress (past II) when an interrupting action occurs (past I), the interruption represents a discrete event portrayed against a continuous background:

Past I and past II

/kwándo‑yó‑◌yamé↑él‑no‑estába↓/

'When I called, he wasn't there.'

Time of day (with /sér/) is reported as background information in a sentence like /éran‑las‑dós↓/ 'It was two o'clock.' But the isolated expression seems truncated unless the context supplies an event occurring against that background, as /éran‑las‑dós|kwándo‑salí↓/ 'It was two o'clock when I left.'

A customary or habitual action in the past creates a background when reported in past II. Thus the sentence /íbamos‑a‑la‑pláya|tódos‑los‑días↓/ 'We went to the beach every day' by implication also says 'at the time I'm referring to.' Otherwise, even an indefinitely repeated action can be reported in past I: /fwímos‑a‑la‑pláya‑múchas‑bó◌es↓/ 'We went to the beach many times.'

Actions planned for occurrence in the past, whether or not the plans were carried out, are reported as background in past II:

/hwán‑íba‑a‑pasár|por‑mí↓ péro‑nó‑pasó↓/

'John was going to come by for me; but he didn't.'

/yó‑pensába|ír‑á‑méhıko↓ ı‑fwí↓/

'I was planning to go to Mexico, and I did.'

Note the contrast in meaning, between what happened and what was intended, in the following two sentences:

/yó‑nó‑súpe|a‑ké‑óra‑◌yegó↓/   /yó‑nó‑sabía|a‑ké‑óra‑◌yegába↓/

'I didn't know what time you arrived.'   'I didn't know when you were arriving (were going to arrive, would arrive).'

Coterminous actions (actions of simultaneous duration) are usually reported in past II, and again the implication is that they are background:

/hwán‑leía|myéntras‑yó‑estudyába↓/ (/así|andubímos‑múy‑byén↓/)

'John read while I studied. This way we got along fine.'

TRECE   19.13

UNIT 19   SPOKEN SPANISH

This discussion has given no 'rules' about the use of past I and past II in Spanish, because it is almost impossible to do so in terms of English, where the distinctions involved are not part of the formal structure of the language. These distinctions are simple and obvious to a native speaker of Spanish; in a very real sense, his language compels him to make them.

One thing is certain: the distinction cannot be taught by simply correlating past I to 'did' (*did speak*) and past II to 'was' (*was speaking*). While this correlation takes care of some occurrences, there are too many like: /yó‑nó‑sabía‑ke‑él‑ablába‑espaṇyól↓/'I didn't know he spoke Spanish,' where both 'did know' and 'spoke' translate past II forms.

A possible correlation of the differences between the two past tenses in Spanish to analogous English constructions might be found in the following pair:

I heard Bill speak.

I heard Bill speaking.

In the first example the implication is that I heard the whole speech; in the second, I imply that I heard only the middle part. The first situation considers Bill's speech as a unit event; the second as a continuing process. The verb constructions of these two English utterances do not parallel the past I and past II tense formations in Spanish, but they may show how English in a roundabout way makes a distinction which in Spanish is normal to all past situations and is accomplished merely by the choice of a past I or a past II tense form.

19.14   CATORCE

SPOKEN SPANISH UNIT 19

19.21.2 Question intonation patterns – Echo questions

A. Presentation of pattern

ILLUSTRATIONS

1 kwántoleđébò↓

I said how much do I owe you?

    kèkwántoleđébò↓

      2   1 1↓
   ¿Cuánto le debo?

         1 2   3 1↓
    ¿Que cuánto le debo?

Where are you from?

2 déđondesustéđ↓

   I said where are you from?

    kéđéđondesustéđ↓

   1 2   11↓
  ¿De dónde es usted?

       1 2   31↓
    ¿Que de dónde es usted?

I said can we see it?

3 póđemozberló↑

    kèsipóđemozberló↓

   1 2   2 2↑
  ¿Podemos verlo?

       1 2   3 1↓
    ¿Que si podemos verlo?

I said do you like the room?

4 lègustạelkwartó↑

    kèsilègustạelkwartò↓

   1 2   2 2↑
  ¿Le gusta el cuarto?

      1   2   3 1↓
    ¿Que si le gusta el cuarto?

EXTRAPOLATION

Information question or statement	Echo question
/1211↓/	/1 231↓/ ke

Yes-no question	Echo question
/1222↑/	/ 1 231↓/ kesı

NOTES

a. Echo questions occur on the contrastive /1231↓/ pattern.

b. Weak stressed /ke.../ precedes an information question, /kesı.../ a yes-no question.

QUINCE 19.15

UNIT 19   SPOKEN SPANISH

19.21.21 Substitution drill — Pattern substitution

1 éŋkeabenidabíbé↓   kéŋkeabenidabíbé↓

2 dondestalasí^ya↓   kédondestalasi^ya↓

3 ákeorabá↓   keákeorabá↓

4 kyenesesachíka↓   kékyenesesachíka↓

5 kyentyenemikópa↓   kékyentyenemikópa↓

6 kwandobamudársè↓   kékwandobamudárse↓

7 kwantostyéne↓   kékwantostyéne↓

```
      1    2        11 ↓                           1     2       3 1 ↓
      ¿En qué avenida vive?                        ¿Que en qué avenida vive?
          2        1 1↓                            1  2           3 1↓
   2  ¿Dónde está la silla?                        ¿Que dónde está la silla?
      1    2   11 ↓                                1     2    31↓
   3  ¿A qué hora va?                              ¿Que a qué hora va?
          2        1 1 ↓                           1    2       3 1↓
   4  ¿Quién es esa chica?                         ¿Que quién es esa chica?
          2        1 1 ↓                           1    2       3 1↓
   5  ¿Quién tiene mi copa?                        ¿Que quién tiene mi copa?
          2        1 1 ↓                           1  2         3 1↓
   6  ¿Cuándo va a mudarse?                        ¿Que cuándo va a mudarse?
          2    1 1↓                                1  2      31↓
   7  ¿Cuántos tiene?                              ¿Que cuántos tiene?
```

19.16   DIECISEIS

SPOKEN SPANISH   UNIT 19

8 dondestalahénṣyà↓   kèdondestalahénṣyà↓

9 sonrrigurosos↑   kèsisonrrigurosós↓

10 àkabandesalir↑   kèsḁàkabandesalir↓

11 e⁀yḁe(s)soltera↑   kèsḁe⁀yḁe(s)solterà↓

12 balṣentro↑   kèsibalṣentrò↓

13 banakomer↑   kèsibanakomer↓

14 bibenunotel↑   kèsibibenunotel↓

```
        2           1  1↓
8  ¿Dónde está la agencia?
```

```
        1      2 2↑
9  ¿Son rigurosos?
```

```
     1 2        22 ↑
10 ¿Acaban de salir?
```

```
       2        22 ↑
11 ¿Ella es soltera?
```

```
       2    2  2↑
12 ¿Va al centro?
```

```
       2       22 ↑
13 ¿Van a comer?
```

```
       2        22 ↑
14 ¿Vive en un hotel?
```

```
   1  2          3  1↓
¿Que dónde está la agencia?
```

```
     1    2     31↓
¿Que si son rigurosos?
```

```
       1    2       31 ↓
¿Que si acaban de salir?
```

```
       1    2      31↓
¿Que si ella es soltera?
```

```
     1    2    3  1↓
¿Que si va al centro?
```

```
     1    2      31↓
¿Que si van a comer?
```

```
       1    2       31↓
¿Que si vive en un hotel?
```

DIECISIETE

jacobeligoodsons.com For Free Audio

UNIT 19   SPOKEN SPANISH

15 éstadesokupadó↑   késįéstadesokupadó↓

16 bálelapéna↑   késíbalelapéna↓

17 éstaseguró↑   késįéstaseguró↓

---

           1 2   2 2 ↑   1   2   3 1 ↓
      15 ¿Está desocupado?   ¿Que si está desocupado?
              2   2 2 ↑   1   2   3 1 ↓
      16 ¿Vale la pena?   ¿Que si vale la pena?
            1 2   2 2 ↑   1   2   3 1 ↓
      17 ¿Está seguro?   ¿Que si está seguro?

B. Discussion of pattern

     Echo questions, questions repeated because they were not heard or understood, normally appear on the contrastive pattern /1231↓/ . The actual repetition is
preceded by the weak stressed forms /kesɪ…/ (for a yes-no question) or /ke…/ (for an information question). These are equivalent to the 'I said' part of a sentence
in English in: 'I said when are you coming?'

     An echo question formed on the above pattern could be expanded as follows:

                    /ke‑kwánto‑le‑débo↓/   'I said how much do I owe you?'

                    /le‑díhe |ke‑kwánto‑le‑débo↓/   'I said how much do I owe you?'

     The difference between English and Spanish on this point is one of construction type. The repetition in English is a direct quotation; in Spanish it is an indirect
quotation, which requires the relator /ke/.

19.18   DIECIOCHO

SPOKEN SPANISH   UNIT 19

19.22   Replacement drills

A   èstúbe |kómọunặórạ |àblándò↓

1 _____ ḍos _____ ↓   èstúbe |kómóḍosóràs |àblándò↓

2 _____ èstúḍyándò↓   èstúbe |kómóḍosóràs |èstúḍyándò↓

3 _____ apénaz _____ ↓   èstúbẹ |apénaz |ḍosóràs |èstúḍyándò↓

4 _____ unạ _____ ↓   èstúbẹ |apénas |unặórạ |èstúḍyándò↓

5 _____ èskríbyéndò↓   èstúbẹ |apénas |unặórạ |èskríbyéndò↓

6 _____ moméntò _____ ↓   èstúbẹ |apénas |unmoméntọ |èskríbyéndò↓

7 _____ ()yàmándò↓   èstúbẹ |apénas |unmoméntò |()yàmándò↓

A   Estuve como una hora hablando.

1 _____ dos _____ .   Estuve como dos horas hablando.

2 _____ estudiando.   Estuve como dos horas estudiando.

3 _____ apenas _____ .   Estuve apenas dos horas estudiando.

4 _____ una _____ .   Estuve apenas una hora estudiando.

5 _____ escribiendo.   Estuve apenas una hora escribiendo.

6 _____ momento _____ .   Estuve apenas un momento escribiendo.

7 _____ llamando.   Estuve apenas un momento llamando.

DIECINUEVE   19.19

UNIT 19   SPOKEN SPANISH

B   éstedifíşyò↓pèrténeşę |alamisyonamerikanat   éstedifíşyò↓pèrténeşę |alministeryodegerrat
1 _____ ministeryodegerrat   àkéỹosedifíşyòs↓pèrténeşen |alministeryode
2 àkéỹos_____t   gerrat

3 _____kásàs_____t   àkéỹaskásàs↓pèrténeşen |alministeryodegerrat
4 _____amerikánost   àkéỹaskásàs↓pèrténeşen |alosamerikánost
5 _____abyón_____t   àkelabyón↓pèrténeşę |alosamerikánost
6 _____algyent   àkelabyón↓pèrténeşę |algyent
7 _____kósà_____t   àkéỹyakósà↓pèrténeşę |algyent

B   Este edificio, ¿pertenece a la Misión Americana?

1 _____, ¿_____Ministerio de Guerra?   Este edificio, ¿pertenece al Ministerio de Guerra?
2 Aquellos___, ¿_____?   Aquellos edificios, ¿pertenecen al Ministerio de Guerra?
3 ___casas, ¿_____?   Aquellas casas, ¿pertenecen al Ministerio de Guerra?
4 _____, ¿_____americanos?   Aquellas casas, ¿pertenecen a los americanos?
5 ___avión, ¿_____?   Aquel avión, ¿pertenece a los americanos?
6 _____, ¿_____a alguien?   Aquel avión, ¿pertenece a alguien?
7 ___cosa, ¿_____?   Aquella cosa, ¿pertenece a alguien?

SPOKEN SPANISH   UNIT 19

C   éz |dèlminustéryod̯egérrà↓

1   pèrtènés̬e̬_ _____↓   pèrtènés̬e̬ |àlmìnìstéryod̯egérrà↓

2   _____misyònàmerikánà↓   pèrtènés̬e̬ |àlàmìsyònàmerikánà↓

3   _____pilotos_____↓   pèrtènés̬e̬ |àlóspìlotos̬àmerikánòs↓

4   són_____↓   són |dèlóspìlotos̬àmerikánòs↓

5   _____espàŋyóles↓   són |dèlóspìlotos̬espàŋyóles↓

6   _____èmbàhad̯a̬_____↓   són |dèla̬èmbàhad̯a̬espàŋyólà↓

7   pèrtènés̬en_____↓   pèrtènés̬en |àla̬èmbàhad̯a̬espàŋyólà↓

C   Es del Ministerio de Guerra.

1 Pertenece _____.   Pertenece al Ministerio de Guerra.

2 _____Misión Americana.   Pertenece a la Misión Americana.

3 _____ pilotos _____.   Pertenece a los pilotos americanos.

4 Son_____.   Son de los pilotos americanos.

5 _____ españoles.   Son de los pilotos españoles.

6 _____ Embajada_____.   Son de la Embajada Española.

7 Pertenecen_____.   Pertenecen a la Embajada Española.

VEINTIUNO   19.21

UNIT 19   SPOKEN SPANISH

D   sólámente |tènemos,akí↑treskwártòs↓   sólo |tènemos,akí↑treskwártós↓

1   sólo _____ ↓   sólo |tènemos,akí↑tres,ofiṣínàs↓

2   _____ ofiṣínàs↓   sólo |tènemos,aⁿyí↑tres,ofiṣínàs↓

3   _____ aⁿyí _____ ↓   sólo |tèníamos |aⁿyí↑tres,ofiṣínàs↓

4   _____ tèníamos _____ ↓   syémpre |tèníamos |aⁿyí↑tres,ofiṣínàs↓

5   syémpre _____ ↓   syémpre |tèníamos |aⁿyí↑nwestras,ofiṣínàs↓

6   _____ nwéstras ___ ↓   syémpre |tèníamos |aⁿyí↑nwestros,abyónès↓

7   _____ abyónès↓

D   Solamente tenemos aquí tres cuartos.

1 Sólo _____ .   Sólo tenemos aquí tres cuartos.

2 _____ oficinas.   Sólo tenemos aquí tres oficinas.

3 _____ allí _____ .   Sólo tenemos allí tres oficinas.

4 _____ teníamos _____ .   Sólo teníamos allí tres oficinas.

5 Siempre _____ .   Siempre teníamos allí tres oficinas.

6 _____ nuestras ___ .   Siempre teníamos allí nuestras oficinas.

7 _____ aviones.   Siempre teníamos allí nuestros aviones.

SPOKEN SPANISH   UNIT 19

E   mírạ |eseʂe |kwaréntạisyété |kèstáterriʂándô↓

1   _____ despegándô↓   mírạ |eseʂe |kwaréntạisyété |kèstadespegándô↓

2   ____ àbyoŋ _____ ↓   mírạ |esẹabyóŋ |kèstadespegándô↓

3   __ esos _____ ↓   mírạ |esosạabyónès |kèstandespegándô↓

4   _____ (yegándô↓   mírạ |esosạabyónès |kèstan(yegándô↓

5   ____ chíkas _____ ↓   mírạ |aesaschíkàs |kèstan(yegándô↓

6   _____ komyéndô↓   mírạ |aesaschíkàs |kèstaŋkomyéndô↓

7   __ aké(yas _____ ↓   mírạ |aké(yaschíkàs |kèstaŋkomyéndô↓

_____

E   Mira ese C—47 que está aterrizando.

1   _____ despegando.   Mira ese C—47 que está despegando.

2   ____ avión _____ .   Mira ese avión que está despegando.

3   ___ esos _____ .   Mira esos aviones que están despegando.

4   _____ llegando.   Mira esos aviones que están llegando.

5   ____ chicas _____ .   Mira a esas chicas que están llegando.

6   _____ comiendo.   Mira a esas chicas que están comiendo.

7   ___ aquellas _____ .   Mira a aquellas chicas que están comiendo.

VEINTITRES   19.23

UNIT 19 SPOKEN SPANISH

F   itàmbyen↑ àbaryoz |delospilótòs↓

1   _____ senyóràs↓   itàmbyen↑ àbaryaz |dela(s)senyóràs↓

2   _____muchaz_____↓   itàmbyen↑ àmuchaz |dela(s)senyóràs↓

3   _____esas_____↓   itàmbyen↑ àmuchaz |desa(s)senyóràs↓

4   _____héfès↓   itàmbyen↑ àmuchoz |desoshéfès↓

5   _____uno_____↓   itàmbyen↑ ąuno |desoshéfès↓

6   _____chíkàs↓   itàmbyen↑ ąuna |desaschíkàs↓

7   _____otra_____↓   itàmbyen↑ ąotra |desaschíkàs↓

F   Y también a varios de los pilotos.

1   _____ señoras.   Y también a varias de las señoras.

2   _____muchas_____.   Y también a muchas de las señoras.

3   _____esas_____.   Y también a muchas de esas señoras.

4   _____jefes.   Y también a muchos de esos jefes.

5   _____uno_____.   Y también a uno de esos jefes.

6   _____chicas.   Y también a una de esas chicas.

7   _____otra_____.   Y también a otra de esas chicas.

SPOKEN SPANISH   UNIT 19

19.23   Variation drills

A   nópudimos |kómůnikárnoskonustéd↓   No pudimos comunicarnos con Ud.

1 We couldn't get in touch with the boss.   nópudimos |kómůnikárnoskonelhéfè↓   No pudimos comunicarnos con el jefe.

2 We couldn't get in touch with you (fam).   nópudimos |kómůnikárnoskontígò↓   No pudimos comunicarnos contigo.

3 We couldn't sit down at the party.   nópudimos |séntarnos₂enlafyéstà↓   No pudimos sentarnos en la fiesta.

4 We couldn't pay attention to the date.   nópudimos |fiharnos₂enlaféchà↓   No pudimos fijarnos en la fecha.

5 We couldn't (go) bathing without   nópudimoz |bàŋyarno(s)simpermísò↓   No pudimos bañarnos sin permiso.
  permission.

6 We couldn't shave right away.   nópudimos |àféytarnos₂ensegídà↓   No pudimos afeitarnos en seguida.

7 We couldn't leave right away.   nópudimos |irnos₂ensegídà↓   No pudimos irnos en seguida.

B   (l)yámamos |pérólálineą |estabąokupádà↓   Llamamos, pero la línea estaba ocupada.

1 We called, but everything was occupied.   (l)yámamos |pérótodǫ |estabąokupádò↓   Llamamos, pero todo estaba ocupado.

2 We arrived, but the house was empty.   (l)yégamos |pérólàkasą |estabądesokupádà↓ Llegamos, pero la casa estaba desocupada.

3 We arrived, but everything was taken.   (l)yégamos |pérótodǫ |estabatomádò↓   Llegamos, pero todo estaba tomado.

4 We arrived, but everyone was (all were)   (l)yègamós |pérótodos |estabaŋkansádòs↓ Llegamos, pero todos estaban cansados.
  tired.

VEINTICINCO   19.25

UNIT 19   SPOKEN SPANISH

5 We returned, but the tables were taken.   bòlbímos |pérólàzmésas |estàbantomádàs↓   Volvimos, pero las mesas estaban tomadas.

6 We returned, but the building was rented.   bòlbímos |pérọèlédifísyọ |estábalkiládò↓   Volvimos, pero el edificio estaba alquilado.

7 We returned, but the car had been (was)   bòlbímos |pérọèlawtọ |yaẹstàbakomprádò↓   Volvimos, pero el auto ya estaba comprado.
   already bought.

C   nọéşelmízmo |kéđèspègàba |kwàndobeníamos↑   ¿No es el mismo que despegaba cuando
                                                                                         veníamos?

1 Isn't it the same one that was taking off   nọéşelmízmo |kéđèspègàba |kwàndọℓℓyegábàmos↑   ¿No es el mismo que despegaba cuando
   as (when) we were arriving?   llegábamos?

2 Isn't it the same one that was landing as   nọéşelmízmo |kẹàtèrrìşàba |kwàndọℓℓyegábàmos↑   ¿No es el mismo que aterrizaba cuando
   (when) we were arriving?   llegábamos?

3 Isn't it the other one that was leaving   nọéşelótro |kèsálìa |kwàndobeníamos↑   ¿No es el otro que salía cuando veníamos?
   as (when) we were coming?

4 Isn't it the other one that was coming as   nọéşelótro |kèbénìa |kwàndosalíamos↑   ¿No es el otro que venía cuando salíamos?
   (when) we were leaving?

5 Isn't it the other one (f) that was arriving nọézlạótra |kéℓℓyègàba |kwàndosalíamos↑   ¿No es la otra que llegaba cuando salíamos?
   as (when) we were leaving?

6 Isn't it the lady who was coming down as   nọézlasèṇyóra |kèbáhàba |kwàndosalíamos↑   ¿No es la señora que bajaba cuando salíamos?
   (when) we were leaving?

7 Isn't it the man who was going up when   nọéşelómbre |kèsúbìa |kwàndobahábamos↑   ¿No es el hombre que subía cuando bajábamos?
   we were coming down?

19.26   VEINTISEIS

SPOKEN SPANISH   UNIT 19

D sí↓ èstámpróbàndo|lozmotórès↓   Sí. Están probando los motores.

1 Yes. They're testing the plane.   sí↓ èstámpróbàndọ|èlabyón↓   Sí. Están probando el avión.

2 Yes. They're testing the car.   sí↓ èstámpróbàndọ|èlkóchè↓   Sí. Están probando el coche.

3 Yes. They're fixing the engine.   sí↓ èstánàrrèglàndọ|èlmotór↓   Sí. Están arreglando el motor.

4 Yes. They're fixing the street.   sí↓ èstánàrrèglàndo|lakáɔ̀yè↓   Sí. Están arreglando la calle.

5 Yes. They're checking the car.   sí↓ èstánrrébisándọ|èlkóchè↓   Sí. Están revisando el coche.

6 Yes. They're checking the bill.   sí↓ èstánrrèbisándo|lakwéntà↓   Sí. Están revisando la cuenta.

7 Yes. They're making (out) the bill.   sí↓ èstánàȿyéndo|lakwéntà↓   Sí. Están haciendo la cuenta.

E pòdríamòs|irabérlo↑   ¿Podríamos ir a verlo?

1 Could we go get acquainted with it?   pòdríamos|irakonoȿérlo↑   ¿Podríamos ir a conocerlo?

2 Could we go look at it?   pòdríamos|iramirárlo↑   ¿Podríamos ir a mirarlo?

3 Could we go out to see it?   pòdríamos|salirabérlo↑   ¿Podríamos salir a verlo?

4 Could we go out and buy it?   pòdríamos|salirakomprárlo↑   ¿Podríamos salir a comprarlo?

VEINTISIETE   19.27

UNIT 19   SPOKEN SPANISH

5 Could we come and do it?   póđríamoz |beniraᶊerlo↑   ¿Podríamos venir a hacerlo?

6 Could we come and look for it?   póđríamoz |benirabuskárlo↑   ¿Podríamos venir a buscarlo?

7 Could we go down and fix it?   póđríamoz |bahararreglárlo↑   ¿Podríamos bajar a arreglarlo?

F dèspwéz |lèsprésénto̜ |àlhefeđelabásè↓   Después les presento al jefe de la base.

1 Afterwards, I'll introduce you to the head   dèspwéz |lèsprésénto̜ |àlhefeđelao̜fiᶊínȧ↓   Después les presento al jefe de la
   (boss) of the office.   oficina.

2 Afterwards, I'll introduce you to the   dèspwéz |lèsprésénto̜ |àlsènyordelakásà↓   Después les presento al señor de la casa.
   gentleman of the house.

3 Afterwards, I'll bring you today's paper.   dèspwéz |lèstraygo̜ |èlpéryođikođe̜óy↓   Después les traigo el periódico de hoy.

4 Before, I'll bring you the suitcases.   ántez |lèstraygolazmalétàs↓   Antes les traigo las maletas.

5 Before, I'll bring (take) you the letters.   ántez |lèzⓁyebolaskártàs↓   Antes les llevo las cartas.

6 Then, I'll bring (take) you the coffee.   èntónᶊez |lèzⓁyebo̜elkafé↓   Entonces les llevo el café.

7 Then, I'll give you the information.   èntónᶊez |lèzđoyla̜imforma̜ᶊyón↓   Entonces les doy la información.

19.28   VEINTIOCHO

SPOKEN SPANISH   UNIT 19

19.24   Review drill — Spanish simple tense for English verb construction in interrogations

    1 When is he coming?   kwándobyéné↓   ¿Cuándo viene?

    2 Is he coming tomorrow?   byénèmáņyanaↃ   ¿Viene mañana?

    3 Who are you going to the party with?   kòņkyembalafyéstá↓   ¿Con quién va a la fiesta?

    4 Are you going with the little plump girl?   bákônlàgòrdita↑   ¿Va con la gordita?

    5 How are you all going?   kómobán↓   ¿Cómo van?

    6 Are you going all going by car? bánénáwtoↃ   ¿Van en auto?

    7 When are you leaving?   kwándosálé↓   ¿Cuándo sale?

    8 Are you leaving tomorrow?   sálèmàņyanaↃ   ¿Sale mañana?

    9 When do you eat?   kwándokómęustéd↓   ¿Cuándo come Ud.?

   10 Do you eat at six?   kómęàlà(s)séysↃ   ¿Come a las seis?

   11 Where do you work?   dondetrabáhà↓   ¿Dónde trabaja?

   12 Do you work downtown?   tràbáhąènélşentroↃ   ¿Trabaja en el centro?

   13 Who do you study with?   kònkyenęstúdyà↓   ¿Con quién estudia?

VEINTINUEVE   19.29

UNIT 19   SPOKEN SPANISH

14 Do you study with Carmen?   èstúɖyákóŋkarmen↑   ¿Estudia con Carmen?

15 Do you drink cuba libre?   tómàkúbálìbre↑   ¿Toma cuba libre?

19.3   CONVERSATION STIMULUS

                                              NARRATIVE 1

1 Jose and Juan were going to visit the   hòseɪhwan↑ibanabisitár |labáse↑ɗóndèlà   José y Juan iban a visitar la base donde
   base where the U. S. Air Force   mísyon |dèlàfwerşaeréa |dèlóséstáɗòsúnìɗos | la Misión de la Fuerza Aérea de los
   Mission has its offices.   tyénesusؚofɪşínàs↓   Estados Unidos tiene sus oficinas.

2 Jose came by for Juan, but Juan wasn't   hòsepasoؚporhwán↓ pèròhwán |noؚęstabalístó | José pasó por Juan, pero Juan no estaba
   ready yet.   tóɗàbíà↓   listo todavía.

3 Jose called him about five times to let   hòseloؙⱡyamó |kómóşiŋkobęşes↑párábisarle | José lo llamó como cinco veces para
   him know he was coming over.   kebenía↓   avisarle que venía.

4 But the line was busy,   pérólálíneạ |estabạọkupáɗà↓   Pero la línea estaba ocupada,

5 because Juan was talking with a   pórkéhwán |estabablando↑kónųnámìạọsụⱱo | porque Juan estaba hablando con un
   friend of his,   amigo suyo,

6 who had just arrived from the States.   kęākábabadęੑੑⱡyegár |dèlòṣéstaɗòṣuníɗòs↓   que acababa de llegar de los Estados Unidos.

19.30   TREINTA

SPOKEN SPANISH   UNIT 19

DIALOG 1

José, pregúntele a Juan si no está listo
todavía.

nǫéstázlísto|tođabía↑

José: ¿No estás listo todavía?

Juan, contéstele que no. Pregúntele que
por qué no le avisó que venía tan temprano.

no↓ pórkénomǫabisaste|kébénías|tán
tempráno↓

Juan: No. ¿Por qué no me avisaste que
venías tan temprano?

José, dígale que Ud. lo llamó como cinco
veces pero la línea estaba ocupada.

téⓁyáme|kómǫsįŋkobéşęs↓ pérólálinęą|
estabǫokupáđà↓

José: Te llamé como cinco veces, pero
la línea estaba ocupada.

Juan, dígale que Ud. estaba hablando con
un amigo suyo que acaba de llegar de los
Estados Unidos.

èstábáblando|kónųnǎmigomio|kęákábađe
Ⓛyegar|dèlòsęstađosunįđòs↓

Juan: Estaba hablando con un amigo
mío que acaba de llegar de los
Estados Unidos.

NARRATIVE 2

1 Colonel Harris, Bob, seems a little
worried.

èlkòrónełharris| bob↑ pàréşę|ùmpóko
pręokupáđò↓

El coronel Harris, Bob, parece un poco
preocupado.

2 Because Juan and José have not arrived
yet.

pórkèhwanįhosé|nǫanⓁyęgáđò|tòđabía↓

Porque Juan y José no han llegado todavía.

3 When they arrive, Jose tells the colonel
that Juan wasn't ready when he came
by for him.

kwándòⓁyęgan↑hóseleđişęalkorónel|kèhwán|
noęstabalístò|kwándòpàsóporél↓

Cuando llegan, José le dice al coronel que
Juan no estaba listo cuando pasó por él.

TREINTA Y UNO   19.31

UNIT 19   SPOKEN SPANISH

4 And that he, Juan, didn't know the colonel   ikǽel| hwán↑ nósabía|kèlkòrónél|lòs   Y que él, Juan, no sabía que el coronel
   was expecting them at ten.   èspérabalaz↓yéṣ↓   los esperaba a las diez.

5 The colonel tells them it's all right, not   èlkòrónél|lèzdíṣe|kestábyén↓kènóse   El coronel les dice que está bien, que
   to worry.   prҽokúpèn↓   no se preocupen.

6 Carmen didn't come. She had to go   kármen|nobínò↓ tènía|kҽírↀèkómpras| Carmen no vino. Tenía que ir de compras
   shopping with the colonel's wife.   kònlҽèsposaↀelkoronél↓   con la esposa del coronel.

                                                                    DIALOG 2

Bob, pregúnteles a José y a Juan que qué   kélespasó↓ pórkeⓎyegáron|tàntárↀè↓   Bob: ¿Qué les pasó? ¿Por qué llegaron
les pasó, que por qué llegaron tan tarde.   tan tarde?

José, contéstele que Juan no estaba listo   hwán|noҽstabalístò|kwándòpàsépórél↓   José: Juan no estaba listo cuando pasé
cuando Ud. pasó por él.   por él.

Juan, dígale a Bob que es que Ud. no sabía   èskèyonosabía|kҽùsteↀ|nòsҽspèrabalaz   Juan: Es que yo no sabía que Ud. nos
que él los esperaba a Uds. a las diez.   dyéʑ↓bób↓   esperaba a las diez, Bob.

Bob, contésteles que está bien, que no se   èstábyén↓ nòseprҽokúpèn↓ nòbínokarmén↑   Bob: Está bien, no se preocupen. ¿No
preocupen. Pregúnteles si no vino Carmen.   vino Carmen?

José, contéstele que no, que le parece que   nó↓ mèpàreṣe|kètènìa|kҽírↀèkómpras|kón   José: No, me parece que tenía que ir de
tenía que ir de compras con la señora de él.   sùsèɲyorà↓   compras con su señora.

Bob, dígale que tiene razón, que ahora   tyénerraṣón↓ àòrarrekwérↀò↓   Bob: Tiene razón. Ahora recuerdo.
recuerda.

SPOKEN SPANISH   UNIT 19

NARRATIVE 3

1 That same evening Jose was talking
with Carmen,

ésàmizmanoche†hósestabablando |koŋkármèn↓

Esa misma noche José estaba hablando
con Carmen,

2 and told her what he and Juan saw at the
air base.

ilèdiho |lòkelihwambyeron |ènlâbaseaérgà↓

y le dijo lo que él y Juan vieron en la
base aérea.

3 They visited the buildings.

bisitaronlosedifísyòs↓

Visitaron los edificios.

4 But they didn't (get to) see many planes.

pěrónobyeron |muchosabyónès↓

Pero no vieron muchos aviones.

5 Only the Mission's C-47 was there.

sólo |èlşekwarentạisyete |delamisyón |èstábáí↓

Sólo el C-47 de la Misión estaba ahí.

6 The others had just taken off when they
arrived at the base.

lósotros |àkàbabandedespegar†kwándoeꝝyoz |
Cyegaronalabásè↓

Los otros acababan de despegar cuando ellos
llegaron a la base.

7 Carmen told Jose that she went shopping
with Mrs. Harris.

karmen |ledihọahose†ke^yafwedekompras |
kònlàsèɲyoradehárris↓

Carmen le dijo a José que ella fué de compras
con la Sra. de Harris.

8 But that they didn't buy anything,

pěrókènokompraro(n)nádá↓

Pero que no compraron nada,

9 because Mrs. Harris thought everything
was too expensive.

pórkẹàlàsèɲyoradeharriz |lèpàrèşyo†kètodọ |
èstábámuykárò↓

porque a la Sra. de Harris le pareció que todo
estaba muy caro.

TREINTA Y TRES   19.33

UNIT 19

SPOKEN SPANISH

DIALOG 3

Carmen, pregúntele a José que cómo les
fué en la base aérea. Que si vieron
muchas cosas.

kómolesfwe |ęnlabaşęáęręà↓ byéronmuchas
kosas↑

Carmen: ¿Cómo les fué en la base aérea?
¿Vieron muchas cosas?

José, contéstele que conocieron los edificios solamente.

kònóşımoz |lòsęḋifişyós |sólámèntè↓

José: Conocimos los edificios, solamente.

Carmen, pregúntele que cuántos aviones
vieron?

kwantos,abyónèz |byéròn↓

Carmen: ¿Cuántos aviones vieron?

José, contéstele que sólo el C—47 que pertenece a la Misión.

sólọęlşękwarèntạisyéte |kèpértènęşęala
mısyón↓

José: Sólo el C—47 que pertenece a la
Misión.

Carmen, pregúntele que dónde estaban los
aviones de guerra, entonces.

iḋondestaban |lòs,àbyonezḋegérrạ |èntónşès↓

Carmen: ¿Y dónde estaban los aviones de
guerra, entonces?

José, contéstele que acababan de despegar
cuando Uds. llegaron. Ahora pregúntele
Ud. a ella si compró muchas cosas con la
Sra. de Harris.

àkàbaban |dèḋèspégar↑kwándọnòsótroz
ⁿyegámòs↓ itú↓ kómprastemuchaskósas |
konlasęꞑoraḋeharris↑

José: Acababan de despegar cuando nosotros llegamos. Y tú, ¿compraste
muchas cosas con la Sra. de Harris?

Carmen, dígale que no compraron nada. Que
a la señora le pareció que todo estaba
muy caro.

nokompramoznáḋà↓ àlàsèꞑóra |lèpàrèşyo↑
kétoḋo |ęstábàmuykáró↓

Carmen: No compramos nada. A la señora
le pareció que todo estaba muy
caro.

19.34

TREINTA Y CUATRO

SPOKEN SPANISH   UNIT 19

19.4   READINGS

19.40   List of cognate loan words

graduado (graduarse)   grádwadô↓ grádwarsê↓

la universidad   la̧-ûnibérsida̧d↓

terminar   tèrminár↓

los estudios   lôs̟-éstudyòs↓

entrado (entrar)   èntradò↓ èntrár↓

el servicio   èl-sêrbi̧s̟yò↓

diplomático   diplômatikô↓

el gobierno   èl-gôbyernò↓

durante   dúrantè↓

el clima   èl-klimà↓

segunda   sêgundâ↓

Florida   flôridà↓

TREINTA Y CINCO   19.35

UNIT 19   SPOKEN SPANISH

19.41   Reading selection

Los Robinson

        Fred Robinson, su esposa, Virginia, y dos hijas, Jane y Ruth, habían llegado a Surlandia dos semanas antes de mudarse a la casa que acababan de alquilar en
Bellavista. El era un hombre de unos treinta años, graduado de la Universidad de Princeton, quien, después de terminar sus estudios en esa universidad, había entrado
al servicio diplomático de los Estados Unidos. Esta era la primera vez que salía de su país como empleado de gobierno, y él y Virginia estaban muy contentos de que
era a Surlandia y no a otra parte adonde su gobierno lo mandaba. Las razones eran dos: primero, que ya ellos conocían este país; habían estado ahí unos días durante
su viaje de bodas y habían quedado encantados con la gente, con las ciudades, con el clima, en fin, con todo. La segunda razón era que Surlandia estaba bastante cerca
de Florida, donde vivía toda la familia de Fred. Sería muy fácil y barato para los Robinson, entonces, ir a menudo a visitar a la familia y a los muchos amigos que tenían
en Florida —un viaje de seis horas por avión.

        Los Robinson empezaron a buscar casa desde el mismo día que llegaron a Las Palmas, la capital de Surlandia, pero ya habían pasado dos semanas, casi tres, y
todavía no habían encontrado una casa como ellos querían. Todo este tiempo estaban viviendo en un hotel carísimo y ya ellos no sabían que iban a hacer para pagar la
cuenta. Todos los días no hacían más que ver casas y más casas. Ya habían visto no menos de veinticinco, pero ninguna les gustaba; unas no les convenían porque eran
demasiado grandes; otras, porque eran demasiado pequeñas o porque estaban muy lejos del centro o en un barrio malo, o porque solamente amuebladas las alquilaban y ellos
las querían sin muebles. En fin, no encontraban lo que ellos buscaban. Pero hace dos o tres días alguien, en la Embajada, les avisó que había una casa magnífica en el
Barrio Bellavista y que la alquilaban sin muebles. En seguida fueron a verla y les gustó mucho. También les gustó el barrio y, sin pensarlo ni un minuto más, fueron y la
tomaron.

19.42   Response drill

    1 ¿Cuál era el nombre del Sr. Robinson?

    2 ¿Cuál era el de su esposa?

    3 ¿Cuántos hijos tenían ellos?

    4 ¿De qué universidad era graduado Fred?

19.36   TREINTA Y SEIS

SPOKEN SPANISH   UNIT 19

5 ¿En qué empezó a trabajar él después de terminar sus estudios?

6 ¿Era ésta la primera o la segunda vez que salía de su país como empleado de gobierno?

7 ¿Por qué estaban contentos ellos de ir a Surlandia?

8 ¿Por qué iba a ser muy fácil para ellos ir a menudo a Florida?

9 ¿Por qué estaban viviendo en un hotel durante los primeros días?

10 ¿Era un hotel barato o caro donde estaban viviendo?

11 ¿Por qué les costó tanto encontrar casa?

12 ¿Querían ellos una casa con muebles o sin muebles?

13 ¿Encontraron por fin la casa que buscaban?

14 ¿Dónde estaba esa casa?

15 ¿Quién les avisó de esa casa?

TREINTA Y SIETE   19.37

jacobeligoodsons.com For Free Audio

jacobeligoodsons.com For Free Audio

SPOKEN SPANISH   UNIT 20

20.1   BASIC SENTENCES.   Visit to Air Mission (continued).

ENGLISH SPELLING   AID TO LISTENING   SPANISH SPELLING

    the provision, supply   là-pròbisyóh↓   la provisión

Molina   Molina
    Do you all buy your supplies here?[1]   kómpran |súspròbisyónes |akí↑   ¿Compran sus provisiones aquí?

    to us them (it) brings   nóz-làs-tráè↓   nos las trae

Harris   Harris
    No. The C—47 brings them in to us once a month.   no↑ nózlàstràe |èlsékwàréntaisyétè↑   No. Nos las trae el C.47 una vez al mes.
                                            únabèsalmés↓

    the runway, the track   là-pìstá↓   la pista

    long   lárgò↓   largo

    the truth   là-bèrdàd↓   la verdad

    isn't it?[2]   bèrdàd↑   ¿verdad?

White   White
    The runway is quite long, isn't it?   làpìsta |ézbàstàntelárgà↓bèrdàd↑   La pista es bastante larga ¿verdad?

    a thousand   míl↓   mil

    five hundred   kínyentòs↓   quinientos

    the meter   èl-métrò↓   el metro

UNO   20.1

jacobeligoodsons.com For Free Audio

UNIT 20   SPOKEN SPANISH

Harris   *Harris*
It's 1500 meters.   tyéné |milkinyéntozmétròs↓   Tiene mil quinientos metros.

        the total   èl—tòtál↓   el total

        altogether   èn—tótál↓   en total

Molina   *Molina*
How many planes are there on the base in all?   èntòtál↑kwántos,abyónes |ayènlabásè↓   En total ¿cuántos aviones hay en la
                                                                                                 base?

        thirty   tréyntà↓   treinta

Harris   (3)   *Harris*
Thirty-three.   tréyntaitrés↓   Treinta y tres.

        the squadron   èl—éskwàdrón↓   el escuadrón

        the bombing   èl—bómbàrdeô↓   el bombardeo

Three bomber squadrons...   tres,eskwadrónez |debombardeô↑   Tres escuadrones de bombardeo...

        the squadron   la—éskwàdriⁿyà↓   la escuadrilla

        the hunt   là—kášà↓   la caza

...and two fighter squadrons.   i↑os |eskwadriⁿyaz |dekášà↓   ...y dos escuadrillas de caza.

White   *White*
That's not many.   nósonmuchós↓   No son muchos.

20.2   DOS

jacobeligoodsons.com For Free Audio

Molina		*Molina*
It's just because it's a small base.	és |kèlábásẹ |èspèkéṇyà↓	Es que la base es pequeña.
(it) flies (to fly)	bwélà↓ bòlár↓	vuela (volar)
the tower	lá—tórrè↓	la torre
the control	èl—kòntról↓	el control
Harris		*Harris*
You see that airplane that's flying over the control tower?	bén‿ésẹabyón |kébwéla |sóbrelatórredekontról↑	¿Ven ese avión que vuela sobre la torre de control?
in it	èn—él↓	en él
the official, officer	èl—òfiṣyál↓	el oficial
the inspection	lạ—inspèkṣyón↓	la inspección
The inspector is coming in it.	èn‿élbyénẹ |èlòfiṣyáldẹinspekṣyón↓	En él viene el oficial de inspección.
to receive	rrèṣibír↓	recibir
Molina		*Molina*
Do you have to go meet him?	tyénekẹír |àrrèṣibírlo↑	¿Tiene que ir a recibirlo?
the lieutenant	èl—tènyéntè↓	el teniente
Harris		*Harris*
Yes. I'll leave you with Lieutenant La Cerda.	sí↓lòzdého |kòn‿èltényéntelaṣérdà↓	Sí, los dejo con el teniente La Cerda.
the sight	lá—bístà↓	la vista

jacobeligoodsons.com For Free Audio

UNIT 20   SPOKEN SPANISH

White
See you later, Colonel.

ástálàbìstà|ķöröŋél↓

White
Hasta la vista, Coronel.

don't itself to you (it) forget
(to forget itself) (4)

nó—se—lg—olbídè↓ ólbidàrsè↓

no se le olvide (olvidarse)

the golf

èl—góíf↓

el golf

And don't forget our golf date.

inó|selg̣olbide|lóḍélgólf↓

Y no se le olvide lo del golf.

20.10   Notes on the basic sentences

     (1) We remind you again that 'you all' is used here as the English second person plural pronoun, a discrimination which all but certain Southern—Midland and Southern dialects of American English lack.

     (2) The form /berdád/ *verdad*, occurring under this particular intonation pattern as a confirmation question after an assertion, must be translated by a wide variety of English phrases like 'isn't it, didn't he, hasn't she, weren't they, can't we, doesn't it' and so on.

     (3) Students whose experience with the military has been sufficiently extensive to make them wonder how there could be only thirty-three planes in three bomber squadrons and two fighter squadrons are hereby reminded of two facts: other countries do not organize their units in the same way we do, though the American Air Force is coming more and more to be used as a model for standardization in Latin America; and it is not uncommon in peacetime to have rather badly undermanned and underequipped squadrons representing only a skeleton of the full force. The difference between /eskwadrón/ *escuadrón* and /eskwadríⱴya/ *escuadrilla* is somewhat elusive: both apparently mean *squadron*, the first of big aircraft and the second of smaller aircraft, just as in English the item *squad* refers to a unit of men and *squadron* to a unit of machines.

     (4) This is an instance of the occurrence of both a reflexive clitic and an indirect clitic in the same construction. It will be examined closely in Unit 25, and in the meanwhile it should not be confused with the examples of direct clitic and indirect clitic that are examined closely in the present unit.

20.4   CUATRO

jacobeligoodsons.com For Free Audio

SPOKEN SPANISH

UNIT 20

20.2   DRILLS AND GRAMMAR

20.21   Pattern drills

20.21.1   Direct and indirect clitics in the same contruction

A. Presentation of pattern

ILLUSTRATIONS

————————————	1	nómèlòbá│rrèbisár↑	¿No *me lo* va a revisar?
Can you change them for me?	2	mélòspwéɖe│kàmbyár↑	¿*Me los* puede cambiar?
He took it for us yesterday.	3	nòzló?yèbogyér↓	*Nos lo* llevó ayer.
————————————	4	nòzlástrag│élşekwarèntaisyétè↓	*Nos las* trae el C-47.
O.K., I'll look it up for you.	5	bwénò↓sèlòbuskó↓	Bueno, *se lo* busco.
O.K., I'll loan it to you.	6	bwénò↓sèlòprèstoaustédès↓	Bueno, *se lo* presto a Uds.
I loaned it to my wife.	7	sèlòprèste│amiespósà↓	*Se lo* presté a mi esposa.
I handed it (f) to him.	8	sèlàpàse│aél↓	*Se la* pasé a él.
I've already given them to them.	9	yá│selosedádò↓	Ya *se los* he dado.
————————————	10	nòsèlodiga│amiespósà↓	No *se lo* diga a mi esposa.
the professor		él—prófèsór↓	el profesor

CINCO

20.5

jacobeligoodsons.com For Free Audio

UNIT 20   SPOKEN SPANISH

I've already brought them to the professor.   11   yásèlòsétráidọ|àlpròfèsór↓   Ya *se los* he traido al profesor.

_____   12   bén|ịtèloprèséntò↓   Ven y *te lo* presento.

EXTRAPOLATION

	Indirect	Direct
sg 1	me	(me)
pl	nos	(nos)
2 fam	te	(te)
sg 2-3	se	lo la
pl		los las

NOTES

a. 1 sg and pl and 2 fam direct forms rarely occur with indirect clitics.

b. 2-3 sg /le/ and 2-3 pl /les/ both appear as /se/ when preceding direct clitics /lo, la, los, las/.

jacobeligoodsons.com For Free Audio

SPOKEN SPANISH

UNIT 20

20.21.11 Substitution drill — Form substitution

1 èlséŋyor |mèrrèbisólazmalétás↓   èlsèŋyor |melazrrebisó↓

2 èlchófer |nò(s)súbyolozmwéblès↓   èlchófer |nozlo(s)subyó↓

3 làsèŋyóra |lɛàlkilólabìtaşyón↓   làsèŋyora |selalkiló↓

4 mínobya |mèmàndoɛlperyóɗìkó↓   mínobya |melomandó↓

5 el |lèsprèsèntolazmorénàs↓   elselaspresentó↓

6 misèkrètarya |mèskribyolos̩anúnşyòs↓   misèkrètarya |melos̩eskribyó↓

7 yó |lèzmàndélrregálô↓   yóselomandé↓

---

1 El señor me revisó *las maletas.*   El señor me las revisó.

2 El chofer nos subió *los muebles.*   El chofer nos los subió.

3 La señora le alquiló *la habitación.*   La señora se la alquiló.

4 Mi novia me mandó *el periódico.*   Mi novia me lo mandó.

5 El les presentó *las morenas.*   El se las presentó.

6 Mi secretaria me escribió *los anuncios.* Mi secretaria me los escribió.

7 Yo les mandé *el regalo.*   Yo se lo mandé.

SIETE

20.7

UNIT 20   SPOKEN SPANISH

20.21.12 Response drill [1]

(Juan le presta el libro al profesor)

1   hwán↓ kemeprestoustéd↓   lèprèsté|g⓪líbró↓

    hósé↓ mèprèstohwàn|e⓪líbro↑   sí↓ sèlóprèstó↓

    hósé↓ kwàndomeloprestó↓   sèlóprèstoạórà↓

    hwán↓ kyénmepresto|g⓪líbró↓   yòseloprèsté↓

    hósé↓ mèlóprèstoustèd↓   nó↓ yonoseloprèsté↓ sèlóprèstohwán↓

(Juan le presta el libro al profesor)

1   Juan, ¿qué me prestó Ud.?   Le presté el libro.

    José, ¿me prestó Juan el libro?   Sí, se lo prestó.

    José, ¿cuándo me lo prestó?   Se lo prestó ahora.

    Juan, ¿quién me prestó el libro?   Yo se lo presté.

    José, ¿me lo prestó Ud.?   No, yo no se lo presté, se lo prestó Juan.

---

[1] Use the names of two students instead of Juan and José, addressing the questions to them after the appropriate activity. Repeat each drill several times until all
     the students have taken both parts.

20.8   OCHO

SPOKEN SPANISH   UNIT 20

(El profesor le presta su lápiz a uno de los estudiantes)

2 hwán↓ keleprestéyó↓   mèprèstoę̇⬭lápi̧ş↓

   hwán↓ yoleprestę̇⬭lápi̧ş↑   si̧↓ ùstedmeloprestó↓

   hosé↓ kelepréstéyo |ạhwán↓   lèprèstóę̇⬭lápi̧ş↓

   hosé↓ yolepreste⬭lápi̧ş̧ahwán↑   si̧↓ ùstedseloprestó↓

   hwán↓ kyénleprestoę̇⬭lápi̧ş |àụstéd↓   ùsted |mèlóprèstó↓

   hwán↓ kwandoseloprèsté↓   mèlóprèsto |àòrà↓

_____

(El profesor le presta su lápiz a uno de los estudiantes)

2 Juan, ¿qué le presté yo?   Me prestó el lápiz.

   Juan, ¿yo le presté el lápiz?   Sí, Ud. me lo prestó.

   José, ¿qué le presté yo a Juan?   Le prestó el lápiz.

   José, ¿yo le presté el lápiz a Juan?   Sí, Ud. se lo prestó.

   Juan, ¿quién le prestó el lápiz a Ud.?   Ud. me lo prestó.

   Juan, ¿cuándo se lo presté?   Me lo prestó ahora.

UNIT 20   SPOKEN SPANISH

(El profesor les presta tres pesos a dos de los estudiantes)

3   hwán↓ kélesprésteyó |aystédès↓   nóspréstó |tréspésòs↓

    hòsé↓ lèspréstéyó |tréspésos |aystédes↑   sí↓ ùstédnozlosprestó↓

    hòsé↓ kwándoselósprésté↓   nòzlósprésto |aorà↓

    hwán↓ kyénlésprésto |lostréspésos |aystédes↑   ùstédnozlosprestó↓

    hòsé↓ kwántospésoz |lèsprésté↓   nóspréstó |tréspésòs↓

_____

(El profesor les presta tres pesos a dos de los estudiantes)

3   Juan, ¿qué les presté yo a Uds.?   Nos prestó tres pesos.

    José, ¿les presté yo tres pesos a Uds.?   Sí, Ud. nos los prestó.

    José, ¿cuándo se los presté?   Nos los prestó ahora.

    Juan, ¿quién les prestó los tres pesos a Uds.? Ud. nos los prestó.

    José, ¿cuántos pesos les presté?   Nos prestó tres pesos.

20.10   DIEZ

SPOKEN SPANISH   UNIT 20

(José le presta al profesor y a Juan cinco monedas)

4 hòsé↓ kénospresto|ustéd↓   lèsprèste|şiŋkomonédàs↓

   hòsé↓ nòsprèstoustéd|şiŋkomonédas↑   si↓ sèlàsprèstè↓

   hòsé↓ kwandonòzlaspréstó↓   sèlàsprèste|àorà↓

   hwán↓ kénosprestohosé↓   nòsprèsto|şiŋkomonédàs↓

   hwán↓ kye(n)nòzlaspréstó↓   nòzlàsprèsto|hòsé↓

_____

(José le presta al profesor y a Juan cinco monedas)

4 José, ¿qué nos prestó Ud?   Les presté cinco monedas.

   José, ¿nos prestó Ud. cinco monedas?   Sí, se las presté.

   José, ¿cuándo nos las prestó?   Se las presté ahora.

   Juan, ¿qué nos prestó José?   Nos prestó cinco monedas.

   Juan, ¿quién nos las prestó?   Nos las prestó José.

ONCE   20.11

UNIT 20   SPOKEN SPANISH

(Juan le presta la pluma a José)

5 hwán↓ kelepresto|ahosé↓   lèprèstélàplumà↓

   hwán↓ lèprèsto|lapluma|ahose↑   si↓ sèlàprèste↓

   hósé↓ keleprestohwan|austéd↓   mèprèstolaplúmà↓

   hósé↓ lèprèstólapluma↑   si↓ mèlàprèsto↑

   hwán↓ kwándo|lèprèstólaplúmà|àhòsé↓   sèlàprèste|àorà↓

   hósé↓ kyénlèprèstólaplúmà↓   hwan|mèlàprèstó↓

───

(Juan le presta la pluma a José)

5 Juan, ¿qué le prestó a José?   Le presté la pluma.

   Juan, ¿le prestó la pluma a José?   Sí, se la presté.

   José, ¿que le prestó Juan a Ud.?   Me prestó la pluma.

   José, ¿le prestó la pluma?   Sí, me la prestó.

   Juan, ¿cuándo le prestó la pluma a José?   Se la presté ahora.

   José, ¿quién le prestó la pluma?   Juan me la prestó.

20.12   DOCE

SPOKEN SPANISH   UNIT 20

20.21.13 Translation drill

1 The menu? I passed it to John.   èlmènu↑ sèlópàsé|àhwán↓   ¿El menú? Se lo pasé a Juan.

2 The drinks? I passed them to the   lóstragòs↑ sèlóspàsé|àló(s)sèɲyorès↓ ¿Los tragos? Se los pasé a los señores.
  gentlemen.

3 The list? They haven't given it to me.   làlìsta↑ nómelàndáđò↓   ¿La lista? No me la han dado.

4 The car? I bought it from Joseph.   èlkàrro↑ sèlókòmpré|àhòsé↓   ¿El carro? Se lo compré a José.

5 The furniture? I bought it (them) from   lózmwéblès↑ sèlóskòmpré|àhwán↓   ¿Los muebles? Se los compré a Juan.
  John.

6 The gifts? I sent them to Carmen.   lózrrègalòs↑ sèlózmàndé|àkármèn↓   ¿Los regalos? Se los mandé a Carmen.

7 The chairs? I sent them to Louise.   là(s)sìɲyas↑ sèlàzmàndé|àlwisà↓   ¿Las sillas? Se las mandé a Luisa.

8 The table? I sent it to my sister.   làmèsa↑ sèlàmàndé|àmɪèrmànà↓   ¿La mesa? Se la mandé a mi hermana.

9 The room? I already rented it to Joseph. èlkwàrto↑ ya|sèlọalkilé|àhòsé↓   ¿El cuarto? Ya se lo alquilé a José.

10 The overnight case? They already   èlmàlétìn↑ ya|nózlòrrèbísarón↓   ¿El maletín? Ya nos lo revisaron.
   checked it for us.

11 The ham? They haven't brought it to me. èlhàmòn↑ nó|mèlọàntráiđò↓   ¿El jamón? No me lo han traído.

12 The prices? They haven't given them   lóspreşyòs↑ nó|selọsạndáđò|tóđàbíà↓ ¿Los precios? No se los han dado todavía.
   to him yet.

13 The names? He wrote them for me.   lóznombrès↑ el|melọseskribyó↓   ¿Los nombres? El me los escribió.

TRECE   20.13

jacobeligoodsons.com For Free Audio

UNIT 20   SPOKEN SPANISH

B. Discussion of pattern

When direct and indirect clitics occur in the same construction with a verb, the indirect always precedes the direct, and both *precede* a conjugated form of the verb (except in affirmative commands, see Unit 29), but *follow* an infinitive or /—ndo/ form (if these are the only verb forms in the phrase, see Unit 29).

The 1 sg and pl and the 2 fam forms rarely if ever occur as direct clitics in the same construction with indirect clitics (these forms are in parentheses in the extrapolation).

The important feature of this pattern is the change of /le/ and /les/ to /se/ when a direct object /lo, la, los, las/ appears in the same construction. Thus /le-dóy-el-líbro/, when /lo/ replaces /el-líbro/, becomes /se-lo-dóy/.

In chart form this change can be shown as follows:

Objects expressed by clitics				
Indirect			Indirect + Direct	
sg	le	become	se	lo la
2-3				
pl	les			los las

It should be noted that the number distinction shown by /le/ and /les/ is lost in /se/, and therefore there is an increased need in many contexts for redundant constructions (presented in Unit 16) to restate the person of /se/. The indirect clitic /se/ can have any of the following possible references: to you, to you all, to it, to him, to her, to them.

In some dialect areas the combination /nos—los/ is avoided.

20.21.2 Exclamatory /ké, kómo/

A. Presentation of pattern

ILLUSTRATIONS

1   kékantidadehénte↓   ¡Qué cantidad de gente!

What tomatoes!   2   kétomátes↓   ¡Qué tomates!

20.14   CATORCE

jacobeligoodsons.com For Free Audio

SPOKEN SPANISH   UNIT 20

What coffee!   3 kékafé↓   ¡Qué café!

————————————   4 kébonítà↓   ¡Qué bonita!

How you talk!   5 komọáblà↓   ¡Cómo habla!

EXTRAPOLATION

ké	what (a)	+ noun
	how	+ adjective
kómo	how	+ verb

NOTES

a. A common pattern for Spanish exclamatory phrases is /ké/ plus a noun or adjective or
    /kómo/ plus a verb.

20.21.21 Translation drill

  1 What a girl!   késeŋyorítà↓   ¡Qué señorita!

  2 What an idea!   keịđéà↓   ¡Qué idea!

QUINCE   20.15

UNIT 20   SPOKEN SPANISH

3 What an order!   keórdèn↓   ¡Qué orden!

4 What a headache!   kedolor|dekabéṣà↓   ¡Qué dolor de cabeza!

5 What women!   kemuhérès↓   ¡Qué mujeres!

6 What water!   keágwà↓   ¡Qué agua!

7 How small!   kepekéŋyà↓   ¡Qué pequeña!

8 How ugly!   keféà↓   ¡Qué fea!

9 How fat!   keǵórdà↓   ¡Qué gorda!

10 How narrow!   kestréchà↓   ¡Qué estrecha!

11 How she talks!   komǫáblà↓   ¡Cómo habla!

12 How she dances!   komobáylà↓   ¡Cómo baila!

13 How she learns!   komǫapréndè↓   ¡Cómo aprende!

14 How she works!   komotrabáhà↓   ¡Cómo trabaja!

15 How she eats!   komokómè↓   ¡Cómo come!

20.16   DIECISEIS

SPOKEN SPANISH   UNIT 20

B. Discussion of pattern

The pattern of the Spanish exclamatory phrases drilled above is somewhat simpler than that of the English equivalents: /ké/ appears with nouns and modifiers, and /kómo/ appears with verbs.

The difference between 'what a' before singular count nouns and 'what' before plural count nouns and mass nouns ('What a man!', but 'what men!, what patriotism!') doesn't occur in Spanish, where the exclamatory modifier is an unvariable /ké/. These Spanish constructions also translate equivalent English expressions with 'some, such' (as 'Some man, such men, such patriotism').

In English, a noun in an exclamatory phrase can be modified by an adjective which precedes it; in the equivalent Spanish phrase the adjective normally follows (except expressions like /ké─grán─ómbre/) and usually is itself always modified by /más/ or /tán/. Thus:

What a pretty girl!	/ké|múchacha|masbonitá↓/
	/ké|múchacha|tambonitá↓/
What good water!	/kęagwa|masbwéná↓/
	/kęagwa|tambwéná↓/

In the second examples /ké/ , when followed by a strong-stressed vowel, may or may not be stressed depending on the relative speed of pronunciation, the 'emotion' with which it is expressed, etc. In a normal, uncolored pronunciation, the first of two adjacent strong-stressed vowels tends to become weak-stressed when they occur in the same intonation phrase. Thus:

Normal	/kęagwa|masbwéná↓/
Deliberate	/ké|agwa|mas|bwená↓/

DIECISIETE   20.17

jacobeligoodsons.com For Free Audio

UNIT 20   SPOKEN SPANISH

20.21.3 Question intonation patterns — Choice questions

A. Presentation of pattern

ILLUSTRATIONS

                                                                      2 2↑2 1 1↓

1 bahątosúbè↓   ¿Baja o sube?

                                                  1   2 2↑ 2 1 1↓

2 dáláka̦yęțalpátyò↓   ¿Da a la calle o al patio?

Are they coming by plane, or by boat?   1   22 ↑2   1 1↓

3 byénémpòràbyon↑oporbárkò↓   ¿Vienen por avión   o por barco?

EXTRAPOLATION

Yes-no question	Choice question
/1222↑/	/1122↑2211↓/

NOTES

a. In essence a choice question is a combination of a yes-no question pattern
followed immediately by an information question pattern.

SPOKEN SPANISH   UNIT 20

20.21.31 Substitution drill

1 ìmbítàlhéfe↑
   ìmbítàsus̪amìços↑   ìmbítàlhéfe↑o̬asus̪amíɡòs↓

2 èmpès̪o̬a̬la (s) séys↑
   èmpès̪o̬a̬las̬ocho↑   èmpès̪ó̬a̬lá (s) séys↑o̬alas̬óchò↓

3 làkás̬a̬esféa↑
   làkás̬a̬ezboníta↑   làkás̬a̬èsféa↑obonítà↓

──

       1 2   22 ↑
1 ¿Invita al jefe?
       1 2   22 ↑   1 1   22 ↑ 2   11↓
   ¿Invita a sus amigos?   ¿Invita al jefe   o a sus amigos?

       1   2   22 ↑
2 ¿Empezó a las seis?
       1   2   2 2↑   1   1   22 ↑ 2   1 1↓
   ¿Empezó a las ocho?   ¿Empezó a las seis   o a las ocho?

       1 2   22 ↑
3 ¿La casa es fea?
       1 2   22↑   1 1   22 ↑ 2   11↓
   ¿La casa es bonita?   ¿La casa es fea   o bonita?

DIECINUEVE   20.19

UNIT 20   SPOKEN SPANISH

4 kómênakı↑
   komenaλyi↑   kómênakı↑gaλyi↓

5 bamos,aóra↑
   bamozdespwes↑   bamos,aóra↑odespwés↓

6 prónunşyabyén↑
   prónunşyamal↑   prónúnşyàbyén↑omál↓

---

        2   22 ↑
4 ¿Comen aquí?
        2   22 ↑   1   22 ↑ 2 11 ↓
   ¿Comen allí?   ¿Comen aquí   o allí?

        2   2 2 ↑
5 ¿Vamos ahora?
        2   22 ↑   1   2 2 ↑ 2   11 ↓
   ¿Vamos después?   ¿Vamos ahora   o después?

        1 2   22 ↑
6 ¿Pronuncia bien?
        1 2   22 ↑   1 1   22 ↑ 2 11 ↓
   ¿Pronuncia mal?   ¿Pronuncia bien   o mal?

SPOKEN SPANISH   UNIT 20

7 lèfáltálgo↑
   lèfáltátódo↑   lèfáltálgǫ↑otódò↓

8 iŋklúyènlálųş↑
   iŋklúyèņelágwa↑   iŋklúyènlálųş↑ǫelágwà↓

9 dálaká͠ye↑
   dálpátyo↑   dálàká͠ye↑ǫalpátyò↓

---

       1 2   2 2↑
7 ¿Le falta algo?
       1 2   2 2↑   1 1   2 2↑2 11↓
   ¿Le falta todo?   ¿Le falta algo   o todo?

       1 2   22↑
8 ¿Incluyen la luz?
       1 2   2 2↑   1 1   22 ↑ 2 1 1↓
   ¿Incluyen el agua?   ¿Incluyen la luz   o el agua?

       2   2 2↑
9 ¿Da a la calle?
       2   2 2↑   1 · 2 2↑ 2 1 1↓
   ¿Da al patio?   ¿Da a la calle   o al patio?

UNIT 20   SPOKEN SPANISH

10 byénèlhwébes↑
    byénèlsábàdo↑   byénèlhwébes↑ọelsábàdo↓

11 báylàbyén↑
    báylàmál↑   báylàbyén↑omál↓

12 dèséạunàbitàṣyón↑
    dèséạunạapartamento↑   dèséạúnàbitàṣyón↑ọunạapartaméntò↓

---

         2   2 2 ↑
10 ¿Viene el jueves?   1   2 2 ↑ 2 1 1↓
         2   2 2↑   ¿Viene el jueves   o el sábado?
    ¿Viene el sábado?

         2   22 ↑
11 ¿Baila bien?   1   22 ↑ 2 11 ↓
         2   22 ↑   ¿Baila bien   o mal?
    ¿Baila mal?

         1 2   22 ↑
12 ¿Desea una habitación?   1 1   22 ↑ 2   1 1↓
         1 2   2 2 ↑   ¿Desea una habitación   o un apartamento?
    ¿Desea un apártamento?

20.22   VEINTIDOS

jacobeligoodsons.com For Free Audio

SPOKEN SPANISH   UNIT 20

13 (l)yégálwegó↑

     (l)yégadespwés↑   (l)yégálwégo↑odespwés↓

---

              2   2 2 ↑
       13 ¿Llega luego?
              2   22 ↑   1   2 2↑ 2   11↓
           ¿Llega después?   ¿Llega luego o después?

B. Discussion of pattern

        Choice questions consist of at least two intonation phrases. The first one is usually /1122↑/ followed immediately by /(2) 211↓/ or /(1) 211↓/ , without
leaving enough time after the /↑/ of the first phrase so that a listener would be able to break in and respond.

        The common yes-no pattern /1222↑/ is changed to /1122↑/ in the first phrase of a choice question, delaying the pitch rise to coincide with the point of
contrast which is established by the choice.

VEINTITRES   20.23

UNIT 20

SPOKEN SPANISH

20.22   Replacement drills

A   nòzlástraę |èlşekwarentaⁱsyétę↑unabeşalmés↓

1   _____abyón_____↓   nòzlástraę |elabyón↑unabeşalmés↓

2   _____semánà↓   nòzlástraę |elabyón↑unabeşalasemánà↓

3   _____ⓁyÉbą_____↓   nòzláz①yebą |elabyón↑unabeşalasemánà↓

4   _____chofér_____↓   nòzláz①yebą |elchofér↑unabeşalasemánà↓

5   mé_____↓   méláz①yebą |elchofér↑unabeşalasemánà↓

6   _____débeşęŋkwándò↓   méláz①yebą |elchofér↑dèbeşęŋkwándò↓

7   _____mandą_____↓   mèlàzmandą |elchofér↑dèbeşęŋkwándò↓

A   Nos las trae el C-47 una vez al mes.

1   _____avión_____ .   Nos las trae el avión una vez al mes.

2   _____ semana.   Nos las *trae* el avión una vez a la *semana*.

3   _____lleva _____ .   Nos las lleva el avión una vez a la semana.

4   _____ chofer _____ .   Nos las lleva el chofer una vez a la semana.

5 Me _____ .   Me las lleva el chofer una vez a la semana.

6   _____ de vez en cuando .   Me las lleva el chofer de vez en cuando.

7   _____ manda _____ .   Me las manda el chofer de vez en cuando.

20.24

VEINTICUATRO

jacobeligoodsons.com For Free Audio

SPOKEN SPANISH   UNIT 20

B   lápistạ |èzbàstantelárgà↓

1 _____ muy _____↓   lápistạ |èzmúylárgà↓

2 _____ ‹ rándè↓   lápistạ |èzmuygrándè↓

3 __èdifíşyọ_____↓   èlèdifíşyọ |èzmúyçrándè↓

4 _____ són _____↓   lòsèdifíşyos |sònmuygrándès↓

5 ésòs_____↓   ésòsèdifíşyos |sònmúygrándès↓

6 _____dèmàsyàdo_↓   ésòsèdifíşyos |sòndèmàsyàdográndès↓

7 _____ pàreşen_____↓   ésòsèdifíşyos |pàreşen |dèmàsyàdográndès↓

_____

B   La pista es bastante larga.

1 _____ muy _____.   La pista es muy larga.

2 _____ grande.   La pista es muy grande.

3 __edificio_____.   El edificio es muy grande.

4 _____ son _____.   Los edificios son muy grandes.

5 Esos _____.   Esos edificios son muy grandes.

6 _____demasiado___.   Esos edificios son demasiado grandes.

7 _____parecen_____.   Esos edificios parecen demasiado grandes.

VEINTICINCO   20.25

UNIT 20   SPOKEN SPANISH

C   kwántos,abyónes |ayenlabáse↓

1 _____ ésa ___↓   kwántos,abyónes |ayenesabáse↓

2 _____ tyénen ___↓   kwántos,abyónes |tyénen |enesabáse↓

3 _____ éskwadrónes _____↓   kwántos,eskwadrónes |tyénen |enesabáse↓

4 _____ país↓   kwántos,eskwadrónes |tyénen |enesepaís↓

5 _____ báses _____↓   kwántazbáses |tyénen |enesepaís↓

6 _____ ákel ___↓   kwántazbáses |tyénen |en,akelpaís↓

7 _____ embahadas _____↓   kwántas,embahadas |tyénen |en,akelpaís↓

_____

C   ¿Cuántos aviones hay en la base?

1 ¿ _____ esa ___?   ¿Cuántos aviones hay en esa base?

2 ¿ _____ tienen ___?   ¿Cuántos aviones tienen en esa base?

3 ¿ _____ escuadrones _____?   ¿Cuántos escuadrones tienen en esa base?

4 ¿ _____ país?   ¿Cuántos escuadrones tienen en ese país?

5 ¿ _____ bases _____?   ¿Cuántas bases tienen en ese país?

6 ¿ _____ aquel ___?   ¿Cuántas bases tienen en aquel país?

7 ¿ _____ embajadas _____?   ¿Cuántas embajadas tienen en aquel país?

20.26   VEINTISEIS

SPOKEN SPANISH   UNIT 20

D   èskèlábasè |èzmúypekéŋyà↓

1   _____àbyon_____↓   èskèlábyon |èzmúypekéŋyò↓

2   _____sòn_____↓   èskè |lòsàbyónès |sònmúypekéŋyòs↓

3   _____gràndès↓   èskè |lòsàbyónès |sònmúygràndès↓

4   _____èskwàdrìŋyas_____↓   èskè |làsèskwàdrìŋyas |sònmúygràndès↓

5   _____ésàs_____↓   èskè |ésàsèskwàdrìŋyas |sònmúygràndès↓

6   _____mòdérnàs↓   èskè |ésàsèskwàdrìŋyas |sònmúymòdérnàs↓

7   _____pàréşén_____↓   èskè |ésàsèskwàdrìŋyas |pàréşènmúymòdérnàs↓

_____

D   Es que la base es muy pequeña.

1   _____avión_____ .   Es que el avión es muy pequeño.

2   _____son_____ .   Es que los aviones son muy pequeños.

3   _____grandes.   Es que los aviones son muy grandes.

4   _____escuadrillas_____ .   Es que las escuadrillas son muy grandes.

5   _____esas_____ .   Es que esas escuadrillas son muy grandes.

6   _____modernas.   Es que esas escuadrillas son muy modernas.

7   _____parecen_____ .   Es que esas escuadrillas parecen muy modernas.

VEINTISIETE

UNIT 20 SPOKEN SPANISH

E tyénékẹir |àrréṣibírlo↑   tyénekẹir |abuskárlo↑
1 _____ buskárlo↑   ténemos |kẹirabuskárlo↑
2 ténemos_____↑   ténemos |kempéṣar |abuskárlo↑
3 _____ empéṣar |a __↑   ténemos |kempéṣar |aṣérlos↑
4 _____ aṣérlos↑   téngo |kempéṣar |aṣérlos↑
5 téngo_____↑   téngo |kẹaprender |aṣérlos↑
6 _____ aprender |a_____↑   áy |kẹaprender |aṣérlos↑
7 áy_____↑

E ¿Tiene que ir a recibirlo?

1 ¿_____ buscarlo?   ¿Tiene que ir a buscarlo?
2 ¿Tenemos _____?   ¿Tenemos que ir a buscarlo?
3 ¿_____ empezar a __?   ¿Tenemos que empezar a buscarlo?
4 ¿_____ hacerlos?   ¿Tenemos que empezar a hacerlos?
5 ¿Tengo _____?   ¿Tengo que empezar a hacerlos?
6 ¿_____ aprender a __?   ¿Tengo que aprender a hacerlos?
7 ¿Hay _____?   ¿Hay que aprender a hacerlos?

SPOKEN SPANISH   UNIT 20

F lòzđeho |kòneltenyéntè↓

1 ___Oyebo _____↓   lòzOyebo |kòneltenyéntè↓

2 _____séɲyormolínà↓   lòzOyebo |kònèlséɲyormolínà↓

3 tè _____↓   té^yebo |kònèlséɲyormolínà↓

4 _____àmɪɡohárris↓   téOyebo |kònèlàmɪɡohárris↓

5 ___đèhamos _____↓   tèđèhamos |kònèlàmɪɡohárris↓

6 là _____↓   làđèhamos |kònèlàmɪɡohárris↓

7 _____nwéstrọ _____↓   làđèhamos |kò(n)nwéstrọàmɪɡohárris↓

_____

F Los dejo con el teniente.

1 ___llevo _____.   Los llevo con el teniente.
2 _____ Sr. Molina.   Los llevo con el Sr. Molina.
3 Te _____.   Te llevo con el Sr. Molina.
4 _____ amigo Harris.   Te llevo con el amigo Harris.
5 ___dejamos _____.   Te dejamos con el amigo Harris.
6 La _____.   La dejamos con el amigo Harris.
7 _____ nuestro ____.   La dejamos con nuestro amigo Harris.

VEINTINUEVE   20.29

UNIT 20   SPOKEN SPANISH

20.23   Variation drills

A kómpran |súspróbisyónes,akí↑   ¿Compran sus provisiones aquí?

   1 Do you buy your vegetables here?   kómpran |súzléǥumbres,akí↑   ¿Compran sus legumbres aquí?

   2 Do you buy your vegetables in the   kómpran |súzléçumbres |enelkámpo↑   ¿Compran sus legumbres en el campo?
      country?

   3 Do you buy your things in that store?   kómpran |súskósas |enesatyénda↑   ¿Compran sus cosas en esa tienda?

   4 Do you buy everything there?   kómpran |tóдoaↄyí↑   ¿Compran todo allí?

   5 Do you pay less there?   paǥan |ménos,aↄyí↑   ¿Pagan menos allí?

   6 Do you pay the same now?   paǥan |ígwalaóra↑   ¿Pagan igual ahora?

   7 Do you charge much now?   kóbran |múchoaóra↑   ¿Cobran mucho ahora?

B tyéné |mílkinyéntozmétròs↓   Tiene mil quinientos metros.

   1 It's one thousand meters.   tyéne |mílmétròs↓   Tiene mil metros.

   2 It's one thousand six hundred meters.   tyéne |mílseys(ş)yéntozmétròs↓   Tiene mil seiscientos metros.

   3 It's one thousand twenty meters.   tyéne |mílbéyntemétròs↓   Tiene mil veinte metros.

20.30   TREINTA

SPOKEN SPANISH   UNIT 20

4 He has two thousand pesos.   tyéne |dózmilpésòs↓   Tiene dos mil pesos.

5 He has eight hundred pesos.   tyéng |óchóşyéntospésòs↓   Tiene ochocientos pesos.

6 He has fifteen dollars.   tyéne |kinşedólárés↓   Tiene quince dólares.

7 He has seventeen dollars.   tyéne |ḍyèşisyétedólárés↓   Tiene diecisiete dólares.

C bén |esçabyoŋ |kèbwéla |sóbrélátorredekontrol↑   ¿Ven ese avión que vuela sobre la torre
                                                                              de control?

   1 Do you see that plane that's flying   bén |esçatyoŋ |kèbwéla |sobrelkampo↑   ¿Ven ese avión que vuela sobre el campo?
      over the field?

   2 Do you see those planes that are   bén |esosạbyónés |kèbwélan |sóbrelapísta↑   ¿Ven esos aviones que vuelan sobre la
      flying over the runway?   pista?

   3 Do you see those cars that are passing   bén |esoskóches |kèpásam |porladérécha↑   ¿Ven esos coches que pasan por la derecha?
      on the right?

   4 Do you see those cars that are passing   bén |esoskóches |kèpásam |porlạişkyérda↑   ¿Ven esos coches que pasan por la izquierda?
      on the left?

   5 Do you see that woman that's going   bén |ạesamuhér |kèbaporaảya↑   ¿Ven a esa mujer que va por allá?
      over there?

   6 Do you see that man that's coming   bén |ạesẹombré |kèbyéneparaká↑   ¿Ven a ese hombre que viene para acá?
      over here?

   7 Do you see that gentleman that's in   bén |ạeseseŋyór |kèstaẹnlạofişına↑   ¿Ven a ese señor que está en la oficina?
      the office?

TREINTA Y UNO   20.31

UNIT 20   SPOKEN SPANISH

D ėnẹlbyénẹ|ėlòfíṣyáldẹinspekṣyón↓   En él viene el oficial de inspección.

1 The customs officer's coming in it.   ėnẹlbyénẹ|ėlòfíṣyáldẹadwánà↓   En él viene el oficial de aduana.

2 The chief of inspection's coming in it.   ėnẹlbyénẹ|ėlhéfėḍẹinspekṣyón↓   En él viene el jefe de inspección.

3 The chief of traffic's arriving in it.   ėnẹlˮyéċạ|ėlhéfėḍetráfikò↓   En él llega el jefe de tráfico.

4 There the fighter squadron's arriving.   àιˮyéċạ|lạệskwàdriˮyàḍekáṣà↓   Ahí llega la escuadrilla de caza.

5 There they're bringing the inspection   àιtráen|lạọrḍendẹinspekṣyón↓   Ahí traen la orden de inspección.
   order.

6 There they're bringing the lettuce salad.   àιtráen|lạệnsàlaḍaḍelechúgà↓   Ahí traen la ensalada de lechuga.

7 They're taking the four o'clock plane   màηyànàtóman|ėlàbyóndelàskwátrò↓   Mañana toman el avión de las cuatro.
   tomorrow.

E ástàlàḅistá|kòrònél↓   Hasta la vista, coronel.

1 See you later, my friend.   ástàlàḅistá|mịàmíçò↓   Hasta la vista, mi amigo.

2 See you this afternoon, Juan.   ástàlàtàrdė|hwán↓   Hasta la tarde, Juan.

3 See you this evening, Juan.   ástàlànochė|hwán↓   Hasta la noche, Juan.

4 See you at four, then.   ástàlàskwatrọ|ėntónṣės↓   Hasta las cuatro, entonces.

20.32   TREINTA Y DOS

SPOKEN SPANISH   UNIT 20

5 See you tomorrow, then.   ástámàŋyàng |èntónşès↓   Hasta mañana, entonces.

6 See you later, then.   ástálwegǫ |èntónşès↓   Hasta luego, entonces.

7 See you soon, then.   ástápronto |èntónşès↓   Hasta pronto, entonces.

F inóseleolbide |lodelgólf↓   Y no se le olvide lo del golf.

1 And don't forget about the car.   inóseleolbide |lodeláwtò↓   Y no se le olvide lo del auto.

2 And don't forget about Saturday.   inóseleolbide |lodelsábàdò↓   Y no se le olvide lo del sábado.

3 And don't forget about the bill.   inóseleolbide |lodelakwéntà↓   Y no se le olvide lo de la cuenta.

4 And don't forget about the house.   inóseleolbide |lodelakásà↓   Y no se le olvide lo de la casa.

5 And don't forget about tomorrow.   inóseleolbide |lodemaŋyánà↓   Y no se le olvide lo de mañana.

6 And don't forget about yesterday.   inóseleolbide |lodeayér↓   Y no se le olvide lo de ayer.

7 And don't forget about Mary.   inóseleolbide |lodemaríà↓   Y no se le olvide lo de María.

TREINTA Y TRES   20.33

UNIT 20   SPOKEN SPANISH

20.24   Review drill — Postposed full-form possessives

   1 He's a friend of mine.   èsúnámigomíó↓   Es un amigo mío.

   2 He's a neighbor of mine.   èsúmbèṣinomíó↓   Es un vecino mío.

   3 It's a check of mine.   èsúnchekemíó↓   Es un cheque mío.

   4 It's a book of mine.   èsúnlibromíó↓   Es un libro mío.

   5 She's a sister of mine.   èsúnảẹrmanamíả↓   Es una hermana mía.

   6 It's a cup of mine.   èsúnátaṣamíả↓   Es una taza mía.

   7 He's a friend of yours.   èsúnámigosúyó↓   Es un amigo suyo.

   8 It's a book of yours.   èsúnlibrosúyó↓   Es un libro suyo.

   9 She's a sister of yours.   èsúnẹẹrmanasúyả↓   Es una hermana suya.

  10 It's a check of yours.   èsúnchekesúyó↓   Es un cheque suyo.

  11 He's a neighbor of yours.   èsúmbèṣinosúyó↓   Es un vecino suyo.

20.34   TREINTA Y CUATRO

SPOKEN SPANISH   UNIT 20

20.3   CONVERSATION STIMULUS

NARRATIVE 1

1 These photos sure are nice!   keḷwenas |estanestasfótòs↓   ¡Qué buenas están estas fotos!

2 They belong to Colonel Harris.   son |delkorónelhárris↓   Son del Coronel Harris.

3 He loaned them to Jose.   elselásprestó |ahosé↓   El se las prestó a José.

4 But Jose has to take them (back)   péróhóse |tyeneke^yebárselas |estanóché↓   Pero José tiene que llevárselas esta
   to him tonight.   noche.

5 This one of Jose in front of that plane   estadehose |emfrénteéésgàbyon↑erlamehór↓   Esta de José, en frente de ese avión,
   is the best.   es la mejor.

6 The Commanding Officer of the base   élhefedelaoase |selatomó↓   El Jefe de la base se la tomó.
   took it for him.

DIALOG 1

Carmen, dígale a José que qué buenas   kebwénas |estánestasfótòs↓ téláspresto |el   Carmen: ¡Qué buenas están estas fotos!
están estas fotos. Pregúntele si se   koronel↑   ¿Te las prestó el Coronel?
las prestó el Coronel.

José, contéstele que sí, pero que tiene sí↓ pérótengo |ke^yebárselas |estanóché↓   José: Sí, pero tengo que llevárselas esta
que llevárselas esta noche.   noche.

TREINTA Y CINCO   20.35

UNIT 20   SPOKEN SPANISH

Carmen, dígale que éste de él (José) en   éstátuyạ |èmfréntẹdésẹabyon↑ezlà   Carmen: Esta tuya en frente de ese avión
    frente de ese avión es la mejor. Pregún-   es la mejor. ¿Quién te la tomó?
    tele que quién se la tomó.   mehór↓ kyentelatomó↓

José, contéstele que el Jefe de la base.   èlhéfèdelabásè↓   José: El Jefe de la base.

                                        NARRATIVE 2

1 They met the Commanding Officer, then.   kònòçyéronạlhéfẹ |èntónçès↓   Conocieron al Jefe, entonces.

2 And some of the pilots, too.   ịàbáryòz |dèlòspìlòtòs |tàmbyén↓   Y a varios de los pilotos, también.

3 Colonel Harris introduced them (to them).   èlkóronèlhárris |sélospresentó↓   El Coronel Harris se los presentó.

4 Carmen wants to know how many planes   kármeņ |kyeresabér↑kwántosạbyónès | Carmen quiere saber cuántos aviones hay
    there are at that base.   ayeņẹsabásè↓   en esa base.

5 'Forty-seven altogether,' says Jose,   kwàréntạịsyétentotál |díçèhòsé↓ sininklwír | Cuarenta y siete en total-dice José, sin
    'not including the C-33 which belongs   incluir el C-33 que pertenece a la Misión.
    to the Mission.'   elçetreyntạịtres |kepertèneçẹ |alamisyón↓

6 He says the CO himself told him so.   éldìçe |kèlhéfémìzmoselodíhò↓   El dice que el Jefe mismo se lo dijo.

7 But it isn't true. He's somewhat confused.   pérònọezberrdád↓ élestá |ụmpókòkòmfúndidò↓   Pero no es verdad. El está un poco
                                                                                               confundido.

8 The CO told him the other way around.   èlhéfe |lèdíhòlókòntraryó↓   El Jefe le dijo lo contrario.

20.36   TREINTA Y SEIS

SPOKEN SPANISH   UNIT 20

9 That there were thirty-three planes,   ke̦åbía |tréynta̦i̦tre̦șa̦byónès↓   Que había treinta y tres aviones, sin
   not including the C-47.   sininklwir |èl̦șékwåréntai̦syetè↓   incluir el C-47.

                                              DIALOG 2

Carmen, pregúntele a José si conocieron al   kònòșyéron |àlhéfe̦d̦è̦lå̦bașe̦ |èntónse̦s↓   Carmen: ¿Conocieron al Jefe de la Base,
   Jefe de la Base, entonces.   entonces?

José, contéstele que sí, y a varios de los   sí↓ i̦åbaryoz |d̦elòspilótòs |tàmbyén↓   José: Sí, y a varios de los pilotos, también.
   pilotos, también. Que se los presentó   nózlòsprèsènto |e̦lkòrònélhárris↓   Nos los presentó el Coronel Harris.
   el Coronel Harris.

Carmen, pregúntele que cuántos aviones   kwántoșa̦byónès |ayene̦sa̦báșè↓   Carmen: ¿Cuántos aviones hay en esa base?
   hay en esa base.

José, contéstele que cuarenta y siete en   kwårénta̦i̦syéte̦ |èntòtál↓ sininklwir | José: Cuarenta y siete en total, sin incluir
   total, sin incluir el C-33 que pertenece a   el̦șe̦treyntai̦trés |kepertene̦șe̦alamisyón↓   el C-33 que pertenece a la Misión.
   la Misión.

Juan, dígale a José que no es verdad, que   nge̦zberd̦á̦d̦ |hòsé↓ èstás |úmpókò   Juan: No es verdad, José. Estás un poco
   está un poco confundido.   kòmfúndi̦d̦ò↓   confundido.

José, dígale que el Jefe mismo se lo dijo.   èlhéfémizmo |mèlòd̦ihò↓   José: El jefe mismo me lo dijo.

Juan, dígale que no, que le dijo lo contrario. nó |tèd̦íhòlòkóntraryó↓ ke̦åbía |tréynta̦   Juan: No, te dijo lo contrario. Que había
   Que había treinta y tres aviones sin incluir i̦tre̦șa̦byónès↓ sininklwir |èl̦șe̦ |kwårénta̦   treinta y tres aviones sin incluir
   el C-47.   i̦syetè↓   el C-47.

José, dígale que tiene razón.   tyénezrra̦șón↓   José: Tienes razón.

TREINTA Y SIETE   20.37
          jacobeligoodsons.com For Free Audio

UNIT 20   SPOKEN SPANISH

NARRATIVE 3

1 This country didn't buy all these planes   éstèpáıʔ↑nólekompro |todos̥estos̥abyónes | Este país no le compró todos estos
  from the United States.   alos̥estados̥uníɗòs↓   aviones a los Estados Unidos.

2 The fighters, yes.   lòzɗèkaṣa |sí↓   Los de caza, sí.

3 But the bombers were bought from the   péról̥òzɗèbòmbárɗeoʔsèlóskômpráron | Pero los de bombardeo se los compraron
  British.   àlós̥inglesès↓   a los ingleses.

4 Carmen doesn't know what they need so   kármen |nòsabeʔpárákeneṣesitan |tántos   Carmen no sabe para qué necesitan tantos
  many war planes for.   abyónez̥degérrá↓   aviones de guerra.

5 This country isn't going to have a war   estèpaıʔ↑nòbáténer |gérràkó(n)náɗyè↓   Este país no va a tener guerra con nadie.
  with anybody.

DIALOG 3

Carmen, pregúntele si este país le compró   éstèpáız |lèkómproʔtodos̥estos̥abyónes | Carmen: Este país le compró todos estos
  todos estos aviones a los Estados Unidos,   alos̥estados̥uníɗós↓n̥ọèzbérɗaɗ↑   aviones a los Estados Unidos,
  que si no es verdad.   ¿no es verdad?

José, contéstele que los de caza sí. Que   lòzɗèkaṣasí↓ lòzɗèbòmbárɗeo |sèlòs   José: Los de caza sí. Los de bombardeo
  los de bombardeo Uds. se los compraron   kòmpramos |àlós̥inglesès↓   se los compramos a los ingleses.
  a los ingleses.

Carmen, dígale que Ud. no sabe para qué   yó |nòsépáráke |neṣesitámós |tántós   Carmen: Yo no sé para que necesitamos
  necesitan Uds. tantos aviones de guerra.   àbyónèz̥degérrá↓ nòsotroz |nobamos̥atener | tantos aviones de guerra.
  Que Uds. no van a tener guerra con nadie.   Nosotros no vamos a tener guerra
                                                 gerrako(n)náɗyè↓   con nadie.

20.38   TREINTA Y OCHO

SPOKEN SPANISH

UNIT 20

20.4   READINGS

20.40   List of cognate loan words

la visita	là-bisítà↓
la sorpresa	là-sórprésà↓
la pronunciación	là-prónùnşyàşyón↓
la oportunidad	là-ópórtúnióàd↓
las conjugaciones	làs-kónhùgàşyonès↓
los verbos	lóz-bérbós↓
la memoria	là-mèmóryà↓
saludar	sàlùdár↓
el desorden	èl-dèsorðèn↓
disgustado (disgustar)	dizgústàðó↓ dizgústár↓
el acento	èl-àşèntò↓

TREINTA Y NUEVE

UNIT 20   SPOKEN SPANISH

20.41   Reading selection

La Primera Visita

—Buenas noches—dijo Virginia de Robinson muy claramente en español y mirando con sorpresa a los señores Fuentes.

Al oír ese 'buenas noches' con tan buena pronunciación, don Ricardo también recibió una sorpresa y en seguida pensó que esa señora no iba a darle oportunidad de hablar en inglés. Eso no le gustó mucho porque el día antes él había estado toda la tarde y toda la noche practicando y estudiando las conjugaciones de los verbos; también había practicado, muchas y muchas veces antes de salir de su casa, y por fin había aprendido completamente de memoria a decir esto: 'Good night. Wee arrr dee neighbors of you that leeve een front of dees house. My naim ees Ricardo Fuentes. She ees my wife, Marta de Fuentes. For shee and for me ees a pleasure to welcome you to Bellavista'. Pero con sólo oír a Virginia decir aquel poquito decidió hablar en español mejor:

—Buenas noches—dijo él también. —Somos la familia de la casa de la esquina que está casi enfrente de la de ustedes y, como vecinos que somos, venimos a saludarlos. Mi nombre es Ricardo Fuentes. Esta es mi señora Marta.

—Encantada de conocerlos y muchísimas gracias por venir a vernos. Yo soy la señora de Robinson, Virginia de Robinson. Pero por favor pasen adelante; están en su casa. Vamos a la sala y dispensen el desorden y todo tan sucio pero, como Uds. saben, acabamos de mudarnos y todavía no hemos tenido tiempo de arreglar nada. Con permiso, voy a llamar a mi esposo...¡Fred!.....¡Oh, Freddie!.....Debe estar en el patio. Dispénsenme un momento, por favor, voy a ver si está ahí.

—Si está ocupado, por favor no lo moleste—dijo Marta —nosotros podemos venir otro día.

—No, no, no, estoy segura de que él va a querer conocerlos a Uds. Vuelvo en seguida —dijo Virginia y salió a buscar a su esposo.

—¿Qué te parece la señora? ¿No te parece que es muy bonita y que habla muy bien el español? —le preguntó Marta a Ricardo cuando quedaron solos en la sala.

Este, que estaba un poco disgustado porque la señora de Robinson en realidad hablaba casi sin acento y no le había dado oportunidad de hablar en inglés, dijo:

—Pensar que estuve todo el día de ayer y todo el día de hoy estudiando inglés cuando tenía tanto trabajo en la oficina. Y ¿para qué? Para venir aquí a hablar sólo español. Pero estoy seguro de que esa señora no habla tan bien como parece. Vas a ver que una vez que....

—Shh...aquí vienen —interrumpió Marta, —no vayas a meter la pata.

20.42   Response drill

    1 ¿Qué tal era el acento de Virginia en español?

    2 ¿Por qué no le gustó mucho a Ricardo oírla hablar con tan buen acento?

20.40   CUARENTA

SPOKEN SPANISH   UNIT 20

3 ¿Cuánto tiempo había estudiado él inglés el día antes?

4 ¿Qué fué lo que estudió más?

5 ¿Tenía él mucho o poco acento español cuando hablaba inglés?

6 ¿Decidió él por fin hablar en español o en inglés?

7 ¿Qué le dijo a la Sra. de Robinson?

8 ¿Qué contestó ella?

9 ¿A qué parte de la casa los llevó ella cuando pasaron adelante?

10 ¿Por qué estaba la casa en desorden?

11 ¿Para qué salió Virginia de la casa?

12 ¿Dónde estaba el esposo de ella?

13 ¿Cuál era el nombre de su esposo?

14 ¿Qué le pareció la Sra. de Robinson a Marta?

15 ¿Le pareció que era fea o que era bonita?

CUARENTA Y UNO   20.41

jacobeligoodsons.com For Free Audio

SPOKEN SPANISH   UNIT 21

21.1   BASIC SENTENCES.   The weather.

          Molina and White continue their visit to the base with Lieutenant La Cerda.

ENGLISH SPELLING   AID TO LISTENING   SPANISH SPELLING

Lieutenant   kéles̮apareṣído|labásè↓   *Teniente*
How did you all like the base? [1]   ¿Qué les ha parecido la base?

     interesting   intèrésántè↓   interesante

White   múyinteresántè↓   *White*
Very interesting.   Muy interesante.

It's the first time I've visited one. [2] èzláprímerabeṣ|kéyobisitǫúná↓   Es la primera vez que yo visito una.

     the cold   èl—fríó↓   el frío
     to be cold (said of the weather)   áṣer—fríó↓   hacer frío

Molina   kefríǫáṣè↓   *Molina*
It sure is cold! [3]   ¡Qué frío hace!

     the weather   èl—tyémpò↓   el tiempo

White   ezberdád↓ kómokámbyaͅeltyémpǫ|àkí↓   *White*
Sure is. The weather is mighty changeable here.   Es verdad. ¡Cómo cambia el tiempo aquí!

     the sun   èl—sól↓   el sol

UNO   21.1

UNIT 21

SPOKEN SPANISH

pleasant, agreeable	àgràdáblé↓	agradable

Molina
Yesterday was a pleasant, sunny day.

àyer |ìşǫundíadesól |muyàgràdáblé↓

Molina
Ayer hizo un día de sol muy agradable.

rather	máz‑byén↓	más bien
the heat	él‑kàlór↓	el calor
to be hot	àşér‑kàlór↓	hacer calor

White
Or rather, it was just plain hot.

ma?byén |ìşókàlór↓

White
Más bien hizo calor.

(we) gave (to give)	dímòs↓ dár↓	dimos (dar)
to take a ride (walk)	dár‑una‑bwéltà↓	dar una vuelta

Molina
We took a ride.

nòsótroz |dímòsúnàbwéltà↓

Molina
Nosotros dimos una vuelta.

(we) went (to go)	fwìmòs↓ ír↓	fuimos (ir)
the country, countryside	él‑kàmpò↓	el campo

We went to the country.

fwìmosạlkámpò↓

Fuimos al campo.

(I) walked (to walk) (I) was out (to be out)	àndubè↓ àndár↓	anduve (andar)

White
I only took a walk through the park.

yó |sólǫandúbè |pòrèlpárkè↓

White
Yo sólo anduve por el parque.

21.2

DOS

SPOKEN SPANISH   UNIT 21

cloudy (to cloud)   núbladó↓ núblarsè↓   nublado (nublarse)

to rain   ʎyóbér↓   llover

Molina
It's cloudy now. Looks like it's going to rain.   áorạestánubládó↓ pàreşé |kèbáʎyóbér↓   *Molina*
Ahora está nublado. Parece que va a llover.

the wind   èl‑byéntò↓   el viento

Lieutenant
And there's considerable wind.   ɹáymuchòbyéntò↓   *Teniente*
Y hay mucho viento.

to enter   èntrár↓   entrar

very, good and   byén↓   bien

warm   kàlyéntè↓   caliente

Why don't we go inside and have a good hot cup of coffee.   pórkenọentrámòs |inòstómamos |ùŋkáfe byeŋkalyéntè↓   ¿Por qué no entramos y nos tomamos un café bien caliente?

to thank   àgrádèşér   agradecer

Molina
Thanks a lot (for the invitation) but we can't.   sèlọàgràdèşémozmúchò↓pèrònopoɗémòs↓   *Molina*
Se lo agradecemos mucho, pero no podemos.

We've got to leave.   tènemoskẹírnòs↓   Tenemos que irnos.

Lieutenant
I'm going to the city.   yóbóy |paralaşyudád↓   *Teniente*
Yo voy para la ciudad.

Do you want to come with me?   kyérembénír |konmígo↑   ¿Quieren venir conmigo?

TRES   21.3

UNIT 21   SPOKEN SPANISH

Molina   *Molina*
You won't need to bother, lieutenant.   nósémólésté |tényénté↓   No se moleste, teniente.

(I) brought (to bring)   tráhé↓ tráér↓   traje (traer)

I brought my car.   yótráhemįáwtó↓   Yo traje mi auto.

21.10   Notes on the basic sentences

   (1)   This sentence more nearly literally says, 'How have you all liked the base,' so that there is some question as to whether a translation in simple present, 'How do you like...' or in simple past, 'How did you like...' is better.

   (2)   Here is a problem of translation which precisely reverses the one just examined: the Spanish says, 'It's the first time I visit one,' which is quite impossible in English. We substitute 'have visited,' and it begins to be clear that the Spanish present perfect verb phrase and the English present perfect verb phrase are likely to appear in rather different situations.

   (3)   This particular sentence and two of those just below (/ayér|işo~un~día.../ *Ayer hizo un día...* and /más~byén|işo~kalór / *Más bien, hizo calor*) illustrate the use of /aşér/ *hacer* in weather expressions. We say, 'It *is* hot', they say, 'It *makes* heat.'

21.2   DRILLS AND GRAMMAR

21.21   Pattern drills

21.21.1 Irregular past I verb forms — an /—ár/ verb taking regular /—ér-ír/ endings

   A.   Presentation of pattern

                                          ILLUSTRATIONS

I gave the old bed.   1   dílakamabyéhà↓   *Di* la cama vieja.

At least you gave something.   2   pòrlómènoz |distęálgó↓   Por lo menos *diste* algo.

21.4   CUATRO

jacobeligoodsons.com For Free Audio

SPOKEN SPANISH   UNIT 21

At last Anna gave us the information.   3 pòrfín↑ ananozđyó |lạimformaşyón↓   Por fin Ana nos *dio* la información.

—————————————————————   4 nòsótroz |dímosunabwéltå↓   Nosotros *dimos* una vuelta.

Actually they didn't give me anything.   5 ènrrẹàliđàđ |nomẹdyéro(n)náđå↓   En realidad, no me *dieron* nada.

EXTRAPOLATION

		d—ár
Stem		d—
Endings		
sg 1		—í
	2 fam	—íste
	2-3	—yó
pl		
	1	—ímos
	2-3	—yéron

NOTES

a. The verb /dár/ is irregular in that it occurs with regular /—ér—ır/ past 1 endings.

CINCO

UNIT 21   SPOKEN SPANISH

21.21.11 Substitution drills — Person-number substitution

1   yóↄı|làrrópabyéhà↓

    márıa _____↓   dyó|larrópabyéhà↓

    hwánıyo _____↓   dímoz|larrópabyéhà↓

    ústedez _____↓   dyéron|larrópabyéhà↓

    él _____↓   dyó|larrópabyéhà↓

2   ústedyo|muchapropínà↓

    márıaıhwàn _____↓   dyérón|muchapropínà↓

    yó _____↓   dímuchapropínà↓

_____

    1 *Yo* di la ropa vieja.

       María _____ .   Dio la ropa vieja.

       Juan y yo _____ .   Dimos la ropa vieja.

       Uds. _____ .   Dieron la ropa vieja.

       El _____ .   Dio la ropa vieja.

    2 *Ud.* dio mucha propina.

       María y Juan _____ .   Dieron mucha propina.

       Yo _____ .   Di mucha propina.

21.6   SEIS

SPOKEN SPANISH   UNIT 21

eʎa _____↓   dyómuchapropíná↓
ústeɗez _____↓   dyérón |muchapropíná↓

3 eʎyoz |dyerondemasyáɗó↓
   ántonyo _____↓   dyoɗemasyáɗó↓
   yo _____↓   diɗemasyáɗó↓
   ústeɗ _____↓   dyoɗemasyáɗó↓
   kármeṇ₁lwísa _____↓   dyérondemasyáɗó↓

_____

   Ella _____.   Dio mucha propina.
   Uds. _____.   Dieron mucha propina.

3 *Ellos* dieron demasiado.

   Antonio _____.   Dio demasiado.
   Yo _____.   Di demasiado.
   Ud. _____.   Dio demasiado.
   Carmen y Luisa _____.   Dieron demasiado.

SIETE

UNIT 21   SPOKEN SPANISH

Tense substitution

1 toḋoz |ḋamospropína↓   toḋoz |ḋimospropína↓

2 yoḋoyrregálòs↓   yoḋirregálòs↓

3 eḽyoz |ḋandemasyáḋò↓   eḽyoz |ḋyerondemasyáḋò↓

4 hwandapropína↓   hwan |ḋyopropína↓

5 yoḋabapókò↓   yoḋipókò↓

6 toḋoz |ḋabandemasyáḋò↓   toḋoz |ḋyerondemasyáḋò↓

7 nòsotroz |noḋabamozrregálòs↓   nòsotroz |noḋimozrregálòs↓

---

1 Todos *damos* propina.   Todos dimos propina.

2 Yo *doy* regalos.   Yo di regalos.

3 Ellos *dan* demasiado.   Ellos dieron demasiado.

4 Juan *da* propina.   Juan dio propina.

5 Yo *daba* poco.   Yo di poco.

6 Todos *daban* demasiado.   Todos dieron demasiado.

7 Nosotros no *dábamos* regalos.   Nosotros no dimos regalos.

21.8   OCHO

SPOKEN SPANISH   UNIT 21

21.21.12 Response drill

	1	ústeɗ |ɗyómúchọ↑opókò↓	dípokò↓
	2	ústeɗez |ɗyérònmúchọ↑opókò↓	dímòzmúchò↓
[éꞎyòs↓]	3	kyénez |ɗyérònmúchò↓	éꞎyòz |ɗyérònmúchò↓
[pròpinà↓]	4	keɗyoél↓	éldyópròpinà↓
[pokò↓]	5	dyoụstéɗmúchò↑	nò↓ dípokò↓
[múchò↓]	6	dyérone̥ꞎyospokò↑	nò↓ dyérònmúchò↓
	7	dyéronụsteɗes |propinà↑	sí|sìɗímòs↓
	8	dyoụstéɗ |propinà↑	sí|sìɗí↓
	9	dyóel |propinà↑	sí| sìɗyó↓

	1	¿Ud. dio mucho o poco?	Di poco.
	2	¿Uds. dieron mucho o poco?	Dimos mucho.
(ellos)	3	¿Quiénes dieron mucho?	Ellos dieron mucho.
(propina)	4	¿Qué dio él?	El dio propina.
(poco)	5	¿Dio Ud. mucho?	No, di poco.
(mucho)	6	¿Dieron ellos poco?	No, dieron mucho.
	7	¿Dieron Uds. propina?	Sí, sí dimos.
	8	¿Dió Ud. propina?	Sí, sí di.
	9	¿Dió él propina?	Sí, sí dio.

NUEVE

UNIT 21   SPOKEN SPANISH

21.21.13 Translation drill

1 He and I gave the sofa to Carmen.   éliyó|lédimos|élsòfakármèn↓   El y yo le dimos el sofá a Carmen.

2 I also gave her a suitcase.   yotambyén|lèdiunamalétá↓   Yo también le di una maleta.

3 They gave her the photos.   é⌒yoz|lèdyéronlasfótòs↓   Ellos le dieron las fotos.

4 What did she give her?   keledyóé⌒yá↓   ¿Qué le dio ella?

5 Who did you give the bill to?   àkyén|lèdyéronlakwéntá↓   ¿A quién le dieron la cuenta?

6 He gave her the key to the car.   é⌒ledyó|lá⌒yabedeláwtò↓   El le dio la llave del auto.

7 I didn't give her permission.   yó|noledipermísò↓   Yo no le di permiso.

B. Discussion of pattern

     The verb /dár/ is unique in the pattern of its past I tense forms. It is the only instance where the stem of a verb of one theme class combines with the regular
endings of another theme class in the conjugation of a verb paradigm.

21.21.2 Irregular past I verb forms — verbs with extended stems

     A. Presentation of pattern

                                                 ILLUSTRATIONS

     _____   1 yóẹstubẹaí|aẹẹunozdíàs↓   Yo estuve ahí hace unos días.

     Were you in the business section?   2 éstúbistẹ|enẹlsektórkomerẹyal↑   ¿Estuviste en el sector comercial?

21.10   DIEZ

jacobeligoodsons.com For Free Audio

SPOKEN SPANISH   UNIT 21

Were you in the Air Force?   3   èstubo̧ |enlafwer̦ṣaér̦e̦a↑   ¿Estuvo en la Fuerza Aérea?

We were at the cathedral.   4   èstúbimos |enlakatedrál↓   Estuvimos en la catedral.

Besides, they were very happy.   5   àd̦emás |èstúbyéronmuykonténtòs↓   Además, estuvieron muy contentos.

_____   6   yo |sólo̧andube |pórèlparkè↓   Yo sólo anduve por el parque.

Apparently you walked a lot.   7   pòrlóbisto̧ |ândúbistemúchò↓   Por lo visto anduviste mucho.

Were you with the fat man?   8   ândubo |kon̦elgórd̦ò↑   ¿Anduvo con el gordo?

We were out with the air attaché.   9   ândúbimos |kón̦élàgrègad̦o̧aérg̦ò↓   Anduvimos con el agregado aéreo.

Weren't they around there?   10   no̧andubyérom |poraí↑   ¿No anduvieron por ahí?

_____   11   yotráhemɪ́áwtò↓   Yo traje mi auto.

Did you bring your new car?   12   tràhiste |tunwebokárro↑   ¿Trajiste tu nuevo carro?

Did you already bring the coffee?   13   yatráho̧elkafé↑   ¿Ya trajo el café?

We brought a million things.   14   tràhimos |ùnmiꞎyondekósàs↓   Trajimos un millón de cosas.

What did they bring today?   15   ketráheronóy↓   ¿Qué trajeron hoy?

ONCE   21.11

UNIT 21   SPOKEN SPANISH

EXTRAPOLATION

	—ár	—ér
Regular stem	est— and—	tra—
Extended stem	est—ub— and—ub—	tra—h—

Alternate endings	
sg	
1	—e
2 fam	—íste
2-3	—o
pl	
1	—ímos
2-3	—yéron (—éron)

NOTES

a. The extension /—ub—/ is added to the stems of /est—ár/ and /and—ár/ before the endings in past I tense forms.

b. The extension /—h—/ is added to the stem of /tra—ér/ before the endings in past I tense forms.

c. The 2-3 pl alternate ending /—yéron/ appears as /—éron/ (the /—y—/ dropping out) after the sound /h—/ in irregular past I tense formations in most dialect areas.

21.12   DOCE

jacobeligoodsons.com For Free Audio

SPOKEN SPANISH   UNIT 21

21.21.21 Substitution drills – Person-number substitution

1 hóse |ęstúbǫá͡yị |tambyén↓

   àntonyǫihosé_____↓   èstúbyéron |á͡yịtambyén↓

   yǫ_____↓   èstúbęà͡yị |tambyén↓

   lwisǫ_____↓   èstúbǫ |á͡yị |tambyén↓

   nósotros_____↓   èstúbímòsá͡yị |tambyén↓

2 kármen |nótráhonáɖà↓

   yǫ_____↓   notráhenáɖà↓

   é͡yọz_____↓   notráhero(n)náɖà↓

_____

      1 *José* estuvo allí también.

         Antonio y José_____.   Estuvieron allí también.

         Yo_____.   Estuve allí también.

         Luisa_____.   Estuvo allí también.

         Nosotros_____.   Estuvimos allí también.

      2 *Carmen* no trajo nada.

         Yo_____.   No traje nada.

         Ellos_____.   No trajeron nada.

TRECE   21.13

UNIT 21   SPOKEN SPANISH

   karmeniyo_____↓   nótráhimoznádà↓

   ùsteđ_____↓   nótráhonádà↓

3 yoạndube |pórlàsàfweràs↓   àndùbyérom |pórlàsàfweràs↓

   ùsteđes_____↓   àndùbyérom |pórlàsàfweràs↓

   hósȩkarmen _____↓   àndúbo |pórlàsàfweràs↓

   éʼyạ _____↓   àndùbimos |pórlàsàfweràs↓

   karmeniyó _____↓

   Carmen y yo _____ .   No trajimos nada.

   Ud. _____ .   No trajo nada.

3 *Yo* anduve por las afueras.

   Uds. _____ .   Anduvieron por las afueras.

   José y Carmen _____ .   Anduvieron por las afueras.

   Ella _____ .   Anduvo por las afueras.

   Carmen y yo _____ .   Anduvimos por las afueras.

SPOKEN SPANISH   UNIT 21

4 àntónyo |noęstubǫ |enlamisyón↓

   yo _____ ↓   noęstubǫ |enlamisyón↓

   àntónyǫiyo _____ ↓   noęstubimos |enlamisyón↓

   é^yaz _____ ↓   noęstubyeron |enlamisyón↓

   ústęd _____ ↓   noęstubǫ |enlamisyón↓

5 é^yostraheron |todokompléto↓

   yo _____ ↓   tráhétodokompléto↓

   ústęd _____ ↓   tráhótodokompléto↓

   lwisaįyo _____ ↓   tràhímòs |todokompléto↓

   é^ya _____ ↓   tráhótodokompléto↓

_____

4 *Antonio* no estuvo en la Misión.

   Yo _____ .   No estuve en la Misión.
   Antonio y yo _____ .   No estuvimos en la Misión.
   Ellas _____ .   No estuvieron en la Misión.
   Ud. _____ .   No estuvo en la Misión.

5 *Ellos* trajeron todo completo.

   Yo _____ .   Traje todo completo.
   Ud. _____ .   Trajo todo completo.
   Luisa y yo _____ .   Trajimos todo completo.
   Ella _____ .   Trajo todo completo.

QUINCE   21.15

UNIT 21   SPOKEN SPANISH

Tense substitution

1   yoǫstóy |eṇelotél↓   yoǫstube̖ |eṇelotél↓

2   eⁿyos |èstanẹnlamisyón↓   eⁿyos |èstúbyeroṇenlamisyón↓

3   elestaǫnmikásà↓   elestube̖ |enmikásà↓

4   nòsótròs |tráiamos̟és̟ò↓   nòsotros |tràhimos̟és̟ò↓

5   eltraia̟ |asy̟íhà↓   eltrahǫ |asy̟íhà↓

6   nòsotros |àndabamosporelşéntrò↓   nòsotros |àndùbimosporelşéntrò↓

7   yoǫndaba |porelpárkè↓   yoǫndube̖ |porelpárkè↓

8   todos |èstabamosa͡ʸy̟í↓   todos |èstùbimosa͡ʸy̟í↓

9   eⁿyos |èstabaṇensukásà↓   eⁿyos |èstúbyeroṇensukásà↓

_____

1 Yo *estoy* en el hotel.   Yo estuve en el hotel.

2 Ellos *están* en la Misión.   Ellos estuvieron en la Misión.

3 El *está* en mi casa.   El estuvo en mi casa.

4 Nosotros *traíamos* eso.   Nosotros trajimos eso.

5 El *traía* a su hija.   El trajo a su hija.

6 Nosotros *andábamos* por el centro.   Nosotros anduvimos por el centro.

7 Yo *andaba* por el parque.   Yo anduve por el parque.

8 Todos *estábamos* allí.   Todos estuvimos allí.

9 Ellos *estaban* en su casa.   Ellos estuvieron en su casa.

21.16   DIECISEIS

SPOKEN SPANISH   UNIT 21

21.21.22 Response drill

```
             1  àndúbyéronustédes |anóche |pòrélşéntrọ↑opòrelpárkè↓     àndúbımos |porélşéntrò↓
             2  àndubọusted |anóche |pòrélşéntrọ↑opòrelpárkè↓          àndube |pòrélşéntrò |tàmbyén↓

[líbròs↓]    3  kétrahọusted |alạeskwélà↓                              trahelíbròs↓
[líbròs↓]    4  kétrahérọnustédès↓                                     tràhımozlíbròs↓
[ànóchè↓]    5  kwándọ |estúbọusted |enẹlşéntrò↓                       ẹstúbẹanóchè↓
 [àyér↓]     6  kwándọ |estúbyéronẹ@yos |enẹlşéntrò↓                   èstúbyeronạyér↓
```

```
             1  ¿Anduvieron Uds. anoche por el centro o por el parque?   Anduvimos por el centro.
             2  ¿Anduvo Ud. anoche por el centro o por el parque?        Anduve por el centro también.

(libros)     3  ¿Qué trajo Ud. a la escuela?                             Traje libros.
(libros)     4  ¿Qué trajeron Uds.?                                      Trajimos libros.
(anoche)     5  ¿Cuándo estuvo Ud. en el centro?                         Estuve anoche.
(ayer)       6  ¿Cuándo estuvieron ellos en el centro?                   Estuvieron ayer.
```

DIECISIETE   21.17

UNIT 21   SPOKEN SPANISH

[èⓁlápiş↓]   7   tráhǫel |laplúma↑   nó↓ tráhǫèⓁlápiş↓

[pokòs↓]   8   tràhérǫnⒶⓎọz |múchozlíbros↓   nó↓ tràhérómpokòs↓

            9   èstuḅǫustèḍakí |ayér↑   sì |sięstúbè↓

           10   èstúbimos |éliyó↑   sí↓ tàmbyénęstubyérón↓

           11   tráhǫustèḍ |sukárro↑   sí |silotráhè↓

_____

(el lápiz)   7 ¿Trajo él la pluma?   No, trajo el lápiz.

(pocos)   8 ¿Trajeron ellos muchos libros?   No, trajeron pocos.

              9 ¿Estuvo Ud. aquí ayer?   Sí, sí estuve.

             10 ¿Estuvimos él y yo?   Sí, también estuvieron.

             11 ¿Trajo Ud. su carro?   Sí, sí lo traje.

21.18   jacobeligoodsons.com For Free Audio   DIECIOCHO

SPOKEN SPANISH   UNIT 21

21.21.23 Translation drill

1	Yesterday I brought the car.	àyér|tráhelkóché↓	Ayer traje el coche.
2	He also brought (one).	él|támbyentráhó↓	El también trajo.
3	On Sunday we didn't bring it.	éldómiŋgo|nolotrahímós↓	El domingo no lo trajimos.
4	They didn't bring anything.	éⁿyoz|nòtráhéró(n)nádá↓	Ellos no trajeron nada.
5	We walked around (the) downtown (section).	àndúbimos|porelṣéntró↓	Anduvimos por el centro.
6	They also walked around there.	éⁿyos|támbyenandubyérom|poraⁿyá↓	Ellos también anduvieron por allá.
7	We were at Immigration.	èstúbimos|eninmigraṣyón↓	Estuvimos en Inmigración.
8	He wasn't there.	él|noҽstúbọaⁿyí↓	El no estuvo allí.
9	Where were they?	dóndҽ|estubyéronéⁿyós↓	¿Dónde estuvieron ellos?

DIECINUEVE   21.19

jacobeligoodsons.com For Free Audio

UNIT 21   SPOKEN SPANISH

B. Discussion of pattern

       Three Spanish verbs have extensions - additional sound(s) - added to their stems when they appear with past I tense endings. They are furthermore irregular in
having a set of alternate past I endings that differ significantly from the endings which occur with regular formations. The alternate endings are like regular /‒ér‒ír/
past I endings in the pl and 2 fam sg forms, but the 1 sg and 2-3 sg forms resemble regular /‒ár/ past I endings except that they appear under weak stress. The
following chart shows these correlations:

		Regular past I endings		Irregular past I endings
		‒ár	‒ér ‒ír	all theme classes
sg				
	1	‒ó	‒í	‒e
	2 fam	‒áste	‒íste	‒íste
	2-3	‒ó	‒yó	‒o
pl				
	1	‒ámos	‒ímos	‒ímos
	2-3	‒áron	‒yéron	‒yéron *

                                                                                           */‒éron/ after /‒ɨr‒/

       These alternate past I endings will also appear with other irregular past I verb stems having different kinds of modifications. **These will be discussed as the
following grammar point.**

21.21.3   Irregular past I verb forms – verbs with modified stems

    A. Presentation of pattern

                                                     ILLUSTRATIONS

    _____   1   nopudímos |kómùnikárnoskoɳustéⱥ↓   No *pudimos* comunicarnos con usted.

    They couldn't find the coin.   2   nopudyéron |èɳkòntrárlamonéⱥⱥ↓   No *pudieron* encontrar la moneda.

21.20   VEINTE

SPOKEN SPANISH   UNIT 21

I translated everything carefully.   3 tráɗuhetoɗo |koŋkwiɗáɗò↓   *Traduje* todo con cuidado.

So you translated everything.   4 èmfín |traɗuhistetóɗò↓   En fin, *tradujiste* todo.

He didn't know how to converse in Spanish. 5 nósupo |kòmbèrsarenespaŋyól↓   No *supo* conversar en español.

You didn't know how to have fun.   6 ústeɗez |nósupyerondibertírsè↓   Ustedes no *supieron* divertirse.

The table didn't fit in the kitchen.   7 làmesa |nokupgenlakoṣínà↓   La mesa no *cupo* en la cocina.

They couldn't all get in the church.   8 nokupyérontoɗos |enlạiglésyà↓   No *cupieron* todos en la iglesia.

And you had to stick your foot in it!   9 itúbiste |kemeterlapátá↓   ¡Y *tuviste* que meter la pata!

They were nice enough to help me.   10 túbyeron |làbònda(ɗ)ɗẹayuɗármè↓   *Tuvieron* la bondad de ayudarme.

I put the book on the table.   11 pusẹ()librọ |enlamésà↓   *Puse* el libro en la mesa.

_____   12 sèpusonerbyósà↓   Se *puso* nerviosa.

_____   13 iṣistebyén |endehárlò↓   *Hiciste* bien en dejarlo.

_____   14 sènòsịṣotárɗé↓   Se nos *hizo* tarde.

_____   15 bíno |konsufamílyaꜛ   ¿*Vino* con su familia?

VEINTIUNO   21.21

jacobeligoodsons.com For Free Audio

UNIT 21   SPOKEN SPANISH

They came with a headache.   16   bínyéroŋ|kòndólordekabéşà↓   *Vinieron* con dolor de cabeza.

He wouldn't (didn't want to) lend me   17   nokíso|prèstarmenáḋà↓   No *quiso* prestarme nada.
anything.

They tried (wanted) to help me.   18   kisyéronayudármè↓   *Quisieron* ayudarme.

He said something horrible.   19   díhọalgorríblè↓   *Dijo* algo horrible.

━━━━━━━━━━━━━━━━━━━━━━━━━   20   mèḋíhéron|késériandós↓   Me *dijeron* que serían dos.

21.22   VEINTIDOS

SPOKEN SPANISH   UNIT 21

EXTRAPOLATION

Past I	/u/stem			/i/stem	
Modification	Vowel	Consonant	Vowel and Consonant	Vowel	Vowel and Consonant
Sample verbs	pod‑ér	traduṣ‑ír	sab‑ér kab‑ér ten‑ér pon‑ér	aṣ‑ér ben‑ír	ker‑ér deṣ‑ír
Modified stems	pud‑	traduh‑(c)	sup‑ kup‑ tub‑ pus‑	iṣ‑ bin‑	kis‑ dih‑(c)
Alternate endings sg 1 2 fam 2‑3 pl 1 2‑3	‑e ‑íste ‑o ‑ímos ‑yéron (‑éron)(c)				

NOTES

a. The common feature of these verb stem changes is a high vowel (/u/ or /i/) in the past I stem.

b. A vowel or a consonant or both may change in the formation of the past I stem.

c. The 2‑3 pl alternate ending /‑yéron/ appears as /‑éron/ (the /‑y‑/ dropping out) after the sound /‑ir‑/ in irregular past I tense formations in most dialect areas.

VEINTITRES   21.23

UNIT 21　　　　　　　　　　　　　　　　　　　　　　　　　　　　　　　　　　　SPOKEN SPANISH

21.21.31 Substitution drills — Person-number substitution

1　hwán |nọíṣónáďayér↓

　nósotroz_____↓　　　　　　　　　　　　　　　　nọíṣimoznáḍạ |àyér↓

　lwísạikármen_____↓　　　　　　　　　　　　nọíṣyero(n)náḍạ |àyér↓

　yo_____↓　　　　　　　　　　　　　　　　　　nọíṣenáḍạ |àyér↓

　ústeď_____↓　　　　　　　　　　　　　　　　nọíṣonáḍạ |àyér↓

1　Juan no hizo nada ayer.

　Nosotros_____.　　　　　　　　　　　　　No hicimos nada ayer.

　Luisa y Carmen_____.　　　　　　　　No hicieron nada ayer.

　Yo_____.　　　　　　　　　　　　　　　　No hice nada ayer.

　Ud._____.　　　　　　　　　　　　　　　　No hizo nada ayer.

SPOKEN SPANISH   UNIT 21

2 yobinembárkò↓
   ústed_____↓   bingembárkò↓
   lósharriz____↓   binyeronembárkò↓
   làsényora____↓   bingembárkò↓
   é^yoz_____↓   binyeronembárkò↓

3 nòsotroz |nopudimozbenír |ànóchè↓
   é^yoz_____↓   nopudyerombenír |ànóchè↓
   hwan_____↓   nopudobenír |ànóchè↓
   yo_____↓   nopudebenír |ànóchè↓
   karmenilwisa_____↓   nopudyerombenír |ànóchè↓

──

   2 *Yo* vine en barco.
      Ud. _____.   Vino en barco.
      Los Harris _____.   Vinieron en barco.
      La señora _____.   Vino en barco.
      Ellos _____ .   Vinieron en barco.

   3 *Nosotros* no pudimos venir anoche.
      Ellos_____.   No pudieron venir anoche.
      Juan _____.   No pudo venir anoche.
      Yo_____.   No pude venir anoche.
      Carmen y Luisa_____.   No pudieron venir anoche.

VEINTICINCO

UNIT 21   SPOKEN SPANISH

4 ántonyo |tràɖúhòtoɖọ |àyér↓
   ústeɖes_____↓   tràɖúhéróntoɖọ |àyér↓
   él_____↓   tràɖúhòtoɖọ |àyér↓
   hóséɟyó_____↓   tràɖuhímóstoɖọ |àyér↓
   yó_____↓   tràɖúhètoɖọ |àyér↓

5 yótúbẹ |únàfyéstạ |ànóchè↓
   éɟyos _____↓   túbyéron |únàfyéstạ |ànóchè↓
   ántónyó_____↓   túbọ |únàfyéstạ |ànóchè↓
   ántónyọɪyó_____↓   túbɪmos |únàfyéstạ |ànóchè↓
   éɟya _____↓   túbọ |únàfyéstạ |ànóchè↓

_____

4 *Antonio* tradujo todo ayer.
   Uds._____.   Tradujeron todo ayer.
   El_____.   Tradujo todo ayer.
   José y yo_____.   Tradujimos todo ayer.
   Yo_____.   Traduje todo ayer.

5 Yo tuve una fiesta anoche.
   Ellos_____.   Tuvieron una fiesta anoche.
   Antonio_____.   Tuvo una fiesta anoche.
   Antonio y yo_____.   Tuvimos una fiesta anoche.
   Ella_____.   Tuvo una fiesta anoche.

SPOKEN SPANISH   UNIT 21

6 élnókiso |kòmprárnáḋà↓
   ùsteḋez _____↓   nokisyeroṇ |kòmprárnáḋà↓
   kármen _____↓   nókiso |kòmprárnáḋà↓
   lwisa̠iyo _____↓   nokisimos |kòmprárnáḋà↓
   yo _____↓   nokise |kòmprárnáḋà↓

7 e̠lyapúso |lòzlíbrosa̠í↓
   àntonyo̠iyo _____↓   púsimoz |lòzlíbrosa̠í↓
   e̠lyos _____↓   pùsyéron |lòzlíbrosa̠í↓
   yo _____↓   puse |lòzlíbrosa̠í↓
   ùsteḋ _____↓   puso |lòzlíbrosa̠í↓

_____

6 *El* no quiso comprar nada.
   Uds. _____.   No quisieron comprar nada.
   Carmen _____.   No quiso comprar nada.
   Luisa y yo _____.   No quisimos comprar nada.
   Yo _____.   No quise comprar nada.

7 *Ella* puso los libros ahí.
   Antonio y yo _____.   Pusimos los libros ahí.
   Ellos _____.   Pusieron los libros ahí.
   Yo _____.   Puse los libros ahí.
   Ud. _____.   Puso los libros ahí.

VEINTISIETE   21.27

UNIT 21   SPOKEN SPANISH

8 àntonyo |noɗıhǫésò↓
   yo_____↓   noɗıhésò↓
   éʊ̀yaz_____↓   noɗıheroṇésò↓
   làmúchachà_____↓   noɗıhǫésò↓
   nòsotroz_____↓   noɗıhımoṣésò↓

9 nòsotros |sùpımozlalekʂyón↓
   hwànıhose_____↓   sùpyeronlalekʂyón↓
   yo_____↓   supelalekʂyón↓
   hòseɪyo_____↓   sùpımozlalekʂyón↓
   èl_____↓   supolalekʂyón↓

_____

8 *Antonio* no dijo eso.
   Yo_____.   No dije eso.
   Ellas_____.   No dijeron eso.
   La muchacha_____.   No dijo eso.
   Nosotros_____.   No dijimos eso.

9 *Nosotros* supimos la lección.
   Juan y José_____.   Supieron la lección.
   Yo_____.   Supe la lección.
   José y yo_____.   Supimos la lección.
   El_____.   Supo la lección.

21.28   VEINTIOCHO

SPOKEN SPANISH   UNIT 21

10 yónokupe̞ |ene̞lkóchȩ↓
    lósharríz_____↓   nokupyéron |ene̞lkóchȩ↓
    lwísa _____↓   nokúpo̞ |ene̞lkóchȩ↓
    lwísa̞ı̯yó _____↓   nokúpimos |ene̞lkóchȩ↓
    ántonyo _____↓   nokúpo̞ |ene̞lkóchȩ↓

11 hóse |túbokesalír |ánóchȩ↓
    éⁿyos_____↓   túbyero̞nkesalír |ánóchȩ↓
    hóse̞ı̯yó _____↓   túbimoskesalír |ánóchȩ↓
    yo _____↓   tubekesalír |ánóchȩ↓
    éⁿya_____↓   túbokesalír |ánóchȩ↓

───

10 *Yo* no cupe en el coche.
    Los Harris _____.   No cupieron en el coche.
    Luisa _____.   No cupo en el coche.
    Luisa y yo_____.   No cupimos en el coche.
    Antonio_____.   No cupo en el coche.

11 *José* tuvo que salir anoche.
    Ellos_____.   Tuvieron que salir anoche.
    José y yo_____.   Tuvimos que salir anoche.
    Yo_____.   Tuve que salir anoche.
    Ella_____.   Tuvo que salir anoche.

VEINTINUEVE

jacobeligoodsons.com For Free Audio

UNIT 21   SPOKEN SPANISH

Tense substitution

1   elnoaşenáɗạ |ėnlȧmisyón↓   elnoişonáɗạ |ėnlȧmisyón↓

2   e͂ɣoz |byenemporabyón↓   e͂ɣoz |bɪnyeromporabyón↓

3   àntonyo |byenembárkó↓   àntonyo |bɪnoembárkó↓

4   nòsotroz |nòpóɗemos,ayuɗár↓   nòsotroz |nòpúɗɪmos,ayuɗár↓

5   yoteŋgọ |úŋkóchėmuybarátò↓   yotubẹ |úŋkóchėmuybarátò↓

6   yo |nòkyero͠ɑȷȧmár↓   yo |nòkise͠ɑȷȧmár↓

7   yopóŋgo |lózlɪbros,enlamésȧ↓   yopuse |lózlɪbros,enlamésȧ↓

8   yoselaleką̇yón↓   yosupelaleką̇yón↓

9   toɗoskaḃémós |ènlȧsálȧ↓   toɗoskupímós |ènlȧsálȧ↓

1 El no *hace* nada en la Misión.   El no hizo nada en la Misión.
2 Ellos *vienen* por avión.   Ellos vinieron por avión.
3 Antonio *viene* en barco.   Antonio vino en barco.
4 Nosotros no *podemos* ayudar.   Nosotros no pudimos ayudar.
5 Yo *tengo* un coche muy barato.   Yo tuve un coche muy barato.
6 Yo no *quiero* llamar.   Yo no quise llamar.
7 Yo *pongo* los libros en la mesa.   Yo puse los libros en la mesa.
8 Yo *sé* la lección.   Yo supe la lección.
9 Todos *cabemos* en la sala.   Todos cupimos en la sala.

21.30   TREINTA

SPOKEN SPANISH   UNIT 21

10 eḻyoz |noạṣia(n̩)náḏà↓   eḻyoz |noạiṣyero(n̩)náḏà↓

11 nósotroz |beniamoshúntòs↓   nósotroz |binimoshúntòs↓

12 yó |nopoḏiaír↓   yó |nopuḏẹír↓

13 eltraḏuṣia |muybyén↓   eltraḏuho |muybyén↓

14 eḻyostenian |únàfyestà↓   eḻyostubyeron |únàfyestà↓

15 nósotroz |nokeriamo(s)salír↓   nósotroz |nokisimo(s)salír↓

16 elponia |toḏẹenlamésà↓   elpuso |toḏẹenlamésà↓

17 nósotrozḏeṣiamos |esotambyén↓   nósotrozdihimos |esotambyén↓

18 eḻyoz |nuŋkasabian |lalekṣyón↓   eḻyoz |nuŋkasupyeron |lalekṣyón↓

19 toḏoskabian |eneldormitóryò↓   toḏoskupyeron |eneldormitóryò↓

---

10 Ellos no *hacían* nada.   Ellos no hicieron nada.

11 Nosotros *veníamos* juntos.   Nosotros vinimos juntos.

12 Yo no *podía* ir.   Yo no pude ir.

13 El *traducía* muy bien.   El tradujo muy bien.

14 Ellos *tenían* una fiesta.   Ellos tuvieron una fiesta.

15 Nosotros no *queríamos* salir.   Nosotros no quisimos salir.

16 El *ponía* todo en la mesa.   El puso todo en la mesa.

17 Nosotros *decíamos* eso también.   Nosotros dijimos eso también.

18 Ellos nunca *sabían* la lección.   Ellos nunca supieron la lección.

19 Todos *cabían* en el dormitorio.   Todos cupieron en el dormitorio.

UNIT 21 SPOKEN SPANISH

21.21.32 Response drill

	1	bínọusté₫ |awáshiṇtom |pórabyón↑ọeṇkárrò↓	bínèṇkárrò↓
	2	binyéronụustéₑₑes |pórabyón↑ọeṇkárrò↓	binimos |pôrábyóh↓
	3	bínọel |pórabyón↑ọeṇkárrò↓	bíngèṇkárrò↓
[múchaskósàs↓]	4	keₐₛọusté₫ |ảyér↓	íṣèmuchaskósàs↓
[múchaskósàs↓]	5	keₐₛyéronụustéₑₑés |ảyér↓	íṣımoz |muchaskósàs↓
[múchaskósàs↓]	6	keₐₛyéronₑyòs |ảyér↓	íṣyéron |múchaskósàs↓
[to₫oz(nosótròs)↓]	7	kyénes |supyéronlalèkṣyón↓	to₫òs |sûpímòzlâlèkṣyón↓
[ênlâmésà↓]	8	dondèpusọusté₫ |lozlíbròs↓	lòspusọ |ênlâmésà↓

---

	1 ¿Vino Ud. a Washington por avión o en carro?	Vine en carro.
	2 ¿Vinieron Uds. por avión o en carro?	Vinimos por avión.
	3 ¿Vino él por avión o en carro?	Vino en carro.
(muchas cosas)	4 ¿Qué hizo Ud. ayer?	Hice muchas cosas.
(muchas cosas)	5 ¿Qué hicieron Uds. ayer?	Hicimos muchas cosas.
(muchas cosas)	6 ¿Qué hicieron ellos ayer?	Hicieron muchas cosas.
(todos [nosotros])	7 ¿Quiénes supieron la lección?	Todos supimos la lección.
(en la mesa)	8 ¿Dónde puso Ud. los libros?	Los puse en la mesa.

SPOKEN SPANISH   UNIT 21

[ènlàmésà↓] 9 dóndepusyéron |ustédez |lózlíbròs↓   lóspùsimos |ènlàmésà↓
[ènlàmésà↓] 10 dóndepuseyo |gⓤlíbrò↓   lópusọ |ènlàmésà↓

[ûnàpàrtè↓] 11 tràdúhọusted |todalaleksyón |ayér↑   nó↓ nolatràduhetódà↓ tràduhẹunapártè↓
[ûnàpàrtè↓] 12 tràdúhéronụstédes |todalaleksyón |ayér↑   nó↓ nolatràduhimostódà↓ tràdúhimosụna
                                                              pártè↓

             13 túbọusted |kestudyar |anóche↑   si↓ ànóche |tubekestudyár↓
             14 túbyeronụstédes |kestudyar |anóche↑   si↓ ànóche |tubimoskestudyár↓
             15 kùpyeronụstédes |enẹstekwàrtọ |ayér↑   si |sikupímòs↓

(en la mesa)   9 ¿Dónde pusieron Uds. los libros?   Los pusimos en la mesa.
(en la mesa) 10 ¿Dónde puse yo el libro?   Lo puso en la mesa.

(una parte)   11 ¿Tradujo Ud. toda la lección ayer?   No, no la traduje toda; traduje una parte.
(una parte)   12 ¿Tradujeron Uds. toda la lección ayer?   No, no la tradujimos toda; tradujimos una parte.

              13 ¿Tuvo Ud. que estudiar anoche?   Sí, anoche tuve que estudiar.
              14 ¿Tuvieron Uds. que estudiar anoche?   Sí, anoche tuvimos que estudiar.
              15 ¿Cupieron Uds. en este cuarto ayer?   Sí, sí cupimos.

TREINTA Y TRES

UNIT 21   SPOKEN SPANISH

21.21.33 Translation drill

1 I didn't say that.   yónódíhg |ésô↓   Yo no dije eso.

2 We didn't say anything.   nòsótroz |nodíhímoznádâ↓   Nosotros no dijimos nada.

3 What did she say?   kédíhoé()yà↓   ¿Qué dijo ella?

4 Last night I didn't want to go out.   ànóche |nókisesalír↓   Anoche no quise salir.

5 What did you do last night?   kéisoustéd |ànóchè↓   ¿Qué hizo Ud. anoche?

6 How many people were able to get   kwántaspérsónas |kupyéronenelâwtô↓   ¿Cuántas personas cúpieron en el auto?
   into (fit in) the car?

7 Why couldn't you go?   pòrké |nopúdoír↓   ¿Por qué no pudo ir?

8 What did you have to do last night?   kétubo |kgagerustéd |ànóchè↓   ¿Qué tuvo que hacer Ud. anoche?

9 We had to work.   túbimosketrabahár↓   Tuvimos que trabajar.

10 Where did you all put the books?   dónde |pusyéronustédez |lozlíbròs↓ ¿Dónde pusieron Uds. los libros?

11 We put them on the table.   lòspúsimos |énlàmesâ↓   Los pusimos en la mesa.

12 Did you translate well?   tráduhoustédbyén↑   ¿Tradujo Ud. bien?

13 Why couldn't you?   pòrkénopúdó↓   ¿Por qué no pudo?

21.34   TREINTA Y CUATRO

SPOKEN SPANISH UNIT 21

B. Discussion of pattern

The above miscellaneous groups of verbs with irregular past I tense forms all appear with the alternate endings listed and discussed in the previous grammar point. None of the formations have strong stress on their final syllable; rather all have strong stress on their next-to-last syllable. So formations which have endings of one syllable (1 and 2-3 sg) have stems under strong stress.

All the resultant modified stems have one of the high vowels /u/ or /ɪ/ in them. Those stems which do not already have /u/ or /ɪ/ change to /u/ or /ɪ/ , though there is no way to predict by general rule which of these vowels will appear in the modified stem. Thus /a/ becomes /u/ in /sab—~sup—,~kab— kup—/ but becomes /ɪ/ in /aş—~ɪş—/; /e/ becomes /u/ in /ten—~tub—/ but /ɪ/ in /ben—~bɪn—, ker—~kɪs—, deş—~dɪh—/. However, /o/ consistently becomes /u/ in /pod—~pud—, pon—~pus—/.

An inspection of these verbs shows great complexity in the consonant changes, which appear to be almost arbitrary and must be learned separately for each individual verb.

Note that no /—ár/ theme class verbs appear in this group of irregular verbs.

21.21.4 Irregular past I verb forms - verbs with suppleted stems

A. Presentation of pattern

ILLUSTRATIONS

I was the last one to leave.	1	fwí ǀelúltimo̦ensalír↓	*Fui* el último en salir.
You were a good neighbor.	2	fwíste̦ ǀúmbwembe̦şínó↓	*Fuiste* un buen vecino.
————————	3	éso ǀnofwenáđà↓	Eso no *fue* nada.
————————	4	ifwímoz ǀlóșultimos ǀenírnòs↓	Y *fuimos* los últimos en irnos.
They were very kind.	5	fwéron ǀmuyamáblès↓	*Fueron* muy amables.
I went to the cashier's desk.	6	fwía̦lakáhà↓	*Fui* a la caja.

TREINTA Y CINCO 21.35

jacobeligoodsons.com For Free Audio

UNIT 21   SPOKEN SPANISH

Did you go to church?   7   fwístęamísa↑   ¿Fuiste a misa?

_____   8   ĭạlósharris↓komolesfwé↓   Y a los Harris ¿cómo les fue?

_____   9   fwímos̬alkámpô↓   Fuimos al campo.

They went all the way downtown.   10 fwéron¦astęelş̧éntro↓   Fueron hasta el centro.

EXTRAPOLATION

Affected verbs	s—ér Ø—ír
Suppleted stem	fw—
Alternate endings sg 1	—í
2 fam	—íste
2-3	—ę́
pl 1	—ímos
2-3	—éron

NOTES

a. Two verbs, /sér/ and /—ír/ have a suppleted (or replaced) stem in past I tense formations.

b. A second set of alternate endings appears with these suppleted stems.

21.36

SPOKEN SPANISH

UNIT 21

21.21.41 Substitution drills — Person-number substitution

1 àntónyo |fwébwéno |konéꝆyàↆ

   yo_____ↆ   fwíbwéno |konéꝆyàↆ

   kármenₗhóse_____ↆ   fwéròmbwénos |konéꝆyàↆ

   ústéd_____ↆ   fwébwéno |konéꝆyàↆ

   hwanₗyo_____ↆ   fwímòzbwénos |konéꝆyàↆ

2 yofwì |ₐlàtyéndàↆ

   ústédes_____ↆ   fwéronₐlàtyéndàↆ

   hóseₗyo_____ↆ   fwímosₐlàtyéndàↆ

_____

1 *Antonio* fue bueno con ella.

   Yo _____.   Fui bueno con ella.

   Carmen y José_____.   Fueron buenos con ella.

   Ud._____.   Fue bueno con ella.

   Juan y yo_____.   Fuimos buenos con ella.

2 *Yo* fui a la tienda.

   Uds._____.   Fueron a la tienda.

   José y yo_____.   Fuimos a la tienda.

TREINTA Y SIETE

UNIT 21   SPOKEN SPANISH

éⁿyos _____↓   fwéronạlatyéndá↓
kármem _____↓   fweạlatyéndá↓

3 éⁿyanófwé|ạlaşyuḍáḍ↓   nófwi|ạlaşyuḍáḍ↓
   yó_____↓   nófwé|ạlaşyuḍáḍ↓
   lwísa_____↓   nófwimos|ạlaşyuḍáḍ↓
   ántonyọiyó_____↓   nófweron|ạlaşyuḍáḍ↓
   ústeḍez_____↓

_____

   Ellos _____.   Fueron a la tienda.
   Carmen _____.   Fue a la tienda.

3 *Ella* no fue a la ciudad.
   Yo _____.   No fui a la ciudad.
   Luisa_____.   No fue a la ciudad.
   Antonio y yo_____.   No fuimos a la ciudad.
   Uds._____.   No fueron a la ciudad.

21.38   TREINTA Y OCHO

SPOKEN SPANISH   UNIT 21

Tense substitution

1   él |èzmuyrrìgurósò↓   él |fwémuyrrìgurósò↓

2   yósoysubeşínò↓   yofwìsubeşínò↓

3   yóboyalşéntrò↓   yofwìạlşéntrò↓

4   nòsotros |tàmbyembámòs↓   nòsotros |tàmbyemfwímòs↓

5   él |éràmuyamìgomíò↓   él |fwémuyamìgomíò↓

6   nòsotros |éramòs |suzbeşínòs↓   nòsotros |fwímo(s)suzbeşínòs↓

7   yó |tàmbyenibà↓   yó |tàmbyemfwí↓

_____

1 El *es* muy riguroso.   El *fue* muy riguroso.

2 Yo *soy* su vecino.   Yo *fui* su vecino.

3 Yo *voy* al centro.   Yo *fui* al centro.

4 Nosotros también *vamos*.   Nosotros también fuimos.

5 El *era* muy amigo mío.   El *fue* muy amigo mío.

6 Nosotros *éramos* sus vecinos.   Nosotros fuimos sus vecinos.

7 Yo también *iba*.   Yo también fui.

TREINTA Y NUEVE

UNIT 21   SPOKEN SPANISH

21.21.42 Response drill

	1	fweẉustéḍ	alṣéntrọ	elsábaḍọt ọeldomíŋgȯ↓	fwí	ẹlsábàḍȯ↓
	2	fweróṇustéḍes	alṣéntrọ	elsábaḍọt ọeldomíŋgȯ↓	fwímos	èldòmíŋgȯ↓
[àlṣéntrȯ↓]	3	àḍónde	fweronéⓎyòs	àẉérↄ↓	fweronạalṣéntrȯ↓
[àlṣéntrȯ↓]	4	àḍondefwél	àẉérↄ↓	fweạlṣéntrȯ↓
[èldómìŋgȯ↓]	5	fweróṇustéḍes	elsábaḍọ	alaṣyuḍáḍ↑	nȯ↓ fwímòsèldòmìŋgȯ↓
[èlsábàḍȯ↓]	6	fweẉustéḍ	eldómìŋgọ	alaṣyuḍáḍ↑	nȯ↓ .fwíẹlsábàḍȯ↓
	7	fwél	alṣéntrȯ↑	sí	sifwéↄ↓
	8	fweronéⓎyos	alaṣyuḍáḍ↑	sí	sifwérȯn↓
	9	fweẉustéḍ	alaṣyuḍáḍ↑	sí	sifwíↄ↓

	1	¿Fue Ud. al centro el sábado o el domingo?	Fui el sábado.
	2	¿Fueron Uds. al centro el sábado o el domingo?	Fuimos el domingo.
(al centro)	3	¿A dónde fueron ellos ayer?	Fueron al centro.
(al centro)	4	¿A dónde fue él ayer?	Fue al centro.
(el domingo)	5	¿Fueron Uds. el sábado a la ciudad?	No, fuimos el domingo.
(el sábado)	6	¿Fue Ud. el domingo a la ciudad?	No, fui el sábado.
	7	¿Fue él al centro?	Sí, así fue.
	8	¿Fueron ellos a la ciudad?	Sí, así fueron.
	9	¿Fue Ud. a la ciudad?	Sí, así fui.

21.40   CUARENTA

SPOKEN SPANISH   UNIT 21

21.21.43 Translation drill

1 We were your neighbors.   nósotrosfwímos |suzbeşínòs↓   Nosotros fuimos sus vecinos.

2 Who was your neighbor?   kyémfwé |subeşínò↓   ¿Quién fue su vecino?

3 She was very good to (with) us.   eĺya |fwémuybwéná |kò(r)nòsótròs↓   Ella fue muy buena con nosotros.

4 They were very good neighbors.   eĺyosfweron |muybwenozbeşínòs↓   Ellos fueron muy buenos vecinos.

5 Who went with you?   kyémfwé |konusté͜d↓   ¿Quién fué con Ud.?

6 I didn't go with them.   yo |nofwikonečyòs↓   Yo no fuí con ellos.

7 Where did you all go?   àdondefweronustédès↓   ¿A dónde fueron Uds.?

B. Discussion of pattern

    The verbs /sér/ and /ír/ have the same stem (/fw—/   ) for past I as well as the same unique endings. The resulting past I forms of these verbs are,
therefore, identical. They are differentiated only by context.

    With this second set of alternate endings, strong stress falls on the first (and in 1 and 2-3 sg the *only*) syllable of the verb form.

CUARENTA Y UNO   21.41
                          jacobeligoodsons.com For Free Audio

UNIT 21   SPOKEN SPANISH

21.21.5   Statement intonation patterns — Deliberate statements

    A. Presentation of pattern

                                              ILLUSTRATIONS

                                                                                    2   1 1↓
    ────────────────   1   fwímosͺalͺ   ː↓   Fuimos al campo.

                                    fwímos |alkámpò↓   22 | 2 1 1↓
                                                                                   Fuimos   al campo.
                                    fwímos |àlkámpó↓   22 | 1 2 1↓
                                                                                   Fuimos   al campo.

                                                                                    1 2   1↓
    We have to leave.   2   ténemoskesalír↓   Tenemos que salir.

                                    ténemos |kesalír↓   1 2 2 | 2   1↓
                                                                                   Tenemos   que salir.
                                    ténemos |kèsàlír↓   1 2 2 | 1 21↓
                                                                                   Tenemos   que salir.

                                                                                    2   1 1↓
    I brought my car.   3   tráhemikóchè↓   Traje mi coche.

                                    tráhe |mikóchè↓   22 | 2 1 1↓
                                                                                   Traje mi coche.
                                    tráhe |mikóchè↓   22 | 1 2 1↓
                                                                                   Traje   mi coche.

21.42   CUARENTA Y DOS

SPOKEN SPANISH

UNIT 21

EXTRAPOLATION

Normal statement	Deliberate statement
/1211↓/	/122|211↓/ /122|121↓/

NOTES

a. A common feature of slow speech, indeed the *distinguishing* feature, is the appearance of more single bar junctures, thus creating several phrases, each short, and introducing modifications into the pitch pattern.

UNIT 21   SPOKEN SPANISH

21.21.51 Substitution drill — pattern substitution

1 bamosalaembaháđà↓   bamos |alaembaháđà↓

2 yasonlas,óchò↓   ya |sonlas,óchò↓

3 èlmioesésè↓   èlmio |es,ésè↓

4 karmena(s)soltérà↓   karmen |e(s)soltérà↓

5 èlótroestakí↓   èlótro |estakí↓

6 àblékonlaseɲyorítà↓   àblé |konlaseɲyorítà↓

```
      2          1 1↓                      2  2 | 2      1 1↓
1 Vamos a la Embajada.                   Vamos    a la Embajada.

      2      1 1↓                          2 | 2    1 1↓
2 Ya son las ocho.                       Ya   son las ocho.

  1  2     1 1↓                            1  2 | 2 1 1↓
3 El mío es ése.                         El mío   es ése.

      2          1 1↓                      2  2 | 2     1 1↓
4 Carmen es soltera.                     Carmen   es soltera.

  1 2      11 ↓                            1 2 2 |  2   11↓
5 El otro está aquí.                     El otro    está aquí.

  1 2        1 1↓                          1  2 | 2      11↓
6 Hablé con la señorita.                 Hablé    con la señorita.
```

SPOKEN SPANISH   UNIT 21

7   pásemę῭líbró↓   pásemę |ę῭líbró↓

8   préstemelaplúmà↓   présteme |laplúmà↓

9   kèremozḍeşírsèló↓   kèremoz |ḍeşírsèló↓

1o màŋyanabenímòs↓   màŋyana |benímòs↓

11 tràbahaŋko(n)nosótròs↓   tràbahaŋ |ko(n)nosótròs↓

12 yabyenemolínà↓   ya |byenemolínà↓

13 sàlyeronaşedíàs↓   sàlyeron |aşedíàs↓

_____

     2   1 1↓   2   2 | 2 1 1↓
7 Páseme el libro.   Páseme   el libro.

     2   1 1↓   2   2 | 2 1 1↓
8 Présteme la pluma.   Présteme   la pluma.

     1 2   1 1↓   1 2 2 | 2 1 1↓
9 Queremos decírselo.   Queremos   decírselo.

     1 2   1 1 ↓   1 2 2 | 2 1 1↓
10 Mañana venimos.   Mañana   venimos.

     1 2   1 1↓   1 2 2 | 2   1 1↓
11 Trabajan con nosotros.   Trabajan   con nosotros.

     2   1 1↓   2 | 2   1 1↓
12 Ya viene Molina.   Ya   viene Molina.

     1 2   11 ↓   1 2 2 | 2   11 ↓
13 Salieron hace días.   Salieron   hace días.

CUARENTA Y CINCO   21.45

UNIT 21

1 bámos,alaembaháða↓

2 yasonlasóchò↓

3 èlmioesésè↓

4 karmene(s)soltérà↓

5 èlótroestakí↓

6 àblekonlaseɲyorítà↓

bámos |álaèmbáhaðá↓

ya |sónlàsòchò↓

èlmio |ès,esè↓

karmen |é(s)sòltérà↓

èlótro |estakì↓

àble |kònlàsèɲyòrità↓

```
      2           1 1↓
1 Vamos a la Embajada.
      2       1 1↓
2 Ya son las ocho.
   1  2    11↓
3 El mío es ése.
      2        11↓
4 Carmen es soltera.
   1 2        11↓
5 El otro está aquí.
   1 2           11↓
6 Hablé con la señorita.
```

```
   2 2 |1      2 1↓
Vamos   a la Embajada.
   2 |1    2 1↓
Ya   son las ocho.
   1  2 |1 1 21↓
El mío  es ése.
   2 2  |1    21↓
Carmen   es soltera.
  1 2 2 | 1   21↓
El otro   está aquí.
  1 2 |1      21↓
Hablé  con la señorita.
```

SPOKEN SPANISH   UNIT 21

7 páseme(l)líbrò↓   páseme |(l)líbrò↓

8 présteme la plúmà↓   présteme |la plúmà↓

9 kèremozdeşírsèlò↓   kèremoz |dèşirsèlò↓

10 mànyanabenímòs↓   mànyana |bènimòs↓

11 tràbahanko(n)nosótròs↓   tràbahan |ko(n)nósótròs↓

12 yabyenemolínà↓   ya |byénèmòlinà↓

13 sàlyeronaşedíàs↓   sàlyeron |áşèdìàs↓

───

```
   2      1 1↓                        2   2 | 1 2 1↓
7 Páseme el libro.                  Páseme   el libro.
   2      1 1↓                        2   2 | 1  2 1↓
8 Présteme la pluma.                Présteme  la pluma.
   1 2    1  1↓                       1 2 2 | 1 2  1↓
9 Queremos decírselo.               Queremos   decírselo.
   1 2     1 1↓                       1 2 2 | 1 2 1↓
10 Mañana venimos.                  Mañana   venimos.
   1 2      1 1↓                      1 2 2 | 1   2 1↓
11 Trabajan con nosotros.           Trabajan   con nosotros.
   2       1 1↓                       2 | 1    2 1↓
12 Ya viene Molina.                 Ya   viene Molina.
   1 2      11                        1 2 2 | 1  21 ↓
13 Salieron hace días.              Salieron   hace días.
```

CUARENTA Y SIETE   21.47

UNIT 21   SPOKEN SPANISH

B. Discussion of pattern

When the normal tempo of conversational Spanish is slowed down, as, for instance, when one is talking to a large group of people, a number of changes occur, both in the *form* of the sounds in sequence and in the *manner* in which they are arranged. For example, a progressive increase in tempo by some speakers might affect adjacent vowels as follows:

/byéne|aórà↓/

/byéngaórà↓/

/byényaórà↓/

/byényórà↓/

The intonation of slower speech is characterized by separation of important syntactical units in the utterance. This separation is signalled by the appearance of single bar junctures, often described by speakers of the language as a 'sort of pause'.

The sentences in the previous drills are examples of points at which a   /|/   enters an utterance when it is slowed down to reach a large audience or simply for emphasis or effect in a conversational situation.

21.48   jacobeligoodsons.com For Free Audio   CUARENTA Y OCHO

SPOKEN SPANISH   UNIT 21

21.22   Replacement drills

A   ké |les‚aparéṣído |labáse↓

1 _____ párké↓   ké |les‚aparéṣído |elpárké↓

2 kétál_____ ↓   kétál |les‚aparéṣído |elpárké↓

3 _____ pareṣyó_____ ↓   kétál |lespareṣyó |elpárké↓

4 _____ ése_____ ↓   kétál |lespareṣyó |esepárké↓

5 _____ ṣyuḓáḓ↓   kétál |lespareṣyó |esaṣyuḓáḓ↓

6 _le_____ ↓   kétál |lepareṣyó |esaṣyuḓáḓ↓

7 _____ paísès↓   kétál |lepareṣyéron |esospaísès↓

_____

A   ¿Qué les ha parecido la base?

1 ¿ _____ parque?   ¿Qué les ha parecido el parque?

2 ¿Qué tal _____ ?   ¿Qué tal les ha parecido el parque?

3 ¿ _____ pareció_____ ?   ¿Qué tal les pareció el parque?

4 ¿ _____ ese _____ ?   ¿Qué tal les pareció ese parque?

5 ¿ _____ ciudad?   ¿Qué tal les pareció esa ciudad?

6 ¿ _le _____ ?   ¿Qué tal le pareció esa ciudad?

7 ¿ _____ paises?   ¿Qué tal le parecieron esos países?

CUARENTA Y NUEVE   21.49

UNIT 21   SPOKEN SPANISH

B   nósotroz |dimosunabwéltá↓

1 _____ chékè↓   nósotroz |dimosunchékè↓

2 _____ kámbyamos _____↓   nósotros |kámbyamosunchékè↓

3 eᶥyos _____↓   eᶥyos |kámbyaronunchékè↓

4 _____ rrèṣibyéron _____↓   eᶥyoz |rrèṣibyéronunchékè↓

5 _____ este _____↓   eᶥyoz |rrèṣibyéron |estechékè↓

6 _____ iṣyeron _____↓   eᶥyos |iṣyeron |estechékè↓

7 yó _____↓   yóiṣę |estechékè↓

_____

B   Nosotros dimos una vuelta.

1 _____ cheque.   Nosotros dimos un cheque.

2 _____ cambiamos _____.   Nosotros cambiamos un cheque.

3 Ellos _____.   Ellos cambiaron un cheque.

4 _____ recibieron _____.   Ellos recibieron un cheque.

5 _____ este _____.   Ellos recibieron este cheque.

6 _____ hicieron _____.   Ellos hicieron este cheque.

7 Yo _____.   Yo hice este cheque.

21.50   CINCUENTA

SPOKEN SPANISH   UNIT 21

C   yó |sólọandúbe |porelpárkẹ↓

1 _____ ṣyuḍáḍ↓   yó |sólọandúbe |porlaṣyuḍáḍ↓

2 _____ én _____ ↓   yó |sólọandúbe |enlaṣyuḍáḍ↓

3 _____ estúbẹ _____ ↓   yó |sólọestúbẹ |enlaṣyuḍáḍ↓

4 nósótros _____ ↓   nósótros |sólọestubímos |enlaṣyuḍáḍ↓

5 _____ ésas ____ ↓   nósótros |sólọestubímos |enẹsa(s) ṣyuḍáḍès↓

6 _____ ápénas _____ ↓   nósótros |ápénasẹestubímós |ènẹsà(s) ṣyúḍáḍès↓

7 tu _____ ↓   tu |ápénasẹestubístẹ |ènẹsà(s) ṣyúḍáḍès↓

_____

C   Yo sólo anduve por el parque.

1 _____ ciudad.   Yo sólo anduve por la ciudad.

2 _____ en _____ .   Yo sólo anduve en la ciudad.

3 _____ estuve _____ .   Yo sólo estuve en la ciudad.

4 Nosotros _____ .   Nosotros sólo estuvimos en la ciudad.

5 _____ esas ____ .   Nosotros sólo estuvimos en esas ciudades.

6 _____ apenas _____ .   Nosotros apenas estuvimos en esas ciudades

7 Tú _____ .   Tú apenas estuviste en esas ciudades.

CINCUENTA Y UNO   21.51

UNIT 21   SPOKEN SPANISH

D   èstánubládò↓ pàréșe |kebá⌢yobér↓

1   _____ pàréșia _____ ↓   èstábanubládò↓ pàréșia |kẹibá⌢yobér↓

2   ___ féò _____ ↓   èstábaféò↓ pàréșia |kẹibá⌢yobér↓

3   _____ àșerfríò↓   èstábaféò↓ pàréșia |kẹibáșerfríò↓

4   éstá _____ ↓   èstáféò↓ pàréșe |kèbáșerfríò↓

5   ___ bwénò _____ ↓   éstábwenò↓ pàréșe |kèbáșerfríò↓

6   _____ àșersól↓   éstábwénò↓ pàréșe |kèbáșersól↓

7   ___ agradáblè _____ ↓   èstagradáblè↓ pàréșe |kèbáșersól↓

───

D   Está nublado. Parece que va a llover.

1   _____. Parecía _____.   Estaba nublado. Parecía que iba a llover.

2   ___ feo. _____.   Estaba feo. Parecía que iba a llover.

3   _____. _____ hacer frío.   Estaba feo. Parecía que iba a hacer frío.

4   Está _____. _____.   Está feo. Parece que va a hacer frío.

5   ___ bueno. _____.   Está bueno. Parece que va a hacer frío.

6   _____. _____ hacer sol.   Está bueno. Parece que va a hacer sol.

7   ___ agradable. _____.   Está agradable. Parece que va a hacer sol.

21.52   jacobeligoodsons.com For Free Audio   CINCUENTA Y DOS

SPOKEN SPANISH   UNIT 21

E   yoboy |paralaşyuđáđ↓

1   _____otél↓   yoboy |paraelotél↓

2   nòsótroz_____↓   nòsótrozbámos |paraelotél↓

3   ____ibamos_____↓   nòsótroşibamos |paraelotél↓

4   _____eşę___↓   nòsótroşibamos |paraeşęotél↓

5   ełyos_____↓   ełyosıbam |paraeşęotél↓

6   _____ofişíná↓   ełyosıbam |paraeşęofişíná↓

7   ____bámos_____↓   nòsótrozbámos |paraeşęofişíná↓

_____

E   Yo voy para la ciudad.

1   _____ hotel.   Yo voy para el hotel.

3   Nosotros_____ .   Nosotros vamos para el hotel.

3   ____ íbamos_____ .   Nosotros íbamos para el hotel.

4   _____ ese____ .   Nosotros íbamos para ese hotel.

5   Ellos_____ .   Ellos iban para ese hotel.

6   _____ oficina.   Ellos iban para esa oficina.

7   ____vamos_____ .   Nosotros vamos para esa oficina.

CINCUENTA Y TRES   21.53

UNIT 21   SPOKEN SPANISH

F   yótrahe |mఝáwtôↆ

1 _____gáfàsↆ   yótrahe |mɪzgáfàsↆ

2 _____ótraz_____ↆ   yòtrahę |otrazgáfàsↆ

3 hwàn _____ↆ   hwàn |tràhotrazgáfàsↆ

4 _____kósàsↆ   hwàn |tràhotraskósàsↆ

5 _dyó_____ↆ   hwàn |dyótraskósàsↆ

6 _____nómbrèↆ   hwàn |dyótronómbrèↆ

7 _pusǫ_____ↆ   hwàm |pusotronómbrèↆ

F   Yo traje mi auto.

1 _____gafas.   Yo traje mis gafas.

2 _____otras_____.   Yo traje otras gafas.

3 Juan_____.   Juan trajo otras gafas.

4 _____cosas.   Juan trajo otras cosas.

5 _dio_____.   Juan dio otras cosas.

6 _____nombre.   Juan dio otro nombre.

7 _puso_____.   Juan puso otro nombre.

21.54   CINCUENTA Y CUATRO

SPOKEN SPANISH   UNIT 21

21.23   Variation drills

A   kéfríọ |áṣè↓   ¡Qué frío hace!

1 It sure is hot!   kékalór |áṣè↓   ¡Qué calor hace!

2 It sure is windy!   kébyéntọ |áṣè↓   ¡Qué viento hace!

3 There's sure a wind!   kébyéntọ |áy↓   ¡Qué viento hay!

4 I sure am hungry!   kẹambrè |téŋgò↓   ¡Qué hambre tengo!

5 I sure am cold!   kéfríó |téŋgò↓   ¡Qué frío tengo!

6 It sure looks good!   kébwénò |ẹstá↓   ¡Qué bueno está!

7 It sure looks pretty!   kébonítò |ẹstá↓   ¡Qué bonito está!

B   kómokámbyạ |eltyémpọ |ảkí↓   ¡Cómo cambia el tiempo aquí!

1 The wind is mighty changeable here.   kómokámbyạ |elbyéntọ |ảkí↓   ¡Cómo cambia el viento aquí!

2 Things are mighty changeable here.   kómokámbyan |laskósàs |ảkí↓   ¡Cómo cambian las cosas aquí!

3 Prices sure do rise here.   kómosúben |lospréṣyòs |ảkí↓   ¡Cómo suben los precios aquí!

CINCUENTA Y CINCO   21.55

jacobeligoodsons.com For Free Audio

UNIT 21   SPOKEN SPANISH

4 People sure do eat here.   kómokome |lahénte |ak↓   ¡Cómo come la gente aquí!

5 People are mighty talkative here.   komoabla |lahénte |akí↓   ¡Cómo habla la gente aquí!

6 Those women are mighty talkative.   komoáblán |ésa(s) señyóràs↓   ¡Cómo hablan esas señoras!

7 What a nuisance that old guy is.   komomolésta |ésèbyéhò↓   ¡Cómo molesta ese viejo!

C àyér |ișǫundiadesol |muyagradáblè↓   Ayer hizo un día de sol muy agradable.

1 Yesterday was a very pretty, sunny day.   àyér |ișǫundiadesol |muybonítò↓   Ayer hizo un día de sol muy bonito.

2 Yesterday was a very quiet, sunny day.   àyér |ișǫundiadesol |muytraŋkílò↓   Ayer hizo un día de sol muy tranquilo.

3 Yesterday was a very nasty (ugly),   àyér |ișǫundiadebyento |muyféò↓   Ayer hizo un día de viento muy feo.
    windy day.

4 Yesterday was a very cold, windy day.   àyér |ișǫundiadebyento |muyfríò↓   Ayer hizo un día de viento muy frío.

5 Yesterday was a very, very cold day.   àyér |ișǫundiadefrio |muygrándè↓   Ayer hizo un día de frío muy grande.

6 Yesterday was a very nasty day.   àyér |ișǫundia |muyféò↓   Ayer hizo un día muy feo.

7 Yesterday was a very pretty day.   àyér |ișǫundia |muybonítò↓   Ayer hizo un día muy bonito.

21.56   CINCUENTA Y SEIS

SPOKEN SPANISH   UNIT 21

D fwímos̩alkámpo↓   Fuimos al campo.

1 We went down town.   fwímos̩als̩éntro↓   Fuimos al centro.

2 We went to the hotel.   fwímos̩alotél↓   Fuimos al hotel.

3 He went to a restaurant.   fwe│aunrrestorán↓   Fue a un restorán.

4 He went to a cafe.   fwe̩aunkafé↓   Fue a un café.

5 They went to the park.   fwéron̩alpárke̩↓   Fueron al parque.

6 They went to the airport.   fwéron│ala̩eropwérto↓   Fueron al aeropuerto.

7 I went to the apartment.   fwi̩ala̩partaménto↓   Fui al apartamento.

E ła̩ymúchobyénto↓   Y hay mucho viento.

1 And there's a whole lot of wind.   ła̩ymúchisimobyénto↓   Y hay muchisimo viento.

2 And there's enough wind.   ła̩ybàstàntebyénto↓   Y hay bastante viento.

3 And there's too much wind.   ła̩yd̥èmàsyḁd̥obyénto↓   Y hay demasiado viento.

CINCUENTA Y SIETE   21.57

UNIT 21   SPOKEN SPANISH

4 And there's little wind.   ¦áypókobyéntò↓   Y hay poco viento.

5 And there's so much sun.   ¦áytantosól↓   Y hay tanto sol.

6 And there's not so much sun.   inǫaytántosól↓   Y no hay tanto sol.

7 And there's very little sun.   ¦áy│muypókosól↓   Y hay muy poco sol.

F   sèlǫảgràdèṣemozmúchò↓pérònopodémòs↓   Se lo agradecemos mucho, pero no podemos.

1 (I) thank you very much, but we can't.   sèlǫảgràdèṣkomúchò↓pérònopodémòs↓   Se lo agradezco mucho, pero no podemos.

2 We're very grateful, but we can't.   èstámòzmuyagradeṣídòs↓pérònopodémòs↓   Estamos muy agradecidos, pero no podemos.

3 Mary's very grateful, but she can't.   mària│ęstámuyagradeṣídà↓pérònopwédè↓   María está muy agradecida, pero no puede.

4 They're very grateful, but they can't.   éȴyos│èstánmuyagradeṣídòs↓péròno   Ellos están muy agradecidos, pero no pueden.
                                              pwédèn↓

5 Thanks a lot, but I can't.   muchazgráṣyàs↓pérònopwédò↓   Muchas gracias, pero no puedo.

6 Thanks an awful lot, but I can't.   múchisimazgráṣyàs↓pérònopwédò↓   Muchísimas gracias, pero no puedo.

7 I'm very sorry, but I can't.   lòsyéntomúchò↓pérònopwédò↓   Lo siento mucho, pero no puedo.

21.58   CINCUENTA Y OCHO

SPOKEN SPANISH   UNIT 21

21.24   Review drill — Theme class in past II tense forms

1 He used to talk and eat a lot.   áblabạ |ikòmiamúchò↓   Hablaba y comía mucho.

2 They studied and ate there.   èstúdyaban |ikòmian̦aí↓   Estudiaban y comían ahí.

3 He worked and ate very little.   tràbáhabạ |ikòmia |muypókò↓   Trabajaba y comía muy poco.

4 We worked and lived there.   tràbáhabamos |ibibiamoșaí↓   Trabajábamos y vivíamos ahí.

5 We worked and ate too much.   tràbáhabamos |ikòmiamozdemasyádò↓   Trabajábamos y comíamos demasiado.

6 We talked and wrote a lot.   áblabamos |ɟ̦èskribiamozmúchò↓   Hablábamos y escribíamos mucho.

7 They talked and wrote very well.   áblaban |ɟ̦èskribian |muybyén↓   Hablaban y escribían muy bien.

8 We went down and up very little.   báhabamos |isúbiamoz |muypókò↓   Bajábamos y subíamos muy poco.

9 He went down and up a lot.   báhabạ |isùbiamúchò↓   Bajaba y subía mucho.

10 They studied and went out also.   èstúdyaban |isàlian |tàmbyén↓   Estudiaban y salían también.

11 We studied but didn't learn.   èstúdyabamos |pèrônoạprendíàmòs↓   Estudiábamos pero no aprendíamos.

CINCUENTA Y NUEVE   21.59

UNIT 21   SPOKEN SPANISH

21.3   CONVERSATION STIMULUS

NARRATIVE 1

1 The weather sure changes in this   kómokámbyą |eltyémpǫ|ènéstèpàís↓   ¡Cómo cambia el tiempo en este país!
   country.

2 It varies from day to day.   kámbya |dèdíadía↓   Cambia de día a día.

3 Yesterday it was warm.   àyér |ìşokalór↓   Ayer hizo calor.

4 Today it's cold.   óy |aşefríó↓   Hoy hace frío.

5 Tomorrow it's going to be warm again.   màņyana |báşérkàlór |otrabéş↓   Mañana va a hacer calor otra vez.

6 Yesterday it was a very nice day.   àyér |ìşǫundía |muyagradáblè↓   Ayer hizo un día muy agradable.

7 And Jose and Mary went to the country. íhóseįmaría |fwerǫnalkámpó↓   Y José y María fueron al campo.

DIALOG 1

Juan, dígale a José que cómo cambia el   kómokámbyą |eltyémpǫ|ènéstèpàís↓   Juan: ¡Cómo cambia el tiempo en este
   tiempo en este país.   país!

José, dígale que así es, que ayer hizo   àsiés↓ àyér|ìşokalór↑óy |aşefrió↑   José: Así es. Ayer hizo calor; hoy hace
   calor; que hoy hace frío; y que mañana ímáņyana↑báşérkálor |otrabéş↓   frío; y mañana va a hacer calor otra
   va a hacer calor otra vez.   vez.

21.60   SESENTA

jacobeligoodsons.com For Free Audio

SPOKEN SPANISH

UNIT 21

Juan, pregúntele que a propósito, qué
hicieron él y Carmen ayer.

àpropósitò↓ ke↓şyeron |tu↓kármèn |àyér↓

Juan: A propósito, ¿qué hicieron tú y
Carmen ayer?

José, contéstele que fueron al campo.

fwimos̩alkámpò↓

José: Fuimos al campo.

NARRATIVE 2

1 Juan and the Harrises went for a walk
through the park.

hwan̩ılosharriz |d̩yeron̩unabwelta |
pòrèlparkè↓

Juan y los Harris dieron una vuelta por el
parque.

2 The Colonel said something to Juan about
Jose.

èlkòrónel |lèd̩ih̩g̩algo |ahwán |dèhósé↓

El Coronel le dijo algo a Juan de José.

3 It was something about some photos, but
Juan doesn't remember what it was.

fwéalgo d̩eunasfótòs↓ pèròhwan |nó
rrekwérd̩a |kèfwé↓

Fue algo de unas fotos, pero Juan no
recuerda qué fue.

4 Jose knows; it's about the photos the
Colonel lent him the other day.

hòsesábè↓ sónlàsfotos |kèlkòrónel |le
prestog̩lotrod̩íà↓

José sabe; son las fotos que el Coronel le
prestó el otro día.

5 He hasn't taken them back yet.

nó |selasa̩ʸebád̩ò |tòd̩àbíà↓

No se las ha llevado todavía.

6 But he'll take them back tomorrow.

péròsèlàzoᵈʸeba |màŋyanà↓

Pero se las lleva mañana.

DIALOG 2

José, pregúntele a Juan que él, a dónde fué.

itú↓ àd̩ondefwístè↓

José: ¿Y tú?, ¿a dónde fuiste?

Juan, contéstele que los Harris y Ud. dieron
una vuelta por el parque.

lòsharris̩ıyó |d̩ımos̩unabwelta |pòrel
párkè↓

Juan: Los Harris y yo dimos una vuelta
por el parque.

SESENTA Y UNO

21.61

UNIT 21   SPOKEN SPANISH

José, pregúntele si el Coronel no le dijo   èlkòrònél |nótèdìhonàdá |dèmi↑   José: ¿El Coronel no te dijo nada de mí?
  nada de Ud.

Juan, contéstele que le dijo algo de unas   mèdìhọalgo |dẹunasfótós↓péró |nó   Juan: Me dijo algo de unas fotos pero no
  fotos pero Ud. no recuerda qué fue.   rrekwerdo |kéfwé↓   recuerdo qué fue.

José, dígale que Ud. sabe; que son las fotos   yósé↓ sònlasfótos |kemepresto |ẹlòtrodíá↓   José: Yo sé; son las fotos que me prestó
  que le prestó el otro día.   el otro día.

Juan, pregúntele si no se las ha llevado   nó |selas̜az̜ọyebado |todabia↑   Juan: ¿No se las has llevado todavía?
  todavía.

José, contéstele que no, que mañana se las   nó↓ màŋyanaselaz̜ọyébò↓   José: No. Mañana se las llevo.
  lleva.

                                              NARRATIVE 3

1 It sure is cold.   kéfriọás̜e↓   ¡Qué frio hace!

2 And it's very cloudy too.   sí↓ ịéstámuynubládò |tàmbyén↓   Sí. Y está muy nublado también.

3 It looks like it's going to rain.   pàres̜e |kebaọyobér↓   Parece que va a llover.

4 It's ten o'clock.   sònlaz̜dyés̜↓   Son las diez.

5 Jose's going to have some coffee.   hò.   ̇tomàrkafé↓   José va a tomar café.

21.62   SESENTA Y DOS

jacobeligoodsons.com For Free Audio

SPOKEN SPANISH   UNIT 21

6 Juan wants to go with him.   hwáŋ |kyéreịirkonél↓   Juan quiere ir con él.

7 But they'll have to be back soon.   pérótyéneŋ |kèbòlbérpróntô↓   Pero tienen que volver pronto.

                                                    DIALOG 3

José, dígale a Juan que qué frío hace.   kéfríọáşè↓   José: ¡Qué frío hace!

Juan, dígale que sí, y que está muy nublado sí↓ ịéstámuynubláṛô |tàmbyén↓   Juan: Sí, y está muy nublado también.
   también. Que parece que va a llover.   pàreşe |kèbá☐ọòbér↓   Parece que va a llover.

José, pregúntele que qué hora es.   kẹorạés↓   José: ¿Qué hora es?

Juan, contéstele que son las diez.   sonlazɖyéş↓   Juan: Son las diez.

José, dígale que Ud. va a tomar café.   boyatomarkafé↓ kyérezbenírkonmigo↑   José: Voy a tomar café. ¿Quieres venir
   Pregúntele si quiere venir con Ud.   conmigo?

Juan, contéstele que muy bien, pero que   muybyén↓ péròtènémos |kèbòlbérpróntô↓   Juan: Muy bien, pero tenemos que volver
   tienen que volver pronto.   pronto.

SESENTA Y TRES   21.63

           jacobeligoodsons.com For Free Audio

UNIT 21   SPOKEN SPANISH

21.4   READINGS

21.40   List of cognate loan words

el plan	èl—plán↓
correctamente	kòrrektaméntè↓
la dificultad	là—difikúltad↓
México	mehikò↓
respondió (responder)	rrèspòndyó↓ rrèspònde'r↓
conjugar	kòŋhùga'r↓
el presente	él—prèsèntè↓
el futuro	èl—fúturò↓
memorizó (memorizar)	mèmòriṣó↓ mèmòriṣa'r↓
prefiero (preferir)	prèfyeró↓ prèférɪ'r↓
el interés	èl—intèrés↓
seria	séryà↓
el entusiasmo	èl—èntúsyazmò↓
la condición	là—kóndiṣyòn↓
las frases	làs—frasès↓
la expresión	la—èsprèsyòn↓
el beisbol	èl—bèyzbòl↓

21.64   SESENTA Y CUATRO

SPOKEN SPANISH   UNIT 21

usa (usar)	usá↓ ùsár↓
indicar	indikár↓
el resultado	èl—rrésúltádó↓
comprendo (comprender)	kòmprèndó↓ kòmprèndér↓

21.41   Reading selection

Plan de Estudiar

——Señores——dijo Virginia——quiero presentarles a mi esposo, Fred Robinson. Fred, éstos son los señores Fuentes, vecinos de nosotros. Han sido muy amables en venir a hacernos esta visita. Ellos viven enfrente, en la casa de la esquina.

——Tanto gusto, señores; por favor dispensen el español tan malo que hablo——dijo Fred correctamente, pero con dificultad y mucho acento.

——No diga eso, Sr. Robinson——exclamó Marta;——habla muy bien. Ya quisiera yo poder decir algo en inglés. ¿Dónde lo aprendieron? Por lo visto ya Uds. dos hablaban español antes de llegar a Surlandia.

——Bueno...mi esposa lo hablaba desde que era niña, porque su familia vivió muchos años en México. Por eso lo habla tan bien; pero yo, en realidad, empecé a estudiarlo hace apenas seis meses en una escuela del gobierno en Washington. Ahí aprendí bastante, pero todavía tengo un acento horrible. Y Ud., Sr. Fuentes, ¿habla inglés?

——Qué va——respondió éste——sólo sé conjugar verbos; eso es todo lo que aprendí en la escuela. Yo le puedo conjugar a Ud. cualquier verbo, en presente, en pasado, y en futuro, si quiere. Pero cuando voy a decir algo, nadie sabe lo que estoy diciendo, ni yo mismo. Ayer y hoy estuve todo el día estudiando en un libro que tengo en casa, pensando que Uds. no hablaban español. Conjugué por lo menos doscientos verbos.

——Y también memorizó una cosa muy bonita para decírsela a Uds.——dijo Marta.

——Queremos oirla——dijeron los Robinson casi al mismo tiempo.

——No, no, no, otro día, ya se me olvidó. Además hoy prefiero hablar en español.

——Podríamos hacer una cosa Ud. y yo, Sr. Fuentes——exclamó Fred. Yo tengo mucho interés en practicar el español con alguien en forma seria, y si Ud. en realidad tiene interés de aprender a hablar inglés, Ud. y yo podríamos reunirnos unas dos o tres veces por semana, en las noches, aquí o en su casa. ¿Qué le parece la idea?

——Me parece estupenda——respondió don Ricardo con entusiasmo. Y mi señora y la suya pueden hacer lo mismo durante el día.

SESENTA Y CINCO

jacobeligoodsons.com For Free Audio

UNIT 21   SPOKEN SPANISH

—Pero con una condición—dijo Fred en tono de broma. —Vamos a practicar repitiendo frases completas, como me hacían estudiar a mí en Washington, sin tener que conjugar verbos, porque conjugando verbos no llegamos ni a primera base, como a veces decimos en inglés.

—¿Qué quiere decir eso de 'no llegamos ni a primera base'?—preguntó don Ricardo.

—Es una expresión tomada del beisbol que se usa para indicar el mal resultado de algo.

—Sí, ya comprendo—dijo don Ricardo.—Sin conjugar verbos, entonces. Ud. y yo queremos llegar por lo menos a primera base.

21.42   Response drill

    1 ¿Cómo habla Fred el español?

    2 ¿Dónde lo estudió?

    3 ¿Cuánto tiempo hace que empezó a estudiarlo?

    4 ¿Por qué lo habla mejor su esposa?

    5 ¿Dónde vivía la familia de ella cuando ella era niña?

    6 ¿Dónde estudió inglés el Sr. Fuentes?

    7 ¿Qué aprendió en la escuela?, ¿aprendió a hablar?

    8 ¿Qué estuvo haciendo él ayer todo el día?

    9 ¿Cuántos verbos conjugó, por lo menos?

   10 ¿Qué memorizó también?

   11 ¿Por qué estuvo practicando inglés todo el día ayer?

   12 ¿Qué plan de estudios tienen Fred y Ricardo?

   13 ¿Cómo lo hacían a Fred estudiar español en Washington?

   14 ¿A qué hora van a reunirse Marta y Virginia a estudiar?

   15 ¿Por qué no es bueno conjugar verbos?

21.66   SESENTA Y SEIS

SPOKEN SPANISH   UNIT 22

22.1   BASIC SENTENCES.   Mrs. Harris wants to go to the market.

Carmen and Mrs. Harris are having a telephone conversation.

ENGLISH SPELLING   AID TO LISTENING   SPANISH SPELLING

continues, follows (to continue, follow) [1]   sígè↓ segír↓   sigue (seguir)

around   pór↓   por

Carmen   Carmen
How's everything going around your house?   komosigetoďo|porsukásà|sèŋyórà↓   ¿Cómo sigue todo por su casa, señora?

even though, although   áwŋkè↓   aunque

very busy (busy)   ókúpàďísimò↓ ókúpàďò↓   ocupadísimo (ocupado)

Mrs. Harris   Sra. Harris
Very well, even though I'm extremely busy.   múybyén↓áwŋkèyo|ęstóyókúpàďísimà↓ Muy bien, aunque yo estoy ocupadísima.

that (I) call (to call) [2]   kè-Ⓛyámè↓ Ⓛyàmár↓   que llame (llamar)

early   tèmpráno↓   temprano

Carmen   Carmen
Forgive me for calling you so early.   pérďone|kelaⓁyámè|tántèmpránò↓   Perdone que la llame tan temprano.

to gladden   àlègrár↓   alegrar

myself (I) am glad (to be glad)   mę-àlègrò↓ àlègrárse↑   me alegro (alegrarse)

Mrs. Harris   Sra. Harris
On the contrary, I'm glad you did.   àlkóntraryò↓mę́àlégromuchò↓   Al contrario, me alegro mucho.

I was just going to call you. [3]   yọibaⓁyamárlá|ạóràmizmò↓   Yo iba a llamarla ahora mismo.

UNO   22.1

UNIT 22   SPOKEN SPANISH

some   àlgún↓ àlgunó↓   algún (alguno)

the problem   èl—próblemá↓   el problema

Carmen
Is something the matter?   tyéngàlgumpróblemá↑   *Carmen*
                                                                   ¿Tiene algún problema?

this (matter) of   èstó—dé↓   esto de...

the market   èl—mèrkadó↓   el mercado

turns, returns (to turn, to return)   bwélbè↓ bòlbér↓   vuelve (volver)

crazy   lókò↓   loco

drives me crazy   mè—bwelbe—lókò↓   me vuelve loco

Mrs. Harris
Yes. This business of the prices in the market   sí↓ ésto|dèlòspréçyos|ènèlmèrkadó↑   *Sra. Harris*
is driving me insane. (4)   Sí. Esto de los precios en el mercado
                                mèbwelbelókà↓   me vuelve loca.

terrible   tèrriblé↓   terrible

Carmen
Oh, yes. That is a mess.   á'|sí↓ éso|èsálgótérriblè↓   *Carmen*
                                                                   Ah, sí. Eso es algo terrible.

If you like, we can leave the other shopping for   sikyéré↑dèhamoz|lòdélástyéndas|páràlà   Si quiere, dejamos lo de las tiendas para
this afternoon and go to the market now. (5)   tardè↑íbamos,almerkadoaórà↓   la tarde y vamos al mercado ahora.

to accompany   àkòmpàŋyár↓   acompañar

Mrs. Harris
Then can you go with me?   éntonçes|pweçeakompaŋyarmé↑   *Sra. Harris*
                                                                   Entonces, ¿puede acompañarme?

22.2   DOS

SPOKEN SPANISH   UNIT 22

for certain, of course   pòr—súpwéstô↓   por supuesto

(I) will show (to show, teach) (6)   ènsèŋyàré↓ ènsèŋyàr↓   enseñaré (enseñar)

Carmen   *Carmen*
Of course, and that way I'll show you where   pòrsùpwéstô↓ ¡ásı |lènsèŋyàre |ḋonde   Por supuesto y así le enseñaré dónde
  there's a very good one.   ay |ůnòmuybwénô↓   hay uno muy bueno.

Mrs. Harris   *Sra. Harris*
Thanks a lot. What time shall I come by for you?(7) muchazgráṣyàs↓ àkęorapásó |pòrùstéḋ↓   Muchas gracias. ¿A qué hora paso por
                                                                                                          usted?

myself (I) dress (to dress oneself)   mè—bıstô↓ bèstırsé↓   me visto (vestirse)

Carmen   *Carmen*
I'll be dressed in half an hour. (8)   yó |ęnmédyąorà |mèbístô↓   Yo en media hora me visto.

(I) dismiss (to dismiss, to see off)   dèspıḋô↓ dèspèdır↓   despido (despedir)

myself (I) take leave (to say goodbye)   mè—dèspıḋô↓ dèspèḋirsé↓   me despido (despedirse)

Mrs. Harris   *Sra. Harris*
Good. I'll say goodbye, then. (9)   bwenò↓ mèḋèspıḋǫ |èntónṣès↓   Bueno, me despido, entonces.

So long.   ástàlwègô↓   Hasta luego.

22.10   Notes on the basic sentences

(1)   Considering its literal meaning, the English speaker is apt to be somewhat surprised a' the variety and extent of usage this word has by comparison with English.
Besides the meaning that appears in this basic sentence, there is also the meaning 'Keep on going,' both literally (as in the sign on doors of business establishments in
Bogotá, meaning 'Come right in') and figuratively (as in the admonition heard when one hesitates in the middle of an anecdote, meaning 'Go on, please'). Still another meaning
appears in a sentence like /ustédsígeseŋyór↓/   *Usted sigue, señor* 'You're next, sir.'

TRES   22.3

UNIT 22   SPOKEN SPANISH

(2) The form /ỵáme/ *llame* is a present subjunctive, 1 sing. The form will be introduced in Unit 36, and this particular usage (in a noun clause) in Unit 37. It is perhaps worth noting, this far in advance, that the form of the present subjunctive 1 - 3 sg is identical with the singular of the polite command, which will be taken up in Unit 27 but which is already to be seen in a form like /perdóne/ *perdone* from /perdonár/ *perdonar* in this same sentence.

(3) Without any special point having been made of it, the *periphrastic future* has been used several times in the dialogs: /bátrabahár|ko(n̩)nosótros↓/ *Va a trabajar con nosotros*, Unit 4; /básér|su̧eskritóryo↓/ *Va a ser su escritorio*, Unit 5; /misbes̩ínos|bán̩amudárse|dekása↓/ *Mis vecinos van a mudarse de casa*, Unit 8; and so on. Here, however, is an example of the *past tense* of the same construction: note that it appears in Past II, not in Past I.

(4) It is worthy of note that English cannot use *this* and *that* with the same degree of nominal status as can Spanish: English permits 'This is driving me insane' but not 'This of the markets is driving me insane.' English must have a busy-word which merely serves to *nominalize* the form *this*: 'This business about...' 'This matter of...'

(5) The construction /...lodelastyéndas.../ *...lo de las tiendas* is taken as the basis for Variation Drill #C later in this unit.

(6) This is an example of *future tense*, which will not be fully examined until Unit 53. Study of it is postponed not because of any special difficulty that accompanies it, but because it is relatively infrequent and unimportant.

(7) Note this use of simple present tense /páso/ *paso* in a context that requires it to be interpreted with future meaning. This is one reason why future tense itself is so rare: present is used instead.

(8) Here, in /mebísto/ *me visto*, is another example of the matter discussed under #7 above.

(9) Still another. It's no wonder the future tense can be postponed.

22.2   DRILLS AND GRAMMAR

22.21   Pattern drills

22.21.1 Present tense irregular verbs — stem vowel changing

   A. Presentation of pattern

                              ILLUSTRATIONS

What time do you have lunch?   1   ák̬e̬orạ|almwérs̬ạ|ústéd↓   ¿A qué hora *almuerza* Ud?

_____   2   ben̩es̬eabyón|kebwéla|sobrela   ¿Ven ese avión que *vuela* sobre la torre
                                               torre̬̩ekontrol↑   de control?

22.4   CUATRO

SPOKEN SPANISH   UNIT 22

———————————————   3   ésto|delóspreşyóz|mèbwélbelóká↓   Esto de los precios me *vuelve* loca.

I can't find the check   4   noęŋkwentro|elchéké↓   No *encuentro* el cheque.

———————————————   5   kwantokwesta|untáksi↓   ¿Cuánto *cuesta* un taxi?

By the way, does it rain much here?   6   àpróposító↓ ⓞ̨wébemucho|akí↑   A propósito, ¿*llueve* mucho aquí?

———————————————   7   nòmèpwedokehár↓   No me *puedo* quejar.

Why don't you try the dessert.   8   pórkénoprweba|elpóstré↓   ¿Por qué no *prueba* el postre?

———————————————   9   kàrambà↓ àora|kerrekwérdo↓   ¡Caramba! Ahora que *recuerdo*.

They take good care of us at the customs   10   ènládwana↑nòsàtyéndembyén↓   En la aduana nos *atienden* bien.
office.

———————————————   11   kyeręusted|agwamineral↑   ¿*Quiere* Ud. agua mineral?

———————————————   12   pyensobuskar|ùn̯àpàrtàmentô↓   *Pienso* buscar un apartamento.

I'm sorry to arrive late.   13   syénto|ⓞ̨yegartárdé↓   Siento llegar tarde.

———————————————   14   lòsyentomúchô↓   Lo *siento* mucho.

      (you) feel (to feel)   syénté↓ sèntír↓   siente (sentir)

Do you feel cold in the living room? 15   syéntefriọ|enlasala↑   ¿*Siente* frio en la sala?

CINCO   22.5

UNIT 22   SPOKEN SPANISH

(they) close (to close)   şyérràn↓ şèrràr↓   cierran (cerrar)

What time do they close the stores?   16   àkẹórașyérran |lastyéndàs↓   ¿A qué hora *cierran* las tiendas?

_____   17   yó |ẹnmẹdyạórà |mebístò↓   Yo en media hora me *visto*.

_____   18   bwénò↓ méđèspíđọ |èntónşès↓   Bueno me *despido*, entonces.

Shall I repeat it again?   19   rrèpítọ |otrabéş↑   ¿*Repito* otra vez?

_____   20   kómosɪgetođo |porsukásà↓   ¿Cómo *sigue* todo por su casa?

                                           EXTRAPOLATION

Stem vowel change	o > wé	e > yé	e > í
Sample verb	pod—ér	ker—ér	seg—ír
sg 1	pwéd—o	kyér—o	síg—o
2 fam	pwéd—es	kyér—es	síg—es
2-3	pwéd—e	kyér—e	síg—e
pl 1	pod—émos	ker—émos	seg—ímos
2-3	pwéd—en	kyér—en	síg—en

                                              NOTES

a. In certain irregular verbs the last stem vowel changes in some present tense forms to a diphthong or another vowel.

b. This change occurs when ever strong stress falls on the stem, ie in sg and 2-3 pl tense forms, but not 1 pl.

SPOKEN SPANISH   UNIT 22

22.21.11 Substitution drills — Person-number substitution

1 nòsotros|àlmòrşamozdemasyádò↓

   yo_____↓   àlmwerşodemasyádò↓

   lwìsaɟantonyo_____↓   àlmwerşandemasyádò↓

   ústed_____↓   àlmwerşademasyádò↓

   éʎʎos_____↓   àlmwerşandemasyádò↓

_____

1 *Nosotros* almorzamos demasiado.

   Yo_____.   Almuerzo demasiado.

   Luisa y Antonio_____.   Almuerzan demasiado.

   Ud._____.   Almuerza demasiado.

   Ellos_____.   Almuerzan demasiado.

UNIT 22   SPOKEN SPANISH

2 nòsótroz |nópóďemosˌɪr |éstanóchė↓   nópwéďenˌɪr |éstanóchė↓
   ústeďez_____↓   nópwéď gɪr |éstanóchė↓
   yó_____↓   nópwéď gɪr |éstanóchė↓
   àntónyo_____↓   nópwéďenˌɪr |éstanóchė↓
   àntónyoˌɪlwísa_____↓

3 nòsótroz |bólbemospróntô↓   bwélbepróntô↓
   èl_____↓   bwélbempróntô↓
   hòseˌkármem_____↓   bwélbepróntô↓
   ústeď_____↓   bwélbempróntô↓
   èˌɣoz_____↓

_____

2 *Nosotros* no podemos ir esta noche.
   Uds. _____ .   No pueden ir esta noche.
   Yo _____ .   No puedo ir esta noche.
   Antonio _____ .   No puede ir esta noche.
   Antonio y Luisa _____ .   No pueden ir esta noche.

3 *Nosotros* volvemos pronto.
   El _____ .   Vuelve pronto.
   José y Carmen_____ .   Vuelven pronto.
   Ud. _____ .   Vuelve pronto.
   Ellos _____ .   Vuelven pronto.

22.8   OCHO

SPOKEN SPANISH   UNIT 22

4 nòsótros |sèntímòsfríọ |àórà↓
   yo _____↓   syéntòfríọ |àórà↓
   lwìsaɨantónyo_____↓   syéntèmfríọ |àórà↓
   éꞵyos _____↓   syéntèmfríọ |àórà↓
   ùstéď_____↓   syéntèfríọ |àórà↓

5 nòsótros |pensamosésò↓
   lwìsa _____↓   pyénsạésò↓
   àntónyọịkármem_____↓   pyénsanésò↓
   ùstéď_____↓   pyénsạésò↓
   éꞵyos_____↓   pyénsanésò↓

_____

4 *Nosotros* sentimos frio ahora.
      Yo _____ .   Siento frío ahora.
      Luisa y Antonio _____ .   Sienten frío ahora.
      Ellos _____ .   Sienten frío ahora.
      Ud. _____ .   Siente frío ahora.

5 *Nosotros* pensamos eso.
      Luisa _____   Piensa eso.
      Antonio y Carmen _____.   Piensan eso.
      Ud. _____ .   Piensa eso.
      Ellos_____ .   Piensan eso.

NUEVE   22.9

UNIT 22   SPOKEN SPANISH

6 nòsótros |segímozďespwés↓

   yo_____↓   sígoďespwés↓

   ústeďes_____↓   sígendespwés↓

   lwísa_____↓   sígeďespwés↓

   èlsènyòr_____↓   sígeďespwés↓

7 nòsótros |tàmbyénrrepetímòs↓

   éḷḷos_____↓   tàmbyénrrepítèn↓

   yo_____↓   tàmbyénrrepítô↓

   lwísa_____↓   tàmbyénrrepítê↓

   ústeďes_____↓   tàmbyénrrepítèn↓

---

6 *Nosotros* seguimos después.

   Yo _____.   Sigo después.

   Uds. _____.   Siguen después.

   Luisa_____.   Sigue después.

   El señor _____.   Sigue después.

7 *Nosotros* también repetimos.

   Ellos_____.   También repiten.

   Yo_____.   También repito.

   Luisa _____.   También repite.

   Uds. _____.   También repiten.

22.10   DIEZ

SPOKEN SPANISH   UNIT 22

Tense substitution

1 yóalmorṣabaemfréntè↓   yóalmwerṣǫemfréntè↓

2 nòsotroz |noǫnkontrábamozlabásè↓   nósotroz |noǫnkontramozlabásè↓

3 éǫyánópòdiạ |abrirelekipáhè↓   éǫyánopweḍę |abrirelekipáhè↓

4 éǫyozbolbian |ensegíḍà↓   éǫyozbwelben |ensegíḍà↓

5 nòsotroz |norrekorḍabamozloznómbrès↓   nòsotroz |norrekorḍamozloznómbrès↓

6 làsèkrètarya |nòkèriạír↓   làsèkretarya |nókyeręír↓

7 todos |sentiamoskalór |àǫụí↓   todo(s) sentimos |kaloraǫụí↓

---

1 Yo *almorzaba* en frente.   Yo almuerzo en frente.

2 Nosotros no *encontrábamos* la base.   Nosotros no encontramos la base.

3 Ella no *podía* abrir el equipaje.   Ella no puede abrir el equipaje.

4 Ellos *volvían* en seguida.   Ellos vuelven en seguida.

5 Nosotros no *recordábamos* los nombres.   Nosotros no recordamos los nombres.

6 La secretaria no *quería* ir.   La secretaria no quiere ir.

7 Todos *sentíamos* calor allí.   Todos sentimos calor allí.

ONCE

8 é(l)yos |nòsátèndianmuymál↓   é(l)yoz |nòsátyendenmuymál↓

9 nòsótros |émpèşabamóstárdè↓   nòsótros |émpèşamostárdè↓

10 é(l)yòzrrèpètian |şıŋkobéşès↓   é(l)yòzrrèpıten |şıŋkobéşès↓

11 nósótroz |rrèpètiamozlaleksyón↓   nósótroz |rrèpètimozlaleksyón↓

12 é(l)yàsègìą |èntónşès↓   é(l)yàsıgę |èntónşès↓

13 nòsótros |sègıamozdespwés↓   nósótros |sègımozdespwés↓

---

8 Ellos nos *atendían* muy mal.   Ellos nos atienden muy mal.

9 Nosotros *empezábamos* tarde.   Nosotros empezamos tarde.

10 Ellos *repetían* cinco veces.   Ellos repiten cinco veces.

11 Nosotros *repetíamos* la lección.   Nosotros repetimos la lección.

12 Ella *seguía*, entonces.   Ella sigue, entonces.

13 Nosotros *seguíamos* después.   Nosotros seguimos después.

SPOKEN SPANISH   UNIT 22

22.21.12 Response drill

          1 kyérẹagwạ↑okafé↓   kyerokafé↓

          2 kyérénạgwạ↑okafé↓   kèremoskaf6↓

          3 sígel↑ọustéd↓   sigél↓

  [ȧkɪ↓] 4 dondẹalmwerṣan|ustédès↓   ȧlmȯrṣamoṣakí↓

[ȇnlȧkásȧ↓] 5 dondẹalmwerṣanℰℂyòs↓   ȧlmwérṣanẹnlȧkásȧ↓

  [ȧkɪ↓] 6 dondẹalmwerṣạ̄ustéɖ↓   ȧlmwérṣɋakíↄ↓

---

          1 ¿Quiere agua o café?   Quiero café.

          2 ¿Quieren agua o café?   Queremos café.

          3 ¿Sigue él o Ud.?   Sigue él.

   (aquí) 4 ¿Dónde almuerzan Uds.?   Almorzamos aquí.

(en la casa) 5 ¿Dónde almuerzan ellos?   Almuerzan en la casa.

   (aquí) 6 ¿Dónde almuerza Ud.?   Almuerzo aquí.

TRECE

UNIT 22   SPOKEN SPANISH

[múchó↓]   7   rrépíteustédpokó↑   nó↓ rrépítómuchó↓

[múchó↓]   8   rrépítenustédes |pokó↑   nó↓ rrépétímózmuchó↓

[múchó↓]   9   rrépítel |pokó↑   nó↓ rrépítèmuchó↓

          10   Qywébèmuchoakí↑   sí↓ àkí |Qywébèmuchó↓

          11   pwédeustéd |ablárespaŋyól↑   sí |sípwéđó↓

          12   pwédenustédes |ablárespaŋyól↑   sí |sípođémòs↓

          13   lósátyéndoyó |byéngustédes↑   sí↓ ùstéd |nòsátyéndèmúybyén↓

(mucho)   7   ¿Repite Ud. poco?   No, repito mucho.

(mucho)   8   ¿Repiten Uds. poco?   No, repetimos mucho.

(mucho)   9   ¿Repite él poco?   No, repite mucho.

          10   ¿Llueve mucho aquí?   Sí, aquí llueve mucho.

          11   ¿Puede Ud. hablar español?   Sí, sí puedo.

          12   ¿Pueden Uds. hablar español?   Sí, sí podemos.

          13   ¿Los atiendo yo bien a Uds.?   Sí, Ud. nos atiende bien.

SPOKEN SPANISH   UNIT 22

22.21.13 Translation drill

1 We can't eat lunch now.	nopoḍémoṣạlmorṣár |aórà↓	No podemos almorzar ahora.
2 She doesn't want to go.	eýa |nokyerẹír↓	Ella no quiere ir.
3 What do you think?	képyenṣạustéd↓	¿Qué piensa Ud.?
4 I don't remember anything.	yó |norrekwerḍonáḍà↓	Yo no recuerdo nada.
5 We plan to go afterwards.	pénsamosịr |despwés↓	Pensamos ir después.
6 We want to send some suits to the cleaners.	kéremóz |mándạrunostrahes |àlàtìntòrèrìà↓	Queremos mandar unos trajes a la tintorería.
7 We're getting along fine.	sègimozmúybyén↓	Seguimos muy bien.
8 How're you getting along?	kómosiggustéd↓	¿Cómo sigue Ud.?
9 What time do we start to work?	ákẹorạ |émpèṣamosạtrabahár↓	¿A qué hora empezamos a trabajar?
10 What time do you start?	ákẹorạempyéṣạustéd↓	¿A qué hora empieza Ud.?
11 Don't you remember?	nórrèkwerḍa↑	¿No recuerda?
12 Are you all coming back tomorrow?	bwélbenụṣtéḍez |maɲyánà↑	¿Vuelven Uds. mañana?
13 No, we aren't (coming back).	nó↓ nòbolbémós↓	No, no volvemos.

QUINCE   22.15

UNIT 22   SPOKEN SPANISH

14 What time do they close the Foreign   ákęoraşyérràn |èlministéryò |đè   ¿A qué hora cierran el Ministerio de
    Office?   rrèlàşyones̩esteryórès↓   Relaciones Exteriores?

15 The colonel doesn't fly in that squadron. èlkòrònél |nòbwelą |eṇẹsèskwađrón↓   El coronel no vuela en ese escuadrón.

B. Discussion of pattern

    The verb patterns described in Units 5, 7, and 8 (/‑ár,‑ér,‑ír/ verbs) are called *regular* because a large majority of Spanish verbs change *according to*
these patterns. Other verbs, then, can conveniently be described in terms of the variations from the established regular patterns that these verbs show. These *irregular*
verbs may have variations that are slight, or they may be very extensive. Sometimes a considerable number of verbs will have the same variations in the same places; others
will have unique or near-unique patterns.

    One rather large group of similarly patterned irregular verbs is presented in this drill section. The irregularity consists of a modification of the last (if more than
one) vowel of the stem, whenever it is stressed. The changes occur in all sg forms and in the 2‑3 pl forms. The infinitive stem re-appears without change only in the 1 pl
form, where the strong stress is on the ending. The three types of change are:

Stem vowel change	Sample stems	endings
o ˃ wé	pod‑	‑ér, ‑émos
	pwéd‑	‑o, ‑es, ‑e, ‑en
e ˃ yé	ker‑	‑ér, ‑émos
	kyér‑	‑o, ‑es, ‑e, ‑en
e ˃ í	seg‑	‑ír, ‑ímos
	síg‑	‑o, ‑es, ‑e, ‑en

22.16   jacobeligoodsons.com For Free Audio   DIECISEIS

SPOKEN SPANISH   UNIT 22

Of course only verbs with /o/ [1] or /e/ in their stems can change in this pattern, though not all do. There is no way to predict which verbs will have stem vowel changes, though one limitation can be stated: verbs from all theme classes may show /o > wé/ or /e > yé/ changes, but only /-ír/ verbs show an /e > í/ change.

The verbs so far presented which follow this irregular pattern are listed below in their infinitive and 2-3 sg present tense forms:

o > wé		e > yé		e > í	
almorşár	almwérşa	atendér	atyénde	bestír	bíste
bolár	bwéla	kerér	kyére	despedír	despíde
bolbér	bwélbe	pensár	pyénsa	rrepetír	rrepíte
enkontrár	enkwéntra	sentár	syénta	segír	síge
kostár	kwésta	sentír	syénte		
(l)yobér	(l)ywébe	şerrár	şyérra		
podér	pwéde				
probár	prwéba				
rrekordár	rrekwérda				

This list is by no means exhaustive; there are many others that pattern the same way. A fuller listing will be found in the appendix. Hereafter when you learn a new verb, you should at once determine whether or not it belongs to this pattern.

_____

(1) One exception is noted in the appendix: /hugár/

DIECISIETE   22.17

UNIT 22   SPOKEN SPANISH

22.21.2   Statement intonation patterns — Sentence modifiers

A.   Presentation of pattern

ILLUSTRATIONS

1   bwénástárdès|sényór↓

   1   2 1 | 1 11↓
   Buenas tardes, señor.

2   nósemolésté|tènyéntè↓

   2   1 1 | 1 1 1↓
   No se moleste, teniente.

3   ástalabístà|kòrònél↓

   2   1 1 | 1 11↓
   Hasta la vista, coronel.

EXTRAPOLATION

English	Spanish
/... |222↑/	/... |111↓/

NOTES

a. In Spanish, sentence modifiers following a sentence are usually a separate phrase on pitch level /1/ with a final falling intonation.

22.18   DIECIOCHO

SPOKEN SPANISH   UNIT 22

22.21.21 Translation drill – Sentence modifiers

   2 3 2 | 2   2 ↑
1 Good morning, gentlemen.   bwénòzđiàs |sènyórès↓   1 21 | 1 1 1 ↓
                                                                   Buenos días, señores.

   2   32 | 2 2 ↑
2 Good afternoon, ladies.   bwénàstarđès |sènyóràs↓   1 2 1 | 1 1 1 ↓
                                                                  Buenas tardes, señoras.

   2 3 2 | 22 ↑
3 Good evening, Miss.   bwénàznochès |sènyòrítà↓   1 2 1 | 1 11 ↓
                                                                  Buenas noches, señorita.

   2 3 2 | 2 22 ↑
4 Good morning, Mr. Molina.   bwénòzđiàs |sènyórmòlínà↓   1 21 | 1 1 1 1↓
                                                                  Buenos días, señor Molina.

   2   32 | 2 22 ↑
5 Come on in, Mr. Molina.   pasçađelántè |sènyórmòlínà↓   2   1 1 | 1 1   11 ↓
                                                                Pase adelante, señor Molina.

   2 32 | 2   22 ↑
6 Come in, Miss Garcia.   pasé |sènyòrítàgàrşíà↓   2 1 | 1   11 ↓
                                                                 Pase, señorita García.

   2 31 | 2   22 ↑
7 Come in, Mrs. Garcia.   àđèlantè |sènyóràgàrşíà↓   1 2 1 | 1 1   11 ↓
                                                                 Adelante, señora García.

   3 2 | 2   22 ↑
8 All right, Miss Gonzalez.   èstàbyén |sènyòrítàgònşálèş↓   1 2 11 | 1 1   11 ↓
                                                                  Está bien, señorita González.

   2 3 2 | 22 ↑
9 Of course, Louise.   pòrsùpwestò |lwísà↓   1   2 1 | 11 ↓
                                                                 Por supuesto, Luisa.

  2 3   2 | 2 2 ↑
10 I can't now, Carmen.   àoranopwéđò |kármèn↓   1 2   11 | 1 1 ↓
                                                                Ahora no puedo, Carmen.

   2   31 | 2 2 ↑
11 Same here, thanks.   igwálmentè |gráşyàs↓   1   2 1 | 1 1 ↓
                                                                Igualmente, gracias.

    31 | 2 22 ↑
12 Yes, Mr. Molina.   sí |sènyórmòlínà↓   21 | 1 1 11 ↓
                                                                 Sí, señor Molina.

DIECINUEVE

UNIT 22   SPOKEN SPANISH

       31 | 2 2 ↑   21 | 1 1 ↓
13 No, thanks.   nó | grá$yàs↓   No, gracias.

      2 3 2 | 2 2↑   1 2 1 | 11 ↓
14 I'm sorry, John.   lósyentò | hwán↓   Lo siento, Juan.

     2   3 . 2   2 22 ↑   1 21 | 1 11 ↓
15 Don't mention it, Colonel.   dènadà | kòrònél↓   De nada, Coronel.

B. Discussion of pattern

    This is one of the really conspicuous errors in intonation frequently occurring when a common English pattern for sentence modifiers is imposed on Spanish pronunciation. A sentence like the greeting 'Good morning, Mr. Jones' pronounced pleasantly is likely to have the Mr. Jones part on a /222↑/ pattern, which sounds strange and inappropriate in a sentence like /bwénosdías | seŋyórmolína↑/, suggesting something akin to effeminacy in a man.

    The common Spanish pattern is /111↓/, as in /bwénosdías | seŋyórmolína↓/. This pattern exists in English, but it usually signals that the

                               2   3 1 | 1   11 ↓   2 | 1 ↓
speakers are from different status levels, as the business-like 'Góod mórning Miss Jónes ' a supervisor offers his secretary, or the compliant 'Yés, sír ' of a

                                                       2   1 | 1 1 ↓
soldier at attention to an officer. Or it may signal arrogance, as with the foreboding 'Côme hére, Jóhnny '.

    Students want to avoid inappropriate status signals, or the appearance of arrogance or disgust. But in doing so they often also avoid the /111↓/ on sentence modifiers, thus distorting a normal and frequent pattern.

SPOKEN SPANISH   UNIT

22.22   Replacement drills

A   múybyén↓ áwŋkèyo |ęstóyókùpáđisimá↓

1   _____ nósotros _____↓   múybyén↓ áwŋkènósotros |éstámòsǫkùpáđisimòs↓

2   _____ ókùpáđòs↓   múybyén↓ áwŋkènósotros |èstámòsǫkùpáđòs↓

3   _____ pórkè _____↓   múybyén↓ pórkènósotros |èstámòsǫkùpáđòs↓

4   _____ eⓁyas _____↓   múybyén↓ pórkeⓁyas |èstánǫkùpáđàs↓

5   _____ listàs↓   múybyén↓ pórkeⓁyas |èstánlistàs↓

6   _____ el _____↓   múybyén↓ pórkel |èstálistò↓

7   _____ dèsòkùpáđos↓   múybyén↓ pórkeⓁyos |èstándèsòkùpáđòs↓

_____

A   Muy bien, aunque yo estoy ocupadísima.

1   _____ , _____ nosotros _____ .   Muy bien, aunque nosotros estamos ocupadísimos.

2   _____ , _____ ocupados.   Muy bien, aunque nosotros estamos ocupados.

3   _____ , porque _____ .   Muy bien, porque nosotros estamos ocupados.

4   _____ , _____ ellas _____ .   Muy bien, porque ellas están ocupadas.

5   _____ , _____ listas.   Muy bien, porque ellas están listas.

6   _____ , _____ él _____ .   Muy bien, porque él está listo.

7   _____ , _____ desocupados.   Muy bien, porque ellos están desocupados.

VEINTIUNO   22.21

UNIT 22   SPOKEN SPANISH

B   yǫíbáǫyamárlạ |áórȧmízmȯ↓

1 _____ màŋyánȧ___↓   yǫíbáǫyamárla |màŋyánȧmízmȯ↓

2 nòsótros_____↓   nòsótros |íbamosạǫyamárla |màŋyánȧmízmȯ↓

3 _____aşerlọ_____↓   nòsótros |íbamosạşerlọ |màŋyánȧmízmȯ↓

4 ___pensábamos_____↓   nòsótros |pensábamosạşerlọ |màŋyánȧmízmȯ↓

5 _____àyér____↓   nòsótros |pensábamosạşerlọ |àyérmízmȯ↓

6 tu_____↓   tu |pensábasạşerlọ |àyérmízmȯ↓

7 _____arreglarlos_____↓   tu |pensábasạarreglarlos |àyérmízmȯ↓

_____

B   Yo iba a llamarla ahora mismo.

1 _____ mañana_____.   Yo iba a llamarla mañana mismo.

2 Nosotros _____.   Nosotros íbamos a llamarla mañana mismo.

3 _____ hacerlo _____.   Nosotros íbamos a hacerlo mañana mismo.

4 _____ pensábamos _____.   Nosotros pensábamos hacerlo mañana mismo.

5 _____ ayer_____.   Nosotros pensábamos hacerlo ayer mismo.

6 Tú _____.   Tú pensabas hacerlo ayer mismo.

7 _____ arreglarlos _____.   Tú pensabas arreglarlos ayer mismo.

SPOKEN SPANISH   UNIT 22

C   tyeṇga̱lgúmpróblemat

1   _____um_____t   tyeṇgumpróblemat

2   _____abyónt   tyeṇguṇabyónt

3   ay_____t   ayuṇabyónt

4   nọay_____t   nọayuṇabyónt

5   _____muchos_____t   nọay |muchosa̱byónest

6   _____mısyónest   nọay |muchazmısyónest

7   _____tyempot   nọay |muchotyempot

_____

C   ¿Tiene algún problema?

1   ¿_____un_____?   ¿Tiene un problema?

2   ¿_____ avión?   ¿Tiene un avión?

3   ¿Hay_____?   ¿Hay un avión?

4   ¿No hay_____?   ¿No hay un avión?

5   ¿_____muchos_____?   ¿No hay muchos aviones?

6   ¿_____misiones?   ¿No hay muchas misiones?

7   ¿_____ tiempo?   ¿No hay mucho tiempo?

VEINTITRES

jacobeligoodsons.com For Free Audio

UNIT 22   SPOKEN SPANISH

D   ésto |dèlóspréşyos |mèbwélbèlòká↓

1   _____ èstádòşùnìdoz _____ ↓   ésto |dèlósèstádòşùnìdoz |mèbwélbèlòká↓

2   àkéⓎo _____ ↓   àkéⓎo |dèlósèstádòşùnìdoz |mèbwélbèlòká↓

3   _____ lòkòs↓   àkéⓎo |dèlósèstádòşùnìdoz |nòzbwélbèlòkòs↓

4   _____ mérkàdo _____ ↓   àkéⓎo |dèlmèrkádo |nòzbwélbèlòkòs↓

5   àkél _____ ↓   àkél |dèlmèrkádo |nòzbwélbèlòkòs↓

6   _____ pàréşèn ____ ↓   àkéⓎoz |dèlmèrkádo |nòspàréşènlòkòs↓

7   _____ lòkàs↓   àkéⓎaz |dèlmèrkádo |nòspàréşènlòkàs↓

_____

D   Esto de los precios me vuelve loca.

1   _____ Estados Unidos _____ .   Esto de los Estados Unidos me vuelve loca.

2   Aquello _____ .   Aquello de los Estados Unidos me vuelve loca.

3   _____ locos.   Aquello de los Estados Unidos nos vuelve locos.

4   _____ mercado _____ .   Aquello del mercado nos vuelve locos.

5   Aquél _____ .   Aquél del mercado nos vuelve locos.

6   _____ parecen ____ .   Aquéllos del mercado nos parecen locos.

7   _____ locas.   Aquéllas del mercado nos parecen locas.

22.24   VEINTICUATRO

SPOKEN SPANISH   UNIT 22

E   lènsènyàré |dóndǥay |únómúybwénò↓

1   _____bonítà↓   lènsènyàré |dóndǥay |únàmúybonítà↓

2   _____únàz_____↓   lènsènyàré |dóndǥay |únàzmúybonítàs↓

3   _____tyénen_____↓   lènsènyàré |dóndetyénen |únàzmúybonítàs↓

4   _____kyénes_____↓   lènsènyàré |kyénestyénen |únàzmúybonítàs↓

5   _____ótròz____↓   lènsènyàré |kyénestyénen |ótròzmúybonítòs↓

6   _____málòs↓   lènsènyàré |kyénestyénen |ótròzmuymálòs↓

7   _____kwál_____↓   lènsènyàré |kwáltyénǥ |ótròzmuymálòs↓

E   Le enseñaré dónde hay uno muy bueno.

1   _____ bonita.   Le enseñaré dónde hay una muy bonita.

2   _____ unas_____.   Le enseñaré dónde hay unas muy bonitas.

3   _____ tienen _____.   Le enseñaré dónde tienen unas muy bonitas.

4   _____ quiénes _____.   Le enseñaré quiénes tienen unas muy bonitas.

5   _____ otros _____.   Le enseñaré quiénes tienen otros muy bonitos.

6   _____ malos .   Le enseñaré quiénes tienen otros muy malos.

7   _____ cuál_____.   Le enseñaré cuál tiene otros muy malos.

VEINTICINCO   22.25

UNIT 22   SPOKEN SPANISH

F   yó |ǫnméɖyạóra |mebístò↓   yó |ǫnméɖyạóra |mebáɳyò↓

1 _____ báɳyò↓   yó |ǫnúnạóra |mebáɳyò↓

2 _____ únạ _____ ↓   yó |ènúnạóra |memúɖò↓

3 _____ múɖò↓   yó |ǫnúndía |memúɖò↓

4 _____ día _____ ↓   yó |ǫnúnòzɖíaz |memúɖò↓

5 _____ únòz _____ ↓   yó |ǫnúnmòmento |memúɖò↓

6 _____ mòmentò _____ ↓   yó |ǫnkwálkyermomento |memúɖò↓

7 _____ kwálkyeř _____ ↓

F   Yo en media hora me visto.

1 _____ baño.   Yo en media hora me baño.

2 _____ una _____ .   Yo en una hora me baño.

3 _____ mudo.   Yo en una hora me mudo.

4 _____ día _____ .   Yo en un día me mudo.

5 _____ unos _____ .   Yo en unos días me mudo.

6 _____ momento _____ .   Yo en un momento me mudo.

7 _____ cualquier _____ .   Yo en cualquier momento me mudo.

22.26   VEINTISEIS

SPOKEN SPANISH   UNIT 22

22.23   Variation drills

A   kómosigetóḍo|pòrsukásà|sènyórà↓   ¿Cómo sigue todo por su casa, señora?

   1 How's everything going around your   kósosigetóḍo|pòrsutyéndà|sènyórfwéntès↓   ¿Cómo sigue todo por su tienda, señor
      store, Mr. Fuentes?   Fuentes?

   2 How's your husband getting along,   kómosíge|sγespósò|màríà↓   ¿Cómo sigue su esposo, María?
      Mary?

   3 How's your family getting along,   kómosíge|súfamílyà|mòlínà↓   ¿Cómo sigue su familia, Molina?
      Molina?

   4 How're things getting along, John?   kómosígen|laskósàs|hwán↓   ¿Cómo siguen las cosas, Juan?

   5 How're things going, John?   kómobán|laskósàs|hwán↓   ¿Cómo van las cosas, Juan?

   6 How's everything going, Harris?   kómobatóḍò|hárris↓   ¿Cómo va todo, Harris?

   7 How's that going?   kómobaésò↓   ¿Cómo va eso?

B   á|sí↓ ésọ|èṣálgòtèrriblè↓   ¡Ah, sí! Eso es algo terrible.

   1 Oh, yes. That's something terrific.   á|sí↓ ésọ|èṣálgòmàgnifikò↓   ¡Ah, sí! Eso es algo magnífico.

   2 Oh, yes. That's something very   á|sí↓ ésọ|èṣálgòmuybarátò↓   ¡Ah, sí! Eso es algo muy barato.
      inexpensive.

VEINTISIETE   22.27

UNIT 22　　　　　　　　　　　　　　　　　　　　　　　　　　　　　　　　SPOKEN SPANISH

3 Oh, sure. That's something very pretty. — á|kláró↓ ésǫ|ès̩álgòmuybonítò↓ — ¡Ah, claro! Eso es algo muy bonito.

4 Oh, sure. That's something very good. — á|kláró↓ ésǫ|ès̩álgòmuybwénò↓ — ¡Ah, claro! Eso es algo muy bueno.

5 Yes, of course. That's not bad at all. — sí|kláró↓ éso|nǫéznadamáló↓ — ¡Sí, claro! Eso no es nada malo.

6 Nonsense. That's nothing. — kebá↓ éso|nǫéznadá↓ — ¡Qué va! Eso no es nada.

7 On the contrary. That's not much. — àlkòntráryó↓ éso|nǫezmúchò↓ — ¡Al contrario! Eso no es mucho.

C　sikyéretdèhamoz|lòdèlástyéndas|páràlàtardè↓ — Si quiere, dejamos lo de las tiendas para la tarde.

1 If you want, we can leave the office (matter) for this afternoon. — sikyéretdèhamoz|lòdèlạófiṣina|páràlátardè↓ — Si quiere, dejamos lo de la oficina para la tarde.

2 If you want, we can leave the golf (date) for Saturday. — sikyéretdèhamoz|lòdèlgólf|párạèlsabádò↓ — Si quiere, dejamos lo del golf para el sábado.

3 If you want, we can leave the Spanish (session) for Monday. — sikyéretdèhamoz|lòdèlèspàŋyol|párạèⓛlunès↓ — Si quiere, dejamos lo del español para el lunes.

4 If you want, we can leave today's (work) for Tuesday. — sikyéretdèhamoz|lòdgoy|párạèlmartés↓ — Si quiere, dejamos lo de hoy para el martes.

5 If you want, we can leave tomorrow's (appointment) for Wednesday. — sikyéretdèhamoz|lòdèmáŋyana|párạèl myerkólès↓ — Si quiere, dejamos lo de mañana para el miércoles.

22.28　　　　　　　　　　　　　　　　　　　　　　　　　　　　　　　　VEINTIOCHO

SPOKEN SPANISH   UNIT 22

6 If you want, we can leave everything for Thursday.

síkyeré↑dèhámóstodo|párąėlhwebės↓

Si quiere, dejamos todo para el jueves.

7 If you want, we can leave everything for Friday.

síkyeré↑dèhámóstodo|párąėlbyérnès↓

Si quiere, dejamos todo para el viernes.

D bámosąalmerkádǫ|áórà↓

Vamos al mercado ahora.

1 Let's go to the restaurant now.

bámosąalrrestorán|áórà↓

Vamos al restorán ahora.

2 Let's go to the park now.

bámosąalpárkę|áórà↓

Vamos al parque ahora.

3 Let's go to the country tomorrow.

bámosąalkámpò|màŋyánà↓

Vamos al campo mañana.

4 Let's go to the house soon.

bámosąalakásà|próntò↓

Vamos a la casa pronto.

5 Let's go to (the) church Sunday.

bámosąaląiglésyą|èldòmíŋgò↓

Vamos a la iglesia el domingo.

6 Let's go to mass Sunday.

bámosąamísą|èldòmíŋgò↓

Vamos a misa el domingo.

7 Let's go for a stroll this afternoon.

bámosąapasęár|èstàtárdè↓

Vamos a pasear esta tarde.

E ėntónsę̀s↓pweɗę|akompaŋyárme↑

Entonces, ¿puede acompañarme?

1 Then, can you wait on me?

ėntónsę̀s↓pweɗę|atendérme↑

Entonces, ¿puede atenderme?

2 Then, can you let me know?

ėntónsę̀s↓pweɗę|abisárme↑

Entonces, ¿puede avisarme?

VEINTINUEVE   22.29

jacobeligoodsons.com For Free Audio

UNIT 22   SPOKEN SPANISH

3 Then, can you introduce me?   èntonşès↓pwéde |présentárme↑   Entonces, ¿puede presentarme?

4 Afterwards, can you take me?   dèspwés↓pwéde |ǫyebárme↑   Después, ¿puede llevarme?

5 Afterwards, can you bring me?   dèspwés↓pwéde |traérme↑   Después, ¿puede traerme?

6 Now, can you receive me?   àorá↓pwéde |rreşíbirme↑   Ahora, ¿puede recibirme?

7 Now, can you hear me?   àorá↓pwédeǫoírme↑   Ahora, ¿puede oírme?

F àkęora |pásoporustéd↓   ¿A qué hora paso por Ud.?

1 What time shall I call by for her?   àkęora |pásopor€ǫyá↓   ¿A qué hora paso por ella?

2 What time shall I come back for you?   àkęora |bwélboporustéd↓   ¿A qué hora vuelvo por Ud.?

3 What time shall I come back for the things?   àkęora |bwélboporlaskósàs↓   ¿A qué hora vuelvo por las cosas?

4 What time shall I come back for the checks?   àkęora |bwélboporloschékès↓   ¿A qué hora vuelvo por los cheques?

5 What time shall I go up for the suitcases?   àkęora |súboporlazmalétàs↓   ¿A qué hora subo por las maletas?

6 When will you come by for the provisions?   kwàndopása |porlasprobisyónès↓   ¿Cuándo pasa por las provisiones?

7 When will you come back for the order?   kwàndobwélbe |porlǫórdèn↓   ¿Cuándo vuelve por la orden?

jacobeligoodsons.com For Free Audio

SPOKEN SPANISH   UNIT 22

22.24   Review drill — Theme class in past I tense forms

1 They came down, but they didn't go up.   báharom↑péronosubyéron↓   Bajaron, pero no subieron.

2 I came down, but I didn't go up.   báhe↑péronosubí↓   Bajé, pero no subí.

3 He called, but he didn't go out.   Oyámo↑péronosalyó↓   Llamó, pero no salió.

4 I called, but I didn't go out.   Oyáme↑péronosalí↓   Llamé, pero no salí.

5 We called, but we didn't go out.   Oyámamos↑péronosalímos↓   Llamamos, pero no salimos.

6 She washed, but she didn't sweep.   lábo↑péronobarryó↓   Lavó, pero no barrió.

7 I washed, but I didn't sweep.   lábe↑péronobarrí↓   Lavé, pero no barrí.

8 We washed, but we didn't sweep.   lábamos↑péronobarrímos↓   Lavamos, pero no barrimos.

9 I worked, but I didn't live there.   trábáhe↑péronobibí|aOyí↓   Trabajé, pero no viví allí.

10 We worked, but we didn't live there.   trábáhamos↑péronobibímós|aOyí↓ Trabajamos, pero no vivimos allí.

11 They worked, but they didn't live there.   trábáharom↑péronobibyéron|aOyí↓ Trabajaron, pero no vivieron allí.

TREINTA Y UNO   22.31

UNIT 22   SPOKEN SPANISH

22.3   CONVERSATION STIMULUS

NARRATIVE 1

1 Today's Friday. The Harrises have   óyezbyérnès↓ lòsharrìs↑tyénénkèir| Hoy es viernes. Los Harris tienen que
  to go to the market.   àlmerkáḋò↓   ir al mercado.

2 Bob's very sorry, but he can't go with   bòb|lòsyéntèmúchò↓ pérònòpwèḋèir|kòn   Bob lo siente mucho, pero no puede ir con
  his wife.   sụespósà↓   su esposa.

3 He always finds some excuse.   élsyémprènkwèntrạ|àlgúmpretéstó↓   El siempre encuentra algún pretexto.

4 It isn't really an excuse.   nọezrrẹalmèntẹ|úmprètéstó↓   No es realmente un pretexto.

5 It's just that in this country men don't   èskènẹstepaìs|àlósọmbrez|nòlezgústạir| Es que en este país, a los hombres no les
  like to go to the market.   àlmerkáḋò↓   gusta ir al mercado.

6 Bob drives Jean crazy with his ideas   bòb|bwélbèlòkàyìŋ|kònsùsiḋèas|ì   Bob vuelve loca a Jean con sus ideas y
  and excuses.   pretéstòs↓   pretextos.

DIALOG 1

Jean, dígale a Bob que hoy es viernes,   óyezbyérnès↓ ténémòskèir|àlmèrkáḋò↓   Jean: Hoy es viernes, tenemos que ir al
  que tienen que ir al mercado.   mercado.

Bob, contéstele que lo siente mucho,   lòsyéntòmúchò↓péròyó|nòpwèḋọ|ìrkòntígò↓   Bob: Lo siento mucho, pero yo no puedo
  pero Ud. no puede ir con ella.   ir contigo.

jacobeligoodsons.com For Free Audio

22.32   TREINTA Y DOS

SPOKEN SPANISH   UNIT 22

Jean, dígale que él siempre encuentra algún
pretexto.

túsyempreŋkwéntras |algumpretéstó↓

Jean: Tú siempre encuentras algún
      pretexto.

Bob, dígale que no es pretexto. Que en este
país a los hombres no les gusta ir al
mercado.

noespretéstó↓ èskénestepaís |álósọmbrez |
nolezgustạir |almerkádó↓

Bob: No es pretexto. Es que en este país
     a los hombres no les gusta ir al
     mercado.

Jean, dígale que él la vuelve loca con sus
ideas y pretextos.

tu |mèbwélbèzlokà |kòntúsịdéàs |iprètéstòs↓

Jean: Tú me vuelves loca con tus ideas
      y pretextos.

NARRATIVE 2

1 Jean calls Carmen up.

yinọ̀yamakármèn↓

Jean llama a Carmen.

2 She wants to ask her if she's going to
   be busy this morning.

kyérepreguntárle |sibáẹstáròkúpaḍạ |
éstàmàɲyánà↓

Quiere preguntarle si va a estar ocupada
esta mañana.

3 Carmen doesn't have to work today. She
   asks Jean if she can be of any help.

karmen |notyéne |kètràbàharóy↓ eọ̀ya |
lèprèguntayin |sipwéḍẹàyúḍarlenálgò↓

Carmen no tiene que trabajar hoy. Ella le
pregunta a Jean si puede ayudarle en algo.

4 Jean wants to know if she can accompany
   her to the market.

yiŋkyeresaber |sipwéḍẹakompaɲyarlạ |
almerkáḍò↓

Jean quiere saber si puede acompañarla al
mercado.

5 Carmen says she'll be delighted.

karmendiṣe |kèŋkàntaḍà↓

Carmen dice que encantada.

6 And that she's ready any time.

ikèstálistạ |èŋkwàlkyermoméntò↓

Y que está lista en cualquier momento.

7 Then Jean'll go by for her right away.

èntonṣez |yim |bápàsárpòreọ̀yạensegíḍà↓

Entonces Jean va a pasar por ella en
seguida.

TREINTA Y TRES   22.33

jacobeligoodsons.com For Free Audio

UNIT 22   *DIALOG 2*   SPOKEN SPANISH

Jean, pregúntele a Carmen si va a estar
ocupada esta mañana.

ùsteḍ |bầẹstáròkùpáḍạ |èstamaṇyána |
karmen↑

Jean: ¿Ud. va a estar ocupada esta
      mañana, Carmen?

Carmen, contéstele que no, que hoy no tiene
que trabajar. Que si puede ayudarle en
algo.

nó↓ oy |noteŋgoketrabahár↓ pweḍọ
ayuḍarlẹ |enạlgo↑

Carmen: No, hoy no tengo que trabajar.
        ¿Puedo ayudarle en algo?

Jean, contéstele que sí, gracias. Pregúntele si quiere hacerle un gran favor.

sí |gráşyàs↓ kyérẹạşẹrmẹ |uŋgrámfabór↑

Jean: Sí, gracias. ¿Quiere hacerme un
     gran favor?

Carmen, contéstele que encantada, que qué
es.

éŋkàntáḍà↓ ké |és↓

Carmen: Encantada, ¿qué es?

Jean, dígale que acompañarla al mercado.

àkómpáṇyarmẹ |àlmérkáḍó↓

Jean: Acompañarme al mercado.

Carmen, dígale que por supuesto, que Ud.
está lista en cualquier momento.

pòrsúpwéstó↓ yọẹstóylìstạ |èŋkwálkyér
moméntó↓

Carmen: Por supuesto. Yo estoy lista en
        cualquier momento.

Jean, dígale que entonces Ud. pasa por
ella en seguida.

èntónşes |pásoporusteḍ |ensegíḍà↓

Jean: Entonces, paso por Ud. en seguida.

NARRATIVE 3

1 Jean always goes to a market (which is)
near the Embassy.

yín |syémprebạ̀ụnmerkáḍo |kèstáşẹrkaḍe
lạembaháḍà↓

Jean siempre va a un mercado que está
cerca de la Embajada.

2 All her American friends go there.

tóḍas |súsạ̀mìgas |àmèrikánaz |bánáí↓

Todas sus amigas americanas van ahí.

22.34   TREINTA Y CUATRO

SPOKEN SPANISH   UNIT 22

3 That's why (for that reason) prices are   pòresarraşon |lòspreşyos |sóntanterríblès | Por esa razón los precios son tan terribles
   so terrible in that market.   ėnѓsèmèrkáɗò↓   en ese mercado.

4 But in the other markets Jean never finds   perǫ |ènlòs̩otrozmerkaɗoz↑nuŋkạ   Pero en los otros mercados nunca encuentra
   what she wants.   eŋkwentra |lokekyérė↓   lo que quiere.

5 Behind Carmen's house there's one where   dètraz |ɗèlàkàsaɗekármen |áyunȯ |ɗóndȯ   Detrás de la casa de Carmen hay uno donde
   they have everything, and it's very cheap.   tyenendetóɗò↓ ˌ̩èzmuybarátò↓   tienen de todo, y es muy barato.

                                                         DIALOG 3

Carmen, pregúntele a Jean que a cuál   ȧkwalmerkaɗo |baụsteɗsyémprė↓   Carmen: ¿A cuál mercado va Ud. siempre?
   mercado va ella siempre.

Jean, contéstele que a uno que está cerca   ạunȯ |kèstạşerkaɗelạembaháɗȧ↓   Jean: A uno que está cerca de la Embajada.
   de la Embajada. Que ahí van todas sus   ȧɪ |bántoɗaz |misȧmɪgas̩amerikánȧs↓   Ahí van todas mis amigas americanas.
   amigas americanas.

Carmen, dígale que por esa razón son tan   pòresarrașon |sóntanterrɪblèz |lòs   Carmen: Por esa razón son tan terribles los
   terribles los precios en ese mercado.   préşyòs |ėnѓsèmèrkáɗò↓   precios en ese mercado.

Jean, dígale que es que en los otros nunca   éskėnlòs̩otroz |nuŋkạeŋkwéntrò |lòkȯ   Jean: Es que en los otros nunca encuentro
   encuentra Ud. lo que quiere.   kyérò↓   lo que quiero.

Carmen, dígale que detrás de su casa hay   dètrazɗemikasạ |áyunȯ |ɗóndȯtyénen   Carmen: Detrás de mi casa hay uno donde
   uno donde tienen de todo y es muy barato.   detóɗò↓ ˌ̩èzmuybarátò↓   tienen de todo y es muy barato.

TREINTA Y CINCO   22.35

UNIT 22   SPOKEN SPANISH

22.4   READINGS

22.40   List of cognate loan words

alarmada (alarmar)   àlármàdá↓ àlármár↓

los platos   lòs—platòs↓

probablemente   pròbáblèmentè↓

las ratas   làz—rratás↓

observó (observar)   òbsérbo↓ òbsèrbár↓

la importancia   là—impòrtançyà↓

la impaciencia   là—impàçyençyà↓

investigar   imbèstigár↓

enormes   énormés↓

la televisión   là—tèlèbisyòn↓

inocentes   inòçentès↓

las voces   làz—boçès↓

inmediatamente   inmédyátàmentè↓

preciosas   prèçyosás↓

las pijamas   làs—piyamás↓

divinas   dibinás↓

la causa   là—káwsá↓

la conmoción   là—kònmóçyòn↓

22.36   TREINTA Y SEIS

SPOKEN SPANISH   UNIT 22

el respeto	èl—rrèspetó↓
la atención	lạ—àtènṣyon↓
indicaba (indicar)	indikabá↓ indikar↓
la educación	lạ—èdúkáṣyon↓
insistido (insistir)	insistidó↓ insistir↓

22.41   Reading selection

Jane and Ruth

Eran casi las diez de la noche y estaban todos muy tranquilos conversando en la sala cuando se oyó un ruido en la cocina.

—¿Qué fue ese ruido?—preguntó Virginia un poco alarmada. —Parece como que se cayeron unos platos.

—Probablemente son las ratas— observó su esposo en tono de broma y sin darle más importancia al ruido.

—¡Ratas....! Tú siempre dices lo mismo cada vez que oyes un ruido—exclamó Virginia con impaciencia. ¿Recuerdas la noche que no quisiste levantarte a investigar qué eran aquellos ruidos en la sala porque tú decías que eran las ratas, recuerdas? Deben haber sido unas ratas enormes porque nos dejaron sin la televisión de trescientos dólares que acabábamos de comprar.

Fred quiso decir algo pero para no discutir con su mujer enfrente de los señores Fuentes se levantó y fue a la cocina a ver qué era el tal ruido. Casi en seguida volvió y dijo:

—Puedes estar tranquila, mujer, no te preocupes. Eran dos ratitas muy bonitas llamadas Jane y Ruth que estaban en la cocina y se les cayeron unos platos que estaban lavando.

—¿Qué están haciendo esas niñas en la cocina?, ¿por qué no están acostadas? ¡Jane y Ruth!!!....

—Yes, mother....? —contestaron dos inocentes y tímidas voces desde la cocina.

—¡Vengan acá inmediatamente!

Dos preciosas niñas en pijamas entraron tímidamente a la sala; la más pequeña, de unos seis años, detrás de la otra que podía tener ocho, más o menos.

TREINTA Y SIETE   22.37

UNIT 22   SPOKEN SPANISH

—Ah, éstas son las dos hijitas de que me hablaban—exclamó la señora de Fuentes.—Mira, Ricardo, qué divinas son.

—Sí, aquí tienen ustedes la causa de toda esa conmoción que oímos en la cocina—dijo Fred— La más grande es Jane y esta otra ratita es Ruth. Niñas, saluden a los señores. Ellos son nuestro vecinos y tienen unas niñitas muy bonitas. Uno de estos días vamos a ir todos a su casa a conocerlas.

Las dos saludaron con mucho respeto y por varios minutos conversaron en español con los señores Fuentes, poniendo mucha atención a todo lo que ellos les decían y contestando a todas las preguntas que les hacían, en forma tal que indicaba la buena educación que habían recibido de sus padres. El español lo hablaban tan bien como su madre, quien desde que eran muy pequeñas había insistido en enseñárselo.

22.42   Response drill

   1 ¿Dónde se oyó el ruido?

   2 ¿Qué hora era cuando eso pasó?

   3 ¿Dónde estaban los señores?

   4 ¿Quién se puso nervioso con el ruido, Fred o su esposa?

   5 ¿Qué dijo él que era la causa del ruido?

   6 ¿Qué dice él cada vez que oye un ruido?

   7 ¿Qué pasó la noche que él no quiso levantarse a investigar?

   8 ¿Cuánto costaba la televisión que acababan de comprar?

   9 ¿Cuál fue la causa del ruido en la cocina esta vez?

  10 ¿Cuál era el nombre de las niñas?

  11 ¿Cuántos años tenían?

  12 ¿Cómo estaban vestidas?

  13 ¿Qué tal hablaban el español?

  14 ¿Desde cuándo lo hablaban?

  15 ¿Quién se lo enseñó a ellas?

22.38   TREINTA Y OCHO

jacobeligoodsons.com For Free Audio

SPOKEN SPANISH   UNIT 23

23.1   BASIC SENTENCES.   Shopping at the market.

        Carmen and Mrs. Harris are at the market.

ENGLISH SPELLING   AID TO LISTENING   SPANISH SPELLING

Carmen   *Carmen*
    What shall we buy?   kékomprámös |sènyórà↓   ¿Qué compramos, señora?

        (I) bring (to bring)   tráygò↓ tràér↓   traigo (traer)

Mrs. Harris   *Sra. Harris*
    I have the list here.   àkitráygo |lalístà↓   Aquí traigo la lista.

        the meat   là—kárnè↓   la carne

    Meat, first.   làkárnè |primérò↓   La carne primero.

        the stand, booth   èl—pwéstò↓   el puesto
        (I) know (to know, be acquainted with) kònóşkò↓ kònóşér↓   conozco (conocer)

Carmen   *Carmen*
    Let's go to a booth that I'm familiar with. bámoş̧aumpwéstó |kèyokonóşkò↓   Vamos a un puesto que yo conozco.

        to sell   bèndér↓   vender
        the fish   èl—pèskaðò↓   el pescado

    Near there they sell fish, too.   şèrkaðęaⱥyi |béndèmpèskaðò |tàmbyén↓   Cerca de allí venden pescado, también.

UNO   23.1

jacobeligoodsons.com For Free Audio

UNIT 23   SPOKEN SPANISH

the green (leafy vegetable)   là—bèrđurà↓   la verdura

fresh   frèskò↓   fresco

how very (fresh)   kè... tàn (frέskàs)↓   que...tan (frescas)

Mrs. Harris   mire|keberrduras|tamfrέskàs↓   Sra. Harris
Look how fresh the green vegetables are! ¡Mire qué verduras tan frescas!

Carmen   nótyenekekómprar↑   Carmen
Don't you have to buy (any)? (1)   ¿No tiene que comprar?

sufficient, enough   súfisyentè↓   suficiente

Mrs. Harris   óynó↓ téngo|súfisyentenkásà↓   Sra. Harris
Not today. I have plenty at home.   Hoy no. Tengo suficiente en casa.

the fruit   là—frutà↓   la fruta

Carmen   ìfrútas↑   Carmen
Fruits, too?   ¿Y frutas?

neither   tàmpokò↓   tampoco

Mrs. Harris   nó↓ tàmpokò↓   Sra. Harris
(I don't need any of them), either.   No, tampoco.

the dozen   là—đòṣènà↓   la docena

the egg   èl—ẏebò↓   el huevo

I need a dozen eggs. (2)   nèṣèsìto|unadòṣena|đeẇébòs↓   Necesito una docena de huevos.

23.2   DOS

SPOKEN SPANISH   UNIT 23

(I) put (to put, place)   póngó↓ ponér↓   pongo (poner)

But where will I put them?   péró |dóndelospóngó↓   ¿Pero dónde los pongo?

the bag, sack   lá‑bólsá↓   la bolsa

Carmen   Carmen
They'll fit here in my bag.   ákı |ęnmìbólsà |kábèn↓   Aquí en mi bolsa caben.

(I) hear (to hear)   óygó↓ óır↓   oigo (oír)

to sing   kàntár↓   cantar

Mrs. Harris   Sra. Harris
I hear them singing over there. What is it? (3)   óygó |kèkántàm |pòráí↓ keés↓   Oigo que cantan por ahí ¿qué es?

the blind (man)   èl‑ęyegó↓   el ciego

Carmen   Carmen
It must be a blind beggar. (4)   débeserunęyégò↓   Debe ser un ciego....

What else do you need to buy?   kémáz |nèęèsìtakomprár↓   ¿Qué más necesita comprar?

the bread   èl‑pán↓   el pan

the butter   là‑màntèkıɥà↓   la mantequilla

the salt   là‑sál↓   la sal

the pepper   là‑pımyéntà↓   la pimienta

Mrs. Harris   Sra. Harris
Bread, butter, salt and pepper.   pan↑màntékıɥa↑sálıpımyéntà↓   Pan, mantequilla, sal y pimienta.

TRES   23.3

UNIT 23   SPOKEN SPANISH

the milk   là—léchè↓   la leche

Carmen   ilechet   *Carmen*
And milk?   ¿Y leche?

the milkman   èl—lècheró↓   el lechero

Mrs. Harris   no↓ mèlǎɥeba̧|eⱲlechéró↓   *Sra. Harris*
No, the milkman brings it to me.   No, me la lleva el lechero.

the food, meal   là—kòmidà↓   la comida

Carmen   àpròpósitò↓ a̧ȩlakomida̧|ustea̧mizmat   *Carmen*
By the way. Do you do your own cooking?   A propósito, ¿hace la comida usted
                                                                          misma?

(I) do, make (to do, make)   agó↓ á̧ȩr↓   hago (hacer)

(I) say (to say)   digó↓ dȩ̀ṣír↓   digo (decir)

the nuisance   là—látà↓   la lata

Mrs. Harris   sí↓ yólágo̧|áwŋkèlèdigo|késu̧nalátà↓   *Sra. Harris*
Yes, I do it even though I must say it's a chore.   Sí, yo la hago, aunque le digo que es una
                                                                          lata.

23.10   Notes on the basic sentences

    (1) The verb /komprár/ *comprar*, like its English counterpart *buy*, can and usually does take an object. But in Spanish, unlike English, if the object has already been mentioned in the immediate context of the utterance, the object need not be repeated in the form of an empty object-substitute like *any* as in the English translation of this sentence.

    (2) Note that *dozen* is a modifier in English — *a dozen eggs* — but a noun in Spanish — *a dozen of eggs*.

    (3) There is no close structural parallel between Spanish and English as regards the use of subordination of clause constructions: here 'I hear them singing' is equated with 'I hear that they are singing.'

    (4) Note the meaning of 'It must be...', which is, of course, 'It probably is...'. The Spanish, literally 'It ought to be...' or 'It must be...', has exactly the same probability notion in it.

23.4   jacobeligoodsons.com For Free Audio   CUATRO

SPOKEN SPANISH   UNIT 23

23.2   DRILLS AND GRAMMAR

23.21   Pattern drills

23.21.1   Present tense irregular verbs — velar stem extensions

    A. Presentation of pattern

ILLUSTRATIONS

I'm very grateful to you.	1	sélọàgrádeşkomúchò↓	Se lo *agradezco* mucho.
_____	2	bamós |aúmpwésto |kèyókonóşkò↓	Vamos a un puesto que yo *conozco*.
I look like (to look like)		mé—pàreşkò↓ pàrèşersè↓	me parezco (parecerse)
I look like my sister.	3	mèpàreşkọ |amįermánà↓	Me *parezco* a mi hermana.
I belong to the Air Force.	4	pértènęşkọ |àlàfwerşaérgà↓	*Pertenezco* a la Fuerza Aérea.
I don't translate very well.	5	nótraďúşkò |múybyén↓	No *traduzco* muy bien.
I'm not worth anything with this headache.	6	nóbàlgonáďà |kònéstèďòlór |ďèkàbéşà↓	No *valgo* nada con este dolor de cabeza.
_____	7	pérò |ďóndelospóŋgò↓	Pero, ¿dónde los *pongo*?
I go out a lot.	8	yósàlgomúchò↓	Yo *salgo* mucho.

CINCO   23.5

UNIT 23   SPOKEN SPANISH

EXTRAPOLATION

Velar stem extension	—k—	—g—
Sample verb	konoṣ —ér	sal —ír
sg 1	konóṣ—k—o	sál—g—o
2 fam	konóṣ —es	sál —es
2-3	konóṣ —e	sál —e
pl 1	konoṣ —émos	sal —ímos
2-3	konóṣ —en	sál —en

NOTES

a. In certain irregular verbs a velar sound (/k/ ∝ /g/) appears between the stem and ending of 1 sg forms.

b. In these verbs, the velar sound /k/ follows a stem final voiceless sound (usually /ṣ/), and the velar
    sound /g/ follows a stem-final voiced sound (usually /n, l/).

23.6

jacobeligoodsons.com For Free Audio

SEIS

SPOKEN SPANISH

UNIT 23

23.21.11 Substitution drills — Person-number substitution

1 yó|nókonoşkọamıbeşínò↓

élténye͝nte _____↓

misảmıgoz _____↓

lwısa _____↓

éĺ yaz _____↓

nókonoşẹ|amıbeşínò↓

nókonoşen|amıbeşínò↓

nókonoşẹ|amıbeşínò↓

nókonoşen|amıbeşínò↓

---

1 *Yo* no conozco a mi vecino.

El teniente _____.

Mis amigos _____.

Luisa _____.

Ellas _____.

No conoce a mi vecino.

No conocen a mi vecino.

No conoce a mi vecino.

No conocen a mi vecino.

SIETE

jacobeligoodsons.com For Free Audio

UNIT 23   SPOKEN SPANISH

2 yotraɖuşko |ɖébeşeŋkwándò↓
   misihos_____↓   trắɖuşen |ɖébeşeŋkwándò↓
   làsèŋyora_____↓   trắɖuşe |ɖébeşeŋkwándò↓
   èỵàỵo_____↓   trắɖúşɪmoz |ɖébeşeŋkwándò↓
   èlkòrònel_____↓   trắɖuşe |ɖébeşeŋkwándò↓

3 nósotros |kónóşemoşeşapártè↓
   yo_____↓   kònòşkọeşapártè↓
   èlchòfer_____↓   kònòşeşapártè↓
   lòsàmèrikanos_____↓   kònòşenẹeşapártè↓
   karmeŋ_____↓   kònòşeşapártè↓

_____

2 *Yo* traduzco de vez en cuando.
   Mis hijos _____.   Traducen de vez en cuando.
   La señora _____.   Traduce de vez en cuando.
   Ella y yo_____.   Traducimos de vez en cuando.
   El coronel_____.   Traduce de vez en cuando.

3 *Nosotros* conocemos esa parte.
   Yo _____.   Conozco esa parte.
   El chofer _____.   Conoce esa parte.
   Los americanos _____.   Conocen esa parte.
   Carmen _____.   Conoce esa parte.

23.8   OCHO

SPOKEN SPANISH   UNIT 23

4 yónuŋkasálgò↓
   làmúchacha___↓   nuŋkasálè↓
   lwisaiyò___↓   nuŋkasalímòs↓
   lòzmúchachoz___↓   nuŋkasálén↓
   èltènyènte___↓   nuŋkasálè↓

5 èčyos|syèmpresalèntárdè↓
   yó___↓   syèmpresalgotárdè↓
   làsèkrétarya___↓   syèmpresaletárdè↓
   lò(s)sènyores___↓   syèmpresalèntárdè↓
   anaiyò___↓   syèmpre|salimostárdè↓

_____

4 *Yo* nunca salgo.
   La muchacha___.   Nunca sale.
   Luisa y yo___.   Nunca salimos.
   Los muchachos___.   Nunca salen.
   El teniente___.   Nunca sale.

5 *Ellos* siempre salen tarde.
   Yo___.   Siempre salgo tarde.
   La secretaria___.   Siempre sale tarde.
   Las señoras___.   Siempre salen tarde.
   Ana y yo___.   Siempre salimos tarde.

NUEVE

UNIT 23   SPOKEN SPANISH

6 yonopóngọ|èlmàlètinẹnlamésȧ↓   nopónen|èlmàlètinẹnlamésȧ↓
   lósẹstúdyantez_____↓   nopónemos|èlmàlètinẹnlamésȧ↓
   nósotroz_____↓   nopónẹ|èlmàlètinẹnlamésȧ↓
   èlsèṇyor_____↓   nopónen|èlmàlètinẹnlamésȧ↓
   éọyaz_____↓

7 el|nòpóne|nacaọyí↓   nòpóngò|nacaọyí↓
   yo_____↓   nòpónè|nacaọyí↓
   làsèṇyora_____↓   nòpónémòz|nacaọyí↓
   làsèṇyorạiyó_____↓   nòpóné(n)|nacaọyí↓
   éọyaz_____↓

---

6 *Yo* no pongo el maletín en la mesa.   No ponen el maletín en la mesa.
   Los estudiantes _____.   No ponemos el maletín en la mesa.
   Nosotros _____.   No pone el maletín en la mesa.
   El señor _____.   No ponen el maletín en la mesa.
   Ellas _____.

7 *El* no pone nada allí.   No pongo nada allí.
   Yo_____.   No pone nada allí.
   La señora _____.   No ponemos nada allí.
   La señora y yo _____.   No ponen nada allí.
   Ellas_____.

23.10   DIEZ
jacobeligoodsons.com For Free Audio

SPOKEN SPANISH   UNIT 23

23.21.11   Tense substitution

1 yokonoşı |àlsèŋyòrmolínà↓   yokonoşkǫ |àlsèŋyórmolínà↓

2 nósotroz |nokonoşimos |alamorénà↓   nósotroz |nokonoşemos |alamorénà↓

3 eltraduhǫe(ļ)líbró↓   eltraduşe(ļ)líbró↓

4 e(ļ)yoz |lótràdúherompriméró↓   e(ļ)yoz |lótràduşempriméró↓

5 yosalí |alazdóşè↓   yosálgǫ |alazdóşè↓

6 nósotroz |nosalímosko(ŋ)nádyè↓   nósotroz |nosalímosko(ŋ)nádyè↓

7 yopusę |e(ļ)líbrǫaí↓   yopóngǫ |e(ļ)líbrǫaí↓

8 e(ļ)yoz |lópúsyèronenlamésà↓   e(ļ)yoz |lóponenenlamésà↓

9 el |nópusolaféchà↓   el |nóponelaféchà↓

---

1 Yo *conocí* al Sr. Molina.   Yo conozco al Sr. Molina.

2 Nosotros no *conocimos* a la morena.   Nosotros no conocemos a la morena.

3 El *tradujo* el libro.   El traduce el libro.

4 Ellos lo *tradujeron* primero.   Ellos lo traducen primero.

5 Yo *salí* a las doce.   Yo salgo a las doce.

6 Nosotros no *salimos* con nadie.   Nosotros no salimos con nadie.

7 Yo *puse* el libro ahí.   Yo pongo el libro ahí.

8 Ellos lo *pusieron* en la mesa.   Ellos lo ponen en la mesa.

9 El no *puso* la fecha.   El no pone la fecha.

ONCE

UNIT 23   SPOKEN SPANISH

23.21.12 Response drill

     1   tráđuʂeusteđ |byénʇomál↓   tráđuʂkobyén↓

     2   tráđuʂenustedez |byénʇomál↓   tráđúʂımozbyén↓

     3   tráđuʂeneʎyoz |byénʇomál↓   tráđuʂembyén↓

[ènlàmésá↓]   4   dondeponeusteđ |lozlíbròs↓   lóspoŋgọenlamésá↓

[ènlàmésá↓]   5   dondeponél |lozlíbròs↓   lósponenlamésá↓

[lózlíbròs↓]   6   keponeneʎyos |enlàmésá↓   ponènlozlíbròs↓

---

     1   ¿Traduce Ud. bien o mal?   Traduzco bien.

     2   ¿Traducen Uds. bien o mal?   Traducimos bien.

     3   ¿Traducen ellos bien o mal?   Traducen bien.

(en la mesa)   4   ¿Dónde pone Ud. los libros?   Los pongo en la mesa.

(en la mesa)   5   ¿Dónde pone él los libros?   Los pone en la mesa.

(los libros)   6   ¿Qué ponen ellos en la mesa?   Ponen los libros.

23.12   jacobeligoodsons.com For Free Audio   DOCE

SPOKEN SPANISH   UNIT 23

[póká↓] 7 kònóşenustedes |amúchahènteakí↑   no↓ kònóşémospóká↓

[póká↓] 8 kònóşgusted |amúchahènteakí↑   no↓ kònóşkopóká↓

[póká↓] 9 kònóşenéỹos |amúchahènteakí↑   no↓ kònóşempóká↓

       10 salgusted |lozdomíngos↑   sí↓ sálgolozdomíngós↓

       11 sálenusteder |lozdomíngos↑   sí↓ sálimozlozdomíngós↓

_____

(poca)   7 ¿Conocen Uds. a mucha gente aquí?   No, conocemos poca.

(poca)   8 ¿Conoce Ud. a mucha gente aquí?   No, conozco poca.

(poca)   9 ¿Conocen ellos a mucha gente aquí?   No, conocen poca.

        10 ¿Sale Ud. los domingos?   Sí, salgo los domingos.

        11 ¿Salen Uds. los domingos?   Sí, salimos los domingos.

TRECE

UNIT 23   SPOKEN SPANISH

23.21.13 Translation drill

1 I'm not acquainted with that district.   yó|nókonóşkǫ|esebárryǒ↓   Yo no conozco ese barrio.

2 Do you know it?   ústedlokonóşe↑   ¿Ud. lo conoce?

3 Is it worth while getting acquainted
      with it?   bálelapéna|konoşerlo↑   ¿Vale la pena conocerlo?
           or
   Is it worth the trouble of seeing it?

4 I'm very grateful to you (for it).
           or   s`lǫágráđeşkomúchǒ↓   Se lo agradezco mucho.
   I thank you very much for it.

5 I go out very little.   yósálgo|muypókǒ↓   Yo salgo muy poco.

6 They go out every week.   ѐ^yǒ(s)sálen|tođazlá(s)semánàs↓ Ellos salen todas las semanas.

7 Where do you put the ashtray?   dóndepónęustéđ|elşenişérǒ↓   ¿Dónde pone Ud. el cenicero?

8 I put it (over) there.   lǒpóņgǫaꞈyí↓   Lo pongo allí.

9 What do you think about it?   kéleparéşęaꞈustéđ↓   ¿Qué le parece a Ud.?

23.14   CATORCE

SPOKEN SPANISH   UNIT 23

B. Discussion of pattern

One pattern of verb irregularity consists in the appearance of a velar stem extension, after the verb stem and before its ending, in 1 sg forms of present tense. There is no way to predict which verbs will belong to this irregular pattern, though certain limitations can be stated: only /‑ér ‑ír/ verbs are involved, and the stem-final consonant is always preceded by a vowel.

The key that determines which velar sound occurs as the extension (i.e., /k/ or /g/) is voicing correlation: voiceless /k/ follows voiceless /ş/, and voiced /g/ follows voiced /n, l/ .

The verbs so far presented which follow this irregular pattern are listed below in their infinitive and 1 sg present tense forms:

—k—		—g—	
agradeş—ér	agradéş—k—o	bal—ér	bál—g—o
konoş—ér	konóş—k—o	pon—ér	pón—g—o
pareş—ér	paréş—k—o	sal—ír	sál—g—o
perteneş—ér	pertenéş—k—o		
traduş—ír	tradúş—k—o		

23.21.2   Present tense irregular verbs — mixed stem-vowel changing and velar stem extensions

A. Presentation of pattern

ILLUSTRATIONS

I almost never come to this building.   1   kásinuŋkabéŋgọ |àestedifíşyò↓   Casi nunca *vengo* a este edificio.

——————————————   2   èspókoloketéŋgò↓   Es poco lo que *tengo*.

——————————————   3   pòrkénobyénes |estanóchè↓   ¿Por qué no *vienes* esta noche?

QUINCE   23.15

UNIT 23   SPOKEN SPANISH

_____   4   tyénezrraşón↓   *Tienes* razón.

_____   5   byénesuswegra|tambyén↑   ¿*Viene* su suegra también?

_____   6   nomekombyéne↓   No me *conviene*.

_____   7   yátyenekasa↑   ¿Ya *tiene* casa?

_____   8   byénen|embárko↑   ¿*Vienen* en barco?

They have a son.   9   tyénenuníhó↓   *Tienen* un hijo.

                                    EXTRAPOLATION

Mixed changes	$\overline{g}$ e > yé	
Verbs	ben —ír	ten —ér
sg 1	bén—g—o	tén—g—o
2 fam	byén —es	tyén —es
2-3	byén —e	tyén —e
pl 1	ben —ímos	ten —émos
2-3	byén —en	tyén —en

                                        NOTES

a. A limited number of verbs have the irregularities of both the velar stem extensions and stem-vowel changes.

23.16   DIECISEIS

SPOKEN SPANISH   UNIT 23

23.21.21 Substitution drills - Person-number substitution

1 yótéŋgolalísta↓
   láséŋyora_____↓   tyénelalísta↓
   lózmúchachos___↓   tyénénlalísta↓
   nósótros_____↓   ténémozlalísta↓
   élséŋyor_____↓   tyénelalísta↓

2 yóbéŋggeŋkárró↓
   mįérmàna_____↓   byéneŋkárró↓
   lwísąįyo_____↓   bénįmoseŋkárró↓

───

1 *Yo* tengo la lista.
   La señora _____.   Tiene la lista.
   Los muchachos _____.   Tienen la lista.
   Nosotros _____.   Tenemos la lista.
   El señor _____.   Tiene la lista.

2 *Yo* vengo en carro.
   Mi hermana _____.   Viene en carro.
   Luisa y yo _____.   Venimos en carro.

DIECISIETE   23.17

UNIT 23   SPOKEN SPANISH

  èltènyénte _____ ↓   byenenkárró↓

  hósełàna _____ ↓   byenenenkárró↓

3 é⁀ŷozbyénentárdè↓

  èlkòrónél _____ ↓   byénetárdè↓

  lózmúchachoz _____ ↓   byénentárdè↓

  yo _____ ↓   bengotárdè↓

  mȧàmiçȯiyo _____ ↓   bènimostárdè↓

  El teniente _____ .   Viene en carro.

  José y Ana _____ .   Vienen en carro.

3 *Ellos* vienen tarde.

  El coronel _____ .   Viene tarde.

  Los muchachos _____ .   Vienen tarde.

  Yo _____ .   Vengo tarde.

  Mi amigo y yo _____ .   Venimos tarde.

SPOKEN SPANISH

UNIT 23

Tense substitution

1 yótubeketrabahár↓   yótengoketrabahár↓

2 éltubokensenyár↓   éltyenekensenyár↓

3 nòsotros |tùbímózmuchosproblémàs↓   nòsotros |tènémózmuchosproblémàs↓

4 yóbingalaúnà↓   yóbenggalaúnà↓

5 eҿyoz |binyeronalafyéstà↓   eҿyoz |byenenalafyéstà↓

_____

1 Yo *tuve* que trabajar.   Yo tengo que trabajar.

2 El *tuvo* que enseñar.   El tiene que enseñar.

3 Nosotros *tuvimos* muchos problemas.   Nosotros tenemos muchos problemas.

4 Yo *vine* a la una.   Yo vengo a la una.

5 Ellos *vinieron* a la fiesta.   Ellos vienen a la fiesta.

DIECINUEVE

23.19

UNIT 23   SPOKEN SPANISH

23.21.22 Response drill

           1 ustedtyene |unapartamentoↄ ọunakásà↓   tengọunakásà↓

           2 ustedestyenen |unapartamentoↄ ọunakásà↓   tenemosunakásà↓

           3 eＱyostyenen |unapartamentoↄ ọunakásà↓   tyenen |unapartaméntò↓

[èŋkárrò↓] 4 komobyenenustedes |alạeskwélà↓   bènimosęŋkárrò↓

[èŋkárrò↓] 5 komobyenęusted |alạeskwélà↓   benggęŋkárrò↓

[èŋkárrò↓] 6 komobyenél↓   byeneŋkárrò↓

---

         1 ¿Ud. tiene un apartamento, o una casa?   Tengo una casa.

         2 ¿Uds. tienen un apartamento, o una casa?   Tenemos una casa.

         3 ¿Ellos tienen un apartamento, o una casa?   Tienen un apartamento.

(en carro) 4 ¿Cómo vienen Uds. a la escuela?   Venimos en carro.

(en carro) 5 ¿Cómo viene Ud. a la escuela?   Vengo en carro.

(en carro) 6 ¿Cómo viene él?   Viene en carro.

SPOKEN SPANISH   UNIT 23

[êmbárkò↓]   7 byénenéQyos |pórabyón↑   nó↓ byénenembárkò↓
[êmbárkò↓]   8 byénel |enabyón↑   nó↓ byénembárkò↓

             9 tyéngustéďkárro↑   sí|sіténgò↓
            10 tyénenųstédeskárro↑   sí|sіtenémòs↓
            11 tyénélkárro↑   sí|sіtyénè↓

_____

(en barco)   7 ¿Vienen ellos por avión?   No, vienen en barco.
(en barco)   8 ¿Viene él en avión?   No, viene en barco.

             9 ¿Tiene Ud. carro?   Sí, si tengo.
            10 ¿Tienen Uds. carro?   Sí, si tenemos.
            11 ¿Tiene él carro?   Sí, sí tiene.

VEINTIUNO

jacobeligoodsons.com For Free Audio

UNIT 23   SPOKEN SPANISH

23.21.23 Translation drill

1 I have to go to the corner.   téngokeír |aląeskínằ↓   Tengo que ir a la esquina.

2 We have lots of dirty shirts.   ténemoz |muchaskamisas(s)úşyàs↓   Tenemos muchas camisas sucias.

3 Do you have to go to the laundry? tyéngustedkeír |alalabanderia↑   ¿Tiene Ud. que ir a la lavandería?

4 He too has to go.   él |támbyentyenekeír↓   El también tiene que ir.

5 I'm coming by car.   yobénggoeŋkárrồ↓   Yo vengo en carro.

6 They're coming on foot.   éꞁyoz |byenénąpyé↓   Ellos vienen a pie.

7 Are you coming on foot?   byeŋgustedapyé↑   Viene Ud. a pie?

B. Discussion of pattern

       Sometimes a verb will show more than one pattern of irregularity in its conjugation. The two verbs in this drill section are examples; the patterns of irregularity are a velar stem extension (in 1 sg) and stem vowel changing (/e > yé/ in 2 fam sg and all 2-3).

       The /–g–/ extension takes precedence, and no other change occurs in the 1 sg form. In other forms where the stem is strong stressed, the diphthongization /e > yé/ occurs.

       The verbs /tenér/ and /benír/ are the important examples of this mixed pattern. Others are compound forms, derived by adding some prefix to these forms, as /kom–/ in /kombenír/.

23.22   jacobeligoodsons.com For Free Audio   VEINTIDOS

SPOKEN SPANISH   UNIT 23

23.21.3 Present tense irregular verbs – mixed miscellaneous /kaér, traér/, /oír/, /aşér, deşír/, /sabér/

    A. Presentation of pattern

                                          ILLUSTRATIONS

—————————————————   1   ȧkítráygo|lalístȧ↓   Aquí *traigo* la lista.

Gosh, I'm falling!   2   kȧrambȧ|kȩmȩ́kaygȯ↓   ¡Caramba, que me *caigo!*

—————————————————   3   nȯzlȧstraȩ|ȩlsȩkwarȩ́ntaisyétȩ↓   Nos las *trae* el C-47.

I'm always dropping something. 4 syémpre|sȩmȩ́kaȩálgȯ↓   Siempre se me *cae* algo.

—————————————————   5   óygo|kȩ́kȧntȧm|pȯráí↓   *Oigo* que cantan por ahí.

Do you hear that noise?   6   óyȩ|esérrwiḍo↑   ¿*Oye* ese ruido?

From time to time we hear it. 7 dȩ̀beşȩŋkwando|loímòs↓   De vez en cuando lo *oímos.*

Do you all hear the traffic? 8   óyenȩltráfɪko↑   ¿*Oyen* el tráfico?

—————————————————   9   sí↓ yólágo↓àwŋkȩlȩ́ḍigo|kesunalátȧ↓   Sí, yo la *hago,* aunque le *digo* que es
                                                                       una lata.

—————————————————   10   pȩrḋóŋ↓kómoḍişȩ̀usté↑   Perdon, ¿cómo *dice* usted?

—————————————————   11   nosé↓ nȯayágwa|ȩnmỵȧpȧrtȧméntȯ↓   No *sé;* no hay agua en mi apartamento.

VEINTITRES   23.23

UNIT 23   SPOKEN SPANISH

EXTRAPOLATION

	palato-velar extension		palato velar-extension palatal extension
Verbs	ka —ér	tra —ér	o —ír
sg 1	ká—yg—o	trá—yg—o	ó—yg—o
2 fam	ká —es	trá —es	ó—y—es
2-3	ká —e	trá —e	ó—y—e
pl 1	ka —émos	tra —émos	o —ímos
2-3	ká —en	trá —en	ó—y—en

	velar consonant changing stem vowel changing		vowel changing shortening
Verbs	aş—ér	deş—ír	sab—ér
sg 1	ág—o	díg—o	sé—
2 fam	áş—es	díş—es	sáb—es
2-3	áş—e	díş—e	sáb—e
pl 1	aş—émos	deş—ímos	sab—émos
2-3	áş—en	díş—en	sáb—en

NOTES

a. The above verbs combine mixed patterns of irregularity into unique combinations.

23.24   VEINTICUATRO

SPOKEN SPANISH   UNIT 23

23.21.31 Substitution drills — Person-number substitution

1 yo|tráyggelkárró↓

   èlkóronel_____↓   tráelkárró↓

   èlsènyoriyó_____↓   tràemosęlkárró↓

   lwisa_____↓   tráelkárró↓

   éÒyos_____↓   tráenęlkárró↓

_____

1 *Yo* traigo el carro.

   El coronel _____.   Trae el carro.

   El señor y yo_____.   Traemos el carro.

   Luisa_____.   Trae el carro.

   Ellos_____.   Traen el carro.

VEINTICINCO   23.25

UNIT 23   SPOKEN SPANISH

2   nôsótroz |nòtràemoznáđà↓   nòtrae(n)náđà↓
    éⓎyoz_____↓   nòtraenáđà↓
    làsèkrètarya_____↓   nòtrae(n)náđà↓
    misàmigoz_____↓   nótraygonáđà↓
    yó_____↓

3   yó |óygòmúybyén↓
    éⓎya_____↓   óyèmúybyén↓
    lwísąikarmen____↓   óyènmúybyén↓
    àntonyọịyó_____↓   óimozmúybyén↓
    hòsé_____↓   óyèmúybyén↓

_____

2   *Nosotros* no traemos nada.
    Ellos_____.   No traen nada.
    La secretaria_____.   No trae nada.
    Mis amigos_____.   No traen nada.
    Yo_____.   No traigo nada.

3   *Yo* oigo muy bien.
    Ella_____.   Oye muy bien.
    Luisa y Carmen____.   Oyen muy bien.
    Antonio y yo_____.   Oimos muy bien.
    José_____.   Oye muy bien.

23.26   VEINTISEIS

SPOKEN SPANISH   UNIT 23

4   yó|ágolomízmô↓
    miérmana_____↓   áşelomízmô↓
    lózmúchachos_↓   áşenlomízmô↓
    éltènyénte___↓   áşelomízmô↓
    élkòróneliyo_↓   áşemozlomízmô↓

5   yó|dígótodoenespanyól↓
    miího_____↓   díşétodoenespanyól↓
    miíhoiyó_____↓   déşimostodo|enespanyól↓
    éⁿyaz_____↓   díşéntodoenespanyól↓
    ana_____↓   díşétodoenespanyól↓

_____

4   *Yo* hago lo mismo.
    Mi hermana_____.   Hace lo mismo.
    Los muchachos____   Hacen lo mismo.
    El teniente_____.   Hace lo mismo.
    El coronel y yo___.   Hacemos lo mismo.

5   *Yo* digo todo en español.
    Mi hijo_____.   Dice todo en español.
    Mi hijo y yo_____.   Decimos todo en español.
    Ellas_____.   Dicen todo en español.
    Ana_____.   Dice todo en español.

VEINTISIETE

UNIT 23   SPOKEN SPANISH

6 yo |syémpre |sélalekşyón↓
   ana_____↓   syémpre |sábelalekşyón↓
   anaiyo_____↓   syémpre |sábemozlalekşyón↓
   éⁿyos_____↓   syémpre |sábenlalekşyón↓
   hwan _____↓   syémpre |sábelalekşyón↓

7 nòsótroz |dèşimos,ésó↓
   el _____↓   dişésó↓
   yo _____↓   digọésó↓
   hwaniyó_____↓   dèşimos,ésó↓
   lòzmúchachoɀ_____↓   dişenésó↓

───

6 *Yo* siempre sé la lección.
   Ana _____.   Siempre sabe la lección.
   Ana y yo_____.   Siempre sabemos la lección.
   Ellos _____.   Siempre saben la lección.
   Juan _____.   Siempre sabe la lección.

7 *Nosotros* decimos eso.
   El _____.   Dice eso.
   Yo_____.   Digo eso.
   Juan y yo_____ .   Decimos eso.
   Los muchachos_____.   Dicen eso.

23.28   VEINTIOCHO

SPOKEN SPANISH   UNIT 23

Tense substitution

1	yótrahe ǀlaşerbéşá↓	yótraygo ǀlaşerbéşá↓
2	nósotros ǀtrahímozlạensaláđà↓	nósotros ǀtráemozlạensaláđà↓
3	yó ǀọịbyén ǀtàmbyén↓	yọygobyén ǀtàmbyén↓
4	yónọịşenáđà↓	yónọạgonáđà↓
5	elíşolalístá↓	elaşelalístá↓
6	nósotroz ǀnọịşimosésò↓	nósotroz ǀnọạşemosésò↓
7	yó ǀtàmpoko ǀđịhenáđà↓	yó ǀtàmpoko ǀđịgonáđà↓
8	nósotrozđịhímos ǀtođomuymál↓	nósotrozđeşimos ǀtođomuymál↓
9	eḷ̂yozdíheron ǀtođọenẹspaŋyól↓	eḷ̂yozdíşen ǀtođọenẹspaŋyól↓
10	yó ǀnosupelalekşyón↓	yó ǀnoselalekşyón↓
11	nósotroz ǀnosupímozloznómbrès↓	nósotroz ǀnosạbemozloznómbrès↓

---

1 Yo *traje* la cerveza.	Yo traigo la cerveza.
2 Nosotros *trajimos* la ensalada.	Nosotros traemos la ensalada.
3 Yo *oí* bien también.	Yo oigo bien también.
4 Yo no *hice* nada.	Yo no hago nada.
5 El *hizo* la lista.	El hace la lista.
6 Nosotros no *hicimos* eso.	Nosotros no hacemos eso.
7 Yo tampoco *dije* nada.	Yo tampoco digo nada.
8 Nosotros *dijimos* todo muy mal.	Nosotros decimos todo muy mal.
9 Ellos *dijeron* todo en español.	Ellos dicen todo en español.
10 Yo no *supe* la lección.	Yo no sé la lección.
11 Nosotros no *supimos* los nombres.	Nosotros no sabemos los nombres.

UNIT 23   SPOKEN SPANISH

23.21.32 Response drill

	1	ùstéd‖díşètódǫ‖ènèspàŋyól↑ǫeninglés↓	dígòtodǫ‖enèspaŋyól↓
	2	ùstédèz‖díşèntódǫ‖ènèspàŋyól↑ǫeninglés↓	dèşímòstodǫ‖enèspaŋyól↓
	3	el‖díşètódǫ‖ènèspàŋyól↑ǫeninglés↓	díşètodǫ‖enèspaŋyól↓
[libròs↓]	4	kétr ̧ǫustéd‖alạeskwélà↓	tráygòlibròs↓
[libròs↓]	5	kétráeňﾟyos‖alạeskwélà↓	tráènlibròs↓
[libròs↓]	6	kétráeɲustédes‖alạeskwélà↓	tráemozlíbròs↓

	1	¿Ud. dice todo en español o en inglés.	Digo todo en español.
	2	¿Uds. dicen todo en español o en inglés?	Decimos todo en español.
	3	¿El dice todo en español o en inglés?	Dice todo en español.
(libros)	4	¿Qué trae Ud. a la escuela?	Traigo libros.
(libros)	5	¿Qué traen ellos a la escuela?	Traen libros.
(libros)	6	¿Qué traen Uds. a la escuela?	Traemos libros.

23.30   TREINTA

SPOKEN SPANISH   UNIT 23

[ènèspànyó1↓]   7   disgusted |tódọeninglés |akí↑   nó↓ àki |dígótodọ |enespanyó1↓

[ènèspànyó1↓]   8   disẹnụstedes |tódọeninglés |akí↑   nó↓ àki |dèṣímòstodọ |enespanyó1↓

               9   sabẹusted |minómbre↑   sí↓ lòsé↓

              10   seyó |ẹldẹusted↑   sí↓ lòsàbė↓

              11   oygusteđbyen↑   sí↓ óygo |múybyén↓

              12   oyenụstedez |byen↑   sí↓ óimoz |múybyén↓

              13   oyenẹllyoz |byen↑   sí↓ óyen |múybyén↓

_____

(en español)   7   ¿Dice Ud. todo en inglés aquí?   No, aquí digo todo en español.

(en español)   8   ¿Dicen Uds. todo en inglés aquí?   No, aquí decimos todo en español.

               9   ¿Sabe Ud. mi nombre?   Sí, lo sé.

              10   ¿Sé yo el de Ud.?   Sí, lo sabe.

              11   ¿Oye Ud. bien?   Sí, oigo muy bien.

              12   ¿Oyen Uds. bien?   Sí, oimos muy bien.

              13   ¿Oyen ellos bien?   Sí, oyen muy bien.

TREINTA Y UNO   23.31

UNIT 23   SPOKEN SPANISH

23.21.33 Translation drill

1 I don't do the cooking at my house.	yoŋgágolakomɨdą	enmɨkásá↓	Yo no hago la comida en mi casa.
2 Who does it in yours?	kyenlaşę	enlasúyá↓	¿Quién la hace en la suya?
3 My wife and I do it.	mįẹsposąiyo	laşémòs↓	Mi esposa y yo la hacemos.
4 Neither he nor I bring the car.	nįelniyó	tráemosąelkárrò↓	Ni él ni yo traemos el carro.
5 I don't bring it either.	yó	tàmpókolotráygò↓	Yo tampoco lo traigo.
6 They bring it once in a while.	ełyozlotraen	dèbeşęŋkwándò↓	Ellos lo traen de vez en cuando.
7 Do you all know my name?	sabenustédez	minombre↑	¿Saben Uds. mi nombre?
8 We do know it.	nòsótros|sį|losabémòs↓	Nosotros sí lo sabemos.
9 Do you know the lesson?	sabęusted	laleķşyon↑	¿Sabe Ud. la lección?
10 I too know it.	yó	tàmbyénlasé↓	Yo también la sé.
11 Do you all hear well?	oyenustédezbyen↑	¿Oyen Uds. bien?
12 We hear very well.	nòsótros	óimozmúybyén↓	Nosotros oímos muy bien.
13 I hear everything very well.	yó|óygòtódo|múybyén↓	Yo oigo todo muy bien.

23.32   TREINTA Y DOS

SPOKEN SPANISH   UNIT 23

B. Discussion of pattern

This section includes several miscellaneous irregular verbs which show very little pattern similarity to other irregular types.

The verbs /traér/ and /kaér/ are similar to each other: each has the palato-velar extension /—yg—/ after the stem and before the ending of their 1 sg forms (/trá—yg—o , ká—yg—o/).

The verb /oír/ , in addition to this irregular feature (/ó—yg—o/) has a palatal extension /—y—/ after the stem of the 2 fam and both 2-3 forms (/ó—y—es ó—y—e. ó—y—en/).

The verbs /aşér/ and /deşír/ have a velar consonant change /ş > g/ in the stem of their 1 sg forms (/áĝ—o , díg—o/), and /deşír/ has the stem vowel change /e > i/ in 2 fam and both 2-3 forms (/díş—es , díş—e , díş—en/).

The verb /sabér/ is irregular only in its 1 sg form when the stem changes to /sé—/ and takes no ending.

Though all these changes can be described, as above, by noting the individual modifications of each irregular form, it is usually more profitable for a student to use and memorize each irregular form as if it were a new vocabulary item, until the verb forms can be related through meaning and distribution, rather than their variance from regular patterns. In other words, these patterns have to be mastered in and of themselves; very limited transfer to similar forms will be possible.

23.21.4 Statement intonation patterns – Leavetakings

A. Presentation of pattern

                                    ILLUSTRATIONS

_____   1   kòmpèrmisó↓   1   21↓
                                                      Con permiso.

_____   2   ástálweĝó↓   1   21↓
                                                      Hasta luego.

_____   3   àđyós↓   1 21 ↓
                                                      Adiós.

TREINTA Y TRES   23.33

UNIT 23   SPOKEN SPANISH

EXTRAPOLATION

English	Spanish
/232↑/	/121↓/

NOTES

a. Leavetakings in Spanish characteristically end in a falling intonation pattern, unlike English.

b. Using an English pattern for leavetakings in Spanish is both conspicuous and inappropriate.

23.21.41 Translation drill — Leavetakings

```
    2      3 2 ↑
1 See you tomorrow.        ástàmàŋyaná↓          1     2 1↓
                                                 Hasta mañana.

    2     3 2 ↑
2 See you later.          ástàlwegó↓             1     2 1↓
                                                 Hasta luego.

    2     3   2 ↑
3 I'll be seeing you.     ástàlàbistá↓           1     2 1↓
                                                 Hasta la vista.

    2      32 ↑
4 See you tonight.        ástàlànoché↓           1     2 1↓
                                                 Hasta la noche.

    2      32 ↑
5 See you soon.           ástàprontó↓            1     2 1↓
                                                 Hasta pronto.

    2     3 2 ↑
6 See you Monday.         ástaéllunès↓           1     2 1↓
                                                 Hasta el lunes.

    2      32 ↑
7 See you at seven.       ástàlà(s)syété↓        1     2 1↓
                                                 Hasta las siete.
```

23.34   TREINTA Y CUATRO

SPOKEN SPANISH   UNIT 23

    2   3 2 ↑
8 Glad to have met you.   muchogusto |dėkȯnȯşerlȯ↓   2   2 2 | 1   2 1 ↓
                                                       Mucho gusto de conocerlo.

    2   3 2 ↑
9 Glad to have seen you.   muchogusto |dėberlȯ↓   2   2 2 | 1 2 1 ↓
                                                         Mucho gusto de verlo.

    2   3 2 ↑
10 Glad to have heard you.   muchogusto |dėȯirlȯ↓   2   2 2 | 1 2 1 ↓
                                                         Mucho gusto de oirlo.

    2 32 ↑
11 Goodbye.   ȧdyȯs↓   1 21 ↓
                                                        Adiós.

    2 32 ↑
12 Good night.   bwėnȧznochės↓   1   2 1 ↓
                                                         Buenas noches.

    2   3 2 ↑
13 Gotta go now.   kȯmpȯrmisȯ↓   1   21 ↓
                                                         Con permiso.

B. Discussion of pattern

    One of the most conspicuous errors that an English speaking student of Spanish can make is to impose an English intonation pattern on Spanish leavetakings. There are several English patterns, nearly all of which are very inappropriate. A listing of these patterns would include: /232↑, 232|, 32↑, 43↑/.

    The common pattern in Spanish, /121↓/, exists in English as an abrupt, discourteous dismissal. It is therefore likely to be avoided by an English-speaking student in favor of a familiar pattern that doesn't make an English speaker feel so uncomfortable.

    In leavetakings as with other features, appropriate patterns must be internalized. But when there is direct interference from similar contexts in the learner's language, special attention should be given to correctly establish the important patterns of the target language.

TREINTA Y CINCO

UNIT 23   SPOKEN SPANISH

23.22   Replacement drills

A   bámos |ạúmpwésto |kèyókonóṣkô↓

1   _____ lábàndèrìa _____↓   bámos |ạúnàlàbàndèrìa |kèyókonóṣkô↓

2   _____ là _____↓   bámos |àlàlàbàndèrìa |kèyókonóṣkô↓

3   _____ él _____↓   bámos |àlàlàbàndèrìa |kélkonóṣè↓

4   _____ díṣè↓   bámos |àlàlàbàndèrìa |kéldíṣè↓

5   _____ ótèl _____↓   bámos |àlótèl |kéldíṣè↓

6   _____ yó _____↓   bámos |àlótèl |kèyódígò↓

7   _____ téṇgó↓   bámos |àlótèl |kéyotéṇgò↓

──

A   Vamos a un puesto que yo conozco.

1   _____ lavandería _____.   Vamos a una lavandería que yo conozco.

2   _____ la _____.   Vamos a la lavandería que yo conozco.

3   _____ él _____.   Vamos a la lavandería que él conoce.

4   _____ dice.   Vamos a la lavandería que él dice.

5   _____ hotel _____.   Vamos al hotel que él dice.

6   _____ yo _____.   Vamos al hotel que yo digo.

7   _____ tengo.   Vamos al hotel que yo tengo.

23.36   TREINTA Y SEIS

jacobeligoodsons.com For Free Audio

SPOKEN SPANISH   UNIT 23

B   șérkadęaʋɪ |béndèmpèskadò |tàmbyén↓

1   _____frutàs_____↓   șérkadęaʋɪ |béndèmfrutàs |tàmbyén↓

2   _____akí_____↓   șérkadęakí |béndèmfrutàs |tàmbyén↓

3   èmfrente_____↓   èmfrente |dęàkɪ|béndèmfrutàs |tàmbyén↓

4   _____kómpràm_____↓   èmfrente |dęàkɪ|kómpràmfrutàs |tàmbyén↓

5   _____àórà↓   èmfrente |dęàkɪ|kómpràmfrutàs |àórà↓

6   _____àɪ_____↓   èmfrente |dęàɪ|kómpràmfrutàs |àórà↓

7   _____lègumbrès_____↓   èmfrente |dęàɪ|kómprànlègumbrès |àórà↓

B   Cerca de allí venden pescado también.

1   _____frutas _____.   Cerca de allí venden frutas también.

2   _____aquí_____.   Cerca de aquí venden frutas también.

3   Enfrente _____.   Enfrente de aquí venden frutas también.

4   _____compran _____.   Enfrente de aquí compran frutas también.

5   _____ahora.   Enfrente de aquí compran frutas ahora.

6   _____ahí _____.   Enfrente de ahí compran frutas ahora.

7   _____legumbres _____.   Enfrente de ahí compran legumbres ahora.

TREINTA Y SIETE

UNIT 23 SPOKEN SPANISH

C   nèṣèsitọ |ùnàdoṣenadewébòs↓

1   teṇgọ _____ ↓   tèṇgọ |ùnàdoṣenadewébòs↓

2   _____ tomátès↓   tèṇgọ |ùnàdoṣenadetomátès↓

3   _____ dóz _____ ↓   teṇgo |dozdoṣenazdetomátès↓

4   tràygo _____ ↓   tràygo |dozdoṣenazdetomátès↓

5   _____ kàhaz _____ ↓ tràygo |doskahazdetomátès↓

6   _____ bínò↓   tràygo |doskahazdebínò↓

7   _____ èstà _____ ↓   tràygọ |èstàkahadebínò↓

C   Necesito una docena de huevos.

1   Tengo _____ .   Tengo una docena de huevos.

2   _____ tomates.   Tengo una docena de tomates.

3   _____ dos _____ .   Tengo dos docenas de tomates.

4   Traigo _____ .   Traigo dos docenas de tomates.

5   _____ cajas _____ . Traigo dos cajas de tomates.

6   _____ vino.   Traigo dos cajas de vino.

7   _____ esta _____ . Traigo esta caja de vino.

SPOKEN SPANISH   UNIT 23

D   ákı|enmibólsakában↓

1   _____ábitášyoŋ___↓   ákı|enmịábitášyoŋkában↓

2   _____éstàs_____↓   ákı|enéstàșábitášyoneskában↓

3   _____áy↓   ákı|enéstàșábitášyonesáy↓

4   áλyı_____↓   áλyı|enésàșábitášyonesáy↓

5   _____dórmitóryọ___↓   áλyı|enésèdórmitóryọáy↓

6   _____éstè_____↓   ákı|enéstèdórmitóryọáy↓

7   _____está↓   ákı|enéstèdórmitóryọestá↓

_____

D   Aquí en mi bolsa caben.

1   _____habitación___.   Aquí en mi habitación caben.

2   _____estas _____.   Aquí en estas habitaciones caben.

3   _____ hay.   Aquí en estas habitaciones hay.

4   Allí_____.   Allí en esas habitaciones hay.

5   _____dormitorio___.   Allí en ese dormitorio hay.

6   _____este _____.   Aquí en este dormitorio hay.

7   _____está.   Aquí en este dormitorio está.

TREINTA Y NUEVE

UNIT 23   SPOKEN SPANISH

E   débesérunşyégò↓   débeser |unabeşíná↓

1   _____beşíná↓   débeserlabeşíná↓

2   _____lá_____↓   débeserelíhó↓

3   _____íhó↓   pweđenser |losíhòs↓

4   pweđen_____↓   pweđesersyíhó↓

5   _____sy_____↓   pweđenser |susamígàs↓

6   _____amígàs↓   pweđenser |nwestrasamígàs↓

7   _____nwestras_↓

E   Debe ser un ciego.   Debe ser una vecina.

1   _____vecina.   Debe ser la vecina.

2   _____la_____.   Debe ser el hijo.

3   _____hijo.   Pueden ser los hijos.

4   Pueden _____.   Puede ser su hijo.

5   _____su_____.   Pueden ser sus amigas.

6   _____amigas.   Pueden ser nuestras amigas.

7   _____nuestras_____.

23.40   jacobeligoodsons.com For Free Audio   CUARENTA

SPOKEN SPANISH   UNIT 23

F   aṣelakomiḍa|ústeḍmizma↑

1   _____ústeḍez___↑   aṣenlakomiḍa|ústeḍezmizmas↑

2   _____trabaho_____↑   aṣeneltrabaho|ústeḍezmizmas↑

3   _____eⁿyoz_____↑   aṣeneltrabaho|eⁿyozmizmos↑

4   ___este_____↑   aṣenestetrabaho|eⁿyozmizmos↑

5   _____kosas_____↑   aṣenestaskosas|eⁿyozmizmos↑

6   benden _____↑   bendenestaskosas|eⁿyozmizmos↑

7   _____eⁿya____↑   bendestaskosas|eⁿyamizma↑

_____

F   ¿Hace la comida usted misma?

1   ¿ _____ustedes ___?   ¿Hacen la comida ustedes mismas?

2   ¿ _____trabajo _____?   ¿Hacen el trabajo ustedes mismas?

3   ¿ _____ellos ____?   ¿Hacen el trabajo ellos mismos?

4   ¿ ___este _____?   ¿Hacen este trabajo ellos mismos?

5   ¿ _____cosas _____?   ¿Hacen estas cosas ellos mismos?

6   ¿Venden _____?   ¿Venden estas cosas ellos mismos?

7   ¿ _____ella ____?   ¿Vende estas cosas ella misma?

CUARENTA Y UNO

UNIT 23   SPOKEN SPANISH

23.23   Variation drills

A   kékomprámòs|sèŋyórà↓   ¿Qué compramos, señora?

1 What'll we take, ma'am?   ké(l)yebámòs|sèŋyórà↓   ¿Qué llevamos, señora?

2 What do you wish, sir?   kédeséà|sèŋyór↓   ¿Qué desea, señor?

3 How much does it cost, Miss?   kwántokwéstà|sèŋyórità↓   ¿Cuánto cuesta, señorita?

4 How much is it worth, Miss?   kwántobálé|sèŋyórità↓   ¿Cuánto vale, señorita?

5 When are you coming back, John? kwándobwélbès|hwán↓   ¿Cuándo vuelves, Juan?

6 How are you, Mary?   kómoęstáz|màríà↓   ¿Cómo estás, María?

7 Where do you live, Mr. Molina? dóndebíbè|sèŋyórmòlínà↓   ¿Dónde vive, señor Molina?

B   ákitráygolalístà↓   Aquí traigo la lista.

1 Here I'm bringing the coffee. ákitráygoęlkafé↓   Aquí traigo el café.

2 Here they're bringing the soup. ákitráenlasópà↓   Aquí traen la sopa.

3 Here comes the girl.   ákibyéne|lamucháchà↓   Aquí viene la muchacha.

23.42   jacobeligoodsons.com For Free Audio   CUARENTA Y DOS

SPOKEN SPANISH   UNIT 23

4 There goes Mary.   áıbamaríá↓   Ahí va María.

5 There go the Harrises.   áıbanloshárrís↓   Ahí van los Harris.

6 There are your friends.   áıẹstán |tusạmígòs↓   Ahí están tus amigos.

7 Here they are.   ákaẹstán↓   Acá están.

C míre |kéberduras |tamfréskàs↓   ¡Mire qué verduras tan frescas!

1 Look how pretty the girls are!   míre |kemucháchas |tambonítàs↓   ¡Mire qué muchachas tan bonitas!

2 Look how expensive (these) things are! míre |kekósas |taŋkáràs↓   ¡Mire qué cosas tan caras!

3 Look how dirty the streets are!   míre |kekáꞥyes |tansúꞩyàs↓   ¡Mire qué calles tan sucias!

4 Look how comfortable the apartment is! míre |keạpartamento |taŋkómódó↓ ¡Mire qué apartamento tan cómodo!

5 Man, what an ugly thing!   ómbre |kekósa |tamféà↓   ¡Hombre, qué cosa tan fea!

6 Man, what awful soup!   ómbre |kesópa |tanmálà↓   ¡Hombre, qué sopa tan mala!

7 Boy, what a long lesson!   chíko |kelekꞩyón |tanlárgà↓   ¡Chico, qué lección tan larga!

CUARENTA Y TRES   23.43

UNIT 23   SPOKEN SPANISH

D nótyéne |kekomprár↑   ¿No tiene que comprar?

1 Don't you have to leave?   nótyéne |kesalír↑   ¿No tiene que salir?

2 Don't you have to study?   nótyéne |kestudyar↑   ¿No tiene que estudiar?

3 Don't you have to eat lunch?   nótyéne |kealmorşar↑   ¿No tiene que almorzar?

4 Don't you have to work?   nótyéne |ketrabahar↑   ¿No tiene que trabajar?

5 Don't you have to come back?   nótyéne |kebolber↑   ¿No tiene que volver?

6 Don't you have to wait?   nótyéne |kesperar↑   ¿No tiene que esperar?

7 Don't you have to go?   nótyéne |keir↑   ¿No tiene que ir?

E kémáz |neşesítakomprár↓   ¿Qué más necesita comprar?

1 What else do you need to declare? kémáz |neşesítadeklarár↓   ¿Qué más necesita declarar?

2 What else do you need to see?   kémáz |neşesítaber↓   ¿Qué más necesita ver?

3 What else do you need to pay for? kémáz |neşesítapagár↓   ¿Qué más necesita pagar?

4 What else do you need to know?   kémáz |neşesítasaber↓   ¿Qué más necesita saber?

23.44   jacobeligoodsons.com For Free Audio   CUARENTA Y CUATRO

SPOKEN SPANISH   UNIT 23

5 What else do you need to carry?   kémaz |neşesitaḽyebár↓   ¿Qué más necesita llevar?

6 What else do you need to change?   kémaz |neşesitakambyár↓   ¿Qué más necesita cambiar?

7 What else do you need?   kémaz |neşesítá↓   ¿Qué más necesita?

F mèlắḽyebạ|eⓌlechéró↓   Me la lleva el lechero.

1 The chauffeur takes it for me.   mèlắḽyebạ|elchofér↓   Me la lleva el chofer.

2 The girl takes it for me.   mèlắḽyeba|lamucháchá↓   Me la lleva la muchacha.

3 The milkman leaves it for me.   mèlắḓehạ|eⓌlechéró↓   Me la deja el lechero.

4 The employee sends them for me.   mèlắzmandạ|elempleáḓò↓   Me las manda el empleado.

5 My wife brings them for me.   mèlắstráe|misenyórà↓   Me las trae mi señora.

6 My secretary writes them for me.   mèlắsèscríbe|misekretáryá↓   Me las escribe mi secretaria.

7 My secretary receives them for me.   mèlắzrrèşíbe|misekretáryá↓   Me las recibe mi secretaria.

CUARENTA Y CINCO   23.45

UNIT 23   SPOKEN SPANISH

23.24   Review drill – The obligatory clause relator /ke/

1 I believe she's American.   kréokéᵭɣạ|es,amerikánà↓   Creo que ella es americana.

2 I believe she doesn't speak Spanish.   kréokéᵭɣa|nọablạespạɲól↓   Creo que ella no habla español.

3 I believe she dances very well.   kréokéᵭɣạ|baylamuybyén↓   Creo que ella baila muy bien.

4 It seems to me he's from the United   mệpárẹ̣ẹkel|ẹzdẹlósẹ̀stạdosụnídòs↓   Me parece que él es de los Estados
   States.   Unidos.

5 It seems to me he's a pilot.   mệpárẹ̣ẹkel|espilótò↓   Me parece que él es piloto.

6 It seems to me he's at the airport.   mệpárẹ̣ẹ|kélestá|ẹnẹḷạeropwértò↓   Me parece que él está en el aeropuerto.

7 It seems to me he's not coming today. mệpárẹ̣ẹkel|nobyeṇọóy↓   Me parece que él no viene hoy.

8 She said she was at (the) school.   eᵭɣadıho|kèstabạenḷạeskwélà↓   Ella dijo que estaba en la escuela.

9 She said she was American.   eᵭɣadıho|kéramerikánà↓   Ella dijo que era americana.

10 She said she wasn't coming.   eᵭɣadıho|kénobeníà↓   Ella dijo que no venía.

11 She said she didn't dance.   eᵭɣadıho|kénobaylábà↓   Ella dijo que no bailaba.

23.46   CUARENTA Y SEIS

SPOKEN SPANISH   UNIT 23

23.3   CONVERSATION STIMULUS

NARRATIVE 1

1 Jean and Carmen are at the market.   yiṇikármen |èstanenelmerkádò↓   Jean y Carmen están en el mercado.

2 They've already bought bread, meat,   yaŋ |kòmprádòpaṇ↑karneṃimantekíỌyà↓   Ya han comprado pan, carne y mantequilla.
   and butter.

3 Jean looks at the list to see what else   yin |míràlàlísta |pàràber |kemas |tyene   Jean mira la lista para ver qué más tiene
   she has to buy.   kekomprár↓   que comprar.

4 She needs some eggs.   nèṣèsitaunozwébòs↓   Necesita unos huevos.

5 But eggs are very expensive at this   pérólòzwébos |sònmuykáròs |ènéstèpwéstò↓ Pero los huevos son muy caros en este
   stand.   puesto.

6 Carmen knows a man who sells them   kármeŋ |kònóṣęàụṇombre |kèlòzbèndemaz   Carmen conoce a un hombre que los vende
   cheaper.   barátòs↓   más baratos.

7 So then, they decide to go there.   àsięntonṣęz↑ḍeṣiḍeniraỌyí↓   Así, entonces, deciden ir allí.

DIALOG 1

Carmen, dígale a Jean que ya tienen el   yatenémos |èlpaṇ↑làkarneṃilamantekíỌyà↓   Carmen: Ya tenemos el pan, la carne y la
pan, la carne y la mantequilla. Pregún-   kemas |tyenekekomprár↓   mantequilla. ¿Qué más tiene que
tele que qué más tiene que comprar.   comprar?

Jean, dígale que aquí trae la lista. Que un àkitraygolalístà↓ unmomento |ile   Jean: Aquí traigo la lista. Un momento
momento y le dice. Ah, sí: huevos, dígale.   dígò↓ a |sí↓ wébòs↓   y le digo. Ah, sí: huevos.

CUARENTA Y SIETE
                                                                                      23.47
jacobeligoodsons.com For Free Audio

UNIT 23   SPOKEN SPANISH

Carmen, dígale que en este puesto son muy
caros. Que Ud. conoce a un hombre que
se los vende a Ud. más baratos.

ė́nėstepwesto |sónmuykárȯs↓ yokonȯ̧kǫ
aynǫmbre |kė̀mė̀lȯ̀zbend̯e̥amí |mazbarátȯs↓

Carmen: En este puesto son muy caros.
Yo conozco a un hombre que me
los vende a mí más baratos.

Jean, dígale que es mejor ir allí, entonces.

ė̀zmė̀hor |íra̧l̯y̧í↓ė́ntóņȩs↓

Jean: Es mejor ir allí, entonces.

NARRATIVE 2

1 The man tells Jean that the eggs are one
twenty-five a dozen.

ė̀lombreled̯i̧ȩay̧ın↑kė̀lȯ̀zwė́bos |ė́stán |
g̯únȯ̀bė̀ynti̧ı̧ŋkȯ́ |lȧd̯ȯ̧ė́nȧ↓

El hombre le dice a Jean que los huevos
están a uno veinticinco la docena.

2 But there's so much noise that Jean can't
hear anything.

pérǫay |tantorrwíd̯ȯt↑kȩ̇yın |nȯ̀pwed̯ȩ |ȯ̀ır
náḋȧ↓

Pero hay tanto ruido que Jean no puede
oír nada.

3 So he has to repeat the price.

ė̀ntóņes↑eltyéne |kė̀rrė̀pėtirelprȩ̇y̧ȯ́↓

Entonces, él tiene que repetir el precio.

4 And he tells her also that they are very
fresh.

iléd̯i̧ȩtambyén |kė̀stánmuyfréskȯs↓

Y le dice también que están muy frescos.

5 Jean buys a dozen and puts them in her
bag.

y̧ın |kómpra̧únȧd̯ȯ̧ȩ́na̧ |ilȯ̀spȯnensubȯ́lsȧ↓

Jean compra una docena y los pone en su
bolsa.

6 There's still room there (for them).

tȯ̀d̯ȧbi̧akábė̀n |ȧı́↓

Todavía caben ahí.

DIALOG 2

Jean, pregúntele al hombre que a cómo
están los huevos.

ȧkomȯȩstánlozwė́bȯs↓

Jean: ¿A cómo están los huevos?

Señor, contéstele que para ella, a uno
veinticinco la docena.

párǫusted̯↑g̯únȯ̀bė̀ynti̧ı̧ŋkȯ́ |lȧd̯ȯ̧ȩ́nȧ↓

Señor: Para Usted, a uno veinticinco la
docena.

23.48   CUARENTA Y OCHO

SPOKEN SPANISH   UNIT 23

Jean, pregúntele otra vez que a cómo. Dígale   àkomoↄ noygonaↄá |kóntántòrɪwíↄò↓   Jean: ¿A cómo? No oigo nada con tanto
    que Ud. no oye nada con tanto ruido.   ruido.

Señor, repítale que a uno veinticinco la   ąuno |bèyntiṣiŋkolaↄoṣéná↓ èstánmuy   Señor: A uno veinticinco la docena. Están
    docena. Dígale que están muy frescos.   muy frescos.
                                                    fréskòs↓

Jean, dígale que una docena, por favor.   únaↄoṣéná |pòrfàbór↓   Jean: Una docena, por favor.

Señor, dígale que aquí tiene. Pregúntele si   àkityéné↓ sèlòspoŋgọenlabolsa↑   Señor: Aquí tiene. ¿Se los pongo en la
    se los pone en la bolsa.   bolsa?

Jean, contéstele que sí, por favor. Que Ud.   sí |pòrfàbór↓ kreo |kètòↄàbɪakáↄèn↓   Jean: Sí, por favor. Creo que todavía caben.
    cree que todavía caben.

                                          NARRATIVE 3

1 The man doesn't have change for the bill   èlombre |nòtyénekámbyo |páràèlbiↄyete | El hombre no tiene cambio para el billete
    Jean hands him.   que Jean le da.
                                                    kèyɪnleↄá↓

2 It's a nuisance because that's all she has.   èsúnàlatá↓pórkesọↄèstoↄo |lòkèↄyatyéné↓   Es una lata porque eso es todo lo que ella
                                                                                                          tiene.

3 She doesn't know what to do now.   nòsabe |keąṣér |àórà↓   No sabe qué hacer ahora.

4 Carmen tells her not to worry.   karmenleↄɪṣe |kènosepreokúpè↓   Carmen le dice que no se preocupe.

5 She can lend her (some).   éↄyapweↄeprestárlè↓   Ella puede prestarle.

CUARENTA Y NUEVE   23.49

UNIT 23   SPOKEN SPANISH

6 Jean tells her she's very kind.   yínlediṣe|kèzmúyamáblè↓   Jean le dice que es muy amable.

7 And that she'll pay her when they   ikeàlⓂ̃yeçaralakasa|lepáçà↓   Y que al llegar a la casa le paga.
   get home.

                                            DIALOG 3

Señor, dígale a Jean que Ud. no tiene cambio   nòtengokámbyo|párⱥesebìⓂ̃yétè|sèⱥóràↆ   Señor: No tengo cambio para ese billete,
para ese billete.   señora.

Jean, dígale que qué lata, que eso es todo lo   keláta↓ esⱥ|èstódoloketéŋgò↓ keágò↓   Jean: ¡Qué lata! Eso es todo lo que
que tiene, que qué hace Ud.   tengo. ¿Qué hago?

Carmen, dígale a Jean que no se preocupe,   nòseprⱥokúpè↓ yolèpwedoprestár↓   Carmen: No se preocupe. Yo le puedo
que Ud. le puede prestar.   prestar.

Jean, dígale que gracias, que qué amable.   graⱥyás↓ keⱥmáblè↓ àlⓂ̃yeçaralakasa|lepágò↓   Jean: Gracias. ¡Qué amable! Al llegar a
Que al llegar a la casa le paga.   la casa le pago.

23.4 READINGS

23.40 List of cognate loan words

           la conversación   là—kòmbèrsàⱥyón↓

           perfectamente   pèrféktaméntè↓

           la mamá   là—màmá↓

23.50   CINCUENTA

SPOKEN SPANISH   UNIT 23

el silencio   èl-silénşyò↓

insistió (insistir)   insistyó↓ insistír↓

la defensa   là-dèfénsà↓

23.41   Reading selection

¿Quién Rompió los Platos?

Los Fuentes estaban encantados al ver que aquellas dos niñas hablaban tan bien el español y que conversaban como dos personas grandes. Pero la conversación fue interrumpida por su madre:

—Bueno, niñas, ahora quiero saber qué estaban haciendo en la cocina a estas horas de la noche. ¿No las mandé a acostarse hace dos horas? ¿Por qué no están en su cama?

—But mother....—dijo Ruth.

—No me hablen en inglés. Ustedes saben perfectamente bien que no deben hablarme en inglés cuando yo les hablo en español.

—Perdón, mamá. Es que teníamos mucha hambre y fuimos a la cocina a comer algo.

—Pero, ¿no comieron lo suficiente antes de acostarse?

—Sí, mamá—contestó Jane esta vez—pero queríamos comer un poquito más del pastel de manzana tan delicioso que hiciste tú.

—¿Y por qué no me llamaron a mí?

—Porque tú estabas en la sala con estos señores y no queríamos molestarte.

—Bueno, está bien. Pero ahora quiero saber qué fue lo que rompieron en la cocina, y no quiero pretextos, quiero la verdad —dijo Virginia en tono riguroso.

Silencio completo; ninguna de las dos niñas hablaba. Pasaron varios segundos y por fin Jane habló:

—Fue una de aquellas tazas feas.

—¿Qué más?—insistió la madre.

CINCUENTA Y UNO   23.51

UNIT 23   SPOKEN SPANISH

—Dos platos también, mamá. Pero no fui yo, fue Ruth.

—Porque ella empezó a molestarme cuando los estaba lavando y entonces se me cayeron —exclamó Ruth en su defensa.

—No es verdad, mamá. Ella fue la que empezó a molestar y a decirme 'gorda fea.' Yo no estaba....

—Bueno, no quiero oír más—interrumpió Virginia rigurosamente. —Vayan a acostarse in-me-dia-ta-men-te. Y si se levantan otra vez, no hay más televisión.

—Sí, mamá—contestaron las dos niñas saliendo de la sala, no sin antes decir buenas noches a sus padres y a los señores Fuentes.

23.42   Response drill

1 ¿Por qué estaban encantados los Fuentes con las niñas?

2 ¿Quién interrumpió la conversación?

3 ¿Qué estaban haciendo ellas en la cocina?

4 ¿Por qué estaban comiendo?

5 ¿Qué estaban comiendo?

6 ¿Quién hizo el pastel?

7 ¿Cómo estaba el pastel?

8 ¿Por qué no llamaron a su mamá?

9 ¿Con quién estaba hablando la Sra. de Robinson en la sala?

10 ¿Cuántas tazas rompieron las niñas en la cocina?

11 ¿Qué más rompieron?

12 ¿Cuál de las dos rompió la taza y los dos platos?

13 ¿Por qué se le cayeron?

14 ¿Qué nombre le estaba diciendo Ruth a Jane?

15 ¿Qué va a pasar si se levantan otra vez de la cama?

23.52   CINCUENTA Y DOS

jacobeligoodsons.com For Free Audio

SPOKEN SPANISH   UNIT 24

24.1   BASIC SENTENCES.   Shopping in the stores.

        Carmen and Mrs. Harris are shopping in the stores.

ENGLISH SPELLING   AID TO LISTENING   SPANISH SPELLING

      the department   èl-dèpàrtàmentò↓   el departamento

Carmen   Carmen
    Shall we go to the women's department? (1)   bámos|aldepartaménto|desenyóras↑   ¿Vamos al departamento de señoras?

      the pair   èl-pár↓   el par

      the shoe   èl-şápatò↓   el zapato

Mrs. Harris   Sra. Harris
    Yes, I have to buy myself a pair of shoes.   sí↓ yoteṇgo|kekomprárme|úmpárdeşapátós↓   Sí, yo tengo que comprarme un par de
                                                                                       zapatos.

      the footwear   èl-kàlşadò↓   el calzado

Carmen   Carmen
    No, the footwear is in another section.   nó↓ èlkàlşadò|estaṇotra|sekşyón↓   No, el calzado está en otra sección.

      the dress   èl-bèstidò↓   el vestido

      the topcoat   èl-àbrigò↓   el abrigo

      the hat   èl-sòmbrerò↓   el sombrero

    There, there are only dresses, topcoats, and hats.   áⁱyı|sólǫáy|bèstidos|àbrigos|ısombréròs↓   Allí sólo hay vestidos, abrigos y sombreros.

UNO   24.1

UNIT 24   SPOKEN SPANISH

made (to make)   échò↓ àşér↓   hecho (hacer)

ready made clothes   lá—rrópạ—échà↓   la ropa hecha

Mrs. Harris   Sra. Harris
  Do you buy ready-made clothes?   ùstéḍ|kómpra|lárrópạéchá↑   ¿Usted compra la ropa hecha?

Carmen   Carmen
  Some times.   álgunạ⁊béşes| Algunas veces.

      the lack   lá—fáltà↓   la falta

      to (make a) lack   àşer—fáltà↓   hacer falta

      the cloth   lá—telà↓   la tela

      the skirt   lá—fáldà↓   la falda

      the blouse   lá—blusà↓   la blusa

  But now I need material for a skirt and a blouse.   pèrọảóra|mẹạşefáltatélá|pàrạûnàfalda| Pero ahora me hace falta tela para una
                                       ¡ûnàblusà↓   falda y una blusa.

      to sew   kòsér↓   coser

Mrs. Harris   Sra. Harris
  Oh, do you sew?   á↓ ùstẹⸯkòse↑   Ah, ¿Usted cose?

      the dressmaker   él—mòḍistà↓ lá—mòḍistà↓   el modista, la modista

Carmen   Carmen
  No, I have a dressmaker.   nó↓ téŋgọunamoḍístà↓   No, tengo una modista.

24.2   DOS

jacobeligoodsons.com For Free Audio

SPOKEN SPANISH   UNIT 24

itself (it) sees (to see itself)[2]   sẽ—bé↓ bèrsé↓   se ve (verse)

Mrs. Harris   sèbé|kèzmúybwénà↓ ùstèdsèbistè|múybyén↓   Sra. Harris
You can see that she's very good. You dress   Se ve que es muy buena. Usted se viste
very well.   muy bien.

Carmen   grásyàs↓   Carmen
Thank you.   Gracias.

       the tie   là—kòrbatà↓   la corbata

       the husband   èl—màridó↓   el marido

Mrs. Harris   kisyerạ|ùnàkòrbata|paramimarídó↓   Sra. Harris
I'd like a tie for my husband.   Quisiera una corbata para mi marido.

       the article   èl—àrtikùlò↓   el artículo

       the gentleman   èl—kàbáɡ̃yeró↓   el caballero

       down   àbahò↓   abajo

Carmen   lós,àrtíkùlós|pàràkàbáɡ̃yerós|èstán   Carmen
Men's clothes are downstairs. Shall we go down?[3]   Los artículos para caballeros están abajo.
                                             àbahò↓ bàhamos↑   ¿Bajamos?

       the exit, way out   là—sálidà↓   la salida

Mrs. Harris   nó↓ àlàsàlida|lozbémós↓   Sra. Harris
No, we'll see them on the way out.   No, a la salida los vemos.

TRES   24.3

UNIT 24   SPOKEN SPANISH

let's go (to go out, away) (4)   bamònós↓ írsè↓   vámonos (irse)

up   àrríbà↓   arriba

Let's go upstairs for your things.   bamonos,arriba|pòrlòsúyó↓   Vámonos arriba por lo suyo.

Carmen   kẹorạés↓   Carmen
  What time is it?   ¿Qué hora es?

Mrs. Harris   son|làs(s)iŋkọ1beyntiṣíŋkô↓   Sra. Harris
  It's five twenty five.   Son las cinco y veinticinco.

Carmen   sinónozdámosprisa↑sènòsạṣetárdè↓   Carmen
  If we don't hurry, we'll be late. (5)   Si no nos damos prisa, se nos hace
                                                                                 tarde.

24.10   Notes on the basic sentences

       (1) This is a typical example of the use of a simple present tense form in Spanish, /bámos/ *vamos*, in a context where the only reasonable translation is
English *shall*.

       (2) Notice that the translation given in the full utterance is 'You can see'. It could also have been 'one can see' or 'it can be seen', or even 'it is obvious',
'it's clear'. That is, the reflexive is here equivalent to what in English would be thought of as impersonal.

       (3) See note (1), above: /bahámos/ *bajamos* is similar here.

       (4) The form /bámonos/ *vámonos* is /bámos/ plus /nos/, with the final /—s/ of /bámos/ dropped in accord with a regular pattern.

       (5) /senosáṣetárde/ *se nos hace tarde* literally means 'it makes itself late for us' or 'it'll get late on us'.

24.4   CUATRO

jacobeligoodsons.com For Free Audio

SPOKEN SPANISH

UNIT 24

24.2   DRILLS AND GRAMMAR

24.21   Pattern drills

24.21.1   Reflexive clitic pronouns

A.   Presentation of pattern

ILLUSTRATIONS

_____	1	mémuđǫelsábáđô↓	*Me mudo* el sábado.
the minute		èl‑minutô↓	el minuto
I'll be dressed in thirty minutes.	2	yó |ǫntreyntaminutoʒ |mebístô↓	Yo en treinta minutos *me visto*.
_____	3	pòrlómenoz |nóʒđibértimozmúchò↓	Por lo menos *nos divertimos* mucho.
We don't worry much.	4	nónorprǫokupamoz |múchò↓	No *nos preocupamos* mucho.
_____	5	kwandotemúđás↓	¿Cuándo *te mudas?*
_____	6	ústeđsebiste |muybyén↓	Ud. *se viste* muy bien.
He pays a lot of attention to the brunette.	7	élsefíha |muchǫenlamorénå↓	El *se fija* mucho en la morena.

CINCO

24.5

jacobeligoodsons.com For Free Audio

UNIT 24   SPOKEN SPANISH

_____   8   misweǫra |sêmàreǫembárkò↓   Mi suegra *se marea* en barco.

You all notice everything.   9   ústedes |sêfihanentóờò↓   Ustedes *se fijan* en todo.

They change apartments almost every year.   10   e^yo(s)sekambyan |dęàpàrtámento | Ellos *se cambian* de apartamento casi
                                         kásitoơozlosáɲyòs↓   todos los años.

Those girls are always getting confused.   11   ésàschikas |syempresekomfúndèn↓   Esas chicas siempre *se confunden.*

EXTRAPOLATION

	sg	pl
1	me	nos
2 fam	te	
2-3	se	

a. Reflexive clitic pronouns repeat the person-number
   form of the subject.

b. The 2-3 form /se/ has no distirction for number.

c. Reflexive clitic forms are not differentiated for gender.

24.6   SEIS

jacobeligoodsons.com For Free Audio

SPOKEN SPANISH   UNIT 24

24.21.11 Substitution drill — Person-number substitution

1 yomemúde |dekásá↓   sèmúdodekásá↓
   èlkòrónel _____↓   sèmúdarondekásá↓
   lósharris _____↓   sèmúdodekásá↓
   mı̨èrmana _____↓   nòzmúdamozdekásá↓
   nòsótroz _____↓

2 eⁿyoz |nuŋkasekéhàn↓   nuŋkasekéhàn↓
   làzmúchacha? _____↓   nuŋkasekéhà↓
   àntónyo _____↓

_____

1 *Yo* me mudé de casa.

   El coronel _____.   Se mudó de casa.
   Los Harris _____.   Se mudaron de casa.
   Mi hermana _____.   Se mudó de casa.
   Nosotros _____.   Nos mudamos de casa.

2 *Ellos* nunca se quejan.
   Las muchachas _____.   Nunca se quejan.
   Antonio _____.   Nunca se queja.

SIETE

UNIT 24   SPOKEN SPANISH

      mįámįçǫiyó_____↓   nuŋkanoskehámôs↓
      yo _____↓   nuŋkamekéhô↓

  3   el˺ya|syempresebaŋyatárɖê↓
      yo _____↓   syempremebaŋyotárɖê↓
      mįsįhos_____↓   syempresebaŋyantárɖê↓
      nósotros_____↓   syempre|nozbaŋyamostárɖê↓
      elįhose_____↓   syempresebaŋyantárɖê↓

      Mi amigo y yo _____.   Nunca nos quejamos.
      Yo _____.   Nunca me quejo.

  3   *Ella* siempre se baña tarde.
      Yo _____ .   Siempre me baño tarde.
      Mis hijos _____ .   Siempre se bañan tarde.
      Nosotros _____ .   Siempre nos bañamos tarde.
      El y José _____.   Siempre se bañan tarde.

24.8   OCHO

SPOKEN SPANISH   UNIT 24

4 èlkòrónel |sèsyéntaǹyí↓

   yo_____↓   mèsyéntọañyí↓

   éꞁyos_____↓   sèsyéntanạñyí↓

   màría_____↓   sèsyéntañyí↓

   karlos_____↓   sèsyéntañyí↓

5 yo |mèdéspèdíđetóđòs↓

   karmen_____↓   sèdèspíđyođetóđós↓

   éꞁyos_____↓   sèdèspíđyerondetóđós↓

   mjàmíga_____↓   sèdèspíđyođetóđòs↓

   mjèrmanạiyo_____↓   nòzdèspèdimozdetóđòs↓

_____

    4 *El Coronel* se sienta allí.

      Yo_____ .   Me siento allí.

      Ellos_____ .   Se sientan allí.

      María_____ .   Se sienta allí.

      Carlos_____ .   Se sienta allí.

    5 *Yo* me despedí de todos.

      Carmen_____ .   Se despidió de todos.

      Ellos_____ .   Se despidieron de todos.

      Mi amiga_____ .   Se despidió de todos.

      Mi hermana y yo_____ .   Nos despedimos de todos.

NUEVE

UNIT 24   SPOKEN SPANISH

24.21.12 Response drill

             1   ùsteđ |sèsyéntàki↑ọaí↓   mèsyéntọakí↓

             2   ùsteđès |sèsyéntánàki↑ọaí↓   nò(s)sèntamọsakí↓

             3   él |sèsyéntàki↑ọaí↓   élsèsyéntakí↓

[àlá(s)syeté↓] 4   àkẹora |selebàntạustéđ↓   mèlèbantọ |àlà(s)syetè↓

[àlà(s)syeté↓] 5   àkẹora |selebàntanẹnsukásà↓   nòzlébántamos |àlà(s)syeté↓

[hwàn↓] 6   kyensemuđođekásà↓   hwan |sèmúđóđèkásà↓

[èlsàbáđó↓] 7   kwandosemuđó↓   sèmúđọ̀ɡlsábàđó↓

[pòrlàmàŋyanà↓] 8   sẹàfeytaṇusteđes |porlanóche↑   nò↓ nòsàféytamos |pòrlàmàŋyanà↓

---

             1 ¿Ud. se sienta aquí o ahí?   Me siento aquí.

             2 ¿Uds. se sientan aquí o ahí?   Nos sentamos aquí.

             3 ¿El se sienta aquí o ahí?   El se sienta aquí.

(a las siete) 4 ¿A qué hora se levanta Ud.?   Me levanto a las siete.

(a las siete) 5 ¿A qué hora se levantan en su casa?   Nos levantamos a las siete.

(Juan) 6 ¿Quién se mudó de casa?   Juan se mudó de casa.

(el sábado) 7 ¿Cuándo se mudó?   Se mudó el sábado.

(por la mañana) 8 ¿Se afeitan Uds. por la noche?   No, nos afeitamos por la mañana.

24.10   DIEZ

SPOKEN SPANISH   UNIT 24

[pòrlàmàŋyánà↓]   9   sèàféytàusteđ |porlanoche↑   nó↓ mèàféytó |pòrlàmàŋyánà↓

  [pòràbyón↓]   10   sèmàreanéʎyos |porbarko↑   nó↓ sèmàream |pòràbyón↓

  [pòràbyón↓]   11   sèmàreael |porbarko↑   nó↓ sèmàrea |pòràbyón↓

                12   sésyèntàusteđ |syémpreai↑   sí↓ syémpre |mèsyéntoàkí↓

                13   sésyéntanusteđes |syémpreai↑   sí↓ syémpre |nó(s)sèntámosˌakí↓

                14   sèkambyahose |muchođerropa↑   sí↓ sèkambyamúchò↓

                15   sèkómfundeusteđ |kónlòʔnombresˌespaŋyoles↑   sí↓ mèkómfundoumpókò↓

                16   sèàkwestàusteđtarđe |lo(s)sábados↑ sí↓ mèàkwesto |muytárđè↓

                17   sèàkwestanéʎyostarđe |lo(s)sábados↑ sí↓ sèàkwestan |muytárđè↓

_____

(por la mañana)   9 ¿Se afeita Ud. por la noche?   No, me afeito por la mañana.

  (por avión)   10 ¿Se marean ellos por barco?   No, se marean por avión.

  (por avión)   11 ¿Se marea él por barco?   No, se marea por avión.

                12 ¿Se sienta Ud. siempre ahí?   Sí, siempre me siento aquí.

                13 ¿Se sientan Uds. siempre ahí?   Sí, siempre nos sentamos aquí.

                14 ¿Se cambia José mucho de ropa?   Sí, se cambia mucho.

                15 ¿Se confunde Ud. con los nombres españoles? Sí, me confundo un poco.

                16 ¿Se acuesta Ud. tarde los sábados?   Sí, me acuesto muy tarde.

                17 ¿Se acuestan ellos tarde los sábados?   Sí, se acuestan muy tarde.

ONCE   24.11

jacobeligoodsons.com For Free Audio

UNIT 24   SPOKEN SPANISH

24.21.13 Translation drill

1 Last night we went to bed late.   ánoche |nós̯akòstanostárdé↓   Anoche nos acostamos tarde.

2 This morning I got up at ten.   éstamáņyana |mèlèbántealazcyéş↓   Esta mañana me levanté a las diez.

3 Yesterday I stayed at home.   àyer |mèkèdenlakásà↓   Ayer me quedé en la casa.

4 They stayed in the city.   éγos |sèkèdaron̩enlaşyudád↓   Ellos se quedaron en la ciudad.

5 We never complain about anything.   nòsótroz |nuŋkanoskehámoz |denádà↓   Nosotros nunca nos quejamos de nada.

6 Now we are used to hearing Spanish   ya |nòs̯akòstúmbramos |aòirablarespaŋyól↓   Ya nos acostumbramos a oír hablar español.
   spoken.

7 She moved last week.   éγa |semudodekasa |làsèmanapasádà↓   Ella se mudó de casa la semana pasada.

8 He didn't say goodbye to us.   nosedespidyo |denosótròs↓   No se despidió de nosotros.

9 Afterward, we got in touch with her.   dèspwez |nòskòmúnikamoskonéγà↓   Después nos comunicamos con ella.

10 I was very happy.   yó |mèalègremúchó↓   Yo me alegré mucho.

11 I never complain.   yónuŋkamekéhò↓   Yo nunca me quejo.

24.12   DOCE

SPOKEN SPANISH   UNIT 24

B. Discussion of pattern

As was pointed out in units 10 and 15, some verbs may appear with direct, some with indirect clitic pronouns. The verbs in the present section appear with a third set of clitic pronouns, called reflexive.

Reflexive clitics always appear identified with the subject of the verb they occur with; i.e., they have the same person and number forms as the subject. Other clitics never refer back to the subject.

Reflexive clitic pronouns may be direct or indirect in function, but they are 'reflexive' in form: that is, although /me/, /nos/ and /te/ look just like direct and indirect clitic forms, /se/ is unique to the reflexive group, and occurs for all 2-3 singular and plural functions. Some of the Spanish reflexive constructions are fairly easy to interpret through English. /sentárse/ 'to sit down' is easily inferred from 'to seat oneself,' /akostárse/ 'to go to bed' from 'to put oneself to bed.' Many times, however, a Spanish construction does not have the support of a possible English construction that is similar, as in the case of /kehárse/ 'to complain.' In English we cannot say 'to complain ourselves.' A verb like /kehárse/ is no less reflexive in Spanish than any other reflexive; it is classified and thought of as being of the same type as /sentárse/.

Translations vary with individual verbs in a reflexive construction, and usually they are quite understandable. There are a couple of patterns, however, that should be illustrated. Occasionally an impersonal or passive construction in English will be the equivalent of a Spanish reflexive construction:

/se‑bé |ke‑es‑múy‑bwéna↓/   It's easy to see she's very good.

/akí‑se‑ábla‑espaŋyól↓/   Spanish is spoken here.

Often a construction similar in type to English 'get ‑‑‑ ed' will equate with a Spanish reflexive construction:

/mi‑swégra |se‑maréa‑em‑bárko↓/   My mother-in-law gets sick on a boat.

/él‑se‑bistyó |en‑médya‑óra↓/   He got dressed in half an hour.

Sometimes a verb will be reflexive or not reflexive, with no apparent change in meaning:

/olbidárse/ ∼ /olbidár/   to forget

/desayunárse/∼/desayunár/   to have breakfast

though a difference in meaning may be carried by a change in the function of the reflexive from direct to indirect:

/komí‑wébos |al‑desayúno↓/   I ate eggs for breakfast.

/me‑komí‑dós‑wébos |al‑desayúno↓/   I ate two eggs for breakfast.

TRECE   24.13

UNIT 24   SPOKEN SPANISH

The function of an indirect reflexive clitic in the second sentence is correlated with the fact that the number of eggs eaten is specifically mentioned, whereas it is *not* mentioned in the first. The difference does not appear in translation.

Perhaps a more important translation equivalent is the correlation between a Spanish reflexive clitic and an English possessive adjective to signal possession:

/me—póngo—el—sombréro↓/   I put on my hat.

/téngo—ke—kambyárme—de—rrópa↓/   I have to change my clothes.

/bámos—a—ꞇyebárnos—el—kárro↓/   Let's take our car.

This construction is very common in Spanish when referring to an object that is normally considered a 'personal' kind of possession, such as parts of the body, articles of clothing, etc.

Since there is not a one-to-one correspondence of Spanish reflexive constructions to any English construction, the context of the entire sentence usually suggests an appropriate translation equivalent. Note some possibilities of the verb /bestírse/ :

/él—se—bistyó|rrápidaménte↓/   'He got dressed quickly.'

/él—se—bíste|múy—byén↓/   'He dresses very well.'

In a verb construction, reflexives always precede other clitics. A full chart of Spanish clitic pronouns, which indicates their position relative to each other, whether preceding or following a verb, is presented below:

	Reflexive	Indirect	Direct
sg 1 pl		me	
		nos	
2 fam		te	
sg 2-3 pl	se	le (se) les	lɔ (le),la los, las

As this chart shows, reflexive, indirect, and direct clitic forms are distinguished only in 2-3 person forms; a single form functions in all three categories for all 1 and 2 fam. forms. Direct clitics (in 2-3 forms) distinguish number and gender, indirect distinguish only number (though even this distinction is lost when indirect /se/ appears), and reflexives fail to distinguish either number or gender.

24.14   CATORCE

SPOKEN SPANISH															UNIT 24

24.21.2   Reflexive clitic pronouns with progressive and periphrastic future verb constructions

   A. Presentation of pattern

ILLUSTRATIONS

I was brushing my teeth.	1	yomestaba│limpyandolozdyéntēs↓	*Yo me estaba limpiando los dientes.*
_____	2	yoęstaba│limpyandomelozdyéntēs↓	Yo *estaba limpiándome* los dientes.
But now I'm getting used to everything.	3	pērǫya│mébóyåkóstúmbrandǫ│atódó↓	Pero ya *me voy acostumbrando* a todo.
_____	4	pērǫya│bóyåkóstúmbrándomę│atódó↓	Pero ya *voy acostumbrándome* a todo.
My neighbors are going to move.	5	mizbęşinos│sębánąmúdardekásá↓	Mis vecinos *se van a mudar* de casa.
_____	6	mizbęşinoz│bánąmúdarsedekásá↓	Mis vecinos *van a mudarse* de casa.
I was going to take a shower too.	7	męíbådar│únåducha│támbyén↓	*Me iba a dar* una ducha también.
_____	8	íbådarmę│únåduchå│támbyén↓	*Iba a darme* una ducha también.

QUINCE															24.15

jacobeligoodsons.com For Free Audio

UNIT 24   SPOKEN SPANISH

EXTRAPOLATION

Progressive				Periphrastic future				
/se/	verb /estár/	/‑ndo/ form		/se/	verb /ír/	/a/	infinitive	
	verb /estár/	/‑ndo/ form	/se/		verb /ír/	/a/	infinitive	/se/

NOTES

a. Any reflexive clitic, symbolized above by /se/, can appear in a construction preceding the conjugated verb
   (here /estár/ or /ír/) or following the /‑ndo/ form or infinitive.

b. Sometimes, other verbs substitute for /estár/ in progressive constructions.

24.16   DIECISEIS

jacobeligoodsons.com For Free Audio

SPOKEN SPANISH   UNIT 24

24.21.21 Substitution drills - Person-number substitution

1   ana |sèstámúdandodekásà↓

    hwan _____↓   sèstámúdandodekásà↓

    misérmanas _____↓   sèstánnúdandodekásà↓

    nòsótroz_____↓   nòsêstamoz |múdandodekásà↓

    yo_____↓   mèstoymúdandodekásà↓

_____

1   *Ana* se está mudando de casa.

    Juan _____.   Se está mudando de casa.

    Mis hermanas_____.   Se están mudando de casa.

    Nosotros_____.   Nos estamos mudando de casa.

    Yo_____.   Me estoy mudando de casa.

DIECISIETE

UNIT 24

2 yo |nomestóykehándȯ↓
    lȧzmúchachaz_____↓
    ȅlsȇŋyor_____↓
    mȧȧmigȧȧyo_____↓
    karmen_____↓

3 ȧntónyo |sȇst ȧbistyéndȯ↓
    yo_____↓
    mȧria_____↓
    nȯsotroz_____↓
    lȯzmúchachos_____↓

nȯsestaŋkehándȯ↓
nȯsestakehándȯ↓
nȯnos̶estamoskehándȯ↓
nȯsestakehándȯ↓

mȇstóybistyéndȯ↓
sȇstȧbistyéndȯ↓
nȯs̶ȇstamozbistyéndȯ↓
sȇstambistyéndȯ↓

---

2 *Yo* no me estoy quejando.
    Las muchachas_____ .
    El señor_____ .
    Mi amiga y yo_____ .
    Carmen_____ .

3 *Antonio* se está vistiendo.
    Yo_____ .
    María_____ .
    Nosotros_____ .
    Los muchachos_____ .

No se están quejando.
No se está quejando.
No nos estamos quejando.
No se está quejando.

Me estoy vistiendo.
Se está vistiendo.
Nos estamos vistiendo.
Se están vistiendo.

24.18   jacobeligoodsons.com For Free Audio   DIECIOCHO

SPOKEN SPANISH   UNIT 24

4 ana│estamuɗándòsè↓
   hwan _____↓   èstamuɗándòsè↓
   mɪ̀érmana _____↓   èstamuɗándòsè↓
   nòsotros _____↓   èstamozmuɗándònòs↓
   yo _____↓   èstoymuɗándòmè↓

5 yó│noestoykehándòmè↓
   làzmùchachaɾ _____↓   noestankehándòsè↓
   èlsèɲyor _____↓   noestakehándòsè↓
   mɪ̀ámiçaɪyo _____↓   noestamoskehándònòs↓
   karmen _____↓   noestakehándòsè↓

_____

   4 Ana está mudándose.
      Juan_____ .   Está mudándose.
      Mi hermana _____ .   Está mudándose.
      Nosotros_____.   Estamos mudándonos.
      Yo_____ .   Estoy mudándome.

   5 Yo no estoy quejándome.
      Las muchachas_____.   No están quejándose.
      El señor_____.   No está quejándose.
      Mi amiga y yo_____.   No estamos quejándonos.
      Carmen _____ .   No está quejándose.

DIECINUEVE   jacobeligoodsons.com For Free Audio   24.19

UNIT 24   SPOKEN SPANISH

6 àntónyọ |èstàbistyéndòsè↓

   yo_____↓   èstoyʰistyéndòmè↓

   máriạ_____↓   èstàbistyéndòsè↓

   nòsotros_____↓   èstàmozbistyéndònòs↓

   lòzmúchachos_____↓   èstàmbistyéndòsè↓

7 ána |sèḃápònernèrḃyósà↓

   éⁿyos_____↓   sèban |àpònernerḃyósòs↓

   kármèn_____↓   sèḃá |àpònernerḃyósà↓

   yo_____↓   mèboy |àpònernerḃyósò↓

   nòsotroz_____↓   nòzbamos |àpònernerḃyósòs↓

---

6 *Antonio* está vistiéndose.

   Yo _____ .   Estoy vistiéndome.

   María _____ .   Está vistiéndose.

   Nosotros _____ .   Estamos vistiéndonos.

   Los muchachos _____ .   Están vistiéndose.

7 *Ana* se va a poner nerviosa.

   Ellos _____ .   Se van a poner nerviosos.

   Carmen _____ .   Se va a poner nerviosa.

   Yo _____ .   Me voy a poner nervioso.

   Nosotros _____ .   Nos vamos a poner nerviosos.

24.20   jacobeligoodsons.com For Free Audio   VEINTE

SPOKEN SPANISH   UNIT 24

8 éᶜyos |sèbánâkèᵈar |enlaşyuᵈáᵈ↓

   karmen _____↓   sèbákèᵈar |enlaşyuᵈáᵈ↓

   lòspilotos _____↓   sòbánâkèᵈar |enlaşyuᵈáᵈ↓

   éltènyéntᵉıyó _____↓   nòzbámósâkèᵈar |enlaşyuᵈáᵈ↓

   yó _____↓   mèbóyâkèᵈar |enlaşyuᵈáᵈ↓

9 yomeboy |âᵈèspèᵈirelhwébès↓

   àntònyo _____↓   sèba |âᵈèspèᵈirelhwébès↓

   mᵢıha _____↓   sèba |âᵈèspèᵈirelhwébès↓

   misámigos _____↓   sèban |âᵈèspèᵈirelhwébès↓

   miswegrᵃıyó _____↓   nòzbamos |âᵈèspèᵈirelhwébès↓

_____

   8 *Ellos* se van a quedar en la ciudad.

      Carmen _____.   Se va a quedar en la ciudad.

      Los pilotos _____.   Se van a quedar en la ciudad.

      El teniente y yo _____.   Nos vamos a quedar en la ciudad.

      Yo _____.   Me voy a quedar en la ciudad.

   9 *Yo* me voy a despedir el jueves.

      Antonio _____.   Se va a despedir el jueves.

      Mi hija _____.   Se va a despedir el jueves.

      Mis amigos _____.   Se van a despedir el jueves.

      Mi suegra y yo _____.   Nos vamos a despedir el jueves.

VEINTIUNO   24.21

UNIT 24   SPOKEN SPANISH

10 ána |bápónersénerbyósá↓

    éꞓyoz _____ ↓   ban |ápónersénerbyósós↓

    kármém _____ ↓   bá |ápónersénerbyósá↓

    yó _____ ↓   boy |ápónermenerbyósó↓

    nósótroz _____ ↓   bámos |ápónernoznerbyósós↓

11 éꞓyoz |bánákéꞓarsénlaꞩyuꞁáꞁ↓

    kármém _____ ↓   bákéꞓarsé |enlaꞩyuꞁáꞁ↓

    lóspílótoz _____ ↓   bánákéꞓarsé |enlaꞩyuꞁáꞁ↓

    éltényéntéꞵyó _____ ↓   bámósꞵkéꞓarnos |enlaꞩyuꞁáꞁ↓

    yó _____ ↓   bóyꞵkéꞓarmé |enlaꞩyuꞁáꞁ↓

---

10 *Ana* va a ponerse nerviosa.

    Ellos _____ .   Van a ponerse nerviosos.

    Carmen _____ .   Va a ponerse nerviosa.

    Yo _____ .   Voy a ponerme nervioso.

    Nosotros _____ .   Vamos a ponernos nerviosos.

11 *Ellos* van a quedarse en la ciudad.

    Carmen _____ .   Va a quedarse en la ciudad.

    Los pilotos _____ .   Van a quedarse en la ciudad.

    El teniente y yo _____ . Vamos a quedarnos en la ciudad.

    Yo _____ .   Voy a quedarme en la ciudad.

24.22   jacobeligoodsons.com For Free Audio   VEINTIDOS

SPOKEN SPANISH   UNIT 24

12 yó |bóyàdèspèdirmelhwébès↓
    àntónyo_____↓   ba |àdèspèdirselhwébès↓
    míìha_____↓   ba |àdèspèdirselhwébès↓
    misàmígoz_____↓   bàn |àdèspèdirselhwébès↓
    miswègrayyó_____↓   bàmos |àdèspèdirnoselhwébès↓

13 eCyoz |bánàkèhársè |dèspwés↓
    mièsposa_____↓   bakehársè |dèspwés↓
    yó_____↓   bòyakèhármè |dèspwés↓
    lòspílótoz_____↓   bànàkehársè |dèspwés↓
    èltènyénte_____↓   bakehársè |dèspwés↓

_____

12 *Yo* voy a despedirme el jueves.
    Antonio _____.   Va a despedirse el jueves.
    Mi hija _____.   Va a despedirse el jueves.
    Mis amigos_____.   Van a despedirse el jueves.
    Mi suegra y yo_____.   Vamos a despedirnos el jueves.

13 *Ellos* van a quejarse después.
    Mi esposa _____.   Va a quejarse después.
    Yo_____.   Voy a quejarme después.
    Los pilotos_____.   Van a quejarse después.
    El teniente_____.   Va a quejarse después.

VEINTITRES   24.23

UNIT 24   SPOKEN SPANISH

Construction substitution

PROBLEM 1:
        ésámúchacha↑sèbístèbyén↓

ANSWER:
        ésámúchacha↑sèstábìstyéndòbyén↓

        ésámúchacha↑èstábìstyéndòsèbyén↓

PROBLEM 2:
        éɟɟos|sèdíbyertènmúchó↓

ANSWER:
        éɟɟoz|sèbánàdìbèrtírmúchó↓

        éɟɟoz|bánàdìbèrtírsèmúchó↓

_____

PROBLEM 1:
             Esa muchacha se viste bien.

ANSWER: Esa muchacha se está vistiendo bien.
             Esa muchacha está vistiéndose bien.

PROBLEM 2:
             Ellos se divierten mucho.

ANSWER:
             Ellos se van a divertir mucho.
             Ellos van a divertirse mucho.

24.24   VEINTICUATRO

SPOKEN SPANISH   UNIT 24

1 mįèspósa|sèkéha|múchọ|àóràↆ   mįèsposa|sèstákèhando|múchọ|àóràↆ
                                                   mįèsposạ|èstákèhandose|múchọ|àóràↆ

2 nòsótróz|nòskèdamos|ènlạófíṣịnạↆ   nòsótroz|nòsẹéstamos|kèdandọ|ènlạófíṣịnạↆástàmuy
   ástàmuytárdèↆ   tárdèↆ
                                                   nòsótros|èstámòskèdandonos|ènlạófíṣịnạↆástàmuy
                                                   tárdèↆ

3 yómẹàféyto|dòzbéṣès|àóràↆ   yó|mèstóyàfèytando|dòzbéṣès|àóràↆ
                                                   yó|ẹstóyàfèytandome|dòzbéṣès|àóràↆ

4 eﬡya|sepónenerbyósàↆ   eﬡya|sèstápònyendonerbyósàↆ
                                                   eﬡyạ|èstápònyendosenerbyósàↆ

---

1 Mi esposa se queja mucho ahora.   Mi esposa se está quejando mucho ahora.
                                              Mi esposa está quejándose mucho ahora.

2 Nosotros nos quedamos en la oficina hasta muy tarde.   Nosotros nos estamos quedando en la oficina hasta muy tarde.
                                                           Nosotros estamos quedándonos en la oficina hasta muy tarde.

3 Yo me afeito dos veces ahora.   Yo me estoy afeitando dos veces ahora.
                                              Yo estoy afeitándome dos veces ahora.

4 Ella se pone nerviosa.   Ella se está poniendo nerviosa.
                                              Ella está poniéndose nerviosa.

VEINTICINCO

UNIT 24   SPOKEN SPANISH

5   mèsyéntɣaḷyí↓   boy|àséntarmɛaḷyí↓
                                                     mèboy|àséntaraḷyí↓

6   syémpre|nózdèspèdimoz|dɛḷyà↓   syémprebamos|àdèspèdirnozdɛḷyà↓
                                                     syémprenozbamos|àdèspèdirdɛḷyà↓

7   eḷyos|sèkèdanɛnɛlkóchè↓   eḷyoz|bánàkèdarsenɛlkóchè↓
                                                     eḷyos|sèbánàkèdarenɛlkóchè↓

8   ána|sèprɛòkúpàmúchò↓   ána|báprɛòkúparsèmúchò↓
                                                     ána|sèbáprɛòkúparmúchò↓

9   yó|mèdèspidodetódòs↓   yó|bóyàdèspèdirme|dètódòs↓
                                                     yó|mèbóyàdèspèdir|dètódòs↓

_____

5 Me siento allí.   Voy a sentarme allí.
                                                    Me voy a sentar allí.

6 Siempre nos despedimos de ella.   Siempre vamos a despedirnos de ella.
                                                    Siempre nos vamos a despedir de ella.

7 Ellos se quedan en el coche.   Ellos van a quedarse en el coche.
                                                    Ellos se van a quedar en el coche.

8 Ana se preocupa mucho.   Ana va a preocuparse mucho.
                                                    Ana se va a preocupar mucho.

9 Yo me despido de todos.   Yo voy a despedirme de todos.
                                                    Yo me voy a despedir de todos.

24.26   VEINTISEIS

SPOKEN SPANISH   UNIT 24

24.21.22 Response drill

1   ústed |sèbásèntáràkitْ o@)ŷí↓   mèbóy|asèntàrakí↓
2   ústedes |sèbánàsèntáràkitْ o@)ŷí↓   nòzbámos|asèntàrakí↓
3   ústed |báfèytàrsẹ|éstànóchẹtْ omaŋyánà↓   bóyàfèytàrmẹ|èstànòchè↓
4   el |báfèytàrsẹ|éstànóchẹtْ omaŋyánà↓   báfèytàrsẹ|èstànòchè↓

[náɟyè↓]   5   kyénẹstàkehándòsè↓   náɟyẹ|èstákèhándòsè↓

───

1   ¿Ud. se va a sentar aquí o allí?   Me voy a sentar aquí.
2   ¿Uds. se van a sentar aquí o allí?   Nos vamos a sentar aquí.
3   ¿Ud. va a afeitarse esta noche o mañana?   Voy a afeitarme esta noche.
4   ¿El va a afeitarse esta noche o mañana?   Va a afeitarse esta noche.

(nadie)   5   ¿Quién está quejándose?   Nadie está quejándose.

VEINTISIETE   24.27

jacobeligoodsons.com For Free Audio

UNIT 24   SPOKEN SPANISH

[àntónyò↓] 6 kyénsestámuďándò↓   àntónyò|sèstámuďándò↓
[únabéş↓]   7 kwántazbéşes|àldía|ęstásafeytándòtè↓   èstoyafeytándomę|unabéş↓

[èlsàbàďò↓] 8 bámúďarsęantónyǫ|eldomingò↑   nò↓ bámúďarsę|elsábàďò↓
[êstànóchê↓] 9 tébasafeytártú|aorà↑   nò↓ mèbóyàfèytár|estanóchê↓

           10 bánàkòstarsęustèďes|tárďę|elsábado↑   si|sìbamos|àkòstarnostárďè↓
           11 sèbákòstarustéď|tárďę|elsábado↑   si|sìmebóy|àkòstartárďè↓

(Antonio)   6 ¿Quién se está mudando?   Antonio se está mudando.
(una vez)   7 ¿Cuántas veces al día estás afeitándote?   Estoy afeitándome una vez.

(el sábado)   8 ¿Va a mudarse Antonio el domingo?   No, va a mudarse el sábado.
(esta noche)   9 ¿Te vas a afeitar tú ahora?   No, me voy a afeitar esta noche.

              10 ¿Van a acostarse Uds. tarde el sábado?   Sí, sí vamos a acostarnos tarde.
              11 ¿Se va a acostar Ud. tarde el sábado?   Sí, sí me voy a acostar tarde.

24.28   VEINTIOCHO

SPOKEN SPANISH   UNIT 24

24.21.23 Translation drill

1 We're going to move to a pretty house.   bámòşàmúdarnos |a̧únàkasabonítà↓   Vamos a mudarnos a una casa bonita.

2 That boy's going to fall and break his   ésèmúchacho |sèbákàer↑ìbárrómpersè | Ese muchacho se va a caer y va a romperse
   head.   lakabȩ́şà↓   la cabeza.

3 I'm getting nervous.   mèstóyponyéndonerbyósò↓   Me estoy poniendo nervioso.

4 Now I'm shaving late.   àorȧ |èstóyàfèytandometárdè↓   Ahora estoy afeitándome tarde.

5 We're staying here every afternoon.   nòşèstamos |kèdándo̧àkí↑todàzlastárdès↓   Nos estamos quedando aquí todas las
                                                                                             tardes.

6 Why are you complaining about the   pórke |sestakehándo̧usted |delozmwéblès↓   ¿Por qué se está quejando Ud. de los
   furniture?   muebles?

7 They are going to change clothes.   él̞yoz |bánȧkàmbyarsederrópà↓   Ellos van a cambiarse de ropa.

8 It's getting late.   sèsta̧şyendotárdè↓   Se está haciendo tarde.

9 We're going to bed.   nòz̧bamoşàkostár↓   Nos vamos a acostar.

10 When are you going to shave?   kwàndo |sebafeytár |ùstéd̞↓   ¿Cuándo se va a afeitar Ud.?

11 Are you all going to get up late tomorrow?   ban |àlèbàntársètarde |mańyȧnȧ↑   ¿Van a levantarse tarde mañana?

12 Tonight I'm going to bed late.   éstànoche↑mèbóyàkòstártárdè↓   Esta noche me voy a acostar tarde.

13 He's going to bed late now.   él |sèstákóstándòtárdȩ |à̧órà↓   El se está acostando tarde ahora.

VEINTINUEVE   24.29

UNIT 24   SPOKEN SPANISH

B. Discussion of pattern

Like other clitic pronouns, reflexives normally precede a conjugated verb, but follow an /—ndo/form or an infinitive, (or an affirmative command: see Unit 29).

When a progressive construction or a periphrastic future construction occurs, thus yielding a conjugated form and an /—ndo/form or an infinitive in a sequence, the clitic may appear either *before* the conjugated form or *after* the nonconjugated form. It apparently makes no difference to the meaning of the resulting verb-clitic construction whether the clitic precedes or follows. The clitic must occur before or after the *whole* construction; it cannot occur *between* the conjugated and nonconjugated verb forms.

/me—bóy—a—labár↓/   'I'm going to get washed.'

/bóy—a—labárme↓/

/me—estóy—labándo↓/   'I'm getting washed.'

/estóy—labándome↓/

The freedom of occurrence which the clitic has is confined to the construction which ends with the 'reflexive' verb. In the following examples, the clitic can precede the conjugated verb or follow the first infinitive, but it cannot follow the second, which is added to the 'reflexive' construction and is not properly a part of it.

/me—bóy—a—ponér—a—trabahár↓/   'I'm going to begin to work.'

/bóy—a—ponérme—a—trabahár↓/

One of the differences between present tense and present progressive is particularly noticeable in reflexive constructions. Present tense tends to signal the customary present (an extension into both the past and the future from the strictly logical present, as in 'She dresses real well'). Present progressive tends to signal a more limited reference to present time, with the implication of a change *to* present conditions in the recent past. Note these differences in the translation equivalents of the following paired sentences:

/maría—se—bíste—byén↓/   Mary dresses well (always).

/maría—se—está—bistyéndo—byén↓/   Mary's starting to dress well (now).

/alíşya—se—póne—nerbyósa↓/   Alice gets nervous (always).

/alíşya—se—está—ponyéndo—nerbyósa↓/   Alice is getting nervous (now).

The difference is between the implication of 'always' or 'generally' in the first sentence and 'now' or 'lately' in the second.

24.30   jacobeligoodsons.com For Free Audio   TREINTA

SPOKEN SPANISH   UNIT 24

These distinctions, however, can be obscured by the occurrence of verb modifiers, which seem to take semantic precedence over the meanings inherent in the tense or construction. Note the modifications in the following examples:

/maría‖se‖bíste‖byén‖aóra↓/   Mary dresses well now (previously didn't).

/maría‖syémpre‖se‖está‖ponyéndo‖nerbyósa↓/   Mary's always getting nervous (habitual).

24.21.3 Expressions for time of day

A. Presentation of pattern

                                    ILLUSTRATIONS

————————	1 keóraés↓	¿Qué hora es?
It's one o'clock.	2 èzlaunà↓	Es la una.
What time is it?	3 keóra(s)són↓	¿Qué horas son?
————————	4 sònlàzdóse↓	Son las doce.
————————	5 sònlàzdóse│ménoskwártó↓	Son las doce menos cuarto.
It's three minutes to two.	6 sònlàzdóz│ménostrés↓	Son las dos menos tres.
It's four fifteen.	7 sònlàskwatro│ikínse↓	Son las cuatro y quince.
It's six thirty.	8 sònlà(s)séys│iméáyà↓	Son las seis y media.

TREINTA Y UNO   24.31

UNIT 24   SPOKEN SPANISH

EXTRAPOLATION

las‑dóṣe‑ménos‑kwárto (kínṣe) un‑kwárto‑para‑las‑dóṣe las‑ónṣe‑ı‑kwarénta‑ı‑ṣínko	las‑dóṣe‑ménos‑ṣínko sínko‑para‑las‑dóṣe	las‑dóṣe	las‑dóṣe‑ı‑ṣínko	las‑dóṣe‑ı‑kwárto (kínṣe)	las‑dóṣe‑ı‑médya (tréynta)

NOTES

a. Time is usually expressed from the nearest hour: /ménos/
    equals 'before' or 'to', and /ı/ equals 'after' or 'past'.

24.32   jacobeligoodsons.com For Free Audio   TREINTA Y DOS

SPOKEN SPANISH   UNIT 24

24.21.31 Translation drill

   1 What time is it?   keóraés↓   ¿Qué hora es?

   2 It's one o'clock.   ézlaúná↓   Es la una.

   3 It's five after one.   ézlaúnaişínko↓   Es la una y cinco.

   4 It's one thirty.   ézlaúnaitréyntá↓   Es la una y treinta.

   5 It's two o'clock.   sónlázdós↓   Son las dos.

   6 It's a quarter after two.   sónlázdosikwárto↓   Son las dos y cuarto.

   7 It's two thirty.   sónlázdosimédyá↓   Son las dos y media.

   8 It's two forty-five.   sónlázdos|ikwaréntaişínkó↓   Son las dos y cuarenta y cinco.

   9 It's three minutes to twelve.   sónlázdoşe|menostrés↓   Son las doce menos tres.

B. Discussion of pattern

   The time is usually asked in Spanish by the question /keóraés↓/, though this may be pluralized to /keóra(s)són↓/. The answer 'one o'clock' is /éslaúna↓/, but two o'clock, etc. are /sónlasdós↓/ etc. The article /la/ always appears in the statement; the noun /óra/ , which, judging from the question is implied by the /la/ , nevertheless never appears.

   When an exact hour is not involved, the time is usually calculated from the nearest hour, though an expression like 'a quarter to...' /las—ónşe—i—kwarénta—i—şínko↓/ is fairly common.

   A twenty-four hour clock is observed in the written schedules of railroads, airlines, in military establishments, etc., but in general conversation the phrase /de—la—maŋyána/ indicates a.m. and /de—la—tárde/ and /de—la—nóche/ indicate p.m.

   Notice that /médya/ 'half' is a modifier and agrees with /óra/ , but that /kwárto/ 'quarter' is a noun and does not show this agreement.

TREINTA Y TRES   24.33

jacobeligoodsons.com For Free Audio

UNIT 24   SPOKEN SPANISH

24.22   Replacement drills

A   bámos |áldèpártámento |desèŋyóras↑

1   _____niŋyos↑   bámos |áldèpártámento |dèniŋyos↑

2   _____sèkṣyon_____↑   bámos |àlàsèkṣyon |dèniŋyos↑

3   boy_____↑   boy |àlàsèkṣyon |dèniŋyos↑

4   _____imformaṣyónes↑   boy |àlàsèkṣyon |dèimformaṣyónes↑

5   _____òfiṣína_____↑   boy |àlạòfiṣína |dèimformaṣyónes↑

6   prègúntọ |èn_____↑   prègúntọ |ènlạòfiṣína |dèimformaṣyónes↑

7   _____ṣéntro_____↑   prègúntọ |ènàlṣéntro |dèimformaṣyónes↑

A   ¿Vamos al departamento de señoras?

1   ¿_____niños?   ¿Vamos al departamento de niños?

2   ¿_____sección_____?   ¿Vamos a la sección de niños?

3   ¿Voy_____?   ¿Voy a la sección de niños?

4   ¿_____informaciones?   ¿Voy a la sección de informaciones?

5   ¿_____oficina_____?   ¿Voy a la oficina de informaciones?

6   ¿Pregunto en_____?   ¿Pregunto en la oficina de informaciones?

7   ¿_____centro_____?   ¿Pregunto en el centro de informaciones?

24.34   TREINTA Y CUATRO

jacobeligoodsons.com For Free Audio

SPOKEN SPANISH   UNIT 24

B   yótengo |kèkómprarmẹụmpár↓

1   él_____↓   éltyéne |kèkómprarsẹụmpár↓

2   _____àkel↓   éltyéne |kèkómprarsẹ |àkélpár↓

3   _____kómprartẹ_____↓   tútyénes |kèkómprartẹ |àkélpár↓

4   _____blúsàs↓   tútyénes |kèkómprartẹ |àkeꞶꞶazblúsàs↓

5   _____ꞶꞶẹbárnos_____↓   nòsótros |tènémoskeꞶꞶẹbárnos |àkeꞶꞶaz
                                         blúsàs↓

6   éꞶꞶa _____↓   eꞶꞶa |tyénèkèꞶꞶèbàrsẹ |àkeꞶꞶazblúsàs↓

7   ____kyéré_____↓   eꞶꞶa |kyéréꞶꞶèbàrsẹ |àkeꞶꞶazblúsàs↓

B   Yo tengo que comprarme un par.

1 El _____ .   El tiene que comprarse un par.

2 _____ aquel__ .   El tiene que comprarse aquel par.

3 _____ comprarte _____ .   Tú tienes que comprarte aquel par.

4 _____ blusas .   Tú tienes que comprarte aquellas blusas.

5 _____ llevarnos _____ .   Nosotros tenemos que llevarnos aquellas blusas.

6 Ella_____ .   Ella tiene que llevarse aquellas blusas.

7 ___quiere _____ .   Ella quiere llevarse aquellas blusas.

TREINTA Y CINCO   24.35

jacobeligoodsons.com For Free Audio

UNIT 24   SPOKEN SPANISH

C   nó↓ èlkálşádo|ęstáęnótrasekşyón↓   nó↓ lòs(ş)ápatos|éstánénótrasekşyón↓

1 _____şápatos_____↓   nó↓ lòs(ş)ápatos|éstánénótrodepartaméntô↓

2 _____departaméntô↓   nó↓ lámóđísta|ęstáęnótrodepartaméntô↓

3 _____móđísta_____↓   nó↓ lámóđísta|tràbáhąęnótrodepartaméntô↓

4 _____tràbáhą_____↓   nó↓ lámóđísta|tràbáhąęnótrakásà↓

5 _____kásà↓   nó↓ lámóđísta|bíbęnótrakásà↓

6 _____bíbè_____↓   nó↓ lámóđísta|bíbęnótrobárryô↓

7 _____bárryô↓

C   No, el calzado está en otra sección.

1 __, __ zapatos _____.   No, los zapatos están en otra sección.

2 __, _____departamento.   No, los zapatos están en otro departamento.

3 __, __modista _____.   No, la modista está en otro departamento.

4 __, _____trabaja _____.   No, la modista trabaja en otro departamento.

5 __, _____casa.   No, la modista trabaja en otra casa.

6 __, _____vive_____.   No, la modista vive en otra casa.

7 __, _____barrio.   No, la modista vive en otro barrio.

24.36   TREINTA Y SEIS

SPOKEN SPANISH   UNIT 24

D   ústed |kompra |larrópaҽchat

1   _____ bestidos_t   ústed |kompra |lozbestidosҽchost

2   ústeɗès _____t   ústeɗès |kompran |lozbestidosҽchost

3   _____ benden _____t   ústeɗèz |benden |lozbestidosҽchost

4   _____ byehost   ústeɗèz |benden |lozbestidozbyehost

5   _____ rropa _____t   ústeɗèz |benden |larropabyehat

6   _____ mucha _____t   ústeɗèz |benden |mucha |rropabyehat

7   _____ artıkuloz _____t   ústeɗèz |benden |muchos |artıkulozbyehost

---

D   ¿Usted compra la ropa hecha?

1   ¿ _____ vestidos _____ ?   ¿Usted compra los vestidos hechos?

2   ¿Ustedes _____ ?   ¿Ustedes compran los vestidos hechos?

3   ¿ _____ venden _____ ?   ¿Ustedes venden los vestidos hechos?

4   ¿ _____ viejos?   ¿Ustedes venden los vestidos viejos?

5   ¿ _____ ropa _____ ?   ¿Ustedes venden la ropa vieja?

6   ¿ _____ mucha _____ ?   ¿Ustedes venden mucha ropa vieja?

7   ¿ _____ articulos _____?   ¿Ustedes venden muchos articulos viejos?

TREINTA Y SIETE   24.37

jacobeligoodsons.com For Free Audio

UNIT 24   SPOKEN SPANISH

E   noↄ téŋgǫunamǫdístà↓

1   _____ báryaz _____↓   noↄ téŋgòbaryazmǫdístàs↓

2   _____ íhòs↓   noↄ téŋgòbaryosíhòs↓

3   sí _____↓   síↄ téŋgòbaryosíhòs↓

4   _____ una _____↓   síↄ teŋgǫunaíhà↓

5   _____ dólàr↓   síↄ teŋgǫundólàr↓

6   _____ algúnoz _____↓   síↄ teŋgǫalgunozdólàrès↓

7   _____ traygǫ _____↓   síↄ traygǫalgunozdólàrès↓

_____

E   No, tengo una modista.

1   ___, _____ varias _____.   No, tengo varias modistas.

2   ___, _____ hijos .   No, tengo varios hijos.

3   Sí, _____.   Sí, tengo varios hijos.

4   ___, _____ una _____   Sí, tengo una hija.

5   ___, _____ dólar.   Sí, tengo un dólar.

6   ___, _____ algunos _____.   Sí, tengo algunos dólares.

7   ___ traigo _____.   Sí, traigo algunos dólares.

24.38   TREINTA Y OCHO

SPOKEN SPANISH   UNIT 24

F   lós‚àrtíkulos |páràkàbáᶜⁱyeros |están‚abáhò↓

1   _____ombres_____↓   lòs‚àrtíkulos |párᶏombres |están‚abáhò↓

2   ____rropa_____↓   làrrópa |párᶏombres |estabáhò↓

3   _____akí↓   làrrópa |párᶏombres |estakí↓

4   ____kosas_____↓   làskósas |párᶏombres |están‚akí↓

5   _____niɲos_____↓   làskósas |páràniɲyos |están‚akí↓

6   toɗazlas_____↓   toɗazlaskósas |páràniɲyos |están‚akí↓

7   ____artikulos_____↓   toɗozlos‚artíkulos |páràniɲyos |están‚akí↓

_____

F   Los artículos para caballeros están abajo.

1   _____hombres_____   Los artículos para hombres están abajo.

2   ____ropa_____.   La ropa para hombres está abajo.

3   _____aquí.   La ropa para hombres está aquí.

4   ____cosas_____.   Las cosas para hombres están aquí.

5   _____niños_____.   Las cosas para niños están aquí.

6   Todas las_____.   Todas las cosas para niños están aquí.

7   ____artículos_____.   Todos los artículos para niños están aquí.

TREINTA Y NUEVE   24.39

jacobeligoodsons.com For Free Audio

UNIT 24   SPOKEN SPANISH

24.23   Variation drills

A   àⁿyi |sólǫáybèstiđos |àbrigosₐₛsombréròs↓   Allí, sólo hay vestidos, abrigos y sombreros.

     1 There, there're only skirts, blouses,   àⁿyi |sólǫáyfáldaz |blusasₐₛsombréròs↓   Allí, sólo hay faldas, blusas y sombreros.
        and hats.

     2 There, there're only shoes, neckties,   àⁿyi |sólǫáyşàpatos |kórbatasₐkamísàs↓   Allí, sólo hay zapatos, corbatas y camisas.
        and shirts.

     3 There, there's only greens, meat and   àⁿyi |sólǫáybérđuras |kárnęₐpeskáđò↓   Allí, sólo hay verduras, carne y pescado.
        fish.

     4 There, there's only milk, coffee, and   àⁿyi |sólǫáyléchè |kàfeₐpán↓   Allí, sólo hay leche, café y pan.
        bread.

     5 Here, there's only cold, wind, and   àki |sólǫáyfrío |byéntǫimazbyéntò↓   Aquí sólo hay frío, viento y más viento.
        more wind.

     6 Here, there's only a living room, a   àki |sólǫay |únàsalą |únđòrmitoryoₐumbáŋyò↓   Aquí sólo hay una sala, un dormitorio y
        bedroom, and a bath.   un baño.

     7 Here you have one, two, three dollars.   àki |tyénęuno |đos |trezđólàrès↓   Aquí tiene uno, dos, tres dólares.

B   pérǫàora |męáşèfáltatélà↓   Pero ahora, me hace falta tela.

     1 But now, I need time.   pérǫàora |męáşèfáltatyémpò↓   Pero ahora me hace falta tiempo.

     2 But now, I need help.   pérǫàora |męáşèfáltayúđà↓   Pero ahora me hace falta ayuda.

24.40   CUARENTA

SPOKEN SPANISH   UNIT 24

3 And now, I need the price.   ↓aóra |mẹásẹèfáltạelpréşyò↓   Y ahora me hace falta el precio.

4 And now, I need the visa.   ↓aóra |mẹásẹèfáltalabísà↓   Y ahora me hace falta la visa.

5 And besides, I need a room.   ↓adèmaz |mẹásẹèfáltạuŋkwártó↓   Y además me hace falta un cuarto.

6 And besides, I need to move.   ↓adèmaz |mẹásẹèfáltamudármè↓   Y además me hace falta mudarme.

7 And often, I need to be quiet.   ↓amènudo |mẹásẹèfálta |ẹstártraŋkílò↓   Y a menudo me hace falta estar tranquilo.

C   kisyérạ |ùnákòrbáta |páramimarídò↓   Quisiera una corbata para mi marido.

1 I'd like something special for my husband.   kisyérạ |álgọèspéşyal |páramimarídò↓   Quisiera algo especial para mi marido.

2 I'd like to be ready by (for) Sunday.   kisyéra |ẹstárlisto |páraẹldomíngò↓   Quisiera estar listo para el domingo.

3 I'd like to be unoccupied by this afternoon. kisyéra |ẹstárdèsókúpado |páraẹstatárdẹ↓   Quisiera estar desocupado para esta tarde.

4 I'd like to sell it soon.   kisyéra |bèndérlopróntò↓   Quisiera venderlo pronto.

5 I'd like to hear it.   kisyérạoírlò↓   Quisiera oírlo.

6 I'd like to arrange it.   kisyérarreqlárlò↓   Quisiera arreglarlo.

7 I'd like to look at it.   kisyéramɪrárlò↓   Quisiera mirarlo.

CUARENTA Y UNO   24.41

UNIT 24   SPOKEN SPANISH

D   nó↓ ȧlȧsȧlíḑa│lozbémòs↓   No, a la salida los vemos.

   1   No, on the way out, we'll buy them.   nó↓ ȧlȧsȧlíḑa│lòskomprámòs↓   No, a la salida los compramos.

   2   No, on the way out, we'll call them.   nó↓ ȧlȧsȧlíḑa│loẑⓨamámòs↓   No, a la salida los llamamos.

   3   No, on the way in, we'll see them.   nó↓ ȧlȧèntrȧḑa│lozbémòs↓   No, a la entrada los vemos.

   4   No, afterwards we'll introduce them.   nó↓ dèspwéz│lóspresentámòs↓   No, después los presentamos.

   5   Yes, afterwards we'll wait on them.   sí↓ dèspwéz│los̬atendémòs↓   Sí, después los atendemos.

   6   Yes, afterwards we'll put them in.   sí↓ dèspwéz│lozmetémòs↓   Sí, después los metemos.

   7   Yes, we'd better buy them.   sí↓ méhor│lòskomprámòs↓   Sí, mejor los compramos.

E   sònlȧs(s)íŋkọ│ıbèyntiṣíŋkò↓   Son las cinco y veinticinco.

   1   It's five thirty.   sònlȧs(s̬)iŋkọ̯ımédyȧ↓   Son las cinco y media.

   2   It's ten past six.   sònlȧ(s)séysıdyés̬↓   Son las seis y diez.

   3   It's a quarter past nine.   sònlȧznwebg̯ıkwártò↓   Son las nueve y cuarto.

   4   It's twenty past two.   sònlȧzḑósıbéyntè↓   Son las dos y veinte.

24.42   CUARENTA Y DOS

SPOKEN SPANISH   UNIT 24

5 It's twenty past twelve.   sónlàzdoşeibéyntè↓   Son las doce y veinte.

6 It's a quarter to four.   sónláskwatró|menoskwártô↓   Son las cuatro menos cuarto.

7 It's a quarter to one.   èzláuna|menoskwártô↓   Es la una menos cuarto.

F   sinonozdamosprisat sènòsaşetárdè↓   Si no nos damos prisa, se nos hace tarde.

1 If we don't hurry, it'll get very late on us.   sinonozdamosprisat sènòsaşe|muytárdè↓   Si no nos damos prisa, se nos hace muy
                                                                                            tarde.

2 If we don't hurry, we'll arrive late.   sinonozdamosprisat(0)yègamostárdè↓   Si no nos damos prisa, llegamos tarde.

3 If we don't hurry, we won't arrive on time.   sinonozdamosprisat nò(0)yègamosatyémpô↓ Si no nos damos prisa, no llegamos a tiempo.

4 If we hurry, we'll arrive on time.   sinózdamosprisat(0)yègamosatyémpô↓   Si nos damos prisa, llegamos a tiempo.

5 If we leave soon, we'll get there on the
   dot (at the hour).   sisálimospronto↑(0)yègamosalaórà↓   Si salimos pronto, llegamos a la hora.

6 If we leave soon, we'll get there early.   sisálimospronto↑(0)yègamostempránô↓   Si salimos pronto, llegamos temprano.

7 If we eat soon, we'll get there on time.   sikòmemospronto↑(0)yègamosatyémpô↓   Si comemos pronto, llegamos a tiempo.

CUARENTA Y TRES   24.43

jacobeligoodsons.com For Free Audio

UNIT 24   SPOKEN SPANISH

24.24   Review drill — Gender class assignment of certain nouns — I

   1 The pencil is here.   ėl̦lápįș|ėstákí↓   El lápiz está aquí.

   2 The taxi is here.   ėltáksı|ęstákí↓   El taxi está aquí.

   3 The check is here.   ėlchékę|ėstákí↓   El cheque está aquí.

   4 The trunk is here.   ėlbául|ėstákí↓   El baúl está aquí.

   5 The suit is here.   ėltráhę|ėstákí↓   El traje está aquí.

   6 The colonel is here.   ėlkóṙȯnėl|ėstákí↓   El coronel está aquí.

   7 The boss is here.   ėlhéfę|ėstákí↓   El jefe está aquí.

   8 The elevator is here.   ėlás(ș)ėnsȯr|ėstákí↓   El ascensor está aquí.

   9 The handbag is here.   ėlmȧlétın|ėstákí↓   El maletín está aquí.

  10 The luggage is here.   ėlėkipáhę|ėstákí↓   El equipaje está aquí.

  11 The ticket is here.   ėlbiⓂyétę|ėstákí↓   El billete está aquí.

  12 The ham is here.   ėlhámón|ėstákí↓   El jamón está aquí.

  13 The dessert is here.   ėlpóstrę|ėstákí↓   El postre está aquí.

24.44   CUARENTA Y CUATRO

SPOKEN SPANISH   UNIT 24

14 The base looks good.   lábase│pareşebwéná↓   La base parece buena.

15 The section looks good.   lásékşyom│pareşebwéná↓   La sección parece buena.

16 The inspection looks good.   lainspékşyom│pareşebwéná↓   La inspección parece buena.

17 The information looks good.   laimfòrmàşyóm│pareşebwéná↓   La información parece buena.

18 The people look good.   láhente│pareşebwéná↓   La gente parece buena.

19 The room looks good.   lábitàşyom│pareşebwéná↓   La habitación parece buena.

20 The city looks good.   làşyúdad│pareşebwéná↓   La ciudad parece buena.

21 The mission looks good.   lámisyom│pareşebwéná↓   La misión parece buena.

22 The tower looks good.   látorre│pareşebwéná↓   La torre parece buena.

23 The street looks good.   láka˄ye│pareşebwéná↓   La calle parece buena.

24 The order looks good.   lạordem│pareşebwéná↓   La orden parece buena.

25 The meat looks good.   lákarne│pareşebwéná↓   La carne parece buena.

26 The milk looks good.   láleche│pareşebwéná↓   La leche parece buena.

27 The salt looks good.   lásal│pareşebwéná↓   La sal parece buena.

CUARENTA Y CINCO   24.45

UNIT 24   SPOKEN SPANISH

24.3   CONVERSATION STIMULUS

                                        NARRATIVE 1

1 It's early. It's only eight o'clock.   éstempránò↓ sònápenaz |lasóchó↓   Es temprano. Son apenas las ocho.

2 But Bob and Jean have to get up.   pèróbóbiyin |tyénenkelebantársé↓   Pero Bob y Jean tienen que levantarse.

3 Even though they went to bed very late   áynkeánoche↑sẹàkòstaron |muytárdè↓   Aunque anoche se acostaron muy tarde.
   last night.

4 They have to go buy some clothes   tyénènkẹir |àkómprarlez |rrópaloznínyòs↓   Tienen que ir a comprarles ropa a los
   for the children.   niños.

5 The children haven't got (a thing)   lózninyoz |nótyénènkeponérsé↓   Los niños no tienen qué ponerse.
   to wear.

6 Bob doesn't want to go.   bób |nókyerẹír↓   Bob no quiere ir.

7 He wants to stay home.   kyérèkèdarsẹ |enlakásá↓   Quiere quedarse en la casa.

8 But he has to go.   pèrótyenekẹír↓   Pero tiene que ir.

9 Because his wife tells him that he also   pórkèsyẹsposa |lédiṣe |kẹàel| Porque su esposa le dice que a él también
   needs a couple of suits.   tàmbyenlẹaṣemfaltạ |umpardetráhès↓   le hacen falta un par de trajes.

24.46   CUARENTA Y SEIS

               jacobeligoodsons.com For Free Audio

SPOKEN SPANISH   UNIT 24

DIALOG 1

Jean, dígale a Bob que son las ocho, que   sònlàsópchò |bób↓ tènemos |kèlèbàntàrnòs↓   Jean: Son las ocho, Bob. Tenemos que
Uds. tienen que levantarse.   levantarnos.

Bob, pregúntele que por qué tan temprano.   pòrketantempránò↓ ànòche |nòsàkòstàmoz | Bob: ¿Por qué tan temprano? Anoche
Dígale que anoche se acostaron muy tarde.   múytardè↓   nos acostamos muy tarde.

Jean, dígale que tienen que ir a comprarles   tènemoskeir |àkòmpràrlezrropa |àlózníɲyòs↓   Jean: Tenemos que ir a comprarles ropa a
ropa a los niños. Que no tienen qué   nótyenen |keponérsè↓   los niños. No tienen qué ponerse.
ponerse.

Bob, pregúntele que por qué no va ella con   pòrkenobastú |kònɛ̀ʎyòs↓ yòmekédò↓   Bob: ¿Por qué no vas tú con ellos? Yo me
ellos. Dígale que Ud. se queda.   quedo.

Jean, contéstele que porque a él también   pòrkeàtì |tàmbyèntɛàɛemfàltạ |umpardetráhès↓   Jean: Porque a ti también te hacen falta
le hacen falta un par de trajes.   un par de trajes.

NARRATIVE 2

1 Bob hasn't dressed yet.   bób |nosɛabestídò |tódàbíà↓   Bob no se ha vestido todavía.

2 And breakfast is on the table.   ɛ̀ldèsàyuno |ɛstaɛnlamésà↓   Y el desayuno está en la mesa.

3 There isn't any hot water.   noạyagwakalyéntè↓   No hay agua caliente.

4 And Bob doesn't want to shave or bathe   ibob |nòkyerɛafeytarse |nibàɲyárse | Y Bob no quiere afeitarse ni bañarse con
  in cold water.   konạgwafríà↓   agua fría.

CUARENTA Y SIETE   24.47

UNIT 24   SPOKEN SPANISH

5 Jean tells him that he has to hurry.   yinlediṣe |kėtyéne |kèḋarseprísȧ↓   Jean le dice que tiene que darse prisa.

6 Then, he says it's all right.   ėntonṣes |ėldiṣe |kèstabyén↓   Entonces él dice que está bien.

7 That he'll bathe and shave later.   késėbaŋyą |isęȧfeytaḋespwés↓   Que se baña y se afeita después.

DIALOG 2

Jean, pregúntele a Bob si no se ha vestido   nótęȧzbėstido |toḋabia↑ ėldėsáyuno | Jean: ¿No te has vestido todavía? El
   todavía, y dígale que el desayuno está   desayuno está en la mesa.
   en la mesa.   ęstaęnlamésȧ↓

Bob, dígale que no puede bañarse, que no   nópweḋobaŋyarmė↓ nǫayagwakalyéntė↓   Bob: No puedo bañarme. No hay agua
   hay agua caliente.   caliente.

Jean, pregúntele si no puede bañarse con   nópweḋezbaŋyarte |konągwafria↑ porfabór↓ Jean: ¿No puedes bañarte con agua fría?
   agua fría. Dígale que por favor, que Uds.   Por favor, tenemos que darnos
   tienen que darse prisa.   tėnemos |kėḋárnòsprisȧ↓   prisa.

Bob, dígale que está bien. Que se baña y se   ėstabyén↓ mėbaŋyǫ |imęȧfeytoḋespwés↓   Bob: Está bien. Me baño y me afeito
   afeita después.   después.

NARRATIVE 3

1 The Harrises are at the store.   lòsharris |estanęnlatyéndȧ↓   Los Harris están en la tienda.

2 Jean looks horrible with a hat she's   yin |sėbęǫrrible |kònųnsòmbrero |kesesta Jean se ve horrible con un sombrero que
   trying on.   se está probando.
                                                  proḃándȯ↓

3 Besides, the hat costs thirty pesos.   àḋėmas |ėlsòmbrerokwesta |tréyntapésòs↓ Además, el sombrero cuesta treinta pesos.

24.48   jacobeligoodsons.com For Free Audio   CUARENTA Y OCHO

SPOKEN SPANISH   UNIT 24

4 And she has bought three already.   ↓ėℓ̣ya↑ya|sẹákȯmpraḋotrés↓   Y ella ya se ha comprado tres.

5 They don't buy anything else, then;   nȯkómpran|nadamás|ėntónṣês↓ ésọ̇ẹstóḋȯ↓   No compran nada más, entonces; eso es todo.
  that's all.

6 Then they go home.   lwego|sėbamparalakásȧ↓   Luego se van para la casa.

                                              DIALOG 3

Jean, pregúntele a Bob que cómo se ve Ud.   komomebéȯ|kȯnéstėsȯmbrérȯ↓   Jean: ¿Cómo me veo con este sombrero?
con este sombrero.

Bob, pregúntele que cuánto cuesta.   kwȧntokwéstȧ↓   Bob: ¿Cuánto cuesta?

Jean, dígale que treinta pesos, apenas.   treyntapésȯs|ȧpénȧs↓   Jean: Treinta pesos, apenas.

Bob, dígale que se ve horrible. Que además   tėbes|ȯrríblė↓ ȧdėmaz|ya|tẹáskȯmpradȯ   Bob: Te ves horrible. Además, ya te has
ya se ha comprado tres.   trés↓   comprado tres.

Jean, dígale que tiene razón. Que eso es   tyénezrraṣón↓ esọestóḋọ|ėntónṣês↓   Jean: Tienes razón. Eso es todo, entonces.
todo, entonces. Pregúntele si se van ya.   nózbamozya↑   ¿Nos vamos ya?

Bob, contéstele que sí, que ¡por favor!   sı|pȯrfȧbȯr↓   Bob: Sí, ¡por favor!

CUARENTA Y NUEVE   jacobeligoodsons.com For Free Audio   24.49

UNIT 24   SPOKEN SPANISH

24.4   READINGS

24.40   List of cognate loan words

    extendió (extender)   [èstèndyó↓ èstèndér↓]

    expresar   [èsprèsár↓]

    la claridad   [là-klàridád↓]

    los tópicos   [lòs-topíkòs↓]

    la política   [là-pólitikà↓]

    internacional   [intèrnàşyónál↓]

    respectivos   [rrèspèktibòs↓]

    permita (permitir)   [pèrmità↓ pèrmitír↓]

    servir   [sèrbír↓]

    la recepción   [là-rrèşèpşyón↓]

    la pausa   [là-pàwsà↓]

24.41   Reading selection

Los Fuentes se Despiden

    La visita se extendió hasta casi medianoche. Ricardo y Marta no habían pensado quedarse tan tarde porque sabían que la primera visita a la casa de una familia que uno acaba de conocer nunca debe ser larga. Pero eran los Robinson, especialmente Fred, quienes no los dejaban irse. Aunque a Fred le costaba bastante expresarse con claridad en español, pudo conversar con don Ricardo sobre muchos tópicos, tales como las relaciones entre su país y Surlandia, política internacional en general, y otros. Las señoras conversaron sobre cosas más interesantes para ellas; hablaron de sus respectivos hijos, sobre los problemas del servicio, de la otra gente que vivía en el barrio, etc. Pero por fin, viendo que en realidad se estaba haciendo demasiado tarde, los Fuentes se levantaron para despedirse.

    —No se pueden ir todavía—dijo Fred al ver que querían irse — no es tarde; permítanme servirles otra copa.

24.50   CINCUENTA

SPOKEN SPANISH

UNIT 24

—No, muchas gracias, más bien creo que ahora sí debemos irnos. Hemos tenido muchísimo gusto de conocerlos y ya saben que nuestra casa está a su disposición. Cualquier cosa que necesiten, avísenos.

—Muy agradecidos, igualmente. Y tienen que volver muy pronto—exclamó Virginia.

—Con mucho gusto—dijo Marta—y ustedes también deben venir a vernos. ¿Por qué no vienen a comer con nosotros uno de estos días y traen a Jane y a Ruth también? Este sábado, por ejemplo.

—Muchas gracias, nosotros encantados—contestó Virginia—sólo que este sábado no podemos, tenemos una recepción en la Embajada; los otros días de esta semana Fred tiene que quedarse trabajando hasta tarde en la oficina, pero la semana que viene, cualquier día.

—Magnífico. ¿Qué les parece el jueves o el viernes?

—Muy bien, muchas gracias. ¿Te parece bien a ti, Fred?—le preguntó su esposa.

—Sí, cómo no, cualquiera de los dos días, aunque para mí es un poco mejor el viernes.

—El viernes, entonces. Yo los llamo antes otra vez para que no se les olvide—exclamó Marta, y después de una pequeña pausa dijo: Bueno, ahora sí nos vamos. Buenas noches y mil gracias por todo.

—A ustedes las gracias, hasta mañana.

24.42   Response drill

1 ¿Hasta qué hora se extendió la visita?

2 ¿Por qué no habían pensado los Fuentes hacer tan larga la visita?

3 ¿De cuánto tiempo, más o menos, deben ser las primeras visitas?

4 ¿Por qué se quedaron tan tarde?

5 ¿Le costaba a Fred expresarse en español?

6 ¿Conversó él de política internacional con Ricardo?

7 ¿De qué otros tópicos conversaron ellos?

8 ¿Por qué no hablaron las señoras de política internacional?

9 ¿De qué conversaron ellas?

10 ¿Por qué no quiso Ricardo tomar otra copa?

11 ¿Los Fuentes invitaron a los Robinson a comer o a almorzar a su casa?

12 ¿Invitaron sólo a los señores o a sus hijas también?

13 ¿Por qué no pueden los Robinson ir esta semana?

14 ¿Para cuál día de la otra semana los invitaron?

15 ¿Cuál de los dos días es mejor para Fred, el jueves o el viernes?

CINCUENTA Y UNO   jacobeligoodsons.com For Free Audio   24.51

jacobeligoodsons.com For Free Audio

SPOKEN SPANISH   UNIT 25

25.1   BASIC SENTENCES.   A visa interview.

        John White is at the Consulate, interviewing a gentleman who wants a visa.

ENGLISH SPELLING   AID TO LISTENING   SPANISH SPELLING

        the visa   là—bìsà↓   la visa

Gentleman
    I'd like a visa for the United States. kisyeraunabisa|pàràlòsèstàdosunídòs↓ Señor
                                                                                  Quisiera una visa para los Estados
                                                                                  Unidos.

        the purpose   èl—pròpósitô↓   el propósito

White   White
    What's the purpose of your trip?   kwaleselproposito|desubyáhè↓   ¿Cuál es el propósito de su viaje?

        over there   àĉyá↓   allá

Gentleman   Señor
    I want to go live there.   dèseǫirmè|àbíbiraĉyá↓   Deseo irme a vivir allá.

        the immigrant   èl—inmigrantè↓   el inmigrante

White   White
    Then you need an immigrant visa.   èntonşez↑nèşèsitạ|ùnábisadẹinmigrántè↓   Entonces necesita una visa de inmigrante.

        to be born   nàşér↓   nacer

    Where were you born?   dondenaşyó↓   ¿Dónde nació?

UNO   jacobeligoodsons.com For Free Audio   25.1

UNIT 25   SPOKEN SPANISH

the father   èl‑pádrè↓   el padre

the parents   lòs‑pádrès↓   los padres

Gentleman   *Señor*
Here. And my parents also.   àkí↓ imíspádrès│támbyén↓   Aquí. Y mis padres también.

White   *White*
Are you going with your family?   séba│kònsúfámilyà↑   ¿Se va con su familia?

divorced (to divorce)   dibòrşyádò↓ dibòrşya'r↓   divorciado (divorciar)

Gentleman   *Señor*
No. I'm divorced and have no children.   nó↓ sóyđibòrşyádo│isiníhòs↓   No. Soy divorciado y sin hijos.

White   *White*
What part of the country do you want to go to?   àképarté│kyérę̇ír↓   ¿A qué parte quiere ir?

Gentleman   *Señor*
Los Angeles, California. (1)   àlòs̩aŋhèlès│kálifórnyà↓   A Los Angeles, California.

at what   èŋ‑ké↓   en qué

White   *White*
What do you intend to work at? (2)   èŋkepyénsatrabahár↓   ¿En qué piensa trabajar?

the engineer   èl‑iŋhènyerò↓   el ingeniero

Gentleman   *Señor*
I'm an engineer.   sóy│iŋhènyerò↓   Soy ingeniero.

jacobeligoodsons.com For Free Audio

25.2   DOS

SPOKEN SPANISH   UNIT 25

the work   èl—tràbahò↓   el trabajo

White
Do you already have a job?   yatyénetrabahó↑   **White**
                                                                          ¿Ya tiene trabajo?

the money   èl—dínéró↓   el dinero
some money   algo—de—dinéró↓   algo de dinero

Gentleman
Not yet. But I'm taking a fair amount of money [3]   tòdàbian6↓ pérò(l)yebo|algodedinéró↓   **Señor**
                                                                          Todavía no. Pero llevo algo de dinero.

White
How much are you taking?   kwanto(l)yéba↓   **White**
                                                                          ¿Cuánto lleva?

Gentleman
Three thousand dollars.   trézmildólàrès↓   **Señor**
                                                                          Tres mil dólares.

itself to me (it) forgot (to forget)   sè—mę—ólbidó↓ ólbidàrsè↓   se me olvidó (olvidarse)
the surname   èl—àpè(l)yidò↓   el apellido

White
Excuse me, but I've forgotten your last name. [4]   pérdónè|sènyór↓ pèròsèmęólbidó| **White**
                                  syape(l)yidó↓   Perdone señor, pero se me olvidó su
                                                                          apellido.

Señor
Moreno Rojas. My full name is José Luis Moreno   mòrenorrohàs↓ minómbrekómpletotès   **Señor**
Rojas.   hòsélwiz |mòrenorróhàs↓   Moreno Rojas. Mi nombre completo es
                                                                          José Luis Moreno Rojas.

TRES   jacobeligoodsons.com For Free Audio   25.3

UNIT 25   SPOKEN SPANISH

25.10   Notes on the basic sentences

(1) Note that in Spanish the preposition /a/ *a*, which was part of the question, /aképárte/ *a qué parte*, must be repeated in the answer, /alosánheles/ *a Los Angeles*. In English the preposition is ordinarily *not* repeated in this situation.

(2) Your attention is called to the preposition /en/ *en* used with working. A similar use of /en/ is this one:

/enkétrabáhaustéd/ *¿En qué trabaja usted?* 'What do you do for a living?'

(3) Note especially the use of the verb /ⱴyebár/ *llevar* in the everyday garden-variety meaning 'take.' Americans at first tend to translate using /tomár/ *tomar.* One student once remarked that he could remember the distinction easily because /ⱴyebár/ means 'carry,' *and he as a southerner was accustomed to using* 'carry' in that sense: 'I'll be glad to carry you all home after work.'

(4) This construction is taken up immediately in the drills.

25.2   DRILLS AND GRAMMAR

25.21   Pattern drills

25.21.1 Reflexive and indirect clitic pronouns in the same construction

A. Presentation of pattern

ILLUSTRATIONS

_____	1	sėmėkȧyo̍ ǀyṅȧtȧ§ȧḋėkȧfe ̍ ịsemerrompyo̍↓	*Se me* cayó una taza de café y *se me* rompió.
_____	2	sėmęó̍lbido̍ ǀsῃapeⱴyido̍↓	*Se me* olvidó su apellido.
We forgot the ad.	3	sėṅóṣó̍lbiḋo̍ ǀȩlanúṅ§yo̍↓	*Se nos* olvidó el anuncio.
We dropped the coins.	4	sėṅóskȧye̍ron ǀlazmoṅéḋȧs↓	*Se nos* cayeron las monedas.

25.4   jacobeligoodsons.com For Free Audio   CUATRO

SPOKEN SPANISH   UNIT 25

Did you drop this pen?	5	sétékáyo ǫstapluma↑	¿Se te cayó esta pluma?
Did you forget the pencils?	6	sétęólbidarón lozlápişes↑	¿Se te olvidaron los lápices?
Did you leave anything in the house?	7	sélékèdoalgǫ enlakasa↑	¿Se le quedó algo en la casa?
Martha left the gift at the office.	8	ámárta sélékèdo ǫlrrègalǫenląofiṣíná↓	A Marta se le quedó el regalo en la oficina.
Did you all forget about the inspection?	9	ápstedés sélęsólbido lódéląinspéksyon↑	¿A ustedes se les olvidó lo de la inspección?
Did they forget the name of the officer?	10	ąeⓁyòs sélęsólbido ǫlnómbredȩlofiṣyal↑	¿A ellos se les olvidó el nombre del oficial?

EXTRAPOLATION

		Reflexive	Indirect
1	sg	—	me
	pl	—	nos
2	fam	—	te
2-3	sg	se	le
	pl		les

a. This typical Spanish construction transposes the subject of an equivalent English sentence to an indirect object.

b. The English object is expressed as a Spanish subject, showing the usual number agreement with the verb.

c. The reflexive clitic is indispensable in the Spanish construction, but has no equivalent in the English sentence.

d. In this Spanish construction, only 'things' occur as subjects (in 3rd person), so 1 and 2 reflexive clitics never occur.

CINCO

jacobeligoodsons.com For Free Audio

25.5

UNIT 25   SPOKEN SPANISH

25.21.11 Substitution drills — Person number substitution

1   àmi│sèmeólbiđólaﬡyábè↓

    àhwan_____↓   sèleólbiđólaﬡyábè↓

    ànósotros_____↓   sènósólbiđólaﬡyábè↓

    àkarmen_____↓   sèleólbiđólaﬡyábè↓

    àeﬡyos_____↓   sèlèsólbiđólaﬡyábè↓

---

1 *A mí* se me olvidó la llave.

   A Juan_____.   Se le olvidó la llave.

   A nosotros_____.   Se nos olvidó la llave.

   A Carmen_____.   Se le olvidó la llave.

   A ellos_____.   Se les olvidó la llave.

SPOKEN SPANISH

UNIT 25

2 àlkòrónél|sèlèkàyèronlaskópàs↓

  àmí _____↓   sèmèkàyèronlaskópàs↓

  àlò(s)sènyorès _____↓   sèlèskàyèronlaskópàs↓

  àlmùchachò _____↓   sèlèkàyèronlaskópàs↓

  ànósotros _____↓   sènóskàyèronlaskópàs↓

3 ànósotros|sènózrròmpyoelbaúl↓

  àmí _____↓   sèmèrròmpyoelbaúl↓

  àlwisa _____↓   sèlèrròmpyoelbaúl↓

  àlòzmùchachos _____↓   sèlèzrròmpyoelbaúl↓

  àhóse _____↓   sèlèrròmpyoelbaúl↓

---

2 *Al coronel* se·le cayeron las copas.

  A mí _____.   Se me cayeron las copas.

  A los señores _____.   Se les cayeron las copas.

  Al muchacho _____.   Se le cayeron las copas.

  A nosotros _____.   Se nos cayeron las copas.

3 *A nosotros* se nos rompió el baúl.

  A mí _____.   Se me rompió el baúl.

  A Luisa _____.   Se le rompió el baúl.

  A los muchachos _____.   Se les rompió el baúl.

  A José _____.   Se le rompió el baúl.

SIETE

jacobeligoodsons.com For Free Audio

UNIT 25   SPOKEN SPANISH

4 álwisa|sèlęólbidaronlasfótòs↓
   àmı_____↓   sèmęólbidaronlasfótòs↓
   àltényente_____↓   sèlęólbidaronlasfótòs↓
   ąęⱡⱡyos_____↓   sèlèsólbidaronlasfótòs↓
   ànósotros_____↓   sènósólbidaronlasfótòs↓

5 ànósotros|sènóskàyólamalétá↓
   ąęⱡⱡyos_____↓   sèlèskàyólamalétá↓
   àmısàmıgos_____↓   sèlèskàyólamalétá↓
   àmıího_____↓   sèlèkàyólamalétá↓
   àmínobya_____↓   sèlèkàyólamalétá↓

---

4 *A Luisa* se le olvidaron las fotos.
   A mí _____.   Se me olvidaron las fotos.
   Al teniente _____.   Se le olvidaron las fotos.
   A ellos _____.   Se les olvidaron las fotos.
   A nosotros _____.   Se nos olvidaron las fotos.

5 *A nosotros* se nos cayó la maleta.
   A ellos_____.   Se les cayó la maleta.
   A mis amigos _____.   Se les cayó la maleta.
   A mi hijo_____.   Se le cayó la maleta.
   A mi novia _____.   Se le cayó la maleta.

jacobeligoodsons.com For Free Audio

SPOKEN SPANISH   UNIT 25

                              Number substitution

1   sémęólbiḋolakorbátà↓   sémęólbiḋaronlaskorbátàs↓

2   sèlérrómpyeronlos(s)apátòs↓   sèlérrómpyoelṣapátò↓

3   sènòsólbiḋoęlnómbrè↓   sènòsólbiḋaronloznómbrès↓

4   sèlérrómpyolakamísà↓   sèlérrómpyeronlaskamísàs↓

5   sèlèskàyeronlozbaúlés↓   sèlèskàyoęlbaúl↓

6   sèmèkàyolafótò↓   sèmèkàyeronlasfótòs↓

7   sèlęólbiḋoęlabrígò↓   sèlęólbiḋaronlosabrígòs↓

_____

1 Se me olvidó *la corbata*.   Se me olvidaron las corbatas.

2 Se le rompieron *los zapatos*.   Se le rompió el zapato.

3 Se nos olvidó *el nombre*.   Se nos olvidaron los nombres.

4 Se le rompió *la camisa*.   Se le rompieron las camisas.

5 Se les cayeron *los baúles*.   Se les cayó el baúl.

6 Se me cayó *la foto*.   Se me cayeron las fotos.

7 Se le olvidó *el abrigo*.   Se le olvidaron los abrigos.

NUEVE   jacobeligoodsons.com For Free Audio   25.9

UNIT 25   SPOKEN SPANISH

25.21.12 Response drill

          1 àystéd↓sèlẹólbída |minómbrẹ↑om̞apeⁿɏídò↓   sèmẹólbída |syápèⁿɏídò↓

          2 ạél↓sèlẹólbída |minómbrẹ↑om̞apeⁿɏídò↓   sèlẹólbída |syápèⁿɏídò↓

[ạél↓]   3 àkyén |selekayeronloⁿlíbròs↓   ạél |sèlèkàyéròn↓

[àmí↓]   4 àkyén |selẹolbidaronlazⁿɏábés↓   àystéd |sèlẹólbidáròn↓

[èⁿlapíş↓]   5 késelekayó|ạél↓   sèlèkàyó |ẹⁿlapíş↓

[làkàmísà↓]   6 késelerrómpyó|ạustéd↓   sèmèrrómpyó |làkàmísà↓

[làlèkşyón↓]   7 késelesọlbidạustédès↓   sènósọlbida |làlèkşyón↓

---

          1 ¿A Ud. se le olvida mi nombre o mi apellido?   Se me olvida su apellido.

          2 ¿A él se le olvida mi nombre o mi apellido?   Se le olvida su apellido.

(a él)   3 ¿A quién se le cayeron los libros?   A él se le cayeron.

(a mí)   4 ¿A quién se le olvidaron las llaves?   A Ud. se le olvidaron.

(el lápiz)   5 ¿Qué se le cayó a él?   Se le cayó el lápiz.

(la camisa)   6 ¿Qué se le rompió a Ud.?   Se me rompió la camisa.

(la lección)   7 ¿Qué se les olvida a Uds.?   Se nos olvida la lección.

jacobeligoodsons.com For Free Audio

SPOKEN SPANISH   UNIT 25

[ðⁿlápiş↓]   8   sêlêkáyo|ael|ðⁿlíbro↑   nó↓ sêlêkáyo|ęⁿlápiş↓

[lózlíbrós↓] 9   sêlêskáyeron|ęⁿyoz|lózlápişes↑   nó↓ sêlêskáyeron|lózlíbrós↓

            10   sêlêsólbiđan|ầustedez|misâpeⁿyidos↑   sí↓ syémpre|senosolbíđàn↓

            11   sêlęólbiđan|ầusted|misâpeⁿyidos↑   sí↓ syémpre|semęolbíđàn↓

            12   sêmęólbiđan|ầmi|sûsâpeⁿyidos↑   sí↓ tâmbyén|selęolbíđàn↓

            13   sêlêrrompen|ầusteđsyémpre|lózlíbros↑ sí↓ syémpre|semerrómpên↓

            14   sêlêskáen|ầustedez|lâzⁿyabesenelkárro↑ sí|sísenoskáên↓

            15   sêlêkaę|akarmen|lâtaşa↑   sí|síselekáê↓

_____

(el lápiz)   8   ¿Se le cayó a él el libro?   No, se le cayó el lápiz.

(los libros) 9   ¿Se les cayeron a ellos los lápices?   No, se les cayeron los libros.

            10   ¿Se les olvidan a Uds. mis apellidos?   Sí, siempre se nos olvidan.

            11   ¿Se le olvidan a Ud. mis apellidos?   Sí, siempre se me olvidan.

            12   ¿Se me olvidan a mi sus apellidos?   Sí, también se le olvidan.

            13   ¿Se rompen a Ud. siempre los libros?   Sí, siempre se me rompen.

            14   ¿Se les caen a Uds. las llaves en el carro? Sí, sí se nos caen.

            15   ¿Se le cae a Carmen la taza?   Sí, sí se le cae.

ONCE   25.11

UNIT 25   SPOKEN SPANISH

25.21.13 Translation drill

1 Carmen's blouse got torn.	àkármen│sèlèrrómpyolablúsà↓	A Carmen se le rompió la blusa.
2 Two cups of Jose's got broken.	àhóse│sèlèrrómpyeron│dóstáṣàs↓	A José se le rompieron dos tazas.
3 My overcoat got torn.	àmi│sèmérrómpyoҫlabrígó↓	A mí se me rompió el abrigo.
4 Ma'am, you dropped something.	sèŋyorà↓ sèlèkáyo│algó↓	Señora, se le cayó algo.
5 Sir, did you drop these checks?	séŋyór↓ sèlèkàyeron│estoschekes↑	Señor, ¿se le cayeron estos cheques?
6 I never drop anything.	àmi↑nuŋka│semekàenáďà↓	A mí nunca se me cae nada.
7 We forgot our hats.	ànósotros│sènòṣòlbidaronlo(s)sombréròs↓	A nosotros se nos olvidaron los sombreros.
8 Do you forget Latin names?	sèlèòlbidanaysteḍ│lòznómbrezlatínos↑	¿Se le olvidan a Ud. los nombres latinos?
9 Darn it! I dropped the ashtray.	kàrambà↓sèmèkáyoҫlҫeniṣérò↓	¡Caramba!, se me cayó el cenicero.
10 The little boy tore his shirt.	álchıko│sèlèrrómpyolakamísà↓	Al chico se le rompió la camisa.
11 Have you all forgotten anything?	sèlèsaҫlbidaḍo│algo↑	¿Se les ha olvidado algo?
12 What did you all forget?	késelesòlbidó↓	¿Qué se les olvidó?
13 Have we dropped anything?	sènòsakaıdo│algo↑	¿Se nos ha caído algo?

25.12   jacobeligoodsons.com For Free Audio   DOCE

SPOKEN SPANISH

UNIT 25

B. Discussion of pattern

The construction drilled in this section is as typical for Spanish as it is strange for English. So even though its mastery is unusually difficult for English speaking students, and even though there are other ways (more similar to English constructions) of expressing the content of sentences that occur in this construction, it is still very important to learn to use it easily.

There is an almost complete transposition of elements in this construction (from the point of view of English). In English we say: 'I broke the cup,' which in Spanish is 'The cup broke itself to (for, on) me.' It is tempting to try to read a desire for evasion of responsibility into the Spanish construction, and perhaps saying it in this way has an effect on how one looks at the incident. Indeed if a Spanish speaker has a strong personal interest in establishing 'who did it', he will probably use another construction, one more like English: /kyén—rrompyó—la—tášaↄ/. The significant point is that the normal usage of English should be equated with the normal usage of Spanish which in essence equates 'He broke the cup' with /se—le—rrompyó—la—tášaↄ/. Broad cultural interpretations based on assumptions drawn from comparative usage, such as 'Spanish speakers are evasive because they prefer the /se—le/ constructions', are dangerously shaky.

The cup, which is the noun object in English, becomes the subject in Spanish (and governs the agreement of the verb). The verb appears in Spanish with a reflexive clitic (always /se/, since only *things* - therefore 3 person - can occur as subjects). The English subject (the person who has primary concern for the incident) is expressed as an indirect object. Thus a change from 'I broke....' to 'You broke....' in the Spanish construction becomes /se—me .../ changing to /se—te .../ .

Some slightly similar constructions exist in certain English dialect areas (usually considered low prestige, hillbilly, etc.) in an expression like 'She up and got married on me,' though here the 'on me' indicates only concern, never the actor. Another similarity can be pointed out in English sentences with the passive 'got,' as 'The cup got broken' (where the former subject 'I' is not expressed).

Much of the difficulty of this construction is due to the absence of a corresponding construction in English, but it is also different from other Spanish constructions by reason of its obligatory inversion of normal subject-verb order. Note well how the substitutability of items is effected in this construction:

I broke the cup.	/se—me—rrompyó—la—taşaↄ/
I broke the cups.	/se—me—rrompyéron—las—tášasↄ/
We broke the cup.	/se—nos—rrompyó—la—tášaↄ/
We broke the cups.	/se—nos—rrompyéron—las—tášasↄ/

Certain verbs have a tendency to appear in this construction. Since the verb is always in a reflexive construction, it must be one that can appear with a **reflexive** clitic (though this stipulation does not eliminate many). Verbs which frequently occur in this construction which have so far appeared in this text include:

kaérse	pareşérse
kasárse	rrompérse
kedárse	salírse
olbɪdárse	

TRECE

25.13

jacobeligoodsons.com For Free Audio

UNIT 25   SPOKEN SPANISH

25.22   Replacement drills

A   kísyéráunabísa |párálós,éstados̥unídos↓

1 _____ mí↓   kisyéráunabísa |paramí↓

2 _____ trabáho _____↓   kisyéráuntrabáho |paramí↓

3 _____ éste _____↓   kisyéra |estetrabáho |paramí↓

4 _____ korbátas _____↓   kisyéra |estaskorbátas |paramí↓

5 _____ ake(l)ya _____↓   kisyéra |ake(l)yakorbáta |paramí↓

6 _____ ṣapátos _____↓   kisyéra |ake(l)yo(s) ṣapátos |paramí↓

7 _____ ótros _____↓   kisyéra |ótro(s) ṣapátos |paramí↓

_____

A   Quisiera una visa para los Estados Unidos.

1 _____ mí.   Quisiera una visa para mí.

2 _____ trabajo _____.   Quisiera un trabajo para mí.

3 _____ este _____.   Quisiera este trabajo para mí.

4 _____ corbatas _____.   Quisiera estas corbatas para mí.

5 _____ aquella _____.   Quisiera aquella corbata para mí.

6 _____ zapatos _____.   Quisiera aquellos zapatos para mí.

7 _____ otros _____.   Quisiera otros zapatos para mí.

25.14   CATORCE

SPOKEN SPANISH   UNIT 25

B   kwál|eselpropósito|desubyáhè↓   kwál|eselpretésto|desubyáhè↓

1 _____pretesto_____↓   kwál|eselpretésto|desuspádrès↓

2 _____pádrès↓   kwál|eselpretésto|desyermánò↓

3 _____ermánò↓   kwál|ezlakása|desyermánò↓

4 _____kása_____↓   kwál|ezlakása|desyamígò↓

5 _____amígò↓   kwál|eselabrígo|desyamígò↓

6 _____abrígo_____↓   kómọ|eselabrígo|desyamígò↓

7 kómọ_____↓

B   ¿Cuál es el propósito de su viaje?   ¿Cuál es el pretexto de su viaje?

1 ¿_____pretexto_____?   ¿Cuál es el pretexto de sus padres?

2 ¿_____padres?   ¿Cuál es el pretexto de su hermano?

3 ¿_____hermano?   ¿Cuál es la casa de su hermano?

4 ¿_____casa_____?   ¿Cuál es la casa de su amigo?

5 ¿_____amigo?   ¿Cuál es el abrigo de su amigo?

6 ¿_____abrigo_____?   ¿Cómo es el abrigo de su amigo?

7 ¿Cómo_____?

QUINCE   25.15

UNIT 25   SPOKEN SPANISH

C   dèséọirmẹ |àbíbírạ̄ỹá↓   dèsẹámosịrnos |àbíbírạ̄ỹá↓

1   _____irnos_____↓   dèsẹámosịrnos |àtràbàharạ̄ỹá↓

2   _____tràbàhar____↓   kyèrẹirsẹ |àtràbàharạ̄ỹá↓

3   kyérẹ_____↓   kyérókèđarmẹ |àtràbàharạ̄ỹá↓

4   _____kèđarmẹ_____↓   bóyàkèđarmẹ |àtràbàharạ̄ỹá↓

5   bóyà_____↓   bámósꓹàkèđarnos |àtràbàharạ̄ỹá↓

6   _____kèđarnos_____↓   bámósꓹàkèđarnos |àbíbírạ̄ỹá↓

7   _____bíbír___↓

C   Deseo irme a vivir allá.   Deseamos irnos a vivir allá.

1   _____irnos_____.   Deseamos irnos a trabajar allá.

2   _____trabajar__.   Quiere irse a trabajar allá.

3   Quiere_____.   Quiero quedarme a trabajar allá.

4   _____quedarme_____.   Voy a quedarme a trabajar allá.

5   Voy a_____.   Vamos a quedarnos a trabajar allá.

6   _____quedarnos_____.   Vamos a quedarnos a vivir allá.

7   _____vivir___.

25.16   DIECISEIS

SPOKEN SPANISH   UNIT 25

D   èntónșez↑nèșèsıtąunabísà↓

1   _____ nèșèsıtan _____↓   èntónșez↑nèșèsıtanųnabísà↓

2   _____ sombrérò↓   èntónșez↑nèșèsıtanųnsombrérò↓

3   àórà _____↓   àór↑nèșèsıtanųnsombrérò↓

4   _____ ótro _____↓   àór↑nèșèsıtan│otrosombrérò↓

5   _____ kósàs↓   àór↑nèșèsıtan│otraskósàs↓

6   _____ áprendę _____↓   àórą↑áprendę│otraskósàs↓

7   _____ léŋgwà↓   àórą↑áprendę│otraléŋgwà↓

_____

D   Entonces necesita una visa.

1   _____ necesitan _____.   Entonces necesitan una visa.

2   _____ sombrero.   Entonces necesitan un sombrero.

3   Ahora _____.   Ahora necesitan un sombrero.

4   _____ otro _____.   Ahora necesitan otro sombrero.

5   _____ cosas.   Ahora necesitan otras cosas.

6   _____ aprende _____.   Ahora aprende otras cosas.

7   _____ lengua.   Ahora aprende otra lengua.

DIECISIETE   25.17

UNIT 25   SPOKEN SPANISH

E   sèbá |konsufamílya↑
1   ⸺tas⸺⸺⸺↑   tèbás |kontufamílya↑
2   ⸺⸺⸺la⸺⸺↑   tèbás |konlafamílya↑
3   nòz⸺⸺⸺↑   nózbamos |konlafamílya↑
4   ⸺⸺⸺níŋyos↑   nòzbamos |konlozníŋyos↑
5   ⸺kéɾamos⸺⸺↑   nóskéɾamos |konlozníŋyos↑
6   tè⸺⸺⸺↑   tèkeɾas |konlozníŋyos↑
7   ⸺⸺⸺estè⸺↑   tèkeɾas |konɛsteníŋyo↑

───

E   ¿Se va con su familia?
1   ¿⸺vas⸺⸺?   ¿Te vas con tu familia?
2   ¿⸺⸺⸺la⸺⸺?   ¿Te vas con la familia?
3   ¿Nos⸺⸺⸺?   ¿Nos vamos con la familia?
4   ¿⸺⸺⸺niños?   ¿Nos vamos con los niños?
5   ¿⸺quedamos⸺⸺?   ¿Nos quedamos con los niños?
6   ¿Te⸺⸺⸺?   ¿Te quedas con los niños?
7   ¿⸺⸺⸺este⸺?   ¿Te quedas con este niño?

25.18   DIECIOCHO

SPOKEN SPANISH   UNIT 25

F   mínombre |kómpletọ†éshósélwiz |mórenorróhàs↓

1   èl _____↓   èlnómbre |kómpletọ†éshóselwiz |mòrenorróhàs↓

2   _____ mìọ _____↓   èlnómbre |mìọ†éshóselwìz |mòrenorróhàs↓

3   _____ ínglés↓   èlnómbre |mìọ†esínglés↓

4   _àpè''yídọ _____↓   èlàpéλyídọ |mìọ†esínglés↓

5   _àmìɡaz _____↓   làsàmìɡaz |mìast soninglésàs↓

6   _____ tùyọ _____↓   èlàmìɡo |tùyọ†esínglés↓

7   _hefés _____↓   lòshefés |tùyọst soninglésès↓

F   Mi nombre completo es José Luis Moreno Rojas.

1   El _____.   El nombre completo es José Luis Moreno Rojas.

2   _____ mío _____.   El nombre mío es José Luis Moreno Rojas.

3   _____ inglés.   El nombre mío es inglés.

4   ___apellido _____.   El apellido mío es inglés.

5   ___amigas _____.   Las amigas mías son inglesas.

6   _____ tuyo _____.   El amigo tuyo es inglés.

7   ___jefes _____.   Los jefes tuyos son ingleses.

DIECINUEVE   25.19

UNIT 25   SPOKEN SPANISH

25.23   Variation drills

A   noↄ́ sòyↄibòrṣyáↄ̧o|isiníhòs↓   No. Soy divorciado y sin hijos.

1 No. I'm married and have no children.   noↄ́ sòykàsàↄ̧ o|isiníhòs↓   No. Soy casado y sin hijos.

2 No. I'm single and have no family.   noↄ́ sòysòlterↄ|isimfamílyà↓   No. Soy soltero y sin familia.

3 Yes. I'm married and have children.   sìↄ́ sòykàsáↄↄ|ikoníhòs↓   Sí. Soy casado y con hijos.

4 Yes. I'm (a) widower and have children.   sìↄ́ sòybyuↄↄ|ikoníhòs↓   Sí. Soy viudo y con hijos.

5 Yes. She's (a) widow and has two little   sìↄ́ èzbyuↄ̧à|ityénéↄòzníɲòs↓   Sí. Es viuda y tiene dos niños.
  boys.

6 Yes. She's (a) widow and has a large-   sìↄ́ èzbyuↄ̧à|ityénémuchafamílyà↓   Sí. Es viuda y tiene mucha familia.
  sized family.

7 Yes. She's (a) widow and has lots of   sìↄ́ èzbyuↄ̧à|ityénémuchoↄinérò↓   Sí. Es viuda y tiene mucho dinero.
  money.

B   àképàrte|kyérↄ̧ír↓   ¿A qué parte quiere ir?

1 Where do you want to go to eat?   àképàrte|kyérↄ̧ir|akomér↓   ¿A qué parte quiere ir a comer?

2 Where do you want to go to work?   àképàrte|kyérↄ̧ir|atraↄ̧ahár↓   ¿A qué parte quiere ir a trabajar?

3 Where do you wish to go to live?   àképàrte|ↄeseↄ̧à|irabibír↓   ¿A qué parte desea ir a vivir?

25.20   VEINTE

SPOKEN SPANISH   UNIT 25

4 What part (of town) do you like to live in?   èŋképárte|legústabibír↓   ¿En qué parte le gusta vivir?

5 What part (of town) do you like to eat in?   èŋképárte|legústakomér↓   ¿En qué parte le gusta comer?

6 Where's the exit?   èŋképárte̦|estalasalíd̦á↓   ¿En qué parte está la salida?

7 Where's the entrance?   èŋképárte̦|estála̦entrád̦á↓   ¿En qué parte está la entrada?

C èŋképyénsà|trábahár↓   ¿En qué piensa trabajar?

1 How (by what means) do you intend to go?   èŋképyénsa̦ír↓   ¿En qué piensa ir?

2 How do you intend to leave?   èŋképyénsasalír↓   ¿En qué piensa salir?

3 How do you intend to come?   èŋképyénsabenír↓   ¿En qué piensa venir?

4 Where do you intend to eat lunch?   dóndepyénsalmorṣár↓   ¿Dónde piensa almorzar?

5 Where do you intend to study?   dóndepyénsa̦estuḑyár↓   ¿Dónde piensa estudiar?

6 Who do you intend to invite?   àkyémpyénsa̦imbitár↓   ¿A quién piensa invitar?

7 Who do you intend to complain to?   àkyémpyénsakehársè↓   ¿A quién piensa quejarse?

VEINTIUNO   25.21

jacobeligoodsons.com For Free Audio

UNIT 25   SPOKEN SPANISH

D pèroᶅyeḅọ|algoᶁeᶁinérò↓   Pero llevo algo de dinero.

1 But I'm taking a fair amount of food.   pèroᶅyeḅọ|algoᶁekomíᶁà↓   Pero llevo algo de comida.

2 But I'm taking a fair amount of provisions.   pèroᶅyeḅọ|algoᶁeproḅisyónès↓   Pero llevo algo de provisiones.

3 But I have a fair amount of money.   pèrótengọ|algoᶁeᶁinérò↓   Pero tengo algo de dinero.

4 But he knows a fair amount about   pèrósabẹ|algoᶁenegóçyòs↓   Pero sabe algo de negocios.
  business.

5 But he knows a fair amount about   pèrósabẹ|algoᶁẹabyónès↓   Pero sabe algo de aviones.
  airplanes.

6 But there's something of truth (in it).   pèrọay|algoᶁeberᶁáᶁ↓   Pero hay algo de verdad.

7 But there's something of reality (in it).   pèrọay|algoᶁerrẹaliᶁáᶁ↓   Pero hay algo de realidad.

E trèzmilᶁólàrès↓   Tres mil dólares.

1 Six thousand dollars.   séyzmildólàrès↓   Seis mil dólares.

2 Seven thousand pesos.   syétèmilpésòs↓   Siete mil pesos.

3 Nine thousand pesos.   nwébèmilpésòs↓   Nueve mil pesos.

25.22   VEINTIDOS

SPOKEN SPANISH   UNIT 25

4 Eleven thousand meters.   ónṣèmilmétròs↓   Once mil metros.

5 Fifteen thousand meters.   kínṣèmilmétròs↓   Quince mil metros.

6 Sixty thousand men.   sèséntàmilómbrès↓   Sesenta mil hombres.

7 Seventy thousand men.   sèténtàmilómbrès↓   Setenta mil hombres.

F pérdoné|sèŋyór↓ pèrósèmèólbido|sụapeřᵧído↓   Perdone, señor, pero se me olvidó su
                                                          apellido.

1 Excuse me, sir; but I've forgotten your   pérdoné|sèŋyór↓ pèrósèmèólbido|sunómbrè↓   Perdone, señor, pero se me olvidó su nombre.
  name.

2 Excuse me, sir; but I forgot the mineral   pérdoné|sèŋyór↓ pèrósèmèólbido|èlaǥwa   Perdone, señor, pero se me olvidó el agua
  water.   minerál↓   mineral.

3 Excuse me, sir; but I forgot to let you know. pérdoné|sèŋyór↓ pèrósèmèólbido|ạbisárlè↓   Perdone, señor, pero se me olvidó avisarle.

4 Excuse me, sir; but I forgot to tell you. pérdoné|sèŋyór↓ pèrósèmèólbido|deṣírlè↓   Perdone, señor, pero se me olvidó decirle.

5 Excuse me, ma'am; but I dropped the milk. pérdoné|sèŋyórà↓ pèrósémèkàyo|laléchè↓   Perdone, señora, pero se me cayó la leche.

6 Excuse me, ma'am; but the cup dropped.   pérdoné|sèŋyórà↓ pèrósémèkàyo|latáṣà↓   Perdone, señora, pero se me cayó la taza.

7 Excuse me, ma'am; but the cup broke.   pérdoné|sèŋyórà↓ pèrósémèrròmpyo|latáṣà↓   Perdone, señora, pero se me rompió la taza.

VEINTITRES   25.23

UNIT 25   SPOKEN SPANISH

25.24   Review drill — Verb-subject order in certain dependent clauses

1 Let's go see when Mary is coming.   bámòsàbér |kwàndobyénèmaríá↓   Vamos a ver cuándo viene María.

2 Let's go see when Jose is coming.   bámòsàbér |kwàndoₒyégahosé↓   Vamos a ver cuándo llega José.

3 Let's go see where Paul works.   bámòsàbér |dóndetrabahapáblò↓   Vamos a ver dónde trabaja Pablo.

4 Let's see where the custom's office is. bámòsàbér |dóndestaladwánà↓   Vamos a ver dónde está la aduana.

5 Let's see where John lives.   bámòsàbér |dóndebìbehwán↓   Vamos a ver dónde vive Juan.

6 Let's go see what Alice needs.   bámòsàbér |kenèșesitalíșyà↓   Vamos a ver qué necesita Alicia.

7 Let's see what Carmen says.   bámosàbér |kedíșekármèn↓   Vamos a ver qué dice Carmen.

8 Let's see what they believe.   bámosàbér |kekręęnₒℓyòs↓   Vamos a ver qué creen ellos.

9 Let's go see what Jose is writing.   bámosàbér |keskríbehosé↓   Vamos a ver qué escribe José.

10 Let's go see how much the bed costs.   bámosàbér |kwántokwéstalakámà↓   Vamos a ver cuánto cuesta la cama.

11 Let's go see how much the suit costs.   bámosàbér |kwántokwéstgelbestídò↓ Vamos a ver cuánto cuesta el vestido.

12 Let's go see how Jose studies.   bámosàbér |komọestudyahosé↓   Vamos a ver cómo estudia José.

13 Let's see how Paul speaks.   bámosàbér |komọablapáblò↓   Vamos a ver cómo habla Pablo.

25.24   VEINTICUATRO

SPOKEN SPANISH   UNIT 25

25.3   CONVERSATION STIMULUS

NARRATIVE 1

1 Chico is talking with his friend, Luis.   chíko |ęstáblando |kònsyàmiɡolwís↓   Chico está hablando con su amigo, Luis.

2 He tells him that he's thinking of going   lédiȿe |kèstápènsandǫirsę |àtràbàhár | Le dice que está pensando irse a trabajar a
   to work in the United States.   àlósę̀stàdosụnídòs↓   los Estados Unidos.

3 In order to work in that country, one   pàrátràbàhár |ènȩsèpàis↑sènèȿèsitatener | Para trabajar en ese país se necesita tener
   has to have an immigrant visa.   bisadęinmiɡrántè↓   visa de inmigrante.

4 But Chico doesn't need (one). He is an   pèróchíko |nóneȿesítà↓ el |ęsàmérikanò↓   Pero Chico no necesita. El es americano.
   American.

5 Luis didn't know that.   lwír |nosabíą |ésò↓   Luis no sabía eso.

6 He thinks it's a joke.   kré |kèsúnàɬromà↓   Cree que es una broma.

7 But it isn't a joke.   pèrónǫès |únàbrómà↓   Pero no es una broma.

8 Chico's been an American (ever)   chíkǫ |àsídǫàmérikano |dèzdèkènàȿyó↓   Chico ha sido americano desde que nació.
   since he was born.

9 He was born in the U. S.   elnaȿyó |ęnlosestadosụnídòs↓   El nació en los Estados Unidos.

VEINTICINCO   25.25

UNIT 25   SPOKEN SPANISH

DIALOG 1

Chico, dígale a Luis que Ud. está pensando irse a trabajar a los Estados Unidos.

èstóypensándǫ |ìrmęatrabàhar |àlos̹estádos

unídòs↓

Chico: Estoy pensando irme a trabajar a los Estados Unidos.

Luis, dígale que está bien, pero que en ese caso necesita visa de inmigrante.

èstàbyém↓pèrǫèn̹ǫsekàso↑nès̹ésitaz |

bísádęinmigràntè↓

Luis: Está bien, pero en ese caso necesitas visa de inmigrante.

Chico, contéstele que Ud. no, que Ud. es americano.

yónó↓ yósóy |àmèrikánò↓

Chico: Yo no, yo soy americano.

Luis, '¿Ah, sí?', dígale. Y pregúntele que desde cuándo es americano.

á|sì↑ dézdékwándǫ |éres̹amerikánò↓

Luis: ¿Ah, sí? ¿Desde cuándo eres americano?

Chico, contéstele que desde que nació. Que Ud. nació en los Estados Unidos.

dézdèkènás̹ì↓ yónás̹i |ęnlòs̹ęstádòsúnidòs↓

Chico: Desde que nací. Yo nací en los Estados Unidos.

Luis, dígale que Ud. no sabía. Que creía que era una broma.

nòsabíá↓ krèía |kér̹ǫúnǫbrómǎ↓

Luis: No sabía. Creía que era una broma.

NARRATIVE 2

1 Chico plans to work at (just) anything.

chíkó |pyénsàtrǎbǎhar |ęŋkwàlkyérkósǎ↓

Chico piensa trabajar en cualquier cosa.

2 It's easy to find work in the United States.

èsfaşíl |èŋkòntrártrǎbáhǫ |ènlòs̹ę̀stádòsúnidòs↓Es fácil encontrar trabajo en los Estados Unidos.

3 Luis would like to go too.

lwís |kìsyérǫ̀irsé |tàmbyén↓

Luis quisiera irse también.

25.26   VEINTISEIS

jacobeligoodsons.com For Free Audio

SPOKEN SPANISH   UNIT 25

4 But he thinks that it wouldn't be so   pérokré|képárael|nòsèriatamfaṣil| Pero cree que para él no sería tan fácil
   easy for him to find a job.   èŋkóntrartrabáhò↓   encontrar trabajo.

5 Because he's not an American, like Chico.   pòrkél| noéznortęamerikanò|kómóchíkò↓   Porque él no es norteamericano, como Chico.

6 It's true, but Luis must remember that he   ézbèrdáð↓ pèrólwíz|ðeberrekordar↑kél| Es verdad, pero Luis debe recordar que él
   is an engineer and Chico (is)n't.   és,iŋhènyerǫ|íchikonó↓   es ingeniero y Chico no.

7 For an engineer it's very easy to find   pàrąúniŋhènyerǫ|ézmuyfáṣil|eŋkóntrár   Para un ingeniero es muy fácil encontrar
   work in the United States.   trabáhǫ|ènlòs,ęstáðòsúníðòs↓   trabajo en los Estados Unidos.

                                                     DIALOG 2

Luis, pregúntele que en qué piensa trabajar.   èŋképyensastrabahár↓   Luis: ¿En qué piensas trabajar?

Chico, contéstele que en cualquier cosa.   èŋkwálkyerkósà↓ èsfaṣíl|eŋkóntrártràbáhǫ| Chico: En cualquier cosa. Es fácil encontrar
   Que es fácil encontrar trabajo en los   ènlósęstáðòsúníðòs↓   trabajo en los Estados Unidos.
   Estados Unidos.

Luis, dígale que Ud. quisiera irse también.   yǫkisyerąírmè|tàmbyén↓ pèròkréǫ|képàramí↑   Luis: Yo quisiera irme también. Pero creo
   Pero Ud. cree que para Ud. no sería tan   nòsèriatamfáṣil|eŋkóntrártràbáhò↓   que para mí no sería tan fácil en-
   fácil encontrar trabajo.   contrar trabajo.

Chico, pregúntele que por qué dice eso.   pòrkéðiçes,ésò↓   Chico: ¿Por qué dices eso?

Luis, contéstele que porque Ud. no es   pórkèyǫ|nòsóynortęamerikanò|kómòtú↑   Luis: Porque yo no soy norteamericano,
   norteamericano, como él.   como tú.

VEINTISIETE   25.27

UNIT 25   SPOKEN SPANISH

Chico, dígale que es verdad, pero que debe   èzbèrđáđ↓péròđebezrrekordár↑kètú| Chico: Es verdad, pero debes recordar
recordar que él es ingeniero y Ud. no.   que tú eres ingeniero y yo no.
                                                    érèsiŋhènyerọ↓iyón6↓

                                            NARRATIVE 3

1 Luis is going to think it (over).   lwíz |bapensárló↓   Luis va a pensarlo.

2 He wants to know what he has to do about élkyéresaber |kétyénekḍaşer |párálóđèlàbìsá↓   El quiere saber qué tiene que hacer para
   the visa problem.   lo de la visa.

3 They can go talk with John White.   pweđen |íràblár |kònyoŋhwáyt↓   Pueden ir a hablar con John White.

4 White is a friend of Chico's who works in hwáyt |èsúnàmígòđèchikò↑kètràbahạ | White es un amigo de Chico que trabaja en
   the Consular Section.   la Sección Consular.
                                            ènlàsèkşyoŋkonsulár↓

5 Luis wants to know what day this week   lwiskyéresàber↑keđía |đéstasemàna | Luis quiere saber qué día de esta semana
   they can go.   pueden ir.
                                            pweđenír↓

6 Chico tells him that Wednesday is a good chíkoleđişe |kélmyérkoles |èsúmbwendíà↓   Chico le dice que el miércoles es un buen
   day.   día.

7 And that he'll call him to let him know. íkél |ló(l)yáma |páràbisàrlè↓   Y que él lo llama para avisarle.

8 Luis tells him not to forget.   lwízleđìşe |kènoselọolbíđè↓   Luis le dice que no se le olvide.

25.28   VEINTIOCHO

SPOKEN SPANISH   UNIT 25

DIALOG 3

Luis, dígale que va a pensarlo. Pregúntele
que qué tiene que hacer para lo de la visa.

bóyapensárlò↓ ketengokeaşer |páràlòdèlà
bìsà↓

Luis: Voy a pensarlo. ¿Qué tengo que
hacer para lo de la visa?

Chico, contéstele que Uds. pueden ir a
hablar con John White, un amigo suyo que
que trabaja en la Sección Consular.

pódemos |íràblár |kónyoŋhwáyt↓únàmìgomìo |
kètrábàhạ |ènlàsèkşyoŋkonsulár↓

Chico: Podemos ir a hablar con John White,
un amigo mío que trabaja en la
Sección Consular.

Luis, pregúntele que qué día de esta
semana.

kedia |déstasèmánà↓

Luis: ¿Qué día de esta semana?

Chico, contéstele que el miércoles es un
buen día. Que Ud. lo llama.

èlmyerkoles |èsúmbwendía↓ yòteⓁyámò↓

Chico: El miércoles es un buen día. Yo
te llamo.

Luis, dígale que muy bien, pero que no
se le olvide.

múybyém↓péròkènosetẹolbíđè↓

Luis: Muy bien, pero que no se le olvide.

25.4   READINGS

25.40   List of cognate loan words

sistemática   sìstèmatìkà↓

metódica   mètoɖìkà↓

la organización   lạ─òrgànişạşyóṅ↓

el sistema   èl─sistemá↓

aceptaba (aceptar)   àşéptàbà↓ àşèptár↓

VEINTINUEVE   25.29

UNIT 25   SPOKEN SPANISH

la canasta   là—kànàstà↓

el bridge   èl—brích↓

dedicado (dedicar)   dèdikàdò↓ dèdikár↓

la excepción   la̱—ès(ṣ)èpṣyóh↓

la experta   la̱—èspèrtà↓

25.41   Reading selection

                                            Señora Sistemática

        Marta de Fuentes era una mujer muy metódica y rigurosa en la organización de su casa. Cada día de la semana era un día de 'algo'; algo diferente a los otros días,
claro, pero el sistema general era el mismo de semana a semana. Solamente por razones muy especiales aceptaba ella hacer algún cambio en este sistema. Por ejemplo,
el lunes era el día de lavar toda la ropa y mandar a la tintorería los trajes de su esposo y de sus hijos, y también algunos de los vestidos y faldas de ella y de las niñas que
no se podían lavar en la casa. Y a la lavandería mandaba solamente las camisas de don Ricardo, porque sólo ahí las sabían lavar a su gusto. El jueves no había ningún
trabajo especial, pero era día de canasta o bridge con las amigas del barrio que casi siempre se reunían en su casa. El sábado estaba dedicado al trabajo general de la casa;
es decir, barrer y limpiar todos los pisos, muebles, lavar ventanas, etc. Aunque los Fuentes tenían dos buenas sirvientas, todos los de la casa ayudaban en algo ese día con
excepción de don Ricardo y dos de los hijos varones que trabajaban en el Ministerio de Relaciones Exteriores. Esas eran las órdenes de su madre y aunque a los niños, especialmente a los otros dos varones, no les gustaba ayudar en nada, nunca se quejaban, o por lo menos, si lo hacían, nunca lo hacían cuando su madre estaba presente, porque
sabían que ella era muy rigurosa y no aceptaba pretextos. Los viernes eran los días de mercado. Marta nunca mandaba a las sirvientas a hacer las compras; prefería ir ella
misma porque nadie como ella sabía dónde y cómo se podía comprar bueno y barato las verduras más frescas, la mejor carne, el mejor pescado.... Esta señora era lo que realmente podríamos llamar una experta en compras.

        Así era Marta de Fuentes, una señora metódica que, aunque a veces demasiado rigurosa, era una magnífica mujer, siempre dedicada a su casa, a su esposo y a sus hijos.

25.42   Response drill

        1 ¿Cómo era la señora de Fuentes en la organización de su casa?

        2 ¿Cambiaba el sistema de semana a semana?

        3 ¿Solamente cuándo aceptaba ella hacer algún cambio?

        4 ¿Qué hacían todos los lunes en su casa?

25.30   jacobeligoodsons.com For Free Audio   TREINTA

SPOKEN SPANISH   UNIT 25

5 ¿Qué mandaba a la tintorería?

6 ¿Por qué mandaba las camisas de su esposo a la lavandería?

7 ¿Cuál era el día de canasta o de bridge?

8 ¿Dónde se reunían ella y sus amigas?

9 ¿Cuántas sirvientas tenían los Fuentes?

10 ¿Hacían las sirvientas todo el trabajo de la casa los sábados?

11 ¿Dónde trabajaban dos de los hijos varones?

12 ¿Qué trabajo había que hacer en la casa los sábados?

13 ¿Por qué no se quejaban enfrente de su madre los otros dos hijos que tenían que ayudar en la casa?

14 ¿Qué hacía Marta los viernes?

15 ¿Por qué no mandaba a sus sirvientas al mercado?

jacobeligoodsons.com For Free Audio

SPOKEN SPANISH   UNIT 26

26.1   BASIC SENTENCES.   A visa interview (continued).

ENGLISH SPELLING   AID TO LISTENING   SPANISH SPELLING

    that (he) answer (to answer, to vouch)   kè-rréspóndà↓ rrèspónde'r↓   que responda (responder)

White   White
    Mister Moreno, do you have anyone who will vouch   sènyòrmòrenó↓ tyéne ̩|algúnapersóna|kè   Señor Moreno, ¿tiene alguna persona que
    for you in the United States? (1)   rréspóndaporustéd ̩|enlos̩estados̩unidos↑   responda por usted en los Estados Unidos?

Gentleman   Señor
    Yes. I know someone who can do it.   si↓kònos̩k̩oalgyen|kepwed̩e̩as̩érló↓   Sí. Conozco a alguien que puede hacerlo.

White   White
    North American?   nòrte̩àmèrikáno↑   ¿Norteamericano?

        the business   èl-nègos̩yó↓   el negocio

        the business man   èl-ombre-de-negós̩yós↓   el hombre de negocios

Gentleman   Señor
    Yes. He's a business man. (2)   si↓ e̩sun̩ombre̩denegós̩yos↓   Sí. Es un hombre de negocios.

        to sign   firmár↓   firmar

        the document   èl-dòkúmentó↓   el documento

    Does he have to sign some type document? (3)   tyéne'l|kefirmar|àlgundokuménto↑   ¿Tiene él que firmar algún documento?

UNO   26.1

                       jacobeligoodsons.com For Free Audio

UNIT 26   SPOKEN SPANISH

(I) will explain (to explain)   èsplikáré↓ èsplikár↓   explicaré (explicar)

White
Of course. I'll explain *that* to you later. (4)   pòrsúpwésto↓ éso |sèlgèsplikáré |dèspwés↓   *White*
                                                                                                Por supuesto. Eso se lo explicaré
                                                                                                después.

for the moment, time being   pòr—lò—prontò↓   por lo pronto

the following   lò—sigyénte↓   lo siguiente

For the moment you need the following: pòrlòpròntò↑nèşèsita |losigyénte↓   Por lo pronto necesita lo siguiente:

the passport   èl—pásàpòrtè↓   el pasaporte

the certificate   èl—şèrtifikàdò↓   el certificado

the vaccination   là—bákuná↓   la vacuna

the health   là—sálud↓   la salud

the conduct   là—kónduktá↓   la conducta

Passport, vaccination certificate, health certificate,   èlpàsàpòrtè↑ şèrtifikàdo |dèbákuná↑   El pasaporte; certificado de vacuna, de
and good conduct certificate.   dèsálud↑idèbwenakonduktá↓   salud y de buena conducta.

the doctor   èl—médikò↓   el médico

Gentleman
The health certificate, can just any doctor give   èldèsálud↓ pwédedàrmelo |kwàlkyérmédikò↑   *Señor*
it to me?   El de salud, ¿puede dármelo cualquier
                                                                                                médico?

to accept   àşèptár↓   aceptar

26.2   DOS

SPOKEN SPANISH   UNIT 26

White
No. It should be from a doctor approved by the Embassy.

nó↓ débésér│deunmediko↑aşeptadoporla embahádá↓

White
No. Debe ser de un médico aceptado por la Embajada.

the application

lá—sólişitúd↓

la solicitud

(you) carry yourself it (to carry, take)

ⓐyebéséla↓ ⓐyébar↓

llévesela (llevar)

(you) fill (to fill)

ⓐyené↓ ⓐyénar↓

llene (llenar)

Take this application. Take it with you, fill it out, and bring it to me tomorrow. (5)

tomestasolişitúd↓ ⓐyebésélá↓ ⓐyénela│iméláтraemanyáná↓

Tome esta solicitud. Llévesela, llénela y me la trae mañana.

Gentleman
Anything else?

álgómas↑

Señor
¿Algo más?

the print

lá—weⓐyá↓

la huella

digital

dihitál↓

digital

the finger print

lá—weⓐya—dihitál↓

la huella digital

at the end

á—lo—ultimó↓

a lo último

White
Yes, your finger prints, but that comes last.

si↑ lázweⓐyazdihitáles↓ péroesoesalo últimó↓

White
Sí, las huellas digitales, pero eso es a lo último.

26.10   Notes on the basic sentences

(1) As in one or two previous sentences, it has been necessary here to use a subjunctive form in the interest of realism and naturalness: /rrespónda/ *responda* from /rresponder/*responder*. A more literal but less accurate English translation would be: '...who may vouch for you....' Full explanation in Units 36 and 40.

(2) A rather important difference between English structure and Spanish structure may be illustrated with this sentence. In Spanish, as you have seen, nearly any word can be *nominalized-i.e.,* used like a noun. That process is much less widespread in English. On the other hand a great diversity of words in English can be caused to function

TRES   26.3

UNIT 26   SPOKEN SPANISH

like modifiers, a much rarer thing in Spanish. Thus in this sentence, *business* appears with *man* in a modifier-plus-head-word construction in English, equivalent in Spanish to a head-word-plus-phrase construction. (In both cases the head-word is the noun modified.)

(3) In English, *some* is functionally the plural of *a, an: He has a book, He has some books.* One cannot say, *He has some book,* at least not without adding '...or other.' Hence /algún/ *algún* places a slight strain on the English translator at this point, and 'some type' is the result. The other alternative would be pluralization: '...sign some documents.'

(4) The emphasis that is indicated by underlining *that* in the English translation (thus showing extra loudness and higher pitch) is obtained in Spanish by word-order: /éso/ *eso* appears first, out of its 'normal' (i.e. unemphatic) position.

(5) It is interesting to note (and a little difficult to account for) that the first three verbs of this sentence are commands in imperative form: /tóme/ *tome,* /ỻyébesela/ *llévesela,* and /ỻyénela/ *llénela;* but the fourth, /tráe/ *trae,* is straight present indicative. The imperative would be /tráygamela/ *tráigamela.* This happens when the person giving the 'orders' wishes to play down, soften, the air of authority: '...and you'll bring it to me tomorrow.'

26.2   DRILLS AND GRAMMAR

26.21   Pattern drills

26.21.1 Reflexive and direct clitic pronouns in the same construction

   A. Presentation of pattern

                                        ILLUSTRATIONS

The milk? I drank it.   1   làléchet mèlàtóméↆ   ¿La leche? *Me la* tomé.

These shoes? I'll take them.   2   éstò(s)ṣàpàtost mèlòzỻyebòↆ   ¿Estos zapatos? *Me los* llevo.

The coffee? We drank it.   3   èlkáfet nòzlòtómàmòsↆ   ¿El café? *Nos lo* tomamos.

The fruit? We ate it.   4   làfrutat nòzlàkòmìmòsↆ   ¿La fruta? *Nos la* comimos.

This overcoat, will you take it?   5   èstḛàbrìgòↆ tèlòỻyebàst   Este abrigo, ¿*te lo* llevas?

26.4   CUATRO

SPOKEN SPANISH																										UNIT 26

The dessert, did you eat it?	6	èlpóstrè↓ ústeɗɑselokómyó↑	El postre, ¿usted *se lo* comió?
The hats? You already took them.	7	ló(s)sómbréros↑ ústeɗez │yáseloz(l)yebárón↓	¿Los sombreros? Ustedes ya *se los* llevaron.
The salad? They (f) ate it.	8	lÿènsàlàɗa↑ sèlàkòmyéronɖ(l)ɥàs↓	¿La ensalada? *Se la* comieron ellas.

EXTRAPOLATION

			Reflexive	Direct	
1		sg	me	———	
		pl	nos	———	
2	fam		te	———	
2 - 3		sg	se	lo	la
		pl		los	las

NOTES

a. All reflexive clitics, but only 3 person direct clitics, occur in this construction.

b. Appearing with reflexives, the direct clitics usually refer to things; occasionally, with verbs like /(l)yebár/ and /traér/, to persons.

CINCO

26.5

jacobeligoodsons.com For Free Audio

UNIT 26   SPOKEN SPANISH

26.21.11 Substitution drill -- Construction substitution

        PROBLEM:

                éÒya |sèkòmyólafrútà↓

        ANSWER:

                éÒyaselakòmyó↓

    1   sètòmo|laléchè↓   sélàtómó↓

    2   sètòmaron|lostrágòs↓   sèlòstòmaròn↓

    3   mèkòmi|lakárnè↓   mélàkómí↓

_____

        PROBLEM:
                Ella se comió *la fruta.*

        ANSWER:
                Ella se la comió.

    1 Se tomó *la leche.*   Se la tomó.

    2 Se tomaron *los tragos.*   Se los tomaron.

    3 Me comí *la carne.*   Me la comí.

26.6   SEIS

SPOKEN SPANISH   UNIT 26

4 nòskómimos|kwàtroɣébòs↓   nòzlòskómimòs↓

5 sèkómyéròn|lɐensaláɖà↓   sèlàkómyéròn↓

6 sèlìmpyáròn|lozɖyéntès↓   sèlózlìmpyaròn↓

7 mèlàbé|lakabéʂà↓   mèlàlàbé↓

8 sèkómpro|ɐltráhè↓   sèlòkómpró↓

9 nòzbébimos|elkafé↓   nòzlòbébimòs↓

---

4 Nos comimos *cuatro huevos.*   Nos los comimos.

5 Se comieron *la ensalada.*   Se la comieron.

6 Se limpiaron *los dientes.*   Se los limpiaron.

7 Me lavé *la cabeza.*   Me la lavé.

8 Se compró *el traje.*   Se lo compró.

9 Nos bebimos *el café.*   Nos lo bebimos.

UNIT 26   SPOKEN SPANISH

26.21.12 Translation drill

1 He ate the whole meal up.   élsékómyó |todalakomída↓   El se comió toda la comida.

   She didn't eat it all up.   eõya |noselakomyotóđá↓   Ella no se la comió toda.

2 I bought myself a car.   mékómpreynkárrò↓   Me compré un carro.

   I bought it cheap.   mélókòmprebarátò↓   Me lo compré barato.

3 They drink two cups of coffee every day.   eõyos |sébébén |dostaşazđekafe |todozlozđíâs↓   Ellos se beben dos tazas de café todos
                                                                                                los días.

   I drink them too.   yó |tambyénmelazbébò↓   Yo también me las bebo.

4 She always eats her green vegetables.   eõya |syémpre |sèkomelazberđúrâs↓   Ella siempre se come las verduras.

   He never eats them.   él |nuŋkaselaskómè↓   El nunca se las come.

5 I ate all the eggs.   mékómi |todozlozwébòs↓   Me comí todos los huevos.

   He ate them too.   él |támbyén |seloskomyó↓   El también se los comió.

B. Discussion of pattern

    In this construction the reflexive clitics function as indirect objects and indicate the concern of the subject of the verb as regards the action. With some verbs, like /tomár, komér/ the reflexive clitic appears only when a direct object (noun or clitic pronoun) appears. These verbs do not usually appear with *any indirect clitics except* reflexive clitics which have this indirect function. Thus /me-lo-kómo↓/ 'I'll eat it' is a normal expression, but /se-lo-kómo↓/, 'I'll eat it for you', while possible, is unusual.

    Other verbs, like /ộyebár, komprár/, and /tomár/ (not meaning 'drink'), can appear in this construction, but they also occur regularly with *any indirect* clitic, not just reflexives with indirect function. Thus /me-lo-ộyébo↓/ 'I'll take it (for myself)' and /se-lo-ộyébo↓/ 'I'll take it for you' are both common expressions.

26.8   OCHO

SPOKEN SPANISH   UNIT 26

    In Spain (except in Madrid, where /le/ can function as a reference to either persons or objects) only /lo/ appears in this construction with an indirect /me/ or /le, se/, even when the reference is to persons.

    Only third person forms (those which begin with /l—/) occur as the direct clitics in this construction.

26.21.2 Reflexives with no designated agents

  A. Presentation of pattern

ILLUSTRATIONS

Spanish is spoken here.	1	ákı |seablaespanyól↓	Aquí *se habla* español.
Chauffeur needed.	2	senesesitachofér↓	*Se necesita* chofer.
Old newspapers bought here.	3	ákı |sekompram |peryodikozbyéhos↓	Aquí *se compran* periódicos viejos.
————————————	4	sebe |kézmuybwéna↓	*Se ve* que es muy buena.
They say everything is expensive in that city.	5	sedíse |ketodoeskáro |enésasyúdád↓	*Se dice* que todo es caro en esa ciudad.
It is believed that (some) bombers are going to arrive.	6	sekree |kebanallyegar |abyonezde bombardéó↓	*Se cree* que van a llegar aviones de bombardeo.

EXTRAPOLATION

	Reflexive clitic	Verb	Subject
3	se	sg verb pl verb	sg noun, clause pl noun

NOTES

  a. This construction is used to state the doing of an action when there is no particular interest in specifying who does it.

  b. The grammatical subject appears after the verb.

NUEVE

UNIT 26   SPOKEN SPANISH

26.21.21 Substitution drill — Construction substitution

PROBLEM:

    áıbénden |rrópaéchá↓

ANSWER:

    áısébénde |rrópaéchá↓

1 ákı |nobáylán↓   ákı |nosébáylá↓

2 áı |áblaınglés↓   áı |seáblaınglés↓

3 áı |aǥembestídòs↓   áı |seǥaǥembestídòs↓

_____

PROBLEM:
    Ahí *venden* ropa hecha.

ANSWER:
    Ahí se vende ropa hecha.

1 Aquí no *bailan*.   Aquí no se baila.

2 Ahí *hablan* inglés.   Ahí se habla inglés.

3 Ahí *hacen* vestidos.   Ahí se hacen vestidos.

26.10   DIEZ

SPOKEN SPANISH   UNIT 26

4 àikompran |mweblezbyéhòs↓   ài |sèkompran |mweblezbyéhòs↓

5 àkı |nobebén |muchaléché↓   àkı |nosebébe |muchaléché↓

6 àkiẹskriben |enẹspaŋyól↓   àkı |sèskribẹ |enẹspaŋyól↓

7 àkı |nokomeŋkárnè↓   àkı |nosekomekárnè↓

_____

4 Ahí *compran* muebles viejos.   Ahí se compran muebles viejos.

5 Aquí no *beben* mucha leche.   Aquí no se bebe mucha leche.

6 Aquí *escriben* en español.   Aquí se escribe en español.

7 Aquí no *comen* carne.   Aquí no se come carne.

ONCE

UNIT 26   SPOKEN SPANISH

26.21.22 Translation drill

1 Nothing is sold there, (they don't sell   ái |nosebéndenáđà↓   Ahí no se vende nada.
   anything).

2 Little is written here, (you write little).   ákí |seskríbepókó↓   Aquí se escribe poco.

3 English lessons are given here, (we give   ákísedán |lékşyónezdęinglés↓   Aquí se dan lecciones de inglés.
   English lessons).

4 Gentlemen's articles are sold here, (we   ákí |sébenden |ártikulosparakabaⱮyéròs↓ Aquí se venden artículos para caballeros.
   sell gentlemen's articles).

5 Children's clothing is sewed here, (we   ákí |sékóse |rropađeníɲyò↓   Aquí se cose ropa de niño.
   sew children's clothing).

6 You don't work on Sundays here.   ákí |nósetrabáha |lozdomíŋgòs↓   Aquí no se trabaja los domingos.

7 Nothing is drunk there, (they don't   ái |nosetómanáđà↓   Ahí no se toma nada.
   drink anything).

8 Chauffeur wanted.   sébuskachofér↓   Se busca chofer.

9 Rooms for rent.   sęálkilaŋkwártòs↓   Se alquilan cuartos.

10 Maid needed.   sénęşésitą |unamucháchà↓   Se necesita una muchacha.

26.12   DOCE

SPOKEN SPANISH   UNIT 26

11 Hats cleaned.   sèlímpyansombréròs↓   Se limpian sombreros.

12 Dancing lessons, (dancing taught).   sènséɲabaylár↓   Se enseña a bailar.

13 Apartment for rent.   sèálkíla|unapartaméntò↓   Se alquila un apartamento.

B. Discussion of pattern

        This construction in Spanish is usually associated with a passive construction in English, especially when no agent appears. Thus a sentence like 'The stores are closed at 6 o'clock' would translate into Spanish as /las—tyéndas—se—ṣyérran—a—las—séys↓/; if the person(s) who close(s) them is/are not mentioned, since in Spanish the statement literally says 'the stores close themselves.'

        Another common English equivalent of this Spanish construction is the impersonal use of pronouns like *you, we, they*. In English, these are usually plural: 'They say he he's rich; You go that way a mile, then you come to a hill...; We should all have an opportunity to go to college; One hopes things will get better.' In Spanish this impersonality can be rendered by a plural verb with no expressed subject, or by casting the sentence to say that it does itself, by means of a third person reflexive clitic.

        Short, laconic signs, especially displayed in store windows, often make use of this reflexive construction: /se—ábla—ınglés↓ se—neṣesíta—muchácha↓ se—áṣem—bestídos↓/, etc.

TRECE

jacobeligoodsons.com For Free Audio

UNIT 26   SPOKEN SPANISH

26.22   Replacement drills

A   kònóṣkǫ│algyeŋ†kepweđǫaṣérló↓

1   _____ yṇǫmbre _____↓   kònóṣkǫ│àyṇǫmbre†kepweđǫaṣérló↓

2   _____ pweđen _____↓   kònóṣkǫ│àyṇòsǫmbres†kepweđenaṣérló↓

3   _____ sèŋyórita _____↓   kònóṣkǫ│àyṇàsèŋyòrita†kepweđǫaṣérló↓

4   kònóṣemos _____↓   kònóṣemos│aúnàsèŋyòrita†kepweđǫaṣérló↓

5   _____ arreglárló↓   kònóṣemos│aúnàsèŋyòrita†kepweđǫarreglárló↓

6   _____ sèŋyóres _____↓   kònóṣemos│aúnò(s)sèŋyores†kepweđenarreglárló↓

7   _____ pweđǫ _____↓   kònóṣemos│aúnsèŋyor†kepweđǫarreglárló↓

A   Conozco a alguien que puede hacerlo.

1   _____ un hombre _____ .   Conozco a un hombre que puede hacerlo.

2   _____ pueden _____ .   Conozco a unos hombres que pueden hacerlo.

3   _____ señorita _____ .   Conozco a una señorita que puede hacerlo.

4   Conocemos _____ .   Conocemos a una señorita que puede hacerlo.

5   _____ arreglarlo.   Conocemos a una señorita que puede arreglarlo.

6   _____ señores _____ .   Conocemos a unos señores que pueden arreglarlo.

7   _____ puede _____ .   Conocemos a un señor que puede arreglarlo.

26.14   CATORCE

SPOKEN SPANISH   UNIT 26

B   èsùnọmbre |đenegóşyòs↓

1 són_____↓   sónùnôsọmbrèz |đenegóşyòs↓

2 _____byahèz_____↓   sónùnôzbyahèz |đenegóşyòs↓

3 páreşẹ_____↓   páreşẹ↑úmbyáhe |đenegóşyòs↓

4 _____àhenşya_____↓   páreşẹ↑únàhenşya |đenegóşyòs↓

5 són_____↓   son↑únàsàhenşyaz |đenegóşyòs↓

6 _____kása_____↓   es↑únàkása |đenegóşyòs↓

7 _____lókós↓   es↑únàkása |đelókós↓

_____

B   Es un hombre de negocios.

1 Son_____.   Son unos hombres de negocios.

2 _____viajes_____.   Son unos viajes de negocios.

3 Parece_____.   Parece un viaje de negocios.

4 _____agencia_____.   Parece una agencia de negocios.

5 Son_____.   Son unas agencias de negocios.

6 _____casa_____.   Es una casa de negocios.

7 _____locos.   En una casa de locos.

QUINCE

UNIT 26   SPOKEN SPANISH

C   tyénel|kefírmar|algundokuménto↑

1   _____kósa↑   tyénel|kefírmar|algúnakósa↑

2   ___yó_____↑   téngoyó|kefírmar|algúnakósa↑

3   _____dokuméntos↑   téngoyó|kefírmar|algúnozdokuméntos↑

4   _____tráer_____↑   téngoyó|ketráer|algúnozdokuméntos↑

5   _____ótro____↑   téngoyó|ketráer|ótrodokúmento↑

6   __ustéd_____↑   tyéngustéd|ketráer|ótrodokúmento↑

7   _____kósas↑   tyéngustéd|ketráer|ótraskósas↑

_____

C   ¿Tiene él que firmar algún documento?

1   ¿ _____cosa?   ¿Tiene él que firmar alguna cosa?

2   ¿ _____yo _____?   ¿Tengo yo que firmar alguna cosa?

3   ¿ _____ documentos?   ¿Tengo yo que firmar algunos documentos?

4   ¿ _____traer_____?   ¿Tengo yo que traer algunos documentos?

5   ¿ _____ otro___?   ¿Tengo yo que traer otro documento?

6   ¿ _____usted_____?   ¿Tiene usted que traer otro documento?

7   ¿ _____ cosas?   ¿Tiene usted que traer otras cosas?

26.16   DIECISEIS

jacobeligoodsons.com For Free Audio

SPOKEN SPANISH   UNIT 26

D   pwéde |dármelo |kwálkyermédiko↑

1   _____ otro _____ ↑   pwéde |dármelo |otromédiko↑

2   _____ persona↑   pwéde |dármelo |otrapersona↑

3   pwéden _____ ↑   pwéden |dármelo |otraspersonas↑

4   _____ bendérmelo _____ ↑   pwédem |bendérmelo |otraspersonas↑

5   _____ usted↑   pwéde |bendérmelousted↑

6   _____ prestármelo _____ ↑   pwéde |prestármelousted↑

7   _____ eĺyos↑   pwédem |prestármeloeĺyos↑

D   ¿Puede dármelo cualquier médico?

1 ¿ _____ otro _____ ?   ¿Puede dármelo otro médico?

2 ¿ _____ persona?   ¿Puede dármelo otra persona?

3 ¿Pueden _____ ?   ¿Pueden dármelo otras personas?

4 ¿ _____ vendérmelo _____ ?   ¿Pueden vendérmelo otras personas?

5 ¿ _____ usted?   ¿Puede vendérmelo usted?

6 ¿ _____ prestármelo __ ?   ¿Puede prestármelo usted?

7 ¿ _____ ellos?   ¿Pueden prestármelo ellos?

DIECISIETE   26.17

jacobeligoodsons.com For Free Audio

UNIT 26   SPOKEN SPANISH

E   debeser |dẹûnmeđikọ↑àşệptađoporlạembahađȧ↓

1   _____ mí↓   debesér |dẹûnmẹđikọ↑àşệptađopormí↓

2   tyéneke_____ ↓   tyénekesér |dẹûnmẹđikọ↑àşệptađopormí↓

3   _____pérsonạ_____ ↓   tyénekesér |dẹûnạpérsonạ↑àşệptađapormí↓

4   _____lȧs_____ ↓   tyénekesér |dẹlȧspérsonas↑àşệptađaspormí↓

5   _____ ȇl↓   tyénekesér |dẹlȧspérsonas↑àşệptađaspor él↓

6   _____inhènyeròs_____ ↓   tyénekesér |dẹlȯsịnhènyeros↑àşệptađospor él↓

7   debèn_____ ↓   debensér |dẹlȯsịnhènyeros↑àşệptađospor él↓

_____

E   Debe ser de un médico aceptado por la Embajada.

1   _____ mí.   Debe ser de un médico aceptado por mí.

2   Tiene que _____ .   Tiene que ser de un médico aceptado por mí.

3   _____persona_____ .   Tiene que ser de una persona aceptada por mí.

4   _____las_____ .   Tiene que ser de las personas aceptadas por mí.

5   _____ él.   Tiene que ser de las personas aceptadas por él.

6   _____ingenieros_____ .   Tiene que ser de los ingenieros aceptados por él.

7   Deben _____ .   Deben ser de los ingenieros aceptados por él.

SPOKEN SPANISH   UNIT 26

F   tomę |estasolis̩itúd↓ ⱥyebèsèlá↓

1   ____ęstas_____↓   tomę |esta(s)solis̩itúdès↓ ⱥyebèsèlàs↓

2   _____dokuméntòs_____↓   tomę |estozdokuméntòs↓ ⱥyebèsèlòs↓

3   _____ⱥyénèló↓   tomę |estedokuméntò↓ ⱥyénèló↓

4   _____kópà_____↓   tomę |estakópà↓ ⱥyénèlá↓

5   _____ⱥyebèsèlàs↓   tomę |estaskópàs↓ ⱥyebèsèlàs↓

6   ____ęsas_____↓   tomę |esaskópàs↓ ⱥyebèsèlàs↓

7   _____líbròs_____↓   tomę |esozlíbròs↓ ⱥyebèsèlòs↓

F   Tome esta solicitud. Llévesela.

1   ____estas_____. ____ .   Tome estas solicitudes. Lléveselas.

2   _____documentos._____ .   Tome estos documentos. Lléveselos.

3   _____. Llénelo.   Tome este documento. Llénelo.

4   _____copa._____ .   Tome esta copa. Llénela.

5   _____. Lléveselas.   Tome estas copas. Lléveselas.

6   ____esas_____ . _____ .   Tome esas copas. Lléveselas.

7   _____libros._____ .   Tome esos libros. Lléveselos.

DIECINUEVE   26.19

jacobeligoodsons.com For Free Audio

UNIT 26   SPOKEN SPANISH

26.23   Variation drills

A   tyéne̞ |algúnapersóna |kḕrrḕspóndapórusté̞a↑   ¿Tiene alguna persona que responda por Ud.?

    1 Does he have some person who will   tyéne̞ |algúnapersóna |kḕrrḕspóndapórel↑   ¿Tiene alguna persona que responda por él?
      vouch for him?

    2 Do you have a friend who will vouch   tyéne̞unamígo |kḕrrḕspóndapórusté̞a↑   ¿Tiene un amigo que responda por Ud.?
      for you?

    3 Does she have a friend who will vouch   tyéne̞unamígo |kḕrrḕspóndapóreﻝya↑   ¿Tiene un amigo que responda por ella?
      for her?

    4 Isn't there someone who will vouch   no̞áyalgyen |kḕrrḕspóndapóreﻝya↑   ¿No hay alguien que responda por ella?
      for her?

    5 Isn't there someone who will vouch   no̞áyalgyen |kḕrrḕspóndapórusté̞a↑   ¿No hay alguien que responda por Ud.?
      for you?

    6 Isn't there anybody who will vouch   no̞áynáᵭye |kḕrrḕspóndapórusté̞de̞s↑   ¿No hay nadie que responda por Uds.?
      for you all?

    7 Isn't there anybody who will vouch   no̞áynáᵭye |kḕrrḕspóndapórusté̞a↑   ¿No hay nadie que responda por Ud.?
      for you?

B   po̞rsúpwésto̞↓ éso |sḕlo̞ḕsplikáre |despwés↓   Por supuesto. Eso se lo explicaré después.

    1 Of course. I'll explain *that* to you   po̞rsúpwésto̞↓ éso |sḕlo̞ḕsplikáre |maɲyáná↓   Por supuesto. Eso se lo explicaré mañana.
      tomorrow.

    2 Of course. I'll explain *that* to you   po̞rsúpwésto̞↓ éso |sḕlo̞ḕsplikáre |e̞nᵿn   Por supuesto. Eso se lo explicaré en un
      in a moment.   mo̞ménto̞↓   momento.

26.20   VEINTE

SPOKEN SPANISH   UNIT 26

3 Sure. I'll explain *that* to you (some)   kláró↓ éso |sèlǫèsplikáre |otrodíá↓   Claro. Eso se lo explicaré otro día.
  other day.

4 Sure. I'm going to give *that* to you (some)   kláró↓ éso |sèlóbóyadar |otrodíá↓   Claro. Eso se lo voy a dar otro día.
  other day.

5 Fine. I'm going to tell *that* to you this   byén↓ éso |sèlóbóyadeşir |estatárdè↓   Bien. Eso se lo voy a decir esta tarde.
  afternoon.

6 Fine. I'm going to send *that* to you on   byén↓ éso |sèlóbóyamandar |eꟷlúnès↓   Bien. Eso se lo voy a mandar el lunes.
  Monday.

7 Wonderful. I'm going to take *that* to you   mágnífikó↓ éso |sèlóbóyaꟷyebár |aórà↓   Magnífico. Eso se lo voy a llevar ahora.
  now.

C pòrlóprontoꜛnèşèsitalosigyéntè↓   Por lo pronto, necesita lo siguiente.

  1 For the time being, you need this.   pòrlóprontoꜛnèşèsitaęéstó↓   Por lo pronto, necesita esto.

  2 For the time being, you need a certificate.   pòrlóprontoꜛnèşèsitaạunşertifikádó↓   Por lo pronto, necesita un certificado.

  3 Apparently, you need a certificate.   pòrlóbistoꜛnèşèsitaạunşertifikádó↓   Por lo visto, necesita un certificado.

  4 Apparently, you need permission.   pòrlóbistoꜛnèşèsitapermísó↓   Por lo visto, necesita permiso.

  5 Apparently, we need an excuse.   pòrlóbistoꜛnèşèsitamoșumpretéstó↓   Por lo visto, necesitamos un pretexto.

  6 Then, you all need to declare the presents.   èntónşezꜛnèşèsitan |dèklàrárlozrregálós↓   Entonces, necesitan declarar los regalos.

  7 Then you all need to check the bills.   èntónşezꜛnèşèsitan |rrèbisárlaskwéntàs↓   Entonces, necesitan revisar las cuentas.

VEINTIUNO   26.21

UNIT 26   SPOKEN SPANISH

D   èlpàsàpórtet ̧èrtifikáɗò |ɗèbàkúnatɗèsálut |iɗèbwènakondúktà↓   El pasaporte, certificado de vacuna, de
                                                                                   salud y de buena conducta.

   1 The passport, health certificate, and   èlpàsàpórtet ̧èrtifikáɗò |ɗèsálut |iɗèbakúná↓   El pasaporte, certificado de salud y de
      vaccination (certificate).   vacuna.

   2 The passport, travel certificate, and   èlpàsàpórtet ̧èrtifikáɗò |ɗèbyahə |iɗəaɗwáná↓   El pasaporte, certificado de viaje y de
      customs (certificate).   aduana.

   3 The passport and immigration documents.   èlpàsàpórtət iɗòkúmentoz |ɗəinmigra ̧yón↓   El pasaporte y documentos de immigración.

   4 The visa and automobile documents.   làbisə |iɗòkúmentozɗelkóchè↓   La visa y documentos del coche.

   5 The visa and special documents.   làbisə |iɗòkúmentoşespe ̧yálès↓   La visa y documentos especiales.

   6 The visa and the purchase order.   làbisə |il ̧orɗendekómprá↓   La visa y la orden de compra.

   7 The purchase certificate and other   èl ̧èrtifikáɗò |ɗèkompra | ̧otrozɗokuméntòs↓   El certificado de compra y otros documentos.
      documents.

E   álgòmast   ¿Algo más?

   1 Do you want something else?   kyèrə |algòmast   ¿Quiere algo más?

   2 Do you wish something else?   dèsèə |algòmast   ¿Desea algo más?

   3 Do you have something else?   tyènə |algòmast   ¿Tiene algo más?

   4 Is there anything else?   áy |algòmast   ¿Hay algo más?

26.22   jacobeligoodsons.com For Free Audio   VEINTIDOS

SPOKEN SPANISH   UNIT 26

5 Don't you wish anything else?   nódèseą |algomást   ¿No desea algo más?

6 Isn't there something else?   nǫay |algomást   ¿No hay algo más?

7 Isn't there anything else?   nǫay |nadamást   ¿No hay nada más?

F   sí↓ làzweỻỵazdihitálès↓ pèrǫesǫ|esạalǫúltimó↓   Sí, las huellas digitales, pero eso es a
                                                            lo último.

   1 Yes, the passport, but that comes last.   sí↓ èlpàsápórté↓ pèrǫesǫ|esạalǫúltimó↓   Sí, el pasaporte, pero eso es a lo último.

   2 Yes, your documents, but that comes last.   sí↓ sùzdókúmentòs↓ pèrǫesǫ|esạalǫúltimó↓   Sí, sus documentos, pero eso es a lo último.

   3 Yes, the bill, but that comes last.   sí↓ làkwentá↓ pèrǫesǫ|esạalǫúltimó↓   Sí, la cuenta, pero eso es a lo último.

   4 Yes, the newspaper, but that's afterwards. sí↓ èlpèryodikó↓ pèrǫesǫ|ezdespwés↓   Sí, el periódico, pero eso es después.

   5 Yes, the ad, but that's afterwards.   sí↓ èlánunsyó↓ pèrǫesǫ|ezdespwés↓   Sí, el anuncio, pero eso es después.

   6 Yes, the car, but that doesn't matter.   sí↓ èlàwtó↓ pèrǫesǫ|nǫimpórtá↓   Sí, el auto, pero eso no importa.

   7 Yes, the gift, but that doesn't matter.   sí↓ èlrrègáló↓ pèrǫesǫ|nǫimpórtá↓   Sí, el regalo, pero eso no importa.

VEINTITRES   jacobeligoodsons.com For Free Audio   26.23

UNIT 26   SPOKEN SPANISH

26.24   Review drill — Gender class assignment certain nouns - II

1 The sector of the city.	èlsèktór |dèlaşyudád↓	El sector de la ciudad.
2 The name of the base.	èlnómbre |dèlabásè↓	El nombre de la base.
3 The chief of the section.	èlhéfè |dèlaseksyón↓	El jefe de la sección.
4 The restaurant of the mission.	èlrrèstórán |dèlamisyón↓	El restorán de la misión.
5 The officer of the tower.	èlòfíşyal |dèlatórrè↓	El oficial de la torre.
6 The lieutenant from the base.	èltènyènte |dèlabásè↓	El teniente de la base.
7 The name of the city.	èlnómbre |dèlaşyudád↓	El nombre de la ciudad.
8 The gentleman from the room.	èlsènyor |dèlabitaşyón↓	El señor de la habitación.
9 The end of the inspection.	èlfín |dèlainspeksyón↓	El fin de la inspección.
10 The room of the gentleman.	làbitáşyon |delsenyór↓	La habitación del señor.
11 The health of the colonel.	làsàlud |dèlkoronél↓	La salud del coronel.
12 The people from the restaurant.	làhénte |dèlrrestorán↓	La gente del restorán.

26.24   VEINTICUATRO

jacobeligoodsons.com For Free Audio

SPOKEN SPANISH

UNIT 26

13 The application of the lieutenant.

làsôlişitud |deltenyéntè↓

La solicitud del teniente.

14 The section of the country.

làsèkşyon |delpaís↓

La sección del país.

15 The milk from the restaurant.

làleche |delrrestorán↓

La leche del restorán.

26.3 CONVERSATION STIMULUS

NARRATIVE 1

1 Chico and Luis are talking.

chikọilwís |estánablándò↓

Chico y Luis están hablando.

2 Luis, without noticing, drops something.

àlwís |simfíharse↑sélékaẹálgò↓

A Luis, sin fijarse, se le cae algo.

3 Chico tells him so.

chikoselodíşè↓

Chico se lo dice.

4 It turns out to be his passport.

rrèsulta |sersupasapórtè↓

Resulta ser su pasaporte.

5 Chico wants to know, by the way, if they finally gave him the visa.

chikokyeresaber |àpropósito↑
sipórfin |ledyéronlabísà↓

Chico quiere saber, a propósito, si por fin le dieron la visa.

6 'Heck no', says Luis.

kebá↓díşèlwís↓

¡Qué va!—dice Luis.

7 He says that now they want a new health certificate.

disekẹaora↑kyérèn |ù(n)nweboşertifíkaďo |
ďesalúď↓

Dice que ahora quieren un nuevo certificado de salud.

VEINTICINCO

26.25

jacobeligoodsons.com For Free Audio

UNIT 26   SPOKEN SPANISH

DIALOG 1

Chico, dígale a Luis que se le cayó algo.

lwís↓ sétèⁱ·àyoálgó↓

Chico: Luis, se te cayó algo.

Luis, dígale que gracias y explíquele que es
el pasaporte.

gráṣyás↓ èṣélpàsàpòrtè↓

Luis: Gracias, es el pasaporte.

Chico, pregúntele, a propósito, si ya le dieron
la visa.

àpróposìtô↓ yátédyeronlàbísa↑

Chico: A propósito, ¿ya te dieron la
visa?

Luis, dígale que qué va, que ahora quieren
un nuevo certificado de salud.

kebà↓ àorakyéren |ù(n)nweboṣertifikado |

desalúd↓

Luis: ¡Qué va! Ahora quieren un nuevo
certificado de salud.

NARRATIVE 2

1 The health certificate he took over the
other day wasn't accepted.

èlṣèrtifikado |desalud |kéⁿyéboṣlotrodía↑

nofweàṣeptádò↓

El certificado de salud que llevó el otro
día no fué aceptado.

2 It was not from one of the doctors approved
by the Embassy.

nọera |deọunodelozmédikos |àṣéptados

porlaembahádà↓

No era de uno de los médicos aceptados por
la Embajada.

3 Luis doesn't know yet if all the other
papers were in order.

lwíz |nosabetodabía |sitodozlosọtroz

dokumentos |èstabanẹnọrdèn↓

Luis no sabe todavía si todos los otros
documentos estaban en orden.

4 Because Mr. White says that he hasn't had
time to check them all.

pórkélsèɲyorhwáyt |dìṣe |kènọatenído

tyémpo |dèrrèbisarlostódòs↓

Porque el Sr. White dice que no ha tenido
tiempo de revisarlos todos.

26.26   VEINTISEIS

SPOKEN SPANISH

UNIT 26

DIALOG 2

Chico, pregúntele que qué pasó con el
certificado de salud que llevó el otro día.

kepaso|konélşèrtifikado|dèsálud|kè

ɯyèbastelotrodía↓

Chico: ¿Qué pasó con el certificado de
salud que llevaste el otro día?

Luis, contéstele que no fué aceptado.

nofweaşeptádò↓

Luis: No fué aceptado.

Chico, pregúntele que por qué.

pórke↓

Chico: ¿Por qué?

Luis, contéstele que porque no era de uno
de los médicos aceptados por la Embajada.

pórkènọera|deúnòdèlózmedikos|àşèptados

porlạembahádá↓

Luis: Porque no era de uno de los médicos
aceptados por la Embajada.

Chico, pregúntele si todos los otros documentos estaban en orden.

todoz|losotrozdokumentos|estabanenordent

Chico: ¿Todos los otros documentos
estaban en orden?

Luis, contéstele que Ud. no sabe todavía.
Que el Sr. White dice que no ha tenido
tiempo de revisarlos todos.

nosé|tódàbíá↓ élsèŋyorhwaytdişe|kènọ

atenidotyempo|dèrrèbisarlostódòs↓

Luis: No sé todavía. El Sr. White dice
que no ha tenido tiempo de
revisarlos todos.

NARRATIVE 3

1 Chico can't understand what's the matter.
It's been two months already since Luis
applied for his visa.

chiko|noọntyéndekepásà↓ yáşèdozméses|kèlwís

işo|làsòlişitudparalabísà↓

Chico no entiende que pasa. Ya hace
dos meses que Luis hizo la solicitud
para la visa.

2 Luis can't understand it either.

lwiz|noọntyende|tampokò↓

Luis no entiende tampoco.

VEINTISIETE

26.27

jacobeligoodsons.com For Free Audio

UNIT 26   SPOKEN SPANISH

3 Sometimes he thinks that it's just that   ábeşęspyénsa |késkènoselakyérendár↓   A veces piensa que es que no se la
  they don't want to give it to him.   quieren dar.

4 Chico's going to talk with White to see   chiko |báblárkòṇhwayt |pàràber |képásà↓ Chico va a hablar con White para ver
  what's the trouble.   qué pasa.

5 That friend of Chico's is driving Luis   ésęàmigo |dechiko↑estábòlbyéndòlokọ |àlwís↓ Ese amigo de Chico está volviendo loco
  crazy.   a Luis.

                                        DIALOG 3

Chico, dígale que Ud. no entiende qué pasa;   noęntyéndo |képásà↓ yáşędozmésés |kęişístè |là Chico: No entiendo que pasa; ya hace dos
  que ya hace dos meses que él hizo la solicitud sòlişitúdpàràlàbísà↓   meses que hiciste la solicitud para
  para la visa.   la visa.

Luis, dígale que Ud. tampoco entiende.   yotampokọ |ęntyéndò↓ àbęşęspyénso | Luis: Yo tampoco entiendo. A veces pienso
  Que a veces Ud. piensa que es que no se   kèskènomelakyérendár↓   que es que no me la quieren dar.
  la quieren dar.

Chico, dígale que Ud. va a hablar con White   boyablár |kòṇhwayt |pàràber |képásà↓   Chico: Voy a hablar con White para ver qué
  para ver qué pasa.   pasa.

Luis, dígale a Chico que ese amigo de él   ésęàmigotuyo |mestábòlbyéndolókò↓   Luis: Ese amigo tuyo me está volviendo
  lo está volviendo loco a Ud.   loco.

26.28   VEINTIOCHO

SPOKEN SPANISH

UNIT 26

26.4   READINGS

26.40   List of cognate loan words

      la formalidad   là—fòrmàlidàd↓

      la coincidencia   là—kòynşiđenşyá↓

26.41   Reading selection

Día de Mercado

Era viernes y Marta estaba haciendo la lista de las cosas que tenía que comprar, cuando oyó el teléfono. Era Virginia de Robinson. Eran como las siete y media de la mañana.

—La llamo para molestarla con un pequeño problema que tengo, Sra. de Fuentes, y perdóneme por haberla llamado tan temprano—le dijo, después de saludarla y preguntarle por don Ricardo y los hijos.

—Primero que todo—interrumpió Marta—mis amigas no me dicen 'Sra. de Fuentes' y por eso Ud. no debe decirme así tampoco. Yo soy Marta para Ud., y si me permite, yo prefiero decirle a Ud. Virginia. Como amigas y vecinas que somos es mejor tratarse por el nombre. Eso de 'Sra. de Robinson' y 'Sra. de Fuentes' es una formalidad horrible, ¿no le parece?

—Sí, claro, tiene toda la razón, Marta; en mi país hacemos lo mismo, pero aquí prefiero no tratar a nadie de 'tú' o por su nombre hasta estar segura de que no voy a meter la pata si lo hago. Muchas gracias por decírmelo y por mi parte Ud. también puede decirme Virginia y no 'Sra. de Robinson.' A mí tampoco me gusta esa formalidad, francamente. Pero lo que sí me preocupa es tener que molestarla con mis problemas.

—No se preocupe por eso, Virginia, al contrario; a mí me alegra mucho poderla ayudar en algo. Como le dije la primera noche que estuvimos en su casa, para eso son los vecinos y aquí nos tienen Uds. para cualquier cosa que necesiten. Nosotros sabemos muy bien que Uds. deben encontrar en este país cosas que son muy diferentes de como son en los Estados Unidos.

—Sí, en realidad hay algunas, pero ya vamos acostumbrándonos poco a poco. El problema con que me encuentro en este momento es el de la comida, y le digo que es una gran lata. Mi marido se queja de que nunca le hago lo que a él le gusta: comida americana. Pero es que no he podido encontrar nada en los mercados de aquí. Ayer fui al mercado de este barrio y luego a otro en el centro, pero en ninguno de los dos encontré nada bueno, y además todo tan caro.... No sé qué hacer. Mi marido me dijo que iba a divorciarse de mí si no le tenía algo bueno para esta noche—Virginia terminó diciendo en broma.

VEINTINUEVE

jacobeligoodsons.com For Free Audio

26.29

UNIT 26   SPOKEN SPANISH

——No se preocupe, Virginia, no vamos a permitirle a su esposo divorciarse de Ud. ——dijo Marta siguiéndole la broma. Yo voy a llevarla a un mercado donde vamos a encontrar de todo lo que Ud. busca y barato. Yo voy allí todos los viernes; vea que coincidencia, en este momento estaba haciendo la lista. Ud. puede ir ahora mismo?

——¡Claro que puedo!——exclamó Virginia. Déme diez minutos para vestirme, por favor.

——Muy bien, llámeme cuando esté lista y yo paso por Ud.

26.42   Response drill

    1 ¿Qué día de la semana era éste?

    2 ¿A dónde iba Marta siempre ese día?

    3 ¿Qué estaba haciendo cuando oyó el teléfono?

    4 ¿Quién era?

    5 ¿Qué hora era?

    6 ¿Para qué la llamaba Virginia?

    7   Cuando la saludó, ¿le dijo 'Sra. de Fuentes' o le dijo 'Marta'?

    8 ¿Le gusta a Marta tratarse con mucha formalidad con sus amigas?

    9 ¿Cómo se debe tratar a las personas que acabamos de conocer, de 'tú' o de 'Ud.'?

    10 ¿Cuándo podemos tratar a otra persona de 'tú'?

    11 ¿Puede uno meter la pata si trata de 'tú' a una persona que uno no conoce muy bien?

    12 ¿Por qué dijo Virginia en broma que su marido iba a divorciarse de ella?

    13 ¿A cuántos mercados fue ella ayer?

    14 ¿Encontró algo bueno en esos mercados?

    15 ¿A dónde va a llevarla Marta?

SPOKEN SPANISH

UNIT 27

27.1   BASIC SENTENCES.   Sports.

Molina and White are talking while they are having lunch.

ENGLISH SPELLING	AID TO LISTENING	SPANISH SPELLING
the sport	él-dėpórtė↓	el deporte
favorite	fåbóritó↓	favorito
White		*White*
What's your favorite sport?	kwal͎èstúdėpórte͎fåbóritó↓	¿Cuál es tu deporte favorito?
the football	èl-fútbôl↓	el fútbol
Molina		*Molina*
Football.	èlfútbôl↓	El fútbol.
(I) lose, miss (to lose, to miss)	pyérdó↓ pèrdér↓	pierdo (perder)
the game	èl-pàrtídó↓	el partido
I never miss a single game. (1)	nópyérdó͎nɪúmpartídó↓	No pierdo ni un partido.
to practice, to participate in	pråktikár↓	practicar
White		*White*
But which one do you *play*?	pèrókwalpraktíkàs↓	Pero ¿cuál practicas?
frankly	frankaméntė↓	francamente

UNO

27.1

UNIT 27   SPOKEN SPANISH

none, not one   ninguno↓   ninguno

Molina   Molina   Molina
Frankly, not a one.   frankamente |ninguno↓   Francamente, ninguno.

to get fat   engordar↓   engordar

White   White   White
You're going to get fat that way.   asi |basaengordar↓   Así vas a engordar.

to play (2)   hugar↓   jugar

Why don't we play some golf tomorrow? (3)   porke |nohugamozgolf |manyana↓   ¿Por qué no jugamos golf mañana?

the (letter) jota (j); jot, tittle   la—hota↓   la jota

Molina   Molina   Molina
I don't know the first thing about golf. (4)   yonose |nihota |deqolf↓   Yo no sé ni jota de golf.

(it) matters (to matter, be important)   importa↓ importar↓   importa (importar)
that (you) know (to know)   ke—sepas↓ saber↓   que sepas (saber)
let's play (to play)   hugemos↓ hugar↓   juguemos (jugar)

White   White   White
It doesn't matter that you don't know how.   noimporta |kenosepas↓   No importa que no sepas.

Let's play. I'll teach you. (5)   hugemos↓ yotensenyo↓   Juguemos. Yo te enseño.

the equipment   el—ekipo↓   el equipo

27.2   jacobeligoodsons.com For Free Audio   DOS

SPOKEN SPANISH   UNIT 27

Molina
But I don't have any equipment, either. (6)   pérǥes |kė |támpōkò |téngǥóékipò↓   *Molina*
                                                                                                  Pero es que tampoco tengo equipo.

    the beginning   èl—prinsipyó↓   el principio

    in the beginning   àl—prinsipyó↓   al principio

White   *White*
To begin with you don't need it. We'll both   àlprinsipyo |noneṣesítâs↓ kǒnlómiò | Al principio no necesitas. Con lo mío
play with mine.   húgamoɔ loɔɖós↓   jugamos los dos.

    to win, earn, gain   gànár↓   ganar

    to convince   kòmbènṣér↓   convencer

Molina   *Molina*
Okay. You win. You convinced me.   bwénò↓ tugánás↓ mékòmbénṣistè↓   Bueno, tú ganas. Me convenciste.

    the hall   èl—pàsíⓄýò↓   el pasillo

White   *White*
Then we'll meet in the hall at six in the   èntónṣez |nòṣénkòntrámosˌeɲèlpasíⓄýọ | Entonces nos encontramos en el pasillo
morning. (7)   àlà(s)séyzɖelamaɲyánà↓   a las seis de la mañana.

Molina   *Molina*
What! At six! Are you mad?   ke↑ àlà(s)séys↑ éstaɔloko↑   ¿Qué? ¿A las seis? ¿Estás loco?

    leave it (to leave)   déhàlò↓ dèhár↓   déjalo (dejar)

Leave it for eleven o'clock.   dehalo |páralas.ónṣè↓   Déjalo para las once.

TRES   jacobeligoodsons.com For Free Audio   27.3

UNIT 27   SPOKEN SPANISH

  lazy, loose   flóhó↓   flojo

  don't be (to be)   nó—seás↓ sér↓   no seas (ser)

White
  Don't be lazy, chum.   nóséasflóhọ|ómbré↓   *White*
                            No seas flojo, hombre.

  be (to be)   sé↓ sér↓   sé (ser)

  punctual   púntwál↓   puntual

  I'll expect you at six. And be on time.   àlà(s)séys|téspéró↓ isépúntwál↓   A las seis te espero. Y sé puntual.

27.10 Notes on the basic sentences

  (1) Literally, 'I do not miss not even one game.' Note doubling of negative.

  (2) /hugár/ *jugar* is the only example of a stem-vowel changing verb which has the change /u> wé/. See Unit 22 for other stem-vowel changing verbs.

  (3) In continental Spanish the equivalent of 'to play golf' is /hugár—al—gólf/ *jugar al golf,* but in American Spanish it is simply /hugár—gólf/ *jugar golf.* Indeed, in American Spanish /hugár—al—gólf/ has the special meaning of 'to play around at golf,' i.e. not to take the game seriously. As in other instances in this text where there was no clear compromise usage that would be acceptable both in Spain and in America, the American usage has been put into the dialogs with a note to indicate the divergent continental usage whenever the data were clear. Students preparing to use the language in Spain should of course substitute the Spanish usage for the American one.

  (4) Literally, 'I don't know not even iota about golf.' As in note (1) above.

  (5) /hugémos/ *juguemos* requires that attention be called to it in two ways: it is an example of the so-called 'hortatory subjunctive,' the command form that includes both speaker and receiver (a form that will be examined closely in the next unit); and it is an instance of a spelling change in the paradigm of the verb that reflects no change of pronunciation (i.e. the *u* is inserted after the *g* before *e* in order that the *g* may not be interpreted as /h/).

  (6) Note that when a negative word other than /nó/ *no* appears before the verb, /nó/ does not occur. /tampóko/ is the negative word here, 'not...either.'

  (7) You will remember that White and Molina live in the same apartment building, hence to meet in the hall.

27.4   CUATRO

SPOKEN SPANISH

UNIT 27

27.2 DRILLS AND GRAMMAR

27.21 Pattern drills

27.21.1 Formal command forms for regular verbs

A. Presentation of pattern

ILLUSTRATIONS

————————————	1. miré |kėlázmúchachaz |lòs̩ės̩tán̩ės̩pėrándó↓
————————————	2. pėrdone |kėláꝶyame |tántempráno↓
Drink more milk.	3. bebamaz léchė↓
Write the following.	4. ėskriba |losigyéntė↓
Take (pl) this application.	5. tomen |estasoliꜱitúd↓
Clean the apartment.	6. limpyen |elapartaméntò↓
Don't sell the car.	7. nobendan |eláwtó↓
Don't live at that hotel.	8. nobiban |enẹsẹotél↓

Mire, que las muchachas los están esperando.
Perdone que la llame tan temprano.
Beba más leche.
Escriba lo siguiente.
Tomen esta solicitud.
Limpien el apartamento.
No *vendan* el auto.
No *vivan* en ese hotel.

EXTRAPOLATION

		‒ár	‒ér‒ír
2	sg	‒e	‒a
	pl	‒en	‒an

NOTES

a. Formal command forms differ from present tense forms only by a trade in theme vowels between /‒ár/ and /‒ér‒ír/ theme classes.

CINCO

jacobeligoodsons.com For Free Audio

27.5

UNIT 27   SPOKEN SPANISH

27.21.11 Substitution drills — Person-tense substitution

    Problem 1:

        karmen│ablaıŋglés↓

    Answer:

        ableıŋglés↓

    Problem 2:

        anaılwısa│komenakí↓

    Answer:

        komanakí↓

    Problem 1:

        Carmen *habla* inglés.

    Answer:

        Hable inglés.

    Problem 2:

        Ana y Luisa *comen* aquí.

    Answer:

        Coman aquí.

SPOKEN SPANISH   UNIT 27

1. anayantónyọ |èstudyanẹspaŋyól↓   èstudyenẹspaŋyól↓

2. élòfişyál |rrèbisàlazmalétàs↓   rrèbiselazmalétàs↓

3. hòsé |ŷébạélkárrọ |alạọfişínà↓   ŷébelkárrọ |alạọfişínà↓

4. àntónyọipàblo |limpyansusẹskritóryòs↓   limpyen |susẹskritóryòs↓

5. pàblo |mànda |làskámisas |alalabandería↓ mànde |laskámisas |alalabandería↓

6. éltényènte |rrèspóndeporél↓   rrèspóndaporél↓

_____

1 Ana y Antonio *estudian* español.   Estudien español.

2 El oficial *revisa* las maletas.   Revise las maletas.

3 José *lleva* el carro a la oficina.   Lleve el carro a la oficina.

4 Antonio y Pablo *limpian* sus escritorios. Limpien sus escritorios.

5 Pablo *manda* las camisas a la lavandería. Mande las camisas a la lavandería.

6 El teniente *responde* por él.   Responda por él.

SIETE

UNIT 27   SPOKEN SPANISH

7. hwan̯lwisa |komeŋko(n̯)nosótròs↓   komaŋko(n̯)nosótròs↓

8. ana |bebeléchè↓   bebaléchè↓

9. làmûchàcha |barrelakoṣínà↓   barralakoṣínà↓

10. lósharriz |nobendensukásà↓   nobendansukásà↓

11. àntónyo |bibekonsuspádrès↓   bibakonsuspádrès↓

12. lwisa |èskribeningléś↓   èskribaeningléś↓

13. pabloihwan |ŋo̯abrenlozlíbròs↓   no̯abran |lozlíbròs↓

----

7 Juan y Luisa *comen* con nosotros.   Coman con nosotros.

8 Ana *bebe* leche.   Beba leche.

9 La muchacha *barre* la cocina.   Barra la cocina.

10 Los Harris no *venden* su casa.   No vendan su casa.

11 Antonio *vive* con sus padres.   Viva con sus padres.

12 Luisa *escribe* en inglés.   Escriba en inglés.

13 Pablo y Juan no *abren* los libros.   No abran los libros.

SPOKEN SPANISH   UNIT 27

Number substitution

1. labelaskamísàs↓   labenlaskamísàs↓

2. fírmeldokuméntò↓   fírmeneldokuméntò↓

3. ǫyamen|aliŋhenyérò↓   ǫyamęaliŋhenyérò↓

4. noęstuđyen|lo(s)sábàđòs↓   noęstuđye|lo(s)sábàđòs↓

5. bendalozmwéblès↓   bendanlozmwéblès↓

6. éskribanlozlúnès↓   éskribalozlúnès↓

7. nobiba|enęlşéntrò↓   nobiban|enęlşéntrò↓

---

1 *Lave* las camisas.   Laven las camisas.

2 *Firme* el documento.   Firmen el documento.

3 *Llamen* al ingeniero.   Llame al ingeniero.

4 No *estudien* los sábados.   No estudie los sábados.

5 *Venda* los muebles.   Vendan los muebles.

6 *Escriban* los lunes.   Escriba los lunes.

7 No *viva* en el centro.   No vivan en el centro.

NUEVE

UNIT 27   SPOKEN SPANISH

8. dèṣiḍanaórá↓   dèṣiḍaórà↓

9. Ⓨyebenlasfúndàs↓   Ⓨyebelasfúndàs↓

10. Ⓨyamę|almédikô↓   Ⓨyamen|almédikô↓

11. nokoma|tantárḍé↓   nokoman|tantárḍé↓

12. bebanménòs↓   bebaménòs↓

13. abrasuzmalétás↓   abransuzmalétás↓

14. sùbanlozbaúlès↓   sùbalozbaúlès↓

15. prònunṣyemehór↓   prònunṣyenmehór↓

---

8 *Decidan* ahora.   Decida ahora.

9 *Lleven* las fundas.   Lleve las fundas.

10 *Llame* al médico.   Llamen al médico.

11 No *coma* tan tarde.   No coman tan tarde.

12 *Beban* menos.   Beba menos.

13 *Abra* sus maletas.   Abran sus maletas.

14 *Suban* los baúles.   Suba los baúles.

15 *Pronuncie* mejor.   Pronuncien mejor.

jacobeligoodsons.com For Free Audio

SPOKEN SPANISH   UNIT 27

27.21.12 Response drill

         1. kòmémos̠akí↑o̦ene̦lrrestorán↓   kóman̠akí↓

         2. kómo̦akí↑o̦ene̦lrrestorán↓   kómakí↓

         3. éskribo̦elsábado↑o̦eldomíŋgò↓   éskriba̦eldomíŋgò↓

         4. èskríbimos│elsábado↑o̦eldomíŋgò↓   èskríban│eldomíŋgò↓

         5. béboléche̠↑okafé↓   bebaléchè↓

[élpàsápórtè↓] 6. kefírmò↓   fírme̦│elpasapórtè↓

[làlèkșyón↓] 7. késplíkò↓   ésplike│lalèkșyón↓

     [kàfé↓] 8. kétomámòs↓   tomeŋkafé↓

[lòzlíbròs↓] 9. ke̦abrímós↓   ábran│lozlíbròs↓

[èlkárrò↓] 10. kebéndò↓   bend̦a̦elkárrò↓

_____

                  1 ¿Comemos aquí o en el restorán?   Coman aquí.
                  2 ¿Como aquí o en el restorán?   Coma aquí.
                  3 ¿Escribo el sábado o el domingo?   Escriba el domingo.
                  4 ¿Escribimos el sábado o el domingo?   Escriban el domingo.
                  5 ¿Bebo leche o café?   Beba leche.

   (el pasaporte) 6 ¿Qué firmo?   Firme el pasaporte.
     (la lección) 7 ¿Qué explico?   Explique la lección.
           (café) 8 ¿Qué tomamos?   Tomen café.
      (los libros) 9 ¿Qué abrimos?   Abran los libros.
        (el carro) 10 ¿Qué vendo?   Venda el carro.

ONCE   27.11

jacobeligoodsons.com For Free Audio

UNIT 27   SPOKEN SPANISH

[ènųnrrèstòrán↓]   11. dóndekómò↓   kómạ|enųnrrestorán↓

[àhósé↓]   12. àkyénⓊyámò↓   Ⓤyamẹahosé↓

[ènẹspàŋyóĺ↓]   13. áblọ|enịnglés↑   nó↓ áblenẹspaŋyóĺ↓

[ènẹspàŋyóĺ↓]   14. àblamos|enịŋglés↑   nó↓ áblen|enẹspaŋyóĺ↓

[èldòmíŋgò↓]   15. èstúɟyámos|elsábaɗo↑   nó↓ èstúɟyen|eldomíŋgò↓

[èldòmíŋgò↓]   16. èstúɟyọ|elsábaɗo↑   nó↓ èstúɟyẹ|eldomíŋgò↓

[làmésà↓]   17. límpyo|los(ṣ)enịṣérós↑   nó↓ límpyèlamésá↓

                   18. bàhoɥa↑   sî|bàhé↓

                   19. bàhamoẓɥa↑   sî|bàhén↓

                   20. súbọaóra↑   sî|subà↓

                   21. súbimos|aóra↑   sî|subán↓

―――

(en un restorán)   11 ¿Dónde como?   Coma en un restorán.

        (a José)   12 ¿A quién llamo?   Llame a José.

     (en español)   13 ¿Hablo en inglés?   No, hable en español.

     (en español)   14 ¿Hablamos en inglés?   No, hablen en español.

     (el domingo)   15 ¿Estudiamos el sábado?   No, estudien el domingo.

     (el domingo)   16 ¿Estudio el sábado?   No, estudie el domingo.

       (la mesa)   17 ¿Limpio los ceniceros?   No, limpie la mesa.

                    18 ¿Bajo ya?   Sí, baje.

                    19 ¿Bajamos ya?   Sí, bajen.

                    20 ¿Subo ahora?   Sí, suba.

                    21 ¿Subimos ahora?   Sí, suban.

27.12   DOCE

SPOKEN SPANISH   UNIT 27

27.21.13 Translation drill

1 Take the shirts to the laundry.   ĺyebe | láskámisas | alalabandería↓   Lleve las camisas a la lavandería.

2 Check (pl) the list.   rrébisen | lalísta↓   Revisen la lista.

3 Rent (pl) the apartment.   álkilen | elapartaménto↓   Alquilen el apartamento.

4 Eat more fruit.   kóma | masfrútás↓   Coma más frutas.

5 Sign (pl) the application.   fírmen | lasolişitúd↓   Firmen la solicitud.

6 Help my friend.   áyuḍę | àmįàmigó↓   Ayude a mi amigo.

7 Call (pl) the agency.   ĺyamen | alahénşyà↓   Llamen a la agencia.

8 Don't vouch (pl) for her.   norrespóndan | poréɑya↓   No respondan por ella.

9 Decide (on) the date.   dèşidalaféchà↓   Decida la fecha.

10 Sell the furniture cheap.   bendalozmwéblez | bàrató↓   Venda los muebles barato.

11 Buy (pl) some meat.   kómprenkárné↓   Compren carne.

12 Buy enough fresh fish.   kómpre | súfişyèntepeskaḍofréskò↓   Compre suficiente pescado fresco.

13 Don't live (pl) in the commercial district.   nobíbàn | ènęlsèktórkòmèrşyál↓   No vivan en el sector comercial.

TRECE   jacobeligoodsons.com For Free Audio   27.13

UNIT 27   SPOKEN SPANISH

14 Go down (pl) in the elevator.   báhen|enelas(ş)ensór↓   Bajen en el ascensor.

15 Invite your neighbors.   ímbíte|asuzbeşínòs↓   Invite a sus vecinos.

16 Don't believe that.   nokréá|ésò↓   No crea eso.

17 Go up (pl) that way.   súbamporaí↓   Suban por ahí.

18 Pay the bill.   págelakwéntà↓   Pague la cuenta.

19 Look for (pl) another house.   búskenotrakásá↓   Busquen otra casa.

B. Discussion of pattern

    Formal command forms for regular verbs show a theme vowel /e/ in verbs from the /-ár/ theme class and a theme vowel /a/ in verbs from the /-ér-ír/ theme class. The final /-n/ after the theme vowel is the typical person-number ending to indicate 2 (or 2-3) pl in all tenses.

    Formal command forms are used to give commands (instructions, directions, requests, etc.) to persons who are addressed with /ustéd/ . Command forms usually do not appear with pronoun subjects, though they may, in which case the pronoun normally follows immediately after the command form of the verb:

        /eskríbansusnómbres↓/   'Write your names.'

        /eskríbanustédes|susnómbres↓/

In English, command forms (except in archaic usage, 'Go ye and do likewise') appear with a pronoun subject only in emphatic or contrastive contexts; they always precede the verb: 'You come here.'   'I don't want to. You do it.' In negative commands, the pronoun subject appears (in emphatic or contrastive contexts) between 'Don't' and the following infinitive form, i.e. before the nucleus verb: 'Don't you dare.'

    Similar constructions are possible in Spanish, though not especially common: /ustéd|báyase-kon-hwán↑ ı-ustéd|kédese-akí↓/

The subject /ustéd/, however, could never occur between the negative /nó/ and the verb, as in English.

27.14   CATORCE

jacobeligoodsons.com For Free Audio

SPOKEN SPANISH																UNIT 27

Spanish clitic pronouns follow all command forms when they express an affirmative command, but precede when they express a negative command, i.e. when /nó/ appears before the verb. Thus:

/mándelas—a—la—labandería↓/ but

/no—las—mánde—a—la—labandería↓/

As the hyphens indicate, in the writing system when the clitics follow they are written together with the verb as one word.

27.21.2   Formal command forms for irregular verbs

A. Presentation of pattern

ILLUSTRATIONS

Remember abc t the golf date.	1. rrékwerde │lodelgólf↓	*Recuerde* lo del golf.
Don't lose the certificate.	2. nópyerda│elşertifikádo↓	No *pierda* el certificado.
—————————	3. rrépita↓	*Repita.*
—————————	4. tráduşká↓	*Traduzca.*
—————————	5. téngalabondad │deàbrir│elbaúl│primérô↓	*Tenga* la bondad de abrir el baúl primero.
Say 'goodbye'.	6. díga│àdyós↓	*Diga* 'adiós'.
For the time being, don't do anything.	7. pòrlópronto│noaganádà↓	Por lo pronto, no *haga* nada.
—————————	8. tráyga│páralozdós↓	*Traiga* para los dos.
Be here at one o'clock.	9. èsteaki│alaúnà↓	*Esté* aqui a la una.
Don't be so nervous.	10. nósean │ta(n)nerbyósòs↓	No *sean* tan nerviosos.
	11. démelaplúmà↓	*Déme* la pluma.

QUINCE																27.15

UNIT 27   SPOKEN SPANISH

_____   12. báyanustédès↓   *Vayan ustedes.*

Know the lesson by this afternoon.   13. sépan│là lèkṣyom│par̦estatárdè↓   *Sepan la lección para esta tarde.*

EXTRAPOLATION

I Irregular types:	—wé—	—yé—	—í—	—k—	—g—	—yg—
1 sg present	bwélb—o	ṣyérr—o	síg—o	tradúṣk—o	sálg—o	tráyg—o
sg command	bwélb—a	ṣyérr—e	síg—a	tradúṣk—a	sálg—a	tráyg—a
pl	bwélb—an	ṣyérr—en	síg—an	tradúṣk—an	sálg—an	tráyg—an

II Individually irregular	aṣér	deṣír	kabér
1 sg present	ág—o	díg—o	kép—o
sg command	ág—a	díg—a	kép—a
pl	ág—an	díg—an	kép—an

III Non-predictable		estár	dár	sér	ír	sabér
command	sg	est—é	d—é	sé—a	báy—a	sép—a
	pl	est—én	d—én	sé—an	báy—an	sép—an

NOTES

a. Most irregular command forms (all except those in chart III) can be derived by adding regular endings to the irregular stem of the 1 sg present tense form.

27.16   DIECISEIS

jacobeligoodsons.com For Free Audio

SPOKEN SPANISH

UNIT 27

27.21.21 Substitution drills - Person-tense substitution

1. kárlos̩alis̩ya|tráduṣembyén↓   tráduṣkambyén↓
2. ántonyo̩ana|bwélbempróntô↓   bwélbampróntô↓
3. márta|nọalmwerṣatárdê↓   nọalmwerṣetárdê↓
4. lwisa|nópiḍenáḍà↓   nópiḍanáḍà↓
5. márta̩anạ|átyéndèmbyén|alozníŋyòs↓   átyendambyén|alozníŋyòs↓
6. hôse|díṣètoḍọenẹspaŋyól↓   dígàtoḍọ|enẹspaŋyól↓
7. ántony̩ọipáblo|traénẹlkóchè↓   tráygan̩ẹlkóchè↓
8. páblo|byénelwégò↓   béŋgalwégò↓

_____

1 Carlos y Alicia *traducen* bien.   Traduzcan bien.
2 Antonio y Ana *vuelven* pronto.   Vuelvan pronto.
3 Marta no *almuerza* tarde.   No almuerce tarde.
4 Luisa no *pide* nada.   No pida nada.
5 Marta y Ana *atienden* bien a los niños. .Atiendan bien a los niños.
6 José *dice* todo en español.   Diga todo en español.
7 Antonio y Pablo *traen* el coche.   Traigan el coche.
8 Pablo *viene* luego.   Venga luego.

DIECISIETE

UNIT 27   SPOKEN SPANISH

9. ánaikármen |ásenlakomíɖà↓   áganlakomíɖà↓

10. lòsèstúɖyantes |pónènlòz libros |enlamésà↓   pongan |lòz librosȩnlamésà↓

11. màría |tyéne |lakomiɖalístạ |àlàskwátrò↓   teṅga |lakomiɖalístạ |alaskwátrò↓

12. ántónyọipàblo |syémpreɖampropínàs↓   dempropínàs↓

13. hòsé |bàlatyéndà↓   bayalatyéndà↓

14. kármen |ṇọeznerbyósà↓   nóseanerbyósà↓

15. àliṣyạihwàn |éstaṅkonténtòs↓   éstéṅkonténtòs↓

---

9 Ana y Carmen *hacen* la comida.   Hagan la comida.

10 Los estudiantes *ponen* los libros en la mesa. Pongan los libros en la mesa.

11 María *tiene* la comida lista a las cuatro.   Tenga la comida lista a las cuatro.

12 Antonio y Pablo siempre *dan* propinas.   Den propinas.

13 José *va* a la tienda.   Vaya a la tienda.

14 Carmen no *es* nerviosa.   No sea nerviosa.

15 Alicia y Juan *están* contentos.   Estén contentos.

27.18   DIECIOCHO

SPOKEN SPANISH   UNIT 27

Person-tense affirmative-negative substitution

Problem 1:

            tràduşkomál↓

Answer:

            nótraduşkamál↓

Problem 2:

            nósébyén|lalekşyón↓

Answer:

            sépabyén|làlěkşyón↓

Problem 1:
            Traduzco mal.

Answer:
            No traduzca mal.

Problem 2:
            No sé bien la lección.

Answer:
            Sepa bien la lección.

DIECINUEVE   27.19

jacobeligoodsons.com For Free Audio

UNIT 27   SPOKEN SPANISH

1. beŋgǫ|ala(s)syétė↓   nóbeŋgala(s)syétė↓
2. sálgotárdė↓   nósalgatárdė↓
3. téngo|dosáwtǒs↓   nótenga|dosáwtǒs↓
4. dígolaberdád↓   nódigalaberdád↓
5. ágolo(s)sáŋwichės↓   nǫagalo(s)sáŋwichės↓
6. póngǫ|èlsòmbrerǫáí↓   nópongǫ|èlsòmbrerǫáí↓
7. óyggesapyéşà↓   nǫoyggesapyéşà↓

8. nǫdóypropínà↓   depropínà↓
9. nóbóyalatyéndà↓   báyalatyéndà↓
10. nǫęstóytraŋkílò↓   èstetraŋkílò↓
11. nosóyamáblè↓   seamáblè↓

──

1 Vengo a las siete.   No venga a las siete.
2 Salgo tarde.   No salga tarde.
3 Tengo dos autos.   No tenga dos autos.
4 Digo la verdad.   No diga la verdad.
5 Hago los sandwiches.   No haga los sandwiches.
6 Pongo el sombrero ahí.   No ponga el sombrero ahí.
7 Oigo esa pieza.   No oiga esa pieza.

8 No doy propina.   Dé propina.
9 No voy a la tienda.   Vaya a la tienda.
10 No estoy tranquilo.   Esté tranquilo.
11 No soy amable.   Sea amable.

27.20   VEINTE

jacobeligoodsons.com For Free Audio

SPOKEN SPANISH   UNIT 27

Number substitution

1. salgaporaí↓   salgamporaí↓

2. tráđuşkanlalekşyón↓   tráđuşkalalekşyón↓

3. poṇga|lózbáulesenelkwártô↓   poṇgan|lózbáulesenelkwártô↓

4. beṇganeldomíṇgô↓   beṇgaeldomíṇgô↓

5. trayganlakwéntâ↓   traygalakwéntâ↓

6. nọagarrwíđô↓   nọaganrrwíđô↓

7. digaṇésọ|ótrâbéş↓   digaésọ|ótrâbéş↓

8. sepalalekşyóm|pârâmâṇyánâ↓   sepanlalekşyóm|pârâmâṇyánâ↓

9. piđamasáqwá↓   piđanmasáqwá↓

10. àlmwerşen|enlạeskwélâ↓   àlmwerşenlạeskwélâ↓

---

1 *Salga* por ahí.   Salgan por ahí.

2 *Traduzcan* la lección.   Traduzca la lección.

3 *Ponga* los baúles en el **cuarto**.   Pongan los baúles en el **cuarto**.

4 *Vengan* el domingo.   Venga el domingo.

5 *Traigan* la cuenta.   Traiga la cuenta.

6 No *haga* ruido.   No hagan ruido.

7 *Digan* eso otra vez.   Diga eso otra vez.

8 *Sepa* la lección para mañana.   Sepan la lección para mañana.

9 *Pida* más agua.   Pidan más agua.

10 *Almuercen* en la escuela.   Almuerce en la escuela.

VEINTIUNO   27.21

UNIT 27   SPOKEN SPANISH

11. prwében lakárnè↓   prwébelakárnè↓

12. bwélbạotrabéş↓   bwélbanọtrabéş↓

13. rrépitanésò↓   rrépitạésò↓

14. àtyendan│amisíhòs↓   àtyendamisíhòs↓

15. téngàtoɗolisto│alaúnà↓   téngàntoɗolisto│alaúnà↓

16. seamáblè↓   seanamáblès↓

17. denmaspropínàs↓   demaspropínàs↓.

18. éstenạkı│ạlaskwátrò↓   ésteạkı│ạlaskwátrò↓

19. bayan│ạúnạéskwelaɗeléngwàs↓   bayạ│ùnạéskwéladeléngwàs↓

---

11 *Prueben* la carne.   Pruebe la carne.

12 *Vuelva* otra vez.   Vuelvan otra vez.

13 *Repitan* eso.   Repita eso.

14 *Atiendan* a mis hijos.   Atienda a mis hijos.

15 *Tenga* todo listo a la una.   Tengan todo listo a la una.

16 *Sea* amable.   Sean amables.

17 *Den* más propinas.   Dé más propinas.

18 *Estén* aquí a las cuatro.   Esté aquí a las cuatro.

19 *Vayan* a una escuela de lenguas.   Vaya a una escuela de lenguas.

jacobeligoodsons.com For Free Audio

SPOKEN SPANISH   UNIT 27

27.21.22 Response drill

          1. àlmòrşámósákı↑ọenụnrrestorán↓   àlmwerşen│enụnrrestorán↓

          2. àlmwérşọákı↑ọenụnrrestorán↓   àlmwérşọ│enụnrrestorán↓

          3. pídòşérbéşa↑owískı↓   pıdaşerbéşà↓

          4. pèdímòs(ş)érbéşa↑owískı↓   pıdanşerbéşà↓

          5. bwélbọáòra↑omaŋyánà↓   bwelbamaŋyánà↓

          6. bòlbémòṣàòra↑omaŋyánà↓   bwélbanmaŋyánà↓

[êlkárrò↓] 7. ketráygò↓   trayggelkárrò↓

[élkárrò↓] 8. ketraémòs↓   traygançlkárrò↓

[lạênsàladà↓] 9. keágò↓   agalạensaláⁿà↓

[lạênsàladà↓] 10. kẹaşémòs↓   aganlạensaláⁿà↓

[làbèrⁿáⁿ↓] 11. keⁿeşímòs↓   dıganlaberⁿáⁿ↓

---

          1 ¿Almorzamos aquı o en un restorán?   Almuercen en un restorán.

          2 ¿Almuerzo aquı o en un restorán?   Almuerce en un restorán.

          3 ¿Pıdo cerveza o whıskey?   Pıda cerveza.

          4 ¿Pedımos cerveza o whıskey?   Pıdan cerveza.

          5 ¿Vuelvo ahora o mañana?   Vuelva mañana.

          6 ¿Volvemos ahora o mañana?   Vuelvan mañana.

(el carro)   7 ¿Qué traıgo?   Traıga el carro.

(el carro)   8 ¿Qué traemos?   Traıgan el carro.

(la ensalada)   9 ¿Qué hago?   Haga la ensalada.

(la ensalada)   10 ¿Qué hacemos?   Hagan la ensalada.

(la verdad)   11 ¿Qué decımos?   Dıgan la verdad.

VEINTITRES   27.23

UNIT 27   SPOKEN SPANISH

[làlékṣyón↓]   12. kétraḍúṣkò↓   tràḍuṣkalaleksyón↓

[ùndólàr↓]   13. kwántoḍoy|ḍepropíná↓   deundólàr↓

[álṣéntrò↓]   14. àḍondebóy↓   bayalṣéntrò↓

[ë̀ŋlunès↓]   15. béŋgeldomìŋgo↑   nó↓ béŋgaë̀ŋlúnés↓

[é̀ŋlunès↓]   16. bènimos|eldomìŋgo↑   nó↓ béŋgaŋé̀ŋlunès↓

[kafé↓]   17. píḍoléche↑   nó↓ píḍakafé↓

[è̀lbyérnès↓]   18. sálgelsábaḍo↑   nó↓ sálgaelbyérnés↓

               19. bámos|alaṣyuḍaḍ↑   sí|bayán↓

               20. sègímoznosótros|aóra↑   sí|sigán↓

               21. sígòyo|aóra↑   sí|sigà↓

──

(la lección)   12 ¿Qué traduzco?   Traduzca la lección.

(un dólar)   13 ¿Cuánto doy de propina?   Dé un dólar.

(al centro)   14 ¿A dónde voy?   Vaya al centro.

(el lunes)   15 ¿Vengo el domingo?   No, venga el lunes.

(el lunes)   16 ¿Venimos el domingo?   No, vengan el lunes.

(café)   17 ¿Pido leche?   No, pida café.

(el viernes)   18 ¿Salgo el sábado?   No, salga el viernes.

                19 ¿Vamos a la ciudad?   Sí, vayan.

                20 ¿Seguimos nosotros ahora? Sí,,sigan.

                21 ¿Sigo yo ahora?   Sí, siga.

27.24   VEINTICUATRO

SPOKEN SPANISH   UNIT 27

27.21.23 Translation drill

1 Don't go out tomorrow.   nosálgà |màŋyánà↓   No salga mañana.

2 Go together to the corner.   báyàŋhuntos |alaeskínà↓   Vayan juntos a la esquina.

3 Go take a walk.   bayadarunabwéltà↓   Vaya a dar una vuelta.

4 Get acquainted with more cities. kônoşkama(s) ş̧yudádès↓   Conozca más ciudades.

5 Put your name, too.   poŋgan |sùnombrè |tàmbyén↓   Ponga su nombre también.

6 Don't think so much.   nopyensetántò↓   No piense tanto.

7 Bring those sheets.   traygaesa(s) sábànàs↓   Traiga esas sábanas.

8 Come once in a while.   beŋga |debeşeŋkwándò↓   Venga de vez en cuando.

9 Don't make (pl) any more noise. noaganmazrrwídò↓   No hagan más ruido.

10 Listen to that piece again.   oygaesapyéş̧a |òtrábéş↓   Oiga esa pieza otra vez.

11 Keep on that way.   sìgaporaí↓   Siga por ahí.

12 Repeat (pl) please.   rrèpitàm |pòrfàbór↓   Repitan por favor.

13 Don't give (pl) any more presents. noden |mazrregálòs↓   No den más regalos.

14 Be (pl) calm here.   éstentraŋkílòs |àkí↓   Estén tranquilos aquí.

VEINTICINCO   27.25

jacobeligoodsons.com For Free Audio

UNIT 27   SPOKEN SPANISH

15 Don't be so nervous.   nóséáta(ŋ)nerbyósó↓   No sea tan nervioso.

16 Take care of my children, too.   àtyéndạ|àmìzniŋyòs|tàmbyén↓   Atienda a mis niños también.

17 Mind you (know that) I'm married.   sépa|késóykasádá↓   Sepa que soy casada.

B. Discussion of pattern

Formal command forms for irregular verbs are similar to the pattern for regular verbs in the distribution of theme vowels and person-number endings. The irregularity is in the stem.

Most irregular formal command forms can be derived by adding regular endings to the irregular stem of the 1 sg present tense form. The following lists of verbs have occurred so far in this text as examples of irregular types:

⁓wé⁓	⁓yé⁓	⁓í⁓	⁓k⁓	⁓g⁓	⁓yg⁓
almorșár	atendér	bestír	agradeșér	*balér	kaér
bolár	*kerér	despedír	konoșér	benír	oír
bolbér	pensár	rrepetír	*nașér	ponér	traér
enkontrár	perdér	segír	*pareșér	salír	
**hugár	sentár		perteneșér	tenér	
kostár	sentír		tradușír		
*Ⓛyobér	șerrár				
*podér					
probár					
rrekordár					

* This is a list of all the irregular verbs which have so far occurred in this text in each type of irregularity. The starred forms are not likely to be used as direct commands, but are included for the sake of completeness.

**The verb /hugár/ has a stem change /u > wé/ . It is the only verb with this particular change; otherwise it is the same pattern as the /o > wé/ changing verbs.

27.26   VEINTISEIS

SPOKEN SPANISH   UNIT 27

    There are five verbs whose command forms cannot be predicted from their 1 sg present tense forms. Two of these, /estár/ and /dár/, suggest regularity; the stem for command forms is the same as the infinitive stem. One, the verb /sér/, has a command form stem /se-/, extended from the infinitive stem /s-/. The other two verbs are more irregular; the verb /ír/ has a new stem (a suppleted stem) /bay-/, and the verb /sabér/ has a command form stem /sep-/. One other verb, /abér/, would be irregular, but it never occurs in direct commands.

    The use of subject pronouns and the position of clitic pronouns is the same for irregular formal command forms as for regular.

27.21.3 Familiar command forms for regular verbs

    A. Presentation of pattern

ILLUSTRATIONS

————————	1. pásadelánte↓	*Pasa* adelante.
Don't come in.	2. nópáses↓	No *pases.*
————————	3. mira│ésésekwarentaisyéte│ kèstaterrisándó↓	*Mira* ese C-47 que está aterrizando.
Don't look now.	4. nomiresaóra↓	No *mires* ahora.
Drink wine.	5. bebebíno↓	*Bebe* vino.
Don't drink water.	6. nóbebaságwa↓	No *bebas* agua.
Write this afternoon.	7. èskribestatárdè↓	*Escribe* esta tarde.
Don't write tomorrow.	8. noeskribasmanyáná↓	No *escribas* mañana.

VEINTISIETE   27.27

UNIT 27   SPOKEN SPANISH

EXTRAPOLATION

	Affirmative		Negative	
	—ár	—ér—ír	—ár	—ér—ír
2 fam	—a	—e	—es	—as

NOTES

a. For 2 sg fam commands there are distinct forms for affirmative and negative.

b. Affirmative command forms for regular verbs are identical with 2-3 sg forms of the present
    tense — they have the same theme vowel as the infinitive, and they lack the final /—s/
    that usually occurs with 2 fam forms.

c. Negative command forms show the same trade in theme vowels as formal commands; in
    addition, they have the typical person-number /—s/ of 2 fam forms in other tenses.

27.28   VEINTIOCHO

SPOKEN SPANISH   UNIT 27

27.21.31 Substitution drills — Person-tense substitution

Problem 1:

kármen |áblaınglés↓

Answer:

kármén↓ áblaınglés↓

Problem 2:

kármen |noáblaınglés↓

Answer:

kármén↓ noáblesınglés↓

Problem 1:
        Carmen *habla* inglés.

Answer:
        Carmen, habla inglés.

Problem 2:
        Carmen no *habla* inglés.

Answer:
        Carmen, no hables inglés.

VEINTINUEVE

UNIT 27   SPOKEN SPANISH

1. ána|estuďyaespaŋyól↓   ánà↓ èstuďyaespaŋyól↓

2. hôse|ȵyebaelkárrọ|alaofiṣínà↓   hôsé↓ ȵyebaelkárrọ|alaofiṣínà↓

3. páblọ|dapropínà↓   páblô↓ dapropínà↓

4. lwísa|komeko(n)nosótròs↓   lwisà↓ komeko(n)nosótròs↓

5. hwambebeléchè↓   hwáȵ↓ bebeléchè↓

6. lwísa|eskribeninglés↓   lwisà↓ éskribeninglés↓

7. páblọ|abrelozlíbròs↓   páblô↓ abrelozlíbròs↓

8. ána|noẹstudyaespaŋyól↓   ánà↓ noẹstuďyeẹespaŋyól↓

9. hôse|noȵyebaelkárrọ|alaofiṣínà↓   hôsé↓ noȵyebes|elkárrọ|alaofiṣínà↓

---

1 Ana *estudia* español.   Ana, estudia español.

2 José *lleva* el carro a la oficina.   José, lleva el carro a la oficina.

3 Pablo *da* propina.   Pablo, da propina.

4 Luisa *come* con nosotros.   Luisa, come con nosotros.

5 Juan *bebe* leche.   Juan, bebe leche.

6 Luisa *escribe* en inglés.   Luisa, escribe en inglés.

7 Pablo *abre* los libros.   Pablo, abre los libros.

8 Ana no *estudia* español.   Ana, no estudies español.

9 José no *lleva* el carro a la oficina.   José, no lleves el carro a la oficina.

27.30   TREINTA

SPOKEN SPANISH   UNIT 27

10. páblo |nomándalaskamísas |alalabandería↓   páblô↓ nomández |laskamísas |alalabandería↓

11. ána |notrabáha |lo(s)sábàdòs↓   ánà↓ notrabáhez |lo(s)sábàdòs↓

12. hwá(n)noða |muchapropíná↓   hwán↓ noðez |muchapropíná↓

13. lwísa |nokomékon̊ε0̥γòs↓   lwísà↓ nokomaskon̊ε0̥γòs↓

14. hwán |nobebeléchè↓   hwán↓ nobebazléchè↓

15. márta |noeskríbeninglés↓   mártà↓ noeskríbaseninglés↓

16. páblo |noabrelozlíbròs↓   páblô↓ noabrazlozlíbròs↓

17. hwán |nobíbenelşéntrò↓   hwán↓ nobíbasenelşéntrò↓

18. kármen |noeskríbelakártà↓   kármèn↓ noeskríbazlakártà↓

19. mária |nosúbe |enelas(ş)ensór↓   máría↓ nosúbas |enelas(ş)ensór↓

---

10 Pablo no *manda* las camisas a la lavandería.   Pablo, no mandes las camisas a la lavandería.

11 Ana no *trabaja* los sábados.   Ana, no trabajes los sábados.

12 Juan no *da* mucha propina.   Juan, no des mucha propina.

13 Luisa no *come* con ellos.   Luisa, no comas con ellos.

14 Juan no *bebe* leche.   Juan, no bebas leche.

15 Marta no *escribe* en inglés.   Marta, no escribas en inglés.

16 Pablo no *abre* los libros.   Pablo, no abras los libros.

17 Juan no *vive* en el centro.   Juan, no vivas en el centro.

18 Carmen no *escribe* la carta.   Carmen, no escribas la carta.

19 Maria no *sube* en el ascensor.   Maria, no subas en el ascensor.

TREINTA Y UNO   27.31

UNIT 27   SPOKEN SPANISH

27.21.32 Response drill

                       1. kómǫàkitǫenǫlrrestorán↓   kómǫakí↓

                       2. èskribǫelsábadǫtǫeldomíngò↓   èskribeldomíngò↓

                       3. bébòlechętokafé↓   bebeléchè↓

[èlpàsàpórtè↓]   4. kéfírmò↓   firmǫelpasapórte↓

[làlèkşyón↓]   5. késplíkò↓   èsplikalalekşyón↓

[èlkárrò↓]   6. kebéndò↓   bendelkárrò↓

[ènųnrréstòrán↓]   7. dóndekómò↓   komǫ|enųnrrestorán↓

---

                   1 ¿Como aquí o en el restorán?   Come aquí.

                   2 ¿Escribo el sábado o el domingo?   Escribe el domingo.

                   3 ¿Bebo leche o café?   Bebe leche.

(el pasaporte)   4 ¿Qué firmo?   Firma el pasaporte.

(la lección)   5 ¿Qué explico?   Explica la lección.

(el carro)   6 ¿Qué vendo?   Vende el carro.

(en un restorán)   7 ¿Dónde como?   Come en un restorán.

SPOKEN SPANISH   UNIT 27

[ènèspàŋyól↓]   8. áblǫeninglést   nó↓ ngábles|eninglés↓ áblạenespaŋyól↓

[éldòmíŋgò↓]   9. èstúɖygelsábaɖot   nó↓ noǫstúɖyes|elsábàɖò↓ èstúɖygeldomíŋgò↓

   [làmésà↓] 10. límpyo|los(ş)eniŝérost   nó↓ nólímpyez|los(ş)eniŝéròs↓ límpyalamésà↓

              11. súbǫaorat   sí|súbé↓

              12. báhǫaorat   sí|báhà↓

              13. èstúɖyomaŋyánat   sí|ǫstúɖyà↓

(en español)   8 ¿Hablo en inglés?   No, no hables en inglés, habla en español.

(el domingo)   9 ¿Estudio el sábado?   No, no estudies el sábado, estudia el domingo.

   (la mesa)   10 ¿Limpio los ceniceros?   No, no limpies los ceniceros, limpia la mesa.

               11 ¿Subo ahora?   Sí, sube.

               12 ¿Bajo ahora?   Sí, baja.

               13 ¿Estudio mañana?   Sí, estudia.

TREINTA Y TRES

UNIT 27   SPOKEN SPANISH

27.21.33 Translation drill

1 Check the list.	rrébísalalístà↓	Revisa la lista.
2 Don't eat much.	nokómazmúchò↓	No comas mucho.
3 Call the agency.	ǫyamalahénsyà↓	Llama a la agencia.
4 Don't work on Sundays.	notrabáhez | lozdomíŋgòs↓	No trabajes los domingos.
5 Buy some meat.	komprakárnè↓	Compra carne.
6 Don't live in the commercial sector.	nobíbas | énélséktórkomersyál↓	No vivas en el sector comercial.
7 Don't arrive late.	noǫyegestárdè↓	No llegues tarde.
8 Go down in the elevator.	bahaenelas(s)ensór↓	Baja en el ascensor.
9 Invite your neighbors.	ímbítatuzbesínòs↓	Invita a tus vecinos.
10 Drink more milk.	bebémazléchè↓	Bebe más leche.
11 Don't believe that.	nokreasésò↓	No creas eso.
12 Pay the bill now.	pagalakwéntạ | àórá↓	Paga la cuenta ahora.
13 Don't look for another apartment.	nobúskes | otrǫapartaméntò↓	No busques otro apartamento.

27.34   TREINTA Y CUATRO

SPOKEN SPANISH   UNIT 27

B. Discussion of pattern

Familiar command forms are used to give commands (requests, instructions, etc.) to persons who are addressed with /tú/ .

As we have seen, clitic pronouns position differently with formal affirmative and negative commands: they follow affirmative and precede negative command forms.

With familiar commands this same difference of arrangement with clitic pronouns occurs, but in addition the command forms themselves are different. Affirmative forms of 2 fam commands are identical with the regular 2-3 sg forms of the present tense, while negative command forms of 2 fam commands are similar to 2 for command forms; but in addition to the vowel trade, the 2 fam command forms add the /-s/ that is typical of 2 fam forms in other tense patterns. These possibilities, illustrated in chart form with common verbs, are:

	-ár		-ér-ír	
	Affirmative	Negative	Affirmative	Negative
2 fam	ábl-a	no ábl-es	kóm-e, bíb-e	no kóm-as, no bíb-as

27.21.4 Familiar command forms for irregular verbs

A. Presentation of pattern

ILLUSTRATIONS

Translate the lesson.	1. tráduṣe │lalekṣyón↓	*Traduce la lección.*
Don't translate the lesson.	2. notráduṣkaz │lalekṣyón↓	No *traduzcas la lección.*
Bring your mother-in-law too.	3. traẹ │átùswegrà │tàmbyén↓	*Trae a tu suegra también.*
Don't bring the children.	4. notráygas │alozníŋyòs↓	No *traigas a los niños.*

TREINTA Y CINCO   27.35

UNIT 27   SPOKEN SPANISH

Know this by tomorrow.   5. sábesto |páramaŋyáná↓   Sabe esto para mañana.

Come back tomorrow, John.   6. bwélbemaŋyáná |hwán↓   Vuelve mañana, Juan.

Don't come back alone.   7. nóbwelba(s)sóló↓   No vuelvas solo.

Don't come back until Thursday.   8. nóbwelbas |ástaélhwebés↓   No vuelvas hasta el jueves.

Close the book.   9. șyerraęⓁlíbró↓   Cierra el libro.

Don't close the office so early.   10. nóșyerrez |laófișina |tántempráno↓ No cierres la oficina tan temprano.

Go on ahead.   11. sígęącęlánté↓   Sigue adelante.

Don't keep on bothering.   12. nósígaz |molestándò↓   No sigas molestando.

_____   13. óyè↓pòrfín |ákyembás |aⓂyebár↓   Oye, por fin ¿a quién vas a llevar?

Don't listen if you don't like it. 14. nóoyças |sínotegústà↓   No oigas si no te gusta.

_____   15. bén↑ itèlòprésentò↓   Ven y te lo presento.

But don't come too early.   16. péró |nobeŋgaz |múytempráno↓   Pero no vengas muy temprano.

Put the cup on the table.   17. pónlakopa |enlamésá↓   Pon la copa en la mesa.

Don't put anything there, please.   18. nópoŋgaz |nadaí |pòrfábór↓   No pongas nada ahi, por favor.

27.36   TREINTA Y SEIS

SPOKEN SPANISH   UNIT 27

Leave early tonight.	19.	sáltempránọ|èstànóchè↓	*Sal* temprano esta noche.
And don't leave late.	20.	inósalgastárdé↓	Y no *salgas* tarde.
Please come with me.	21.	tén|làbóndadẹakómpaɲyármè↓	*Ten* la bondad de acompañarme.
Don't be in a hurry.	22.	noténgaspŕisâ↓	No *tengas* prisa.
Do what I told you.	23.	aṣ|lokétedíhè↓	*Haz* lo que te dije.
Don't make so much noise.	24.	nọaɡas|tántorrwídò↓	No *hagas* tanto ruido.
Tell the truth.	25.	dilabeɾdád↓	*Di* la verdad.
Don't say that in English.	26.	nódigaséso|ènínglés↓	No *digas* eso en inglés.
You go if you want.	27.	bétú|síkyérès↓	*Ve* tú, si quieres.
_____	28.	kwídadò↓ nóbayas|àmètérlapátà↓	Cuidado, no *vayas* a meter la pata.
_____	29.	àlà(s)séys|tèspéró↓isépuntwál↓	A las seis te espero; y *sé* puntual.
_____	30.	nóséasflóhọ|ómbrè↓	No *seas* flojo, hombre.

TREINTA Y SIETE   27.37

UNIT 27

SPOKEN SPANISH

EXTRAPOLATION

	Affirmative forms	Negative forms
Verb types	No irregularity	Command form irregularities
/—k—/ stem extension	tradúṣ—e	no tradúṣk—as
/—yg—/ stem extension	trá—e	no tráyg—as
Individual verbs		
/kabér/	káb—e	no kép—as
/sabér/	sáb—e	no sép—as

Verb types	Present tense irregularities	Command form irregularities
Stem vowel changing	bwélb—e	no bwélb—as
	ṣyérr—a	no ṣyérr—es
	síg—e	no síg—as
Individual verbs		
/oír/	óy—e	no óyg—as

27.38

jacobeligoodsons.com For Free Audio

TREINTA Y OCHO

SPOKEN SPANISH   UNIT 27

	Affirmative forms	Negative forms
Verb types	Command form irregularities	
/–g–/ stem extension	bál	no bálg–as
	bén	no béng–as
	pón	no póng–as
	sál	no sálg–as
	tén	no téng–as
Stem final /ş > g/	áş	no ág–as
	dí	no díg–as
Individual verbs		
/ír/	b–é	no báy–as
/sér/	s–é	no sé–as
/abér/	–é	no áy–as

NOTES

a. All irregular negative familiar command forms are like formal command forms with the addition of the final /–s/ of 2 fam forms.

b. Affirmative familiar command forms do not have a final /–s/ as do most other 2 fam forms.

c. Compared with irregular negative forms, the corresponding affirmative forms may be (1) regular, (2) irregular in the same way as their corresponding present tense forms, or (3) uniquely irregular.

d. Verbs with a /–g–/ stem extension or modification are uniquely irregular; they usually consist of a form identical with the infinitive stem.

TREINTA Y NUEVE   27.39

jacobeligoodsons.com For Free Audio

UNIT 27   SPOKEN SPANISH

27.21.41 Substitution drill — Person-tense substitution

1. àlíşya|tráduşelaleksyón↓   àlíşyà↓ tráduşelaleksyón↓

2. àna|bwélbęotrabéş↓   anà↓ bwélbęotrabéş↓

3. hwán|àlmwerşakí↓   hwàn↓ àlmwerşakí↓

4. martą|àtyendęalozníŋyòs↓   martà↓ àtyendęalozníŋyòs↓

5. pablo|traelkóchè↓   pàblò↓ traelkóchè↓

6. hòse|dişètodęeninglés↓   hòsé↓ ditodęeninglés↓

7. karmém|byenelwégò↓   karmèn↓ benlwégò↓

8. aną|aşelakomíđà↓   anà↓ aşlakomíđà↓

_____

1 Alicia *traduce* la lección.   Alicia, traduce la lección.

2 Ana *vuelve* otra vez.   Ana, vuelve otra vez.

3 Juan *almuerza* aquí.   Juan, almuerza aquí.

4 Marta *atiende* a los niños.   Marta, atiende a los niños.

5 Pablo *trae* el coche.   Pablo, trae el coche.

6 José *dice* todo en inglés.   José, di todo en inglés.

7 Carmen *viene* luego.   Carmen, ven luego.

8 Ana *hace* la comida.   Ana, haz la comida.

27.40   CUARENTA

SPOKEN SPANISH   UNIT 27

9. hwampone|lòzlibrosenlamésà↓   hwàn↓ ponlozlibros|enlamésà↓

10. màriatyene|làkòmiɖalístà↓   màría↓ tenlakomiɖalístà↓

11. hòsebalatyéndà↓   hòse↓ beɑlatyéndà↓

12. angeṣamáblè↓   anà↓ seamáblè↓

13. àliʂyaɛstakí|ɑla(s)syétè↓   àliʂyà↓ èstakí|ɑla(s)syétè↓

14. àliʂya|notraɖuʂelaleksyón↓   àliʂyà↓ notraɖuʂkaz|laleksyón↓

15. ana|nobwelbe|otrabéʂ↓   anà↓ nobwelbas|otrabéʂ↓

16. marta|nɑatyénde|alozníɳyòs↓   martà↓ noɑtyéndas|alozníɳyòs↓

17. hòse|noɖiʂetoɖo|eninglés↓   hòse↓ noɖigastoɖo|eninglés↓

───

  9 Juan *pone* los libros en la mesa.   Juan, pon los libros en la mesa.

 10 María *tiene* la comida lista.   María, ten la comida lista.

 11 José *va* a la tienda.   José, ve a la tienda.

 12 Ana *es* amable.   Ana, sé amable.

 13 Alicia *está* aquí a las siete.   Alicia, está aquí a las siete.

 14 Alicia no *traduce* la lección.   Alicia, no traduzcas la lección.

 15 Ana no *vuelve* otra vez.   Ana, no vuelvas otra vez.

 16 Marta no *atiende* a los niños.   Marta, no atiendas a los niños.

 17 José no *dice* todo en inglés.   José, no digas todo en inglés.

CUARENTA Y UNO   27.41

jacobeligoodsons.com For Free Audio

UNIT 27　　　　　　　　　　　　　　　　　　　　　　　　　　　　　SPOKEN SPANISH

18. páblo|notráelkóchè↓　　　　　　　　　páblò↓ notráygaṣelkóchè↓

19. kármèn|nobyènetárdè↓　　　　　　　　kármèn↓ nobeŋgastárdè↓

20. ána|ŋọaṣelakomídà↓　　　　　　　　　ánà↓ ŋọagazlakomídà↓

21. hwán|nopóne|lózlibrosenlamésà↓　　　hwán↓ nopóŋgas|lózlibrosenlamésà↓

22. hòsé|notyènechofér↓　　　　　　　　hòsé↓ noteŋgaschofér↓

23. hòsé|nobàlatyéndà↓　　　　　　　　hòsé↓ nobayas|alatyéndà↓

24. ána|ŋọeznerbyósà↓　　　　　　　　　ánà↓ nóseaznerbyósà↓

25. àlişya|noẹstapreokupádà↓　　　　　　àlişyà↓ noẹstespreokupádà↓

---

18 Pablo no *trae* el coche.　　　　　　　　Pablo, no traigas el coche.

19 Carmen no *viene* tarde.　　　　　　　　Carmen, no vengas tarde.

20 Ana no *hace* la comida.　　　　　　　　Ana, no hagas la comida.

21 Juan no *pone* los libros en la mesa.　　　Juan, no pongas los libros en la mesa.

22 José no *tiene* chofer.　　　　　　　　　José, no tengas chofer.

23 José no *va* a la tienda.　　　　　　　　José, no vayas a la tienda.

24 Ana no *es* nerviosa.　　　　　　　　　Ana, no seas nerviosa.

25 Alicia no *está* preocupada.　　　　　　Alicia, no estés preocupada.

27.42

SPOKEN SPANISH   UNIT 27

27.21.42 Response drill

               1. àlmwérşǫakí↑ǫeŋunrrestorán↓   àlmwérşakí↓

               2. píđòkàfé↑oléchè↓   píđekafé↓

               3. bwélboy↑omaŋyánà↓   bwelbemaŋyánà↓

[èlkárrò↓]   4. ketráygò↓   traelkárrò↓

[ląènsàlàđà↓]   5. keágò↓   aźląensaláđà↓

[làbèrđàđ↓]   6. keđígò↓   dilaberđáđ↓

[lálékşyón↓]   7. ketrađúşkò↓   tráđuşelalekşyón↓

[àlàunà↓]   8. àkęórasálgò↓   salalaúnà↓

[àlşèntrò↓]   9. àđondebóy↓   bęalşéntrò↓

---

               1 ¿Almuerzo aquí o en un restorán?   Almuerza aquí.

               2 ¿Pido café o leche?   Pide café.

               3 ¿Vuelvo hoy o mañana?   Vuelve mañana.

(el carro)   4 ¿Qué traigo?   Trae el carro.

(la ensalada) 5 ¿Qué hago?   Haz la ensalada.

(la verdad)   6 ¿Qué digo?   Di la verdad.

(la lección) 7 ¿Qué traduzco?   Traduce la lección.

(a la una)   8 ¿A qué hora salgo?   Sal a la una.

(al centro)   9 ¿A dónde voy?   Ve al centro.

CUARENTA Y TRES

UNIT 27   SPOKEN SPANISH

[ð̩lunès↓]   10. benggeldomingò   nobengas|eldomíngò↓ benⓔllónès↓
[kàfé↓]   11. pidolèchet   nopidazléchè↓ pidekafé↓
[élbyérnès↓] 12. salggelsábadot   nosalgas|elsábàdò↓ salelbyérnès↓

              13. boyalçentrot   sí|bé↓
              14. bengomanyanat   sí|bén↓
              15. pidgagwat   sí|pidé↓

(el lunes)   10 ¿Vengo el domingo?   No vengas el domingo, ven el lunes.
(café)   11 ¿Pido leche?   No pidas leche, pide café.
(el viernes) 12 ¿Salgo el sábado?   No salgas el sábado, sal el viernes.

              13 ¿Voy al centro?   Sí, ve.
              14 ¿Vengo mañana?   Sí, ven.
              15 ¿Pido agua?   Sí, pide.

jacobeligoodsons.com For Free Audio

SPOKEN SPANISH   UNIT 27

27.21.43 Translation drill

1 Put your name, too.   pontunómbrè |tàmbyén↓   Pon tu nombre también.

2 Go take a walk.   beađar |unabwéltà↓   Ve a dar una vuelta.

3 Don't put those trunks there. nopoŋgas |esozbaúlès |àí↓   No pongas esos baúles ahí.

4 Bring your girl friend.   traђatunóbyà↓   Trae a tu novia.

5 Don't go to school today.   nobayas |alɐeskwélɐ |óy↓   No vayas a la escuela hoy.

6 Don't bring the car tomorrow. notraygas |elkárrò |ṃaŋyánà↓ No traigas el carro mañana.

7 Don't make a lot of noise.   noагaz |muchorrwíđò↓   No hagas mucho ruido.

8 Listen to the same piece again. oye |lamizmapyéѕɐ |ótràbéѕ↓ Oye la misma pieza otra vez.

9 Get the meal.   aѕlakomíđà↓   Haz la comida.

10 Keep on this way.   sigeporaí↓   Sigue por ahí.

CUARENTA Y CINCO   27.45

UNIT 27   SPOKEN SPANISH

11 Repeat please.   rrépité |pòrfàbór↓   Repite por favor.

12 Be less strict.   semenozrrigurósô↓   Sé menos riguroso.

13 Don't be so nervous.   noseas |tannerbyósô↓   No seas tan nervioso.

B. Discussion of pattern

    Irregular familiar command forms comprise a very complex pattern, since affirmative and negative forms belong to two different systems with independent patterns of irregularities.

    The negative familiar command forms follow the same patterns (have the same irregularities) as the corresponding formal command forms. Negative familiar command forms always end in /‑s/ , the typical person-number ending of 2 fam forms.

    Affirmative familiar forms usually follow the patterns of 3 sg present tense. There are a number of exceptions, however, all listed in the third chart in the extrapolation. These forms (which can usually be associated with a /‑g‑/ stem modification in 1 sg of the present tense) are usually identical with the infinitive stem. It is interesting to note that in some dialect areas there is a tendency to restructure some of these irregular familiar command forms by adding a theme vowel; so forms like /sál‑e,pón‑e,áş‑e/ are used. This restructuring seems to occur only when similar forms can appear in the present tense.

    A couple of these forms, /bál/ and /é/ , are unlikely to occur in conversational Spanish. They are included here for the sake of completeness.

SPOKEN SPANISH															UNIT 27

27.22   Replacement drills

A   kwál|estudeportè|faborítò↓

1, kwáles_____↓   kwáles|sóntuzdepórtes|faborítòs↓

2. _____komídas_____↓   kwáles|sóntuskomídas|faborítàs↓

3. _____sus_____↓   kwáles|sónsuskomídas|faborítàs↓

4. _____nómbre_____↓   kwál|e(s)sunómbre|faborítò↓

5. _____komplétò↓   kwál|e(s)sunómbre|kompléto↓

6. komọ_____↓   komọ|e(s)sunómbre|kompléto↓

7. _____sepronunşya_____↓   komo|sepronunşya|sunómbrekompléto↓

A   ¿Cuál es tu deporte favorito?

1 ¿Cuáles_____?   ¿Cuáles son tus deportes favoritos?

2 ¿_____comidas_____?   ¿Cuáles son tus comidas favoritas?

3 ¿_____sus_____?   ¿Cuáles son sus comidas favoritas?

4 ¿_____nombre_____?   ¿Cuál es su nombre favorito?

5 ¿_____completo?   ¿Cuál es su nombre completo?

6 ¿Cómo_____?   ¿Cómo es su nombre completo?

7 ¿_____se pronuncia_____?   ¿Cómo se pronuncia su nombre completo?

CUARENTA Y SIETE

UNIT 27   SPOKEN SPANISH

B   àsí |bas̩a̩eŋgordár↓

1. _____akostumbrárte↓   àsí |bas̩akostumbrárte↓

2. ____boy_____↓   àsí |boyakostumbrárme↓

3. nuŋka_____↓   nuŋka |boyakostumbrárme↓

4. _____sentárnòs↓   nuŋka |bamos̩asentárnòs↓

5. àora_____↓   àora |bamos̩asentárnòs↓

6. ____ban_____↓   àora |ban̩asentárse↓

7. _____lebantárte↓   àora |bas̩a̩lebantárte↓

_____

B   Así vas a engordar.

1 _____acostumbrarte.   Así vas a acostumbrarte.

2 ____voy_____.   Así voy a acostumbrarme.

3 Nunca_____.   Nunca voy a acostumbrarme.

4 _____sentarnos.   Nunca vamos a sentarnos.

5 Ahora_____.   Ahora vamos a sentarnos.

6 ____van_____.   Ahora van a sentarse.

7 _____levantarte.   Ahora vas a levantarte.

27.48   CUARENTA Y OCHO

jacobeligoodsons.com For Free Audio

SPOKEN SPANISH   UNIT 27

C   yónòsé |nihòtaɖególf↓

1. _____espaɲyól↓   yónòse |nihòtaɖespaɲyól↓

2. tú_____↓   túnòsàbez |nihòtaɖespaɲyól↓

3. ___ab̯lamoz_____↓   nòsótroz |nóab̯lamoz |nihòtaɖespaɲyól↓

4. _____inglés↓   nòsótroz |nóab̯lamóz |nihótaɖeinglés↓

5. él_____↓   élnɡab̯la |nihótaɖeinglés↓

6. ___ȧ |apréndiɖo_____↓   élnɡa |apréndiɖo |nihótaɖeinglés↓

7. nòsótroz_____↓   nòsótroz |nɡemos̯apréndiɖo|nihótaɖeinglés↓

_____

C   Yo no sé ni jota de golf.

1 _____ español.   Yo no sé ni jota de español.

2 Tú _____ .   Tú no sabes ni jota de español.

3 _____ hablamos_____.   Nosotros no hablamos ni jota de español.

4 _____ inglés.   Nosotros no hablamos ni jota de inglés.

5 El_____.   El no habla ni jota de inglés.

6 _____ ha aprendido_____.   El no ha aprendido ni jota de inglés.

7 Nosotros _____.   Nosotros no hemos aprendido ni jota de inglés.

CUARENTA Y NUEVE   27.49

UNIT 27   SPOKEN SPANISH

D èntonşez↑nòsènkòntramos │enelpasílↄyó↓

1. _____ kásâ↓   èntonşez↑nòsènkòntramos │enlakásâ↓

2. _____ bémos _____ ↓   èntonşez↑nòzbémos │enlakásâ↓

3. dèspwéz _____ ↓   dèspwez↑nòzbémos │enlakásâ↓

4. _____ otél ↓   dèspwez↑nòzbémos │enelotél↓

5. _____ kéɗamos _____ ↓   dèspwez↑nòskéɗamos │enelotél↓

6. _____ mè _____ ↓   dèspwez↑mèkeɗọ │enelotél↓

7. _____ bóy │al _____ ↓   dèspwez↑mèbóy │alotél↓

_____

D Entonces, nos encontramos en el pasillo.

1 _____ casa.   Entonces, nos encontramos en la casa.

2 _____ vemos _____ .   Entonces, nos vemos en la casa.

3 Después, _____ .   Después, nos vemos en la casa.

4 _____ hotel.   Después, nos vemos en el hotel.

5 _____ quedamos _____ .   Después, nos quedamos en el hotel.

6 _____ me _____ .   Después, me quedo en el hotel.

7 _____ voy al _____ .   Después, me voy al hotel.

27.50   CINCUENTA

SPOKEN SPANISH   UNIT 27

E   nóséasflóhǫ|ómbrè↓

1. _____ómbrés↓   nòseamflóhòs|ómbrès↓

2. _____lókǫ_____↓   nòsealókǫ|ómbrè↓

3. _____chíkàs↓   nòseanlókàs|chíkàs↓

4. _____así_____↓   nòseanasí|chíkàs↓

5. _____chíkò↓   nòseasasí|chíkò↓

6. __dígas_____↓   nòdigas,así|chíkò↓

7. _____ésò_____↓   nòdigasésò|chíkò↓

_____

E   No seas flojo, hombre.

1 _____, hombres.   No sean flojos, hombres.

2 _____loco , _____   No sea loco, hombre.

3 _____, chicas.   No sean locas, chicas.

4 _____así, _____ .   No sean así, chicas.

5 _____, chico.   No seas así, chico.

6 ___digas _____ .   No digas así, chico.

7 _____eso, _____.   No digas eso, chico.

CINCUENTA Y UNO   27.51

jacobeligoodsons.com For Free Audio

UNIT 27   SPOKEN SPANISH

F   àlà(s)séys|tespéró↓ ísepuntwál↓

1. _____ los _____↓   àlà(s)séyz|los̮espéró↓ íseampuntwálès↓

2. ___úna_____↓   àláúna|los̮espéró↓ íseampuntwálès↓

3. _____bwénàs↓   àláúna|las̮espéró↓ íseambwénàs↓

4. ___şíŋko_____↓   àlàs(ş)íŋko|las̮espéró↓ íseambwénàs↓

5. ___ɷ̮yámò_____↓   àlàs(ş)íŋko|laz̮ɷ̮yámò↓ íseambwénàs↓

6. ___la_____↓   àlàs(ş)íŋko|laɷ̮yámò↓ íseabwénà↓

7. _____puntwálés↓   àlàs(ş)íŋko|laz̮ɷ̮yámò↓ íseampuntwálès↓

F   A las seis te espero. Y sé puntual.

1 _____los_____. _____.   A las seis los espero. Y sean puntuales.

2 ___una_____. _____.   A la una los espero. Y sean puntuales.

3 _____. ___buenas.   A la una las espero. Y sean buenas.

4 ___cinco_____. _____.   A las cinco las espero. Y sean buenas.

5 _____llamo. _____.   A las cinco las llamo. Y sean buenas.

6 ___la_____. _____.   A las cinco la llamo. Y sea buena.

7 _____. ___puntuales.   A las cinco las llamo. Y sean puntuales.

27.52   CINCUENTA Y DOS

SPOKEN SPANISH   UNIT 27

27.23   Variation drills

A   nópyérdo|niumpartídó↓   No pierdo ni un partido.

     1 I don't miss a single day.   nópyérdo|niundíá↓   No pierdo ni un día.

     2 I don't miss a single weekend.   nópyérdo|niumfindesémáná↓   No pierdo ni un fin de semana.

     3 I don't miss a single business (deal). nópyérdo|niu(n)negósyó↓   No pierdo ni un negocio.

     4 He doesn't miss a single trip.   nópyérde|niumbyáhé↓   No pierde ni un viaje.

     5 He doesn't miss a single mass.   nópyérde|niunamísá↓   No pierde ni una misa.

     6 He doesn't miss a single (musical) nópyérde|niunapyéşá↓   No pierde ni una pieza.
        piece.

     7 He doesn't miss a single party.   nòpyérde|niunafyéstá↓   No pierde ni una fiesta.

B   noimpórta|kenosépás↓   No importa que no sepas.

     1 It doesn't matter that you don't know   noimpórta|kénosépashugár↓   No importa que no sepas jugar.
        how to play.

     2 It doesn't matter that you don't know   noimpórta|kénosépazbaylár↓   No importa que no sepas bailar.
        how to dance.

     3 It doesn't matter that you don't know   noimpórta|kénosépasensenyár↓ No importa que no sepas enseñar.
        how to teach.

CINCUENTA Y TRES   27.53

UNIT 27   SPOKEN SPANISH

4 It doesn't matter that you don't know
   how to translate.

noįmpórta |kénòsepastraðuşír↓   No importa que no sepas traducir.

5 It doesn't matter that you don't know
   how to do that.

noįmpórta |kénòsepas̩aşérésò↓   No importa que no sepas hacer eso.

6 It doesn't matter that you don't know
   how to speak English.

noįmpórta |kénòsepas̩ablaringlés↓   No importa que no sepas hablar inglés.

7 It doesn't matter that you don't know
   English.

noįmpórta |kénòsepas̩inglés↓   No importa que no sepas inglés.

C pérọ |éskètámpòko |téŋgọèkipò↓   Pero es que tampoco tengo equipo.

1 But I'm not hungry either.

pérọ |éskètámpòko |téŋgọ̀ambré↓   Pero es que tampoco tengo hambre.

2 But I'm not cold either.

pérọ |éskètámpòko |téŋgòfrió↓   Pero es que tampoco tengo frío.

3 But I'm never cold.

pérọ |éskènuŋka |téŋgòfrió↓   Pero es que nunca tengo frío.

4 But I never have any money.

pérọ |éskènuŋka |téŋgòdineró↓   Pero es que nunca tengo dinero.

5 But I hardly have any clothes.

pérọ |éskẹàpenas |téŋgòrropá↓   Pero es que apenas tengo ropa.

6 But I hardly have any time.

pérọ |éskẹàpenas |téŋgotyémpò↓   Pero es que apenas tengo tiempo.

7 But I always have enough.

pérọ |éskèsyémpre |téŋgòsùfişyéntè↓   Pero es que siempre tengo suficiente.

SPOKEN SPANISH   UNIT 27

D àlprinşipyo |noneşesítàs↓   Al principio no necesitas.

1 At first you don't need anything.   àlprinşipyo |noneşesitaznádà↓   Al principio no necesitas nada.

2 Afterwards you don't need anything.   dèspwéz |noneşesitaznádà↓   Después no necesitas nada.

3 Afterwards you don't do anything.   dèspwéz |noaşeznádà↓   Después no haces nada.

4 You still don't owe anything.   tòdàbía |nodebeznádà↓   Todavía no debes nada.

5 You still don't know anything.   tòdàbía |nòsabeznádà↓   Todavía no sabes nada.

6 We still don't know anything.   tòdàbía |nòsàbemoznádà↓   Todavía no sabemos nada.

7 We still haven't eaten anything.   tòdàbía |ngemos |komidonádà↓   Todavía no hemos comido nada.

E bwenò↓tugánàs↓ mèkòmbènşiste↓   Bueno, tú ganas. Me convenciste.

1 OK, you pay. You convinced me.   bwenò↓tupágàs↓ mèkòmbènşiste↓   Bueno, tú pagas. Me convenciste.

2 OK, you go. You convinced me.   bwenò↓tubás↓ mèkòmbènşiste↓   Bueno, tú vas. Me convenciste.

3 OK, I lose. *You* won from me.   bwenò↓yopyérdò↓ tumeganáste↓   Bueno, yo pierdo. Tú me ganaste.

4 OK, I win. You lost.   bwenò↓yogánò↓ tuperdíste↓   Bueno, yo gano. Tú perdiste.

CINCUENTE Y CINCO   27.55

UNIT 27   SPOKEN SPANISH

5 OK, let's go. You've already eaten.   bwénò↓bámòs↓ yákomístè↓   Bueno, vamos. Ya comiste.

6 OK, let's go. You've already paid.   bwénò↓bámòs↓ yápagástè↓   Bueno, vamos. Ya pagaste.

7 OK, let's go. You've already put   bwénò↓bámòs↓ yámetiste│lapátà↓   Bueno, vamos. Ya metiste la pata.
   your foot in it.

F   déhalo│pàràlásonșè↓   Déjalo para las once.

   1 Leave (frml) it for one o'clock.   déhelo│pàràláunà↓   Déjelo para la una.

   2 Open (fam) it right away.   ábrelopróntò↓   Ábrelo pronto.

   3 Open (frml) it right away.   ábralopróntò↓   Ábralo pronto.

   4 Translate (fam) it right now.   tráduşelọaórà↓   Tradúcelo ahora.

   5 Translate (frml) it right now.   tráduşkalọaórà↓   Tradúzcalo ahora.

   6 Say (fam) it right now.   dílọaórà↓   Dilo ahora.

   7 Say (frml) it right now.   dígalọaórà↓   Dígalo ahora.

27.56   CINCUENTA Y SEIS

SPOKEN SPANISH   UNIT 27

27.24   Review drill. — Nominalized possessives

1 My car is the green one. How about
   yours?
mikárroęsęlbérdé↓ ięlsúyo↑
Mi carro es el verde, ¿y el suyo?

2 His last name is Molina. How about hers?
syápéɰyięoęzmolína↓ ięldęɰya↑
Su apellido es Molina, ¿y el de ella?

3 Your-mother-in-law isn't here. How
   about John's?
súswegra|noęstakí↓ iláđéhwan↑
Su suegra no está aquí, ¿y la de Juan?

4 My wife isn't here. How about yours?
mięsposa|noęstakí↓ iláđęústeđ↑
Mi esposa no está aquí, ¿y la de Ud?

5 My house has five bedrooms. How
   many does yours have?
mikása|tyénéęiŋkoęormitóryòs↓ iláđęústeđ↑
Mi casa tiene cinco dormitorios, ¿y la de
usted?

6 Here's your pencil. Where's mine?
ákięstatulápię↓ ięondestaęlmíó↓
Aquí está tu lápiz, ¿y dónde está el mío?

7 Here's my pen. Where's yours?
ákięstamiplúmà↓ ięondesta|laęęústéđ↓
Aquí está mi pluma, ¿y dónde está la de Ud?

8 Is this my drink or yours?
éstáęzmikópạ↑olatúya↓
¿Esta es mi copa o la tuya?

9 Are these my books or yours?
éstós|sònmizlíbros↑olo(s)súyòs↓
¿Estos son mis libros o los suyos?

10 Is this my pencil or yours?
éstézmilápię↑ęelsúyò↓
¿Este es mi lápiz o el suyo?

11 Are these my shirts or yours?
éstás|sònmiskàmisas↑olastúyàs↓
¿Estas son mis camisas o las tuyas?

UNIT 27

SPOKEN SPANISH

27.3   CONVERSATION STIMULUS

NARRATIVE 1

1 Jaime and his friend Pedro are talking about sports.

háymęisyamígo |ęstánàblandoɾeɾepórtès↓

Jaime y su amigo Pedro están hablando de deportes.

2 Jaime plans to go play soccer tomorrow.

háymepyénsa↑íráhúgar |àlfútbòl |màŋyánà↓

Jaime piensa ir a jugar al fútbol mañana.

3 He hasn't played for a long time.

áşęmúchótyémpo |kènohwégà↓

Hace mucho tiempo que no juega.

4 Pedro tells him that he shouldn't go.

peɾroleɾįşę |kènoɾebęír↓

Pedro le dice que no debe ir.

5 He's crazy if he goes.

èsùnlókosıbá↓

Es un loco si va.

6 It may be hard on him.

lępweɾę |àşéɾɾaŋyó↓

Le puede hacer daño.

7 'Nonsense,' says Jaime.

kebá |ɾįşęháymè↓

Qué va--dice Jaime.

8 He says he has very good health.

díşękeltyéne |muybwénasalúɾ↓

Dice que él tiene muy buena salud.

9 Pedro says that may be true.

peɾrodįşę |késopweɾe |sérberɾáɾ↓

Pedro dice que eso puede ser verdad.

10 But that he's too old for that game.

pérókel |yáęstámuybyehò |pàrąésęɾępórtè↓

Pero que él ya está muy viejo para ese deporte.

27.58

jacobeligoodsons.com For Free Audio

CINCUENTA Y OCHO

SPOKEN SPANISH   UNIT 27

DIALOG 1

Pedro, pregúntele a Jaime que qué va
   a hacer mañana.

    kébas̩a s̩er |maɲyánà↓

Pedro: ¿Qué vas a hacer mañana?

Jaime, contéstele que piensa ir a jugar
   al fútbol. Que hace mucho tiempo que
   no juega.

    pyens̩oir |àhúgaralfutból↓
    ás̩ēmuchotyempo |kenohwégò↓

Jaime: Pienso ir a jugar al fútbol. Hace
   mucho tiempo que no juego.

Pedro, dígale que no sea loco, que no
   vaya. Que le puede hacer daño.

    nóseazlóků↓nobáɏàs↓ tèpwed̩e |ás̩èrd̩aɲò↓

Pedro: No seas loco, no vayas. Te puede
   hacer daño.

Jaime, dígale que qué va, que Ud. tiene
   muy buena salud.

    kebá↓ yotengo |múybwénasalúd̩↓

Jaime: Qué va. Yo tengo muy buena salud.

Pedro, dígale que sí, pero que ya él está
   muy viejo para ese deporte.

    sí |péró |ɏátúes̩táz |múybyéhò |pàra̩ésè
    d̩epórtè↓

Pedro: Sí, pero ya tú estás muy viejo para
   ese deporte.

NARRATIVE 2

1 It isn't good for Jaime to play football,
   really.

    àháyme |rre̩àlmente↑nólekombyéne |hugárfútból↓

A Jaime realmente no le conviene jugar
   fútbol.

2 He ought to play something else, like
   golf.

    eldèbehugar |otrakósà↓kómógólf↓

El debe jugar otra cosa, como golf.

3 Golf isn't harmful to old people.

    èlgolf |nolę s̩a s̩ed̩aɲo̧ |àlòzbyéhòs↓

El golf no les hace daño a los viejos.

CINCUENTA Y NUEVE   27.59

UNIT 27   SPOKEN SPANISH

4 The trouble is that he doesn't like that   lómalo |ęskęáęl↑nólęgustạ |ésędępórtę↓   Lo malo es que a él no le gusta ese
  game.   deporte.

5 So he says.   ésòdíşę́l↓   Eso dice él.

6 But Pedro asks him how he can tell (know)   pèrópedro |lęprègúnta↑kèkomopwédel| Pero Pedro le pregunta que cómo puede
  whether he likes it or not.   saber |silègústạonó↓   él saber o no.

7 Without having ever played it.   sinàberlo |hùgádònuŋkà↓   Sin haberlo jugado nunca.

8 Pedro asks him why doesn't he go play   pędrolępregúnta↑kèpòrke |nòbàhugárkonę́l| Pedro le pregunta que por qué no va a
  with him tomorrow.   mȧŋyáná↓   jugar con él mañana.

9 And he'll be glad to teach him.   ḭél |kònmúchogusto |lènsę́ŋyà↓   Y él con mucho gusto le enseña.

10 Jaime says all right, he'll try.   haymelèdiȿę |kèstabyén↓ kèbàtratár↓   Jaime le dice que está bien, que va a tratar.

                                        DIALOG 2

Pedro, dígale que a él realmente no le   àti↑rręȧlmente |nòtèkòmbyènè |hùgárfútbòl↓ Pedro: A ti realmente no te conviene jugar
  conviene jugar fútbol. Que debe jugar   tudèbeshugar |otrakósá↓   fútbol. Tú debes jugar otra cosa.
  otra cosa.

Jaime, pregúntele que cómo qué.   kómòkḗ↓   Jaime: ¿Cómo qué?

Pedro, dígale que como golf. Que el golf   kómògólf↓ èlgolf |nòles̩ąȿędȧŋyọ |àlòȥbyéhòs↓ Pedro: Como golf. El golf no les hace daño
  no les hace daño a los viejos.   a los viejos.

27.60   SESENTA

SPOKEN SPANISH   UNIT 27

Jaime, dígale que lo malo es que a Ud. no   lómaloęskęamí |nòmęgustą |ésèdèpórtè↓   Jaime: Lo malo es que a mí no me gusta
le gusta ese deporte.   ese deporte.

Pedro, pregúntele que cómo puede saber si   komopwędę(s)saber |sitegustạonó↓   Pedro: ¿Cómo puedes saber si te gusta o
le gusta o no, sin haberlo jugado nunca.   sinąberlo |húgádònuŋká↓   no, sin haberlo jugado nunca?

Jaime, dígale que sí, es verdad, que tiene   sí |ęzberdád↓ tyénezrrașón↓   Jaime: Sí, es verdad, tienes razón.
razón.

Pedro, pregúntele que por qué no viene a   pòrke |nobyenesạhugar |konmigomaŋyáná↓   Pedro: ¿Por qué no vienes a jugar conmigo
jugar con Ud. mañana; que Ud. le enseña.   yotenséŋyò↓   mañana? Yo te enseño.

Jaime, dígale que está bien, que va a tratar,   éstabyém↓bóyàtràtár↓ ()yámametempránò↓   Jaime: Está bien, voy a tratar. Llámame
que lo llame a Ud. temprano.   temprano.

NARRATIVE 3

1 Pedro calls Jaime up very early.   pedro |()yámàhaymet muytempránò↓   Pedro llama a Jaime muy temprano.

2 He calls him up at five in the morning.   ló()yamę |àlá(s)șiŋkodelamaŋyáná↓   Lo llama a las cinco de la mañana.

3 Jaime doesn't want to get up.   hayme |nokyerelebantársè↓   Jaime no quiere levantarse.

4 He says he's too tired.   dișę |kèstámuykansádò↓   Dice que está muy cansado.

5 And that he has a headache, besides.   ikęademás |tyéneçdólordekabéșá↓   Y que, además, tiene dolor de cabeza.

SESENTA Y UNO   27.61

UNIT 27																											SPOKEN SPANISH

6 He wants to put it off for (some) other day.

kyéreɗehárlo|pàrɑotrɑ ì↓

Quiere dejarlo para otro día.

7 'Don't be lazy, don't complain so much and get dressed', Pedro tells him.

noseasflóhò↓ notekehestánto|ibístètè|
lèɗíşèpéɗrò↓

No seas flojo, no te quejes tanto y vístete —le dice Pedro.

8 Jaime gets up, then.

háyme|sèlébàntɑ|éntónşès↓

Jaime se levanta, entonces.

9 But he says it'll be the first and last time.

péròɗişè†kèsprimérɑ|¡últimabéş↓

Pero dice que es primera y última vez.

DIALOG 3

Pedro, dígale a Jaime que se levante, que son las cinco.

lèbántàté|háymè↓ sónlá(s)şiŋkò↓

Pedro: ¡Levántate, Jaime! Son las cinco.

Jaime, dígale que no lo moleste. Que Ud. está muy cansado.

nomemoléstés↓ èstóymuykansáɗò↓

Jaime: No me molestes. Estoy muy cansado.

Pedro, dígale que no sea flojo, que ya es tarde.

noseasflóhò↓ ɣáẹstarɗè↓

Pedro: No seas flojo, ya es tarde.

Jaime, dígale que mejor lo deje para otro día. Que además Ud. tiene dolor de cabeza.

mèhorɗehalo|párɑotroɗíà↓ àɗèmás|
tengoɗolorɗekabéşà↓

Jaime: Mejor déjalo para otro día. Además, tengo dolor de cabeza.

Pedro, dígale que no se queje tanto y que se vista.

notekehestánto|ibístètè↓

Pedro: No te quejes tanto y vístete.

Jaime, dígale que bueno, que se va a levantar, pero que es primera y última vez.

bwenò↓ mèboyalebantár↓ péròẹsprimérɑ|
¡últimabéş↓

Jaime: Bueno, me voy a levantar; pero es primera y última vez.

27.62																											SESENTA Y DOS

SPOKEN SPANISH   UNIT 27

27.4   READINGS

27.40   List of cognate loan words.

la técnica	lá‑tekniká↓
exótico	éksotikó↓
los productos	lòs‑pròduktós↓
importados (importar)	impòrtaდòs↓ impòrtár↓
el aspecto	èl‑àspektó↓
la actitud	la‑àktitúd↓
desinteresada (desinteresar)	dèsintèrèsađá↓ dèsintèrèsár↓
standard	éstandárd↓
competir	kòmpétir↓

27.41   Reading selection

La Técnica de Comprar

—¿Ha estado usted en la parte antigua de la ciudad, Virginia?—le preguntó Marta a la Sra. de Robinson cuando pasó por ella para llevarla al mercado.

—No—respondió ella—pero he oído hablar mucho de ese sector y me dicen que es muy interesante y exótico. ¿Por qué? ¿Vamos a ir allí?

—Sí, porque allí hay un mercado donde se encuentra de todo lo que uno necesita, incluyendo productos importados y todo muy fresco, muy barato y muy bueno, va a ver. El edificio tiene un aspecto viejo y sucio, como todo ese sector de la ciudad que está tan abandonado, pero, como le digo, todas las cosas que allí venden son siempre mucho más baratas que en cualquier otra parte...eso es, si uno sabe comprar, porque si no, puede resultar más bien muy caro. Lo que quiero decir con ésto es que, para poder comprar barato en ese mercado, hay que saber decir que sí, cuando conviene, y que no, cuando no conviene, ya va a ver Ud. la técnica que tengo yo. Yo voy a un puesto donde venden por ejemplo, unos huevos grandes y que parecen muy frescos, yo los miro y le pregunto al hombre, con actitud desinteresada, que a cómo están. Si él me dice que están a tres pesos la docena, inmediatamente le digo que no me conviene, que están carísimos, muy pequeños y además que no parecen ser frescos, y que mejor voy a otro puesto donde me los venden más baratos. Entonces va a ver Ud. que el hombre va a decirme que me los deja a dos cincuenta. Yo lo pienso un momento y luego le digo que no, que no le puedo dar más de uno cincuenta por la docena, y así seguimos. Él me dice una cosa y yo le digo otra, hasta que por fin termina dándomelos a mi precio, o casi a mi precio.

SESENTA Y TRES   27.63

UNIT 27   SPOKEN SPANISH

—Ay, qué interesante—dijo Virginia—yo quisiera poder hacer lo mismo en los Estados Unidos, pero allá casi no se puede hacer eso. Allá los mercados grandes generalmente pertenecen a grandes compañías que tienen precios standard para todos los productos, y la gente que trabaja en esos mercados son solamente empleados que no pueden vender ni más barato ni más caro del precio fijado para cada cosa.

—Pues aquí sí pueden porque cada puesto pertenece a una persona y esa persona puede competir con los otros puestos. Así pues, Ud. tiene que acostumbrarse a comprar en esa forma porque si no, todo le resulta carísimo. Pero no se preocupe, yo le enseñaré cómo se hace. Esta vez Ud. no va a comprar nada; dígame lo que quiere comprar y yo se lo compro.

—Muy bien, entonces; aquí tengo la lista y mejor se la doy ahora. Y si quiere, nos vamos, yo ya estoy lista. ¿Vamos a pie?

—No, porque está bastante lejos de aquí. Yo llamé un taxi y, a propósito, creo que ya está aquí—dijo Marta, mirando por la ventana de la sala—sí, ahí está. El taxi nos deja a la entrada de la parte antigua y de ahí tenemos que ir a pie hasta el mercado porque las calles son muy estrechas y los carros no pueden pasar.

Las dos señoras subieron al taxi y veinte minutos después estaban allá.

27.42   Response drill

  1 ¿A qué parte de la ciudad van a ir las dos señoras?

  2 ¿Por qué van a ir allí?

  3 ¿Ha estado la Sra. de Robinson en ese sector?

  4 ¿Qué aspecto tiene el edificio del mercado?

  5 ¿Qué hay que tener para saber comprar barato en ese mercado?

  6 ¿Es la Sra. de Fuentes experta en compras?

  7 Si en un puesto venden huevos a tres pesos la docena, ¿qué le dice ella al hombre que los vende?

  8 ¿En cuánto termina dándoselos por fin?

  9 ¿Por qué no se puede usar esa técnica en los Estados Unidos?

  10 ¿A quién pertenecen generalmente los grandes mercados en los Estados Unidos?

  11 ¿Por qué tiene Virginia que acostumbrarse a seguir la técnica de Marta?

  12 ¿Quién le va a hacer las compras a Virginia esta vez?

  13 ¿Por qué no van a ir a pie hasta el mercado?

  14 ¿Hasta dónde las puede dejar el taxi?

  15 ¿Por qué no pueden llegar en el taxi hasta el mercado?

27.64   jacobeligoodsons.com For Free Audio   SESENTA Y CUATRO

SPOKEN SPANISH   UNIT 28

28.1   BASIC SENTENCES.   At the golf course.

        Molina and White happen to meet Colonel Harris at the golf course.

ENGLISH SPELLING   AID TO LISTENING   SPANISH SPELLING

        the boy   èl-múchachô↓   el muchacho

        early rising   mádrúgádór↓   madrugador

Harris   Harris
Hi, lads! You're up mighty early! (1)   ólá|múchachôs↓ ké|mádrúgádórès↓   ¡Hola, muchachos! ¡Qué madrugadores!

Molina, I didn't know you played golf.   mòliná↓ nósabiá|kèustédhùgábàgólf↓   Molina, no sabía que usted jugaba golf.

        to commit oneself, obligate oneself kòmpròmétersè↓   comprometerse

Molina   Molina
I don't play. But White has promised to teach   nóhwégò↓ péróhwáyt|sèákòmpròmétidò| No juego. Pero White se ha comprometido
me.   áensenyármè↓   a enseñarme.

        the player   èl-húgàdór↓   el jugador

Harris   Harris
Ah! He's a fine player.   á↓ él|ésúmbwenhúgadór↓   ¡Ah! El es un buen jugador.

        to stop, to leave off   déhar-dè↓   dejar de

        stop joking   dehese-de-brómàs↓   déjese de bromas

UNO   jacobeligoodsons.com For Free Audio   28.1

UNIT 28   SPOKEN SPANISH

White
Stop pulling my leg, colonel. With you I always lose.

dehèsêḋébrómáz |kòrònél↓ kònústeḋ↑
syemprepyérḋò↓

White
Déjese de bromas, coronel. Con usted siempre pierdo.

Harris
Hadn't you been here before, Molina?

nọ̀àbịạestàḋọakí |antez |mòlínà |

Harris
¿No había estado aquí antes, Molina?

the club

èl—klúḃ↓

el club

Molina
Yes, in the club. At several evening parties. (2)

ènẹ̀lklúḃ |sí↓ èmbaryasfyestàzḋenóché↓

Molina
En el club, sí. En varias fiestas de noche.

the course, field

èl—kampò↓

el campo

Harris
Hadn't you seen the course? (3)

èlkampò↓ nólọàbíàbistò↑

Harris
El campo, ¿no lo había visto?

Molina
No, and it's worth the trouble seeing it.

nó↓ ibalelapéna |bérlò↓

Molina
No, y vale la pena verlo.

beautiful

èrmosò↓

hermoso

the grass

èl—ṣespèḋ↓

el césped

to care for

kwiḋár↓

cuidar

It's very beautiful, and they take good care of the grass.

èzmuyermósò |ḷèlṣespèḋ↑èsta |múybyeŋkwiḋáḋò↓

Es muy hermoso y el césped está muy bien cuidado.

Harris
They sure do.

ézberḋáḋ↓

Harris
Es verdad.

SPOKEN SPANISH   UNIT 28

than	keˊ↓	que
the hole	èl—oyòˊ↓	el hoyo
Well, I'll leave you now. I'm only going to play nine holes.	bwenóˊ↓ lózdehòˊ↓ nóboyahugaˊr |máskènwebè óyòsˊ↓	Bueno, los dejo. No voy a jugar más que nueve hoyos.
to leave, go away	márcharsèˊ↓	marcharse
I have to leave early.	téngokemárcharme|tempránòˊ↓	Tengo que marcharme temprano.
that (she) remember (to remember)	kè—rrékwerdèˊ↓ rrékòrdáˊr↓	que recuerde (recordar)
the tennis	èl—tenisˊ↓	el tenis

Molina
Please tell your wife to remember the tennis date with Carmen.

pòrfabóˊr↓ digalè \|àsyèsposàˊtkèrrékwerdè \| lódèltenis \|kòŋkármènˊ↓

Molina
Por favor. Dígale a su esposa que recuerde lo del tenis con Carmen.

Harris
Of course. Glad to.

komonóˊ↓ kònmuchogústòˊ↓

Harris
Cómo no. Con mucho gusto.

that to you (it) go (to go)	kè—léz—bayàˊ↓ íˊr↓	que les vaya (ir)

Take it easy, gentlemen.

kèlézbayabyén \|sèŋyórèsˊ↓

Que les vaya bien, señores.

28.10 Notes on the basic sentences

  (1) /madrugadór/ *madrugador* is an adjective meaning literally 'dawn-rising.' In this sentence it is nominalized, literally 'What dawn-rising (characters you are).'

  (2) It was remarked in an earlier note that the correspondence between Spanish prepositions and English prepositions is not very considerable. Here is an instance of *en* meaning 'at,' a rather common correspondence.

TRES   28.3

UNIT 28   SPOKEN SPANISH

(3) The word order of this Spanish sentence seems quite dramatic, indeed even exaggerated, if translate literally into English: 'The field, hadn't you seen it?'
Such inversion is, however, quite frequent and not particularly emphatic in Spanish.

28.2   DRILLS AND GRAMMAR

28.21   Pattern drills

28.21.1   Indirect command forms — regular and irregular

    A. Presentation of pattern

                                              ILLUSTRATIONS

Hope you rent the house.   1. keálkilezlakásá↓   Que *alquiles* la casa.

Hope you sell the car.   2. kébendaselkárrò↓   Que *vendas* el carro.

Don't let Mary talk English.   3. kémária|noablęinglés↓   Que María no *hable* inglés.

Have them take my clothes to the cleaners. 4. kéOyeben|mirropalatintorería↓   Que *lleven* mi ropa a la tintorería.

Have the gentleman come up.   5. késubạelseņyór↓   Que *suba* el señor.

Don't let them open the books.   6. kénọabranlozlíbròs↓   Que no *abran* los libros.

Hope you get everything soon.   7. kérrệsiba|todoprôntô↓   Que *reciba* todo pronto.

Let the girls go out.   8. késalganlazmucháchàs↓   Que *salgan* las muchachas.

28.4   CUATRO

SPOKEN SPANISH   UNIT 28

And may it be worth while.   9. ikébalgalapéná↓   Y que *valga* la pena.

Make him tell the truth.   10. kédigalaberdád↓   Que *diga* la verdad.

Hope it's the last time.   11. kèséa|laụltimabéș↓   Que *sea* la última vez.

——————————————   12. kèlézbayabyén|sèŋyórès↓   Que les *vaya* bien, señores.

EXTRAPOLATION

	sg		pl	
	‑ár	‑ér‑ír	‑ár	‑ér‑ír
2 fam	‑es	‑as		
2 ‑ 3	‑e	‑a	‑en	‑an

NOTES

a. Indirect command forms for all second and third person forms are
    identical with (negative) direct command forms.

b. In function, they differ by the placement of /ke/ before the verb
    (and subject), and they either express instructions to be carried
    out by a person not present or a hope that a stated desire may be
    fulfilled for someone (whether present or not).

CINCO   28.5

UNIT 26   SPOKEN SPANISH

28.21.11 Substitution drills — Tense substitution — 3rd person

        Problem 1:
                ána │ lábalarrópá↓

        Answer:
                kélábelarrópá↓

        Problem 2:
                ánǎilwísa │ límpyanlakásǎ↓

        Answer:
                kélímpyenlakásǎ↓

_____

        Problem 1:
                Ana *lava* la ropa.

        Answer:
                Que lave la ropa.

        Problem 2:
                Ana y Luisa *limpian* la casa.

        Answer:
                Que limpien la casa.

28.6   jacobeligoodsons.com For Free Audio   SEIS

SPOKEN SPANISH   UNIT 28

1. hôsé |komprálaşerbéşà↓   kèkomprelaşerbéşà↓

2. anąımarią |ablanespaŋyól↓   kęablenespaŋyól↓

3. hwan |trȧbahaí↓   kȅtrȧbahęaí↓

4. lóznıŋyoz |nokoméntárdè↓   kȅnokomántárdè↓

5. lwisa |barrelasálà↓   kȅbarralasálà↓

6. éltènyénte |bendelkárrò↓   kȅbendąelkárrò↓

7. lósęstúdyántez |noęskríbenąkí↓   kȅnoęskríbanąkí↓

---

1 José *compra* la cerveza.   Que compre la cerveza.
2 Ana y María *hablan* español.   Que hablen español.
3 Juan *trabaja* ahi.   Que trabaje ahi.
4 Los niños no *comen* tarde.   Que no coman tarde.
5 Luisa *barre* la sala.   Que barra la sala.
6 El teniente *vende* el carro.   Que venda el carro.
7 Los estudiantes no *escriben* aquí.   Que no escriban aquí.

SIETE   jacobeligoodsons.com For Free Audio   28.7

UNIT 28   SPOKEN SPANISH

8. karlos│tráduşelalekşyón↓   kètráduşka│lalekşyón↓

9. àntonyoana│nopide(n)náđà↓   kènopida(n)náđà↓

10. marta│nodişésò↓   kènođigaésò↓

11. pabloantonyo│traenelkóchè↓   kètrayganelkóchè↓

12. mària│byengalazdós↓   kèbengalazdós↓

13. martailwisa│aşenelpóstrè↓   kèaganelpóstrè↓

_____

8 Carlos *traduce* la lección.   Que traduzca la lección.

9 Antonio y Ana no *piden* nada.   Que no pidan nada.

10 Marta no *dice* eso.   Que no diga eso.

11 Pablo y Antonio *traen* el coche.   Que traigan el coche.

12 María *viene* a las dos.   Que venga a las dos.

13 Marta y Luisa *hacen* el postre.   Que hagan el postre.

28.8   OCHO

SPOKEN SPANISH   UNIT 28

Tense substitution -- 2nd person

Problem 1:

        ûsteđ |bárrelakásá↓

Answer:

        kébarralakásá↓

Problem 2:

        tú |bárrezlakásá↓

Answer:

        kébarrazlakásá↓

_____

Problem 1:
        Ud. *barre* la casa.

Answer:
        Que barra la casa.

Problem 2:
        Tú *barres* la casa.

Answer:
        Que barras la casa.

NUEVE   28.9

UNIT 28   SPOKEN SPANISH

1. ústed |abrelazmalétàs↓   kǫabralazmalétàs↓

2. ústed |subelozbaúlès↓   késubalozbaúlès↓

3. ústedes |traenḁlkóchè↓   kètraygaṇḁlkóchè↓

4. ústedes |komenḁnḁlpátyò↓   kèkoman |enḁlpátyò↓

5. ústed |èskribelakártà↓   kèskribalakártà↓

6. tú |abrezlazmalétàs↓   kǫabrazlazmalétàs↓

7. tú |subezlozbaúlès↓   kèᵒubazlozbaúlès↓

---

1 Ud. *abre* las maletas.   Que abra las maletas.

2 Ud. *sube* los baúles.   Que suba los baúles.

3 Uds. *traen* el coche.   Que traigan el coche.

4 Uds. *comen* en el patio.   Que coman en el patio.

5 Ud. *escribe* la carta.   Que escriba la carta.

6 Tú *abres* las maletas.   Que abras las maletas.

7 Tú *subes* los baúles.   Que subas los baúles.

28.10   DIEZ

SPOKEN SPANISH   UNIT 28

8. tú |traeselkóchè↓   kètráygaselkóchè↓

9. tukomes |enelpátyò↓   kèkomas |enelpátyò↓

10. tueskribez |lakártà↓   kèskribaz |lakártà↓

11. tukompraz |laskokakólàs↓   kèkomprez |laskokakólàs↓

12. tutraduşez |lalekşyón↓   kètráduşkaz |lalekşyón↓

13. tubas |almerkáďò↓   kèbayas |almerkáďò↓

14. tulimpyaz |lamésà↓   kèlimpyez |lamésà↓

15. tú |noestudyaz |lo(s)sábàďòs↓   kènoestudyez |lo(s)sábàďòs↓

---

8 Tú *traes* el coche.   Que traigas el coche.

9 Tú *comes* en el patio.   Que comas en el patio.

10 Tú *escribes* la carta.   Que escribas la carta.

11 Tú *compras* las coca-colas.   Que compres las coca-colas.

12 Tú *traduces* la lección.   Que traduzcas la lección.

13 Tú *vas* al mercado.   Que vayas al mercado.

14 Tú *limpias* la mesa.   Que limpies la mesa.

15 Tú no *estudias* los sábados.   Que no estudies los sábados.

ONCE   28.11

UNIT 28   SPOKEN SPANISH

Construction substitution

Problem 1:

    keana│limpyelozmwébles↓

Answer:

    aná↓ limpyelozmwébles↓

Problem 2:

    kélwis│trabahestatárde↓

Answer:

    lwís↓ trabahaestatárde↓

_____

Problem 1:
        Que Ana *limpie* los muebles.

Answer:
        Ana, limpie los muebles.

Problem 2:
        Que Luis *trabaje* esta tarde.

Answer:
        Luis, trabaja esta tarde.

28.12   jacobeligoodsons.com For Free Audio   DOCE

SPOKEN SPANISH   UNIT 28

1. kęáli̧yạ |áblen̦espan̦yól↓   àlisyà↓ áblen̦espan̦yól↓

2. kėkarmen |eskríbalakártȧ↓   karmèn↓ èskríbalakártȧ↓

3. kėkárlos |subạesebaúl↓   karlòs↓ subạesebaúl↓

4. kęántonyo |bahelazmalétȧs↓   àntónyò↓ bahelazmalétȧs↓

5. kėmåria |ben̦gaman̦yánȧ↓   màriȧ↓ ben̦gaman̦yánȧ↓

6. kėlwis |estu̧dyęaórȧ↓   lwís↓ èstu̧dyęaórȧ↓

7. kėrrosa |traygạelkafé↓   rrosȧ↓ traygạelkafé↓

8. kėhóse |komamás↓   hòsé↓ kómemás↓

───

1 Que Alicia *hable* en español.   Alicia, hable en español.

2 Que Carmen *escriba* la carta.   Carmen, escriba la carta.

3 Que Carlos *suba* ese baúl.   Carlos, suba ese baúl.

4 Que Antonio *baje* las maletas.   Antonio, baje las maletas.

5 Que María *venga* mañana.   María, venga mañana.

6 Que Luis *estudie* ahora.   Luis, estudíe ahora.

7 Que Rosa *traiga* el café.   Rosa, traiga el café.

8 Que José *coma* más.   José, come más.

TRECE

UNIT 28   SPOKEN SPANISH

9. kèkarloz |beŋgatempránò↓   karlós↓ bentempránò↓

10. kẹàliṣyạ |estuḍyemás↓   àliṣyà↓ èstuḍyamás↓

11. kẹ̀anạ |abrạẹⓁlíbrò↓   anà↓ abreⓁlíbrò↓

12. kèlwiz |bendạẹlawtobyéhò↓   lwís↓ bendelawtobyéhò↓

13. kéhòsé |bebabínò↓   hòsé↓ bebebínò↓

14. kèmária |komprẹótrobestíơò↓   màrià↓ komprạótrobestíơò↓

15. kèlwisa |Ⓛyamẹalozmolínà↓   lwìsà↓ Ⓛyamalozmolínà↓

---

9 Que Carlos *venga* temprano.   Carlos, ven temprano.

10 Que Alicia *estudie* más.   Alicia, *estudia más.*

11 Que Ana *abra* el libro.   Ana, abre el libro.

12 Que Luis *venda* el auto viejo.   Luis, vende el auto viejo.

13 Que José *beba* vino.   José, bebe vino.

14 Que María *compre* otro vestido.   María, compra otro vestido.

15 Que Luisa *llame* a los Molina.   Luisa, llama a los Molina.

28.14   CATORCE

SPOKEN SPANISH   UNIT 28

Number substitution

1. kẹabralozbaúlès↓   kẹabranlozbaúlès↓

2. kènọẹstudyen │lozdomíngòs↓   kènọẹstudye │lozdomíngòs↓

3. kẹablekonẹlhéfè↓   kẹablenkonẹlhéfè↓

4. kẹimbitẹalkoronél↓   kẹimbiten │alkoronél↓

5. kènobeban │mazléchè↓   kènobeba │mazléchè↓

6. kèskribalakártà↓   kèskriban │lakártà↓

7. kènopoŋgan │là(s)siɱyasẹnẹlkwártò↓   kènopoŋga │là(s)siɱyasẹnẹlkwárto↓

8. kèden │larropabyéhà↓   kèdelarropabyéhà↓

9. kèbayamísà↓   kèbayanamísà↓

10. kèstenakì │ẹnlanóchè↓   kèsteạkì │ẹnlanóchè↓

11. kèsea │menozrrigurósò↓   kèsean │menozrrigurósòs↓

---

1 Que *abra* los baúles.   Que abran los baúles.

2 Que no *estudien* los domingos.   Que no estudie los domingos.

3 Que *hable* con el jefe.   Que hablen con el jefe.

4 Que *invite* al coronel.   Que inviten al coronel.

5 Que no *beban* más leche.   Que no beba más leche.

6 Que *escriba* la carta.   Que escriban la carta.

7 Que no *pongan* las sillas en el cuarto.   Que no ponga las sillas en el cuarto.

8 Que *den* la ropa vieja.   Que de la ropa vieja.

9 Que *vaya* a misa.   Que vayan a misa.

10 Que *estén* aquí en la noche.   Que esté aquí en la noche.

11 Que *sea* menos riguroso.   Que sean menos rigurosos.

QUINCE   28.15

UNIT 28

SPOKEN SPANISH

28.21.12 Translation drill

1 Have Louise sweep the bedrooms.	kélwísa |bárralozdormitóryòs↓	Que Luisa barra los dormitorios.
2 Have Ana wash the cups.	keana |labelastáşàs↓	Que Ana lave las tazas.
3 Have Ana bring the children.	keana |traygalozníŋyòs↓	Que Ana traiga a los niños.
4 Let Ana and Martha wait here.	keanaimartạ |espérenakí↓	Que Ana y Marta esperen aquí.
5 Let her get the meal.	keeỌyạ |agalakomídà↓	Que ella haga la comida.
6 May they come right away.	kébeŋgan |ensegídà↓	Que vengan en seguida.
7 (See that) you clean the desk.	keustéd |limpyeleskritóryó↓	Que Ud. limpie el escritorio.
8 (See that) you don't talk so much English.	keustéd |ŋọable |tantọiŋglés↓	Que Ud. no hable tanto inglés.
9 (See that) you all get the meal this afternoon.	keustédes |aganlakomídạ |éstâtárdé↓	Que Uds. hagan la comida esta tarde.
10 (See that) you buy the bread and butter.	keustédes |komprenẹlpán |ilâmântékiỌyà↓	Que Uds. compren el pan y la mantequilla.
11 (See that) you work tomorrow too.	keustédes |tràbahenmaŋyánà |tâmbyén↓	Que Uds. trabajen mañana también.
12 (See that) you come too, Alice.	kébeŋgas |tutambyén |álişyà↓	Que vengas tú también, Alicia.
13 (See that) you don't get dinner today, Mary.	kéŋọagaskomídạ |óy |máríà↓	Que no hagas comida hoy, María.

28.16

DIECISEIS

SPOKEN SPANISH

UNIT 28

14 (I hope) you make out OK, Joseph.

ké tèbayabyéŋ |hòsé↓

Que te vaya bien, José.

15 (I hope) you learn enough, Carmen.

kęåprendazbastántè |kårmèn↓

Que aprendas bastante, Carmen.

B. Discussion of pattern

Indirect commands in Spanish can often be translated more or less literally into English by an expression with 'may': /ke⸗le⸗báya⸗byén↓/ 'may it go well with you (him).' This hope could be expressed more informally as 'I hope you make out OK,' which does not at all correlate structurally with the Spanish construction.

A more frequent correlation of meaning is with an English construction using 'let' or 'have': /ke⸗éntre↓/ 'Have him come in,' /ke⸗lo⸗ɑ̨ɣébe |entónꜱes↓/ 'Let him take it, then.' In English this is a direct command to one person giving instructions to another person. The Spanish indirect command, as this rubric implies, indirectly gives instructions to a person not present (and therefore a person that cannot be directly addressed), or expresses a hope. This hope might be directed in second or even in first person if the fulfillment is imminent, as /ke⸗gáne↓ke⸗gáne↓/ 'I hope I win, I hope I win.'

Indirect command constructions are actually another function of the same forms given for negative direct commands, and show, therefore, the same stem irregularities.

In a chant, the usual introductory /ke⸗/ may be omitted; thus: /bíba⸗el⸗koronél⸗hárrıs↓/ 'Long live colonel Harris!'

28.21.2 Hortatory command forms

A. Presentation of pattern

ILLUSTRATIONS

Let's sign the documents.

1. firmémoz |lozɗokuméntòs↓

Firmemos los documentos.

Let's use tú forms.

2. tràtémonozɗetú↓

Tratémonos de tú.

Let's eat in a restaurant.

3. kòmamos |enʉnrrestorán↓

Comamos en un restorán.

DIECISIETE

28.17

UNIT 28   SPOKEN SPANISH

_____   4. bèamoselmenú↓   *Veamos* el menú.

Let's go up now.   5. súbamosaórà↓   *Subamos* ahora.

Let's translate the letter.   6. tràdúṣkamozlakártà↓   *Traduzcamos* la carta.

Let's put the coffee on.   7. pòngamoselkafé↓   *Pongamos* el café.

Let's tell the truth.   8. digamozlaberdád↓   *Digamos* la verdad.

      let's sleep (to sleep)   dúrmamòs↓ dòrmír↓   durmamos (dormir)

Let's sleep another hour.   9. dúrmamos|unaoramás↓   *Durmamos* una hora más.

Let's not feel so sorry about it.   10. nolosintamostántò↓   No lo *sintamos* tanto.

Let's keep on with the same lesson. 11. siqamos|kònlàmizmaleksyón↓   *Sigamos* con la misma leccion.

EXTRAPOLATION

		Affirmative	Negative
		—ár —ér—ír	
	form	—émos —ámos	
(1 pl) Hortatory			
	construction	/bámos—a___'r/	xxxx

NOTES

a. Hortatory means exhorting; these expressions are usually translated by the English equivalent 'Let's....'

b. Hortatory forms are like formal command forms, with the 1 pl person-number ending /—mos/ occurring.

c. The hortatory construction /bámos—a—(infinitive)/ usually occurs with this meaning only in affirmative utterances.

d. Clitic pronouns follow affirmative hortatory forms (final /—s/ drops before /n/ : /sentémonos/), but precede negative hortatory forms.

SPOKEN SPANISH   UNIT 28

28.21.21 Substitution drills — Tense substitution

1. kántamos |enespaŋyól↓   kántemos |enespaŋyól↓

2. trábáhamos |ochóràs↓   trábáhemos |ochóràs↓

3. limpyamoz |la(s)siǫyàs↓   limpyémoz |la(s)siǫyàs↓

4. nopraktikamos |eliŋglés↓   nopraktikémos |eliŋglés↓

5. nokreemoznáđà↓   nokreamoznáđà↓

6. kòmemos |enlakásà↓   kòmamos |enlakásà↓

7. bàrremos |todalakásà↓   bàrramos |todalakásà↓

8. béndemoz |lozmwéblès↓   bèndamoz |lozmwéblès↓

_____

1 *Contamos* en español.   Cantemos en español.

2 *Trabajamos* ocho horas.   Trabajemos ocho horas.

3 *Limpiamos* las sillas.   Limpiemos las sillas.

4 No *practicamos* el inglés.   No practiquemos el inglés.

5 No *creemos* nada.   No creamos nada.

6 *Comemos* en la casa.   Comamos en la casa.

7 *Barremos* toda la casa.   Barramos toda la casa.

8 *Vendemos* los muebles.   Vendamos los muebles.

DIECINUEVE   28.19

UNIT 28   SPOKEN SPANISH

9. ábrimoz|lozlíbròs↓   ábramoz|lozlíbròs↓

10. éskríbimospókò↓   éskríbamospókò↓

11. tráɗúṣimoz|lalekṣyón↓   tráɗúṣkamoz|lalekṣyón↓

12. nopeɗimoznáɗà↓   nopíɗamoznáɗà↓

13. nóɗeṣimoṣésò↓   nóɗigamoṣésò↓

14. tráemoz|lozlíbròs↓   tráygamoz|lozlíbròs↓

15. bénimoṣentáksi↓   béŋgamos|entáksi↓

16. áṣemoz|lakomíɗà↓   àgamoz|lakomíɗà↓

17. éstamosakí|àḷaunà↓   éstemosakí|àḷaunà↓

_____

9 *Abrimos* los libros.   Abramos los libros.

10 *Escribimos* poco.   Escribamos poco.

11 *Traducimos* la lección.   Traduzcamos la lección.

12 No *pedimos* nada.   No pidamos nada.

13 No *decimos* eso.   No digamos eso.

14 *Traemos* los libros.   Traigamos los libros.

15 *Venimos* en taxi.   Vengamos en taxi.

16 *Hacemos* la comida.   Hagamos la comida.

17 *Estamos* aquí a la una.   Estemos aquí a la una.

28.20   VEINTE

SPOKEN SPANISH   UNIT 28

Person-number substitution

Problem:

álkiléusteđ |lakásá↓

_____ nòsótroz_____

Answer:

álkilémoz |nòsótroz |lakásá↓

1. ábléusteđ |konelhéfé↓

_____ nòsótros_____   áblémoz |nòsótros |konelhéfé↓

2. imbítéusteđ |alkoronél↓

_____ nòsótros_____   imbítémoz |nòsótros |alkoronél↓

_____

Problem:
    Alquile Ud. la casa.
    _____ nosotros_____.

Answer:
    Alquilemos nosotros la casa.

    1 Hable Ud. con el jefe.
       _____ nosotros_____.   Hablemos nosotros con el jefe.

    2 Invite Ud. al coronel.
       _____ nosotros_____.   Invitemos nosotros al coronel.

VEINTIUNO   28.21

UNIT 28   SPOKEN SPANISH

3. kómąustéđ |aórà↓
   _____nòsótros_____   kòmámoz |nòsótros |aórà↓

4. ábrąustéđ |lozbaúlès↓
   _____nósótroz_____   ábrámoz |nòsótroz |lozbaúlès↓

5. póŋgąustéđ |làmàlétaí↓
   _____nósótroz_____   pòŋgámoz |nòsótroz |làmàlétaí↓

6. deųstéđ |lapropínà↓
   _____nósótroz_____   démoz |nòsótroz |lapropínà↓

7. noséąustéđ |ta(n)nerbyósò↓
   _____nòsótros_____   noseámoz |nòsótros |ta(n)nerbyósòs↓

_____

3 Coma Ud. ahora.
  _____nosotros_____   Comamos nosotros ahora.

4 Abra Ud. los baúles.
  _____nosotros_____   Abramos nosotros los baúles.

5 Ponga Ud. la maleta ahí.
  _____nosotros_____   Pongamos nosotros la maleta ahí.

6 De Ud. la propina.
  _____nosotros_____   Demos nosotros la propina.

7 No sea Ud. tan nervioso.
  _____nosotros_____   No seamos nosotros tan nerviosos.

28.22   VEINTIDOS

SPOKEN SPANISH   UNIT 28

Construction substitution

Problem:

bámos |alkilár |unapartaméntô↓

Answer:

álkilémos |unapartaméntô↓

1 bámos |aestuɗyár |aórà↓   èstúɗyémòs |aórà↓

2 bámos |abuskárkásà↓   búskémoskásà↓

3 bámos |akómprármwéblès↓   kómprémozmwéblès↓

4 bámos |ablár |konálgyèn↓   áblémoskonálgyèn↓

_____

Problem:
    Vamos a alquilar un apartamento.

Answer:
    Alquilemos un apartamento.

    1 Vamos a estudiar ahora.   Estudiemos ahora.
    2 Vamos a buscar casa.   Busquemos casa.
    3 Vamos a comprar muebles.   Compremos muebles.
    4 Vamos a hablar con alguien.   Hablemos con alguien.

VEINTITRES   jacobeligoodsons.com For Free Audio   28.23

UNIT 28   SPOKEN SPANISH

5 bámos|abarrér|labitaşyón↓   bárramoz labitaşyón↓

6 bámos|akomeráí↓   kòmamos̩aí↓

7 bámos|aẹskribír|enẹspaŋyól↓   èskribamos|enẹspaŋyól↓

8 bámos|asubír|enẹlas(ş)ensór↓   sùbamos|enẹlas(ş)ensór↓

9 bámos|àténerunafyéstå↓   téŋgamosụnafyéstå↓

10 bámos|ọóires̩apyéşå↓   òygamos̩es̩apyéşå↓

11 bámos|àbénirmaŋyáná↓   béŋgamozmaŋyáná↓

12 bámos|àşerlo(s)sáŋwichès↓   àgamoz lo(s)sáŋwichès↓

13 bámos|àtràeralozníŋyòs↓   tráygamos̩alozníŋyòs↓

---

5 Vamos a barrer la habitación.   Barramos la habitación.

6 Vamos a comer ahí.   Comamos ahí.

7 Vamos a escribir en español.   Escribamos en español.

8 Vamos a subir en el ascensor.   Subamos en el ascensor.

9 Vamos a tener una fiesta.   Tengamos una fiesta.

10 Vamos a oír esa pieza.   Oigamos esa pieza.

11 Vamos a venir mañana.   Vengamos mañana.

12 Vamos a hacer los sándwiches.   Hagamos los sándwiches.

13 Vamos a traer a los niños.   Traigamos a los niños.

jacobeligoodsons.com For Free Audio

SPOKEN SPANISH

UNIT 28

28.21.22 Response drill

	1.	éstúdyamos↑ablámòs↓	éstúdyemòs↓
	2.	kòmemos↑obebémòs↓	kòmamòs↓
	3.	limpyamos↑obarrémòs↓	limpyemòs↓
[àki↓]	4.	dondekomémòs↓	kòmamos̩aki↓
[làbérdàd↓]	5.	kedes̩ímòs↓	dìgamoz laberdàd↓
[làkòmida↓]	6.	keas̩émòs↓	àgamoz lakomída↓
[èlkárrò↓]	7.	ketraémòs↓	tràygamos̩elkárrò↓

---

	1 ¿Estudiamos o hablamos?	Estudiemos.
	2 ¿Comemos o bebemos?	Comamos.
	3 ¿Limpiamos o barremos?	Limpiemos.
(aquí)	4 ¿Dónde comemos?	Comamos aquí.
(la verdad)	5 ¿Qué decimos?	Digamos la verdad.
(la comida)	6 ¿Qué hacemos?	Hagamos la comida.
(el carro)	7 ¿Qué traemos?	Traigamos el carro.

UNIT 28   SPOKEN SPANISH

[màŋyánà↓] 8. kwándobenímòs↓   bèŋgamózmaŋyánà↓

[làkòmíđà↓] 9. tráemoz|laskókakólas↑   nó↓ tráygamoz|làkòmíđà↓

[léchè↓] 10. bèbemoskafé↑   nó↓ bèbámoz|léchè↓

[àkarmén↓] 11. bìsítamosahóse↑   nó↓ bisítemos|àkármèn↓

        12. kántamos|enespaŋyól↑   sì↑|kántemòs↓
        13. sùbìmos|enelas(ş)ensór↑   sì↑|sùbamòs↓
        14. èmpèşamos|aestuđyár↑   sì↑|ǫmpèşémòs↓
        15. àlmòrşamoz|ya↑   sì↑|ạlmòrşémòs↓

(mañana)   8 ¿Cuándo venimos?   Vengamos mañana.

(la comida)   9 ¿Traemos las coca colas?   No, traigamos la comida.
(leche)   10 ¿Bebemos café?   No, bebamos leche.
(a Carmen)   11 ¿Visitamos a José?   No, visitemos a Carmen.

        12 ¿Cantamos en español?   Sí, cantemos.
        13 ¿Subimos en el ascensor?   Sí, subamos.
        14 ¿Empezamos a estudiar?   Sí, empecemos.
        15 ¿Almorzamos ya?   Sí, almorcemos.

SPOKEN SPANISH

UNIT 28

28.21.23 Translation drill

1	Let's clean the table.	límpyémoz lamésà↓	Limpiemos la mesa.
2	Let's help Mary.	àyúdemos,amaríà↓	Ayudemos a María.
3	Let's check the luggage.	rrébisémos |elekipáhè↓	Revisemos el equipaje.
4	Let's never do that.	núŋkạ |agámos,ésò↓	Nunca hagamos eso.
5	Let's ask for the visa.	pídamoz labísà↓	Pidamos la visa.
6	Let's study some more this week.	èstúdyemozmás |éstàsèmánà↓	Estudiemos más esta semana.
7	Let's say everything in Spanish.	dígamos tódọ |enẹspaɲól↓	Digamos todo en español.
8	Let's write the letter.	èskríbamoz |lakártà↓	Escribamos la carta.
9	Let's rent a furnished house.	àlkilémos |únàkasamwebládà↓	Alquilemos una casa amueblada.
10	Let's look for another excuse.	búskemos |otropretéstò↓	Busquemos otro pretexto.
11	Let's not buy antique furniture.	nókómpremoz |mwéblesạntígwòs↓	No compremos muebles antiguos.
12	Let's go down in the elevator.	bàhemos |enẹlas(s)ensór↓	Bajemos en el ascensor.
13	Let's not put anything there.	nópoŋgamoz |nadaí↓	No pongamos nada ahí.

VEINTISIETE

28.27

jacobeligoodsons.com For Free Audio

UNIT 28   SPOKEN SPANISH

14 Let's not bring the children.   nótraygámós|alozníɲyòs↓   No traigamos a los niños.

15 Let's be here with her.   éstemos̩akí|koné()yà↓   Estemos aquí con ella.

B. Discussion of pattern

Hortatory forms are first person plural equivalents of second person direct commands; that is, they are like a direct command given, usually in the form of a suggestion, to a group that includes the speaker. They are usually translated in English by an expression beginning with 'Let's...'

The hortatory form for the verb /ír/ is /bámos/, in affirmative constructions, but the expected form /bayámos/ in negative constructions.

In addition to the hortatory *forms*, there is a hortatory *construction*, consisting of /bámos—a/ plus an infinitive, which is usually used only in affirmative utterances. Actually there is probably a slight difference between the meaning of hortatory forms and that of hortatory constructions, but this does not often affect their distribution:

/bámos—a—komér↓/   'Let's go eat.'   (spoken on the street)

/komámos↓/   'Let's eat.'   (spoken at the table)

There are certain stem irregularities in hortatory forms, mostly corresponding to patterns already presented. These include verbs with /—k—/ or /—g—/ modified stems (such as /traduşkámos, salgámos, traygámos, agámos, digámos/), and most of the verbs previously listed as uniquely irregular (/seámos, sepámos/).

One additional feature of irregularity occurs with some stem vowel changing verbs. In /—ár/ and /—ér/ verbs the hortatory form has the same stem as the infinitive; thus /bolbámos, şerrémos/. With /—ír/ verbs, however, there is a different stem unless the stem vowel change is /e ⟩í/, in which case this change is extended to the hortatory forms. The change is a vowel change, either /o⟩u/ or /e⟩ı/. The pattern of change is as follows:

Infinitive stem	Present tense singular and 2-3 stem	Hortatory stem
o	wé	u
e	yé	ı
e	í	ı

This same pattern illustrated by sample verbs is:

	Infinitive	1 sg present	Hortatory
o ⟩ wé ⟩ u	dorm—ír	dwérm—o	durm—ámos
e ⟩ yé ⟩ i	sent—ír	syént—o	sint—ámos
e ⟩ i	seg—ír	síg—o	sig—ámos

28.28   VEINTIOCHO

jacobeligoodsons.com For Free Audio

SPOKEN SPANISH

UNIT 28

28.22   Replacement drills

A   nósabía|kẹústẹđ|húgabagólf↓

1. _____tántò↓   nósabía|kẹústẹđ|húgabatántò↓

2. _____ênséŋyaba____↓   nósabía|kẹústẹđ|ênséŋyabatántò↓

3. _____espaŋyól↓   nósabía|kẹústẹđ|ênséŋyabạespaŋyól↓

4. _____hóse_____↓   nósabía|kẹhòse|ọnséŋyabạespaŋyól↓

5. _____âblabạ____↓   nósabía|kẹhòse|âblabạespaŋyól↓

6. _____ústẹđes____↓   nósabía|kẹústẹđes|âblabanespaŋyól↓

7. _____êran____↓   nósabía|kẹústẹđes|êranẹspaŋyólès↓

A   No sabía que usted jugaba golf.

1 _____tanto.   No sabía que usted jugaba tanto.

2 _____enseñaba___.   No sabía que usted enseñaba tanto.

3 _____español.   No sabía que usted enseñaba español.

4 _____José_____.   No sabía que José enseñaba español.

5 _____hablaba____.   No sabía que José hablaba español.

6 _____ustedes_____.   No sabía que ustedes hablaban español.

7 _____eran_____.   No sabía que ustedes eran españoles.

VEINTINUEVE

28.29

jacobeligoodsons.com For Free Audio

UNIT 28   SPOKEN SPANISH

B   hwáyt|seákòmpròmètiđọ|aẹnseŋyármè↓

1. ústeđes_____↓   ústeđes|seáŋkòmpròmètiđọ|aẹnseŋyármè↓

2. _____ẹnseŋyárlès↓   ústeđes|seáŋkòmpròmètiđọ|aẹnseŋyárlès↓

3. ____émos_____↓   nòsótroz|nòs,emos|kòmpròmètiđọaẹnseŋyárlès↓

4. _____ír↓   nòsótroz|nòs,emos|kòmpròmètiđọaír↓

5. ____kòmpròmètimos____↓   nòsótroz|nòskòmpròmètimos|aír↓

6. tú_____↓   tú|tèkòmpròmètistẹaír↓

7. _____ẹnseŋyármé↓   tú|tèkòmpròmètistẹ|aẹnseŋyármè↓

B   White se ha comprometido a enseñarme.

1 Ustedes _____ .   Ustedes se han comprometido a enseñarme.

2 _____enseñarles.   Ustedes se han comprometido a enseñarles.

3 ____hemos_____ .   Nosotros nos hemos comprometido a enseñarles.

4 _____ ir.   Nosotros nos hemos comprometido a ir.

5 ____comprometimos_____ .   Nosotros nos comprometimos a ir.

6 Tú _____ .   Tú te comprometiste a ir.

7 _____ enseñarme.   Tú te comprometiste a enseñarme.

28.30   TREINTA

jacobeligoodsons.com For Free Audio

SPOKEN SPANISH   UNIT 28

C   él |ésúmbweɲhugadór↓

1. éʎyos_____↓   éʎyos |sónúnòȥbwenoshugadórès↓

2. _____amígòs↓   éʎyos |sónúnòȥbwénosˌamígòs↓

3. tú_____↓   tú |érèsˌúmbwenˌamígò↓

4. _____mál_____↓   tú |érèsˌúnmalamígò↓

5. éʎyạ_____↓   éʎyạ |èsúnạmalamígà↓

6. _____ótrạ_____↓   éʎyạ |ès̮ótrạmalamígà↓

7. _____hugadórà↓   éʎyạ |ès̮ótrạmalahugadórà↓

_____

C   El es un buen jugador.

1 Ellos_____ .   Ellos son unos buenos jugadores.

2 _____amigos.   Ellos son unos buenos amigos.

3 Tú_____.   Tú eres un buen amigo.

4 _____mal_____.   Tú eres un mal amigo.

5 Ella_____.   Ella es una mala amiga.

6 _____otra_____.   Ella es otra mala amiga.

7 _____jugadora.   Ella es otra mala jugadora.

TREINTA Y UNO   jacobeligoodsons.com For Free Audio   28.31

UNIT 28   SPOKEN SPANISH

D   ėlşėspeḋ↑ėstá |múybyėŋkwiḋáḋó↓

1. __parkes_____↓   lósparkes↑ėstán |múybyėŋkwiḋáḋòs↓

2. _____arregláḋò↓   ėlparke↑ęsta |múybyėn‚arregláḋó↓

3. __niŋyas_____↓   lázniŋyas↑ėstán |múybyėn‚arregláḋàs↓

4. _____bestíḋàs↓   lazniŋyas↑ėstán |múybyėmbestíḋàs↓

5. _____mal_____↓   lázniŋyas↑ėstán |múymalbestíḋàs↓

6. __niŋyo_____↓   ėlniŋyo↑ęsta |múymalbestíḋò↓

7. éstòz_____↓   éstòzniŋyos↑ėstán |múymalbestíḋòs↓

D   El césped está muy bien cuidado.

1 __parques_____.   Los parques están muy bien cuidados.

2 _____arreglado.   El parque está muy bien arreglado.

3 __niñas_____.   Las niñas están muy bien arregladas.

4 _____vestidas.   Las niñas están muy bien vestidas.

5 _____mal_____.   Las niñas están muy mal vestidas.

6 __niño_____.   El niño está muy mal vestido.

7 Estos_____.   Estos niños están muy mal vestidos.

28.32   jacobeligoodsons.com For Free Audio   TREINTA Y DOS

SPOKEN SPANISH   UNIT 28

E   óy |nobóyahúgar |máskènwèbęóyòs↓

1. _____bamos_____↓   óy |nobámos |ähúgar |máskènwèbęóyòs↓

2. _____kęustédès↓   óy |nobámos |ähúgar |maskęustédès↓

3. máɲyaná_____↓   máɲyana |nobámos |ähúgar |maskęustédès↓

4. _____trábáhar_____↓   máɲyana |nobámos |átrábáhar |maskęustédès↓

5. tenemos_____↓   máɲyana |notenémos |kétrábáhar |maskęustédès↓

6. débemos_____↓   máɲyana |nodébemos |trábáhar |maskęustédès↓

7. _____ménos_____↓   máɲyana |nodébemos |trábáhar |menoskęustédès↓

_____

E   Hoy no voy a jugar más que nueve hoyos.

1 _____vamos_____.   Hoy no vamos a jugar más que nueve hoyos.

2 _____que ustedes.   Hoy no vamos a jugar más que ustedes.

3 Mañana_____.   Mañana no vamos a jugar más que ustedes.

4 _____trabajar_____.   Mañana no vamos a trabajar más que ustedes.

5 _____tenemos_____.   Mañana no tenemos que trabajar más que ustedes.

6 _____debemos_____.   Mañana no debemos trabajar más que ustedes.

7 _____menos_____.   Mañana no debemos trabajar menos que ustedes.

TREINTA Y TRES   jacobeligoodsons.com For Free Audio   28.33

UNIT 28   SPOKEN SPANISH

F   téngo |kèmàrchármetempránò↓

1. tyéne _____↓   tyéne |kèmàrcharsetempránò↓

2. _____ensegíđà↓   tyéne |kèmàrcharsẹ |ensegíđà↓

3. _____írnos _____↓   ténemos |kẹirnosẹnsegíđà↓

4. áy_____↓   áykẹirsẹ |ensegíđà↓

5. _____bèstirsẹ_____↓   áy |kèbéstirsẹ |ensegíđà↓

6. téngo_____↓   téngo |kébèstirmẹ |ensegíđà↓

7. _____bàɲyárnos_____↓   ténemos |kèbàɲyárnos |ensegíđà↓

F   Tengo que marcharme temprano.

1 Tiene _____.   Tiene que marcharse temprano.

2 _____ en seguida.   Tiene que marcharse en seguida.

3 _____ irnos _____.   Tenemos que irnos en seguida.

4 Hay_____.   Hay que irse en seguida.

5 _____vestirse _____.   Hay que vestirse en seguida.

6 Tengo _____.   Tengo que vestirme en seguida.

7 _____bañarnos_____.   Tenemos que bañarnos en seguida.

SPOKEN SPANISH   UNIT 28

28.23   Variation drills

A   kemadrugadóres↓   ¡Qué madrugadores!

    1 You sure are crazy!   kelókòs↓   ¡Qué locos!

    2 You sure are lazy!   keflóhòs↓   ¡Qué flojos!

    3 You sure are punctual!   kepuntwálès↓   ¡Qué puntuales!

    4 You sure are strict!   kerrigurósòs↓   ¡Qué rigurosos!

    5 You sure are nervous!   kenerbyósòs↓   ¡Qué nerviosos!

    6 You sure are calm!   ketraŋkílòs↓   ¡Qué tranquilos!

    7 You sure are nice!   keamáblès↓   ¡Qué amables!

B   dehesedebrómàs↓ kónusted|syémprepyérdò↓   Déjese de bromas. Con Ud. siempre pierdo.

    1 Stop joking. I always win with you.   dehesedebrómàs↓ kónusted|syempregánò↓   Déjese de bromas. Con Ud. siempre gano.

    2 Stop joking. I never win with him.   dehesedebrómàs↓ kónel|nuŋkagánò↓   Déjese de bromas. Con él nunca gano.

    3 Stop joking. I never go with him.   dehesedebrómàs↓ kónel|nuŋkabóy↓   Déjese de bromas. Con él nunca voy.

    4 Stop joking. I never dance with her.   dehesedebrómàs↓ kóneOya|nuŋkabáylò↓   Déjese de bromas. Con ella nunca bailo.

TREINTA Y CINCO   28.35

UNIT 28   SPOKEN SPANISH

5 Stop joking. I never go out with her.   dehesedebrómàs↓ kònⱥⱺⱥa̧|nuⱨkasálgò↓   Déjese de bromas. Con ella nunca salgo.

6 Stop joking. I never study with them.   dehesedebrómàs↓ kòneⱥꙨoz|nuⱨkaⱥstúᵭyò↓   Déjese de bromas. Con ellos nunca estudio.

7 Stop joking. I never practice with them.   dehesedebrómàs↓ kòneⱥⱥoz|nuⱨkapraktíkò↓   Déjese de bromas. Con ellos nunca practico.

C   nọábiaⱥstaⱷọaki|àntest   ¿No había estado aquí antes?

1 Hadn't you been there before?   nọábiaⱥstaⱷọaꙨya|àntest   ¿No había estado allá antes?

2 Hadn't you ever been there?   nuⱨkabiaⱥstaⱷọ|aꙨyát   ¿Nunca había estado allá?

3 Hadn't you ever eaten there?   nuⱨkabiakomiⱷọ|aꙨyát   ¿Nunca había comido allá?

4 Hadn't you ever gone out with Mary?   nuⱨkabiasaliⱷọ|konmaríat   ¿Nunca había salido con María?

5 Hadn't you ever danced with Mary?   nuⱨkabiabaylaⱷọ|konmaríat   ¿Nunca había bailado con María?

6 Hadn't you ever lost anything?   nuⱨkabiaperⱷiⱷọ|naⱷat   ¿Nunca había perdido nada?

7 Hadn't you ever won before?   nuⱨkabiaganaⱷọ|àntest   ¿Nunca había ganado antes?

D   èlkampò↓ nólọàbíàbistot   El campo, ¿no lo había visto?

1 Hadn't you seen the park?   èlparkè↓ nólọàbíàbistot   El parque, ¿no lo había visto?

2 Hadn't you seen the church?   lₐiglésyà↓ nólàbíàbistot   La iglesia, ¿no la había visto?

28.36   jacobeligoodsons.com For Free Audio   TREINTA Y SEIS

SPOKEN SPANISH   UNIT 28

3 Hadn't you seen the cathedral?   làkàtèdrál↓ nólábíábìsto↑   La catedral, ¿no la había visto?

4 Hadn't you eaten that (kind of) meat?   èsàkàrnè↓ nólàbíàkòmìdo↑   Esa carne, ¿no la había comido?

5 Hadn't you eaten that (kind of) fruit?   èsàfrutá↓ nólàbíàkòmìdo↑   Esa fruta, ¿no la había comido?

6 Hadn't you eaten that (kind of) fish?   èsèpèskàdò↓ nólọàbíàkòmìdo↑   Ese pescado, ¿no lo había comido?

7 Hadn't you decided on that business (deal)? èsènègosyò↓ nólọàbíàdèsìdìdo↑   Ese negocio, ¿no lo había decidido?

E   nó↓ ìbàlèlàpéna|bérlò↓   No, y vale la pena verlo.

1 No, and it's worth the trouble buying it.   nó↓ ìbàle|làpéna|komprárlò↓   No, y vale la pena comprarlo.

2 No, and it's worth the trouble including it.   nó↓ ìbàlelàpéna|ìŋklwírlò↓   No, y vale la pena incluirlo.

3 No, and it's worth the trouble getting   nó↓ ìbàlelàpéna|konosérlò↓   No, y vale la pena conocerlo.
  acquainted with it.

4 No, and it's worth the trouble collecting it.   nó↓ ìbàlelàpéna|kobrárlò↓   No, y vale la pena cobrarlo.

5 No, and it's worth the trouble having a   nó↓ ìbàlelàpéna|dìbertírsè↓   No, y vale la pena divertirse.
  good time.

TREINTA Y SIETE   28.37

UNIT 28   SPOKEN SPANISH

6 No, and it's not worth the trouble   nó↓ inóbalelapéna |komfundírsé↓   No, y no vale la pena confundirse.
  getting confused.

7 No, and it's not worth the trouble moving.   nó↓ inóbalelapéna |mudársé↓   No, y no vale la pena mudarse.

F   dígalę |àsyèspósa↑kèrrèkwérde |lodelténis↓   Dígale a su esposa que recuerde lo
                                                                              del tenis.

1 Tell your wife to remember about the   dígalę |àsyèspósa↑kèrrèkwérde |lodelmerkádó↓   Dígale a su esposa que recuerde lo
  market.   del mercado.

2 Tell her to clean the house.   dígalę |àe0yà↑kèlímpyelakásà↓   Dígale a ella que limpie la casa.

3 Tell her to go soon.   dígalę |àe0yà↑kèbayaprónto↓   Dígale a ella que vaya pronto.

4 Tell John to finish soon.   dígalę |àhwàn↑kęàkabeprónto↓   Dígale a Juan que acabe pronto.

5 Tell Maria to come tomorrow.   dígalę |àmària↑kèbengamanyáná↓   Dígale a Maria que venga mañana.

6 Tell Louis to bring the prices.   dígalę |àlwis↑kètráygalospréşyòs↓ Dígale a Luis que traiga los precios.

7 Tell Louis to do something.   dígalę |àlwis↑kęagálgò↓   Dígale a Luis que haga algo.

28.38   jacobeligoodsons.com For Free Audio   TREINTA Y OCHO

SPOKEN SPANISH

UNIT 28

28.24   Review drill — Review of past I tense forms

Problem:

nòbátòmárkafé↑

Answer:

yátomé↓

1	nòbaysteď	àęstúďyár↑	yáęstuďyé↓
2	nòbaysteď	àlmòrşar↑	yalmorşé↓
3	nòbaysteď	àkòmprá(r)rrópa↑	yakòmpré↓
4	nòbaysteď	àlímpyár↑	yalìmpyé↓

Problem:

¿No va a tomar café?

Answer:

Ya tomé.

1	¿No va Ud. a estudiar?	Ya estudié.
2	¿No va Ud. a almorzar?	Ya almorcé.
3	¿No va Ud. a comprar ropa?	Ya compré.
4	¿No va Ud. a limpiar?	Ya limpié.

TREINTA Y NUEVE

UNIT 28   SPOKEN SPANISH

5 nòbaʉsteđ|åblár|koŋelhéfe↑   ʏáblé↓

6 nòbáel|åtòmarkafé↑   ʏatomó↓

7 nòbáel|àlmórşar↑   ʏalmorşó↓

8 nòbáel|åkómpra(r)rrópa↑   ʏakompró↓

9 nòbáel|åblár|koŋelhéfe↑   ʏábló↓

10 nòbaŋusteđes|álimpyár↑   ʏálimpyámòs↓

11 nòbaŋusteđes|åkómpra(r)rrópa↑   ʏakomprámòs↓

12 nòbaŋusteđes|åtòmarkafé↑   ʏatomámós↓

13 nòbáneʎyos|àlmórşar↑   ʏálmorşáròn↓

_____

5 ¿No va Ud. a hablar con el jefe?   Ya hablé.

6 ¿No va él a tomar café?   Ya tomó.

7 ¿No va él a almorzar?   Ya almorzó.

8 ¿No va él a comprar ropa?   Ya compró.

9 ¿No va él a hablar con el jefe?   Ya habló.

10 ¿No van Uds. a limpiar?   Ya limpiamos.

11 ¿No van Uds. a comprar ropa?   Ya compramos.

12 ¿No van Uds. a tomar café?   Ya tomamos.

13 ¿No van ellos a almorzar?   Ya almorzaron.

SPOKEN SPANISH   UNIT 28

14 nóbanéčyos |àlimpyár↑   yàlimpyáròn↓
15 nóbanéčyos |àblár |konẹlhéfe↑   yàbláròn↓
16 nóbanéčyos |àkómprá(r)rrópa↑   yàkompráròn↓

17 nóbaysteđ |àkómer↑   yàkomí↓
18 nóbaysteđ |àbèberágwa↑   yàbebí↓
19 nóbaysteđ |aèskríbir↑   yàẹskribí↓
20 nóbaysteđ |àsúbir↑   yàsubí↓
21 nóbael |àkómér↑   yàkomyó↓
22 nóbael |àbèbérágwa↑   yàbebyó↓

_____

14 ¿No van ellos a limpiar?   Ya limpiaron.
15 ¿No van ellos a hablar con el jefe?   Ya hablaron.
16 ¿No van ellos a comprar ropa?   Ya compraron.

17 ¿No va Ud. a comer?   Ya comí.
18 ¿No va Ud. a beber agua?   Ya bebí.
19 ¿No va Ud. a escribir?   Ya escribí.
20 ¿No va Ud. a subir?   Ya subí.
21 ¿No va él a comer?   Ya comió.
22 ¿No va él a beber agua?   Ya bebió.

CUARENTA Y UNO   28.41

UNIT 28   SPOKEN SPANISH

23 nòbael|aèskribir↑   yaeskriby6↓

24 nòbael|àsúbir↑   yasuby6↓

25 nòbanustedes|àkómer↑   yakomímòs↓

26 nòbanustedes|àbèberagwa↑   yabebímòs↓

27 nòbanustedes|aèskribir↑   yaeskribímòs↓

28 nòbanustedes|àsúbir↑   yasubímòs↓

29 nòbaneꞌyos|àkòmer↑   yakomyéròn↓

30 nòbaneꞌyos|àbèberagwa↑   yabebyéròn↓

31 nòbaneꞌyos|aèskribir↑   yaeskribyéròn↓

---

23 ¿No va él a escribir?   Ya escribió.
24 ¿No va él a subir?   Ya subió.
25 ¿No van Uds. a comer?   Ya comimos.
26 ¿No van Uds. a beber agua?   Ya bebimos.
27 ¿No van Uds. a escribir?   Ya escribimos.
28 ¿No van Uds. a subir?   Ya subimos.
29 ¿No van ellos a comer?   Ya comieron.
30 ¿No van ellos a beber agua?   Ya bebieron.
31 ¿No van ellos a escribir?   Ya escribieron.

28.42   CUARENTA Y DOS

SPOKEN SPANISH   UNIT 28

28.3   CONVERSATION STIMULUS

NARRATIVE 1

1 Pedro and Jaime are at the golf course.   pédrọihàymẹ |èstàn |ènẻlkampodẹgólf↓   Pedro y Jaime están en el campo de golf.

2 Pedro sees a friend of his there and   pédrobé |àụnàmígòsuyọ |àλyí↓↓léprèséntaháymẻ↓   Pedro ve a un amigo suyo allí y le presenta
   introduces Jaime to him.   a Jaime.

3 His name is Victor Blanco.   sẻλyama |biktorblánkò↓   Se llama Víctor Blanco.

4 Jaime's last name is Ortiz.   èlàpẻλyido |dèhaymẹ |esọrtíṣ↓   El apellido de Jaime es Ortiz.

5 Pedro tells Victor Jaime is just learning.   pédro |lèdíṣẹabiktor↑kèhaymẹ |èstápenas   Pedro le dice a Víctor que Jaime está
                                                  aprendyéndò↓   apenas aprendiendo.

6 Jaime likes golf, although it's very   àhayme |legustạelgólf↓àwŋkẻlẻkwẻstamúchò↓   A Jaime le gusta el golf, aunque le cuesta
   difficult for him.   mucho.

7 But Pedro has promised to teach him.   péròpédro |sẹákómpròmètidọaẹnsẹŋyárlé↓   Pero Pedro se ha comprometido a enseñarle.

8 Victor tells Jaime not to worry, then.   biktor |lẻdíṣẹàhaymẻ↑kènosepreokúpẹ |èntónṣès↓   Víctor le dice a Jaime que no se preocupe,
                                                                                              entonces.

9 He'll learn soon.   baprendérpróntò↓   Va a aprender pronto.

10 Because Pedro knows a lot about golf.   pórkèpédro |sábèmúchisimó |dẻgólf↓   Porque Pedro sabe muchísimo de golf.

11 Pedro tells Victor to stop joking.   pédro |lèdíṣẹabiktor |kèsèdehedebrómás↓   Pedro le dice a Víctor que se deje de bromas.

CUARENTA Y TRES   28.43

UNIT 28   SPOKEN SPANISH

DIALOG 1

Pedro, dígale a Víctor que le deje presentarle a un amigo, Jaime Ortiz. Que Jaime está aprendiendo a jugar.

déhame |présèntartéaunamígò↓ háyméortís↓
haymé |éstáprèndyendóahugár↓

Pedro: Déjame presentarte a un amigo, Jaime Ortiz. Jaime está aprendiendo a jugar.

Víctor, dígale que mucho gusto y déle su nombre, Víctor Blanco.

muchogústò↓bíktorbláŋkò↓

Víctor: Mucho gusto, Víctor Blanco.

Jaime, dígale que igualmente y repítale su nombre, Jaime Ortiz.

igwalménté↓haymçortís↓

Jaime: Igualmente, Jaime Ortiz.

Víctor, pregúntele a Jaime que qué le parece el golf; si le gusta.

kéleparéçelgólf↓ légustà↑

Víctor: ¿Qué le parece el golf?, ¿le gusta?

Jaime, dígale que sí, aunque le cuesta mucho. Pero que Pedro se ha comprometido a enseñarle.

sí↓áwŋkè |mèkwèstamúchò↓ pérópedro |
sçákòmpròmètidç |àçnsèŋyarmé↓

Jaime: Sí, aunque me cuesta mucho. Pero Pedro se ha comprometido a enseñarme.

Víctor, dígale que entonces no se preocupe. Que pronto va a aprender. Que Pedro sabe muchísimo de golf.

éntonçez |nosepreokúpè↓ prontobaprendér↓
pedro |sábèmùchisimò |dègólf↓

Víctor: Entonces no se preocupe. Pronto va a aprender. Pedro sabe muchísimo de golf.

Pedro, dígale a Víctor que se deje de bromas.

déhatedebrómáz |bíktór↓

Pedro: Déjate de bromas, Víctor.

NARRATIVE 2

1 It's obvious that a lot of people like golf.

sèbèkelgólf |légustą |àmuchahéntè↓

Se ve que el golf le gusta a mucha gente.

2 The course is full.

èlkampo |çstáũyenò↓

El campo está lleno.

3 It's a great game, particularly for businessmen.

èsúŋgrandepórtç↓énèspéçyal |pàrą
ombrezdenegóçyòs↓

Es un gran deporte, en especial para hombres de negocios.

28.44   jacobeligoodsons.com For Free Audio   CUARENTA Y CUATRO

SPOKEN SPANISH   UNIT 28

4 Players can be playing and at the same   lòshúgáɗores |pwéɗenǝstárhúgandoↄ   Los jugadores pueden estar jugando y al
   time discussing other subjects.   ⱬàlmɪzmotyempo |kòmbèrsandoɗɛotraskósàsↄ   mismo tiempo conversando de otras cosas.

5 Golf is an excuse for getting together and èlgolf |èsǫmprètesto↑pàràrrèwnírsǝ |à   El golf es un pretexto para reunirse a
   discussing business.   kòmbèrsarɗenegóʂyòsↄ   conversar de negocios.

6 Although most of the time it is just the   áwŋkè |kásisyemprǝ↑èstoɗolokontráryòↄ   Aunque casi siempre es todo lo contrario.
   opposite.

7 Discussing business is an excuse for   kòmbèrsar |ɗenégoʂyost↑èsǫmprètesto | Conversar de negocios es un pretexto para
   playing golf.   pàràhúgargólfↄ   jugar golf.

                                               DIALOG 2

Jaime, dígale a Víctor que se ve que el golf sèbekelgólftlègustǝ |àmuchahéntèↄ   Jaime: Se ve que el golf le gusta a mucha
   le gusta a mucha gente. Que el campo   èlkampo |ǝstáↄⱬenòↄ   gente. El campo está lleno.
   está lleno.

Víctor, dígale que es un gran deporte, en   és |úngrandepórtǝↄènǝspèʂyal |párⱬombrez | Víctor: Es un gran deporte, en especial
   especial para hombres de negocios.   ɗènégoʂyòsↄ   para hombres de negocios.

Jaime, pregúntele que por qué en especial   pòrkénespèʂyal |parⱬombrezɗenegóʂyòsↄ   Jaime: ¿Por qué en especial para hombres
   para hombres de negocios.   de negocios?

Víctor, contéstele que porque los jugadores   pórkèlòshúgáɗores |pwéɗenǝstárhúgandoↄ   Víctor: Porque los jugadores pueden estar
   pueden estar jugando y al mismo tiempo   ⱬàlmɪzmotyempo↑kòmbèrsandoɗɛotraskósàsↄ   jugando y al mismo tiempo con-
   conversando de otras cosas.   versando de otras cosas.

Jaime, dígale que claro, que entonces el   klaroↄ èntónʂes |èlgolf |èsǫmprètestoↄ   Jaime: Claro. Entonces el golf es un
   golf es un pretexto para reunirse a con-   pàràrrèwnírsǝ |àkòmbèrsárɗenègóʂyòsↄ   pretexto para reunirse a conversar
   versar de negocios.   de negocios.

Víctor, dígale que sí, que aunque casi   sí |áwŋkè |kásisyemprǝ |èstoɗo |lòkóntráryòↄ Víctor: Sí, aunque casi siempre es todo lo
   siempre es todo lo contrario.   contrario.

CUARENTA Y CINCO   28.45

UNIT 28   SPOKEN SPANISH

Jaime, dígale que cómo, que no entiende.   komó↓ nóęntyendó↓   Jaime: ¿Cómo? No entiendo.

Victor, explíquele que conversar de negocios   kòmbèrsarđenegóşyos |èşùmprétèstó | Victor: Conversar de negocios es un
es un pretexto para jugar golf.   pàràhúgárgólf↓   pretexto para jugar golf.

                                          NARRATIVE 3

1 'Let's play only nine holes today', says   húgemos |sólónwebęóyòs |óy |đíşèpéđrò↓   Juguemos sólo nueve hoyos hoy —dice
  Pedro.   Pedro.

2 He has to leave early.   tyéne |kèmàrcharsetempránò↓   Tiene que marcharse temprano.

3 'Let's come and play again tomorrow',   bęngamosˌahugar |otrabéẓ |manyáná |đíşè   Vengamos a jugar otra vez mañana —dice
  says Jaime.   háymè↓   Jaime.

4 He wants to learn.   él |kyéręaprendér↓   El quiere aprender.

5 Pedro says he'll call him up at five, then.   pedrodişe |kèlóóˈyamą |àlà(s)şiŋkǫ |èntónşès↓ Pedro dice que lo llama a las cinco, entonces.

6 Because if Jaime wants to learn, he has   pórkèsìhayme |kyéręáprendér↑   Porque si Jaime quiere aprender, tiene que
  to be an early bird.   tyenekeser |mađrugađór↓   ser madrugador.

                                          DIALOG 3

Pedro, dígale a Jaime que jueguen sólo nueve   húgemos |sólónwebęóyòs |óy↓   Pedro: Juguemos sólo nueve hoyos hoy.
hoyos hoy. Que Ud. tiene que marcharse   tęngo |kèmàrcharmetempránò↓   Tengo que marcharme temprano.
temprano.

Jaime, dígale que vengan a jugar otra vez   bęngamosˌahugar |otrabéẓ |mànyáná↓   Jaime: Vengamos a jugar otra vez mañana.
mañana. Que Ud. quiere aprender.   yòkyerǫ |àprêndér↓   Yo quiero aprender.

28.46   jacobeligoodsons.com For Free Audio   CUARENTA Y SEIS

SPOKEN SPANISH   UNIT 28

Pedro, dígale que muy bien. Que Ud. lo   múybyén↓ téꞔyamo│ala(s)ṣíŋkó↓   Pedro: Muy bien. Te llamo a las cinco.
llama a las cinco.

Jaime, pregúntele si está loco, que tan   èstázloko↑ tántèmprano↑   Jaime: ¿Estás loco? ¿Tan temprano?
temprano.

Pedro, dígale que sí, que tiene que ser   sí↓ tyénéskèser│màdrúgàdor│sikyéres   Pedro: Sí, tienes que ser madrugador si
madrugador si quiere aprender.   quieres aprender.
                                              aprendér↓

28.4   READINGS

28.40   List of cognate loan words

            físico   físikò↓

            el contraste   èl—kòntrasté↓

            tradicional   tràdiṣyòná'l↓

            enteras   ènteràs↓

            la variedad   là—báryèdàd↓

            los estilos   lós—èstilòs↓

            arquitectónicos   àrkitèktónikòs↓

            la época   là—epòkà↓

            colonial   kòlònya'l↓

            el núcleo   èl—núklęó↓

            urbano   ûrbanò↓

            adobe   àdobè↓

            las mansiones   làz—mánsyónès↓

CUARENTA Y SIETE   jacobeligoodsons.com For Free Audio   28.47

UNIT 28   SPOKEN SPANISH

aristocráticas	àristòkratikàs↓
la plaza	lá—plaşà↓
las armas	làs—armás↓
el tipo	èl—tipó↓
existe (existir)	èksistè↓ èksistir↓
progresiva	prògrèsibà↓
la industrialización	la̦—indústryàli̦a̦şyoʼn↓
aumentar	àwmèntar↓
la población	là—pòblàşyoʼn↓
las clases	làs—klasès↓
ricas	rrikàs↓
construir	kònstrwir↓
el detalle	èl—dètàn̦yè↓
la aristocracia	la̦—àristòkra̦şyà↓
los vestigios	lóz—bèstihyòs↓
desaparecer	dèsàpàrèşeʼr↓

28.41 Reading selection

Ciudades Latinoamericanas

Observando el aspecto físico de las ciudades latinoamericanas, podemos ver que muchas de ellas presentan un gran contraste de lo viejo con lo nuevo, lo tradicional con lo moderno. En algunas ciudades este contraste es muy claro porque hay allí secciones enteras muy antiguas que todavía están casi igual a como estaban hace muchos años. Estos son los barrios antiguos que encontramos en las ciudades de la América Latina y aun en algunas de los Estados Unidos, tales como Nueva Orleans y Washington.

28.48   jacobeligoodsons.com For Free Audio   CUARENTA Y OCHO

SPOKEN SPANISH   UNIT 28

En el barrio antiguo encontramos una gran variedad de estilos arquitectónicos que va desde el principio de la época colonial hasta el fin de la misma. Este sector representa generalmente el núcleo urbano de otros tiempos. Las calles allí son estrechas y se ven muchísimas casas pequeñas de adobe; pero también existen otros edificios mejores y más grandes que en otros tiempos probablemente fueron mansiones aristocráticas. En el centro del sector se encuentra una plaza generalmente llamada Plaza de Armas. Este tipo de plan urbano todavía existe en muchas de las ciudades pequeñas de la América Latina..

Como resultado de la progresiva industrialización en estos países durante los últimos cincuenta años, al aumentar la población de estos centros urbanos, las nuevas clases ricas buscaron otros sectores donde construir sus casas y poco a poco se formaron nuevos barrios de tipo más moderno.

Pero en algunas ciudades, el sector antiguo, por otras razones que no vamos a explicar ahora para no entrar en mucho detalle, continúa siendo el barrio donde aun viven familias de la antigua aristocracia. En otras, esta parte es ahora un sector comercial. Pero en otros casos, especialmente en las grandes ciudades capitales, quedan apenas algunos vestigios de la parte antigua; y como resultado de construcciones modernas de edificios comerciales y casas de apartamentos, aun estos últimos vestigios tienen que desaparecer algún día.

28.42   Response drill

1 ¿Qué se refleja en el aspecto físico de algunas ciudades latinoamericanas?

2 ¿Por qué es tan claro este contraste en algunas ciudades?

3 ¿Cuál es una ciudad en los Estados Unidos muy conocida por su barrio antiguo?

4 ¿Son estos barrios antiguos solamente de un estilo arquitectónico?

5 ¿Cómo son las calles de esos barrios?

6 ¿Cómo son las casas?

7 ¿Cómo se llamaba generalmente la plaza que está en el centro del barrio?

8 ¿Existe todavía este tipo de plan urbano?

9 ¿Por qué se formaron nuevos barrios de tipo más moderno?

10 ¿Qué hicieron las nuevas clases ricas al aumentar la población?

11 ¿Existen todavía barrios antiguos donde aun viven las familias de la antigua aristocracia?

12 ¿En otros casos, ¿en qué se han convertido esos barrios?

13 ¿Qué ha pasado en otras ciudades?

14 ¿Especialmente en cuáles ciudades ha pasado eso?

15 ¿Por qué hay sólo vestigios del sector antiguo?

CUARENTA Y NUEVE

jacobeligoodsons.com For Free Audio

SPOKEN SPANISH

UNIT 29

29.1   BASIC SENTENCES.   At the tennis court.

    Carmen and Mrs. Harris have just completed a set of tennis.

ENGLISH SPELLING

AID TO LISTENING

SPANISH SPELLING

to congratulate

félișitár↓

felicitar

Mrs. Harris
Congratulations, Carmen. You play very well. [1]

làfélișitó|kármèn↓ hwégàmúybyén↓

Sra. Harris
La felicito Carmen. Juega muy bien.

    the service, serve

èl—sákè↓

    el saque

    very good

bwénìsimò↓

    buenisimo

You've got an exceptional serve.

tyéngùnsake|bwénìsimò↓

Tiene un saque buenisimo.

Carmen
You're very kind, Jean.

ùstéd|èzmúyamáblè|yín↓

Carmen
Usted es muy amable, Jean.

    to handle, to drive (a car)

mànéhár↓

    manejar

    the racquet

là—rràketà↓

    la raqueta

But *you're* the one who can really handle a racquet.

pérólákèmànèha|lárrràketa|múybyén↑èsústéd↓

Pero la que maneja la raqueta muy bien es usted.

    the practice

là—praktikà↓

    la práctica

Mrs. Harris
Nonsense! I need practice. [2]

kèbá↓ mèáșèfalta|práktikà↓

Sra. Harris
¡Que vá! Me hace falta práctica.

UNO

29.1

UNIT 29   SPOKEN SPANISH

from now on, henceforth   dǫ—áki—ęn—adelántě↓   de aqui en adelante

(we) will be able (to be able)   pǒdremòs↓ pǒde'r↓   podremos (poder)

to see ourselves (each other) [3] bérnòs↓   vernos

the court   lå—kanchå↓   la cancha

the frequency   là—frékwenšyå↓   la frecuencia

frequently, often   kòm—frékwenšyå↓   con frecuencia

Carmen   Carmen
From now on, we'll be able to meet on the court   dǫáki|ęnádelantě↑pǒdremozbérnos| De aqui en adelante podremos vernos en la
often, won't we?   énlàkanchà↑kòmfrékwenšyå↓ not   cancha con frecuencia, ¿no?

the maid   là—kryadå↓   la criada

competent   kòmpéténtě↓   competente

difficult   difíšil↓   dificil

Mrs. Harris   Sra. Harris
Yes, because now I've got a very competent maid,   si|pòrkęàora|téŋgǫûnåkryada|muy   Si, porque ahora tengo una criada muy
and it's not so difficult for me.   kompéténtě↓inómes|tandifíšil↓   competente, y no me es tan dificil.

Carmen   Carmen
Shall we come Sunday afternoon?   bénimos|éldòmiŋgo|porlatarde↑   ¿Venimos el domingo por la tarde?

Mrs. Harris   Sra. Harris
It can't be this Sunday.   éstedǫmiŋgo|nòpwedesér↓   Este domingo no puede ser.

the entrance, admission ticket   lą—éntradå↓   la entrada

29.2   jacobeligoodsons.com For Free Audio   DOS

SPOKEN SPANISH   UNIT 29

the bull   él—toró↓   el toro

the bullfights   lòs—toròs↓   los toros

Carmen   *Carmen*
Oh, yes. Jose already bought tickets for the   á|sí↓ yahóse|kómprolasentraɗas|para   ¡Ah, sí! ya José compró las entradas
bullfights.   lostóròs↓   para los toros.

to remain   kèɗarsé↓   quedarse

to miss going   kèɗarse—sin—ír↓   quedarse sin ir

the bullfight   lâ—kòrriɗá↓   la corrida

the world   èl—mundô↓   el mundo

Mrs. Harris   *Sra. Harris*
And I wouldn't miss going to that fight for   iyo|nomekeɗo|sinir|ɡesakorriɗa↑   Y yo no me quedo sin ir a esa corrida
anything in the world.   pòrnaɗaɗelmúndô↓   por nada del mundo.

29.10   Notes on the basic sentences

   (1) It should be noted that the equivalent of English 'Congratulations' is actually 'I congratulate you.'

   (2) Literally, of course, 'Practice is lacking to me.'

   (3) This verb, especially in 1 pl /nos—bémos/ *nos vemos*, is very common as a parting expression. 'I'll be seeing you' or 'We'll be seeing you' is its closest
       equivalent.

TRES   29.3

UNIT 29   SPOKEN SPANISH

29.2   DRILLS AND GRAMMAR

29.21   Pattern drills

29.21.1 Clitic pronouns with command forms

    A. Presentation of pattern

ILLUSTRATIONS

_____	1. syéntésè↓	*Siéntese.*
Don't sit down.	2. nosesyénté↓	*No se siente.*
_____	3. súbamela│despwés↓	*Súbamela después.*
_____	4. noselodiga│amįespósà↓	*No se lo diga a mi esposa.*
_____	5. syéntátè↓	*Siéntate.*
Don't sit down.	6. notesyéntès↓	*No te sientes.*
Tell me the truth.	7. díme│laberdác↓	*Dime la verdad.*
_____	8. nomedígàs↓	*No me digas.*

EXTRAPOLATION

Commands	
Affirmative	Command form — clitic(s)
Negative	/nó/ — clitic(s) — command form

NOTES

a. Clitic pronouns follow command forms of verbs used affirmatively.

b. They precede (and are themselves preceded by /nó/) command forms of verbs used negatively.

SPOKEN SPANISH   UNIT 29

29.21.11 Substitution drills — Pronominal substitution

Problem:

abrae(ll)líbro↓

Answer:

abrálo↓

1. éskriba|lakárta↓   éskribála↓
2. trayga|laz(ll)yábes↓   traygálas↓
3. kómpre|elsofá↓   komprélo↓
4. kámbye|loschékes↓   kámbyelos↓

_____

Problem:

Abra *el libro.*

Answer:

Abralo.

1 Escriba *la carta.*   Escríbala.
2 Traiga *las llaves.*   Tráigalas.
3 Compre *el sofá.*   Cómprelo.
4 Cambie *los cheques.*   Cámbielos.

CINCO   29.5

UNIT 29   SPOKEN SPANISH

5. bénda|lamésà↓   bendàlà↓

6. mire|loṣabrígòs↓   mirèlòs↓

7. èstudye|laleksyón↓   èstudyèlà↓

8. kwiḍe|elsésped↓   kwiḍèlò↓

9. barra|loẓḍormitóryòs↓   barràlòs↓

10. èskribe|lakártà↓   èskribèlà↓

11. tráe|laẓⱡyábès↓   tràèlàs↓

---

5 Venda *la mesa.*   Véndala.
6 Mire *los abrigos.*   Mírelos.
7 Estudie *la lección.*   Estúdiela.
8 Cuide *el césped.*   Cuídelo.
9 Barra *los dormitorios.*   Bárralos.

10 Escribe *la carta.*   Escríbela.
11 Trae *las llaves.*   Tráelas.

jacobeligoodsons.com For Free Audio

SPOKEN SPANISH   UNIT 29

12. kómpra|elsofá↓   kómprálô↓
13. kámbya|loschékês↓   kámbyálôs↓
14. bénde|lamésá↓   béndêlá↓
15. míra|losabrígôs↓   mírálôs↓
16. kwída|elséspéd↓   kwídálô↓
17. bárre|lozdormitóryôs↓   bárrélôs↓

Cómpralo.
Cámbialos.
Véndela.
Míralos.
Cuidalo.
Bárrelos.

SIETE

UNIT 29   SPOKEN SPANISH

29.21.11   Affirmative — negative substitution

       Problem 1:
                     dígáséló↓
       Answer:
                     nóseloᴅígá↓

       Problem 2:
                     nomelotráygá↓
       Answer:
                     tráygámėló↓

_____

            Problem 1:
                    Digaselo.

            Answer:
                       No se lo diga.

            Problem 2:
                       No me lo traiga.

            Answer:
                       Tráigamelo.

29.8   jacobeligoodsons.com For Free Audio   OCHO

SPOKEN SPANISH   UNIT 29

1. dígásèló↓   nóseloðígà↓
2. págémèlà↓   nómelapágè↓
3. èskríbàsélàs↓   nóselaşeskríbà↓
4. mandènózlà↓   nónozlamándè↓
5. lèbàntèsè↓   nóselebántè↓
6. àféytèsé↓   nósȩaféytè↓
7. kómprèmèlòs↓   nómeloskómprè↓
8. nóselazbéndà↓   bendàsèlàs↓
9. nómeloȩsplíkè↓   èsplíkèmèlò↓
10. nóselatráygá↓   traygàsélà↓
11. nónozloðígà↓   dígànòzlò↓
12. nóselaðé↓   desélà↓

---

1 Dígaselo.   No se lo diga.
2 Páguemela.   No me la pague.
3 Escríbaselas.   No se las escriba.
4 Mándenosla.   No nos la mande.
5 Levántese.   No se levante.
6 Aféitese.   No se afeite.
7 Cómpremelos.   No me los compre.
8 No se las venda.   Véndaselas.
9 No me lo explique.   Explíquemelo.
10 No se la traiga.   Tráigasela.
11 No nos lo diga.   Díganoslo.
12 No se la dé.   Désela.

UNIT 29   SPOKEN SPANISH

13. nómelospágè↓   pagémélòs↓

14. èskríbémèlà↓   nomelaęskríbas↓
15. mándàmèlà↓   nomelamándés↓
16. traémèlà↓   nomelatráygàs↓
17. dímélò↓   nomelodígàs↓
18. lèbàntàtè↓   notelebántés↓
19. àfeytàtè↓   notęaféytés↓
20. nómelakómprès↓   komprámèlà↓
21. nóselabéndàs↓   bendésélà↓
22. nóselǫsplíkès↓   èsplíkàsèlò↓
23. nónozlatráygàs↓   traénòzlà↓

_____

        13 No me los pague.   Páguemelos.

        14 Escríbemela.   No me la escribas.
        15 Mándamela.   No me la mandes.
        16 Tráemela.   No me la traigas.
        17 Dímelo.   No me lo digas.
        18 Levántate.   No te levantes.
        19 Aféitate.   No te afeites.
        20 No me la compres.   Cómpramela.
        21 No se la vendas.   Véndesela.
        22 No se lo expliques.   Explícaselo.
        23 No nos la traigas.   Tráenosla.

SPOKEN SPANISH UNIT 29

29.21.12 Response drill

1. póŋgolozlíbros |ènlámesa↑ọenọleskritóryò↓   póngalos |ènlamésà↓
2. tráygolasfotos |àorạ↑omaŋyánà↓   tráygalas |aórà↓
3. lèsplíkolalekşyon |àorạ↑omaŋyánà↓   èsplíkemelaórà↓
4. lèḍoyelrregaḷo |àkarmen |àorạ↑omaŋyánà↓   déselo |maŋyánà↓
5. lèstrayḡọelkafé |àorạ↑oḍespwés↓   tráyganozlọ |aórà↓
6. tèsplíkolalekşyon |àorạ↑omaŋyánà↓   èsplíkamelaórà↓
7. tèḍoyelrregaḷo |àorạ↑omaŋyánà↓   dameḷọaórà↓
8. tètrayḡọelkafé |àorạ↑oḍespwés↓   tráemelo |ḍespwés↓

[yá↓] 9. kwando |lestrayḡọelkafé↓   tráyganozlo |yá↓
[màŋyánà↓] 10. kwando |lelímpyọelkárró↓   límpyemelo |maŋyánà↓

---

1 ¿Pongo los libros en la mesa o en el escritorio?   Póngalos en la mesa.
2 ¿Traigo las fotos ahora o mañana?   Tráigalas ahora.
3 ¿Le explico la lección ahora o mañana?   Explíquemela ahora.
4 ¿Le doy el regalo a Carmen ahora o mañana?   Déselo mañana.
5 ¿Les traigo el café ahora o después?   Tráiganoslo ahora.
6 ¿Te explico la lección ahora o mañana?   Explícamela ahora.
7 ¿Te doy el regalo ahora o mañana?   Dámelo ahora.
8 ¿Te traigo el café ahora o después?   Tráemelo después.

(ya) 9 ¿Cuándo les traigo el café?   Tráiganoslo ya.
(mañana) 10 ¿Cuándo le limpio el carro?   Límpiemelo mañana.

ONCE

jacobeligoodsons.com For Free Audio

UNIT 29   SPOKEN SPANISH

[déspwés↓]   11.   lètráygọelkafe|aora�t   nó↓ tráygamelo|despwés↓

[mànyáná↓]   12.   lèzlìmpyọelkárrọ|aora↑   nó↓ lìmpyenozlo|mànyáná↓

             13.   mẹàfeyto↑   sí↓ àfeytèsé↓

             14.   lèsplìkolalèkşyon|aeⓁya↑   sí↓ èsplìkèsèlá↓

             15.   léɗiggaeⓁya|laberɗaɗ↑   sí↓ digàsèlá↓

             16.   lèmandolakártạ|ael↑   sí↓ mandèsèlá↓

             17.   lèzɗoyaeⓁyos|èlrrégalọ|aora↑   sí↓ dèsèló↓

             18.   téɗigolaberɗaɗ↑   sí↓ dimèlá↓

             19.   tétráygọ|elşenişero↑   sí↓ traémèló↓

_____

(después)   11 ¿Le traigo el café ahora?   No, tráigamelo después.

(mañana)   12 ¿Les limpio el carro ahora?   No, limpienoslo mañana.

             13 ¿Me afeito?   Sí, aféitese.

             14 ¿Le explico la lección a ella?   Sí, explíquesela.

             15 ¿Le digo a ella la verdad?   Sí, dígasela.

             16 ¿Le mando la carta a él?   Sí, mándesela.

             17 ¿Les doy a ellos el regalo ahora?   Sí, déselo.

             18 ¿Te digo la verdad?   Sí, dímela.

             19 ¿Te traigo el cenicero?   Sí, tráemelo.

jacobeligoodsons.com For Free Audio

29.12   DOCE

SPOKEN SPANISH   UNIT 29

29.21.13 Translation drill

1 The book? Give it to them.   éllibro↑ déselǫaéⱳⱳòs↓   ¿El libro? Déselo a ellos.

2 The coffee? Bring it to me now.   élkåfe↑ tráygamelǫ|aórå↓   ¿El café? Tráigamelo ahora.

3 The children? Don't bring them.   lózniɲyos↑ nólostráygå↓   ¿Los niños? No los traiga.

4 The keys? Take them to Paul.   låzⱳⱳabes↑ ⱳⱳebéselas|apáblò↓   ¿Las llaves? Lléveselas a Pablo.

5 The ash tray? Don't put it there.   élșeníșero↑ nólopǫɲgas,aí↓   ¿El cenicero? No lo pongas ahí.

6 The milk? Don't bring it to me yet. låleche↑ nómelatráygås|tòđåbíå↓ ¿La leche? No me la traigas todavía.

7 The salad? Make it now.   lȿénsåladå↑ ågålå|yá↓   ¿La ensalada? Hágala ya.

8 The letters? Write them now.   låskartas↑ éskríbalas|aórå↓   ¿Las cartas? Escríbalas ahora.

9 The furniture? Sell it to my sister. lózmwebles↑ béndaselos|åmȿèrmanå↓ ¿Los muebles? Véndaselos a mi hermana.

10 The handbag? Send it to me tomorrow. élmålètin↑ mándemelo|maɲyánà↓   ¿El maletín? Mándemelo mañana.

11 The list? Check it.   lålista↑ rrébiséla↓   ¿La lista? Revísela.

12 The lawn? Take care of it.   élșespeđ↑ kwiđélò↓   ¿El césped? Cuídelo.

13 The photos? Ask Mary.   låsfotos↑ piđaselas|amaríå↓   ¿Las fotos? Pídaselas a María.

TRECE

UNIT 29   SPOKEN SPANISH

14 The living room? Don't sweep it   làsálat nólabárrą|óy↓   ¿La sala? No la barra hoy.
   today.

15 The chairs? Clean them now.   là(s)sílyast límpyelas|aórà↓   ¿Las sillas? Límpielas ahora.

B.   Discussion of pattern

        Clitic pronouns immediately follow command forms expressing affirmative commands. They immediately precede command forms expressing negative commands. In
either case they are included in the stress and intonation pattern of the verb; that is to say, they are like 'endings,' becoming part of the same phonological phrase (or
word) as the verb form.

        If two clitic pronouns appear together, they have the same order relative to each other (as discussed in units 20, 25, and 26) regardless of whether they precede
or follow the verb.

        The close linking of verb and clitic is recognized in the writing system of Spanish when the clitic follows the verb (they are written together as one word), but
when the clitic precedes, they appear as separate words, even though the same close relationship prevails.

        With some command form and clitic combinations, certain transpositions of sounds are made by many speakers. For example:

                   /dénmelaplúma↓/   becomes   /démenlaplúma↓/

                   /dénselo|ąéⓁyos↓/   becomes   /désenlo|ąéⓁyos↓/

        These analogical re-formations (where the person-number ending of the verb is placed *after* the clitic) underscore the **closeness of the verb-clitic relation**. Though
widely used, these changes are considered a mark of substandard usage by many educated speakers of Spanish.

29.21.2   Clitic pronouns in constructions with infinitives and with /—ndo/ forms

    A.   Presentation of pattern

                                                        ILLUSTRATIONS

Having so much fun, you're never going   1. dibirtyéndotetanto|nuŋkabásaprendér↓   Divirtiéndote tanto, nunca vas a aprender.
   to learn.

─────────────────────────   2. éŋkántaɖa|ɖekonoşérlà↓   Encantada de conocerla.

29.14   jacobeligoodsons.com For Free Audio   CATORCE

SPOKEN SPANISH   UNIT 29

I was brushing my teeth.	3.	yómestába|límpyándolozdyéntés↓	Yo *me* estaba limpiando los dientes.
———————————	4.	yóęstába|límpyándomelozdyéntés↓	Yo estaba limpiándome los dientes.
———————————	5.	nómelobarrebisár↑	¿No *me lo* va a revisar?
Aren't you going to check it for me?	6.	nóbárrébisármelo↑	¿No va a revisár*melo?*

EXTRAPOLATION

infinitive – clitic
/...ndo/ – clitic

Sample verb constructions	
Periphrastic future	las—bóy—a—komprár↓
	bóy—a—komprár—las↓
Progressive	las—estóy—eskrıbyéndo↓
	estóy—eskrıbyéndo—las↓

NOTES

a. Clitic pronouns follow infinitives and /—ndo/ forms.

b. When infinitives and /—ndo/ forms occur in constructions with conjugated verbs, clitic pronouns may appear
    before the conjugated verb or after the non-conjugated form (infinitive or /—ndo/ form), but never between
    them.

QUINCE   jacobeligoodsons.com For Free Audio   29.15

UNIT 29   SPOKEN SPANISH

29.21.21 Substitution drills — Pronominal substitution

    Problem 1:

        éstoy│éskribyéndolaskártàs↓

    Answer:

        éstoy│éskríbyéndòlàs↓

        làs,èstóyeskribyéndò↓

    Problem 2:

        bóy│àkòmprárlaschulétàs↓

    Answer:

        bóyakomprárlàs↓

        làzbóyakomprár↓

      Problem 1:

        Estoy escribiendo *las cartas.*

      Answer:

        Estoy escribiéndolas.

        Las estoy escribiendo.

      Problem 2:

        Voy a comprar *las chuletas.*

      Answer:

        Voy a comprarlas.

        Las voy a comprar.

29.16   jacobeligoodsons.com For Free Audio   DIECISEIS

SPOKEN SPANISH   UNIT 29

1. èstóybyéndolakásà↓   èstóybyéndòlà↓
                                                         làèstoybyéndò↓

2. èstamoz |bèndyéndọelkárrò↓   èstamozbèndyéndòlò↓
                                                         lòẹstamozbèndyéndò↓

3. èstas |kwiḍándọalozníŋyòs↓   èstaskwiḍándòlòs↓
                                                         lòsẹstaskwiḍándò↓

_____

1 Estoy viendo *la casa*.   Estoy viéndola.
                                                         La estoy viendo.

2 Estamos vendiendo *el carro*.   Estamos vendiéndolo.
                                                         Lo estamos vendiendo.

3 Estás cuidando *a los niños*.   Estás cuidándolos.
                                                         Los estás cuidando.

DIECISIETE   jacobeligoodsons.com For Free Audio   29.17

UNIT 29   SPOKEN SPANISH

4. ėstá|bȧrryéndoloskwártȯs↓   ėstabarryéndȯlȯs↓
                                                           lȯs,ėstabarryéndȯ↓

5. ėstáz|byéndolasfótȯs↓   ėstazbyéndȯlȧs↓
                                                           lȧs,ėstazbyéndȯ↓

6. ėstáşyéndolasópá↓   ėstaşyéndȯlȧ↓
                                                           lȧ,ȩstaşyéndȯ↓

---

4 Está barriendo *los cuartos*.   Está barriéndolos.
                                                          Los está barriendo.

5 Estás viendo las fotos.   Estás viéndolas.
                                                          Las estás viendo.

6 Está haciendo *la sopa*.   Está haciéndola.
                                                          La está haciendo.

29.18   jacobeligoodsons.com For Free Audio   DIECIOCHO

SPOKEN SPANISH   UNIT 29

7. bóy|àkómprárlazlegúmbrès↓   bóyakomprárlàs↓
                                                 làzbóyakomprár↓

8. bás|àęskríbírlaskártàs↓   bás‚aęskríbírlàs↓
                                                 làzbás‚aęskríbír↓

9. bamós|àpàgárlakwéntà↓   bámos‚apaɡárlà↓
                                                 làbamos‚apaɡár↓

_____

7 Voy a comprar *las legumbres.*   Voy a comprarlas.
                                                 Las voy a comprar.

8 Vas a escribir *las cartas.*   Vas a escribirlas.
                                                 Las vas a escribir.

9 Vamos a pagar *la cuenta.*   Vamos a pagarla.
                                                 La vamos a pagar.

DIECINUEVE

UNIT 29   SPOKEN SPANISH

10.   bás|àkòmprárlos(ş)apátòs↓   básˌakomprárlòs↓
                                                    lózbasˌakomprár↓

11.   pwéde|límpyárlasálà↑   pwéɗelimpyárlà↑
                                                    làpwéɗelimpyár↑

12.   kyéro|kòmprárelrregálò↓   kyérokomprárlò↓
                                                    lòkyérokomprár↓

13.   bán|àlimpyárlozɗormitóryòs↓   banˌalimpyárlòs↓
                                                    lózbanˌalimpyár↓

───

10 Vas a comprar *los zapatos.*   Vas a comprarlos.
                                                    Los vas a comprar.

11 ¿Puede limpiar *la sala?*   ¿Puede limpiarla?
                                                    La puede limpiar.

12 Quiero comprar *el regalo.*   Quiero comprarlo.
                                                    Lo quiero comprar.

13 Van a limpiar *los dormitorios.*   Van a limpiarlos.
                                                    Los van a limpiar.

29.20   jacobeligoodsons.com For Free Audio   VEINTE

SPOKEN SPANISH   UNIT 29

Construction substitution

Problem:

    sèláďoygél↓

Answer:

    sèlàęstoyďandǫaél↓
    sèlàbóyaďargél↓

1. sèlóďięgapáblô↓   sèlóęstaďięyéndǫ|apáblô↓
                                                 sèlóbaďeşir|apáblô↓

_____

Problem:
        Se la doy a él.

Answer:
        Se la estoy dando a él.

        Se la voy a dar a él.

        1 Se lo dice a Pablo.   Se lo está diciendo a Pablo.

                                                 Se lo va a decir a Pablo.

VEINTIUNO   29.21

UNIT 29   SPOKEN SPANISH

2. sélàséskríbǫ |aéꝏyòs↓   sélàsèstaǝskribyéndǫ |aéꝏyòs↓
                                                          sélàzbaǝskríbìr |aéꝏyós↓

3. télósèskríbél↓   télósèstaǝskribyéndǫ |él↓
                                                          télózbaǝskríbìr |él↓

4. sélàzmándan |amaríâ↓   sélàséstanmandándǫ |amaríâ↓
                                                          sélàzbanamandár |amaríâ↓

_____

2 Se las escribe a ellos.   Se las está escribiendo a ellos.
                                                   Se las va a escribir a ellos.

3 Te los escribe él.   Te los está escribiendo él.
                                                   Te los va a escribir él.

4 Se las mandan a María.   Se las están mandando a María.
                                                   Se las van-a mandar a María.

29.22   jacobeligoodsons.com For Free Audio   VEINTIDOS

SPOKEN SPANISH   UNIT 29

5. sèlózlímpyàn |múybyén↓   sèlòséstánlimpyándo |múybyén↓
                                              sèlózbánalimpyár |muytyén↓

6. sèlàkwiđa |lasèŋyórà↓   sèláestákwiđándo |lasèŋyórà↓
                                              sèlàbákwiđar |lasèŋyórà↓

7. tèlàzlímpyambyén↓   tèlàsèstánlimpyándo |byén↓
                                              tèlázbánalimpyár |byén↓

_____

5 Se los limpian muy bien.   Se los están limpiándo muy bien.

                                               Se los van a limpiar muy bien.

6 Se la cuida la señora.   Se la está cuidando la señora.

                                               Se la va a cuidar la señora.

7 Te las limpian bien.   Te las están limpiando bien.

                                               Te las van a limpiar bien.

VEINTITRES   29.23

UNIT 29   SPOKEN SPANISH

29.21.22 Translation drill

1	The old clothing? I'm giving it to Louise.	làrrópábyéhá↑ sèlàҽstóyɗandǫ｜alwísá↓	¿La ropa vieja? Se la estoy dando a Luisa.
2	The books? I'm loaning them to John.	lòzlíbrost èstoyprestándoselos｜ahwán↓	¿Los libros? Estoy prestándoselos a Juan.
3	The pencil? I'm going to give it to Carmen.	él)lápįṣt sélòbóyáɗár｜àkarmén↓	¿El lápiz? Se lo voy a dar a Carmen.
4	The letter? I'm going to send it to her.	làkártat sèlàboy｜àmàndàraé(l)ýá↓	¿La carta? Se la voy a mandar a ella.
5	The letters? I'm going to write them for you.	làskártast bóyҽéskríbírsélàs↓	¿Las cartas? Voy a escribírselas.
6	The photo? I want to see it.	làfótot làkyéróbér↓	¿La foto? La quiero ver.
7	The shoes? They're cleaning them.	lòs(ṣ)ápátost lòsҽèstánlimpyandò↓	¿Los zapatos? Los están limpiando.
8	The luggage? They're checking it for us.	élékípáhet nòzlóҽstánrrèbísandò↓	¿El equipaje? Nos lo están revisando.
9	The names? I'm going to write them.	lòznómbrest bóyҽéskríbírlòs↓	¿Los nombres? Voy a escribirlos.

B.   Discussion of pattern

When an infinitive is used as a noun, and when an /—ndo/ form is used as a modifier, any associated clitic pronouns must follow these verb forms.

When an infinitive or /—ndo/ form appears in a construction with a conjugated verb, any associated clitics either precede the conjugated verb or follow the infinitive or /—ndo/ form. A clitic may occur between these construction elements only when certain command forms occur with non-conjugated forms, as in /permítame—ablár↓/.

Apparently there is no meaning difference reflected in the occurrence of the clitic before or after the entire verb construction, other than stylistic variation. Two clitics normally either both precede or both follow.

29.24   VEINTICUATRO

SPOKEN SPANISH   UNIT 29

29.22   Replacement drills

A   tyénęúnsake |bwénisimò↓

1. _____rráketa_____↓   tyénęúnàrràketa |bwénisimà↓

2. _____fántastikà↓   tyénęúnàrràketa |fántastikà↓

3. _____kósas_____↓   tyénęúnàskosas |fántastikàs↓

4. èskríbę_____↓   èskríbę |ùnàskósas |fántastikàs↓

5. _____muyagradáblès↓   èskríbę |ùnàskósaz |muyagradáblès↓

6. áşę_____↓   áşęúnàskosaz |muyagradáblès↓

7. _____día_____↓   áşęúndia |muyagradáblè↓

_____

A   Tiene un saque buenísimo.

1 _____raqueta_____.   Tiene una raqueta buenísima.

2 _____fantástica.   Tiene una raqueta fantástica.

3 _____cosas_____.   Tiene unas cosas fantásticas.

4 Escribe_____.   Escribe unas cosas fantásticas.

5 _____ muy agradables.   Escribe unas cosas muy agradables.

6 Hace_____.   Hace unas cosas muy agradables.

7 _____día_____.   Hace un día muy agradable.

VEINTICINCO   29.25

UNIT 29   SPOKEN SPANISH

B   ústeđ |ézmúyamáblè |yín↓

1. _____ séŋyóres↓   ùsteđes |sónmúyamáblès |sèŋyórès↓

2. _____puntwáles_____↓   ùsteđes |sónmúypuntwáles |sèŋyórès↓

3. _____séŋyòrítà↓   ùsteđ |ézmúypuntwál |sèŋyòrítà↓

4. _____rrigurósà_____↓   ùsteđ |ézmúyrrigurósà |sèŋyòrítà↓

5. ústeđes _____↓   ùsteđes |sónmúyrrigurósàs |sèŋyòrítàs↓

6. _____sèŋyór↓   ùsteđ |ézmúyrrigurósò |sèŋyór↓

7. _____pàréşè_____↓   ùsteđ |pàréşèmúyrrigurósò |sèŋyór↓

B   Usted es muy amable, Jean.

1 _____, señores.   Ustedes son muy amables, señores.

2 _____puntuales , _____.   Ustedes son muy puntuales, señores.

3 _____, señorita.   Usted es muy puntual, señorita.

4 _____rigurosa, _____.   Usted es muy rigurosa, señorita.

5 Ustedes_____ , _____.   Ustedes son muy rigurosas, señoritas.

6 _____, señor.   Usted es muy riguroso, señor.

7 _____ parece_____, _____.   Usted parece muy riguroso, señor.

29.26   VEINTISEIS

SPOKEN SPANISH   UNIT 29

C   kebá↓ me̞ás̷e̞fálta |práktika↓

1. kláró_____↓   kláró↓ me̞ás̷e̞fálta |práktika↓

2. _____nós_____↓   kláró↓ nós̷ás̷e̞fálta |práktika↓

3. _____práktikár↓   kláró↓ nós̷ás̷e̞falta |práktikár↓

4. _____byem_____↓   kláró↓ nós̷ás̷e̞byem |práktikár↓

5. dézde̞lwego̞_____↓   dézde̞lwego̞↓ nós̷ás̷e̞byem |práktikár↓

6. _____te̞_____↓   dézde̞lwego̞↓ te̞ás̷e̞byem |práktikár↓

7. _____hûgár↓   dézde̞lwego̞↓ te̞ás̷e̞byeŋ |hûgár↓

_____

C   ¡Qué va! Me hace falta práctica.

1 ¡Claro!_____.   ¡Claro! Me hace falta práctica.

2 ¡____! Nos_____.   ¡Claro! Nos hace falta práctica.

3 ¡____! _____practicar.   ¡Claro! Nos hace falta practicar.

4 ¡____! _____bien_____.   ¡Claro! Nos hace bien practicar.

5 ¡Desde luego!_____.   ¡Desde luego! Nos hace bien practicar.

6 ¡_____! Te_____.   ¡Desde luego! Te hace bien practicar.

7 ¡_____! _____jugar.   ¡Desde luego! Te hace bien jugar.

VEINTISIETE

UNIT 29   SPOKEN SPANISH

D   téŋgọùnàkriaɗa |múykompeténtè↓

1. _____ɗos_____↓   téŋgòɗoskriaɗaz |múykompeténtès↓

2. _____bwénàs↓   téŋgòɗoskriaɗaz |muybwénàs↓

3. _____kriaɗo_____↓   téŋgọùŋkriaɗo |muybwénò↓

4. kònóşkọ_____↓   kònóşkọ |ùŋkriaɗo |muybwénò↓

5. _____hénte_____↓   kònóşkọ |ùnàhénte |muybwénà↓

6. _____amáblè↓   kònóşkọ |ùnàhénte |muyamáblè↓

7. _____kàbàУèroz_____↓   kònóşkọ |ùnòskàbàУèroz |múyamáblès↓

_____

D   Tengo una criada muy competente.

1 _____dos_____.   Tengo dos criadas muy competentes.

2 _____buenas.   Tengo dos criadas muy buenas.

3 _____criado_____.   Tengo un criado muy bueno.

4 Conozco_____.   Conozco un criado muy bueno.

5 _____gente_____.   Conozco una gente muy buena.

6 _____amable.   Conozco una gente muy amable.

7 _____caballeros_____.   Conozco unos caballeros muy amables.

29.28   VEINTIOCHO

SPOKEN SPANISH   UNIT 29

E   hòsé|kòmprólas̬entrádàs↓

1. tú_____↓   tú|kòmprástelas̬entrádàs↓

2. _____líbròs↓   tú|kòmprásteloz líbròs↓

3. ____pérdimoz_____↓   nòsótros|pérdimoz loz líbròs↓

4. _____partídò↓   nòsótros|pérdimos̬el partídò↓

5. _____otro_____↓   nòsótros|pérdimos|otro partídò↓

6. _____kósàs↓   nòsótros|pérdimos|otraskósàs↓

7. ____gánastę_____↓   tú|gánastę|otraskósàs↓

_____

E   José compró las entradas.

1 Tú_____.   Tú compraste las entradas.

2 _____libros.   Tú compraste los libros.

3 ____perdimos_____.   Nosotros perdimos los libros.

4 _____partido.   Nosotros perdimos el partido.

5 _____otro_____.   Nosotros perdimos otro partido.

6 _____cosas.   Nosotros perdimos otras cosas.

7 ____ganaste_____.   Tú ganaste otras cosas.

VEINTINUEVE   29.29

UNIT 29 SPOKEN SPANISH

F yó |nomekeđo |sinịr |ạesakorríđà↓

1. él_____↓   él |nosekeđa |sinịr |ạesakorríđà↓

2. _____partíđò↓   él |nosekeđa |sinịr |ạesepartíđò↓

3. _____ber_____↓   él |nosekeđa |simber |esepartíđò↓

4. _____keđamos_____↓   nòsótroz |nonoskeđamos |simber |esepartíđò↓

5. _____iglésyà↓   nòsótroz |nonoskeđamos |simber |esạiglésyà↓

6. _____boy_____↓   yó |nomeboy |simber |esạiglésyà↓

7. _____konoşer_____↓   yó |nomeboy |sinkonoşer |esạiglésyà↓

F Yo no me quedo sin ir a esa corrida.

1 El_____ .   El no se queda sin ir a esa corrida.

2 _____partido.   El no se queda sin ir a ese partido.

3 _____ver_____ .   El no se queda sin ver ese partido.

4 _____quedamos_____ .   Nosotros no nos quedamos sin ver ese partido.

5 _____iglesia.   Nosotros no nos quedamos sin ver esa iglesia.

6 _____voy_____ .   Yo no me voy sin ver esa iglesia.

7 _____conocer_____ .   Yo no me voy sin conocer esa iglesia.

29.30   TREINTA

SPOKEN SPANISH   UNIT 29

29.23   Variation drills

A   làfélíṣítò|kármèn↓ hwégàmuybyén↓   La felicito, Carmen. Juega muy bien.

        1 Congratulations, Carmen. You dance   làfélíṣítò|kármèn↓ báylàmuybyén↓   La felicito, Carmen. Baila muy bien.
          very well.

        2 Congratulations, Carmen. You drive   làfélíṣítò|kármèn↓ mànéhàmuybyén↓   La felicito, Carmen. Maneja muy bien.
          very well.

        3 Congratulations, Lieutenant. You fly   lòfélíṣítò|tènyénté↓ bwélàmuybyén↓   Lo felicito, Teniente. Vuela muy bien.
          very well.

        4 Congratulations, Jose. You play golf   lòfélíṣítò|hòsé↓ hwégàgolf|muybyén↓   Lo felicito, José. Juega golf muy bien.
          very well.

        5 Congratulations, Juan. You play tennis lòfélíṣítò|hwán↓ hwégàteniz|muybyén↓   Lo felicito Juan. Juega tenis muy bien.
          very well.

        6 Congratulations, Mr. White. You speak   lòfélíṣítò|sènyórhwáyt↓ áblàéspànyol|muybyén↓ Lo felicito, Sr. White. Habla español muy
          Spanish very well.   bien.

        7 Congratulations, Carmen. You speak   làfélíṣítò|kármèn↓ áblàinglez|muybyén↓   La felicito, Carmen. Habla inglés muy bien.
          English very well.

B   péròlàkèmànehà|làrràketa|muybyén|ésùstéd↓   Pero la que maneja la raqueta muy bien es
                                                                                            usted.

        1 But she's the one who can really drive péròlàkèmàneha|elkoche|muybyén|ésèlyà↓   Pero la que maneja el coche muy bien es
          a car.   ella.

        2 But Carmen's the one who can really   péròlàkèprònunṣyà|éspànyol|muybyén|éskármèn↓ Pero la que pronuncia español muy bien
          pronounce Spanish.   es Carmen.

        3 But I'm the one who always loses   pérgèlkèpyerde|dinerosyempre|sòyyó↓   Pero el que pierde dinero siempre soy yo.
          money.

TREINTA Y UNO   jacobeligoodsons.com For Free Audio   29.31

UNIT 29   SPOKEN SPANISH

4 But *you're* the one who complains   péro̧élkésékéha |to̧dóz lozdías |éşústéd↓   Pero el que se queja todos los días es Ud.
  every day.

5 But *we're* the ones who get up at seven.   pérólóskésélébántan |àlá(s)syéte |sómóznósótrós↓   Pero los que se levantan a las siete somos
                                                                                                  nosotros.

6 But *they're* (f) the ones that notice   pérólàskéséfíhan |èntódo̧ |sónéo̧y̧às↓   Pero las que se fijan en todo son ellas.
  everything.

7 But *my wife* is the one that forgets   pérólàkéşo̧lbída |dȩtódo̧ |èzmi̧éşpóşà↓   Pero la que se olvida de todo es mi esposa.
  everything.

C dȩáki |ȩnádélánte |pódrémozbérnos |ȩnlákanchà↓no↑   De aquí en adelante, podremos vernos en
                                                                la cancha, ¿no?

1 From now on, we'll be able to see each   dȩáki |ȩnádélánte |pódrémozbérnos |ȩnélklúb↓no↑   De aquí en adelante, podremos vernos en
  other at the club, won't we?   el club, ¿no?

2 From now on, we'll be able to see each   dȩáki |ȩnádélánte |pódrémozbérnoz |débeşȩn   De aquí en adelante, podremos vernos de
  other from time to time, won't we?   kwándò↓no↑   vez en cuando, ¿no?

3 From now on, we'll be able to see each   dȩáki |ȩnádélánte |pódrémozbérnos |àménúdò↓no↑   De aquí en adelante, podremos vernos a
  other often, won't we?   menudo, ¿no?

4 From now on, we'll be able to go out   dȩáki |ȩnádélánte |pódrémo(s)salír |àménúdò↓no↑   De aquí en adelante, podremos salir a
  often, won't we?   menudo, ¿no?

5 Apparently, we'll be able to leave early, pòrlóbisto |pódrémosi̧rnos |tèmpranò↓no↑   Por lo visto, podremos irnos temprano,
  won't we?   ¿no?

6 Apparently, we'll be able to return early, pòrlóbisto |pódrémozbolbérnos |tèmpranò↓no↑   Por lo visto, podremos volvernos temprano,
  won't we?   ¿no?

7 Apparently, we'll be able to say goodbye   pòrlóbisto |pódrémozdespedírnos |prontò↓no↑   Por lo visto, podremos despedirnos pronto,
  soon, won't we?   ¿no?

SPOKEN SPANISH   UNIT 29

D ínomés |tándifíṣíl↓   Y no me es tan difícil.

   1 And it's not so easy for me.   ínomés |tàmfáṣíl↓   Y no me es tan fácil.

   2 And it's not so easy for us.   ínonoșes |tàmfáṣíl↓   Y no nos es tan fácil.

   3 And it's not so comfortable for them. ínoleșes |tàŋkómòḍò↓   Y no les es tan cómodo.

   4 And it's very comfortable for him.   ílesmuykómòḍò↓   Y le es muy cómodo.

   5 And it seems very comfortable to him. ílépàreṣemuykómòḍò↓   Y le parece muy cómodo.

   6 And it seems excellent to us.   ínòspàreṣeks(ș)elénté↓   Y nos parece excelente.

   7 And it seems terrific (stupendous) to me. ímépàreṣestupéndò↓   Y me parece estupendo.

E   bênímos |èldómìŋgo |pórlatárdé↑   ¿Venimos el domingo por la tarde?

   1 Shall we come Saturday evening?   bênímos |èlsábaḍo |pórlanoché↑   ¿Venimos el sábado por la noche?

   2 Shall we leave Friday morning?   sálímos |èlbyérnes |pórlamaŋyáná↑ ¿Salimos el viernes por la mañana?

   3 Shall we go Thursday of this week?   bámos |èlhwèḅez |ḍestasemaná↑   ¿Vamos el jueves de esta semana?

   4 Shall we eat tonight at my house?   kômemos |éstànoche |enmíkása↑   ¿Comemos esta noche en mi casa?

TREINTA Y TRES   29.33

UNIT 29   SPOKEN SPANISH

5 Shall we close this afternoon at six?   șȇrramos |éstàtardȩ |ala(s)séys↑   ¿Cerramos esta tarde a las seis?

6 Shall we open tomorrow early?   àbrimoz |mȧŋyanatempranó↑   ¿Abrimos mañana temprano?

7 Shall we dance this number now?   bȧylamos |éstȧpyeșaóra↑   ¿Bailamos esta pieza ahora?

F   éstȇdòmiŋgò |nòpwȇḓȇsér↓   Este domingo, no puede ser.

1 It's impossible *this* Saturday.   éstȇsábado |nòpwȇḓȇsér↓   Este sábado, no puede ser.

2 It's impossible *this* Friday.   éstébyérnez |nòpwȇḓȇsér↓   Este viernes, no puede ser.

3 It's impossible *this* Thursday.   éstȇhwébez |nòpwȇḓȇsér↓   Este jueves, no puede ser.

4 It's impossible *this* afternoon.   éstȧtarḓe |nòpwȇḓȇsér↓   Esta tarde, no puede ser.

5 It's impossible tonight.   éstȧnóche |nòpwȇḓȇsér↓   Esta noche, no puede ser.

6 It's impossible *this* week.   éstȧsȇmána |nòpwȇḓȇsér↓   Esta semana, no puede ser.

7 It's impossible tomorrow.   mȧŋyana |nòpwȇḓȇsér↓   Mañana, no puede ser.

29.34   jacobeligoodsons.com For Free Audio   TREINTA Y CUATRO

SPOKEN SPANISH   UNIT 29

29.24   Review drill — Review of present perfect construction

Problem:

          yálmòrṣó|ustéd↑

Answer:

          nó↓ noeạlmorṣádò|tòdàbíà↓

    1. yáẹstúdyo|ustéd↑   nó↓ noẹstudyádò|tòdàbíà↓
    2. yáẹstúdyaron|ustédes↑   nó↓ noẹmosẹstudyádò|tòdàbíà↓
    3. yáẹstúdyaron|éⓄyos↑   nó↓ noạnẹstudyádò|tòdàbíà↓
    4. yálmòrṣaste|tú↑   nó↓ noẹạlmorṣádò|tòdàbíà↓

_____

        Problem:
            ¿Ya almorzó Ud.?

        Answer:
            No, no he almorzado todavía.

        1 ¿Ya estudió Ud.?   No, no he estudiado todavía.
        2 ¿Ya estudiaron Uds.?   No, no hemos estudiado todavía.
        3 ¿Ya estudiaron ellos?   No, no han estudiado todavía.
        4 ¿Ya almorzaste tú?   No, no he almorzado todavía.

TREINTA Y CINCO   jacobeligoodsons.com For Free Audio   29.35

UNIT 29   SPOKEN SPANISH

5. yálmòrṣáron |ustéđest   nó↓ ṇǫemos,almorṣáđò |tòđàbíà↓

6. yákòmyo |ustéđt   nó↓ ṇǫekomíđò |tòđàbíà↓

7. yákòmiste |tút   nó↓ ṇǫekomíđò |tòđàbíà↓

8. yákòmyó |élt   nó↓ ṇǫakomíđò |tòđàbíà↓

9. yákòmyéron |ustéđest   nó↓ ṇǫemoskomíđò |tòđàbíà↓

10. yákòmyéron |eⱷyost   nó↓ ṇǫaŋkomíđò |tòđàbíà↓

11. yárrèpètiste |tút   nó↓ ṇǫerrepetíđò |tòđàbíà↓

12. yárrèpityó |ustéđt   nó↓ ṇǫerrepetíđò |tòđàbíà↓

13. yárrèpìtyéron |eⱷyost   nó↓ ṇǫanrrepetíđò |tòđàbíà↓

---

5 ¿Ya almorzaron Uds.?   No, no hemos almorzado todavía.

6 ¿Ya comió Ud.?   No, no he comido todavía.

7 ¿Ya comiste tú?   No, no he comido todavía.

8 ¿Ya comió él?   No, no ha comido todavía.

9 ¿Ya comieron Uds.?   No, no hemos comido todavía.

10 ¿Ya comieron ellos?   No, no han comido todavía.

11 ¿Ya repetiste tú?   No, no he repetido todavía.

12 ¿Ya repitió Ud.?   No, no he repetido todavía.

13 ¿Ya repitieron ellos?   No, no han repetido todavía.

29.36

SPOKEN SPANISH   UNIT 29

29.3   CONVERSATION STIMULUS

NARRATIVE 1

1 Jean and Carmen played tennis this
morning.

yíniká̀rmen |húgárònténis |éstàmànyáná↓

Jean y Carmen jugaron tenis esta mañana.

2 Jean won, and her husband congratulated
her.

yíngano|ìsuèspósolafelìsitó↓

Jean ganó y su esposo la felicitó.

3 They played two sets.

húgáròndospartídòs↓

Jugaron dos partidos.

4 Jean won both of them.

yín |gànólozdós↓

Jean ganó los dos.

5 She beat Carmen 6-1, 6-2.

légàno|àkármen↑séysùno|séyzdós↓

Le ganó a Carmen 6-1, 6-2.

DIALOG 1

Bob, pregúntele a Jean si jugó tenis con
Carmen esta mañana.

húgàsteténis↑kònkármen |estámanyana↑

Bob: ¿Jugaste tenis con Carmen esta
mañana?

Jean, contéstele que sí, y que Ud. le ganó.
Pregúntele que qué le parece.

sí|ìlègáné↓ ketèparésè↓

Jean: Sí, y le gané. ¿Qué te parece?

Bob, dígale que le parece muy bien, que la
felicita. Pregúntele que cuántos partidos jugaron.

mèpàré̢sè |múybyén↓tèfèli̢sitó↓
kwántospartídos |hugárón↓

Bob: Me parece muy bien, te felicito.
¿Cuántos partidos jugaron?

Jean, contéstele que dos; y que Ud. le
ganó los dos: 6-1, 6-2.

dós↓ilègáné lozdós↓ séysùno|séyzdós↓

Jean: Dos; y le gané los dos: 6-1, 6-2.

TREINTA Y SIETE   jacobeligoodsons.com For Free Audio   29.37

UNIT 29   SPOKEN SPANISH

NARRATIVE 2

1 Carmen handles the racquet fairly well.   kármen |mánehalarrakéta |bástantebyén↓   Carmen maneja la raqueta bastante bien.

2 But she lacks a good serve.   péròlęáşèfáltạ |úmbwensákè↓   Pero le hace falta un buen saque.

3 They played at the club.   húgaronenęlklúb↓   Jugaron en el club.

4 They have grass courts at that club.   tyénènkanchaz |dèşéspèd |ènęsèklúb↓   Tienen canchas de césped en ese club.

5 Jean thought they were excellent.   àyín |lèpàrèşyéron |èks(ş)èlentés↓   A Jean le parecieron excelentes.

6 It's the first time she's played on grass courts.   èzlàprimérabeş |kèhwègạ |ènkánchazdeşéspèd↓   Es la primera vez que juega en canchas de césped.

DIALOG 2

Bob, dígale a Jean que Ud. creía que Carmen jugaba muy bien.   yókréía |kèkármeŋ |húgábàmúybyèn↓   Bob: Yo creía que Carmen jugaba muy bien.

Jean, dígale que Carmen maneja la raqueta bastante bien; pero que le hace falta un buen saque.   kármen |mánéhàlárrákéta |bàstántebyém↓ péròlęáşefáltạ |úmbwensákè↓   Jean: Carmen maneja la raqueta bastante bien, pero le hace falta un buen saque.

Bob, pregúntele que qué le parecieron las canchas.   kéteparèşyeron |laskánchàs↓   Bob: ¿Qué te parecieron las canchas?

Jean, contéstele que excelentes, que es la primera vez que Ud. juega en canchas de césped.   èks(ş)èlentès↓ èzlàprimérabeş |kèhwègạ | ènkanchazdeşéspèd↓   Jean: Excelentes. Es la primera vez que juego en canchas de césped.

29.38   jacobeligoodsons.com For Free Audio   TREINTA Y OCHO

SPOKEN SPANISH   UNIT 29

NARRATIVE 3

1 Changing the subject, Bob already bought
  the tickets for the bullfight.

àblandodҫotrakosa↓ bobyakompro |làsҫéntradas |
párálàkòrridadetórós↓

Hablando de otra cosa, Bob ya compró las
entradas para la corrida de toros.

2 The bullfight is this coming Sunday.

làkòrrida |èsҫéstédòmingokebyéné↓

La corrida es este domingo que viene.

3 Jean says she can't go, really.

yindiҫe |kènópwedgír |ènrrҫálidád↓

Jean dice que no puede ir, en realidad.

4 Because she and Bob told the children
  they'd take them to the country.

pórkeҫyҫibòb↑lédiheron |àlózninyos↑
kélósҫiban |àCyèbaralkámpò↓

Porque ella y Bob le dijeron a los niños
que los iban a llevar al campo.

5 'Let's tell them we'll take them some
  other day', says Bob.

digamozles |kélózuyébamos |otrodía |diҫèbób↓

Digámosles que los llevamos otro día-
dice Bob.

6 But Jean can't tell them that now.

péróyin |nópwederҫҫírlesҫésҫo |àórà↓

Pero Jean no puede decirles eso, ahora.

7 *She'll* have to take them, then.

eCyà |tyénèkèCyèbárlòs |èntónҫès↓

Ella tiene que llevarlos, entonces.

8 Because Bob says he wouldn't miss the
  fight for anything in the world.

pórkébob |diҫékel |nosekeda |simberlakorrida↑
pòrnadadelmúndò↓

Porque Bob dice que él no se queda sin ver
la corrida por nada del mundo.

DIALOG 3

Bob, dígale a Jean, hablando de otra cosa,
que Ud. ya compró las entradas para la
corrida de toros.

àblandodҫotrakosa↓yàkòmprélasҫéntradas |
párálàkòrridadetórós↓

Bob: Hablando de otra cosa, ya compré las
     entradas para la corrida de toros.

Jean, pregúntele que para cuándo.

párákwandò↓

Jean: ¿Para cuándo?

TREINTA Y NUEVE   29.39

UNIT 29   SPOKEN SPANISH

Bob, contéstele que para este domingo que viene. Y que no le diga que no puede ir.

párģéstéđòmingokebyéné↓inomeđigas|

kenopweđesír↓

Bob: Para este domingo que viene. Y no me digas que no puedes ir.

Jean, dígale que Ud. no puede ir, en realidad.

nòpweđọír|ènrrẹàliđáđ↓

Jean: No puedo ir, en realidad.

Bob, pregúntele que qué pretexto tiene para no ir.

kepretestotyénès|páràngír↓

Bob: ¿Qué pretexto tienes para no ir?

Jean, contéstele que ya Uds. les dijeron a los niños que los iban a llevar al campo.

yanosótroz|lèzđíhimos|àlòzniŋyost

kélòsibamos|ầ(l)yẹbáràlkampò↓

Jean: Ya nosotros les dijimos a los niños que los íbamos a llevar al campo.

Bob, dígale que Uds. les digan que los llevan otro día.

digámozles|kelòz(l)yẹbamos|otrođíá↓

Bob: Digámosles que los llevamos otro día.

Jean, dígale que Uds. no pueden decirles eso ahora.

nòpóđemóz|đẹșírlèșésọ|áórà↓

Jean: No podemos decirles eso ahora.

Bob, dígale que los lleve ella, entonces. Que Ud. no se queda sin ver la corrida por nada del mundo.

(l)yẹbalostú|ẹntónșès↓ yonomekéđo|

simberlakorriđat pòrnađađelmúndò↓

Bob: Llévalos tú, entonces. Yo no me quedo sin ver la corrida por nada del mundo.

29.4   READINGS

29.40   List of cognate loan words

originalmente   òrihinalméntè↓

fundada (fundar)   fúndaďá↓ fúndár↓

públicos   públikòs↓

la atracción   lạ–àtràkșyón↓

el turista   èl–túristà↓

principal   prinșipá'l↓

exclusivamente   èsklúsibaméntè↓

SPOKEN SPANISH   UNIT 29

los propietarios   lôs—pròpyétàryòs↓

prohibido (prohibir)   pròybídò↓ pròybír↓

la distancia   là—distànṣyà↓

el kilómetro   èl—kilométrò↓

29.41   Reading selection

El Barrio Viejo de Las Palmas

        Toda la parte norte de Las Palmas, capital de Surlandia, es lo que la gente en general llama 'barrio viejo'. Todo este sector es lo que originalmente fue la ciudad de Las Palmas cuando fue fundada por los españoles hace muchos años, y su aspecto físico ha cambiado muy poco desde entonces. De calles estrechas y casas y edificios públicos de un estilo colonial español, esta sección es hoy día un centro de gran atracción para el turista norteamericano. Por esta razón en la calle principal hay ahora cantidades de pequeñas tiendas que venden casi exclusivamente cosas típicas del país. En el centro del barrio, en lo que hace muchos años fue una plaza, hay ahora un mercado muy grande donde la mayor parte de la gente que vive por ahí hace sus compras. El edificio mismo del mercado no se puede decir que es exactamente un edificio; es más bien una serie de pequeños puestos, juntos unos a otros, que pertenecen a diferentes propietarios. Todo por ahí tiene un aspecto feo, sucio y viejo, pero vale la pena comprar en ese mercado porque, como le decía Marta a su vecina Virginia de Robinson, es ahí donde se compra mejor y más barato, y por eso fue a ese mercado adonde las señoras fueron a hacer sus compras ese día.

        El taxi las había dejado a la entrada del barrio, es decir, donde las calles se hacen tan estrechas que está prohibido el tráfico. De ahí en adelante tuvieron que ir a pie hasta el mercado, una distancia de casi un kilómetro. Pero a Virginia no le importó eso ni se cansó de andar; al contrario, estaba encantada de ver la cantidad de cosas tan bonitas y típicas que vendían en todas las tiendas por donde pasaban. En cada una de ellas quería entrar y comprar todo lo que ahí tenían; pero aunque le costó mucho convencerla, Marta no la dejó comprar nada y por fin llegaron al mercado.

29.42   Response drill

    1 ¿Cómo se llama la capital de Surlandia?

    2 ¿En qué parte de la ciudad está situada la parte antigua?

    3 ¿Por cuál otro nombre conoce la gente ese sector también?

    4 ¿Qué fue originalmente la parte antigua de Las Palmas?

    5 ¿Por quién y cuándo fue fundada esa ciudad?

CUARENTA Y UNO   29.41

UNIT 29   SPOKEN SPANISH

6 ¿Por qué hay muchas tiendas de productos típicos en la calle principal?

7 ¿Dónde está el mercado de ese barrio?

8 ¿Qué había antes donde está ahora ese mercado?

9 ¿Cómo es el mercado en su aspecto físico?

10 ¿Pertenece todo el mercado a un solo propietario?

11 Si todo es viejo, sucio y feo por ahí, ¿por qué fueron las dos señoras a ese mercado?

12 ¿Dónde las dejó el taxi?

13 ¿Por qué está prohibido el tráfico en las calles de ese barrio?

14 ¿Qué distancia tuvieron que andar Virginia y Marta para llegar al mercado?

15 ¿Qué quería hacer Virginia en todas las tiendas por donde pasaba?

SPOKEN SPANISH

UNIT 30

30.1   BASIC SENTENCES.   Bullfighting.

The Harrises, Carmen, Molina, and White are sitting in a bar discussing the bullfight.

ENGLISH SPELLING

AID TO LISTENING

SPANISH SPELLING

phenomenal

fènòmènál↓

fenomenal

Harris
What a terrific bullfight!

ké |kòrríđà |támfénòmènál↓

Harris
¡Qué corrida tan fenomenal!

by little, almost, nearly

pòr‑pókò↓

por poco

to faint

dèsmáyarsè↓

desmayarse

Mrs. Harris
Don't say that. I wasn't far from fainting. [1]

nòđigaşéṣò↓ yó |pòrpokomeđezmáyò↓

Sra. Harris
No digas eso. Yo por poco me desmayo.

to behave, conduct oneself

pórtarsè↓

portarse

valiant

bàlyèntè↓

valiente

Carmen
Arruza acted like a hero.

àrruşa |sèpórtó |kómọùmbàlyèntè↓

Carmen
Arruza se portó como un valiente.

the bullfighting

èl‑tòrèò↓

el toreo

cruel

krwé'l↓

cruel

White
I think bullfighting's a very cruel sport.

yòkréò |kèltòrèọ |èsùndèpórtè |múykrwél↓

White
Yo creo que el toreo es un deporte muy cruel.

UNO

30.1

UNIT 30   SPOKEN SPANISH

the game   èl→hwégò↓   el juego

the art   èl→artè↓   el arte

Molina   Molina
The thing is that it's not a game. It's an art. [2]   és |kênǫesͺunhwégò↓ èsúnͺartè↓   Es que no es un juego. Es un arte.

the bullfighter   èl→tòrèrò↓   el torero

to play, to gamble   húgàr↓   jugar

the life   là→bíđà↓   la vida

The bullfighter risks his life. [3]   èltòréro |sèhwégalabíđà↓   El torero se juega la vida.

poor   pòbrè↓   pobre

Mrs. Harris   Sra. Harris
And the poor bull?   ₁élpòbretóro↑   ¿Y el pobre toro?

to die   mòrír↓   morir

to defend   dèfèndèr↓   defender

Molina   Molina
The bull dies defending himself.   èltoro |mwéređefendyéndòsè↓   El toro muere defendiéndose.

the liveliness, animation   lạ→ànimàşyón↓   la animación

the plaza   là→plaşà↓   la plaza

30.2   DOS

Carmen The thing that *I* like **best is the excitement** in the plaza.	àmí | lòkèmázmegústa̧↑èzlànimàşyóndelapláşà↓	*Carmen* A mí lo que **más me gusta** es **la animación** de la plaza.
well	pwés↓	pues
exciting, touching	èmòşyónantè↓	emocionante
the race	là-kàrrérà↓	la carrera
the horse	èl-kàbáʎyò↓	el caballo
White Well, for *me* the most exciting thing is horseracing.(4)	pwés | pàràmí | lòmásemoşyonánte↑sónlàs kàrrérazdekabáʎyòs↓	*White* Pues para mí lo **más emocionante** son las carreras de caballos.
Carmen It's not bad to go once in a while.	dèbéşeŋkwándo↑noestámal | ír↓	*Carmen* De vez en cuando no **está mal** ir.
to bet	àpòstár↓	apostar
White Why don't we go the 15th and place a few bets?	pòrké | nobámosélkínşe↑ȧàpòstámòs↓	*White* ¿Por qué no vamos el quince y apostamos?
that...(they) may leave	kè-déhèn↓	que...dejen
clean	límpyò↓	limpio
Mrs. Harris You go on, and I hope they clean you out.	bayaustéd | ikélòdéhenlímpyò↓	*Sra. Harris* Vaya usted y que lo dejen limpio.
the luck	là-swérte↓	la suerte
as for us	lò-ke-éz-nosótròs↑	lo que es **nosotros**

UNIT 30   SPOKEN SPANISH

       to get bored   ábúrrirsè↓   aburrirse

Harris   *Harris*
  As for us, we just aren't lucky. (5)   lókeznosotroz↑nótènemo(s)swértè↓   Lo que es nosotros, no tenemos suerte.
                                                                  Y yo no quiero aburrirme.
  And I'd just as soon not be bored.   iyó|nòkyérọàbùrrirmè↓

30.10   Notes on the basic sentences

     (1) Literally 'I'm almost fainting,' or 'I don't lack much of fainting.' From context, however, it appears that it was during the fight that she felt this way, so that 'I wasn't far from fainting' is evidently the sense of the utterance.

     (2) This statement is typical, and is entirely serious. Bullfighting is not thought of as a sport in the same sense as horseracing or football (soccer). It is conceived of as an art and so defended when an American reacts unfavorably to the cruelty (from our 'be kind to dumb animals' point of view) of killing the bulls. In some places, the death of the bull is further justified by the argument that the meat is subsequently sold cheaply or given away in charity. To what extent this is generally true is not known by your commentator.

     (3) Note the use of the reflexive pronoun in a simple possessive sense: the bullfighter risks the life that belongs to him.

     (4) Note that the agreement of the verb /son/ *son is with* /las-karréras/ *las carreras* rather than with /lo-más-emoşyonánte/ *lo más emocionante.* Given a nominalized phrase on one side and a singular or plural noun on the other, the number of the latter dominates.

     (5) /lo-kẹ-és...../ *lo que es...* followed by a noun or pronoun literally says 'that which is (us)...' A more normal English translation is 'As far as (we)'re concerned...'

30.2   DRILLS AND GRAMMAR

30.21   General review

30.21.1   Verb review

30.21.11 Translation-substitution drill [1] — verb forms

    1 Are you going down in the elevator?   baha|enẹlas(ş)ensor↑   ¿Baja en el ascensor?

       Were you going down in the elevator?   bàhaba|enẹla(ş)ensór↑   ¿Bajaba en el ascensor?

       Did you go down in the elevator?   bàho|ẹnẹlas(ş)ensór↑   ¿Bajó en el ascensor?

[1] In the following translation drill, change basic sentences to reflect verb tense patterns previously drilled.

30.4   CUATRO

SPOKEN SPANISH   UNIT 30

2 Do you speak English, Mr. Molina?   áblaustedíngles |señyormolinat   ¿Habla Ud. inglés, señor Molina?

   Were you speaking English, Mr. Molina?   áblabaustedíngles |señyormolinat   ¿Hablaba Ud. inglés, señor Molina?

   Did you speak English, Mr. Molina?   ábloustedíngles |señyormolinat   ¿Habló Ud. inglés, señor Molina?

3 They live in an apartment just like mine. biben |énunápàrtàmento |ìgwalalmíó↓   Viven en un apartamento igual al mío.

   They were living in an apartment just like mine.   bibían |énunápàrtàmento |ìgwalalmíó↓   Vivían en un apartamento igual al mío.

   They lived in an apartment just like mine. bibyéron |énunápàrtàmento |ìgwalalmíó↓ Vivieron en un apartamento igual al mío.

4 I have to change my clothes.   téngo |kèkámbyarmederrópà↓   Tengo que cambiarme de ropa.

   I had to (was supposed to) change my clothes. ténía |kèkámbyarmederrópà↓   Tenía que cambiarme de ropa.

   I had to change my clothes.   túbe |kékámbyarmederrópà↓   Tuve que cambiarme de ropa.

5 Where do you send your laundry?   dondemándas |turrópà↓   ¿Dónde mandas tu ropa?

   Where did you (use to) send your laundry? dondemandábas |turrópà↓   ¿Dónde mandabas tu ropa?

   Where did you send your laundry?   dondemandáste |turrópà↓   ¿Dónde mandaste tu ropa?

6 It's not convenient for me.   nomekombyéné↓   No me conviene.

   It wasn't (didn't use to be) convenient
   for me.   nomekombeníà↓   No me convenía.
   It wasn't convenient for me.   nomekombínó↓   No me convino.

7 What's the matter, John?   ketepásà |hwán↓   ¿Qué te pasa, Juan?

   What was (used to be) the matter, John?   ketepasábà |hwán↓   ¿Qué te pasaba, Juan?

   What happened to you, John?   ketepasó |hwán↓   ¿Qué te pasó, Juan?

CINCO   jacobeligoodsons.com For Free Audio   30.5

UNIT 30   SPOKEN SPANISH

8 We barely have half an hour to get   àpenastenémoz |meɖyạóra |parabestírnòs↓   Apenas tenemos media hora para vestirnos.
   dressed.

   We barely had (used to have) half an hour   àpenasteniámoz |meɖyạóra |parabestírnòs↓   Apenas teníamos media hora para vestirnos.
   to get dressed.

   We barely had half an hour to get dressed.   àpenastubímoz |meɖyạóra |parabestírnòs↓   Apenas tuvimos media hora para vestirnos.

9 Are they coming by boat?   byenenẹmbarkot↑   ¿Vienen en barco?

   Were they coming by boat?   bènianẹmbarkot↑   ¿Venían en barco?

   Did they come by boat?   binyeronẹmbarkot↑   ¿Vinieron en barco?

10 Yes, she's coming with my wife and the   si↓ byéne |kònmɪ̀espósạ |ilozníɲyòs↓   Sí, viene con mi esposa y los niños.
   children.

   Yes, she was coming with my wife and   si↓ bènía |kònmɪ̀espósạ |ilozníɲyòs↓   Sí, venía con mi esposa y los niños.
   the children.

   Yes, she came with my wife and the   si↓ bíno |kònmɪ̀espósạ |ilozníɲyòs↓   Sí, vino con mi esposa y los niños.
   children.

11 A married sister of mine lives there.   ùnạ̀ermanamía |kàsáɖa |bibẹaⱭyí↓   Una hermana mía casada vive allí.

   A married sister of mine used to live there.   ùnạ̀ermanamía |kàsáɖa |bibíaⱭyí↓   Una hermana mía casada vivía allí.

   A married sister of mine lived there.   ùnạ̀ermanamía |kàsáɖa |bibyoaⱭyí↓   Una hermana mía casada vivió ahí.

12 No ma'am, it's not necessary.   nosèɲyórà↓ nɡ̀ezneṣesáryò↓   No señora, no es necesario.

   No ma'am, it wasn't necessary.   nosèɲyórà↓ nɡ̀eraneṣesáryò↓   No señora, no era necesario.

   No ma'am it wasn't (didn't turn out to be)   nosèɲyórà↓ nòfweneṣesáryò↓   No señora, no fue necesario.
   necessary.

13 It isn't worth while.   nóbalelapénà↓   No vale la pena.

   It wasn't worth while.   nòbàlíalapénà↓   No valía la pena.

   It wasn't (didn't turn out to be) worth while.   nòbàlyolapénà↓   No valió la pena.

30.6   jacobeligoodsons.com For Free Audio   SEIS

SPOKEN SPANISH   UNIT 30

15 This building here...Does it belong to   éstedıfíşyó↓ pértěněşę|alamısyonamerikana↑   Este edificio ¿pertenece a la Misión
    the American Mission?   Americana?

    This building here...Did it (use to) belong éstedıfíşyó↓ pértěněşıą|alamısyonamerikana↑   Este edificio ¿pertenecía a la Misión
    to the American Mission?   Americana?

    This building here...Did it belong to the   éstedıfíşyó↓ pértěněşyo|alamısyonamerikana↑   Este edificio ¿perteneció a la Misión
    American Mission?   Americana?

15 Do you buy your supplies here?   kómpran|súsprǒbısyóneșakı↑   ¿Compran sus provisiones aquí?

    Did you (used to) buy your supplies here?   kómpraban|súsprǒbısyóneșakı↑   ¿Compraban sus provisiones aquí?

    Did you buy your supplies here?   kǒmpraron|súsprǒbısyóneșakı↑   ¿Compraron sus provisiones aquí?

16 I can be dressed in half an hour.   yo↑ěnmědyą̧ora|mebístó↓   Yo, en media hora me visto.

    I used to get dressed in half an hour.   yo↑ěnmědyą̧ora|mebestíą̀↓   Yo, en media hora me vestía.

    I got dressed in half an hour.   yo↑ěnmědyą̧ora|mebestí↓   Yo, en media hora me vestí.

17 By the way, do you do your own cooking?   ápróposító↓ aşelakomı́dą|ustedmizma↑   A propósito, ¿hace la comida Ud. misma?

    By the way, were you doing your own   ápróposító↓ áşıalakomı́dą|ustedmizma↑   A propósito, ¿hacía la comida Ud. misma?
    cooking?
    By the way, did you do your own cooking?   ápróposító↓ ışolakomı́dą|ustedmizma↑   A propósito, ¿hizo la comida Ud. misma?

18 What's the purpose of your trip?   kwal|eșelproposito|desubyáhě↓   ¿Cuál es el propósito de su viaje?

    What was (to be) the purpose of your trip?   kwal|erą̧elproposito|desubyáhě↓   ¿Cuál era el propósito de su viaje?

    What was the purpose of your trip?   kwal|fwélproposito|desubyáhě↓   ¿Cuál fue el propósito de su viaje?

19 Are you going with your family?   sěba|konsufamílya↑   ¿Se va con su familia?

    Were you going with your family?   sę̌ıba|konsufamílya↑   ¿Se iba con su familia?

    Did you go with your family?   sěfwe|konsufamílya↑   ¿Se fue con su familia?

SIETE   jacobeligoodsons.com For Free Audio   30.7

UNIT 30   SPOKEN SPANISH

30.21.12 Translation substitution drill — Verb construction

1 Do you speak English, Mr. Molina?   ablaustedingles |senyormolina↑   ¿Habla Ud. inglés, señor Molina?

   Have you spoken English, Mr. Molina?   abladgusted |ingles |senyormolina↑   ¿Ha hablado Ud. inglés, señor Molina?

   Are you speaking English, Mr. Molina?   estáblandgusted |ingles |senyormolina↑   ¿Está hablando Ud. inglés, señor Molina?

   Are you going to speak English,   báblarusted |ingles |senyormolina↑   ¿Va a hablar Ud. inglés, señor Molina?
   Mr. Molina?

2 They live in an apartment just like mine. biben |enunapàrtámento |igwalalmió↓   Viven en un apartamento igual al mío.

   They have lived in an apartment just like ambibidọ |enunapàrtámento |igwalalmió↓ Han vivido en un apartamento igual al mío.
   mine.
   They are living in an apartment just like estámbibyendọ |enunapàrtámento |igwalalmió↓ Están viviendo en un apartamento igual al
   mine.   mío.
   They are going to live in an apartment   bánabibir |enunapàrtámento |igwalalmió↓ Van a vivir en un apartamento igual al mío.
   just like mine.

3 Where do you send your laundry?   donde |mandasturrópà↓   ¿Dónde mandas tu ropa?

   Where have you sent your laundry?   dondẹ |azmandadoturrópà↓   ¿Dónde has mandado tu ropa?

   Where are you sending your laundry?   dondẹ |estazmandandoturrópà↓   ¿Dónde estás mandando tu ropa?

   Where are you going to send your   donde |bas,amandárturrópà↓   ¿Dónde vas a mandar tu ropa?
   laundry?

4 What's the matter, John?   ketepásà |hwán↓   ¿Qué te pasa, Juan?

   What has happened to you, John?   keteapasádo |hwán↓   ¿Qué te ha pasado, Juan?

   What is happening to you, John?   ketestapasándò |hwán↓   ¿Qué te está pasando, Juan?

   What's going to happen to you, John?   ketebapasár |hwán↓   ¿Qué te va a pasar, Juan?

30.8   OCHO

SPOKEN SPANISH   UNIT 30

5 Hey, do they throw these parties here
   often?

   oyè↓dan |éstàsfyestas,akí |muyamenuɗot

   Oye, ¿dan estas fiestas aquí muy a menudo?

   Hey, have they given these parties here
   often?

   oyè↓ándaɗo |éstàsfyestas,akí |muyamenuɗot

   Oye, ¿han dado estas fiestas aquí muy a
   menudo?

   Hey, are they giving these parties here
   often?

   oyè↓èstándandọ |éstàsfyestas,akí |muyamenuɗot

   Oye, ¿están dando estas fiestas aquí muy a
   menudo?

   Hey, are they going to give these parties
   here often?

   oyè↓bánáɗar |éstàsfyestas,akí |muyamenuɗot

   Oye, ¿van a dar estas fiestas aquí muy a
   menudo?

6 A married sister of mine lives there.

   ùnaèrmanamía |kàsaɗa |bíbeằ℩yí↓

   Una hermana mía casada vive allí.

   A married sister of mine has lived there.

   ùnaèrmanamía |kàsaɗạ |ábibíɗoằ℩yí↓

   Una hermana mía casada ha vivido allí.

   A married sister of mine is living there.

   ùnaèrmanamía |kàsaɗa |ẹstábibyéndoằ℩yí↓

   Una hermana mía casada está viviendo allí.

   A married sister of mine is going to live
   there.

   ùnaèrmanamía |kàsaɗa |bábibírÀ℩yí↓

   Una hermana mía casada va a vivir allí.

7 Do you all buy your supplies here?

   kompran |susprobisyones,akít

   ¿Compran sus provisiones aquí?

   Have you all bought your supplies here?

   áŋkòmpraɗo |sùspróbisyones,akít

   ¿Han comprado sus provisiones aquí?

   Are you all buying your supplies here?

   éstaŋkomprando |sùspróbisyones,akít

   ¿Están comprando sus provisiones aquí?

   Are you all going to buy your supplies here?

   bánákòmprar |sùspróbisyones,akít

   ¿Van a comprar sus provisiones aquí?

8 Do you buy ready-made clothes?

   ùstéɗkompra |larropạechat

   ¿Ud. compra la ropa hecha?

   Have you bought ready-made clothes?

   ústéɗ |àkòmpraɗo |larropạechat

   ¿Ud. ha comprado la ropa hecha?

   Are you buying ready-made clothes?

   ùstéɗèstákòmprando |larropạechat

   ¿Ud. está comprando la ropa hecha?

   Are you going to buy ready-made clothes?

   ústéɗbákòmprar |larropạechat

   ¿Ud. va a comprar la ropa hecha?

NUEVE   30.9

UNIT 30   SPOKEN SPANISH

9 Do you sew?   ùstéɑkóse↑   ¿Ud. cose?

  Have you sewed?   ùstéɑàkòsiɑo↑   ¿Ud. ha cosido?

  Are you sewing?   ùstédèstákòsyéndo↑   ¿Ud. está cosiendo?

  Are you going to sew?   ùstéɑbákòser↑   ¿Ud. va a coser?

30.21.2 Response drill — Clitic pronoun review

A Pancho, Luis y Pablo van a ir esta tarde a conocer la ciudad. Van a ver el sector comercial, la catedral y el Ministerio de Relaciones Exteriores. Luego van a
   visitar los mejores cafés. Pablo no va con ellos porque ya los conoce. Además, tiene que trabajar.

  1 kwándo |bánɑir |éꞮyos |àkònòꞅerlaꞅyuɑáɑ↓   làbànɑir |àkònòꞅer |estatárɑé↓

  2 bánàber |elsektórkomerꞅyál↑   si↓ lòbanɑbér↓

  3 bánàber |lakateɑral↑   si↓ làbanɑbér↓

  4 bánàber |élministeryo |ɗèrrélàꞅyones,esteryòres↑ si↓ lòbanɑbér↓

  5 bánàbisitar |lozmehoreskafés↑   si↓ lòzbanàbisitár↓

  6 lózbàbisitár |pablo↑   no↓ pablo |nolozbàbisitár↓

  7 pórke |nolozbàbisitár↓   pórkě |yáloskonóꞅé↓

──

  A   1 ¿Cuándo van a ir ellos a conocer la ciudad?   La van a ir a conocer esta tarde.

      2 ¿Van a ver el sector comercial?   Sí, lo van a ver.

      3 ¿Van a ver la catedral?   Sí, la van a ver.

      4 ¿Van a ver el Ministerio de Relaciones Exteriores? Sí, lo van a ver.

      5 ¿Van a visitar los mejores cafés?   Sí, los van a visitar.

      6 ¿Los va a visitar Pablo?   No, Pablo no los va a visitar.

      7 ¿Por qué no los va a visitar?   Porque ya los conoce.

jacobeligoodsons.com For Free Audio

SPOKEN SPANISH   UNIT 30

B Ayer llegó mi suegra de los Estados Unidos. Nos trajo muchas cosas. A mi esposa le trajo un vestido que le pareció muy bonito. A mis hijos les trajo unas camisas
   que a ellos les gustaron mucho. A mí me trajo un par de zapatos.

1 kénostraho|miswégrà↓   lèstraho|muchaskósàs↓

2 kéletraho|amįespósà↓   lètrahoumbestído↓

3 kéleparęyó↓   lèpàręyo|muybonító↓

4 kélestraho|amisɹ́hòs↓   lèstraho|unaskamísàs↓

5 lèzgústaronaęl̨yoz|laskamísas↑   sí↓ lèzgústaronmúchò↓

6 ɹ̨ámi↓kemetráhò↓   lètraho|umpardeȿapátòs↓

7 mètrahoami|kàmisas↑   nó↓ àusteḋ|noletráhokamísàs↓

_____

B 1 ¿Qué nos trajo mi suegra?   Les trajo muchas cosas.

  2 ¿Qué le trajo a mi esposa?   Le trajo un vestido.

  3 ¿Qué le pareció?   Le pareció muy bonito.

  4 ¿Qué les trajo a mis hijos?   Les trajo unas camisas.

  5 ¿Les gustaron a ellos las camisas?   Sí, les gustaron mucho.

  6 ¿Y a mí que me trajo?   Le trajo un par de zapatos.

  7 ¿Me trajo a mi camisas?   No, a Ud. no le trajo camisas.

ONCE   30.11

UNIT 30   SPOKEN SPANISH

C   Todos los lunes, Luisa le presta el carro a su amigo Carlos. El se lleva el carro por la mañana y lo trae por la noche. El le cuida mucho el carro a Luisa.

1   keléprestalwísa |asuamígȯ↓   léprestaͅelkárrȯ↓

2   léprestalwísa |elkárrȯ |asuamigo |lozdomíŋgȯs↑   nȯ↓ noseloprésta |lozdomíŋgȯs↓

3   kéđías |seloprésta↓   sèlóprésta |lozlúnès↓

4   kwándoselọͺyéba↓   sèlóͺyeba |porlamaŋyáná↓

5   kwándo |lètraͅekárlos |èlkárrọalwísa↓   sèlótraͅe |porlanóchè↓

6   sèlókwiđa↑   sí↓ sèlókwiđamúchȯ↓

7   ùstéd↓léprestaͅelkárrọ |asusͺamígos↑   nȯ↓ noselopréstȯ↓

C 1 ¿Qué le presta Luisa a su amigo?   Le presta el carro.

   2 ¿Le presta Luisa el carro a su amigo los domingos?   No, no se lo presta los domingos.

   3 ¿Qué días se lo presta?   Se lo presta los lunes.

   4 ¿Cuándo se lo lleva?   Se lo lleva por la mañana.

   5 ¿Cuándo le trae Carlos el carro a Luisa?   Se lo trae por la noche.

   6 ¿Se lo cuida?   Sí, se lo cuida mucho.

   7 ¿Ud. le presta el carro a sus amigos?   No, no se lo presto.

30.12   DOCE

SPOKEN SPANISH   UNIT 30

D   Francisco le escribió una carta en inglés a su novia que estaba en California. Mandó la carta por avión. En la carta le decía que la iba a ver muy pronto.

1   àkyén|lèskribyófrançískó↓   lèskríbyo|ạsunóbyà↓

2   keléskribyó↓   lèskríbyo|ụnakártà↓

3   lèskríbyólakártạ|enẹspaṇyól↑   nó↓ nóselạẹskríbyo|enẹspaṇyól↓

4   lèskríbyólakártạ|eninglés↑   sí↓ sèlạẹskríbyo|ẹninglés↓

5   sèlàmándo|porabyón↑   sí↓ sèlàmándo|porabyón↓

6   kómoselamandó↓   sèlàmándo|pòrábyón↓

7   kéleçeçịạ|enlakártà↓   kèlạịbabér|muypróntò↓

D 1 ¿A quién le escribió Francisco?   Le escribió a su novia.

  2 ¿Qué le escribió?   Le escribió una carta.

  3 ¿Le escribió la carta en español?   No, no se la escribió en español.

  4 ¿Le escribió la carta en inglés?   Sí, se la escribió en inglés.

  5 ¿Se la mandó por avión?   Sí, se la mandó por avión.

  6 ¿Cómo se la mandó?   Se la mandó por avión.

  7 ¿Qué le decía en la carta?   Que la iba a ver muy pronto.

TRECE

UNIT 30   SPOKEN SPANISH

E   Esta mañana se me olvidó decirles algo a Uds. Anoche, en la fiesta de Carmen, a Luis se le cayó una copa y se le rompió, y después se le cayeron las gafas y
    también se le rompieron.

1   késeme̦olbido |de̦s̱írlés |éstàma̦ŋyána̱↓   sèle̦ólbido |de̦s̱irnos̱álgô↓

2   késelekayo̧alwís |ànóchê̱↓   sèlékàyo̧unakópa̱↓

3   sèlèrrómpyo↑   si↑ sèlèrrómpyo↓

4   kémas |selekayó↓   sèlékàyeron |lazgáfàs↓

5   sèlèkàyeron |laz̧çafas |alwís↑   si↑ sèlèkàyeron↓

6   sèlèrrómpyeron↑   si↑ sèlèrrómpyerôn↓

7   dondeselekayérôn↓   sèlékàyeron |enlafyésta̱↓

8   kwando |selerrompyeronlazgáfàs |àlwís↓   sèlèrrómpyero̦nanóchê↓

9   késemekayó |a̦mí↓   a̧ustèd |nóselekayó |náda̱↓

10 késelerrompyó |akármèn↓   àkarmen |noselerrompyó |náda̱↓

E 1 ¿Qué se me olvidó decirles esta mañana?   Se le olvidó decirnos algo.

  2 ¿Qué se le cayó a Luis anoche?   Se le cayó una copa.

  3 ¿Se rompió?   Sí, se rompió.

  4 ¿Qué más se le cayó?   Se le cayeron las gafas.

  5 ¿Se cayeron las gafas a Luis?   Sí, se le cayeron.

  6 ¿Se le rompieron?   Sí, se le rompieron.

  7 ¿Dónde se le cayeron?   Se le cayeron en la fiesta.

  8 ¿Cuándo se le rompieron las gafas a Luis?   Se le rompieron anoche.

  9 ¿Qué se me cayó a mí?   A Ud. no se le cayó nada.

 10 ¿Qué se le rompió a Carmen?   A Carmen no se le rompió nada.

30.14   jacobeligoodsons.com For Free Audio   CATORCE

SPOKEN SPANISH   UNIT 30

30.21.3   Response drill — Content review

1   lėgústoęlkwárto |delotél |àlsèŋyórhwáyt↑   sí↓ lėgústomúchò↓

2   dėspwéz |dèⁿyėgaralkwártò↓kėlesubyoęlmóşò↓   lėsúbyo |agwaminerál↓

3   báhoęlsęŋyorhwáyt |alprímerpísò↑   sí↓báhó↓

4   kęişǫentónşęs↓   kámbyo |ynchékebyahérò↓

5   dėspwéz |dėkambyarelchékę↓àdondefwé↓   fweęlęembahádà↓

6   kómofwęęlęembahádà↓   fwentáksi↓

7   kwántolędyo |depropína |àlchòfér↓   lėdyoųmpésó↓

8   kyęmfwe |súprimeramígǫ |ènlęęmbáhádà↓   hòsemolínà↓

9   éŋkėsékşyon |ıbatrabahár↓   ènlàsékşyoŋkonsulár↓

10 kėtal |fwelbyahe |délsęŋyorhwáyt↓   fweks(ş)eléntè↓

---

1 ¿Le gustó el cuarto del hotel al Sr. White?   Sí, le gustó mucho.
2 Después de llegar al cuarto, ¿qué le subió el mozo? Le subió agua mineral.
3 ¿Bajó el señor White al primer piso?   Sí, bajó.
4 ¿Qué hizo entonces?   Cambió un cheque viajero.
5 Después de cambiar el cheque, ¿a dónde fue?   Fue a la Embajada.
6 ¿Cómo fue a la Embajada?   Fue en taxi.
7 ¿Cuánto le dió de propina al chofer?   Le dió un peso.
8 ¿Quién fue su primer amigo en la Embajada?   José Molína.
9 ¿En qué sección iba a trabajar?   En la sección consular.
10 ¿Qué tal fué el viaje del Sr. White?   Fue excelente.

QUINCE   30.15

UNIT 30   SPOKEN SPANISH

11   dondȩ |àprèndyóel |espaŋyól↓   ènúnąȩskwela |dèleŋgwas |ènlòsȩ̀staḋosųníḋos↓

12   dèképarte |dèlòsȩ̀stáḋosúnidos |erąél↓   dèsàmfrànşiskò↓kàlifornyà↓

13   éràkàsaḋo↑   no↓ érásòlteró↓

14   èlprimerdią |enląȩmbahádà↓   sì↓ àlmòrşaroŋhúntòs↓
     àlmòrşaroŋhuntos |hwaytimolína↑

15   kebebyeroŋ |konlakomíḋà↓   hwayt |bèbyóşèrbeşą↑imòlína |bebyobínó↓

16   iḋépostrè↓ kèkomyéròn↓   kòmyerom |pàsteldemanşánà↓

17   dèspwezḋekomér↓ sètràtaron |dȩųstedoḋetú↓   sètràtaron |dètú↓

18   hwáyt↓àlkilóyŋàkasa↑oųnąapartàméntò↓   àlkilo |yŋąpàrtàméntò↓

19   lǫàlkilo |sinmwebles↑ǫamwebláḋò↓   lǫàlkiloąmwebláḋò↓

20   kyeņera |làmúchachaḋelafoto |kèbyohwáyt | era |lànobyąḋehosé↓
     ènȩ̀làpàrtàméntoḋemolínà↓

21   èstàbąȩstúḋyandǫ |eˇyą↑   no↓ èstàbatrabahándò↓

_____

11   ¿Dónde aprendió él español?   En una escuela de lenguas en los Estados Unidos.

12   ¿De qué parte de los Estados Unidos era él?   De San Francisco, California.

13   ¿Era casado?   No, era soltero.

14   El primer día en la Embajada, ¿almorzaron juntos White y Molina?   Sí, almorzaron juntos.

15   ¿Qué bebieron con la comida?   White bebió cerveza y Molina bebió vino.

16   Y de postre, ¿qué comieron?   Comieron pastel de manzana.

17   Después de comer, ¿se trataron de Ud. o de tú?   Se trataron de tú.

18   ¿White alquiló una casa o un apartamento?   Alquiló un apartamento.

19   ¿Lo alquiló sin muebles o amueblado?   Lo alquiló amueblado.

20   ¿Quién era la muchacha de la foto que vió White en el apartamento de Molina?   Era la novia de José.

21   ¿Estaba estudiando ella?   No, estaba trabajando.

30.16   DIECISEIS

SPOKEN SPANISH   UNIT 30

22 donde |mandabalostrahez |molínà↓   àlàtintòréría |kestabaemfréntè↓

23 ilàskàmisas↑   àlàlàbàndèria |delaeskína↓
                                                          ùnàmúchachà↓
24 kyénlelimpyabạ |èlàpàrtàmentọ |àmòlínà↓

25 komoẹstubọ |laprimérafyestạ |àkèfweron | èstubọ |èstùpéndà↓
    hwàytimolínà↓

26 àkyén(y)ebo |hwáyt↓   àlàgòrdita |dèlàzgafás↓

27 dondekonoçyohwáyt |àlkòrónelhárris↓   lòkònòşyo |ẹnụnafyéstà↓

28 (y)ègó |lafəmilyadeharris |pòrbárko↑   nó↓ (y)ègoporabyón↓

29 kwantosịhos |tènia |èlkòrònelhárris↓   tréz↓dozbaronés |ụunaníŋyà↓

30 komọatendyeron |àlàsényòraharris |enladwánà↓   làténdyeron |muybyén↓

31 (y)èbohosé |àlòsharris |àkònòşerlaşyudad↑   sí↓ lóz(y)èbó↓

32 kómosẹpusó |lasẹnyórà↓   sẹpusó |nèrbyosà↓

---

22 ¿Dónde mandaba los trajes Molina?   A la tintorería que estaba en frente.

23 ¿Y las camisas?   A la lavandería de la esquina.
                                                          Una muchacha.
24 ¿Quién le limpiaba el apartamento a Molina?

25 ¿Cómo estuvo la primera fiesta a que fueron White y Molina?   Estuvo estupenda.

26 ¿A quién llevó White?   A la gordita de las gafas.

27 ¿Dónde conoció White al coronel Harris?   Lo conoció en una fiesta.

28 ¿Llegó la familia de Harris por barco?   No, llegó por avión.

29 ¿Cuántos hijos tenía el coronel Harris?   Tres, dos varones y una niña.

30 ¿Cómo atendieron a la Sra. Harris en la Aduana?   La atendieron muy bien.

31 ¿Llevó José a los Harris a conocer la ciudad?   Sí, los llevó.

32 ¿Cómo se puso la señora?   Se puso nerviosa.

DIECISIETE   30.17

UNIT 30   SPOKEN SPANISH

33 àkyénesimbito |ę1kòrònelhárris |àbisitárlamisyón |
    dèláfwerşaéręà↓   àhóse |àkármen |ąahwáyt↓

34 puḍǫir |karmen↑   nó↓ nòpúḍǫír↓

35 pòrke |nopúḍǫir↓   pòrkètènia |kèsálirḍekómpras |kònlàsèŋyóra
                                                                hárris↓

36 komosę́ḷyamabą |elseŋyór |kèkèria |làbisa |párálòs
    èstaḍos̭unídòs↓   hóselwiz |mòrénorróhàs↓

37 era |tènyénte↑   nó↓ éraįnhènyeró↓

38 kwalerą |èlḍèpórtefaborito |ḍemolíná↓   èlfutbòl↓

39 kwalpraktikábà↓   niŋunò↓

40 sàbia |hugargolf |molina↑   nó↓ nosabíá↓

41 kyénlenseŋyo |ąhugarḍespwés↓   hwayt |lènsèŋyó↓

42 kéhugabaŋ |kármen |ìlàsèŋyoráhárris↓   húgabanténis↓

43 kéleparęşyo |làkòrriḍaḍetoros |àlkòrònelhárris↓   lèpàręşyó |fènòmènáĺ↓

---

33 ¿A quiénes invitó el coronel Harris a visitar la Misión de la Fuerza Aérea?   A José, a Carmen y a White.

34 ¿Pudo ir Carmen?   No, no pudo ir.

35 ¿Por qué no pudo ir?   Porque tenía que salir de compras con la Sra. Harris.

36 ¿Cómo se llamaba el señor que quería la visa para los Estados Unidos?   José Luis Moreno Rojas.

37 ¿Era teniente?   No, era ingeniero.

38 ¿Cuál era el deporte favorito de Molina?   El fútbol.

39 ¿Cuál practicaba?   Ninguno.

40 ¿Sabía jugar golf Molina?   No, no sabía.

41 ¿Quién le enseñó a jugar después?   White le enseñó.

42 ¿Qué jugaban Carmen y la Sra. Harris?   Jugaban tenis.

43 ¿Qué le pareció la corrida de toros al coronel Harris?   Le pareció fenomenal.

SPOKEN SPANISH   UNIT 30

30.22   Replacement drills

A   yó |pòrpókomeđezmáyò↓

1. _____ noz _____↓   nòsotros |pòrpóko |nozđezmayámòs↓

2. tú _____↓   tu |pòrpókoteđezmáyás↓

3. _____ mwérés↓   tu |pòrpókotemwérès↓

4. ___kàsi _____↓   tú |kàsitemwérès↓

5. _____káęs↓   tú |kàsitekáęs↓

6. ùsteđ _____↓   ùsteđ |kàsisekáę↓

7. _____káygò↓   yó |kàsimekáygò↓

_____

A   Yo por poco me desmayo.

1 _____ nos _____.   Nosotros por poco nos desmayamos.

2 Tú _____.   Tú por poco te desmayas.

3 _____ mueres.   Tú por poco te mueres.

4 ___casi _____.   Tú casi te mueres.

5 _____ caes.   Tú casi te caes.

6 Usted _____.   Usted casi se cae.

7 _____ caigo.   Yo casi me caigo.

UNIT 30   SPOKEN SPANISH

B   árruṣa |sèpòrtó |kómọûmbàlyèntè↓

1. ùsteđes_____↓   ùsteđes |sèpòrtaroŋ |kómọûnòzbàlyèntès↓

2. _____flohòs↓   ùsteđes |sèpòrtaroŋ |kómọûnòsflohòs↓

3. _____mè_____↓   yó |mèpórtè |kómọûmflohò↓

4. _____ombrè↓   yó |mèpórtè |kómọûnọmbrè↓

5. tú_____↓   tú |tèpòrtàstè |kómọûnọmbrè↓

6. _____mûhe'r↓   tú |tèpòrtàstè |kómọûnàmûhe'r↓

7. _____niŋyò↓   tú |tèpòrtàstè |kómọû(n)niŋyò↓

B   Arruza se portó como un valiente.

1 Ustedes_____.   Ustedes se portaron como unos valientes.

2 _____flojos.   Ustedes se portaron como unos flojos.

3 _____me_____.   Yo me porté como un flojo.

4 _____hombre.   Yo me porté como un hombre.

5 Tú_____.   Tú te portaste como un hombre.

6 _____mujer.   Tú te portaste como una mujer.

7 _____niño.   Tú te portaste como un niño.

30.20   VEINTE

SPOKEN SPANISH   UNIT 30

C   èltòreọ |ésûndèpórte |múykrwél↓

1. _____kósa_____↓   èltòreọ |ésûnàkósa |múykrwél↓

2. _____emoşyonántè↓   èltòreọ |ésûnàkósa |múyemoşyonántè↓

3. esọ_____↓   esọ |ésûnàkósa |múyemoşyonántè↓

4. _____féà↓   esọ |ésûnàkósa |múyféà↓

5. estạ_____↓   estạ |ésûnàkósa |múyféà↓

6. _____fáşil↓   estạ |ésûnàkósa |múyfáşil↓

7. _____bíđa_____↓   estạ |ésûnàbíđa |múyfáşil↓

_____

C   El toreo es un deporte muy cruel.

1 _____cosa_____.   El toreo es una cosa muy cruel.

2 _____emocionante.   El toreo es una cosa muy emocionante.

3 Eso _____.   Eso es una cosa muy emocionante.

4 _____fea.   Eso es una cosa muy fea.

5 Esta_____.   Esta es una cosa muy fea.

6 _____fácil.   Esta es una cosa muy fácil.

7 _____vida_____.   Esta es una vida muy fácil.

VEINTIUNO

UNIT 30　　　　　　　　　　　　　　　　　　　　　　　　　　　　　SPOKEN SPANISH

D　　èltòréro |sèhwégalabídà↓

1. nòsótroz＿＿＿＿＿＿＿＿＿↓　　　　　nòsótroz |nòshùgámozlabídà↓

2. ＿＿＿＿＿＿＿＿＿tódò↓　　　　　　nòsótroz |nòshùgámostódò↓

3. ＿＿＿＿＿kàmbyámos＿＿↓　　　　　nòsótroz |nòskàmbyámostódò↓

4. ＿＿＿＿＿＿＿＿＿larrópà↓　　　　　nòsótroz |nòskàmbyámozlarrópà↓

5. ùstèdes＿＿＿＿＿＿＿＿＿↓　　　　　ùstèdes |sèkàmbyanlarrópà↓

6. ＿＿＿＿＿pónen＿＿＿＿↓　　　　　ùstèdes |sèpónenlarrópà↓

7. yó＿＿＿＿＿＿＿＿＿＿＿↓　　　　　yó |mèpoŋgolarrópà↓

D　El torero se juega la vida.

1 Nosotros＿＿＿＿＿＿＿＿.　　　　　Nosotros nos jugamos la vida.

2 ＿＿＿＿＿＿＿＿todo.　　　　　　　Nosotros nos jugamos todo.

3 ＿＿＿＿＿cambiamos＿＿.　　　　　Nosotros nos cambiamos todo.

4 ＿＿＿＿＿＿＿la ropa.　　　　　　Nosotros nos cambiamos la ropa.

5 Ustedes＿＿＿＿＿＿＿＿.　　　　　Ustedes se cambian la ropa.

6 ＿＿＿＿＿ponen＿＿＿.　　　　　　Ustedes se ponen la ropa.

7 Yo＿＿＿＿＿＿＿＿＿＿.　　　　　Yo me pongo la ropa.

30.22　　　　　　　　　　jacobeligoodsons.com For Free Audio　　　　　　　　VEINTIDOS

SPOKEN SPANISH   UNIT 30

E   ėltóro |mwéreɖefendyéndȯsė↓

1. ___ombrez _____↓   lós,ombrez |mwérendefendyéndȯsė↓

2. _____èstán_____↓   lós,ombres |ėstandefendyéndȯsė↓

3. nȯsótros_____↓   nȯsótros |ėstamozɖefendyéndȯnȯs↓

4. naɖyę _____↓   naɖyę |ėstaɖefendyéndȯsė↓

5. _____ɖezmayándȯsė↓   naɖyę |ėstaɖezmayándȯsė↓

6. álgyen_____↓   álgyen |ėstaɖezmayándȯsė↓

7. _____kayéndȯsė↓   álgyen |ėstakayéndȯsė↓

E   El toro muere defendiéndose.

1 ___hombres _____.   Los hombres mueren defendiéndose.

2 _____están_____.   Los hombres están defendiéndose.

3 Nosotros _____.   Nosotros estamos defendiéndonos.

4 Nadie _____.   Nadie está defendiéndose.

5 _____ desmayándose.   Nadie está desmayándose.

6 Alguien_____.   Alguien está desmayándose.

7 _____ cayéndose.   Alguien está cayéndose.

UNIT 30   SPOKEN SPANISH

F   nòsotroz |nótenémo(s) swértè↓

1. yó _____ ↓   yó |nótengoswértè↓

2. _____ náđà↓   yó |nótengonáđà↓

3. _____ ágo _____ ↓   yó |ngagonáđà↓

4. kármen _____ ↓   kármen |ngaşenáđà↓

5. _____ múchò↓   kármen |ngaşemúchò↓

6. _____ đişe _____ ↓   kármen |nođişemúchò↓

7. tú _____ ↓   tú |nođişezmúchò↓

F   Nosotros no tenemos suerte.

1 Yo_____ .   Yo no tengo suerte.

2 _____ nada.   Yo no tengo nada.

3 _____ hago _____ .   Yo no hago nada.

4 Carmen _____ .   Carmen no hace nada.

5 _____ mucho.   Carmen no hace mucho.

6 _____ dice _____ .   Carmen no dice mucho.

7 Tú _____ .   Tú no dices mucho.

SPOKEN SPANISH   UNIT 30

30.23   Variation drills

A   kékorriđa |tamfenomenál↓   ¡Qué corrida tan fenomenal!

     1 What a terrific idea!   kei̯đea |tamfenomenál↓   ¡Qué idea tan fenomenal!

     2 What terrific weather!   kétyempo |tamfenomenál↓   ¡Qué tiempo tan fenomenal!

     3 What a fine bullfighter!   kétorero |tambwénò↓   ¡Qué torero tan bueno!

     4 What a dirty business deal!   kenegoşyo |tansúşyò↓   ¡Qué negocio tan sucio!

     5 What a competent servant!   kekryađa |taŋkompeténtè↓   ¡Qué criada tan competente!

     6 What an exciting race!   kekarrera |taṇemoşyonántè↓   ¡Qué carrera tan emocionante!

     7 What a punctual man!   ke̦ombre |tampuntwál↓   ¡Qué hombre tan puntual!

B   éskě |no̦esu̯ŋhwégò↓ ėșúna̦rtè↓   Es que no es un juego. Es un arte.

     1 But it's not a sport. It's an art.   éskěnǥes |undepórtè↓ éșúna̦rtè↓   Es que no es un deporte. Es un arte.

     2 But it's not a restaurant. It's a club. éskěnǥes |unrrestorán↓ ėșúŋklub↓   Es que no es un restorán. Es un club.

     3 But it's not a check. It's a bill.   éskěnǥesunchékè↓ ésúmbiḽḽetè↓   Es que no es un cheque. Es un billete.

VEINTICINCO   30.25

UNIT 30   SPOKEN SPANISH

4 But it's not a month. It's two months.   pèrònǫésunmés↓ sòndozmésés↓   Pero no es un mes. Son dos meses.

5 But it's not agreeable. It's a nuisance.   pèrònǫés|agraḍáblé↓ ésúnàlatà↓   Pero no es agradable. Es una lata.

6 But it's not pretty. It's ugly.   pèrònǫézbonítò↓ èsfeò↓   Pero no es bonito. Es feo.

7 But it's not just stupendous. It's fantastic. pèrònósolǫ|esestupéndò↓ èsfàntastikò↓ Pero no sólo es estupendo. Es fantástico.

C   àmí|lókèmazmegustą↑èzlànìmàşyón|delaplàşà↓   A mí, lo que más me gusta es la animación
                                                       de la plaza.

1 The thing I like best is the excitement of àmí|lókèmazmegustą↑èzlànìmàşyón|dela   A mí, lo que más me gusta es la animación
   the party.   fyéstà↓   de la fiesta.

2 The thing I like best is the activity in the àmí|lókèmazmegustą↑èsélmòbimyentǫ|enlas A mí, lo que más me gusta es el movimiento
   stores.   tyéndàs↓   en las tiendas.

3 The thing I like least in the movement of àmí|lókèmenozmegustą↑èsélmòbimyento|del   A mí, lo que menos me gusta es el movimiento
   the ship.   bárkò↓   del barco.

4 The thing she likes least is the bad luck àeǜya|lókèménozlegustą↑èzlàmálaswérte|del A ella, lo que menos le gusta es la mala
   of the bull.   tóró↓   suerte del toro.

5 The thing that bothers him most is the   àel|lókèmázlemoléstą↑èsélrrwiḍoḍeltráfikò↓ A él, lo que más le molesta es el ruido del
   noise of the traffic.   tráfico.

jacobeligoodsons.com For Free Audio   VEINTISEIS

SPOKEN SPANISH   UNIT 30

6 The thing that bothers *John* most is
waiting for a person.

àhwàn |lòkèmàzlemolestà↑èsèspèrár |ₐunapersónà↓

A Juan, lo que más le molesta es esperar
a una persona.

7 The thing that bothers *us* most is
traveling by plane.

ànòsótroz |lòkèmàznozmolestà↑èzbyàharpòrabyón↓

A nosotros, lo que más nos molesta es viajar
por avión.

D   pàràmì↑lòmasₑemoşyonante↑sònlàskàrrèrás↓

Para mí, lo más emocionante son las carreras.

1 For *me* the most exciting thing is the
bullfights.

pàràmì↑lòmasₑemoşyonante↑sònlàskòrrídàs↓

Para mí, lo más emocionante son las corridas.

2 For *her* the most pleasant thing is the
sunny days.

pàrₐeˢyà↑lòmasₐagradable↑sònlòꝝdìazdesól↓

Para ella, lo más agradable son los días de sol.

3 For *John* the most pleasant thing is the
trips by boat.

pàràhwàn↑lòmasₐagradable↑sònlòzbyàhesporbárkò↓

Para Juan, lo más agradable son los viajes por
barco.

4 For *him* the most difficult thing is
convincing his wife.

pàrₐel↑lòmazdifiṣil↑èskòmbènşerasyespósà↓

Para él, lo más difícil es convencer a su
esposa.

5 For *them* the most difficult thing is
translating the lesson.

pàrₐeˢyoz↑lòmazdifiṣil↑èstràdùṣirlalekşyón↓

Para ellos, lo más difícil es traducir la lección.

6 For *them* (f) the easiest thing is putting
their foot in it.

pàrₐeˢyaz↑lòmasfaṣil↑èzmèterlapátà↓

Para ellas, lo más fácil es meter la pata.

7 For *us* the most expensive thing is the gas.

pàrànòsótroz↑lòmaskàrₒ↑esₑelgàs↓

Para nosotros, lo más caro es el gas.

E   pòrké |nobámosₑelkinşe↑ₐapostámós↓

¿Por qué no vamos el quince y apostamos?

1 Why don't we go the 20th and play?

pòrké |nobámosₑelbéynte↑ₐihuᶃámós↓

¿Por qué no vamos el veinte y jugamos?

2 Why don't we come tomorrow and play?

pòrké |nobenìmozmaŋyanₐ↑ihuᶃámòs↓

¿Por qué no venimos mañana y jugamos?

VEINTISIETE   jacobeligoodsons.com For Free Audio   30.27

UNIT 30   SPOKEN SPANISH

3 Why don't we come tomorrow and eat?   pòrke |nobenimoʂmaɲyanạ↑ikomémòs↓   ¿Por qué no venimos mañana y comemos?

4 Why don't we leave word now and go out?   pòrke |noabisamos̩aorạ↑isalímòs↓   ¿Por qué no avisamos ahora y salimos?

5 Why don't we leave now and go by your   pòrke |nosalimos̩aorạ↑ípàsamos̩atukáså↓   ¿Por qué no salimos ahora y pasamos a tu
   house?   casa?

6 Why don't we go up now and look for the   pòrke |nosubimos̩aorạ↑ibùskamozlakártå↓   ¿Por qué no subimos ahora y buscamos la
   letter?   carta?

7 Why don't we come back afterwards and   pòrke |nobolbemozdespwés↑ɹàrrèglàmoz   ¿Por qué no volvemos después y arreglamos
   settle (arrange) the bills?   laskwéntås↓   las cuentas?

F bayạustéd |ikèlòdèhenlímpyò↓   Vaya Ud., y que lo dejen limpio.

1 You go on, and I hope they leave you   bayạustéd |ikèlòdèhenạí↓   Vaya Ud., y que lo dejen ahí.
   there.

2 You go on, and I hope they leave you   bayạustéd |ikèlòdèhen |sin̩umpésò↓   Vaya Ud., y que lo dejen sin un peso.
   without a nickel.

3 You go on, and I hope they leave you   bayạustéd |ikèlòdèhen |sindinérò↓   Vaya Ud., y que lo dejen sin dinero.
   without any money.

4 You go on, and I hope they leave you   bayạustéd |ikèlòdèhen |si(n)nádå↓   Vaya Ud., y que lo dejen sin nada.
   without anything.

5 You go on, and I hope they drive you crazy. bayạustéd |ikèlòbwelbanlókò↓   Vaya Ud., y que lo vuelvan loco.

6 You go on, and I hope they make you   bayạustéd |ikèlópoŋga(n)nerbyósò↓   Vaya Ud., y que lo pongan nervioso.
   nervous.

7 You go on, and I hope they put you out   bayạustéd |ikèlópongan |enlakáᶜyè↓   Vaya Ud., y que lo pongan en la calle.
   in the street.

30.28   jacobeligoodsons.com For Free Audio   VEINTIOCHO

SPOKEN SPANISH

UNIT 30

30.3   CONVERSATION STIMULUS

NARRATIVE 1

1 Bob mustn't make any engagements for this Sunday.

bob |noðebekomprométerse |párạestedomíngò↓

Bob no debe comprometerse para el domingo.

2 He wants to go to the bullfights again.

kyérẹir |àlàkòrriðadetóròs |ótràbéṣ↓

Quiere ir a la corrida de toros otra vez.

3 But Jean tells him he can't.

péròyin |lèðiṣekenopwéðè↓

Pero Jean le dice que no puede.

4 Because last Sunday they told the children they were going to take them out to the country.

pòrkèldòmingopasaðot lézdihéron |àlóznìṇyost kèlòs̪iban |àḷyèbaralkámpò↓

Porque el domingo pasado les dijeron a los niños que los iban a llevar al campo.

5 And they didn't take them.

inolozûyebáròn↓

Y no los llevaron.

6 Then, they'll have to take them this Sunday.

èntonṣes |tyénenkẻỵebárlos |éstedomíngò↓

Entonces, tienen que llevarlos este domingo.

7 It's true that the children can go with the maid.

èzbérdad |kèlóznìṇyos |pweðenị̀r |kònlàkryádà↓

Es verdad que los niños pueden ir con la criada.

8 But they want to go with their parents, not with the maid.

pérgeûyos |kyerenị̀r |kònṣùspadrèṣ↓ nokonlakryáðà↓

Pero ellos quieren ir con sus padres, no con la criada.

9 And Bob shouldn't be so mean.

ibob |noðebiasertaṇkrwél↓

Y Bob no debía ser tan cruel.

VEINTINUEVE

jacobeligoodsons.com For Free Audio

30.29

UNIT 30   SPOKEN SPANISH

DIALOG 1

Jean, dígale a Bob que no se comprometa para
este domingo.

nótekompromḗtas |párạestẹḍomíŋgò |bób↓

Jean: No te comprometas para este
domingo, Bob.

Bob, pregúntele que por qué. Que Ud. quiere
ir otra vez a la corrida de toros.

pòrké↓ yókyẹrọir |ótràbẹṣ |àlàkòrríḍàḍẹtoròs↓

Bob: ¿Por qué? Yo quiero ir otra vez a
la corrida de toros.

Jean, dígale que no puede, que Uds. tienen
que llevar a los niños al campo.

nópwéḍès↓ tènẹmoskẹⁿyebár |àlòzníŋyọsₐlkámpò↓

Jean: No puedes. Tenemos que llevar
a los niños al campo.

Bob, dígale que vayan con la criada.

kébayaŋkọnlakryáḍà↓

Bob: Que vayan con la criada.

Jean, dígale que no sea tan cruel. Que ellos
quieren ir con sus padres, no con la
criada.

nóséastaŋkrwél↓ eⁿyostkyérénịr |kònsúspaḍrès↓
nokọnlakryáḍà↓

Jean: No seas tan cruel. Ellos quieren
ir con sus padres, no con la
criada.

NARRATIVE 2

1 Besides, Jean thinks that bullfighting is
an awful and cruel thing.

àḍḗmastॣàyₙₑ inlepareṣe |kéltòréotèsúnàkosạ |
órríblẹikrwél↓

Además, a Jean le parece que el toreo es
una cosa horrible y cruel.

2 But Bob thinks it's very exciting.

pérọàbób |lépàreṣe |kéꝯmúyemọṣyọnántḕ↓

Pero a Bob le parece que es muy emocionante.

3 And that Sunday's fight was terrific.

ikèlàkòrríḍa |ḍeldomíŋgotẹstubo |fénòmḕnäl↓

Y que la corrida del domingo estuvo fenomenal.

4 Jean doesn't see how Bob can say such
a thing.

yín |nòbékọmòbób |pwéḍẹḍẹṣir |talkósà↓

Jean no ve cómo Bob puede decir tal cosa.

5 She got so nervous she almost fainted.

eⁿyạ |sèpúsòtá(n)nerbyósa╵tẹpòrpókosẹḍesmáyà↓

Ella se puso tan nerviosa que por poco se
desmaya.

30.30   TREINTA

SPOKEN SPANISH   UNIT 30

6 Bob believes that happened to her
  because it was the first bullfight
  she'd seen.

bobkreę |kesolepaso |pòrkėzlâprimera
korriđa |keḷḷyabístò↓

Bob cree que eso le pasó porque es la
primera corrida que ella ha visto.

7 It may be, but as for Jean, she doesn't
  want to see any more bullfights.

pwęđesér↓ péròlòkęzyin↑nòkyéreber |
maskorríđàs↓

Puede ser, pero lo que es Jean, no quiere
ver más corridas.

                                      DIALOG 2

Jean, dígale a Bob que además el toreo es
una cosa horrible y cruel.

àđémàs |ėltóreǫ |ės̨únàkos̨ạ |òrríbleįkrwél↓

Jean: Además, el toreo es una cosa
       horrible y cruel.

Bob, dígale que a Ud. le parece que es muy
emocionante. Que la corrida del domingo
estuvo fenomenal.

àmı |mėpc̨reşę |kėzmuyemoşyonántė↓
làkòrriđadeldomiŋgǫ |èstúbòfènòmènal↓

Bob: A mí me parece que es muy emocio-
       nante. La corrida del domingo estuvo
       fenomenal.

Jean, pregúntele que cómo puede decir tal
cosa. Que Ud. se puso tan nerviosa que
por poco se desmaya.

kómopwéđez |đeçırtalkósà↓ yo |mépúsė |ta(n)
nerbyosa↑kėpòrpokomeđezmáyò↓

Jean: ¿Cómo puedes decir tal cosa? Yo me
       puse tan nerviosa que por poco me
       desmayo.

Bob, dígale que eso le pasó porque es la
primera corrida que ha visto.

esotepaso |pòrkėzlâprimerakorriđa |kęazbístò↓

Bob: Eso te pasó porque es la primera
       corrida que has visto.

Jean, contéstele que puede ser, pero lo que
es Ud., no quiere ver más corridas.

pwęđesér↓ pèròlòkézyo↑nòkyerober |
maskorríđàs↓

Jean: Puede ser, pero lo que es yo, no
       quiero ver más corridas.

TREINTA Y UNO   30.31

UNIT 30   SPOKEN SPANISH

NARRATIVE 3

1 Bob and Jean want to go to the races
this evening.

bòbìyìŋ|kyérenⁱr|àláskárrerazdekabáↄyòs|
éstànóchè↓

Bob y Jean quieren ir a las carreras de
caballos esta noche.

2 But Jean doesn't know whom to leave
the children with.

pèròyⁱn|nòsabe|kòŋkyéndeháralozníɲyòs↓

Pero Jean no sabe con quién dejar a
los niños.

3 'Let them stay with the maid,' says Bob.

kèsékeden|kònlákryaɗà|dìṣèbób↓

Que se queden con la criada—dice Bob.

4 But Jean tells him that's not possible.

pèròyⁱnledⁱṣe|kénosepwéɗè↓

Pero Jean le dice que no se puede.

5 Because the maid wants to go out this
evening.

pórkèlàkryaɗa|kyéresalír|éstànóchè↓

Porque la criada quiere salir esta noche.

6 'Well, don't let her go out this evening, let
her go out tomorrow; it's the same thing,'
says Bob.

pwés|kènosálgą|éstànóchè↓kèsalga|máɲyanà↓
èzlómⁱzmò|dìṣèbób↓

Pues, que no salga esta noche, que salga
mañana; es lo mismo—dice Bob.

DIALOG 3

Bob, pregúntele a Jean si quiere ir a las
carreras de caballos esta noche.

kyéresⁱr|àláskàrrerazdekabáↄyos|éstanóche↑

Bob: ¿Quieres ir a las carreras de caballos
esta noche?

Jean, contéstele que bueno, pero que con
quién dejan a los niños.

bwenò|pèròkòŋkyéndehámos|àlozníɲyòs↓

Jean: Bueno, pero ¿con quién dejamos a
los niños?

Bob, dígale que se queden con la criada.

kèsékeden|kònlákryaɗà↓

Bob: Que se queden con la criada.

Jean, dígale que es que la criada quiere
salir esta noche.

éskèlàkryaɗa|kyérèsálⁱr|éstànóchè↓

Jean: Es que la criada quiere salir esta
noche.

Bob, dígale que pues que no salga esta
noche, que salga mañana; que es lo
mismo.

pwés↑kènosálgą|éstànóchè↓kèsálgàmáɲyanà↓
èzlómⁱzmò↓

Bob: Pues que no salga esta noche, que
salga mañana; es lo mismo.

30.32   jacobeligoodsons.com For Free Audio   TREINTA Y DOS

SPOKEN SPANISH   UNIT 30

30.4   READINGS

30.40   List of cognate loan words

las ofertas	làs—ófértàs↓
el comentario	èl—kòméntaryò↓
simplemente	sìmpléméntè↓
el gesto	èl—héstò↓
significaba (significar)	sìgnifikàbà↓ sìgnifikár↓
etcétera	è(t)ṣètèrá↓
el italiano	èl—itàlyanò↓
Italia	itàlyà↓
la cliente	lá—klyèntè↓
los empleados	lós—èmpleàdòs↓
inteligente	intèlihèntè↓
la cuestión	là—kwéstyòn↓
pretendiendo (pretender)	prètèndyendò↓ prètèndér↓
depende (depender)	dèpèndè↓ dèpèndér↓
los kilos	lòs—kilòs↓
los céntimos	lòs—ṣèntimós↓
la calidad	là—kàlidàd↓
ofende (ofender)	óféndè↓ ófèndér↓
cultiva (cultivar)	kúltibà↓ kùltibár↓

TREINTA Y TRES   30.33

UNIT 30   SPOKEN SPANISH

produce (producir)   próduṣè↓ próduṣír↓

imitando (imitar)   imitandò↓ imitár↓

la desesperación   là—déséspéràṣyón↓

la discusión   là—diskúsyón↓

la curiosidad   là—kúryòsidàd↓

pacientemente   pàṣyéntemèntè↓

las ocasiones   làs—òkàsyònès↓

furioso   fùryósò↓

el asilo   èl—àsilò↓

la aspirina   là—àspirinà↓

la experiencia   là—éspèryenṣyà↓

adaptar   àdàptár↓

representar   rrèprèsèntár↓

sincero   sinṣèrò↓

actuar   àktwár↓

los surlandeses   lòs—súrlàndesès↓

populares   pòpúlarès↓

la colonia   là—kòlonyà↓

30.34   jacobeligoodsons.com For Free Audio   TREINTA Y CUATRO

SPOKEN SPANISH   UNIT 30

30.41   Reading selection

                                             En el Mercado

—¡Venga para acá, señora! ¿Qué le damos hoy? ¡Mire estas verduras tan frescas! Me las acaban de traer, ¡mire qué tomates, qué lechugas...! ¿Qué busca Ud.?
Dígame qué busca que aquí tenemos de todo, fresco y barato. Un momento, señora, no se vaya, vea estos huevos que acaban de llegar, y a tres pesos la docena solamente;
un regalo, ¿no cree Ud.? Pero señora, ¿cómo cree que los puedo dar a uno cincuenta cuando a mí me costaron dos y medio? No gano casi nada; pero venga, no se vaya,
se los dejo un poco más baratos. ¿Cuánto me da? Le apuesto que no va a encontrar nada mejor en todo el mercado. Tómelos, se los doy a dos cincuenta...dos cuarenta,
entonces...¡señora!...¡venga, no se vaya!

Esto mismo le decían a Marta o a Virginia en cada puesto por donde pasaban, y todo el mundo parecía hablar al mismo tiempo. El ruido era enorme, aquello parecía
una casa de locos. Pero Marta, que estaba acostumbrada a estas cosas, seguía andando muy tranquila sin poner atención a las ofertas que le hacían; y Virginia, que sólo
iba ese día para aprender, tomaba la misma actitud de su amiga. De vez en cuando Marta preguntaba el precio de alguna cosa, y cuando se lo decían, contestaba con un
pequeño comentario, tal como 'carísimo', 'no me gusta', etc., o simplemente hacía un gesto que significaba lo mismo. Otras veces no decía nada y seguía muy tranquila,
dejando a la persona que vendía, llamándola y diciéndole la misma cosa de siempre: 'Un momento, señora, no se vaya, hágame una oferta, se lo dejo más barato, etcétera,
etcétera.'

Por fin llegaron a un puesto, que se llamaba 'El Regalo.' El propietario era un italiano que hacía muchos años que vivía en Surlandia y que siempre estaba hablando
de volver a Italia para pasar allá los últimos años de su vida. Su nombre era Vittorio Martini, y aunque había vivido muchos años en Surlandia nunca había podido, o no se
había preocupado, de aprender a hablar bien en español; hablaba con un acento tan grande que a veces no se sabía si era en italiano o en español que estaba hablando. Don
Vittorio sabía que a la *signora Fonti*, como le decía él a la Sra. Fuentes, aunque era buena cliente, le gustaba mucho discutir por los precios y fácilmente podía confundir y
convencer a cualquiera de sus empleados. Por eso él mismo en persona prefería atenderla cada vez que ella venía a comprar.

—Don Vittorio—dijo Pedro, un empleado, llamando a su jefe—allá viene la Sra. Fuentes. ¿La atiendo yo? Va a ver que a mí no me confunde.

—Estás loco, *bambino*, la *signora Fonti* es *molto intelligente* para ti—responde don Vittorio con una ensalada de italiano y español.—Esta *signora* es *buona* cliente,
pero hay que tener mucho cuidado con la cuestión de los precios. Ah, pero yo, Vittorio Martini, también soy *molto intelligente*. Déjame, yo mismo la voy a atender.

—Aquél es el puesto, Virginia, aquél que dice 'El Regalo'—le dijo la Sra. Fuentes a su amiga americana, indicándole el puesto del italiano. —El propietario es una
persona muy amable, y aunque discute mucho por los precios y cuesta un poco convencerlo, siempre termina vendiéndome todo más barato que en cualquiera otra parte. Déjeme
ver lo que tengo en la lista; arroz, carne, huevos, mantequilla y algunas verduras. Voy a comprar las cosas mías primero y luego compro las suyas. Aquí estamos. Ahora
observe con mucho cuidado para que aprenda.

---

signora Fonti	señora Fuentes
bambinos	niño
molto intelligente	muy inteligente
buona	buena

TREINTA Y CINCO   30.35

UNIT 30   SPOKEN SPANISH

—Buenos días, don Vittorio— le dijo —¿Cómo le va y qué tal la señora y los *bambinos?*

—¡*Signora Fonti!*, ¿Qué sorpresa tan agradable!, -¡*molto piacere* de verla por aquí! —contestó el italiano pretendiendo no haberla visto cuando venía. —Los *bambinos*
y la *signora* están *molto bene, grazie, grazie.* ¿Y qué le vendemos hoy, *signora?*

—Tengo mucho que comprarle, pero eso depende del precio. Primero, necesito diez kilos de arroz.

—*Molto bene,* signora, mire Ud. que arroz tan bonito tenemos, no hay otro mejor en todo el mercado. Y le voy a dar un precio especial, a cincuenta céntimos el kilo,
pero sólo a Ud. por ser tan buena cliente nuestra.

—¡Cincuenta céntimos! Ni loca. ¿Eso llama Ud. precio especial? Además, este arroz no parece de muy buena calidad.

—*Signora,* Ud. ofende a Vittorio Martini al decir tal cosa. ¿Cómo puede decir que no es de *buona qualitá* cuando es importado directamente de Italia donde se cultiva
el mejor arroz de *tutto il mondo?* Italia produce *tutto....*

—Sí, sí, sí, ya lo sé, no me diga. Italia produce *tutto* lo mejor de *tutto il mondo*— le interrumpió Marta imitando su acento,y en un tono que indicaba haber oído a
don Vittorio decir muchas veces la misma cosa. —Está bien, no vamos a discutir la calidad, pero tiene que darme un precio mejor. Si me lo da a treinta el kilo, bueno; si no, no.

—¡*Mamma* mía!, ¡*impossibile!* A treinta céntimos mejor cierro el negocio y me voy para Italia. A cuarenta y cinco es lo menos, pero 'shhh', no se lo diga a nadie. —Y
sin esperar más, empezó a llenar una bolsa.

—Un momento, don Vittorio, yo dije treinta, ni un céntimo más.

—¡Pero *signora, per favore!*, ¡son diez *bambinos* los que tengo! Mire esta foto si no me cree— exclamó don Vittorio con desesperación, al mismo tiempo que le enseñaba
una foto de él con su señora y diez hijos. —Algo tengo que ganar.

—Bueno, está bien, se lo voy a pagar a treinta y cinco el kilo, pero eso sí es lo último.

—Cuarenta, por ser Ud.

—No, a treinta y cinco.

bambinos	niños	*tutto il mondo*	todo el mundo
Signora Fonti	señora Fuentes	*tutto*	todo
molto piacere	mucho gusto	*mamma*	mamá
molto bene	muy bien	*impossibile*	imposible
grazie	gracias	*signora*	señora
buona qualitá	buena calidad	*per favore*	por favor

30.36   TREINTA Y SEIS

SPOKEN SPANISH   UNIT 30

—No puedo, *signora*, lo siento mucho.

—Voy a comprarlo a otra parte, entonces. Vamos, Virginia.

—Bueno, bueno, no se vaya, no vamos a discutir más, Ud. gana otra vez, y yo pierdo.

—Muchas gracias, don Vittorio, Ud. es muy amable. Ahora vamos a ver, necesito unas buenas chuletas de cerdo pero....

Etcétera, etcétera. Empezó la misma discusión con la cuestión de la carne, y luego lo mismo con los huevos, y la mantequilla, y todas las otras cosas que **Marta tenía que** comprar: 'que le doy tanto, que imposible, que me voy, que si, que no, que mis *bambinos*, que *Mamma* mia, que Italia...etc.' La Sra. Robinson observaba con **curiosidad** y esperaba pacientemente, poniendo mucha atención para aprender a hacer lo mismo que su amiga en ocasiones futuras.

Por fin, una hora después terminó Marta de comprar todo y muy contenta le dijo adiós a don Vittorio. Este apenas pudo contestarle el adiós; se sentía cansado y con *'molto'* dolor de cabeza de tanta discusión por los precios. Estaba además furioso porque sabía que la *'signora Fonti'* había salido ganando una vez más.

—¿Cómo le fue, don Vittorio?— le preguntó Pedro, el empleado—¿Hicimos buen negocio esta vez?

—¿¡Buen negocio!?, con diez clientes más como esta mujer, Vittorio Martini acaba sus días en un asilo de locos. ¡*Mamma* mia!, ¡qué dolor de cabeza! **Dame una** aspirina, *bambino, per favore.*

Esta experiencia en el mercado fue una de las muchas cosas nuevas, o por lo menos diferentes, que los Robinson encontraron en Surlandia. A veces les parecía que **algunas de esas cosas** eran bastante difícil de comprender, pero ellos las aceptaban porque querían adaptarse al sistema de vida en Surlandia. Para representar mejor los **intereses de su país,** Estados Unidos, era necesario ser aceptado como amigo sincero de la gente de Surlandia, y para esto, era necesario aprender a vivir y a actuar como los **surlandeses.** Y asi fue: poco a poco todos los Robinson, padres e hijas, fueron acostumbrándose y adaptándose a todo lo que era nuevo o diferente y, en menos de tres meses después de haber llegado, Fred, Virginia y sus hijas Jane y Ruth eran los más populares de toda la colonia norteamericana en Las Palmas.

signora	señora
bambinos	niños
mamma	mamá
molto	mucho
signora Fonti	señora Fuentes
per favore	por favor

TREINTA Y SIETE   jacobeligoodsons.com For Free Audio   30.37

UNIT 30   SPOKEN SPANISH

30.42   Response drill

    1 ¿A dónde fueron ese día las dos señoras?

    2 ¿Qué les decían en cada puesto por donde pasaban?

    3 ¿Qué parecía el mercado con tanto ruido?

    4 ¿Para qué iba la Sra. Robinson al mercado?

    5 ¿Qué comentarios hacía Marta cuando no le gustaba el precio de algo?

    6 ¿A cuál puesto llegaron por fin?

    7 ¿Cómo se llamaba ese puesto?

    8 ¿Cómo se llamaba el propietario?

    9 ¿De dónde era él?

   10 ¿Cuánto tiempo hacía que vivía en Surlandia?

   11 ¿Cómo hablaba el español?

   12 ¿Por qué no había aprendido a hablarlo bien?

   13 ¿Cuántos hijos tenía él?

   14 ¿Cómo le decía él a la Sra. Fuentes?

   15 ¿Por qué prefería él mismo en persona atender a esa señora?

   16 ¿Que tenía que comprar la señora ese día?

   17 ¿Iba a comprar las cosas de su amiga primero o las de ella?

   18 ¿Empezó por la carne, por la mantequilla, o por el arroz?

   19 ¿Cuántos kilos tenía que comprar?

   20 ¿A cómo quería vendérselo don Vittorio?

   21 ¿A cómo quería pagárselo ella?

   22 ¿Discutieron mucho por el precio?

   23 ¿A cómo se lo dejó, don Vittorio, por fin?

   24 ¿Qué pasó después con la cuestión de la carne, la mantequilla, etc.?

   25 Mientras la Sra. Fuentes y don Vittorio discutían, ¿qué hacía Virginia?

   26 ¿Por qué ponía atención y observaba con curiosidad?

   27 ¿Por qué estaba furioso don Vittorio después de acabar el negocio con Marta?

   28 ¿Por qué querían los Robinson adaptarse al sistema de vida en Surlandia?

   29 ¿Qué tenían que hacer ellos para poder adaptarse a ese sistema de vida?

   30 ¿En cuánto tiempo llegaron a ser ellos los más populares de la colonia norteamericana en Las Palmas?

30.38   jacobeligoodsons.com For Free Audio   TREINTA Y OCHO

SPOKEN SPANISH   APPENDIX II

AII.1   Vocabulary

         Units 16–30

         The following vocabulary list includes all words presented in Units 16-30. The format of presentation is the same as in the preceding volume.

         Items which first appear in the basic dialogs are indicated by a figure one after the unit designation, as 16.1; items which first appear in illustration drills, by a figure two, as 16.2. New items in the readings, which in this volume are limited to cognate loan words, are indicated by a figure four, as 16.4.

         The following abreviations are used:

(f)	feminine
(fam)	familiar
(frml)	formal
(m)	masculine
(n)	neuter
(neg)	negative
(pl)	plural
(sg)	singular

/a/

a

a—lo—últımo		at the end	26.1
al—prınşípyo		in the beginning	27.1
a—tyémpo		on time	19.1
abáho	(abajo)	down	24.1

UNO   AII.1

jacobeligoodsons.com For Free Audio

VOCABULARY   SPOKEN SPANISH

/aba/

	abandonádo, —a	(abandonado)	neglected	16.1
	abandonár	(abandonar)	to neglect, to abandon	16.1
	abér			
	abía		there was, there were	17.1
el	abrígo	(abrigo)	topcoat	24.1
	aburrír	(aburrir)		
	aburrírse		to get bored	30.1
	adaptár	(adaptar)	to adapt	30.4
	adelánte			
	de—akí—en—adelánte		from now on, henceforth	29.1
el	adóbe	(adobe)	adobe	28.4
	aéreo, —a	(aéreo)	aerial	19.1
la	aerolínea	(aerolínea)	airline	18.1
	ága (see aşér)			
	ágas (see aşér)			
	ágo (see aşér)			
	agradáble, —∅	(agradable)	pleasant, agreeable	21.1
	agradeşér	(agradecer)	to thank	21.1
	agradéşko		(I) thank	23.2
el	agregádo	(agregado)	attaché	19.1
	aká	(acá)	here	16.1
	akabár	(acabar)	to finish	16.1
	akabár—de		to have just	16.1
	akí			
	de—akí—en—adelánte		from now on, henceforth	29.1

AII.2   DOS

SPOKEN SPANISH

VOCABULARY

/aŋy/

	akompaŋyár	(acompañar)	to accompany	22.1
	akostár	(acostar)		
	akostárse		to go to bed	17.1
	akostumbrár	(acostumbrar)	to accustom	17.1
	akostumbrárse		to accustom oneself	17.1
la	aktɪtúd	(actitud)	attitude	27.4
	aktwár	(actuar)	to act	30.4
	alarmádo, —a	(alarmado)	alarmed	22.4
	alarmár	(alarmar)	to alarm	22.4
	alegrár	(alegrar)	to gladden	22.1
	alegrárse		to be glad	22.1
	algúno, —a	(alguno)	some	22.1
	algún		some	22.1
	almorşár			
	almwérşa		(you) have lunch	22.2
	aⓁyá	(allá)	over there	25.1
	andár	(andar)	to walk, to be out	21.1
	andúbe		(I) walked, was out	21.1
	andubímos		(we) were out	21.2
	andubíste		(you) walked (fam)	21.2
	andúbo		(you) were	21.2
	andubyéron		(they) were	21.2
la	anɪmaşyón	(animación)	liveliness, animation	30.1
	antígwo, —a	(antiguo)	old, ancient	16.1
el	áŋyo	(año)	year	16.1

TRES

AII.3

VOCABULARY   SPOKEN SPANISH

/ape/

el	apeⓁyído	(apellido)	surname	25.1
	apostár	(apostar)	to bet	30.1
la	arıstokráşya	(aristocracia)	aristocracy	28.4
	arıstokrátıko, —a	(aristocrático)	aristocratic	28.4
	arkıtektónıko, —a	(arquitectónico)	architectural	28.4
el	árma (f)	(arma)	arm	28.4
	arríba	(arriba)	up	24.1
el	árte	(arte)	art	30.1
el	artíkulo	(artículo)	article	24.1
el	asílo	(asilo)	asylum	30.4
el	aspékto	(aspecto)	aspect	27.4
la	aspırína	(aspirina)	aspirin	30.4
	ásta			
	ásta—la—bísta		see you later	20.1
	áş (see aşér)			
el	aşénto	(acento)	accent	20.4
	aşeptádo, —a	(aceptado)	approved, accepted	26.1
	aşeptár	(aceptar)	to accept	25.4
	aşér			26.1
	ága		do	27.2
	ágas		do (fam neg)	27.2
	ágo		(I) do	23.1
	áş		do (fam)	27.2
	écho		made	24.1
	ışíste		(you) did (fam)	18.1

AII.4   CUATRO

SPOKEN SPANISH   VOCABULARY

/bar/

	íṣo		(it) made	17.1
	áṣe-(unos-días)		(a few days) ago	16.1
	aṣér-dáŋyo		to be harmful, to harm	17.1
	aṣér-fálta		to (make a) lack	24.1
	aṣér-frío		to be cold (weather)	21.1
	aṣér-kalór		to be hot (weather)	21.1
	aṣérse-tárde		to become late	19.1
	désde-áṣe-múcho-tyémpo		for quite a while	18.1
	atendér			
	atyénden		(they) take care	22.2
la	atenṣyón	(atención)	attention	22.4
	aterriṣár	(aterrizar)	to land	19.1
la	atrakṣyón	(atracción)	attraction	29.4
	atyénden (see atendér)			
	aún	(aún)	even	17.1
	awmentár	(aumentar)	to increase, to augment	28.4
	áwnke	(aunque)	even though, although	22.1

/b/

la	bakúna	(vacuna)	vaccination	26.1
	balér			
	bálga		(it may) be worth	28.2
	bálgo		(I) am worth	23.2
	balyénte, -∅	(valiente)	valiant	30.1
la	baryedád	(variedad)	variety	28.4

CINCO   AII.5

jacobeligoodsons.com For Free Audio

VOCABULARY   SPOKEN SPANISH
/bar/

	báryos, —as	(varios)	several	19.1
la	báse	(base)	base	19.1
	báya (see ír)			
	báyan (see ír)			
	bé (see ír)			
	beía (see bér)			
	beíamos (see bér)			
	beían (see bér)			
	beías (see bér)			
	bendér	(vender)	to sell	23.1
	benír			
	béngas		come (fam neg)	27.2
	béngo		(I) come	23.2
	bınyéron		(they) came	21.2
	(el—sábado)—ke—byéne		next (Saturday)	18.1
	bér			
	beía		(I) saw, was seeing	18.1
	beíamos		(we) saw, were seeing	18.2
	beían		(they) saw, were seeing	18.2
	beías		(you) saw, were seeing (fam)	18.2
	bísto		seen	16.1
	bérse		to see itself	24.1
	por—lo—bísto		from appearances, apparently	16.1
el	bérbo	(verbo)	verb	20.4
la	berdád	(verdad)	truth; is it, does it, can't we, etc.	18.2

jacobeligoodsons.com For Free Audio

SPOKEN SPANISH   VOCABULARY
                                                                                      /boş/

la   berdúra   (verdura)   green (leafy vegetable)   23.1
el   bestído   (vestido)   dress   24.1
el   bestíhyo   (vestigio)   vestige, trace   28.4
      bestír
            bísto   (I) dress   22.1
el   beysból   (beisbol)   baseball   21.4
la   bída   (vida)   life   30.1
      bɪnyéron (see benír)
la   bísa   (bisa)   visa   25.1
la   bɪsíta   (visita)   visit   20.4
      bɪsɪtár   (visitar)   to visit   18.1
la   bísta   (vista)   sight   20.1
            ásta-la-bísta   see you later   20.1
      bísto (see bér, bestír)
la   blúsa   (blusa)   blouse   24.1
      bolár   (volar)   to fly   20.1
            bwéla   (it) flies   20.1
      bolbér   (volver)   to turn, to return   22.1
            bwélbas   come back (fam neg)   27.2
            bwélbe   come back (fam)   27.2
                                                 (it) turns, returns   22.1
la   bólsa   (bolsa)   bag, sack   23.1
el   bombardéo   (bombardeo)   bombing   20.1
la   bóş   (voz)   voice   22.4

SIETE   AII.7

VOCABULARY   SPOKEN SPANISH

/brɪ/

el	brích	(bridge)	bridge	25.4
	bwéla (see bolár)			
	bwélbas (see bolbér)			
	bwélbe (see bolbér)			
la	bwélta			
	dár—una—bwélta		to take a ride (walk)	21.1
	bwéno, —a			
	bwenísɪmo, —a		very good	29.1
	byén	(bien)	very, good and	21.1
	más—byén		rather	21.1
el	byénto	(viento)	wind	21.1

/d/

el	dáɲyo	(daño)	damage, hurt	17.1
	aşér—dáɲyo		to be harmful, to harm	17.1
	dár			
	dí		(I) gave	21.2
	dímos		(we) gave	21.1
	díste		(you) gave (fam)	21.2
	dyéron		(they) gave	21.2
	dyó		(she) gave	21.2
	dár—una—bwélta		to take a ride (walk)	21.1
	de			
	akabár—de		to have just	16.1

AII.8   OCHO

SPOKEN SPANISH   VOCABULARY
                                                                                      /des/

	de—akí—en—adelánte		from now on, henceforth	29.1
	dedikádo, —a	(dedicado)	dedicated	25.4
	dedikár	(dedicar)	to dedicate	25.4
el	defékto	(defecto)	defect	16.4
	defendér	(defender)	to defend	30.1
la	defénsa	(defensa)	defense	23.4
	dehár			
	dehár—de		to leave off, to skip, to miss	17.1
			to stop	28.1
	dehárse—de—brómas		to stop joking	28.1
	delisyóso, —a	(delicioso)	delicious	17.4
el	departaménto	(departamento)	department	24.1
	dependér	(depender)	to depend	30.4
el	depórte	(deporte)	sport	27.1
	desapareşér	(desaparecer)	to disappear	28.4
el	desayúno	(desayuno)	breakfast	17.1
	désde			
	désde—áşe—mucho—tyémpo		for quite a while	18.1
la	desesperaşyón	(desesperación)	desperation	30.4
	desinteresádo, —a	(desinteresado)	disinterested	27.4
	desinteresár	(desinteresar)	to disinterest	27.4
	desmayár	(desmayar)		
	desmayárse		to faint	30.1
el	desórden	(desorden)	disorder	20.4
	despedír	(despedir)	to dismiss, to see off	22.1

NUEVE   AII.9

VOCABULARY   SPOKEN SPANISH
/des/

		despído		(I) say goodbye	22.1
		despedírse		to say goodbye	22.1
		despegár	(despegar)	to take off	19.1
		despído (see despedír)			
		deṣénte, —∅	(decente)	decent	16.4
		deṣír			
			dí	tell (fam)	27.2
			díga	(he may) say	28.2
			dɪgámos	(let's) tell	28.2
			dígas	say (fam neg)	27.2
			dígo	(I) say	23.1
			dího	(he) said	18.1
	el	detáॻye	(detalle)	detail	28.4
		dí (see dár, deṣír)			
		dɪbertír	(divertir)		
			dɪbertírse	to enjoy oneself	17.1
		dɪbíno, —a	(divino)	divine	22.4
		dɪborṣyádo, —a	(divorciado)	divorced	25.1
		dɪborṣyár	(divorciar)	to divorce	25.1
		dɪferénte, —∅	(diferente)	different	18.4
	la	dɪfɪkultád	(dificultad)	difficulty	21.4
		dɪfíṣɪl, —∅	(difícil)	difficult	29.1
		díga (see deṣír)			
		dɪgámos (see deṣír)			
		dígas (see deṣír)			
		dígo (see deṣír)			

SPOKEN SPANISH   VOCABULARY
                                                                          /dyo/

	díhitál, —∅	(digital)	digital	26.1
	dího (see deşír)			
	dímos (see dár)			
el	dinéro	(dinero)	money	25.1
	diplomátiko, —a	(diplomático)	diplomatic	19.4
	diréktaménte	(directamente)	directly	18.4
	disgustádo, —a	(disgustado)	displeased	20.4
	disgustár	(disgustar)	to displease	20.4
la	diskusyón	(discusión)	discussion	30.4
	diskutír	(discutir)	to discuss	17.4
la	distánşya	(distancia)	distance	29.4
	díste (see dár)			
el	dokuménto	(documento)	document	26.1
el	dolór	(delor)	pain	17.1
	dolór—de—kabéşa		headache	17.1
	dormír	(dormir)	to sleep	28.2
	durmámos		(let's) sleep	28.2
la	doşéna	(docena)	dozen	23.1
	duránte	(durante)	during	19.4
	durmámos (see dormír)			
	dyéron (see dár)			
	dyó (see dár)			

ONCE   AII.11

jacobeligoodsons.com For Free Audio

VOCABULARY   SPOKEN SPANISH
/echo/

/e/

	écho (see aşér)			
la	edukaşyón	(educación)	education	22.4
el	ehémplo	(ejemplo)	example	18.4
el	ekípo	(equipo)	equipment	27.1
	eksıstír	(existir)	to exist	28.4
	eksótıko, —a	(exótico)	exotic	27.4
	e(k)steryór, —∅	(exterior)	exterior	16.1
	emoşyonánte, —∅	(emocionante)	exciting, touching	30.1
el	empleádo	(empleado)	employee	30.4
	en			
	en—totál		altogether	20.1
	engordár	(engordar)	to get fat	27.1
	enkontrár			
	enkwéntro		(I) find	22.2
	enórme, —∅	(enorme)	enormous	22.4
	enseŋyár	(enseñar)	to show, to teach	22.1
	entéro, —a	(entero)	whole	28.4
la	entráda	(entrada)	admission ticket	29.1
	entrár	(entrar)	to enter	19.4
				21.1
el	entusyásmo	(entusiasmo)	enthusiasm	21.4
la	époka	(época)	epoch	28.4
	éra (see sér)			
	éramos (see sér)			

AII.12   DOCE

jacobeligoodsons.com For Free Audio

SPOKEN SPANISH   VOCABULARY
                                                                        /est/

	éras (see sér)			
	ermóso, —a	(hermoso)	beautiful	28.1
	esáktaménte	(exactamente)	exactly	17.4
	esklamár	(exclamar)	to exclaim	17.4
	esklusíbaménte	(exclusivamente)	exclusively	29.4
la	eskwadríĝya	(escuadrilla)	squadron	20.1
el	eskwadrón	(escuadrón)	squadron	20.1
	espérto, —a	(experto)	expert	25.4
la	esperyénşya	(experiencia)	experience	30.4
	espeşyál, —ø	(especial)	special	16.1
	(nada)—en—espeşyál		(nothing) special	16.1
	esplıkár	(explicar)	to explain	26.1
	espresár	(expresar)	to express	24.4
la	espresyón	(expresión)	expression	21.4
la	es(ş)epşyón	(excepción)	exception	25.4
	es(ş)épto	(excepto)	except	18.4
el	estándard	(standard)	standard	27.4
	estár			
		esté	be	27.2
		estúbe	(I) was	16.1
		estubímos	(we) were	21.2
		estubíste	(you) were (fam)	21.2
		estúbo	(you) were	21.2
		estubyéron	(they) were	21.2

TRECE   AII.13

VOCABULARY   SPOKEN SPANISH
/est/

	estendér	(extender)	to extend	24.4
el	estílo	(estilo)	style	28.4
	estrécho, —a	(estrecho)	narrow	16.1
	estúbe (see estár)			
	estubímos (see estár)			
	estubíste (see estár)			
	estúbo (see estár)			
	estubyéron (see estár)			
el	estudyánte	(estudiante)	student	17.2
el	estúdyo	(estudio)	study	19.4
	e(t)şétera	(etcétera)	etcetera	30.4

/f/

	faboríto, —a	(favorito)	favorite	27.1
la	fálda	(falda)	skirt	24.1
la	fálta	(falta)	lack	24.1
	aşér—fálta		to (make a) lack	24.1
	fantástıko, —a	(fantástico)	fantastic	17.1
	felışıtár	(felicitar)	to congratulate	29.1
	fenomenál, —∅	(fenomenal)	phenomenal	30.1
	féo, —a	(feo)	ugly	16.2
	fırmár	(firmar)	to sign	26.1
	físıko, —a	(físico)	physical	28.4
	flóho, —a	(flojo)	lazy, loose	27.1

AII.14   CATORCE

jacobeligoodsons.com For Free Audio

SPOKEN SPANISH

VOCABULARY

/fwı/

la	fórma	(forma)	form	18.4
la	formalıdád	(formalidad)	formality	26.4
	formár	(formar)	to form	18.4
	fránkaménte	(francamente)	frankly	18.4 27.1
la	fráse	(frase)	phrase	21.4
la	frekwénşya	(frecuencia)	frequency	29.1
	kom-frekwénşya		frequently, often	29.1
	frésko, —a	(fresco)	fresh	23.1
el	frío	(frio)	cold	21.1
	aşér-frío		to be cold (weather)	21.1
la	frúta	(fruta)	fruit	23.1
	fundádo, —a	(fundado)	founded	29.4
	fundár	(fundar)	to found	29.4
	furyóso, —a	(furioso)	furious	30.4
el	fútbol	(fútbol)	football	27.1
el	futúro	(futuro)	future	21.4
	fwé (see ír, sér)			
	fwéron (see ír, sér)			
la	fwérşa-aérea	(Fuerza Aérea)	Air Force	18.1
	fwí (see ír, sér)			
	fwímos (see ír, sér)			
	fwíste (see ír, sér)			

QUINCE

AIL.15

jacobeligoodsons.com For Free Audio

VOCABULARY   SPOKEN SPANISH

/gan/

                                        /g/

              ganár   (ganar)   to win, to earn, gain   27.1
      la   gérra   (guerra)   war   19.1
      el   gobyérno   (gobierno)   government   19.4
      el   gólf   (golf)   golf   20.1
              gradwádo, —a   (graduado)   graduated   19.4
              gradwár   (graduar)
                 gradwárse   to graduate   19.4

                                        /h/

      el   héfe   (jefe)   boss, chief, manager   18.1
      el   henerál   (general)   general   18.4
      la   hénte   (gente)   people   16.1
      el   hésto   (gesto)   gesture   30.4
      la   hóta   (jota)   the (letter) jota (j); jot, tittle   27.1
      el   hugadór   (jugador)   player   28.1
              hugár   (jugar)   to play   27.1
                                               to gamble   30.1
                 hwégo   (I) play   28.1
      el   hwégo   (juego)   game   30.1

AII.16   DIECISEIS

SPOKEN SPANISH   VOCABULARY
                                                                           /ınt/

                                    /i/

        íbamos (see ír)
        íban (see ír)
        íbas (see ír)
    la ıglésya   (iglesia)   church   16.1
        ımbestıgár   (investigar)   to investigate   22.4
        ımbıtár   (invitar)   to invite   18.1
        ımıtár   (imitar)   to imitate   30.4
    la ımpaşyénşya   (impaciencia)   impatience   22.4
        ımportádo, —a   (importado)   imported   27.4
    la ımportánşya   (importancia)   importance   22.4
        ımportánte, —∅   (importante)   important   17.4
        ımportár   (importar)   to matter, be important 27.1
        ımportár   (importar)   to import   27.4
        ındıkár   (indicar)   to indicate   21.4
    la ındustryalışaşyón   (industrialización)   industrialization   28.4
    el ınhenyéro   (ingeniero)   engineer   25.1
        ınmedyátaménte   (inmediatamente)   immediately   22.4
    el ınmıgránte   (inmigrante)   immigrant   25.1
        ınoşénte, —∅   (inocente)   innocent   22.4
        ınsıgnıfıkánte, —∅   (insignificante)   insignificant   17.4
        ınsıstír   (insistir)   to insist   22.4
    la ınspekşyón   (inspección)   inspection   20.1
        ıntelıhénte, —∅   (inteligente)   intelligent   30.4

DIECISIETE   AII.17

VOCABULARY   SPOKEN SPANISH
/int/

el	interés	(interés)	interest	21.4
	interesánte, —∅	(interesante)	interesting	21.1
	internaşyonál, —∅	(internacional)	international	24.4
	interrumpír	(interrumpir)	to interrupt	17.4
	ír			
	báya		(it may) go	28.1
	báyan		go (pl)	18.1
	bé		go (fam)	27.2
	fwé		(it) went	17.1
	fwéron		(they) went	21.2
	fwí		(I) went	21.2
	fwímos		(we) went	21.1
	fwíste		(you) went (fam)	21.2
	íbamos		(we) went, were going	18.2
	íban		(they) went, were going	18.2
	íbas		(you) went, were going (fam)	18.2
	ír—a—pyé		to go by foot	16.1
	ír—de—kómpras		to go (of) shopping	18.1
	ké—bá		nonsense	16.1
	ke—les—báya—byén		take it easy	28.1
	irritádo, —a	(irritado)	irritated	18.4
	irritár	(irritar)	to irritate	18.4
	işíste (see aşér)			
	íşo (see aşér)			
()	itálya	(Italia)	Italy	30.4

AII.18   DIECIOCHO

SPOKEN SPANISH

VOCABULARY

/kan/

	italyáno, —a	(italiano)	Italian	30.4

/k/

el	kaballyéro	(caballero)	gentleman	24.1
el	kabállyo	(caballo)	horse	30.1
	kabér			
	kúpo		(it) fit	21.2
	kupyéron		(they) fit	21.2
la	kabéṣa	(cabeza)	head	17.1
	dolór-de-kabéṣa		headache	17.1
	kaér	(caer)		
	káygo		(I) fall	23.2
	kaérse		to fall	17.1
el	kafé	(café)	cafe	16.1
el	kafé	(café)	coffee	16.1
la	kalɪdád	(calidad)	quality	30.4
el	kalór	(calor)	heat	21.1
	aṣér-kalór		to be hot (weather)	21.1
el	kalṣádo	(calzado)	footwear	24.1
	kalyénte, —∅	(caliente)	warm	21.1
el	kámpo	(campo)	course	28.1
la	kanásta	(canasta)	basket	25.4

DIECINUEVE

AII.19

VOCABULARY   SPOKEN SPANISH

/kan/

la	káncha	(cancha)	court	29.1
	kansádo, —a	(cansado)	tired	18.2
	kansár	(cansar)	to tire	18.2
	kantár	(cantar)	to sing	23.1
la	kapıtál	(capital)	capital	16.4
la	kárne	(carne)	meat	23.1
la	karréra	(carrera)	race	30.1
la	káʂa	(caza)	hunt	20.1
la	katedrál	(catedral)	cathedral	16.1
la	káwsa	(causa)	cause	22.4
	káygo (see kaér)			
	ke	(que)	than	28.1
	pórke		because	16.1
	ké, —∅			
	ké—bá		nonsense	16.1
	kedár	(quedar)		
	kedár—en		to agree to, to decide on	18.1
	kedárse		to stay, to remain	18.1
	kedárse—sın—(ír)		to miss (going)	29.1
	kerér			
	kíso		(he) wanted	21.2
	kısyéra		(I) would like	16.1

AII.20   VEINTE

SPOKEN SPANISH

VOCABULARY

/kom/

	kısyéron		(they) wanted	21.2
el	kílo	(kilo)	kilo	30.4
el	kilómetro	(kilómetro)	kilometer	29.4
	kınyéntos, —as	(quinientos)	five hundred	20.1
	kíso, (see kerér)			
	kısyéra (see kerér)			
	kısyéron (see kerér)			
la	klarıdád	(claridad)	brightness	24.4
la	kláse	(clase)	class	28.4
el	klíma	(clima)	climate	19.4
el	klúb	(club)	club	28.1
la	klyénte	(cliente)	client	30.4
la	kolónya	(colonia)	colony	30.4
	kolonyál, —ø	(colonial)	colonial	28.4
el	kolór	(color)	color	16.4
	kombenír	(convenir)	to be advantageous	18.1
	kombenşér	(convencer)	to convince	27.1
	kombersár	(conversar)	to converse, to chat	16.1
la	kombersaşyón	(conversación)	conversation	23.4
	komentár	(comentar)	to comment	17.4
el	komentáryo	(comentario)	commentary	30.4
	komerşyál, —ø	(comercial)	commercial	16.1
la	komída	(comida)	food, meal	23.1
	komo	(como)	about, around	19.1
la	kompaŋyía	(compañía)	company	18.1
	kompeténte, —ø	(competente)	competent	29.1

VEINTIUNO

AII.21

VOCABULARY   SPOKEN SPANISH

/kom/

	kompetír	(competir)	to compete	27.4
la	kómpra	(compra)	purchase	18.1
	ír—de—kómpras		to go (of) shopping	18.1
	komprendér	(comprender)	to understand	21.4
	komprometér	(comprometer)		
	komprometérse		to commit oneself, obligate oneself	28.1
	komunıkár	(comunicar)		
	komunıkárse		to communicate	19.1
	kon			
	kom—frekwénşya		frequently, often	29.1
la	kondışyón	(condición)	condition	21.4
la	kondúkta	(conducta)	conduct	26.1
	konhugár	(conjugar)	to conjugate	21.4
la	konhugaşyón	(conjugación)	conjugation	20.4
la	konmoşyón	(conmoción)	commotion	22.4
	konoşér			
	konóşko		(I) know	23.1
	konstrwír	(construir)	to construct	28.4
la	kontınwaşyón	(continuación)	continuation	18.4
el	kontráste	(contraste)	contrast	28.4
el	kontról	(control)	control	20.1
la	korbáta	(corbata)	tie	24.1
	korréktaménte	(correctamente)	correctly	21.4
la	korrída	(corrida)	bullfight	29.1
	kosér	(coser)	to sew	24.1

AII.22   VEINTIDOS

SPOKEN SPANISH

VOCABULARY

/lok/

	kostár	(costar)	to be difficult	18.1
la	koynşıdénşya	(coincidencia)	coincidence	26.4
	krwél, —∅	(cruel)	cruel	30.1
la	kryáda	(criada)	maid	29.1
	kultıbár	(cultivar)	to cultivate	30.4
	kúpo (see kabér)			
	kupyéron (see kabér)			
la	kuryosıdád	(curiosidad)	curiosity	30.4
	kwarénta, —∅	(cuarenta)	forty	19.1
la	kwestyón	(cuestión)	question	30.4
	kwıdár	(cuidar)	to care for	28.1

/l/

	lárgo, —a	(largo)	long	20.1
la	láta	(lata)	nuisance	23.1
	latínoamerıkáno, —a	(Latinoamericano)	Latinamerican	16.4
	lebantár	(levantar)		
	lebantárse		to arise	17.1
la	léche	(leche)	milk	23.1
el	lechéro	(lechero)	milkman	23.1
la	lekşyón	(lección)	lesson	17.2
	límpyo, —a	(limpio)	clean	30.1
la	línea	(línea)	line	19.1
	lóko, —a	(loco)	crazy	22.1

VEINTITRES

VOCABULARY   SPOKEN SPANISH
/ǉyen/

		/ǉy/		
	ǉyenár	(llenar)	to fill	26.1
	ǉyéno, —a	(lleno)	full	16.1
	ǉyobér	(llover)	to rain	21.1
	ǉywébe		(it) rains	22.2

		/m/		
	madrugadór, —ø	(madrugador)	early rising	28.1
	magnífıko, —a	(magnifico)	magnificent	16.1
	málo, —a			
	ménos—mál		luckily; it could have been worse	17.1
la	mamá	(mamá)	mother	23.4
	manehár	(manejar)	to handle, to drive (a car)	29.1
la	manéra	(manera)	manner	18.4
la	mansyón	(mansión)	mansion	28.4
la	mantekíǉya	(mantequilla)	butter	23.1
	marchár	(marchar)		
	marchárse		to leave, go away	28.1
el	marído	(marido)	husband	24.1
	más			
	más—byén		rather	21.1
el	médıko	(médico)	doctor	26.1
( )	méhıko	(México)	Mexico	21.4
	mehór, —ø	(mejor)	better, best	16.1

AII.24   VEINTICUATRO

SPOKEN SPANISH

VOCABULARY

/mye/

		memorışár	(memorizar)	to memorize	21.4
	la	memórya	(memoria)	memory	20.4
		ménos			
		ménos—mál		luckily, less injury; it could have been worse	17.1
		por—lo—ménos		at least	17.1
	el	merkádo	(mercado)	market	22.1
	el	més			
		el—més—pasádo		last month	17.1
		metódıko, —a	(metódico)	methodic	25.4
	el	métro	(metro)	meter	20.1
		míl, —∅	(mil)	a thousand	20.1
	el	mınıstéryo	(ministerio)	ministry	16.1
	el	mınúto	(minuto)	minute	17.4 24.2
	la	mísa	(misa)	mass	16.1
	la	mısyón	(misión)	mission	18.1
el,	la	modísta	(modista)	dressmaker	24.1
		morír	(morir)	to die	30.1
	el	motór	(motor)	motor, engine	19.1
	el	muchácho	(muchacho)	boy	28.1
	la	muhér	(mujer)	woman	17.1
	el	múndo	(mundo)	world	29.1
		myéntras	(mientras)	while	19.2

VEINTICINCO

VOCABULARY   SPOKEN SPANISH

/naş/

                                         /n/

         naşér   (nacer)   to be born   25.1
         naşyonál, —∅   (nacional)   national   18.1
   el   negóşyo   (negocio)   business   26.1
         nerbyóso, —a   (nervioso)   nervous   17.1
             ponérse—nerbyóso   to get nervous   17.1
         ní   (ni)   not even   17.1
         nıngúno, —a   (ninguno)   none, not one   27.1
   el   nórte   (norte)   north   16.4
         norteamerıkáno, —a (Norteamericano)   North American   16.4
                                                                  26.1
         nubládo, —a   (nublado)   cloudy   21.1
         nublár   (nublar)
             nublárse   to cloud   21.1
   el   núkleo   (núcleo)   nucleus   28.4

                                         /o/

         obserbár   (observar)   to observe   22.4
         ofendér   (ofender)   to offend   30.4
   la   oférta   (oferta)   offer   30.4
   la   ofışína   (oficina)   office   18.1
   el   ofışyál   (oficial)   official, officer 20.1
         oír
             óye   (you) hear   23.2

AII.26   VEINTISEIS

SPOKEN SPANISH   VOCABULARY
                                                                                          /pad/

	óyen		(you) hear (pl)	23.2
	óygas		listen (fam neg)	27.2
	óygo		(I) hear	23.1
la	okasyón	(ocasión)	occasion	30.4
	okupádo, —a			
	okupadísımo, —a		very busy	22.1
	olbıdár	(olvidar)		
	olbıdárse		to forget itself	20.1
la	opınyón	(opinión)	opinion	18.4
la	oportunıdád	(oportunidad)	opportunity	20.4
la	organışaşyón	(organización)	organization	25.4
	orıhınálménte	(originalmente)	originally	29.4
	orríble, —∅	(horrible)	horrible	17.1
	ótro, —a	(otro)	next	18.1
	óy	(hoy)	today	16.1
	óye (see oír)			
	óyen (see oír)			
	óygas (see oír)			
	óygo (see oír)			
el	óyo	(hoyo)	hole	28.1

                                            /p/

| el | pádre | (padre) | father | 25.1 |
| | | | (pl) parents | 25.1 |

VOCABULARY   SPOKEN SPANISH

/pag/

	pagár	(pagar)	to pay	18.1
el	país	(país)	country	19.1
el	pán	(pan)	bread	23.1
el	pár	(par)	pair	24.1
	pareşér			
	paréşko		(I) look like	23.2
	pareşérse		to look like	23.2
el	partído	(partido)	game	27.1
	pasádo, —a	(pasado)	passed	17.1
	el—més—pasádo		last month	17.1
el	pasapórte	(pasaporte)	passport	26.1
	paseár	(pasear)	to stroll	16.1
el	pasíĺyo	(pasillo)	hall	27.1
	paşyénteménte	(pacientemente)	patiently	30.4
la	páwsa	(pausa)	pause	24.4
	peór	(peor)	worse	17.1
	perdér	(perder)	to lose, to miss	27.1
	pyérda		lose	27.2
	pyérdo		(I) lose	27.1
	perdonár	(perdonar)	to pardon	19.1
	perféktaménte	(perfectamente)	perfectly	23.4
	permitír	(permitir)	to permit	24.4
la	persóna	(persona)	person	17.4
				18.1
	perteneşér	(pertenecer)	to pertain, to belong	19.1

AII.28   VEINTIOCHO

SPOKEN SPANISH   VOCABULARY
                                                                                             /pon/

                          pertené ş ko   (I) belong   23.2
        el   peskádo   (pescado)   fish   23.1
        el   pılóto   (piloto)   pilot   19.1
        la   pımyénta   (pimienta)   pepper   23.1
        la   písta   (pista)   runway, track   20.1
        la   pıyáma   (pijama)   pajama(s)   22.4
        el   plán   (plan)   plan   21.4
        la   pláşa   (plaza)   plaza   28.4
                                                                                          30.1
        el   pláto   (plato)   plate, dish   22.4
        la   poblaşyón   (población)   population   28.4
              póbre, ‐ɸ   (pobre)   poor   30.1
              podér
                    podrémos   (we) will be able   29.1
                    pudímos   (we) could, were able 19.1
                    pudyéron   (they) could, were able 21.2
              póko, ‐a
                    por‐póko   by little, almost, nearly 30.1
        la   polítıka   (politica)   politics   24.4
              ponér
                    pón   put (fam)   27.2
                    pongámos   (let's) put   28.2
                    póngas   put (fam neg)   27.2
                    póngo   (I) put   23.1
                    púse   (I) put   21.2

VEINTINUEVE   AII.29

VOCABULARY   SPOKEN SPANISH

/pop/

	púso		(she) put	17.1
	ponérse		to get, to become	17.1
	populár, —∅	(popular)	popular	30.4
	pór		around	22.1
	por—ehémplo		for example	18.4
	pórke		because	16.1
	por—lo—bísto		from appearances, apparently	16.1
	por—lo—ménos		at least	17.1
	por—lo—prónto		for the moment, time being	26.1
	por—póko		by little, almost, nearly	30.1
	por—supwésto		for certain, of course	22.1
	portár	(portar)		
	portárse		to behave, conduct oneself	30.1
la	práktıka	(práctica)	practice	29.1
	praktıkár	(practicar)	to practice, to participate in	27.1
	preferír	(preferir)	to prefer	21.4
	prefyéro		(I) prefer	21.4
	preokupár	(preocupar)		
	preokupárse		to worry	19.1
el	presénte	(presente)	present	21.4
	preşyóso, —a	(precioso)	precious	22.4
el	preté(k)sto	(pretexto)	pretext, excuse	16.1
	pretendér	(pretender)	to pretend	30.4
	prınşıpál, —∅	(principal)	principal	29.4

AII.30   TREINTA

jacobeligoodsons.com For Free Audio

SPOKEN SPANISH   VOCABULARY

/pwe/

el	prınşípyo	(principio)	beginning	27.1
	al—prınşípyo		in the beginning	27.1
	probáblemente	(probablemente)	probably	22.4
	probár			
	prwéba		(you) try	22.2
la	probısyón	(provisión)	provision, supply	20.1
el	probléma	(problema)	problem	22.1
el	prodúkto	(producto)	product	27.4
	produşír	(producir)	to produce	30.4
el	profesór	(profesor)	professor	20.2
	progresíbo, —a	(progresivo)	progressive	28.4
	prónto			
	por—lo—prónto		for the moment, time being	26.1
la	pronunşyaşyón	(pronunciación)	pronunciation	20.4
el	propyetáryo	(propietario)	proprietor	29.4
	proybído, —a	(prohibido)	prohibited	29.4
	proy˙ír	(prohibir)	to prohibit	29.4
	prwéba (see probár)			
	públiko, —a	(público)	public	29.4
	pudímos (see podér)			
	pudyéron (see podér)			
	puntwál, —ø	(puntual)	punctual	17.4
				27.1
	púse (see ponér)			
	púso (see ponér)			
	pwés	(pues)	well	30.1

TREINTA Y UNO   AII.31

jacobeligoodsons.com For Free Audio

VOCABULARY   SPOKEN SPANISH

/pwe/

el	pwésto	(puesto)	stand, booth	23.1
el	pyé	(pie)	foot	16.1
	ír a pyé		to go by foot	16.1
	pyérda (see perdér)			
	pyérdo (see perdér)			
la	pyéşa	(pieza)	piece (of music)	17.1

/r/

la	rrakéta	(raqueta)	racquet	29.1
la	rráta	(rata)	female rat	22.4
	rrekordár			
	rrekwérde		remember	27.2
	rrekwérde		(she may) remember	28.1
la	rrelaşyón	(relación)	relation	16.1
	rrepetír			
	rrepíto		(I) repeat	22.2
	rrepresentár	(representar)	to represent	30.4
la	rrepúblıka	(república)	republic	16.4
	rrespektíbo, —a	(respectivo)	respective	24.4
el	rrespéto	(respeto)	respect	22.4
	rrespondér	(responder)	to answer	21.4
			to vouch	26.1
el	rresultádo	(resultado)	result	21.4
	rresultár	(resultar)	to result, turn out	17.1

AII.32   TREINTA Y DOS

SPOKEN SPANISH

VOCABULARY

/sal/

la	rreşepşyón	(recepción)	reception	24.4
	rreşıbír	(recibir)	to receive	20.1
	rrewnír	(reunir)		
	rrewnírse		to get together, to assemble	16.1
	rríko, —a	(rico)	rich	28.4
	rrompér	(romper)		
	rrompérse		to break	17.1
la	rrópa			
	rrópa—écha		ready made clothes	24.1
el	rrwído	(ruido)	noise	17.1

/s/

	sabér			
	sépan		know (pl)	27.2
	sépas		(you may) know	27.1
	súpo		(he) knew	21.2
	supyéron		(they) knew	21.2
el	sáke	(saque)	service, serve	29.1
	sál (see salír)			
la	sál	(sal)	salt	23.1
	sálgan (see salír)			
	sálgas (see salír)			
	sálgo (see salír)			
la	salída	(salida)	exit, way out	24.1
	salír			

TREINTA Y TRES

AII.33

VOCABULARY   SPOKEN SPANISH

/sal/

	sál		leave (fam)	27.2
	sálgan		(they may) go out	28.2
	sálgas		leave (fam neg)	27.2
	sálgo		(I) go out	23.2
la	salúd	(salud)	health	26.1
	saludár	(saludar)	to greet	20.4
el	sarkásmo	(sarcasmo)	sarcasm	17.4
	se—	(se)	to her	16.1
			to you (sg and pl), him, them	20.2
	sé (see sér)			
	séa (see sér)			
	séan (see sér)			
	séas (see sér)			
	segír	(seguir)	to continue, to follow	22.1
	sıgámos		(let's) keep on	28.2
	sígas		continue (fam neg)	27.2
	síge		(it) continues, follows	22.1
			continue (fam)	27.2
	kómo—síge—tódo		how's everything going	22.1
	segúndo, —a	(segundo)	second	19.4
el	sektór	(sector)	sector, section	16.1
	sentár			
	syénto		(I) seat	22.2

AII.34   TREINTA Y CUATRO

SPOKEN SPANISH

VOCABULARY

/sıg/

sentír			
sıntámos		(let's) feel	28.2
syénte		(you) feel	22.2
sépan (see sabér)			
sépas (see sabér)			
sér			
éra		(he) was, was being	18.1
éramos		(we) were, were being	18.2
éras		(you) were, were being (fam)	18.2
fwé		(it) was	17.1
fwéron		(they) were	21.2
fwí		(I) was	21.2
fwímos		(we) were	17.1
fwíste		(you) were (fam)	21.2
sé		be (fam)	27.1
séa		(it may) be	28.2
séan		be (pl)	27.2
séas		be (fam neg)	27.1
serbír	(servir)	to serve	24.4
el serbíşyo	(servicio)	service	19.4
séryo, —a	(serio)	serious	21.4
sıgámos (see segír)			
sígas (see segír)			
síge (see segír)			

TREINTA Y CINCO

AII.35

VOCABULARY   SPOKEN SPANISH

/sıg/

	sıgnıfıkár	(significar)	to signify	30.4
	sıgyénte	(siguiente)		
	lo—sıgyénte		the following	26.1
el	sılénşyo	(silencio)	silence	23.4
	símpleménte	(simplemente)	simply	30.4
	sín			
	kedárse—sın—(ír)		to miss (going)	29.1
	sınşéro, —a	(sincero)	sincere	30.4
	sıntámos (see sentír)			
el	sıstéma	(sistema)	system	25.4
	sıstemátıko, —a	(sistemático)	systematic	25.4
	sıtwádo, —a	(situado)	situated	16.4
	sıtwár	(situar)	to situate	16.4
el	sól	(sol)	sun	21.1
	sólaménte	(solamente)	only	19.1
la	solışıtud	(solicitud)	application	26.1
el	sombréro	(sombrero)	hat	24.1
la	sorprésa	(sorpresa)	surprise	20.4
	sufışyénte, —∅	(suficiente)	sufficient, enough	23.1
	superyór, —∅	(superior)	superior	18.4
	súpo (see sabér)			
	supwésto	(supuesto)		
	por—supwésto		for certain, of course	22.1
	supyéron (see sabér)			

AII.36   TREINTA Y SEIS

SPOKEN SPANISH   VOCABULARY

/tar/

el	surlandés	(Surlandés)	Surlandian	30.4
la	swérte	(suerte)	luck	30.1
	syénte (see sentír)			
	syénto (see sentár)			

/ş/

el	şapáto	(zapato)	shoe	24.1
el	şéntımo	(céntimo)	centime (monetary unit)	30.4
	şerrár	(cerrar)	to close	22.2
	şyérra		close (fam)	27.2
	şyérran		(they) close	22.2
	şyérres		close (fam neg)	27.2
el	şertıfıkádo	(certificado)	certificate	26.1
el	şésped	(césped)	grass	28.1
el	şyégo	(ciego)	blind (man)	23.1
	şyérra (see şerrár)			
	şyérran (see şerrár)			
	şyérres (see şerrár)			
la	şyudád	(ciudad)	city	16.1

/t/

	tampóko	(tampoco)	neither	23.1
	tán	(tan)	so	16.1
	tárde			

TREINTA Y SIETE   AII.37

jacobeligoodsons.com For Free Audio

VOCABULARY   SPOKEN SPANISH
/taş/

	aşérse—tárde		to become late	19.1
la	táşa	(taza)	cup	17.1
la	téknıka	(técnica)	technique	27.4
la	téla	(tela)	cloth	24.1
la	telebısyón	(televisión)	television	22.4
el	teléfono	(teléfono)	telephone	17.4
	tempráno	(temprano)	early	22.1
	tenér			
	tén		have (fam)	27.2
	téngas		have (fam neg)	27.2
	tubíste		(you) had (fam)	21.2
	tubyéron		(they) had	21.2
	tyénen		(they) have	23.2
el	ténıs	(tenis)	tennis	28.1
el	tenyénte	(teniente)	lieutenant	20.1
	termınár	(terminar)	to terminate	19.4
	terríble, —Ø	(terrible)	terrible	22.1
	tímıdo, —a	(tímido)	bashful, timid	18.4
	típıko, —a	(típico)	typical	16.4
el	típo	(tipo)	type	28.4
	tomár	(tomar)	to drink	16.1
el	tóno	(tono)	tone	17.4
el	tópıko	(tópico)	topic	24.4
el	toréo	(toreo)	bullfighting	30.1

AII.38   TREINTA Y OCHO

jacobeligoodsons.com For Free Audio

SPOKEN SPANISH

VOCABULARY

/tra/

el	toréro	(torero)	bullfighter	30.1
el	tóro	(toro)	bull	29.1
			(pl) bullfights	29.1
la	tórre	(torre)	tower	20.1
el	totál	(total)	total	20.1
	en—totál		altogether	20.1
el	trabáho	(trabajo)	work	25.1
	tradışyonál, —∅	(tradicional)	traditional	28.4
	traduşír			
	tradúhe		(I) translated	21.2
	traduhíste		(you) translated (fam)	21.2
	traduşkámos		(let's) translate	28.2
	tradúşkas		translate (fam neg)	27.2
	tradúşko		(I) translate	23.2
	traér			
	tráhe		(I) brought	21.1
	trahéron		(they) brought	21.2
	trahímos		(we) brought	21.2
	trahíste		(you) brought (fam)	21.2
	tráho		(you) brought	21.2
	tráygas		bring (fam neg)	27.2
	tráygo		(I) bring	23.1
el	tráfıko	(tráfico)	traffic	17.1
	tráhe (see traér)			
	trahéron (see traér)			

TREINTA Y NUEVE

AII.39

VOCABULARY   SPOKEN SPANISH

/tra/

		trahímos (see traér)			
		trahíste (see traér)			
		tráho (see traér)			
		tráygas (see traér)			
		tráygo (see traér)			
		tréynta, —∅	(treinta)	thirty	20.1
		tubíste (see tenér)			
		tubyéron (see tenér)			
el,	la	turísta	(turista)	tourist	29.4
	el	tyémpo	(tiempo)	weather	21.1
		a—tyémpo		on time	19.1
				here	
	la	tyénda	(tienda)	store	16.1
		tyénen (see tenér)			

/u/

		últımo, —a	(último)	last	17.1
		a—lo—últımo		at the end	26.1
	la	unıbersıdád	(universidad)	university	19.4
		urbáno, —a	(urbano)	urban	28.4
		usár	(usar)	to use	21.4

/w/

		wébo	(huevo)	egg	23.1
	el				
	la	wéⓁya	(huella)	print	26.1

SPOKEN SPANISH   INDEX

AII.2   INDEX

ADJECTIVES   IMPERSONAL CONSTRUCTIONS (see clitic)

   Demonstratives   INDIRECT COMMANDS (see verb constructions)

      Masculine forms   16.24   INDIRECT CLITICS (see pronouns)

   Possessives   INTONATION (see pronunciation)

      Postposed full-forms   20.24   INVERSION (see word order)

      Nominalized   27.24   IRREGULAR (see verb forms)

COGNATE (see loan words)   JUNCTURE (see pronunciation)

CLITICS (see pronouns)   LOAN WORDS

COMMANDS (see verb forms, verb constructions)   Cognate loan words   16.4

DEMONSTRATIVES (see adjectives)   MASCULINE GENDER (see adjectives)

DEPENDENT CLAUSES (see word order)   MODIFIED STEMS (see verb forms)

DIPHTHONG (see verb forms)   NEGATIVE PARTICLE   27.10(1,6)

DIRECT CLITICS (see pronouns)   NOMINALIZED POSSESSIVES (see adjectives)

EXCLAMATORY PHRASES   NOUNS

   Exclamatory /kómo/ + verbs   20.21.2   Gender class in nouns   24.24
                                                                                   26.24
   Exclamatory /ké/ + nouns and modifiers 20.21.2 PALATAL EXTENSION (see verb forms)

FAMILIAR (see verb forms)   PALATO-VELAR EXTENSION (see verb forms)

FORMAL (see verb forms)   PASSIVE CONSTRUCTION (see clitic pronouns)

FUTURE (see verbs, verb constructions)   PAST I (see verbs, verb forms)

GENDER (see adjectives, nouns, pronouns)   PAST II (see verbs, verb forms)

HOURS (see time of day)   PERIPHRASTIC FUTURE (see verb constructions)

HORTATORY COMMANDS (see verb forms,   PHRASES (see exclamatory phrases, pronunciation,
   verb constructions)   relators)

CUARENTA Y UNO   AII.41

jacobeligoodsons.com For Free Audio

INDEX   SPOKEN SPANISH

POSITION (see adjectives, clitic pronouns,   Reflexives with no designated agents   26.21.2
  word order)
                                                     Reflexives in impersonal use   25.21.2B
POSSESSION (see reflexive clitic pronouns)
                                                     Reflexives with progressive and
POSSESSIVES (see adjectives, relators)   periphrastic future constructions   24.21.2

PROGRESSIVE CONSTRUCTIONS (see verb   Reflexives to signal possession   24.21.1B
  constructions)
                                                   PRONUNCIATION
PRESENT (see verbs, verb forms)
                                                     Intonation patterns
PRONOUNS
                                                       Echo questions   19.21.2
  Clitics review   30.21.2
                                                       Choice questions   20.21.3
  Clitics
                                                       Choice question intonation phrases   20.21.3B
    Position   20.21.1B
                                       27.21.1B   No questions   16.21.2
                                       29.21.1
                                       29.21.2   Affirmative confirmation questions 17.21.2

    Position of reflexives with   Negative confirmation questions   18.21.3
    progressive and periphrastic
    future constructions   24.21.2   Deliberate statements   21.21.5

    With command forms   29.21.1   Sentence modifiers for statements   22.21.2

    In constructions with infinitives   Leavetaking statements   23.21.4
    and /-ndo/ forms   29.21.2   Stress

    Direct and indirect in the same   Strong stress on Past I endings   17.21.1
    construction   25.21.1   Juncture

    Reflexive and direct in the same   Single Bar   21.21.5
    construction   26.21.1   Tempo

    Indirect /le, les/ changes to /se/ 16.10(2)   Slower speech tempo   21.21.5B
                                       20.21.1   READINGS   16.4

    Reflexives   24.21.1   REDUNDANT CONSTRUCTIONS (see relators)
                                       26.21.1B

AII.42   CUARENTA Y DOS

jacobeligoodsons.com For Free Audio

SPOKEN SPANISH INDEX

REFLEXIVE (see clitic pronouns, verb
  constructions)

REGULAR (see verb forms)

RELATORS

  Phrase relators

    /a/ with nonclitic pronoun   16.21.1B

    Redundant construction with indirect
    clitic pronouns   16.21.1

    Possessive phrases with /kyén/   17.24

  Clause relator

    Obligatory clause relator /ke/   23.24

SENTENCE (see pronunciation)

SHORTENING (see verb forms)

STEMS (see verb forms)

STEM VOWEL (see verb forms)

STRESS (see pronunciation)

SUPPLETED (see verb forms)

TEMPO (see pronunciation)

TENSE (see verbs, verb forms)

THEME CLASS (see verbs)

TIME OF DAY EXPRESSIONS   24.21.3

VELAR (see verb forms)

VERBS

  Tense

Future   19.21.1B

Present   19.21.1B

Spanish simple tense for English
verb constructions in interrogations   19.24

Past I   19.21.1B

  Past I theme class   22.24

Past II   19.21.1B

  Past II theme class   21.24

Past I and Past II in the same
construction   19.21.1

VERB FORMS

  Verb forms review   30.21.11

  Regular   22.21.1B
               30.21.1

    Formal command forms   27.21.1

    Familiar command forms   27.21.3

    Past I tense forms   17.21.1
               28.24

    Past II tense forms   18.21.1

  Irregular   22.21.1B
               30.21.1

    Formal command forms   27.21.2

    Familiar command forms   27.21.4

    Present tense

      Stem vowel changing   22.21.1
                         28.21.2

CUARENTA Y TRES

jacobeligoodsons.com For Free Audio

INDEX

SPOKEN SPANISH

Diphthongization in stem vowel changing verbs	22.21.1 23.21.2
Velar stem extension	23.21.1
Voicing correlation in velar stem extensions	23.21.1B
Mixed stem vowel changing and velar stem extensions	23.21.2
Palato-velar extension /kaér, traér/	
Palato-velar extension and palatal extension /oír/	
Velar consonant changing /apér/	
Velar consonant changing and stem vowel changing /depír/	
Vowel changing and shortening in one form /sabér/	23.21.3
Past I tense forms /dár/	21.21.1
Verbs with extended stems	21.21.2
Verbs with modified stems	21.21.3
Verbs with suppleted forms	21.21.4
Past II tense forms	18.21.2
/bér, sér, ir/	18.21.2
Hortatory command forms	28.21.2

VERB CONSTRUCTIONS

Verb constructions review	30.21.12
/abía-ké/	17.10(2)
Command forms	
Indirect — regular and irregular	28.21.1
Command constructions	
Hortatory	28.21.2B
Periphrastic future construction	24.21.2
Present perfect	29.24
Progressive construction	24.21.2

VOICING CORRELATION (see verb forms)
VOWEL (see verb forms)
WORD ORDER

Information questions	18.24
Inversion of normal subject-verb order	25.21.1B
Verb subject in certain dependent clauses	25.24

AII.44

CUARENTA Y CUATRO

* U S GOVERNMENT PRINTING OFFICE 1961 O—398864

For sale by the Superintendent of Documents, U.S. Government Printing Office, Washington 25, D.C. - Price per set of 2 Volumes - $7.50

jacobeligoodsons.com For Free Audio

Manufactured by Amazon.ca
Bolton, ON